9. Save the configuration and reload. r1#**copy run start** (or **wr mem**) r1#**reload** r1#**sh version**	3. Type **flash_init** and then type **load_helper**. You can list the files in flash with **dir flash:**, and the default configuration is config.text.
	4. Type **more flash:config.text** to view the passwords. If not encrypted, you are done. If encrypted, go to Step 5.
	5. Rename the configuration file as follows: **rename flash:config.text flash:config.old.**
	6. Boot the system with the **boot** command. Answer **n** for no to start setup. Go to enable mode by typing **enable**, but do not exit.
	7. Rename the configuration file to its original name as follows: **rename flash:config.old flash:config.text.**
	8. Copy the configuration file to memory with the **config mem** or **copy flash:config.text system:running-config** command. Accept config.text as the source and running-config as the destination filenames.
	9. Change the passwords. **enable password** *donna* **enable secret** *harrington*
	10. Save your configurations. **copy run start** (or **wr mem**)

CCNP Self-Study

CCNP Practical Studies: Troubleshooting

Donna L. Harrington

Cisco Press

Cisco Press
201 West 103rd Street
Indianapolis, IN 46290 USA

CCNP Self-Study
CCNP Practical Studies: Troubleshooting
Donna L. Harrington

Copyright© 2003 Cisco Systems, Inc.

Published by:
Cisco Press
201 West 103rd Street
Indianapolis, IN 46290 USA

Printed in the United States of America 1 2 3 4 5 6 7 8 9 0

Library of Congress Cataloging-in-Publication Number: 2001095270

First Printing March 2003

ISBN: 1-58720-057-0

Warning and Disclaimer

This book is designed to provide information about Cisco troubleshooting. Every effort has been made to make this book as complete and as accurate as possible, but no warranty or fitness is implied.

The information is provided on an "as is" basis. The authors, Cisco Press, and Cisco Systems, Inc., shall have neither liability nor responsibility to any person or entity with respect to any loss or damages arising from the information contained in this book or from the use of the discs or programs that may accompany it.

The opinions expressed in this book belong to the author and are not necessarily those of Cisco Systems, Inc.

Trademark Acknowledgments

All terms mentioned in this book that are known to be trademarks or service marks have been appropriately capitalized. Cisco Press or Cisco Systems, Inc. cannot attest to the accuracy of this information. Use of a term in this book should not be regarded as affecting the validity of any trademark or service mark.

Feedback Information

At Cisco Press, our goal is to create in-depth technical books of the highest quality and value. Each book is crafted with care and precision, undergoing rigorous development that involves the unique expertise of members from the professional technical community.

Readers' feedback is a natural continuation of this process. If you have any comments regarding how we could improve the quality of this book, or otherwise alter it to better suit your needs, you can contact us through e-mail at feedback@ciscopress.com. Please make sure to include the book title and ISBN in your message.

We greatly appreciate your assistance.

Publisher	John Wait
Editor-in-Chief	John Kane
Executive Editor	Brett Bartow
Cisco Representative	Anthony Wolfenden
Cisco Press Program Manager	Sonia Torres Chavez
Manager, Marketing Communications, Cisco Systems	Scott Miller
Cisco Marketing Program Manager	Edie Quiroz
Production Manager	Patrick Kanouse
Acquisitions Editor	Michelle Grandin
Development Editor	Andrew Cupp
Copy Editor	Keith Cline
Technical Editors	Marty Adkins
	Rick Burts
	Chris Heffner
	Scott Morris
	Mark Olivo
Configuration Reviewer	Charles Mann
Team Coordinator	Tammi Ross
Cover Designer	Louisa Adair
Production Team	Mark Shirar
Indexer	Larry Sweazy

CISCO SYSTEMS

Corporate Headquarters
Cisco Systems, Inc.
170 West Tasman Drive
San Jose, CA 95134-1706
USA
www.cisco.com
Tel: 408 526-4000
 800 553-NETS (6387)
Fax: 408 526-4100

European Headquarters
Cisco Systems International BV
Haarlerbergpark
Haarlerbergweg 13-19
1101 CH Amsterdam
The Netherlands
www-europe.cisco.com
Tel: 31 0 20 357 1000
Fax: 31 0 20 357 1100

Americas Headquarters
Cisco Systems, Inc.
170 West Tasman Drive
San Jose, CA 95134-1706
USA
www.cisco.com
Tel: 408 526-7660
Fax: 408 527-0883

Asia Pacific Headquarters
Cisco Systems, Inc.
Capital Tower
168 Robinson Road
#22-01 to #29-01
Singapore 068912
www.cisco.com
Tel: +65 6317 7777
Fax: +65 6317 7799

Cisco Systems has more than 200 offices in the following countries and regions. Addresses, phone numbers, and fax numbers are listed on the
Cisco.com Web site at www.cisco.com/go/offices.

Argentina • Australia • Austria • Belgium • Brazil • Bulgaria • Canada • Chile • China PRC • Colombia • Costa Rica • Croatia • Czech Republic
Denmark • Dubai, UAE • Finland • France • Germany • Greece • Hong Kong SAR • Hungary • India • Indonesia • Ireland • Israel • Italy
Japan • Korea • Luxembourg • Malaysia • Mexico • The Netherlands • New Zealand • Norway • Peru • Philippines • Poland • Portugal
Puerto Rico • Romania • Russia • Saudi Arabia • Scotland • Singapore • Slovakia • Slovenia • South Africa • Spain • Sweden
Switzerland • Taiwan • Thailand • Turkey • Ukraine • United Kingdom • United States • Venezuela • Vietnam • Zimbabwe

About the Author

Donna L. Harrington, MS, CCNP, has more than 20 years experience in the information systems, telecommunications, business management, and electronics fields. She is also a certified Cisco Systems instructor. Donna specializes in networking and the delivery of TCP/IP and CCNP courses. She has taught Cisco, Microsoft, and Novell certified courses for several years. Donna is currently employed as an internetworking specialist in Annapolis Junction, Maryland. Previously she was with Mentor Technologies (Chesapeake Computer Consultants) and certified to deliver CCNP-related courses. She developed, delivered, and maintained Mentor's TCP/IP Networking course. Although they were long hours at times, she enjoyed assisting with Mentor's ECP1, the CCIE preparation course. She found it particularly fun to break things for the students to fix. Donna has developed and delivered courses for the information and telecommunication systems for business and the police executive leadership graduate programs at John Hopkins University and consulted and trained for numerous well-known businesses throughout her career.

About the Technical Reviewers

Scott Morris, CCIE No. 4713, has more than 15 years experience in telecommunications, network design, and installation. He is a triple CCIE (Routing and Switching, ISP/Dial, and Security) and has specialties in various fields of technology, including security, IP telephony, and cable (RF) internetworking. Scott is a certified Cisco Systems instructor and has taught classes on many advanced topics in his specialty areas and other advanced routing, MPLS, and troubleshooting topics. Currently, Scott is an independent contractor with Uber-Geek Networks (www.uber-geek.net). Previously, he was with Mentor Technologies along with Donna and traveled all over the world delivering Cisco curricula. These days, in addition to delivering Cisco courses, Scott also works on developing courses within his specialty areas.

Rick Burts, CCIE No. 4615, has more than 20 years experience with computers and computer networks. Rick is a certified Cisco Systems instructor. In addition to having taught a variety of Cisco courses, including the Cisco Internetwork Troubleshooting course, Rick has taught with Donna at Mentor Technologies. Since then, Rick joined Chesapeake NetCraftsmen (www.netcraftsmen.net) where he is a senior consultant. In his current position, Rick deals with network design, implementation, and troubleshooting issues in addition to teaching courses.

Marty Adkins, CCIE No. 1289, is a senior consultant with Chesapeake NetCraftsmen, LLC, based in the Washington, D.C., metro area (www.netcraftsmen.net). He is an electrical engineer with more than 25 years experience in networking and telecommunications. Previously, he was with Chesapeake Computer Consultants (a.k.a, Mentor Technologies) for eight years as a senior consultant and certified Cisco Systems instructor, where he delighted in teaching the Cisco Internetwork Troubleshooting course.

Mark T. Olivo has been in the computer field for more than 26 years, with more than 20 years of teaching experience. He has more than 70 different computer industry certifications from 12 different vendors, including CCNP and CCDP. Mark is currently employed as a technical trainer and courseware developer for SMARTS (System Management Arts) and works on outside projects as time allows. Mark has known Donna for many years and has worked with her at three different companies.

Christopher M. Heffner, CCIE No. 8211, has been in the networking, telecommunications, and design fields for more than 19 years. He is a certified Cisco Systems instructor and contract instructor for the past eight years in the Cisco, Microsoft, Novell, and Lotus Notes curricula. Chris earned his CCIE in Routing and Switching in September 2001, and is currently working on his CCIE in Security. Chris is the owner of Certified Labs and Strategic Network Solutions, Inc., which offers Cisco certification preparation including remote labs access, practical lab scenarios, exam prep guides, and web-based practice exams for Cisco CCIE, CCNP, CCSP, and CCNA certifications. Chris can be reached at cheffner@certified-labs.com and at www.certified-labs.com.

Acknowledgments

Internetworking must be built around the business at hand in order to provide easy access to pertinent information regardless of location, time, or system. Much of the information included in this book is based on questions I have received in class. I have to send out a special thanks to all of my students and coworkers from TCP/IP to CCNA to CCNP and others over the years who have kept me on my toes. I wouldn't want to forget my technical reviewers, who have helped me make this book what it is today. Thank you Scott Morris, Rick Burts, Marty Adkins, Mark Olivo, and Chris Heffner. I would also like to thank Charlie Mann for testing the hands-on scenarios and Trouble Tickets.

Contents at a Glance

Contents

Foreword

CCNP Practical Studies: Troubleshooting is designed to provide you with another vehicle to obtain hands-on experience, which is a critical component of any preparation program for the Cisco Certified Network Professional exams. The detailed lab scenarios contained in this book illustrate the application of key support and troubleshooting concepts covered on the CCNP Troubleshooting exam, helping you master the advanced practical skills you need to install, configure, and operate LAN, WAN, and dial access services for networks from 100 to more than 500 nodes. With the introduction of performance-based testing elements to the CCNP exams, these hands-on skills are of critical importance to succeeding on the exam and in your daily job as a CCNP professional. This book was developed in cooperation with the Cisco Internet Learning Solutions Group. Cisco Press books are the only self-study books authorized by Cisco for CCNP exam preparation.

Cisco and Cisco Press present this material in text-based format to provide another learning vehicle for our customers and the broader user community in general. Although a publication does not duplicate the instructor-led or e-learning environment, we acknowledge that not everyone responds in the same way to the same delivery mechanism. It is our intent that presenting this material via a Cisco Press publication will enhance the transfer of knowledge to a broad audience of networking professionals.

Cisco Press will present lab manuals on existing and future exams through these Practical Studies titles to help achieve Cisco Internet Learning Solutions Group's principal objectives: to educate the Cisco community of networking professionals and to enable that community to build and maintain reliable, scalable networks. The Cisco Career Certifications and classes that support these certifications are directed at meeting these objectives through a disciplined approach to progressive learning. To succeed on the Cisco Career Certifications exams, as well as in your daily job as a Cisco-certified professional, we recommend a blended learning solution that combines instructor-led, e-learning, and self-study training with hands-on experience. Cisco Systems has created an authorized Cisco Learning Partner program to provide you with the most highly qualified instruction and invaluable hands-on experience in lab and simulation environments. To learn more about Cisco Learning Partner programs available in your area, please go to: www.cisco.com/go/training.

The books that Cisco Press creates in partnership with Cisco Systems meet the same standards for content quality demanded of our courses and certifications. It is our intent that you will find this and subsequent Cisco Press certification and training publications of value as you build your networking knowledge base.

Thomas M. Kelly
Vice-President, Internet Learning Solutions Group
Cisco Systems, Inc.
March 2003

Introduction

CCNP Practical Studies: Troubleshooting is part of the Practical Studies series of Cisco Press books designed to prepare readers for the CCNP exams and real-world application of LAN and WAN technologies. Unfortunately, life is not just a checklist and neither is supporting networks. However, if you know how things are supposed to work, use a consistent troubleshooting method and layered approach, apply your skills through hands-on application, and have a positive attitude, you are most certainly on your way to shooting trouble before it shoots you.

Troubleshooting skills are a must-have for every CCNA, CCNP, and CCIE today. There is an increasing demand for practical application of the knowledge learned in Cisco and other internetworking classes. People learn by doing. Practice makes perfect. Employers want people with degrees and certifications, but they really need people who can perform the job that their resume says they can. This book gives you a practical advantage over the competition through real-world application of internetworking topics. It is designed for CCNAs and CCNPs as well as the want-to-be seeking practical experience in the topics covered on the CCNP Troubleshooting exam. Because material in this book is very helpful for anyone in or pursuing a support career, even CCIEs and other support professionals may enjoy reviewing the book to sharpen their troubleshooting skills. The scope is limited to TCP/IP and routing and switching and to a lesser extent Novell IPX troubleshooting.

Cisco Career Certifications

Cisco CCNA, CCNP, and CCIE certifications coupled with field experience ensure high standards of technical expertise and can lead to outstanding opportunities. To learn more about the Associate, Professional, and Expert certification paths, go to www.cisco.com/en/US/learning/index.html.

Beyond being an excellent troubleshooting training tool, this book helps prepare you for the Cisco Internetwork Troubleshooting (CIT) Troubleshooting exam, which is one of the exams required to achieve CCNP certification. Review the published support exam topics at www.cisco.com/en/US/learning/index.html (click Professional, then CCNP, and then Troubleshooting exam).

To schedule an exam in the United States and Canada, visit Prometric online at www.prometric.com or VUE at www.vue.com. Alternatively, call 1-800-829-6387 (NETS) to register for an exam.

Goals of This Book

Cisco Systems, Cisco Press, and I strongly recommend that you supplement instructor-led training with additional practical experience to prepare for Cisco certification exams and gain the knowledge necessary to work in the field. Cisco is starting to make sure of that by including simulations on their certification tests.

This book assumes a CCNA level of knowledge. Many times when students get to the CCNP curriculum, however, they fail to understand the basics of TCP/IP networking and lack a methodology to troubleshoot basic issues. This will not be an issue for readers of this troubleshooting guide because supporting TCP/IP and Cisco internetworks are essential goals of this book.

This book is a strong companion to the Cisco Internetwork Troubleshooting course as well as other Cisco Press and third-party materials, including the Cisco System website, www.cisco.com. It is an essential resource to prepare you for the *real-world* CCNP Troubleshooting certification. It helps you test yourself before your employers do.

To meet these goals, this book helps you do the following:

- Establish a baseline and document your physical and logical internetwork.

- Take step-by-step approaches to troubleshooting.

- Understand protocol characteristics and tools to help identify how technologies work so that you know when they are broken.

- Experience coverage of IP over Ethernet and the WAN.

- Apply your troubleshooting skills firsthand through practical chapter scenarios, detailed figures, and examples.

- Set up a test lab or at least walk through the solutions to solve real-world situations via Trouble Tickets. People learn by doing. Hands-on labs assist you in quickly recognizing common issues so that you avoid just applying the swap-till-you-drop approach to troubleshooting.

In addition, this book provides supporting resources and files including troubleshooting checklists and charts, tools, Sniffer Pro protocol analyzer captures, downloadable configurations, review questions, and the appendix materials.

How to Use This Book

To get the maximum benefit from this book, when reading engage yourself in the chapter scenarios and practical approaches to supporting the LAN and WAN. It is critical to learn to identify trouble spots using a layered approach—however, this cannot be accomplished via memorization techniques. This book shows you how to apply theoretical knowledge and skills to practical scenarios. Each chapter includes a scenario that forms the practical hands-on basis for a review of the applicable technology. Each chapter ends with real-world Trouble Tickets designed to give you further practical experience. Having your own equipment or access to equipment is the ideal way to profit from this book (see Appendix C), but if that is not possible, the appropriate information is delivered through figures, configuration examples, and text, so you can still follow along with the practical exercises.

Troubleshooting commands such as **cdp**, **ping**, **trace**, **set**, **show**, **clear**, and **debug** are used extensively in the printed examples in this book so that you can follow along with or without the appropriate equipment. Captures from Sniffer Pro protocol analyzer traces and other tools emphasize important concepts and trouble spots as required. Each chapter suggests additional references such as utilities, labs, websites, and supplemental reading as it relates. Refer to Appendix C if you need to get started right away on acquiring the equipment for your lab.

I sincerely wish you the best with applying this book to your specific requirements. I recommend that you use the first couple of chapters to review the topics you think you already know. Use Chapter 10 as both a pre-test and a post-test for the book. It includes a comprehensive set of self-guided Trouble Tickets that enable you to assess your support skills before and after reading the book. If you want, turn to it now to get familiar with what to expect throughout the book. Then you can return to the beginning of the book and spend as much or as little time needed on the topics included.

My experiences and studies have given me the challenges and opportunities needed to live and work in our technologically advancing society. Providing technical expertise, leadership, and support to my employer, coworkers, family, and friends gives me the challenge, encouragement, and enthusiasm required to utilize today's technology for tomorrow's competitive advantage. Please help me continue that by sending your feedback to donna@shoretraining.com.

Supporting Files

You can find files and links to utilities that support this book on the Cisco Press website at www.cisco-press.com/1587200570. Even if you do not have a lab, you can take advantage of the supporting configuration files including the logs to understand device input and output. The files are listed throughout the chapters in italics.

In order to be able to read and work with some of the supporting files offered at www.ciscopress.com/1587200570, you may want to download some of the programs listed in Table I-1.

Table I-1 *Useful Programs for Reading and Using This Book's Supporting Files at www.ciscopress.com/1587200570.*

Software	Website link	Evaluation copy available?	Description
Protocol Analyzers			
Network Associates Sniffer Pro	www.sniffer.com	No	Protocol analyzer used throughout this book.
Ethereal	www.ethereal.com	Free	Protocol analyzer.
WildPackets EtherPeek	www.wildpackets.com	Yes	Protocol analyzer.
Terminal Emulation Programs			
SecureCRT	www.vandyke.com	Yes	Terminal emulator used throughout this book. Supports Telnet/SSH.
HyperTerminal	www.hilgraeve.com	Comes with Windows operating systems.	Update your Windows terminal emulator to the private edition for free.
PuTTY	www.chiark.greenend.or g.uk/~sgtatham/putty/ download.html	Free	Telnet/SSH SCP SFTP
FTP/TFTP/Syslog Programs			
PumpKin TFTP	www.klever.net/kin	Yess	TFTP client and server.
3CDaemon	support.3com.com/ infodeli/swlib/ utilities_for_windows_3 2_bit.htm	Free	TFTP FTP Syslog
Cisco TFTP server	www.cisco.com/pcgi-bin/tablebuild.pl/tftp	Free	TFTP server.

Command Syntax Conventions

Command syntax in this book conforms to the following conventions:

- Commands, keywords, and actual values for arguments are **bold**.

- Arguments (which need to be supplied with an actual value) are *italic*.

- Optional keywords and arguments are in brackets [].

- A choice of mandatory keywords and arguments is in braces {}.

Note that these conventions are for syntax only.

Icons Used in This Book

Throughout this book, you will see the following icons used for networking devices:

Router

Bridge

Hub

DSU/CSU

Catalyst
Switch

Multilayer
Switch

ATM
Switch

ISDN/Frame Relay
Switch

Communication
Server

Gateway

Access
Server

The following icons are used for peripherals and other devices:

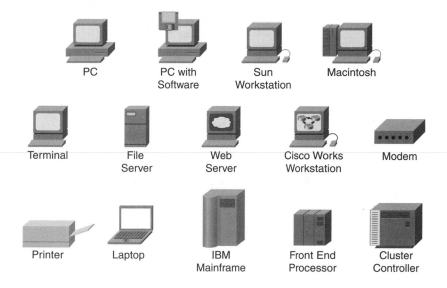

The following icons are used for networks and network connections:

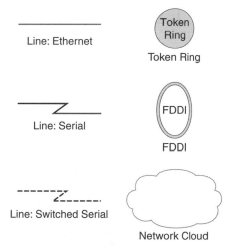

Protocol Characteristics and Tools

CHAPTER 1

Shooting Trouble

This chapter serves as the basis for the troubleshooting exercises throughout this book. In addition to a solid understanding of specific technologies, effective troubleshooting requires that you follow consistent procedures that are based on industry standards and reliable methods. The Open System Interconnection (OSI) model and the TCP/IP suite can help you methodically divide and conquer a problem or learn a new internetworking topic (by taking a layer-by-layer approach, for instance). This chapter presents an introduction to troubleshooting; a review of standards, protocols, and industry models; and practical troubleshooting, including baselining and documentation techniques. These standards, models, and techniques are covered in this chapter so that you can refer to them as you work through the specific troubleshooting tasks in this book. This chapter includes a Trouble Ticket designed to give you practical experience in solving real-world issues using Cisco's troubleshooting approach.

This chapter covers the following topics:

- Do You Shoot Trouble or Does Trouble Shoot You?
- Standards and Protocols
- Models and Methods
- Practical Troubleshooting

Do You Shoot Trouble or Does Trouble Shoot You?

Troubleshooting is all about reducing guesswork and eliminating the obvious. Following a systematic method is essential during the troubleshooting process. Methodical problem solving is the core of the CIT course, the CCNP Troubleshooting test, and this book, regardless of technical intricacies. Many times, whether or not you use a systematic method determines if you shoot trouble or if trouble shoots you.

Shooting trouble is often about questions. Do you ask the equipment or the user? Who is waiting for the results? What has happened? When did it occur? Why? Where did it happen? Are you using 10/100-Mbps Ethernet to the desktop; 155-Mbps ATM; or carrier services such as cable modems, digital subscriber line (DSL), wireless, ISDN, Frame Relay, Switched Multimegabit Data Service (SMDS), ATM, or long-haul Ethernet? The protocols, technologies, media, and topologies entail lots of complexity and the only thing constant is change. So where do you begin?

NOTE   Appendix A material from the Cisco instructor-led Cisco Internetwork Troubleshooting (CIT) course for the CCNP Support exam is covered throughout this chapter and in more detail in the relevant chapters of this book. Consider this chapter fertile with test material; even more importantly, it makes an excellent practical review.

The first topic is standards and protocols. Think back for a moment to the last time you chatted with a friend. Certainly you and your friend had something to share, regardless of the method used to communicate. If you made a phone call, you were listening to each other talk. If you sent an e-mail or used a chat client, you were sending data back and forth. Whether it was your home phone, wireless phone, or PC, communications media was in place nonetheless. I assume that you waited for the friend to say hello first and that you took turns talking. You spoke the same language or understood multiple languages. Hopefully, you were polite enough to not talk while the other person was talking. You may have had to troubleshoot some issues while talking with the friend. Perhaps a lightning storm hit your phone line or you dialed the wrong number. Maybe you didn't pay your phone bill and the service was turned off. The friend may not have answered or the phone may have been busy. Maybe your friend had caller ID and picked up right away because it was you. Regardless of your exact scenario, throughout the contact you had to decide your next step.

NOTE   Continue to think about your communications with your friend as you read through this chapter. You may begin to see how a different perspective or an analogy can help you to simplify complex topics. Throughout this book, I include occasional analogies I have found to be very helpful to my students learning in the classroom.

Standards and Protocols

Communication rules are referred to as *standards* and *protocols*. Playing with the right rules to the game normally means you are more apt to communicate well in the networking game. Standards are rules, conditions, and requirements that can be de jure, de facto, proprietary, or open. *De jure standards* are official; by legislation they are endorsed by a standards body, such as those listed in Table 1-1.

Table 1-1   *Standards Bodies*

Standards Body	Acronym	Examples
American National Standards Institute www.ansi.org	ANSI	C Cobol Fortran X3T9.5
International Telecommunication Union www.itu.int	ITU	V.22 V.32 V.34 V.42
Institute of Electrical and Electronic Engineers standards.ieee.org www.ieee.org	IEEE	802.2 LLC* 802.3 Ethernet 802.5 Token Ring
International Organization for Standardization www.iso.org	ISO (not an acronym)	OSI IS-IS
Electronic Industries Alliance/ Telecommunications Industry Association www.eia.org www.tiaonline.org	EIA/TIA	EIA/TIA 568 Commercial Building Telecommunications Wiring Standard RS-232 EIA/TIA 232
Internet Engineering Task Force www.ietf.org	IETF	RFCs
Internet Assigned Numbers Authority www.iana.org	IANA	Port and protocol numbers

*LLC = Logical Link Control

TCP/IP and OSI are examples of nonproprietary open standards that are widely used today. Standards are wonderful things; that's why we have so many. Webopedia (www.webopedia.com) defines standard as a definition or format that has been approved by a recognized standards organization or is accepted as a de facto standard by the industry. Standards exist for programming languages, operating systems, data formats, communications protocols, and electrical interfaces.

As an example of an evolution of technology through standards, consider the creation of the Internet. According to "20 Questions: How the Net Works," by Scot Finnie at www.scotfinnie.com/20quests/hownet.htm#Q1, no one person or group can claim this fame; however, in 1962 a series of memos discussed the "Galactic Network Concept" from MIT's J.C.R. Licklider. Licklider later became the head of the Department of Defense (DoD)

Advanced Research Projects Agency (ARPA). TCP/IP research began in 1961, and in 1967 ARPA's Lawrence Roberts published his plan for the worldwide network. Tests were conducted for several years, and e-mail and the Internet made their first public appearances in 1972. TCP/IP protocols and services made their way into the network in the 1970s. The World Wide Web (WWW) was born in the late 1980s. The National Science Foundation (NSF) took over the management of ARPANET in 1990. In the mid-1990s, NSFnet was turned over to a consortium of public providers we know today as Internet service providers (ISPs). Many standards bodies are responsible for the Internet's existence and maintenance, including the following:

- Internet Society (ISOC), which includes the Internet Architecture Board (IAB) for broad direction and overall architecture and the Internet Engineering Steering Group (IESG).

- Internet Assigned Numbers Authority (IANA) and Internet Network Information Center (InterNIC) for IP addresses, domain names, and other numbers.

- World Wide Web Consortium (WC3) for HTML and web standards.

- Internet Engineering Task Force (IETF) for RFCs and smooth operations.

- Internet Research Task Force (IRTF) for ongoing research.

TCP/IP open standards (nonproprietary) are based on Request For Comments (RFCs); whereas, proprietary standards are vendor-specific. Refer to www.rfc-editor.org to read RFCs and for more detail on the RFC process, including a tribute to Jon Postel who was *the* RFC Editor. Figure 1-1 shows the RFC Editor. Also refer to www.ietf.org/rfc/rfc2026.txt for particulars.

Anyone can propose a new standard, which then goes through various levels toward maturity. All RFCs start out as drafts, but not all drafts mature to RFCs. When published, RFCs do not change. Updates get a new RFC number. You can review private addressing in RFC 1918, for example, which obsoletes the original RFC 1597.

De facto standards include examples such as the Hayes command set for controlling modems, the Kermit and Xmodem communications protocols, and the printer control language (PCL) and postscript for laser printers. Although numerous de facto standards may have started as proprietary implementations, by the time they are regarded as de facto standards there are many different vendor implementations. One example of this is quite relevant to Chapter 7, "Shooting Trouble with VLANs on Routers and Switches"; the example is the two different ways that Ethernet trunking can occur:

- InterSwitch Link (ISL), which is the Cisco proprietary method

- 802.1Q, which is the IEEE standard

Standards are important. They enable different people (and different vendors) to approach a task in a similar way to achieve a similar solution that works. Standards can be categorized by how they are recognized: proprietary or open. Proprietary beginnings tend to produce de facto standards (Hayes, Kermit, and PCL). Open beginnings tend to produce de jure standards (TCP/IP and RFCs). If it is truly a proprietary solution and other vendors cannot use it, it probably is not a standard. A standard really refers to a solution available to multiple vendors.

Figure 1-1   *RFC Editor*

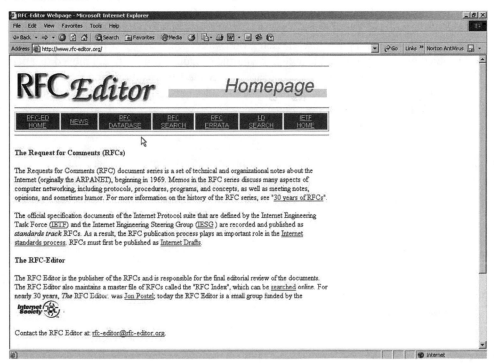

Now that I have defined standards and the standards process, what about the need for protocols? *Communications protocols* are rules governing the transmitting (Tx) and receiving (Rx) of data so that different end systems or applications can communicate with one another. A *protocol* is an agreed-upon format for transmitting data between two devices. The protocol determines how the sending and receiving devices communicate, such as the indicator for sending and receiving a message. The protocol also defines the type of error-checking and data-compression methods if any are used.

Examples of protocol suites include TCP/IP, OSI, IEEE, AppleTalk, DECnet, Novell Internetwork Packet Exchange (IPX), and IBM Systems Network Architecture (SNA). A protocol suite or stack is like many subcontractors building a house. Brick layers take care of the foundation, the electricians put in the wires, the plumbers install the pipes, the framers frame it up, roofers carry out their part, and finally the homeowners do their own finishing touches. In networking, different protocols operate at each layer to carry out fundamental functions such as encapsulation, segmentation and re-assembly, connection control (connection-oriented or connectionless), flow control, error control, multiplexing, and delivery.

These protocols use rules to dictate how communication is established. Unless everyone plays by the same rules, communication is not possible. As a fun demonstration of the importance of standards and protocols, I gave several groups of technology students a card game to play. The rules were on a piece of paper given to each group. Unbeknownst to them, each group was given a slightly different set of rules. (One sheet said ace is high, another said the joker is a wildcard, and yet another said joker loses.) Each group was instructed to play by the rules and not to talk. When they were comfortable in their own little groups of four or five, I moved one person from each team to another group. It was chaos, to say the least, as they tried to play the game with different understandings of the rules. They finally figured it out and agreed that a standard set of rules (protocol) is definitely beneficial.

NOTE   Understanding standards and protocols and their layered approach will assist you in applying internetworking skills and shooting trouble in a practical environment. In addition, with such understanding you will be on your way to passing many certification tests.

Models and Methods

Models are guidelines for communications and methods for troubleshooting. This section covers the ISO's OSI model, the DoD's TCP/IP suite, and Cisco's seven-step approach to troubleshooting.

The OSI Model

You have probably dealt with the OSI model more times than you care to remember. Hopefully, however, this review will make the OSI model meaningful to you. Use it to troubleshoot the practical lab scenarios that follow as well as to understand and review internetworking topics.

ISO began work on the OSI model in the late 1970s and published the OSI reference model in 1984 to facilitate interoperability among vendors. It is one of the best troubleshooting models around, and every certification vendor will test to make sure you are an expert in this area. Be aware, however, that every vendor has its own approach to OSI. (I write from experience here; I have been heavily involved in not only Cisco, but also Microsoft, Novell, and CompTIA (A+/ Network+) certification course delivery over the years.)

Although the focus here is on understanding the OSI model and using it to troubleshoot, the OSI model provides other benefits as well (such as interoperability and standardization, and it enables you to subdivide developer tasks without having to alter other layers). For example, network interface card (NIC) vendors really don't want to be concerned with what upper-layer applications and protocols run over the hardware. However, NIC vendors must be concerned with LAN technologies such as Ethernet, Token Ring, and what physical specifications (cable and connectors) to follow.

Please Do Not Threaten Support People Again

I love mnemonics. They may seem simple, but they can be surprisingly effective in helping commit principles to memory. In this case, **Please Do Not Threaten Support People Again** is a tool to help you remember the seven layers of the OSI model, as displayed in Table 1-2. Note the layers and protocol data units (PDUs) in Table 1-2. Although often referred to as just plain old packets, PDUs actually came from the ISO.

Table 1-2   *OSI Layers and PDUs*

OSI Layer Number	OSI Layer Name	PDU	Mnemonic
7	**A**pplication	Messages (data, voice, video)	**A**gain
6	**P**resentation	Messages (data, voice, video)	**P**eople
5	**S**ession	Messages (data, voice, video)	**S**upport
4	**T**ransport	Segments (TCP*)/datagrams (UDP*)	**T**hreaten
3	**N**etwork	Packets/datagrams	**N**ot
2	**D**ata Link	Frames	**D**o
1	**P**hysical	Bits	**P**lease

*TCP = Transport Control Protocol
*UDP = User Datagram Protocol

Take each layer and examine the services provided to or from the next layer. It is helpful to draw a picture of two end systems communicating to understand the layers. (See Figure 1-2.) Often you miss a lot of important host-to-host activity if you look only at the source or the destination host of one protocol stack. Figure 1-2 shows GroupWise hosta, which sends e-mail to Exchange hostb. The general layered approach is presented here, not all the application details.

Figure 1-2   *End-System Data Flow*

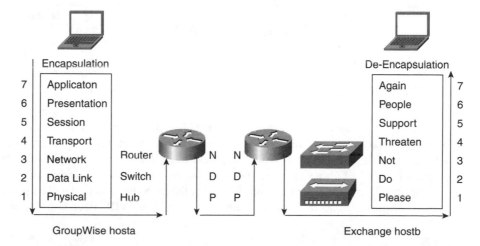

Notice how the source GroupWise hosta encapsulates the message as it works its way from Layer 7 to Layer 1 across the wire. Assuming that the destination Exchange hostb is on another network, lots of encapsulation/de-encapsulation occurs between Layers 1 through 3 until the packet gets to the destination host (router-to-router operations). The destination host pulls the frames off the wire and processes (de-encapsulates) them up the stack from Layer 1 to Layer 7 so that the e-mail application can read the e-mail. The processing includes any necessary re-ordering and re-assembly of packets that result from packet routing and fragmentation.

Understanding a layered approach and packet flows is critical to being a good troubleshooter. That's why vendors put all that theory stuff in their courses. If you don't know how things work correctly, how in the world do you know what is wrong? End system–to–end system Exchange and GroupWise messaging is the main example I share with students in many of my classes. Take a look again at Figure 1-2 and then at Figure 1-3 (on encapsulation) to review the packet flow and layer operations. For more detail, refer to materials on CCNA and CCNP from Cisco Press and other publishers. I particularly like Jeff Doyle's *Routing TCP/IP*, Volumes I and II, and think they belong on everyone's shelf.

Figure 1-3 *Encapsulation*

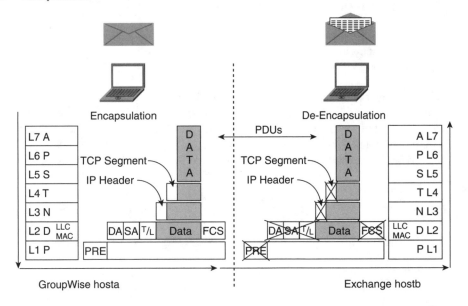

Encapsulation (framing) is like wrapping presents for someone else so that he or she can tear the wrapping paper off. Another analogy many people use when referring to encapsulation is that it is like writing a letter and stuffing the letter in an IP envelope to be delivered to a destination. Think of encapsulation as placing a letter in your mailbox and putting the flag up to let the postal worker know to pick up and deliver the letter; this analogy will help you analyze the fields of the IP header in Chapter 3, "Shooting Trouble with IP." Each hop (Layer 3 device)

along the way strips off the packaging (Layer 2 framing/encapsulation) and repackages (Layer 2 framing/encapsulation) for the next hop closer to the destination (Layer 3). Figure 1-3 illustrates the encapsulation /de-encapsulation process for Ethernet, including the destination address (DA), source address (SA), type or length field (T/L), and the frame check sequence (FCS), all of which are examined in more detail in Chapter 5, "Shooting Trouble with Ethernet."

Each layer adds a *header*, which is nothing more than a set of instructions for its peer layer. With TCP/IP, for example, the upper-layer messages (data, voice, or video packets) get encapsulated (stuffed) inside of a TCP segment or UDP datagram at the Transport Layer for delivery. The Transport Layer segment (connection-oriented) or datagram (connectionless) gets encapsulated (stuffed) inside of the Network Layer IP packet or datagram (connectionless). The number of segments sent before acknowledgement is required may vary (windowing). The IP packet gets encapsulated (stuffed) inside of the Data Link Layer frame. In Ethernet, for instance, the preamble (PRE) starts the frame and the trailer (cyclic redundancy check [CRC] or FCS) ends the frame. If necessary, an Address Resolution Protocol (ARP) packet is broadcast (local broadcast) to resolve the destination IP address (Layer 3) to its equivalent Media Access Control (MAC) address (Layer 2). If the destination host is on the same subnet, the MAC is the destination host's address. If the destination host is on a different subnet, the resulting resolution is generally the default gateway (local router interface) MAC address. ARP is not necessary across a serial point-to-point link because it is not a broadcast segment like Ethernet. The IP packet destination IP address doesn't change during normal destination-based routing; however, the Layer 2 MAC addresses change each hop along the way.

NOTE   The preceding paragraph discusses IP, but this layered approach certainly applies to various protocol stacks (such as Novell IPX, IBM SNA, AppleTalk, and so on).

Networking is limited by the standards that prevail. Even though 10-MB, 100-MB, and Gigabit Ethernet standards are available today, for example, the frame size is still limited to 1500 bytes. What if everything doesn't fit into the frame? Think of it like sending a box of Christmas gifts rather than just a Christmas card. You could get a bigger box to put all the presents in or send lots of smaller ones. Just like the Christmas box, if everything doesn't fit in the frame, IP fragments the data into smaller packets (chunks) each hop along the way according to the frame type or the maximum transmission unit (MTU) set on the interface. The initial packet ID number may be randomly generated, but the subsequent packet IDs are sequential in nature for re-ordering and re-assembly purposes. Some Layer 3 protocols, such as IPX, don't fragment the data at all. The Physical Layer requires bits (0s and 1s) to traverse the wire. A lot of activity occurs among the lower layers until the packets reach the destination host.

De-encapsulation is like opening envelopes or presents. Each layer reads and carries out the instructions from its peer layer, discards the header (instructions), and sends the packets up the stack for further processing. Each layer receives services from the layer below and provides services to the layer above it.

The following sections cover the OSI model layer by layer. It is assumed that you are somewhat familiar with the layers and abbreviations and acronyms discussed with regards to each layer. If not, you can find more information at websites such as www.acronymfinder.com, www.shoretraining.com, www.learntcpip.com, www.computerlanguage.com, www.whatis.com, www.amazon.com, www.certificationzone.com, and www.cisco.com.

NOTE   Remember that protocols and applications are written to perform functions, and the focus here is using the OSI model as a *model* to understand and troubleshoot them. If you really want to know the technical details (for an engineering standpoint), you should read the ISO documents.

Layer 7: The Application Layer

Layer 7, the Application Layer, is all about servers providing services and users requesting to use those services. Servers provide shared services, such as file, print, message, database, network management, communications, and application services. Clients request the same services. This reminds me of going out to eat. The restaurant hostess seats you with the menus, and a server comes to the table to take your order (providing you with services). You, as a customer (client), order your food (request services) and indulge as usual.

Application Layer examples include the user interface, X.400 Mail services, X.500 Directory services, Simple Mail Transport Protocol (SMTP), Internet Message Access Protocol (IMAP), Post Office Protocol (POP), Simple Network Management Protocol (SNMP), FTP, TFTP, HTTP, telnet, Domain Name System (DNS), Bootstrap Protocol/Dynamic Host Configuration Protocol (BOOTP/DHCP*), Network File System (NFS), gateways, Border Gateway Protocol (BGP*), Routing Information Protocol (RIP*), and so on. Rout**ing** protocols are generally thought of at the Network Layer (Layer 3). Because BGP operates over TCP port number 179 and RIP operates over UDP port 520, however, many people choose to list them here. DHCP operates over UDP ports 67 and 68.

NOTE   Many different opinions exist as to how to best classify routing protocols. It is important to keep in mind that many management and control type protocols obviously support Layer 3 functions rather than transfer data. Examples include such services as DHCP, BGP, and RIP, which I have marked with an asterisk (*) in the preceding paragraph. It is impossible to make everything fit nicely into the layers.

Layer 6: The Presentation Layer

Layer 6, the Presentation Layer, is the *translator*. Presentation is everything. How about that big hunk of cheesecake for desert with strawberry glaze on the plate? The waiter wrote down your order, but can the person serving the desert interpret it?

Think of translation from one application to another application (translation of, for example, such things as character codes and syntax, encryption, and compression). In the Cisco environment, compression is often thought to relate to Layer 2; I will cover that detail in the WAN chapters (Chapter 8, "Shooting Trouble with Frame Relay," and Chapter 9, "Shooting Trouble with HDLC, PPP, ISDN BRI, and Dial Backup"). Presentation Layer examples include ASCII, Extended Binary Coded Decimal Interchange Code (EBCDIC), Tagged Image File Format (TIFF), Joint Photographic Experts Group (JPEG), Musical Instrument Digital Interface (MIDI), MPEG-I Audio Layer III (MP3), Moving Picture Experts Group (MPEG), Rivest Shamir Adleman (RSA), Data Encryption Standard (DES), Secure Sockets Layer (SSL), and Transport Layer Security (TLS).

Layer 5: The Session Layer

Layer 5, the Session Layer, is the operator or dialog layer. It establishes, maintains, and tears down communication sessions within the operating system using protocols such as remote-procedure calls (RPCs), Lightweight Directory Access Protocol (LDAP), Network Basic Input/Output System (NetBIOS), sockets, Server Message Block (SMB), or Network Control Program (NCP). Communications examples include the following:

- Simplex (one way, like a television or radio broadcast)
- Half-duplex (one way at a time, like my Nextel walkie-talkie phone)
- Full-duplex (simultaneous, like telephones and networks)

NOTE   The upper three layers of the OSI model are referred to as the Application Layer in the TCP/IP suite of protocols. From a troubleshooting standpoint, these layers typically relate to software problems in end systems and name resolution issues.

Layer 4: The Transport Layer

Layer 4, the Transport Layer, is all about host-to-host delivery. This layer hides lower-layer problems from upper layers in that it provides error detection and correction on the receiving end (host). In addition, it segments and re-assembles data for upper-layer applications based on various TCP and UDP port numbers. Application multiplexing is common (just like when you press Alt+Tab to cycle through your open programs in Windows). For example, you may be running a web browser (HTTP port 80), telnetted into a router (TCP port 23), and copying configurations to a TFTP server (UDP port 69) or FTP server (TCP ports 20 and 21) all at the same time. Normally, systems run out of resources before they run out of *ports* (pointers to applications).

TCP and UDP are the most common examples at Layer 4 for TCP/IP; the equivalent IPX/Sequenced Packet Exchange (SPX) transport is SPX. TCP is *connection-oriented*, which means the host must establish a logical connection, such as a 3-way handshake, before communications can occur. Flow control occurs through windowing, and TCP is *reliable* in that it uses acknowledgements (acks) and negative acknowledgements (naks). UDP is *connectionless*, which means it does not require an established connection before communications can occur. It is unreliable at the Transport Layer, which means that the reliability is left up to the Application Layer. TCP is like the certified mail protocol; whereas, UDP is like the regular mail protocol.

Rou**ting** protocols are generally thought of as relating to the Network Layer (Layer 3). Because Interior Gateway Routing Protocol (IGRP, protocol number 9), Enhanced IGRP (EIGRP, protocol number 88), and Open Shortest Path First (OSPF, protocol number 89) operate side-by-side with TCP and UDP, however, they are often discussed as Layer 4 protocols. This leaves reliability up to the upper-layer protocols.

NOTE   Protocol numbers and port numbers are different. Port numbers link the Transport Layer to the upper layers. FTP is an application that operates based on TCP ports 20 and 21; TFTP is an application that operates based on UDP port 69. Protocol numbers link the Network Layer to the Transport Layer, whereas service access points (SAPs) or type codes link the Layer 2 frame to point to Layer 3. You can access an excellent site for details on protocol and port numbers by the layers at www.networksorcery.com/enp/topic/ipsuite.htm.

Layer 3: The Network Layer

Layer 3, the Network Layer, is where routers or Layer 3 switches operate. By the way, Layer 3 switches are routers, and Layer 2 switches are bridges. Path determination and routing is all about moving things from one place to another. You do it every day with the telephone, mail, planes, trains, cars, boats, busses, subways, and so on. Do you take the fastest route, the best roads, the scenic route, or do you figure it out as you go? The routing table directs the packets as to where to go and drops them in the bit bucket if it doesn't know what to do with them. Do you use a map (link-state rou**ting** protocols) or do you just stop at the gas stations along the way (distance vector rou**ting** protocols)? Either way, your car or other form of transportation (rout**ed** protocol such as IP or IPX) carries you (the data) and any upper-layer instructions (headers) hop-by-hop to your destination. The router strips off the old framing (Layer 2 packaging) and re-encapsulates the packet for the outbound interface according to the destination IP address in the data packet header. Layer 2 addresses change from hop-to-hop, but the Layer 3 addresses stay the same assuming normal destination-based routing.

NOTE   According to the ISO documents, rou**ting** protocols stand outside the basic protocol stack in a management plane and provide management services for the Network Layer. Although this discussion focuses on the OSI model as a model, it is more than just any old model. It is a set of ISO documents. Spend the money and read the ISO documents. Alternately, for a small fee you can subscribe to www.certificationzone.com for some very comprehensive OSI study guides by Howard Berkowitz and Katherine Tallis.

As displayed in Figure 1-4, routers route using a hop-to-hop relay system to get packets one step closer to their destination. Routers accept a frame on one interface, strip off the Layer 2 header, and select an outbound interface closer to the destination. The router adds a new Layer 2 header (re-encapsulates the packet) and switches (forwards) from the inbound interface to the outbound interface within the router to transmit the packet.

Figure 1-4   *Routing and Switching Process (Within the Router)*

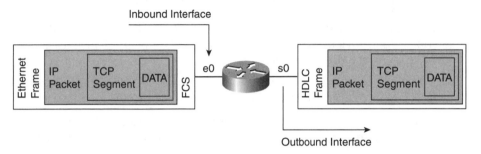

Figure 1-4 illustrates how the router accepts the Ethernet frame on inbound interface e0 and strips off the Layer 2 Ethernet frame leaving the upper-layer data intact. According to the destination IP address in the IP header, the router does a route table lookup to see which outbound interface will get the packet closer to its destination network. The router adds a new Layer 2 header to encapsulate the data and forwards it to its next hop. Next-hop reachability is not only a key point in getting packets to their destination network, it is also a key point in troubleshooting.

Routers *route* to the destination network address. They buffer and *switch* packets from the inbound interface to the outbound interface within the router. Performance is definitely affected by the switching type. *Fast switching* refers to when a router does a route table lookup for the first packet toward a destination and caches it so that it doesn't have to perform a route table lookup on each and every packet. (Imagine the overhead if a router actually performs a route table lookup on each and every packet, which is called *process switching* and is used when you perform such tasks as debug commands.) Newer devices offer Cisco Express Forwarding (CEF) as a switching type, whereby even the first packet gets cached. Remember these important points: Routers *route* hop-to-hop, and routers *switch* from the inbound interface to the outbound interface of the router at Layer 3. Chapters 6, "Shooting Trouble with CatOS and IOS," and 7, "Shooting Trouble with VLANs on Routers and Switches," discuss switching types (architectures) in more detail.

Much activity occurs at Layer 3. IP, the connectionless Internet Protocol, is the heart of TCP/ IP-based applications. Connectionless is unplanned and without prior coordination (as is UDP at Layer 4). Each packet stands alone; no negotiation occurs. Think about this when you travel to various locations and mail postcards to people you haven't seen for a while.

IP and IPX are rout**ed** protocols responsible for delivery of packets, including rout**ing** protocol packets that are based on IP and IPX respectively. Rout**ing** protocols exchange routes with other routers. Rout**ed** protocols deliver packets; they send user data. This section briefly reviews rout**ing**/rout**ed** protocols for troubleshooting purposes.

NOTE	Refer to the book *CCNP Practical Studies: Routing* (Cisco Press) or ACRC/BSCN/BSCI-related courses and books for more details on routing protocols. Although they all have good information, Building Switched Cisco Internetworks (BSCI) replaces Building Scalable Cisco Networks (BSCN), which replaced Advanced Cisco Router Configuration (ACRC).

Routed protocols transport packets through routers. Routing is a relay system, a hop-by-hop paradigm from one network to another. Routers filter based on Layer 3 logical network addresses. The router strips and rebuilds the Layer 2 framing according to the outbound interface. Route filters, such as access control lists (ACLs), distribution lists, route maps, and prefix lists, allow further filtering.

TCP handles end-to-end connectivity, whereas the transport of the data is handled by the connectionless IP. Each router from the source to the destination makes a decision.

Rout**ing** protocols *route* rout**ed** protocols. Rout**ing** protocols give directions; rout**ed** protocols carry the data. Rout**ing** protocols are used by routers to exchange data. Table 1-3 gives a brief comparison of routing protocols.

Besides learning from routing protocols, routers know about directly connected routes. Directly connected routes are like your arms and legs; they are attached networks. Basically, the router needs driving directions just as you and I need them. For example, you know where your immediate family and friends live. They might be in the same state, town, or even on the same street. You can also learn of other locations; perhaps the location you're looking for is right next door (directly connected routes), perhaps you look up an address on a website such as Yahoo! Maps (link-state routing protocols), or perhaps someone else gives you directions (distance vector routing protocols).

Table 1-3   *Routing Protocol Comparison*

Feature	IP RIP	IGRP	EIGRP	OSPF	IS-IS	BGP
Open or Proprietary	Open	Proprietary	Proprietary	Open, but IP support only	Open	Open
Network size	Small	Medium	Large	Large	Very Large	Very Large
Distance vector or link state	Distance vector (Routing by rumor)	Distance vector (Routing by rumor)	Advance distance vector (hybrid) (Routing by rumor)	Link-state (Routing by map)	Link-state (Routing by rumor)	Path vector (Routing between autonomous systems)
Interior or exterior	IGP	IGP	IGP	IGP	IGP	EGP
Updates	30-second broadcast updates RIPv2 is 224.0.0.9	90-second broadcast updates	Triggered updates 224.0.0.10	224.0.0.5 224.0.0.6 Link-state packets	Triggered updates Link-state Packets	Triggered unicast updates

Table 1-3   *Routing Protocol Comparison (Continued)*

Feature	IP RIP	IGRP	EIGRP	OSPF	IS-IS	BGP
Port or protocol number	UDP port 520	Protocol number 9	Protocol number 88	Protocol number 89	Protocol I CLNP (81) ES-ES (82) IS-IS (83) IP (CC)	TCP port 179
Administrative distance	120	100	90/170	110	115	200/20
Metrics	Hop count	Bandwidth Delay Reliability Load MTU (**Big Dogs Really Like Meat**)	Bandwidth Delay Reliability Load MTU (**Big Dogs Really Like Meat**)	Cost	Default (optional) Delay Expense Error	Attributes: Weight Local pref MED Origin AS-path Next-hop Community Others
Algorithm	Bellman-Ford algorithm	Bellman-Ford algorithm	DUAL algorithm	Dijkstra/SPF* algorithm	Dijkstra/ S algorithm	Shortest AS* path
Support for VLSM* and summarization	VLSM and summarization (in RIPv2)	N/A	VLSM and summarization Automatic classful summarization by default Manual summarization per interface	VLSM and summarization Manual summarization at ABR*/ ASBR* only	VLSM and summarization	VLSM and summarization

*AS = Autonomous system   ABR = Area Border Router
SPF = Shortest Path First   VLSM = Variable-Length Subnet Masking
ASBR = Autonomous System Boundary Router (or Border)

The routing table is also populated by static and default routes, which are not always automatically propagated to other routers by default. Default routes are very useful in stub network scenarios where there is only one way in and one way out. Static and default routes can eliminate routing update traffic in many cases—but don't be tricked into packets getting sent but not returned because they don't have a return route.

At this point in your CCNP preparation, you should be very comfortable with routing, IP addressing, subnetting, and summarizing. The labs in later chapters will certainly determine whether you have mastered these concepts. In the meantime, some IP examples appear here for your review.

IP version 4 mathematically allows for 4.2 billion addresses (2^{32}). Base 2, 32-bit, dotted-decimal addresses such as 172.16.1.1 are used. Figure 1-5 shows all 4 octets, which are comprised of a total of 32 bits (8 bits each). It is common to see the subnet mask listed as /*number* in the routing table to illustrate the number of network bits in the mask (as shown in the bitwise notation row). The next row is a power of two for the binary place value. The last row is the decimal equivalent or base 10 representation of the binary place value above it. Use a graphic such as this to assist you with subnetting and summarizing.

Figure 1-5   *Binary Place Values*

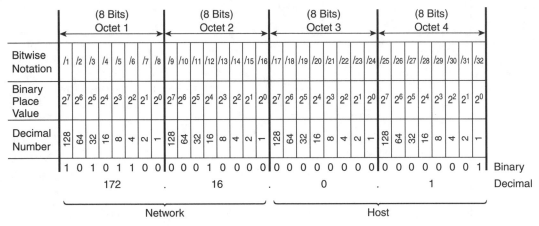

NOTE   IP version 4 addresses are in a 4-octet, dotted-decimal, 32-bit format, whereas version 6 is 128 bits written as 8 groups of 4 hex digits separated by colons (such as 0000:AAAA:1111:BBBB:2222:CCCC:3333:DDDD).

By the way, IP version 4 still has a long life ahead of it because of address-exhaustion solutions such as private addresses, proxy servers, Network Address Translation (NAT), and Classless Interdomain Routing (CIDR). For a valid public address, contact your ISP or www.arin.net in the Americas for details. ARIN is one of the three regional internet registries the authority in the U.S. RIPE NCC is for Europe, the Middle East, North Africa, and parts of Asia. APNIC is the Asia Pacific Network Information Centre.

Private addresses are not routed on the Internet and fall within the following ranges:

- 10.0.0.0/8

- 172.16.0.0 through 172.31.0.0/12

- 192.168.0.0 through 192.168.255.0/16

NOTE   Private addresses are used throughout the rest of the chapters so that I don't step on anyone's toes.

Table 1-4 displays Class A, B, and C addresses, which are available for hosts, and also shows Class D and E addresses, which are reserved for other purposes. Notice the pattern of **0, 10, 110** in the first octet binary range. You may be familiar with the Jackson 5 "A-B-C" song; the first octet follows that tune precisely: "A-B-C, it's easy as 1-2-3…" where the 1-2-3 is the bit position of the 0. (Thank you Glenn Tapley.)

Table 1-4   *Classes, Masks, Networks, and Hosts*

Class	First Octet Binary Range	First Octet Decimal Range	Default or Natural Mask	Number of Networks	Number of Hosts
A	00000001 01111111	1–127*	/8 255.0.0.0	126 $2^7 - 2$	16,777,214 $2^{24} - 2$ $(256 \times 256 \times 256) - 2$
B	10000000 10111111	128–191	/16 255.255.0.0	16,384 2^{14}	65,534 $2^{16} - 2$ $(256 \times 256) - 2$
C	11000000 11011111	192–223	/24 255.255.255.0	2,097,152 2^{21}	254 $2^8 - 2$ $(256) - 2$
D	11100000 11101111	224–239	Multicast		
E	11110000 11111111	240–255	Experimental		

* 127.0.0.0/8 denotes loopback addressing

Table 1-4 illustrates the classes of networks. It is essential to recognize the class by the first octet range so that you are familiar with the default or natural mask. When subnetting, you must borrow bits from the host portion; if you know the default mask, the host portion is where the 0 bits are. For example, 10.0.0.1/8 is a Class A address with a default subnet mask of 255.0.0.0 or /8. If you need more networks, you subnet by borrowing the required number of bits from the host octets 2, 3, and 4 contiguously. To determine the number of bits to borrow, use the following formula:

$2^x >=$ the number of subnets you need

Solve for *x* to know how many bits to borrow. It is not wrong to use the formula $2^x - 2$, but the minus 2 is for the 0 subnet and the all 1s subnet (broadcast), which are certainly valid today. Suppose you need 250 subnets. The formula to solve is $2^x >= 250$. In this example, you borrow 8 bits to give you a new subnet mask of 255.255.0.0 or /16. The class is still a Class A, however, not a Class B.

Default subnet masks, class ranges, networks, hosts, and their associated logical addresses are important practical topics that will help you with troubleshooting. Shortcuts are nice, but the binary really tells all. Check out www.learntosubnet.com for a refresher on subnetting and Chapter 3 of this book for practical application thereof. In the meantime, look at a couple of examples of subnetting and summarization here. Practice makes perfect, and Cisco tests aren't as lenient as others in allowing you to use a calculator. Use Figure 1-5 and Table 1-4 to assist in your calculations.

1 How many hosts are on 172.16.0.0/16? What are they?

Answer: 172.16.0.0 is one big network (broadcast domain) with 65,534 hosts ($2^{16} - 2$). The first host is 172.16.0.1. The last host is 172.16.255.254, and the broadcast is 172.16.255.255. The binary representation of this is critical to understanding bits and boundaries. Often it is helpful to write out the hosts in ranges, such as the following:

- 172.16.0.1 through 172.16.0.255

- 172.16.1.0 through 172.16.1.255

- 172.16.2.0 through 172.16.2.255

- ...

- 172.16.255.0 through 172.16.255.254

- 172.16.255.255 (broadcast)

Figure 1-6 illustrates the calculations using binary place values. Notice how the first host is the network address plus one; the broadcast address is the same as turning all bits on (1) for the hosts portion; and the last host is the broadcast address minus one.

Figure 1-6 *Binary Place Values (Question 1 Answer)*

	Octet 1 (8 Bits)	Octet 2 (8 Bits)	Octet 3 (8 Bits)	Octet 4 (8 Bits)	
Bitwise Notation	/1 /2 /3 /4 /5 /6 /7 /8	/9 /10 /11 /12 /13 /14 /15 /16	/17 /18 /19 /20 /21 /22 /23 /24	/25 /26 /27 /28 /29 /30 /31 /32	Mask (Bitwise)
Binary Place Value	2^7 2^6 2^5 2^4 2^3 2^2 2^1 2^0	2^7 2^6 2^5 2^4 2^3 2^2 2^1 2^0	2^7 2^6 2^5 2^4 2^3 2^2 2^1 2^0	2^7 2^6 2^5 2^4 2^3 2^2 2^1 2^0	
Decimal Number	128 64 32 16 8 4 2 1	128 64 32 16 8 4 2 1	128 64 32 16 8 4 2 1	128 64 32 16 8 4 2 1	
Network	1 0 1 0 1 1 0 0	0 0 0 1 0 0 0 0	0 0 0 0 0 0 0 0	0 0 0 0 0 0 0 0	
	172	16	0	0	

Network (Broadcast Domain) | Hosts $2^{16} - 2 = 65,534$

172.16.0.1 → 0 0 0 0 0 0 0 0 . 0 0 0 0 0 0 0 1 First Host
172.16.255.254 → 1 1 1 1 1 1 1 1 . 1 1 1 1 1 1 1 0 Last Host
172.16.255.255 → 1 1 1 1 1 1 1 1 . 1 1 1 1 1 1 1 1 Broadcast

2 How many networks and hosts are on 172.16.0.0/24? What are they?

Answer: 172.16.0.0 is 1 subnet (broadcast domain) with 254 hosts ($2^8 - 2$). The first host for this subnet is 172.16.0.1. The last host for this subnet is 172.16.0.254, and the broadcast address is 172.16.0.255. The binary representation of this is critical to understanding bits and boundaries. Often it is helpful to write out the hosts in ranges, such as the following:

- 172.16.0.1 through 172.16.0.254 (hosts on subnet 172.16.0.0/24)

- 172.16.0.255 (broadcast on subnet 172.16.0.0/24)

This is a Class B address with a default subnet mask of /16. The given mask is /24, which means that 8 host bits were borrowed to provide more networks (subnets). This is subnetting. There are $2^8 = 256$ available subnets in this scenario with 254 hosts ($2^8 - 2$) on each one. These subnets increment by 1 because the lowest 1 (network) bit is in the 1 or 2^0 binary position. The next two subnets are 172.16.1.0/24 and 172.16.2.0/24.

Use Figure 1-7 to verify your calculations and to relate the following general rules:

- The rightmost available host bit is turned on (1) for the first host. All other host bits are off (0).

- The rightmost available host bit is turned off (0) for the last host. All other host bits are on (1).

- All host bits are on (1) for the broadcast address. The broadcast for a subnet is one less than the next subnet.

- Subnets increment by the lowest 1 bit (rightmost bit) in the mask. The subnet increment and the first two subnets are circled in Figure 1-7.

Figure 1-7 *Binary Place Values (Question 2 Answer)*

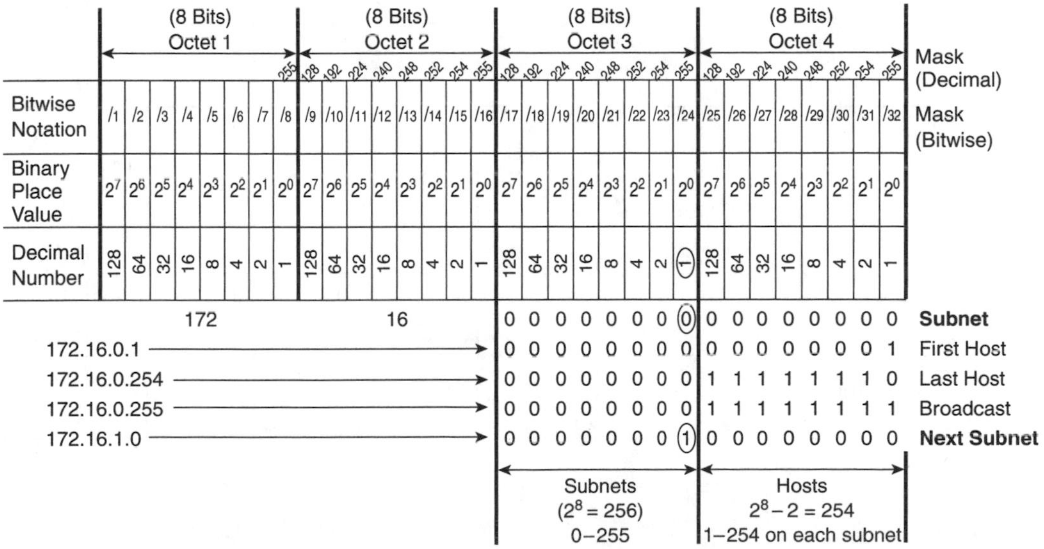

> **3** How many networks and hosts are on 172.16.1.4/30? What are they? What is the next available subnet?

Answer: 172.16.1.4 is one subnet (broadcast domain) with two hosts ($2^2 - 2$). The first host for this subnet is 172.16.1.5. The last host for this subnet is 172.16.1.6, and the broadcast address is 172.16.1.7. The binary representation of this is critical to understanding bits and boundaries. Often it is helpful to write out the hosts in ranges, such as the following:

- 172.16.1.5 through 172.16.1.6 (hosts on subnet 172.16.1.4/30)

- 172.16.1.7 (broadcast on subnet 172.16.1.4/30)

- 172.16.1.8/30 (next subnet)

This is a Class B address with a default subnet mask of /16. The given mask is /30, which means that 14 host bits were borrowed to give more networks (subnets). This is subnetting. There are $2^{14} = 16,384$ possible subnets in this scenario with 2 hosts ($2^2 - 2$) on each one. The subnet increment is circled in Table 1-5. These subnets increment by 4 because the lowest 1 (network) bit is in the 4 or 2^2 binary position. The next two subnets are 172.16.1.8/30 and 172.16.1.12/30. The shading in Table 1-5 indicates the subnet portion. Only the last octet is shown.

Table 1-5 *Binary Place Values for the Last Octet (Question 3 Answer)*

Subnet	Subnet	Subnet	Subnet	Subnet	Subnet	Hosts	Hosts	
/25	**/26**	**/27**	**/28**	**/29**	**/30**	**/31**	**/32**	**Mask (Bitwise)**
128	192	224	240	248	252	254	255	Mask (Decimal)
2^7	2^6	2^5	2^4	2^3	2^2	2^1	2^0	**Binary**
128	64	32	16	8	④	2	1	Subnet increment
0	0	0	0	0	1	0	0	(Subnet) **172.16.1.4**
0	0	0	0	0	1	0	1	(First host) 172.16.1.5
0	0	0	0	0	1	1	0	(Last host) 172.16.1.6
0	0	0	0	0	1	1	1	(Broadcast) 172.16.1.7
0	0	0	0	1	0	0	0	(Subnet) **172.16.1.8**
0	0	0	0	1	0	0	1	(First host) 172.16.1.9

Table 1-5   *Binary Place Values for the Last Octet (Question 3 Answer) (Continued)*

Subnet	Subnet	Subnet	Subnet	Subnet	Subnet	Hosts	Hosts	
0	0	0	0	1	0	1	0	(Last host) 172.16.1.10
0	0	0	0	1	0	1	1	(Broadcast) 172.16.1.11
0	0	0	0	1	1	0	0	(Subnet) **172.16.1.12**

4 How many networks and hosts are on 10.1.1.0/28? What are they? List the hosts and broadcast address for the next available subnet.

Answer: 10.1.1.0 is 1 subnet (broadcast domain) with 14 hosts ($2^4 - 2$). The first host for this subnet is 10.1.1.1. The last host for this subnet is 10.1.1.14, and the broadcast address is 10.1.1.15. The binary representation of this is critical to understanding bits and boundaries. Often it is helpful to write out the hosts in ranges, such as the following:

- 10.1.1.1 through 10.1.1.14 (hosts on subnet 10.1.1.0/28)

- 10.1.1.15 (broadcast on subnet 10.1.1.0/28)

- 10.1.1.16 (next subnet)

- 10.1.1.17 through 10.1.1.30 (hosts on subnet 10.1.1.16/28)

- 10.1.1.31 (broadcast on subnet 10.1.1.16/28)

- 10.1.1.32 (next subnet)

This is a Class A address with a default subnet mask of /8. The given mask is /28, which means that 20 host bits were borrowed to give more networks. This is subnetting. There are $2^{20} = 1,048,576$ possible subnets in this scenario with 14 hosts ($2^4 - 2$) on each one. These subnets increment by 16 because the lowest 1 (network) bit is in the 16 (2^4) binary position. The next two subnets are 10.1.1.16/28 and 10.1.1.32/28. The shading in Table 1-6 indicates the subnet portion. Only the last octet is shown.

NOTE   If you have ever taken any of my classes, you know that all 4 octets with all 32 bits get drawn on the board first. Then I write out only the octets where the mask is less than 255 or 8 bits. One student suggested I actually write the last 2 octets on the back of my business card and hand them out to future students.

Table 1-6 *Binary Place Values for the Last Octet (Question 4)*

Subnet /25	Subnet /26	Subnet /27	Subnet /28	Hosts /29	Hosts /30	Hosts /31	Hosts /32	Mask (Bitwise)
128	192	224	240	248	252	254	255	Mask (Decimal)
2^7	2^6	2^5	2^4	2^3	2^2	2^1	2^0	**Binary**
128	64	32	⑯	8	4	2	1	Subnet increment
0	0	0	**0**	0	0	0	0	(Subnet) **10.1.1.0**
0	0	0	**0**	0	0	0	1	(First host) 10.1.1.1
0	0	0	**0**	1	1	1	0	(Last host) 10.1.1.14
0	0	0	**0**	1	1	1	1	(Broadcast) 10.1.1.15
0	0	0	**1**	0	0	0	0	(Subnet) **10.1.1.16**
0	0	0	**1**	0	0	0	1	(First host) 10.1.1.17
0	0	0	**1**	1	1	1	0	(Last host) 10.1.1.30
0	0	0	**1**	1	1	1	1	(Broadcast) 10.1.1.31
0	0	**1**	**0**	0	0	0	0	(Subnet) **10.1.1.32**

5 Assuming you have all point-to-point serial links to assign addresses to and that you are given the network 10.1.1.0/28, can you squeeze any more subnets out of it? If so, how many and what are they? What is this called?

Answer: VLSM is just subnetting again. You move the bit boundary to the right to get more subnets. In this example, the subnet boundary is at /28. Because point-to-point serial links never need more than 2 host addresses, you can borrow out to a /30 or 255.255.255.252 subnet mask. This gives $2^2 = 4$ VLSM subnets (0, 4, 8, and 12) with 2 hosts each. *Caution*: No overlap is allowed with VLSM! If subnet 0 has already been assigned, for instance, you *cannot* subnet that subnet. VLSM is common practice on WAN links, but the routing protocol must support it.

- 10.1.1.0/30 (VLSM subnet)

- 10.1.1.4/30 (VLSM subnet)

- 10.1.1.8/30 (VLSM subnet)

- 10.1.1.12/30 (VLSM subnet)

Table 1-7 illustrates subnet 10.1.1.0/28, its VLSM subnets (0, 4, 8, 12), and its hosts. The first host on VLSM subnet 0 is 10.1.1.1/30, for example, the last host is 10.1.1.2/30, and the broadcast is 10.1.1.3.30. The next VLSM subnet is 10.1.1.4/30. Its first host is 10.1.1.5, the last host is 10.1.1.6/30, and the broadcast is 10.1.1.7/30. The next VLSM subnet is 10.1.1.8/30 and so on. The lighter shading indicates subnets, and the darker shading indicates VLSM subnets.

Table 1-7   *Binary Place Values for the Last Octet (Question 5)*

Subnet	Subnet	Subnet	Subnet	VLSM Subnet	VLSM Subnet	Hosts	Hosts	
/25	**/26**	**/27**	**/28**	**/29**	**/30**	**/31**	**/32**	**Mask (Bitwise)**
128	192	224	240	248	252	254	255	Mask (Decimal)
2^7	**2^6**	**2^5**	**2^4**	**2^3**	**2^2**	**2^1**	**2^0**	**Binary**
128	64	32	16	8	④	2	1	Subnet increment
0	0	0	0	0	0	0	0	(Subnet) **10.1.1.0**
0	0	0	0	0	0	0	1	(First host) 10.1.1.1
0	0	0	0	0	0	1	0	(Last host) 10.1.1.2
0	0	0	0	0	0	1	1	(Broadcast) 10.1.1.3
0	0	0	0	0	1	0	0	(Subnet) **10.1.1.4**
0	0	0	0	0	1	0	1	(First host) 10.1.1.5
0	0	0	0	0	1	1	0	(Last host) 10.1.1.6
0	0	0	0	0	1	1	1	(Broadcast) 10.1.1.7
0	0	0	0	1	0	0	0	(Subnet) **10.1.1.8**

Table 1-7 *Binary Place Values for the Last Octet (Question 5) (Continued)*

Subnet	Subnet	Subnet	Subnet	VLSM Subnet	VLSM Subnet	Hosts	Hosts	
0	0	0	0	1	0	0	1	(First host) 10.1.1.9
0	0	0	0	1	0	1	0	(Last host) 10.1.1.10
0	0	0	0	1	0	1	1	(Broadcast) 10.1.1.11
0	0	0	0	1	1	0	0	(Subnet) **10.1.1.12**
0	0	0	0	1	1	0	1	(First host) 10.1.1.13
0	0	0	0	1	1	1	0	(Last host) 10.1.1.14
0	0	0	0	0	0	1	1	(Broadcast) 10.1.1.15

6 Summarize the following into the fewest number of statements possible.

- 192.168.168.0/24
- 192.168.169.0/24
- 192.168.170.0/24
- 192.168.171.0/24
- 192.168.172.0/24
- 192.168.173.0/24
- 192.168.174.0/24
- 192.168.175.0/24

Answer: 192.168.168.0/21

Table 1-8 illustrates the third octet in binary so that you can easily identify the best pattern as to summarize in the fewest number of statements. As the darker shading shows, all bits match from bit /1 through /21; therefore you can capture eight lines into one. Although not as efficient, you can summarize using two statements (192.168.168.0/22 and 192.168.172.0/22) or four statements (192.168.168.0/23, 192.168.170.0/23, 192.168.172.0/23, and 192.168.174.0/23).

Table 1-8 *Summarization (Question 6 Answer)*

Mask (Bitwise)	/17	/18	/19	/20	/21	/22	/23	/24
Mask (Decimal)	128	192	224	240	248	252	254	255
Binary Place Value	2^7	2^6	2^5	2^4	2^3	2^2	2^1	2^0
Decimal Number	128	64	32	16	8	4	2	1
168	1	0	1	0	1	0	0	0
169	1	0	1	0	1	0	0	1
170	1	0	1	0	1	0	1	0
171	1	0	1	0	1	0	1	1
172	1	0	1	0	1	1	0	0
173	1	0	1	0	1	1	0	1
174	1	0	1	0	1	1	1	0
175	1	0	1	0	1	1	1	1

NOTE   If you think you need more review and practical application of subnetting, see Chapter 3. Additionally, review the *CCNA Practical Studies* and *CCNP Practical Studies: Routing* titles as well as the www.learntosubnet.com website.

So what else happens at Layer 3? IP is responsible for delivery and fragmentation at Layer 3 and it has various helper protocols to accomplish these tasks. Internet Control Message Protocol (ICMP) is for status and error reporting. Address Resolution Protocol (ARP) resolves an IP address to MAC on a broadcast-based network such as a LAN. Network cards and router interfaces have burned-in addresses (BIAs) for the MAC. By the way, ARP is not needed for IPX addressing because the MAC is the host address on the wire in Novell. ARP is also not required on point-to-point media either. ARP is initiated with a local broadcast, but the reply is a unicast. Think of it this way: I have the IP, but I need the MAC. You experiment and learn a little more about ARP in Chapter 3 in the section titled "Protocols and Packets." Until then, think about what would happen in the following circumstances:

- **Local ARP request**—If you were to ping a host on a local network and look at the ARP cache (**arp –a**), what would you expect to see?

- **Remote ARP request**—If you were to ping a host on a different network and look at the ARP cache, what would you expect to see?

I would expect to see the host MAC address for the destination host in the ARP table for a local ARP request. If I were to ping a host on a different network and look at the ARP cache, however, I would expect to see the MAC address associated with the local interface of the router (default gateway). Learning to follow the ARP is quite beneficial in troubleshooting.

Now turn your attention to RARP, which sounds like something out of the TV show *Mork & Mindy*. RARP is Reverse Address Resolution Protocol. First there was RARP, then BOOTP, and now DHCP too. You explore DHCP in one of the later labs.

NOTE   The Transport Layer is often referred to as the host-to-host layer and the Network Layer as the Internet layer. If you can't ping the destination host but can ping another local host and your default gateway, the problem may be in the path from the source to the destination. Use **traceroute** (**tracert**) to help you determine exactly where the problem is.

Layer 2: The Data Link Layer

Layer 2, the Data Link Layer, is where bridges and switches operate. Bridges and switches are covered in much more detail in Chapters 5, 6, and 7.

The IEEE Layer 2-defined sublayers include Logical Link Control (LLC) and Media Access Control (MAC) as represented in Figure 1-8. LLC is responsible for synchronization and connection services via Service Access Points (SAPs) to the upper layers. MAC is responsible for physical (hardware) addressing, logical topology, and shared media access.

Digital Intel Xerox (DIX) Ethernet II uses a Type field to point to the Layer 3 protocol (0800 is IP), but IEEE 802.3 Ethernet uses a valid length field and 802.2 LLC SAPs to link to the Layer 3 protocol. SAPs are pointers or software controls to manage multiple Layer 3 protocols. For example, the hex SAP value of 06 is a link to IP; the hex SAP value of e0 is a link to IPX. Table 1-9 provides more detail on LLC types.

Table 1-9   *LLC Types*

LLC Type	Connection	Reliability	Description
LLC Type 1	Connectionless	Unacknowledged	Does not confirm data transfers Used in LANs
LLC Type 2	Connection-oriented	Acknowledged	Establishes logical connection and confirms data upon receipt Used in IBM SNA
LLC Type 3	Connectionless	Acknowledged	Confirms data upon receipt but does not establish logical connection Used in factory automation

Figure 1-8   *LLC and MAC*

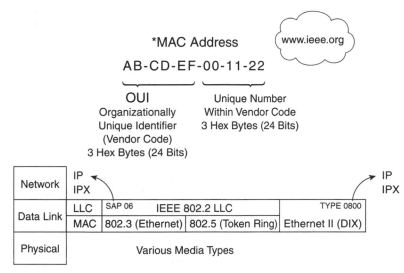

*48 Bits/12 Hex Characters/6 Hex Bytes

IEEE-assigned MAC addresses are often referred to as hardware addresses, Layer 2 addresses, BIAs, or physical addresses that are coded into the network card or interface on a router. A 3-byte IEEE-assigned Organizationally Unique Identifier (OUI) is used to generate universal MAC addresses for vendors. Table 1-10 offers some examples from Cisco, 3Com, Intel, DEC, and Madge. This is not by any means a comprehensive list; see www.ieee.org for more details. Download them all in a text file from standards.ieee.org/regauth/oui/oui.txt.

Table 1-10   *IEEE-Assigned MAC Addresses*

Vendor	Identification (OUI)
Cisco	00-00-0C
	00-01-42
	00-01-43
	00-01-63
	00-01-64
	00-E0-F7
	00-E0-F9
	00-E0-FE
	08-00-58

Table 1-10   *IEEE-Assigned MAC Addresses (Continued)*

Vendor	Identification (OUI)
3Com	00-01-02
	00-01-03
	02-C0-8C
	08-00-4E
Intel	00-01-2A
	00-02-B3
	00-AA-01
	00-AA-02
DEC	AA-00-00
	AA-00-01
	AA-00-02
	AA-00-03
	AA-00-04
Madge	00-00-6F
	00-00-C1
	00-80-E9

The MAC sublayer is for taking turns on the wire as well as error checking and addressing. It is like the traffic cop on the medium. Table 1-11 provides a brief review of access methods.

Table 1-11   *Access Methods*

Access Method	Description	Examples
CSMA/CD*	Polite conversation at a cocktail party. You listen (carrier sense) and if you and another person talk simultaneously (multiple access), you both wait a random amount of time and talk again.	Ethernet II IEEE Ethernet 802.3
CSMA/CA**	Collision avoidance Signal the intent to transmit	AppleTalk
Token Passing	Must hold the token to talk	IBM Token Ring IEEE 802.5 Token Ring ANSI X3T9.5 FDDI

*CSMA/CD = Carrier sense multiple access with collision detection

**CSMA/CA = Carrier sense multiple access with collision avoidance

Ethernet, whether a physical star or bus, uses the carrier sense multiple access collision detect (CSMA/CD) logical access method because logically it acts like a bus. Token Ring and FDDI use a token-passing access method in a logical ring topology over a physical star or ring. Collisions do not occur in Token Ring because a device must have the token to talk. Access methods are nothing you and I set; they are a function of the network architecture, such as Ethernet or Token Ring, that allows devices to share the media.

Topologies encompass the Data Link (logical) and Physical Layers. Ethernet is typically a physical star, logical bus; whereas Token Ring is a physical star, logical ring topology. (See Figure 1-9.)

Figure 1-9   *Topology*

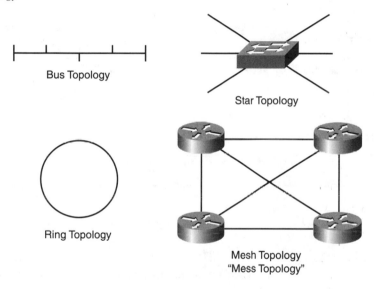

The PDU for Layer 2 is frames. Control bits mark the beginning and end of frames just as picture frames mark the edges of a picture. Layer 2 is the LAN/WAN layer in many respects. You have seen how it allows different devices to take turns on the media and how the network works (logical topologies). But how is the data actually packaged at Layer 2? Figures 1-10 (Ethernet), 1-11 (Token Ring), and 1-12 (FDDI) show some basic frame format (encapsulation) examples. Use the following legend for the abbreviations:

PRE = Preamble

DA = Destination address

SA = Source address

T/L = Type or length

FCS = Frame check sequence

DEL = Delimiter

FS = Frame status

Figure 1-10 *Ethernet Frame Format*

Ethernet Frame Format					
PRE	DA	SA	T/L	DATA	FCS

Figure 1-11 *Token Ring Frame Format*

Token Ring Frame Format							
START DEL	ACCESS CTRL	FRAME CTRL	DA	SA	DATA	FCS	END DEL

Figure 1-12 *FDDI Frame Format*

FDDI Format								
PRE	START DEL	FRAME CTRL	DA	SA	DATA	FCS	END DEL	FS

NOTE   Ethernet dominates typical LAN topologies today and is further discussed in Chapter 5.

While I discuss other Layer 2 activities, think back to the earlier analogy of the waiter who took your order. Did you get the big-endian cheesecake or the little-endian cheesecake…ekaceseehc for desert? *Big-endian* systems, such as IBM, RISC, and Motorola processors, read left to right, or high-order to low-order bits and bytes. *Little-endian* systems, such as Intel processors and DEC Alphas, read right to left, or low-order to high-order bits and bytes. Likewise, Ethernet is canonical and Token Ring is noncanonical. Use Table 1-12 to review the hex calculations (base 16) used in Figure 1-13. Also remember that A = 10, B = 11, C = 12, D = 13, E = 14, and F = 15 in hexadecimal.

Table 1-12   *Hex Place Values*

2^3	2^2	2^1	2^0	2^3	2^2	2^1	2^0
8	4	2	1	8	4	2	1

NOTE   According to www.whatis.com, "Big-endian and little-endian derive from Jonathan Swift's *Gulliver's Travels* in which the Big Endians were a political faction that broke their eggs at the large end ("the primitive way") and rebelled against the Lilliputian King who required his subjects (the Little Endians) to break their eggs at the small end."

Figure 1-13   *Canonical Names*

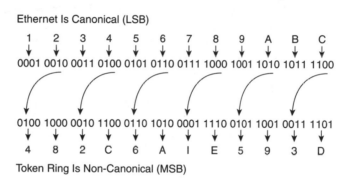

Ethernet Is Canonical (LSB)

1 2 3 4 5 6 7 8 9 A B C

0001 0010 0011 0100 0101 0110 0111 1000 1001 1010 1011 1100

0100 1000 0010 1100 0110 1010 0001 1110 0101 1001 0011 1101

4 8 2 C 6 A I E 5 9 3 D

Token Ring Is Non-Canonical (MSB)

*Hexadecimal 0–9, A–F

Figure 1-13 illustrates that Ethernet is canonical, and the least significant bit (LSB) is read first. In contrast, Token Ring is noncanonical, and the most significant bit (MSB) is read first. The picture also is a great review of binary-to-hex conversion, but most people use calculators for that anyhow.

NOTE   Cisco offers a tool on their website that enables you to automatically convert canonical to noncanonical and vice versa. Search for the "bitswap tool" on www.cisco.com to see for yourself.

Layer 1: The Physical Layer

Layer 1, the Physical Layer, is all about the shape of the network. How things work is more a matter of Layer 2 logical topologies, but Layer 1 is concerned with physical topologies such as star, bus, ring, or mesh. Ethernet is typically a physical star, logical bus (10BASE-T/100BASE-T/1000BASE-T). Token Ring and FDDI are typically wired as a physical star, logical ring. Without a concentrator, FDDI is truly a physical ring topology.

Hubs are Layer 1 devices that repeat or regenerate the signal to allow connectivity and assist with attenuation issues. Layer 1 devices just extend the network; they do no filtering. Hubs spit bits, including collisions and broadcasts. Switches (Layer 2 devices) assist with collisions and make filtering decisions based on physical addresses. Routers (Layer 3 devices or VLANs) assist with collisions and broadcasts; they make filtering decisions based on logical addresses. A collision domain is a separate CSMA/CD network in Ethernet or a separate ring in Token Ring where devices are taking turns for use of the wire. Collision domains exist between two Layer 2 devices and for each user-dedicated port on a switch. Broadcast domains are subnets in TCP/IP. They exist between routers and for each Layer 3 interface. Figure 1-14 shows collision domains and broadcast domains. Technically there are no collisions on the serial links, so you shouldn't count them as collision domains as you examine Figure 1-14.

Figure 1-14 *Collision and Broadcast Domains*

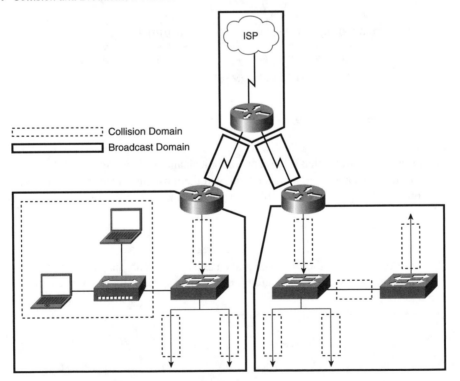

*The broadcast domains assume one VLAN per switch here.

Hubs with any intelligence at all (such as multiple speeds or network management capabilities) are not just Layer 1 devices; they move up the OSI stack according to the built-in intelligence. Most people know hub and repeater as the same thing; however, repeater is an IEEE term. When selecting a hub or any connectivity device for that matter, consider network architecture (such as Ethernet or Token Ring, or FDDI; port density and speed; management; cable types; and modularity).

Physical star topologies are easier to troubleshoot but take more cable. Failure of one device doesn't usually interfere with another. If a user calls and says the network is down, you can start your troubleshooting between the user and the hub or switch port connection. Switches are typically used rather than hubs today because the price per port is declining all the time. The big advantage is that each port is a separate collision domain; whereas all hub ports are in the same collision domain. After all, you don't need too many packet fights. Cat5E unshielded twisted-pair cable is still by far the most common.

Frozen yellow garden hose and vampire taps come to mind when I think of the old 10BASE5 Ethernet backbones using RG-8 or RG-11 standard Ethernet coax cable rated at 50-ohms impedance. 10BASE2 could be a bus or star depending on whether hubs are in the picture. Think of a two-pole clothesline setup on which you hang your clothes out to dry. The poles at each end are the terminators connecting one of the RG-58 family of cables. Although inexpensive to implement, the disadvantages include heavy traffic patterns on the bus and tedious troubleshooting, to say the least, unless you have a time domain reflectometer (TDR) to help you find the fault within the coax cable. Without the proper test equipment, carrying the terminator from one station to another is about as exciting as relocating your clothesline poles. Today the backbone is normally twisted-pair or fiber cable, so these issues are not as relevant; be aware, however, that many certification tests think you should know the specifications.

FDDI and Token Ring are typically a physical star, logical ring topology. The *active monitor* monitors the token circulating around the ring. Problem isolation and network reconfiguration are issues. It used to be that Token Ring wiring was all shielded twisted-pair Type 1, 2, 3, 6, and so on with hermaphroditic connectors, but now it is primarily UTP with RJ-45 connectors.

In meshes, fault tolerance may be maximized, but from the troubleshooting perspective, it is often a mess. I refer to the mesh topology as the *mess topology*, and it is more often used for backup links on the WAN (for example, ISDN backup for Frame Relay links).

Installation, reconfiguration, and cost normally lead us to some hybrid of the preceding topologies in a practical environment.

The PDU for Layer 1 is bits. Remember that the Physical Layer is responsible for transmitting bits (0s and 1s) and coordinating rules for transmitting (Tx) and receiving (Rx) them. Mechanical, electrical, optical, and signaling are among the many specifications at Layer 1. Layer 1 is a good place for trouble to shoot you if you are not careful.

NOTE

I had to laugh at myself the other day when I connected my PC to the hub in the front of the classroom. I had lights on the hub, but not on the PC dongle. "This is a little strange," I thought to myself. I thought maybe I had the wrong cable type, because I didn't know what was on the other side of the wall. I thought I would eliminate the hub and plug directly into the wall. Neither a straight-through nor a crossover cable worked. I even tried different cables. Finally I picked up the laptop PC, took it to another room, and connected it fine. So I returned to the classroom, connected up again, but still no dongle light. I decided to just test things from the laptop PC anyhow and found I could ping and use the Internet, which is all I originally wanted to do. The funny part was that I had put a red mark on this dongle to trick a student who needed a little more of a challenge. Refer back to this scenario as I discuss using models and methods to troubleshoot by the layers.

Do you work with the physical aspects or is that done for you? (I have thrown brooms through the ceiling and used slingshots to get the cable a little farther down the hall when I didn't have any other tools at hand.) Because you are in a physical mindset at the moment, take a minute to look at a list of what uses RJ-45 (see Table 1-13). Only the active pins are displayed.

Table 1-13 *What Uses RJ-45?*

What Uses RJ-45?	Active Pins
10BASE-T Ethernet	1–2 3–6
100BASE-TX UTP (2 pair Category 5)*	1–2 3–6
Token Ring	4–5 3–6
Console cable	All pins rolled 1–8 2–7 3–6 4–5
T-1	1–2 4–5
ISDN U (North America; *U* for *unpowered*)	4–5 single pair
ISDN S/T	1–2(pwr) 4–5(data) 7–8(pwr)

*Although not commonly used, 100BASE-T4 uses 4 pair of Category 3, 4, or 5 cabling.

Figure 1-15 shows the RJ-45 connector. When you point the clip toward the floor, pin 1 is on the left and pin 8 is on the right. Compare it to the smaller RJ-11 connector.

Figure 1-15 *RJ-11 and RJ-45 Connectors*

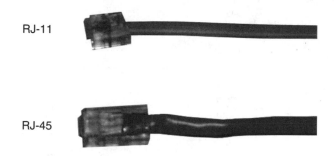

RJ-11

RJ-45

Back in the mid-1980s, companies were concerned with cabling standards in particular. EIA/TIA has definitely permeated the cabling industry, particularly with EIA/TIA 568, and has very high recognition among users and vendors alike. Various committees have developed cabling standards and continue to provide updates with Technical Service Bulletins (TSBs) as the industry evolves. 568A and 568B are technically identical, as you can verify in Table 1-14. 568B is very widespread because it is basically the same as AT&T 258A; however, 568A allows two pairs for voice to make it a little more compatible in the telco environment.

Table 1-14   *568A and 568B Standards*

568A (EIA/TIA Where Orange and Green Are Reversed to Be More Compatible with Telco)	568B (The Old AT&T Standard That Is Very Widespread Today)
Pin	Pin
1 white/green (Rx+)	1 white/orange (Tx+)
2 green (Rx–)	2 orange (Tx–)
3 white/orange (Tx+)	3 white/green (Rx+)
6 orange (Tx–)	6 green (Rx–)

NOTE   Although only one pair is used for Tx and one pair for Rx, the RJ-45 connector, which holds four pair (eight wires) is standard. Compare it to the RJ-11 connector back in Figure 1-15, which only physically holds two pair (four wires).

Besides the connectors and the pinouts, the wire thickness varies too according to the American Wire Gauge (AWG). For example, one-pair UTP 16 AWG speaker wire for my outside BOSE speakers is much larger than the four-pair UTP 24-gauge running my network.

Figure 1-16 shows a DB-60 to DB-25 serial cable used for WAN connectivity.

Figure 1-16 *EIA/TIA-232 Cable Assembly*

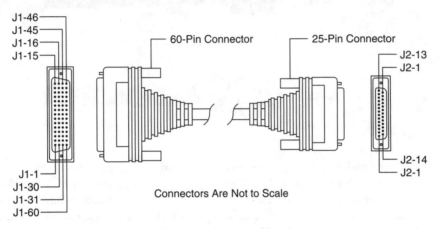

Part II, "Supporting IP and IPX," and Part III, "Supporting Ethernet, Switches, and VLANs," of this book discuss the Physical Layer and Data Link Layer as they relate to LANs/WANs in more detail. In addition, you can check out the following cable sites on your own:

- www.cisco.com

- www.belden.com

- www.belkin.com

- www.stonewallcable.com

- www.amp.com

Now look at some practical application of the Physical Layer. Do you know when to use a straight-through cable compared to a crossover cable? Perhaps a better question is what is a crossover cable? A straight-through cable is wired pin 1 to 1, 2 to 2, 3 to 3, and 6 to 6. A crossover is 1 to 3 and 2 to 6; it crosses between active pairs. Generally speaking, *unlike devices* require a *straight-through cable*, whereas *like devices* require a *crossover cable*. Repeat this rule to yourself as you review Table 1-15. As with any rule, exceptions apply. Therefore, check the cable documentation that comes with your switch or router. For example, a hub may have an uplink port and when in the normal position it requires a crossover cable to connect two devices together. When in the uplink position, the cross is already performed in the device hardware and a straight-through cable is appropriate. Many of the Cisco switch ports are designated with an X above the port or a media dependent interface (MDI/MDI-X) toggle and some are not. Connecting two devices with Xs normally means they are like; therefore you need which kind of cable? Check your answer in Table 1-15.

Table 1-15   *Do You Need a Straight-Through or Crossover Cable?*

Straight-Through (Unlike Devices)	Crossover (Like Devices)	Rollover	T1-Crossover
1-1	1-3	1-8	1-4
2-2	2-6	2-7	
3-3	3-1	3-6	
4-4	4-4	4-5	2-5
5-5	5-5	5-4	
6-6	6-2	6-3	
7-7	7-7	7-2	
8-8	8-8	8-1	
PC to hub PC to switch Switch to router	PC to PC (PC to server) Hub to hub Switch to switch Hub to switch* Router to router PC to router*	Console cable	T1 - RJ-45 jack

*Doesn't follow the general rule of like devices use crossover cable and unlike use straight-through cable. The devices marked with an asterisk require a crossover.

The examples marked with an asterisk are exceptions to the general rule of like devices needing a crossover cable and unlike requiring a straight-through cable. If you draw a line between Layer 2 and Layer 3, however, any device on the same side of the line uses crossover cables.

NOTE   I think of hubs and switches as Access Layer devices; because you use them to connect users, in the cabling respect they are the same. I think of PCs and routers as being the same for cabling purposes because both can route using routing protocols.

Wireless media is hot these days and is going to get hotter. It is great for places where wires are not possible (when you can't dig up the street because you don't have the right-of-way, for instance, or over a body of water where you choose not to lay cable or cable is just not feasible). It is becoming conveniently popular in schools, universities, and homes. Some examples follow. Infrared technologies enable you to transfer files or print as easily as you flip TV channels. Spread-spectrum radio is a cost-effective way to divide frequencies into channels instead of leasing lines from the service providers. Encrypted full-duplex data is carried at a fraction of the cost. Cellular digital packet data (CDPD) uses the network for data when not used for voice. Microwave is still very widespread. Take a trip to Maryland's NASA Goddard Space Flight Center sometime or check out the towers at Chincoteague Island, Virginia. New cars are coming out with what rental cars have had for some time; global positioning systems (GPSs) are more popular than ever. If you are out on a boat, your latitude and longitude location is pretty significant to your whereabouts on the bay.

Table 1-16 provides a concise yet comprehensive review of the OSI model.

Table 1-16   *The OSI Reference Model*

A g a i n	Application (Layer 7)	Messages, data, packets (User interface) (Services)	Telnet, NFS, FTP/ TFTP, HTTP, DNS, X.400, X.500, *RIP, *BGP, *DHCP	Service advertisement Service use Name resolution (DNS)	File, print, message, application, database, user interface, file transfer, e-mail
P e o p l e	Presentation (Layer 6)	Messages, data packets (Translator)	ASCII, EBCDIC, JPEG, MIDI, MPEG	Translation, encryption, compression	Bit order/byte order, character codes, file syntax, public key/ private key
S u p p o r t	Session (Layer 5)	Messages, data packets (Operator/dialog)	NetBIOS, Sockets, RPC, LDAP, drive mappings	Dialog Session administration	Simplex, half-duplex, full-duplex connection establishment/data transfer
T h r e a t e n	Transport (Layer 4)	Datagrams, segments, packets (Certified mail)	*OSPF, *IGRP, *EIGRP, SPX, TCP, UDP	Addressing, sequencing Connection services Disassembly/re-assembly Delivery/ acknowledgment	Segment sequencing Error/flow control (end-to-end) Guaranteed delivery Hides lower layer intricacies from upper layers

Table 1-16   *The OSI Reference Model (Continued)*

N o t	Network (Layer 3) L3 Switch Router	Datagrams, packets (Path determination) (Routing)	IP, *ARP, RARP, ICMP, IGMP	Logical addressing Address resolution (ARP) Switching, sequencing Route discovery/ selection Connection services Gateway services	Unique IP/IPX (internal network number) Packet/message/circuit Distance vector/link state Static/dynamic Flow/error/sequence control Network Layer translation
D o	Data Link (Layer 2) L2 Switch N I C	Frames (Carpenter/framer) (Data packaging) (Encapsulation)	Ethernet, Token Ring, FDDI, Frame Relay, HDLC, SDLC, PPP, ISDN, LAPD	LLC sublayer Synchronization Connection services Logical topology Media access Physical addressing MAC sublayer	Logical link control Asynchronous/ synchronous/ isochronous Flow/error control Organizes 0s and 1s into frames Media Access Control Bus/ring Contention/token passing/polling MAC address (physical device address)
P l e a s e	Physical (Layer 1) Hub	Bits (0s and 1s) (Coordinate rules for bit transmission)	UTP/Cat5E, HSSI, RJ-45, coax, fiber, wireless	Connection types Physical topology Digital/analog signaling Bit synchronization Bandwidth use Multiplexing	Point-to-point/ multipoint Cable layout (bus,ring, star, mesh, cellular) Current state/transition Asynchronous/ synchronous Bascband (TDM)/ broadband (FDM)

*Protocols and applications are written to perform functions. Analyze the layers by looking at protocol analyzer traces. Routing in general is discussed in more detail with regard to Layer 3 (although many ride on TCP/UDP or contain their own reliability mechanisms).

As you work through this book, you will encounter more detailed information and investigate specific troubleshooting targets. At all times, remember that although it is certainly helpful to understand how things work when you are shooting trouble, a methodical approach to troubleshooting is actually more important.

Troubleshooting by Layers

You must train yourself to systematically analyze, resolve, and escalate problems. Troubleshooting by OSI layers is certainly one way to accomplish this. The OSI layers are built and stacked for a reason. For troubleshooting, start at the Physical Layer and work your way up to the Application Layer. A layer problem will lead you to a box and a solution. It is pretty frustrating to just compare what works to what doesn't (the swap-til-you-drop approach), especially when you don't have anything left to swap. Use Table 1-17 to help you troubleshoot by layers.

Table 1-17 *Troubleshooting by Layers*

OSI Layer Number	OSI Layer Name	Basic Troubleshooting
7	Application	Software problem in end system
6	Presentation	Software problem in end system
5	Session	Software problem in end system Host name (Sockets) or NetBIOS name issue
4	Transport	Software problem in end system Cisco/UNIX Traceroute tests up to L4
3	Network	Ping tests up to L3 Microsoft Tracert tests up to L3
2	Data Link	Ping tests up to and through L3
1	Physical	Ping tests up to and through L3

The reality of it all is that the OSI layers are a good approach to discussing networking and internetworking technologies and provide a very good foundation from which to troubleshoot. Be aware, however, that they do not necessarily answer all interoperability issues. As you can see, many industry standards and protocols exist, and obviously there is a lot more to know.

NOTE   Perhaps the ISO should have included a Layer 0 for Power and Layers 8, 9, and 10 for Finance, Politics, and Religion. Should I dare say lowest bid wins again, many decisions are quite political in nature, and the methodology (religion) is because we have always done it that way? Although these layers are not part of the ISO specifications, they do appear to be part of most practical environments (whether anyone actually admits it or not).

Many internetworking topics can be examined by reviewing the technical details of the OSI model. I have tried to give you a taste of them in this chapter and to introduce the importance of troubleshooting by layers. My OSI model examples have purposely been IP-related due to the practical application of the book, but they certainly didn't have to be. I could have just as easily used another protocol stack.

The DoD TCP/IP Suite

Other industry standard models, such as the DoD TCP/IP suite, provide a way to take a systematic approach to troubleshooting. Table 1-18 compares the DoD TCP/IP suite with the OSI model.

Table 1-18   *Comparing the ISO's OSI Model to the DoD's TCP/IP Suite*

OSI Layer Number	OSI Layer Name	PDU	DoD TCP/IP Suite
7	Application	Messages	Application
6	Presentation	Messages	
5	Session	Messages	
4	Transport	Segments (TCP)	Transport
		Datagrams (UDP)	Host-to-host
3	Network	Packets/datagrams	Internet
2	Data Link	Frames	Data Link
1	Physical	Bits	Physical

TCP/IP came from ARPANET. It is old, but definitely not outdated. Prior to the acceptance of the TCP/IP suite, single-vendor solutions, such as IBM SNA and Novell IPX, prevailed. TCP/IP allows for heterogeneous operating systems, platforms, and hardware, hence open systems. Many vendors and resources discuss the TCP/IP suite using four layers (see Figure 1-17); however, the DoD standards call for five layers, dividing the Network Interface Layer into separate Physical and Link Layers (see Table 1-18).

Figure 1-17   *Upper, Host-to-Host, and Lower Layers*

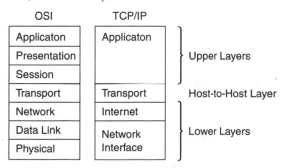

This model gives you more mnemonics from the bottom up: **N**ever **I**gnore **T**eacher's **A**dvice:

- **Application**
- **Transport**
- **Internet**
- **Network Interface**

Industry models enable you to take a layered approach to understanding technology and troubleshooting it. Cisco even recommends a layered approach to design. The *Access Layer* (user layer) is typically comprised of low-end switches operating at 10/100 Mbps. The *Distribution Layer* (decision-making layer) is typically comprised of 100-Mbps routers, whereas the *Core Layer* is typically a 100/1000-Mbps backbone of multilayer switches to switch packets as fast as possible from the source to the destination network. Knowing the layers and your network is a big part of troubleshooting. Compare the models once again in Figure 1-18 before you move on to the Cisco approach to troubleshooting.

Figure 1-18 *Compare the Models*

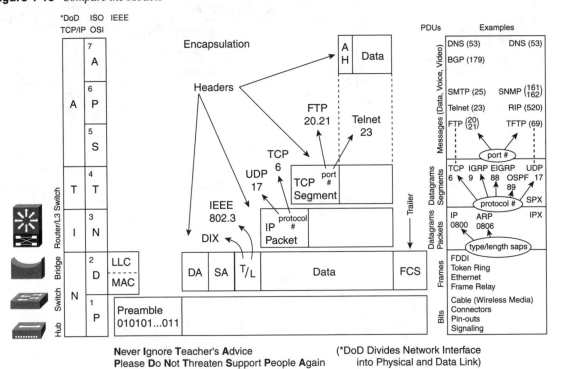

As you work through the scenarios and Trouble Tickets throughout the rest of the book, and particularly when you tackle problems in real life, it will become more and more apparent that you need an understanding of standards and protocols as well as systematic models and methods to effectively support your LANs and WANs. The OSI model and TCP/IP suite certainly offer a layered approach to understanding and troubleshooting complex internetworks. However, there are many other approaches. As a matter of fact, Cisco offers a systematic approach of their own. Take the time to review the Cisco troubleshooting model. You can find it on the Documentation CD-ROM or search at Cisco.com for "Internetwork Troubleshooting Guide, Troubleshooting Overview" to find the Cisco approach to troubleshooting.

The Cisco Troubleshooting Approach

The Cisco approach to shooting trouble can be an effective way to troubleshoot, particularly if you don't already have a working method. This method is *critical* to the CCNP Support exam objectives, so you should study Figure 1-19 very carefully. From a practical viewpoint, you do not need to change to the Cisco strategy if the troubleshooting method/model you have works.

Figure 1-19 *The Cisco Approach to Troubleshooting*

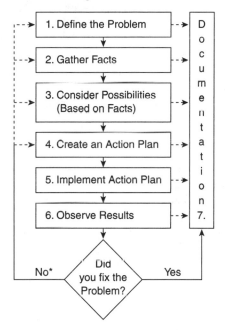

*Always undo any previous changes
before you iterate the process or
attempt your next plan of action.

The Cisco troubleshooting approach includes seven steps for resolving problems. (See Figure 1-19.) First you define the problem. Next you gather facts and then consider possibilities based on those facts. This is another way of saying evaluate your alternatives. Create an action plan, which may be kind of an if-then-else action plan. Implement the plan, observe the results, and verify that you and everyone involved thinks you fixed the problem at hand. If you did not fix the problem, be sure to undo any previous changes before you continue with the next plan of action. If you have exhausted all your if-then-else courses of action in your action plan, you may have to start at the top of the Cisco ladder to ensure you defined the right problem. Cisco suggests step seven as the place to document the solution. However, documentation is very important at each step in this process (as indicated on Figure 1-19). I define some examples at each step in the following list. Use them to apply this method to your own environment and to work through the chapter Trouble Ticket.

1   Define the problem.

   For example, an end user calls in and reports the network is down. You should identify the symptoms, isolate the problem, and document the findings.

2   Gather facts.

   Perform pertinent tests. For example, can you ping or trace? From the PC? From the router? Can you use another application such as HTTP or FTP? Can you telnet to the port?

   Find out when it last worked, if it ever worked, and whether it is a recurring problem. What has changed since it last worked?

   Determine how many people/devices are affected. Is it a local or remote issue? If you did a network baseline up front, you have some comparison information. See the "Practical Troubleshooting" section for more on baselining and documentation.

   Work as a team; collaborate with other engineers and colleagues. Contact users, network administrators, managers, and other key people.

   Use your tools. For example, network management systems (NMS) such as CiscoWorks or Cisco Info Center (CIC) enable you to map your network and track changes. Take advantage of protocol analyzer captures from programs such as Sniffer or NetMon. Monitor syslog or other logs. Interpret Cisco **show** and **debug** output and research Cisco.com and other sites and tools. Time and date stamps are valuable for troubleshooting; Network Time Protocol (NTP) is free, so you should take advantage of it and show the clock while gathering facts. Answer the questions that help you identify which tool to use; remember that different tools operate at different layers.

NOTE   Chapter 2, "What's in Your Tool Bag," covers tools relevant to the CCNP Support exam objectives and the practical world of internetworking.

   The most important thing about this step is to determine what the "real" and "full" problem is. If you open Trouble Tickets based on user complaints, remember to consider the user's description of the problem in light of the user's technical expertise and understanding.

Document the findings.

3 Consider possibilities (based on facts).

Brainstorm and narrow down the possibilities so that you can focus on what is relevant. Find out whether anyone else has tried to fix the problem. Just as you did in the fact-gathering step, work with the people on your team, not against them.

Document the findings. More times than one I have been the victim of my own circumstance because I did not document the relevant possibilities or make a checklist of what had and had not been completed. Documentation should be so good that someone should be able to immediately pick up where you left off in a Trouble Ticket.

4 Create an action plan.

Determine what has to be done to fix the problem. Take a divide-and-conquer approach. List the most likely cause first and plan to change *only* one variable at a time so that you know what change has what impact. Identify any special resource requirements. Prioritize possibilities so that you start with the most likely solution first. Who or what will be affected as a result of your action plan?

Document the findings.

5 Implement action plan.

Follow a step-by-step approach to carrying out the action plan. Change only *one thing at a time* and measure the results; *always* maintain a fallback plan. Make sure you don't make things worse or add additional problems. Documenting each step of the way and following your plan systematically and meticulously will assist with this.

Limit the impact on others as required. For example, shops that work around the clock (7×24) are more likely to have a more stringent change process.

Call or e-mail TAC if you can't resolve a problem after putting it through the rigorous online tests that Cisco gives you at Cisco.com.

There's nothing worse than trying to troubleshoot more than one problem at a time — particularly if the embedded problem is something you have helped create! This is why you undo a plan when it does not solve the problem.

Document the findings.

6 Observe results.

Determine whether you permanently solved the problem or whether you just implemented a temporary solution.

Make sure the affected party/parties think you fixed the problem. Then document the results and action plan. If you did not fix the problem, go back and try the next item on your action plan. *Always* undo any previous changes before you iterate the process or attempt your next plan of action.

If you have not fixed the problem, consider taking time away from the problem; you might be able to come back with a fresh perspective. *Always* have a backup plan.

Document the findings.

7 Document the solution.

Document each step along the way and the final solution to improve overall expertise as you support your internetwork. Many people forget this step.

Whether manual or automated, maintain a database and change log for each piece of equipment. For example you should do things such as maintain version control, comment your configurations, add descriptions to your interfaces, and capture your logs for later review. Include change notes for yourself and others in the configurations with **remark**, !, or # for comments. If you are capturing your logs, show the clock a couple of times to show when things happened.

Record what you have done, have a fallback plan, and provide a history for yourself and others.

Plan for people and equipment upgrades (future expansion). Emergency changes to fix problems are one thing, but planned changes should be coordinated properly to assess the risk, plan for the change, communicate the change, implement the change, test the change, and document it.

One of the major goals of the CIT course and the Support exam is to make sure you establish a methodical mindset for troubleshooting so that your network operates with a minimum amount of downtime. The Cisco generic systematic approach is meticulous, disciplined, and optimistic. Any method that you are already used to is probably fine for practical purposes, as long as you are sure it takes advantage of the benefits a systematic approach can bring. For exam purposes, however, be very familiar with the Cisco problem-solving method.

NOTE   Cisco offers another method called VISTA (View, Isolate, Solve, Test, Apply), which may be a little easier to recall in the real world of troubleshooting. Cisco's latest methodology says, "Define the problem, then Isolate, and Correct."

The following Trouble Ticket gives you a chance to apply the Cisco model to a sample network problem. The objectives are twofold. I want you to troubleshoot a particular technology by applying the seven-step Cisco troubleshooting approach presented earlier in this chapter. Figure 1-20 shows a graphic view of the scenario. Walk through the Trouble Ticket with me as I use the Cisco method to solve the problem and summarize some important technical concepts.

NOTE   Even though the issue is not something previously discussed in the book, it is something you should be familiar with in a Cisco environment.

Trouble Ticket: Users Are Not Losers

An end user (hosta) calls in and reports, "I can't get to the FTP server."

This and Figure 1-20 is all the information you have been given, so you must brainstorm accordingly. Check your thoughts against the Trouble Ticket solution that follows.

Figure 1-20 *Users Are Not Losers*

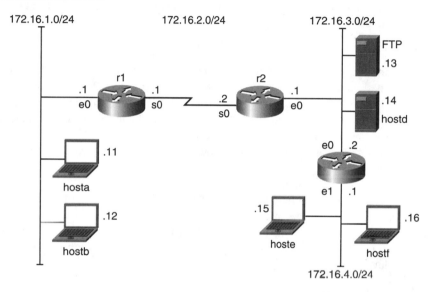

Trouble Ticket Solution: Users Are Not Losers

1 Define the problem.

hosta can't get to the FTP server, or at least that is what the user is telling you.

2 Gather facts.

Fact gathering requires you to ask lots of questions of users and devices and to collaborate with others. As long as you are systematic and methodical, you can divide and conquer a bit while you are gathering facts to eliminate checking everything. For example, hosta can't get to the FTP server. Instead of asking too many questions of the users, you can try a simple ping and tracert from hosta to both of the servers on network 172.16.3.0. If you can't ping, you know you must test for Physical, Data Link, and/or Network Layer issues between the source and destination networks. Perhaps you don't have a route to the destination network; but if you can ping, you can move your testing above the Network Layer. Maybe there is a problem with a router in the path. Tracert (or traceroute) is helpful there. You should have gathered and documented facts such as the following:

- hosta can ping hostb, its gateway 172.16.1.1, both devices on remote network 172.16.3.0, and everything on network 172.16.4.0.

- hosta can tracert to all hosts on its local network and all remote networks shown in Figure 1-20.

- hosta and hostb on network 172.16.1.0 can't FTP to the FTP server on network 172.16.3.0. Other remote hosts and routers can FTP to the FTP server on network 172.16.3.0.

- You are not sure whether this ever worked because you don't have any other documentation.

3 Consider possibilities (based on facts).

Narrow down the facts and possibilities so that you can focus on what is relevant. Your facts should help you further define the original problem. The real issue is that hosta can't FTP to the FTP server 172.16.3.13. Because r1, r2, r3, and the hosts on network 172.16.4.0 can FTP, you know the issue is not with the FTP services on the server; instead the problem more likely involves the 172.16.1.0 network off of r1. You also know that your problem is not a Physical or Data Link Layer issue because all pings are successful.

4 Create an action plan.

Start with the most likely cause and change only one variable at a time. r1 is a very likely target, and everyone on the local 172.16.1.0 network is affected. Your action plan should include further investigation of r1. Save your configurations and write down every step you intend to perform. The Cisco IOS **show access-lists** command is by far the most relevant here.

5 Implement action plan.

The **show access-lists** command reveals the following on r1:

```
r1#sh access-lists
Extended IP access list ftp
    deny tcp any any (16 matches)
    permit icmp any any (4 matches)
    permit tcp any 0.0.0.0 255.255.0.0 eq ftp-data
    permit tcp any 0.0.0.0 255.255.0.0 eq ftp
```

The access list is the reason hosta can't FTP to the server. After you found the access list, you determined that it was applied outbound on interface s0 by examining the running configuration. You verified this by typing **show ip interface s0**, and sure enough the FTP access list was applied outbound.

Your analysis requires that you further define your action plan. You may temporarily decide to remove the statement off the interface so that the access list is not applied (**no ip access-group ftp out**). If this allows hosta to FTP, you should fix the access list for a more permanent solution. You should shut the interface down until all changes have been made. Note that the access list denies all TCP communications from anywhere to anywhere outbound. Your pings should succeed because of the ICMP statement. However, the two **permit tcp** statements don't accomplish a thing because they use the subnet mask rather than the necessary wildcard mask. In this example, it is probably easiest to completely remove the old access list and create another one. You may need to go back to the top of the Cisco troubleshooting ladder on this one to gather more facts to determine exactly what the access list should do. Assume you did that and hosta, hostb, and any other hosts except host 172.16.1.13 added to network 172.16.1.0 should be able to FTP to 172.16.3.13. Although host 172.16.1.13 should not be able to FTP, all other IP-related commands should be allowed. You also want to determine whether host 172.16.1.13 ever attempts to FTP to the FTP server. Your new action plan should attempt to create and apply the following access list on r1:

```
r1(config)#ip access-list extended ftp
r1(config-ext-nacl)#deny tcp host 172.16.1.13 host 172.16.3.13 eq 20
r1(config-ext-nacl)#deny tcp host 172.16.1.13 host 172.16.3.13 eq 21
r1(config-ext-nacl)#permit ip any any

r1(config-ext-nacl)#interface serial 0
r1(config-if)#ip access-group ftp out
r1(config-if)#end
r1#copy running-config startup-config
```

6 Observe results.

Test your new access list by making sure that hosta and hostb can ping and FTP to the FTP server. If possible, add host 172.16.1.13 to ensure that it can't FTP to the FTP server; it should, however, be able to ping and tracert. It is critical to make sure you fixed the problem at hand and did not introduce any others. In addition, everyone must be content with your solution; otherwise it is still a problem. Make sure you save your configurations and document the findings. Now that things are working, you may consider revisiting your action plan. Alternatively, you could place this ACL inbound on interface e0 to filter the traffic closer to the source.

7 Document the solution.

Document all changes and your new configurations.

```
r1#show access-lists
Extended IP access list ftp
    deny tcp host 172.16.1.13 host 172.16.3.13 eq ftp-data
    deny tcp host 172.16.1.13 host 172.16.3.13 eq ftp
    permit ip any any
r1#show ip interface serial 0
Serial0 is up, line protocol is up
  Internet address is 172.16.2.1/24
  Broadcast address is 255.255.255.255
  Address determined by non-volatile memory
  MTU is 1500 bytes
  Helper address is not set
  Directed broadcast forwarding is disabled
  Multicast reserved groups joined: 224.0.0.10
  Outgoing access list is ftp
  Inbound  access list is not set
  Proxy ARP is enabled
```

This Trouble Ticket has provided you with the opportunity to practice solving a problem using the Cisco seven-step approach and to review the following about access lists:

- When coding your ACLs, use top-down processing. Place the more specific items at the top and the general items at the bottom. Don't rely on a particular version of the IOS to order things for you.

- At least one **permit** statement is required; otherwise the implicit default of **deny any any** applies.

- Wildcard masks are used in ACLs. They predate subnet masks. Many people write a 0 with a line through it anyhow, so just draw a checkmark over it so that you remember that 0 means check. Think of the 1 with a dot above it so it looks more like the letter *i*, for *ignore*. For example, 172.16.1.13 0.0.0.0 means check all bits if this statement is in the ACL. Instead of spelling out the 0.0.0.0, I used the keyword **host** in my revised access list. By the same token, 172.16.0.0 0.0.255.255 implies to check the first 16 bits and ignore the last 16. 172.16.0.0 255.255.255.255 is the same as ignore all bits or the keyword **any**; an example being **permit ip any any**, which says permit all IP traffic from anywhere to anywhere.

- An ACL will not block traffic originating from the router. You observed this when you could FTP from r1 to 172.16.3.13 but not from hosta, where you had to go through the affected router.

- Named ACLs enable you to remove individual lines of code; although in this example, it was just as easy to delete it and start again.

- To delete an ACL, it is best practice to type **no** in front of the lines to create and apply the ACL to take care of any version inconsistencies. An empty ACL that is applied to an interface used to deny everything; now it permits everything. Just don't apply an empty ACL. Always create before you apply and use third-party tools for editing because you can't add or delete lines within the ACL in the Cisco command-line interface (CLI). However, you can delete lines within a named ACL.

- When troubleshooting ACLs, use **debug** and **log**; matches are also helpful. For example, the **log** keyword is how you can determine whether the host you wanted to deny ever attempts to FTP anyhow.

- Although not apparent in this example, you should not have problems modifying an outbound ACL remotely. However, you could potentially lock yourself out of the router with an inbound.

- Remember, one ACL per protocol, per interface, per direction. This would have been an issue if you would not have temporarily issued the **no ip access-group** statement so that the incorrect ACL wasn't applied.

- Now that you have gone through the entire exercise and technically solved the implied problem, you probably should have asked yourself whether the user was *supposed to* have access to the FTP server! Be aware of any policies in place outside the actual configuration of networking equipment. This should be part of your "gathering facts" step.

Practical Troubleshooting

One day you will get a call that says the network is down. Be very prepared to divide and conquer to get to the real problem. Work through the affected layers. Remember that shooting trouble is often about questions. Do you ask the equipment or the user? Who is waiting for the results? What has happened? When did it occur? Why? Where did it happen? Plug it in; turn it on. Make sure you have lights and power. Did it ever work? What has changed since it last worked? Check the obvious. Who is complaining? Is it an end-system issue? Check the application and configuration if it is an individual person or machine. Is it a group of people or machines? Check connectivity and performance. Run through the OSI layers; remember ping and trace; check the routing tables. Is it a local segment issue or does it extend through routers? Is a bad NIC, cable, or device causing performance degradation? Ping yourself, ping someone local, ping the default gateway, or start by pinging a remote network to test all of these. Trace the problem. What is slow: cabling, link, devices? Do you have a baseline comparison? Use ping, trace, a protocol analyzer, and other tools on an ongoing basis. Did someone else try to fix the problem? Never be too proud to ask for help.

Actually it is quite helpful to have people with different backgrounds on your team, whether it be in a test lab or practical environment. You must be able to prioritize problem areas and people for that matter. Normally if the CEO has a problem, you take care of it immediately; if everyone else in the company is *down*, however, obviously they take precedence (one of those 8, 9, 10 layer things—finance, politics, and religion). Modern day prioritization says let the CEO wait so that when you ask for more people or resources the CEO recognizes the need.

Models and Methods

I would like to credit my REDI model source, but it is something I learned about in college while at Johns Hopkins. I think it came from a systems design or database textbook. In any case, the REDI model gives me a systematic mindset for whatever I am doing. It is quite effective yet easy to remember. The basic tenants of the REDI model are as follows:

- Define Your **R**equirements
- **E**valuate the Alternatives
- **D**esign and Develop
- **I**mplement (and then do it all over again)

If the design and development work is done, you are probably troubleshooting or starting the life cycle all over again. Whether it is taking a certification test, a new consulting gig, or applying for a job, taking a structured approach and documenting appropriately are of utmost importance.

Baselining and Documentation

Baselining and documentation are crucial to your long-term success with internetwork troubleshooting. This is not just theory; for if you don't know what is normal, how do you know where to begin with troubleshooting. What if you get the call saying the network is slow? Slow compared to what? Did you collect any data when the network was installed and running properly, do you audit it from time to time, or have you just taken the put-out-the-fire approach to network management? You should know what information to collect, how to store it, and who is affected by what. Utilization (CPU and bandwidth); memory; error statistics; protocol distribution; traffic statistics; changes in hardware, software, and configuration; and past troubleshooting documentation are all important aspects for troubleshooting. Track patterns and trends. When you find out who or what is affected, time of day, day of week, and month of year, you can compare this to your baseline.

In the form of pictures, charts, maps, tables, and databases, your baseline should include items such as the following:

Model number	Serial number
RAM/Flash memory	IOS version
Config-register settings	Interface statistics
Bandwidth/speed	Clocking
Encapsulation	Duplex
Descriptions	Addresses
Passwords	Spanning-tree portfast
VLANs	Routed protocols
Routing protocols	Bridged protocols

In practical application, other things that are valuable to document include the detailed location of equipment (down to the country, state, city, building, wiring closet, rack, and position). Store this information in a log book, on your network, or your personal digital assistant (PDA) for that matter.

From a practical viewpoint, pictures are wonderful resources. Physical layouts, logical maps, lists of protocols (routed, bridged, and routing including redistribution and filtering) can aid you in the process. Include your Internet connections, addressing plans, DHCP, NAT, security plans, and application implementations in your diagrams. What is normal for you may not be what is normal for the next person, so documentation and diagrams are invaluable. Change is truly the only thing constant in this industry—software, hardware, and configuration. Doctors keep records on your children from the time they are born throughout their life, documenting such things as shots, diseases, symptoms, cures, operations, and so on. Do the same for your network. The answer to your problem will be easier to find if it happened before and you documented it in a database of some kind.

Practical troubleshooting is all about taking the previous methods and models and applying them to the real world. Regardless of the model/method you follow, if you take a systematic approach you will be able to narrow the problem down. Amateurs and pros alike should be able to analyze new and complex problems with an effective strategy. It is not necessary to be a know-it-all to be an effective troubleshooter. A successful troubleshooter is a logical thinker with common sense and people skills. Divide and conquer as you did with the access list Trouble Ticket; narrow possibilities down by the layers. Analyze and resolve. If you can't, escalate the issue to the team that can.

An unsystematic approach is time-consuming and costly. This concept is stressed on the CCNP Troubleshooting exam, CCIE exams, and CCSI exams. Troubleshooting models and methods help reduce a large set of causes to a smaller set of causes or, better yet, a single cause. Then you can solve the problem and document it for future reference to help mitigate the pressures of supporting critical complex internetworks. Remember, however, that vendor interoperability is far less smooth than theory models pretend it to be.

Review Questions

Use this chapter and your practical troubleshooting knowledge and skills to answer the following questions. The answers are located in Appendix A, "Answers to Review Questions."

1 The Transport Layer is the host-to-host layer in the OSI model and the TCP/IP suite. It is in-between the upper and lower layers and depending on the protocol is responsible for delivery, error detection, and correction. Describe the upper layers of the OSI model and include examples.

2 Describe the lower layers of the OSI model and include examples.

3 Draw a picture showing the differences between OSI layers and TCP/IP layers.

4 Explain encapsulation using the appropriate protocol data unit terminology.

5 Explain de-encapsulation, including how Layer 2 hands off to Layer 3, how Layer 3 hands off to Layer 4, and so on.

6 What is the difference between a hub, switch, and router?

7 What is the difference between routed and routing protocols? Give examples of each.

8 Describe packet flows through routers.

9 How can the OSI model assist in troubleshooting?

10 List the seven steps of the Cisco troubleshooting model?

Summary

This chapter presented an introduction to troubleshooting, a review of standards and protocols, industry models, troubleshooting methods, baselining, and documentation techniques. The chapter covered the OSI model and included information on how an understanding of that model can aid you in the troubleshooting process. The DoD TCP/IP suite was also covered and compared to the OSI model. The Trouble Ticket offered you an opportunity to apply the Cisco troubleshooting method and other techniques you learned in this chapter. Now that you have reviewed and studied a systematic approach to troubleshooting, you should determine whether you really have the right tools for the job.

CHAPTER 2

What's in Your Tool Bag?

One of your objectives thus far is for you to shoot trouble rather than let trouble shoot you. When confronted with network problems, it is of utmost importance for you to define the problem, gather facts, and consider various possibilities based on those facts. The connection may not be possible, for example, or perhaps the data transfer is just slow. Higher-level processes may provide error-checking issues, retransmission problems, routed and routing protocol issues, and other problems. Lower-level data-link targets are basically interfaces and controllers. This chapter reviews the output of some basic IOS commands to assist you in identifying trouble-shooting targets and to prove this bottom-up troubleshooting theory before you adventure into the detailed troubleshooting Trouble Ticket-based chapters to follow.

This chapter focuses on many of the CCNP Troubleshooting objectives and is just as critical to your overall certification and practical success as the preceding chapter. This chapter specifically addresses what you need in your tool bag for Cisco troubleshooting. The chapter starts by reviewing IOS commands and goes on to discuss other hardware- and software-related tools you need in your bag.

This chapter covers the following topics:

- IOS Troubleshooting Tools
- Cisco Connection Online
- Project DOTU
- Network Management
- Hardware Tools and Media Testers
- Network Monitors
- Protocol Analyzers
- Desktop Tools

Supporting Website Files

You can find files and links to utilities that support this book on the Cisco Press website at www.ciscopress.com/1587200570. Even if you do not have a lab, you can take advantage of the supporting configuration files including the logs to understand device input and output. The files are listed throughout the chapters in italics.

In order to be able to read and work with some of the supporting files offered at www.ciscopress.com/1587200570, you may want to download some of the programs listed in Table I-1 in the Introduction.

IOS Troubleshooting Tools

Cisco is more than just a hardware company. Cisco IOS provides you with powerful diagnostic programs such as **show**, **ping**, **trace**, **log**, and **debug** commands. Mastering them is important because some of these can be simple tools that can still save you a great deal of time.

Table 2-1 and the following sections review some basic IOS troubleshooting tools. The objectives here are to review the output and summarize the importance of the commands so that you can put them to practical use. Many times it is advantageous if you can physically inspect the hardware, such as the equipment, cables, and connectors; but maybe you can't. Lots of times you are remote to the problem, depending on your scenario, so it is critical to know the tools innate to the IOS to assist you.

NOTE   Review Chapter 1, "Shooting Trouble," to make sure you have an understanding of protocol technical characteristics and a systematic method for troubleshooting.

Table 2-1   *IOS Troubleshooting Tools*

Cisco Command	Description
show	A snapshot of what is occurring to monitor status. The show commands enable you to detect neighbors, spot performance issues, and isolate problems.
ping	Determine end-to-end connectivity and reachability.
traceroute	Hop-by-hop approach to finding the problem.
log	Monitor and view messages that record real-time events, such as errors, warnings, and state transitions.
debug	Use for troubleshooting traffic flow or misconfigurations; *not* for normal daily operations.

Cisco Show Commands

Cisco show commands give a snapshot of what is occurring to monitor status, detect neighbors, spot performance issues, and isolate problems. This discussion covers several show commands to prepare you for the chapter practical exercise, various Trouble Tickets throughout the book, and for your overall real-world troubleshooting needs. Feel free to use the question mark (**?**) for help or more detail. Be aware that **show ?** yields different results according to whether you are in user mode or privileged (enable) mode. In addition, you can use **show cdp ?** to display the optional keywords available with that particular command.

NOTE   The following examples and screen shots were captured with little or no traffic, but are some of the commands you should use to set up a baseline. Any time you see ... I have cut part of the output.

Use **show controllers** for Ethernet, Token Ring, FDDI, or T1 to see DTE/DCE, clocking, bandwidth, and to determine whether the cable is plugged in properly. Narrow the command output by specifying an interface, such as s0. Remember, however, to put a space between the s and the 0. This is the only IOS command I can think of where you must put the space (but, in fact, this is an IOS release-dependent behavior). Examples 2-1 through 2-3 show the output of **show controllers serial 0**.

Example 2-1   **show controllers** *on DCE End with serial 0 Up and Running*

```
r2>show controllers serial 0
HD unit 0, idb = 0xDFE7C, driver structure at 0xE52F8
buffer size 1524  HD unit 0, V.35 DCE cable, clockrate 64000
...
```

The shaded line emphasizes the V.35 DCE cable with a clock rate of 64000. The DCE end of a serial line always provides clocking (timing synchronization). Normally you receive the clock from the service provider, but in a lab scenario a back-to-back 60-pin serial cable is used (in which the DCE end requires the **clock rate** command). You can order these cables for your lab from such places as Ebay.com or Stonewallcable.com. Search for "cable assemblies and pinouts" on Cisco.com for a picture of the DB60 60-pin, male, back-to-back EIA-530 type used for the practical examples in this book.

Example 2-2 shows what happens when you unplug the cable. If you can, set up two routers of your own with the back-to-back serial cable and give it a try.

Example 2-2   **show controllers** *and* **show interfaces** *with serial 0 Unplugged*

```
r2#
00:59:36: %LINK-3-UPDOWN: Interface Serial0, changed state to down
00:59:37: %LINEPROTO-5-UPDOWN: Line protocol on Interface Serial0, changed state
  to down
r2#show controllers serial 0
HD unit 0, idb = 0xDFE7C, driver structure at 0xE52F8
buffer size 1524  HD unit 0, No cable, clockrate 64000
...
r2#show interfaces serial 0
Serial0 is down, line protocol is down
  Hardware is HD64570
  Description: r2 s0 DCE to r1 s0 DTE
  Internet address is 192.168.2.2/24
  MTU 1500 bytes, BW 64 Kbit, DLY 20000 usec, rely 255/255, load 1/255
  Encapsulation HDLC, loopback not set, keepalive set (10 sec)
  Last input 00:03:31, output 00:03:35, output hang never
  Last clearing of "show interface" counters never
  Input queue: 0/75/0 (size/max/drops); Total output drops: 0
Queueing strategy: weighted fair
```

continues

Example 2-2 **show controllers** *and* **show interfaces** *with serial 0 Unplugged (Continued)*

```
   Output queue: 0/1000/64/0 (size/max total/threshold/drops)
      Conversations  0/2/256 (active/max active/max total)
      Reserved Conversations 0/0 (allocated/max allocated)
   5 minute input rate 0 bits/sec, 0 packets/sec
   5 minute output rate 0 bits/sec, 0 packets/sec
      390 packets input, 22659 bytes, 0 no buffer
      Received 367 broadcasts, 0 runts, 0 giants, 0 throttles
      0 input errors, 0 CRC, 0 frame, 0 overrun, 0 ignored, 0 abort
      389 packets output, 23296 bytes, 0 underruns
      0 output errors, 0 collisions, 26 interface resets
      0 output buffer failures, 0 output buffers swapped out
      7 carrier transitions
      DCD=down  DSR=down  DTR=down  RTS=down  CTS=down
r2#
01:06:38: %LINK-3-UPDOWN: Interface Serial0, changed state to up
01:06:39: %LINEPROTO-5-UPDOWN: Line protocol on Interface Serial0, changed state
   to up
...
```

The **show controllers** output "no cable" on r2 indicates that the cable is unplugged. Hence, the status of serial0 in Example 2-2 is that s0 is down and the line protocol is down. Notice the last couple of lines of the display for **show interfaces serial0**. These indicate carrier transitions; all modem control leads are down, too. This is obviously a Layer 1 issue. Now plug the cable back in and take a look at the DTE end on r1 in Example 2-3.

Example 2-3 **show controllers** *on DTE End with serial 0 Up and Running*

```
r1>show controllers serial 0
HD unit 0, idb = 0xFC1A8, driver structure at 0x101628
buffer size 1524  HD unit 0, V.35 DTE cable
cpb = 0xE2, eda = 0x4064, cda = 0x4078
RX ring with 16 entries at 0xE24000
00 bd_ptr=0x4000 pak=0x104A60 ds=0xE2F240 status=80 pak_size=45
01 bd_ptr=0x4014 pak=0x103E60 ds=0xE2C9D8 status=80 pak_size=45
r1>
```

It is often difficult to discuss one IOS command without mentioning another. For example, it is almost impossible to discuss the **show controllers** command without mentioning the **show interfaces** command because they are both very important lower-level troubleshooting target commands.

The **show interfaces** command shows the statistics for all the Ethernet, Token Ring, FDDI, ATM, BRI, PRI, High-Speed Serial Interface (HSSI), or serial interfaces on a particular box. However, it is normally more helpful to clear the counters and look at just a particular interface to hone in on the problem. The **clear counters** command resets the counters, enabling you to look at the interface from a certain time forward; however, it does not reset things such as Simple Network Management Protocol (SNMP) parameters. Example 2-4 illustrates these interface commands.

Example 2-4   show interfaces *and* clear counters

```
r2>show interfaces
Ethernet0 is up, line protocol is up
  Hardware is Lance, address is 0000.0c38.a05d (bia 0000.0c38.a05d)
  Description: r2 e0 to HostC Win98Dell
  Internet address is 192.168.3.1/24
  MTU 1500 bytes, BW 10000 Kbit, DLY 1000 usec, rely 255/255, load 1/255
  Encapsulation ARPA, loopback not set, keepalive set (10 sec)
  ARP type: ARPA, ARP Timeout 04:00:00
  Last input 00:04:22, output 00:00:03, output hang never
  Last clearing of "show interface" counters never
Queueing strategy: fifo
  Output queue 0/40, 0 drops; input queue 0/75, 0 drops
  5 minute input rate 0 bits/sec, 0 packets/sec
  5 minute output rate 0 bits/sec, 0 packets/sec
     15 packets input, 3026 bytes, 0 no buffer
     Received 10 broadcasts, 0 runts, 0 giants, 0 throttles
     0 input errors, 0 CRC, 0 frame, 0 overrun, 0 ignored, 0 abort
     0 input packets with dribble condition detected
     554 packets output, 55751 bytes, 0 underruns
     0 output errors, 0 collisions, 2 interface resets
     0 babbles, 0 late collision, 0 deferred
     0 lost carrier, 0 no carrier
     0 output buffer failures, 0 output buffers swapped out
Serial0 is up, line protocol is up
...
r2#clear counters
Clear "show interface" counters on all interfaces [confirm]
r2#
01:22:56: %CLEAR-5-COUNTERS: Clear counter on all interfaces by console
r2#show interfaces ethernet 0
Ethernet0 is up, line protocol is up
  Hardware is Lance, address is 0000.0c38.a05d (bia 0000.0c38.a05d)
  Description: r2 e0 to HostC Win98Dell
  Internet address is 192.168.3.1/24
  MTU 1500 bytes, BW 10000 Kbit, DLY 1000 usec, rely 255/255, load 1/255
  Encapsulation ARPA, loopback not set, keepalive set (10 sec)
  ARP type: ARPA, ARP Timeout 04:00:00
  Last input 00:00:43, output 00:00:04, output hang never
  Last clearing of "show interface" counters 00:00:19
  Queueing strategy: fifo
  Output queue 0/40, 0 drops; input queue 0/75, 0 drops
  5 minute input rate 0 bits/sec, 0 packets/sec
  5 minute output rate 0 bits/sec, 0 packets/sec
     0 packets input, 0 bytes, 0 no buffer
     Received 0 broadcasts, 0 runts, 0 giants, 0 throttles
     0 input errors, 0 CRC, 0 frame, 0 overrun, 0 ignored, 0 abort
     0 input packets with dribble condition detected
     2 packets output, 120 bytes, 0 underruns
     0 output errors, 0 collisions, 0 interface resets
     0 babbles, 0 late collision, 0 deferred
     0 lost carrier, 0 no carrier
     0 output buffer failures, 0 output buffers swapped out
r2>
```

Example 2-4 displays **clear counters** and has me confirm that I want to clear the counters on *all* interfaces. From a troubleshooting perspective, it is advantageous to clear *only* the affected interface counters. Also note the description section in Example 2-4. The **description** command is an optional interface command that is extremely helpful for troubleshooting. A good example would be to type **description fa2/0 to headquarters fa1/2 room 101**. The description is like naming the port; it is all part of good documentation techniques that successful troubleshooters need.

Example 2-5 shows the **show ip interface brief** command output. It is not just an IP command; it also works for other Layer 3 protocols. It gives you a glimpse of the status of your interfaces and addresses. Although this command may suit your requirements when you don't need to see all that other stuff, be aware that this output doesn't even show you subnet mask details, which you often need to see in troubleshooting scenarios.

Example 2-5   **show ip interface brief**

```
r2>show ip interface brief
Interface           IP-Address      OK? Method Status                 Protocol
Ethernet0           192.168.3.1     YES manual up                     up
Serial0             192.168.2.2     YES manual up                     up
Serial1             unassigned      YES unset  administratively down down
r2>
```

"Administratively down" always indicates that you need to perform the **no shut** command on the interface; in Example 2-5 I am really not using s1, however, so it is not a worry here. In general, the Status column indicates the Layer 1 status, and the Protocol column indicates the Layer 2 status.

Two other interface commands are **show interfaces ethernet0** and **show ip interface ethernet0**. Although these look similar, they differ significantly. (See Example 2-6.) The **show ip interface ethernet0** command displays the IP settings and defaults, whereas **show interfaces ethernet0** (or any other type of interfaces for that matter) shows statistics for packets that go to, through, or are generated by the router. When checking to determine whether an access list has been applied on the interface, type **show ip interface ethernet 0**. If, on the other hand, you are looking for interface errors, **show interfaces ethernet0** offers more help.

Example 2-6   **show ip interface ethernet 0** *Compared to* **show interfaces ethernet 0**

```
r2>show ip interface e0
Ethernet0 is up, line protocol is up
  Internet address is 192.168.3.1/24
  Broadcast address is 255.255.255.255
  Address determined by setup command
  MTU is 1500 bytes
  Helper address is not set
  Directed broadcast forwarding is disabled
  Outgoing access list is not set
  Inbound  access list is not set
  Proxy ARP is enabled
  Security level is default
  Split horizon is enabled
  ICMP redirects are always sent
  ICMP unreachables are always sent
  ICMP mask replies are never sent
```

Example 2-6   **show ip interface ethernet 0** *Compared to* **show interfaces ethernet 0** *(Continued)*

```
    IP fast switching is enabled
    IP fast switching on the same interface is disabled
    IP Fast switching turbo vector
    IP multicast fast switching is enabled
    IP multicast distributed fast switching is disabled
    Router Discovery is disabled
    IP output packet accounting is disabled
    IP access violation accounting is disabled
    TCP/IP header compression is disabled
    RTP/IP header compression is disabled
    Probe proxy name replies are disabled
    Policy routing is disabled
    Network address translation is disabled
    Web Cache Redirect is disabled
    BGP Policy Mapping is disabled

r2>show interfaces e0
Ethernet0 is up, line protocol is up
    Hardware is Lance, address is 0000.0c38.a05d (bia 0000.0c38.a05d)
    Description: r2 e0 to HostC Win98Dell
    Internet address is 192.168.3.1/24
    MTU 1500 bytes, BW 10000 Kbit, DLY 1000 usec, rely 255/255, load 1/255
    Encapsulation ARPA, loopback not set, keepalive set (10 sec)
    ARP type: ARPA, ARP Timeout 04:00:00
    Last input 00:00:45, output 00:00:04, output hang never
    Last clearing of "show interface" counters 00:22:51
    Queueing strategy: fifo
    Output queue 0/40, 0 drops; input queue 0/75, 0 drops
    5 minute input rate 0 bits/sec, 0 packets/sec
    5 minute output rate 0 bits/sec, 0 packets/sec
        3 packets input, 750 bytes, 0 no buffer
        Received 3 broadcasts, 0 runts, 0 giants, 0 throttles
        0 input errors, 0 CRC, 0 frame, 0 overrun, 0 ignored, 0 abort
        0 input packets with dribble condition detected
        160 packets output, 15281 bytes, 0 underruns
        0 output errors, 0 collisions, 0 interface resets
        0 babbles, 0 late collision, 0 deferred
        0 lost carrier, 0 no carrier
        0 output buffer failures, 0 output buffers swapped out
r2>
```

Look for lights (LEDs) to help troubleshoot Layer 1 problems, and check things such as encapsulation, input and output drops and errors, carrier transitions, and interface resets to assist with Layer 1 and Layer 2 issues. IOS interface and controller commands prove quite helpful in this respect. You will examine more specifics in the chapters to come. For now, turn your attention to Cisco Discovery Protocol (CDP).

The **show cdp neighbors [detail]** command shows only directly connected Cisco devices because it is a Layer 2 proprietary protocol. However, you can telnet to other devices and use **show cdp ?** from there to draw a physical map of your Cisco devices. As many of the other IOS commands, **cdp** even works from user mode to give you information for ports, holdtime, device and capabilities codes, and so on. In addition, you can use **clear cdp** rather than wait the three minutes for it to completely disappear, if necessary. CDP sends and receives neighbor advertisements over multicast address 01-00-0c-cc-cc-cc. It uses a proprietary High-Level Data Link Control (HDLC) type value, so it must run on media that supports the Subnetwork Access Protocol (SNAP) format.

Example 2-7 illustrates **show cdp neighbors** with and without the optional **detail** keyword.

Example 2-7   **show cdp neighbors [detail]**

```
r2>show cdp neighbors
Capability Codes: R - Router, T - Trans Bridge, B - Source Route Bridge
                  S - Switch, H - Host, I - IGMP, r - Repeater
Device ID        Local Intrfce     Holdtme    Capability  Platform  Port ID
r1                  Ser 0           178           R        2516      Ser 0
r2>show cdp neighbors detail
Device ID: r1
Entry address(es):
  IP address: 192.168.2.1
Platform: cisco 2516,  Capabilities: Router
Interface: Serial0,  Port ID (outgoing port): Serial0
Holdtime : 168 sec
Version :
Cisco Internetwork Operating System Software
IOS (tm) 2500 Software (C2500-IS-L), Version 12.0(5), RELEASE SOFTWARE (fc1)
```

Notice the holdtime parameter in the preceding example and how it changed from 178 to 168. This is how long you remember CDP parameters from your neighbor. Use **show cdp** as in Example 2-8 to check the defaults of 180 seconds for the holdtime, which is 3 times the advertising interval of 60 seconds. Interestingly enough, if you turn off CDP on your router interface, it still learns about other neighbors in its CDP table, but doesn't forward its own information.

Example 2-8   **show cdp** *Defaults*

```
r2>show cdp
Global CDP information:
        Sending CDP packets every 60 seconds
        Sending a holdtime value of 180 seconds
r2>
```

Review **show cdp neighbors** and **show cdp neighbors detail** output until you are very comfortable with them, or better yet until you can draw a complete map of your environment. Look back at Example 2-7 once more. **show cdp neighbors** shows the local interface and the remote port ID. **show cdp neighbors detail** shows the local interface as port ID and the remote interface as outgoing port.

NOTE	In troubleshooting CDP, look for lines such as **no cdp run** (global) or **no cdp enable** (interface) in your configurations. Also, IP unnumbered does not pass your IP information through CDP.

Although many problems are physical in nature, if the lower layers check out you must move up to protocol connections as troubleshooting targets. Some examples include routing processes, switching processes, routing protocols, routed protocols, and so on.

You certainly can start with **show ip route**, assuming you are using IP as a routed protocol, to see whether you have a route to your destination network. However, do not underestimate the power of **show protocols** and **show ip protocols** (see Example 2-9).

Example 2-9   **show protocols** *and* **show ip protocols**

```
r2>show protocols
Global values:
  Internet Protocol routing is enabled
Ethernet0 is up, line protocol is up
  Internet address is 192.168.3.1/24
Serial0 is up, line protocol is up
  Internet address is 192.168.2.2/24
Serial1 is administratively down, line protocol is down
r2>show ip protocols

r2>show ip route
Codes: C - connected, S - static, I - IGRP, R - RIP, M - mobile, B - BGP
       D - EIGRP, EX - EIGRP external, O - OSPF, IA - OSPF inter area
       N1 - OSPF NSSA external type 1, N2 - OSPF NSSA external type 2
       E1 - OSPF external type 1, E2 - OSPF external type 2, E - EGP
       i - IS-IS, L1 - IS-IS level-1, L2 - IS-IS level-2, * - candidate default
       U - per-user static route, o - ODR
Gateway of last resort is not set
C    192.168.2.0/24 is directly connected, Serial0
C    192.168.3.0/24 is directly connected, Ethernet0
r2>
```

Example 2-9 certainly illustrates that IP routing is enabled by default, but it is possible for someone to issue **no ip routing**. To re-enable the IP routing process, use the global command **ip routing**. To enable IPX routing, you must issue **ipx routing**.

Perhaps you have figured out by now that in Example 2-9 both **show ip protocols** and **show ip route** indicate that no routing protocols are turned on.

If you are following along with me in your own practical lab, you can take a look at Figure 2-1 for a picture of my test lab that I plan to build upon throughout this book. Although I am using a 2516 and 2501 for the examples in this chapter, you can certainly use any router that has at least one Ethernet and one serial interface. Take a look at Cisco.com to get a list of routers that meet these criteria.

Figure 2-1 *Chapter 2 Scenario*

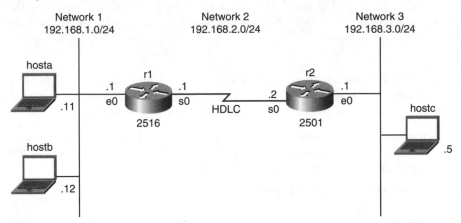

Next I configure RIP on r1 and r2 to allow r1 to reach the far side of r2 and vice versa. Example 2-10 shows the configuration, and Example 2-11 shows the testing.

Example 2-10 *Adding a Routing Protocol to r1 and r2*

```
r1(config)#router rip
r1(config-router)#network 192.168.1.0
r1(config-router)#network 192.168.2.0
r1(config-router)#end
r2(config)#router rip
r2(config-router)#network 192.168.2.0
r2(config-router)#network 192.168.3.0
r2(config-router)#end
r2#
```

Example 2-11 *Testing the Routing Protocol*

```
r2#show protocols
Global values:
  Internet Protocol routing is enabled
Ethernet0 is up, line protocol is up
  Internet address is 192.168.3.1/24
Serial0 is up, line protocol is up
  Internet address is 192.168.2.2/24
Serial1 is administratively down, line protocol is down
r2#show ip protocols
Routing Protocol is "rip"
  Sending updates every 30 seconds, next due in 20 seconds
  Invalid after 180 seconds, hold down 180, flushed after 240
  Outgoing update filter list for all interfaces is
  Incoming update filter list for all interfaces is
  Redistributing: rip
  Default version control: send version 1, receive any version
    Interface      Send  Recv    Key-chain
    Ethernet0       1     1 2
    Serial0         1     1 2
```

Example 2-11 *Testing the Routing Protocol (Continued)*

```
 Routing for Networks:
   192.168.2.0
   192.168.3.0
 Routing Information Sources:
   Gateway          Distance       Last Update
   192.168.2.1          120        00:00:25
 Distance: (default is 120)

r2#show ip route
Codes: C - connected, S - static, I - IGRP, R - RIP, M - mobile, B - BGP
       D - EIGRP, EX - EIGRP external, O - OSPF, IA - OSPF inter area
       N1 - OSPF NSSA external type 1, N2 - OSPF NSSA external type 2
       E1 - OSPF external type 1, E2 - OSPF external type 2, E - EGP
       i - IS-IS, L1 - IS-IS level-1, L2 - IS-IS level-2, * - candidate default
       U - per-user static route, o - ODR
Gateway of last resort is not set
R    192.168.1.0/24 [120/1] via 192.168.2.1, 00:00:11, Serial0
C    192.168.2.0/24 is directly connected, Serial0
C    192.168.3.0/24 is directly connected, Ethernet0
r2#exit
r2>ping 192.168.1.1
Type escape sequence to abort.
Sending 5, 100-byte ICMP Echos to 192.168.1.1, timeout is 2 seconds:
!!!!!
Success rate is 100 percent (5/5), round-trip min/avg/max = 28/30/32 ms
```

show protocols indicates that the IP routing process (routed protocol) is enabled as well as the interface address and status. **show ip protocols** identifies exactly which routing protocols are running and what networks are advertised. The routing table now contains the missing Network 1, and the user ping output in Example 2-11 confirms that r2 can now reach the far side of r1.

NOTE   When changes are made with routes, it is often helpful to issue the **clear ip route** command to clear a particular route and force the network to converge. In a lab environment, I tend to not worry about specifics and just type **clear ip route ***, but this is definitely one of those possible career-limiting moves (CLMs) in the practical world. Best practice is to replace the * with a specific network address to clear an *individual* route.

Recall from Chapter 1 and from your own networks that on broadcast media, an Address Resolution Protocol (ARP) packet is broadcast (local broadcast) to resolve the destination IP address (Layer 3) to its corresponding MAC address (Layer 2). If the destination host is on the same subnet, the MAC is the destination host's address. If the destination host is on a different subnet, the resulting resolution is generally the default gateway (local router interface) MAC address. The output in Example 2-12 shows the MAC address of interface Ethernet 0 on my r2 router, which I verified with **show ip interface ethernet 0**. The other address in the ARP table is the host MAC address for 192.168.3.5, because it is on the local Ethernet segment of the r2 router. There is no difference between **show arp** and **show ip arp** in the example because IP is the only routed protocol currently running.

Example 2-12   **show arp** *and* **show ip arp**

```
r2>ping 192.168.3.5
Type escape sequence to abort.
Sending 5, 100-byte ICMP Echos to 192.168.3.5, timeout is 2 seconds:
.!!!!
Success rate is 80 percent (4/5), round-trip min/avg/max = 1/3/4 ms
r2>ping 192.168.3.5
Type escape sequence to abort.
Sending 5, 100-byte ICMP Echos to 192.168.3.5, timeout is 2 seconds:
!!!!!
Success rate is 100 percent (5/5), round-trip min/avg/max = 1/2/4 ms
r2>show arp
Protocol  Address          Age (min)  Hardware Addr   Type   Interface
Internet  192.168.3.1           -     0000.0c38.a05d  ARPA   Ethernet0
Internet  192.168.3.5           0     0050.04df.5f3c  ARPA   Ethernet0
r2>show ip arp
Protocol  Address          Age (min)  Hardware Addr   Type   Interface
Internet  192.168.3.1           -     0000.0c38.a05d  ARPA   Ethernet0
Internet  192.168.3.5           0     0050.04df.5f3c  ARPA   Ethernet0
r2>show interfaces e0
Ethernet0 is up, line protocol is up
  Hardware is Lance, address is 0000.0c38.a05d (bia 0000.0c38.a05d)
  Description: r2 e0 to HostC Win98Dell
  Internet address is 192.168.3.1/24
  MTU 1500 bytes, BW 10000 Kbit, DLY 1000 usec, rely 255/255, load 1/255
  Encapsulation ARPA, loopback not set, keepalive set (10 sec)
  ARP type: ARPA, ARP Timeout 04:00:00
r2>show arp
Protocol  Address          Age (min)  Hardware Addr   Type   Interface
Internet  192.168.3.1           -     0000.0c38.a05d  ARPA   Ethernet0
Internet  192.168.3.5          13     0050.04df.5f3c  ARPA   Ethernet0
r2>show arp
Protocol  Address          Age (min)  Hardware Addr   Type   Interface
Internet  192.168.3.1           -     0000.0c38.a05d  ARPA   Ethernet0
Internet  192.168.3.5          14     0050.04df.5f3c  ARPA   Ethernet0
```

NOTE   The router keeps an ARP entry for four hours by default, whereas a PC retains this information for only a couple of minutes. Microsoft Windows default ARP cache timeout is two minutes.

Refer to the Age (min) column in the preceding example to watch the numbers increase. ARP is dynamic in nature; if the wrong information was learned or you move a device, however, you may sometimes need to clear the ARP cache with the **clear arp-cache** command when you are troubleshooting. First, you should **shut/no shut** the particular interface to see if that clears the issue at hand.

Other helpful show commands include **show version**, **show running-config**, **show startup-config**, **show flash**, various memory commands, and **show tech-support**. Examples 2-13 through 2-22 illustrate and explain these commands.

NOTE	Example 2-13 displays the output of **show version**. Even when you are at your wits' end, you better pay attention to it. Too many times, I have exhausted my bottom-up troubleshooting skills and still been stumped by this one. In other words, I worked my way up from the Physical Layer to the Application Layer, and the real problem was the IOS version I was using.

Example 2-13   show version

```
r2>shver
Translating "shver"...domain server (255.255.255.255)
% Unknown command or computer name, or unable to find computer address
r2>show version
Cisco Internetwork Operating System Software
IOS (tm) 2500 Software (C2500-IS-L), Version 12.0(5), RELEASE SOFTWARE (fc1)
Copyright  1986-1999 by cisco Systems, Inc.
Compiled Tue 15-Jun-99 19:57 by phanguye
Image text-base: 0x0303D744, data-base: 0x00001000
ROM: System Bootstrap, Version 11.0(10c)XB1, PLATFORM SPECIFIC RELEASE SOFTWARE
     (fc1)
BOOTFLASH: 3000 Bootstrap Software (IGS-BOOT-R), Version 11.0(10c)XB1,
     PLATFORM SPECIFIC RELEASE SOFTWARE (fc1)
r2 uptime is 6 hours, 15 minutes
System restarted by power-on
System image file is "flash:c2500-is-l.120-5.bin"
cisco 2500 (68030) processor (revision D) with 16384K/2048K bytes of memory.
Processor board ID 01507529, with hardware revision 00000000
Bridging software.
X.25 software, Version 3.0.0.
1 Ethernet/IEEE 802.3 interface(s)
2 Serial network interface(s)
32K bytes of non-volatile configuration memory.
16384K bytes of processor board System flash (Read ONLY)
Configuration register is 0x2102
>r2
```

Notice in Example 2-13 how the router is attempting to resolve the host name to an IP address. I could have just typed **no ip domain-lookup** so that the router didn't keep looking for a Domain Name System (DNS) server, but I didn't. The shortcut **sh ver** would have worked just fine had I inserted the space. I have shaded some of the output of interest, such as hardware and software config files, boot images, and version, but you can always research the details at Cisco.com. You will do that in later sections of this chapter. **show version** shows 16384K/2048K, which is the amount of RAM/shared packet memory on the router. The command also helps you identify any known bugs with a particular IOS version or release. For example, the current IOS version on r1 and r2 is 12.0(5), which is read Version 12.0 Release 5. However, 12.0 code did not reach General Deployment (GD) until 12.0(8).

NOTE	The router takes almost a minute to attempt DNS lookups for *every* unknown phrase that may be a telnet attempt. On a practical note, also keep in mind that DNS name resolution is via a User Datagram Protocol (UDP) broadcast packet.

From a support standpoint, it is very helpful to understand not only the command structure of the IOS but also how the versions and releases work. You may use new IOS releases in a test bed, but GD is more common in a production environment. Table 2-2 describes the release designations. Also, Cisco makes use of Technology release train letters such as E for Enterprise feature set, S for Service Provider, and T for Consolidated Technology followed by another sequential character such as A or B at the end of its filenames.

Table 2-2 *The IOS Life Cycle*

Release Designation	Description
FCS	First Commercial Shipment. Initial release that delivers new functionality to the market.
CCO FCS Date	Commercially available to customers for electronic download from Cisco.com.
MFG FCS Date	Commercially available to customers from Cisco manufacturing (normally a week after CCO FCS).
Product Bulletin#	ID number of product bulletin describing the new features.
Major Release	Delivers significant platform and feature support to market. No new features are added to a Major Release after the initial FCS to protect stability.
GD	Reaches the General Deployment milestone when Cisco announces that it is suitable for deployment anywhere in customer networks where features and functionality of the release are required. The GD milestone is reached after Cisco considers criteria such as customer feedback, bug reports, and reported field experience. Only Major Releases are GD candidates.
LD	Limited Deployment is the life cycle phase between the initial FCS and the GD milestones.
GD Release	Maintenance release at which the Major Release became GD.
ED Release	Early Deployment Releases offer new feature, platform, or interface support.
End of Sales	Can't order after this date, but still available on Cisco.com.
End of Engineering	Although no more scheduled maintenance releases for the Major Release, it is still available on Cisco.com.
End of Life	Software is no longer officially supported. Removed from Cisco.com. Approximately 3 years following the FCS of the Major Release.
Obsolete	Can't order, but can be made available on Cisco.com under certain conditions.

Example 2-14 shows the output of **show running-config**. Compare this to Example 2-15, which covers **show startup-config**.

Example 2-14   **show running-config** (**write terminal**) *Command Output*

```
r2>show run
 ^
% Invalid input detected at '^' marker.
r2>en
r2#show run
r2#show running-config
Building configuration...
Current configuration:
version 12.0
service timestamps debug uptime
service timestamps log uptime
no service password-encryption
hostname r2
ip subnet-zero
ip host r1 192.168.2.1
ip host hostA 192.168.1.11
ip host hostB 192.168.1.12
ip host hostC 192.168.3.5
ip host r2 192.168.2.2
process-max-time 200
interface Ethernet0
 description r2 e0 to hostC Win98Dell
 ip address 192.168.3.1 255.255.255.0
 no ip directed-broadcast
interface Serial0
 description r2 s0 DCE to r1 s0 DTE
 bandwidth 64
 ip address 192.168.2.2 255.255.255.0
 no ip directed-broadcast
 no ip mroute-cache
 clockrate 64000
interface Serial1
 no ip address
 no ip directed-broadcast
 shutdown
router rip
 network 192.168.2.0
 network 192.168.3.0
ip classless
line con 0
 transport input none
line aux 0
line vty 0 4
 password donna
 login
end
r2#
```

NOTE   Note that **show run** is not available in user mode. I typed **show run** from enable mode and pressed Tab to complete the command so that you could view the full command. I do the same for **show start** in the next example. Command completion is not necessary and normally I do not bother. *Always* pay attention to commands and modes, however, because Cisco CCNP tests in general cover them. The commands in this book follow the Cisco and Cisco Press conventions of spelling them out entirely so that you can get comfortable with the full command. In a practical environment, shortcuts are just fine.

It is definitely not good practice that I haven't saved my configuration for a while. I will save just as soon as you take a look at **show startup-config** in Example 2-15.

Example 2-15   **show start** *(show config) Command Output*

```
r2#show start
r2#show startup-config
Using 764 out of 32762 bytes
version 12.0
service timestamps debug uptime
service timestamps log uptime
no service password-encryption
hostname r2
ip subnet-zero
ip host r1 192.168.2.1
ip host hostA 192.168.1.11
ip host hostB 192.168.1.12
ip host hostC 192.168.3.5
ip host r2 192.168.2.2
process-max-time 200
interface Ethernet0
 description r2 e0 to hostC Win98Dell
 ip address 192.168.3.1 255.255.255.0
 no ip directed-broadcast
interface Serial0
 description r2 s0 DCE to r1 s0 DTE
 bandwidth 64
 ip address 192.168.2.2 255.255.255.0
 no ip directed-broadcast
 no ip mroute-cache
 clockrate 64000
interface Serial1
 no ip address
 no ip directed-broadcast
 shutdown
ip classless
line con 0
 transport input none
line aux 0
line vty 0 4
 password donna
 login
end
r2#wr
```

Example 2-15 shows that you are using 764 out of 32762 bytes of the NVRAM. Many people confuse NVRAM and Flash, but they are quite different. NVRAM is writable permanent storage for your startup configuration, whereas Flash provides permanent storage for the Cisco IOS software image(s), backup configurations, or other files. I saved my configuration on r2 with the **write memory** command because **wr** is easy to type (same as **copy run start**). If I were to compare the running configuration to the startup configuration, now they should both know about what I have configured.

NOTE   Many Cisco troubleshooters are still attached to the old commands that are left over from IOS pre-10.3 code, such as **write**; however, Cisco says the commands will eventually go away. **write memory** saves the running configuration to the startup configuration, **write terminal** is like **show running-config**, and **show config** is like **show startup-config**. In a practical sense, I have had to use **show config** when not enough memory was available to type **show running-config** or **show startup-config**.

Example 2-16 demonstrates **show flash** on a 2500 series router.

Example 2-16   **show flash** *on a 2500 Series Router*

```
r2>show flash
System flash directory:
File  Length    Name/status
  1   7567500   c2500-is-l.120-5.bin
[7567564 bytes used, 9209652 available, 16777216 total]
16384K bytes of processor board System flash (Read ONLY)
r2>
```

The shaded lines indicate that there is one file in Flash that takes up 7 MB out of the existing 16 MB available. The last line shows that the system Flash is read-only. The 2500 series routers run the IOS from Flash because they were designed at a time when Cisco was trying to save users money. The image file is relocatable and is indicated as such by the letter *l* in the filename. To upgrade the IOS image on this router, I would need to get into rxboot mode by changing the config register to 0x2101 as a consequence of the Flash being read-only. However, newer images and routers automate this for you with Flash load helper. Compare Example 2-16 to the Flash on a 3600 series router in Example 2-17.

Example 2-17   **show flash** *on a 3600 Series Router*

```
3620>show flash
System flash directory:
File  Length    Name/status
  1   3971288   c3620-d-mz.113-9.T
[3971352 bytes used, 12805864 available, 16777216 total]
16384K bytes of processor board System flash (Read/Write)
3620>
```

Notice the read/write status of Flash on the 3620. Like hard drives, Flash can be partitioned. Therefore, you may need to check the partitions, in which case the question mark (**?**) will help you through. Always check for additional Flash in slot0: and slot1: on routers with Flash memory cards. For example, the 6509s may have additional Flash memory cards on the supervisor module.

Assuming you had an updated IOS file handy that you had verified would work in your network, you could take the time to upgrade the IOS. Copying configurations and upgrading IOS versions is somewhat assumed knowledge here. If you do need some practice, however, refer to the practical troubleshooting worksheets in Appendix B, "Troubleshooting Resources," or see Cisco.com for more information. A good starting place is the Cisco IOS Roadmap available at www.cisco.com/warp/public/620/roadmap.shtml. Alternatively, search for "cisco roadmap."

Now turn your focus to some memory show commands, such as **show memory**, **show processes**, **show stacks**, and **show buffers** to monitor memory leaks and utilization issues.

In Example 2-18, I issued a **show mem** on my router and the Tab key to complete the command. I pressed the Spacebar to display the output screen-by-screen instead of just pressing Enter to see line-by-line. Many times I find what I need before the end of the display, so I tap the Esc key, Q key, or any key for that matter to stop where I am. Depending on the scroll buffer size, I scroll back to find the required detail. In situations such as this where you are trying to capture output, log the session so that you can refer back to it later. The specifics depend on the terminal program. Because I am using SecureCRT for mine, I can go to the File menu and turn on the logging functionality, clear the screen, and start again. After I finish logging, I just turn it off so that I can open the saved session file in my SecureCRT directory. Then I rename the file to something relevant so that I can refer back to it later. Example 2-18 shows the available options for **show memory** and **show memory ?**.

Example 2-18 **show memory** *Output*

```
r2>show mem
r2>show memory
                Head     Total(b)    Used(b)     Free(b)   Lowest(b)  Largest(b)
Processor      94DC8    16163384    1578748    14584636   14437208    14437896
      I/O     4000000     2097152     336376     1760776    1760776     1760556
            Processor memory
  Address  Bytes Prev.     Next     Ref  PrevF   NextF   Alloc PC  What
  94DC8    1064  0         9521C     1                   31AB1C4   List Elements
  9521C    2864  94DC8     95D78     1                   31AB1C4   List Headers
  95D78    3992  9521C     96D3C     1                   314C830   TTY data
  ...
            I/O memory
  Address  Bytes Prev.     Next     Ref  PrevF   NextF   Alloc PC  What
  4000000  260   0         4000130   1                   3187E70   *Packet Data*
  4000130  260   4000000   4000260   1                   3187E70   *Packet Data*
  ...
r2>show memory ?
  allocating-process   Show allocating process name
  dead                 Memory owned by dead processes
  fast                 Fast memory stats
```

Example 2-18   **show memory** *Output (Continued)*

```
 free                  Free memory stats
 io                    IO memory stats
 multibus              Multibus memory stats
 pci                   PCI memory stats
 processor             Processor memory stats
 summary               Summary of memory usage per alloc PC
 <cr>
r2>
```

show memory gives a block-by-block display of memory usage, which is why I had to stop the command and give you only a partial capture in Example 2-18. There are many processes running on the CPU that are allocated a certain amount of memory each. Consider the processor memory, for instance. You had better have at least 1 MB free, and if running Border Gateway Protocol (BGP), you should consider more like 5 to 10 MB free working space to handle route flaps and convergence. From a troubleshooting standpoint, if a process doesn't de-allocate the memory it had and it is being allocated more memory, that is reason to watch it. Actually, this is referred to as a *memory leak* and normally the fix is to upgrade the IOS. For memory allocation errors, about all you can do temporarily is power cycle the box; for a more permanent fix, upgrade the IOS. Check Cisco.com or report the problem if you are the first to find it so that the rest of us don't have to suffer.

Example 2-19 illustrates **show process**, which gives you the CPU utilization and memory usage.

Example 2-19   **show process** *Output*

```
r2>show process
CPU utilization for five seconds: 21%/19%; one minute: 28%; five minutes: 23%
 PID QTy       PC Runtime (ms)    Invoked   uSecs     Stacks TTY Process
   1 Csp  31C05CC         648       6436     100   736/1000   0 Load Meter
   2 M*         0         124         14    8857  2792/4000   0 Exec
   3 Lst  31B0DDA       70276       4864   14448  3704/4000   0 Check heaps
   4 Cwe  31B70F6           0          1       0  3732/4000   0 Pool Manager
...
r2>show process memory
Total: 18260536, Used: 1915000, Free: 16345536
 PID TTY  Allocated      Freed    Holding    Getbufs    Retbufs Process
   0   0      35668       1252    1641800          0          0 *Init*
   0   0        484     109420        484          0          0 *Sched*
   0   0    3219684    1348972       1720     323940          0 *Dead*
   1   0        268        268       1748          0          0 Load Meter
   2   0        312          0      56696          0          0 Exec
   3   0          0          0       4748          0          0 Check heaps
...
 PID TTY  Allocated      Freed    Holding    Getbufs    Retbufs Process
                                  1914160 Total
r2>
```

I cut most of the output from the commands in Example 2-19 because the main emphasis here is on the beginning shaded lines dealing with the CPU utilization and memory usage. **show process** shows the average CPU utilization for intervals of 5 seconds, 1 minute, and 5 minutes. After you have taken several snapshots of this command, you can then compare the relative instances that a particular process has been invoked. The one that has been invoked the most is more than likely responsible for the load on the CPU. The **show process memory** command offers a more detailed display on how each process allocates, frees, and holds memory.

NOTE   It is *extremely important* not to overload the router with **debug packet**-type commands if any of these utilization values are greater than 50%. Perhaps you can use **debug event**-type commands, for a little less overhead, to aid you in your troubleshooting.

Example 2-20 shows the output of **show stacks**, which is used to monitor router processes and interrupts. This command is not a daily routine. If you use **show version** and see that the box reloaded because of a crash, however, use the **show stacks** command so that the Technical Assistance Center (TAC) can assist. It may be helpful if you dump the output to the Cisco Stack Decoder Tool before you reload a crashed router. If the output doesn't appear to be helpful to you, it may be of value to the Cisco TAC engineer; many times they have different versions of tools from what you and I have.

Example 2-20   **show stacks** *Output*

```
r2>show stacks
Minimum process stacks:
 Free/Size    Name
 2348/4000    Init
 3468/4000    RADIUS INITCONFIG
 3388/4000    DHCP Client
 1964/4000    Exec
 3500/4000    Router Init
Interrupt level stacks:
Level    Called Unused/Size  Name
  3          3    2772/3000  Serial interface state change interrupt
  4      13976    2576/3000  Network interfaces
  5     171009    2864/3000  Console Uart
r2>
```

Example 2-21 shows the output of **show buffers**, including the size of the various buffer pools. The router is pretty smart in serving its customers (or should I say allocating buffers and reallocating as necessary), especially if you use the faster switching modes. Overruns occur when the hardware can't send received data to a buffer because the input rate exceeded its capability to handle the data. Underruns are when the transmitter is running faster than the router can process. However, interface buffers can fall back on system buffers as needed, which makes them pretty self-tuning.

NOTE   Newer versions of IOS do a much better job of tuning buffers on their own than earlier versions did. This is a case where tweaks, knobs, and adjustments are great if you *know* the impact of the defaults you are changing. Defaults are set for a reason, and when it comes to buffers, always consult TAC before you arbitrarily adjust them.

Example 2-21   **show buffers** *Output*

```
r2>show buffers
Buffer elements:
     500 in free list (500 max allowed)
     18734 hits, 0 misses, 0 created
Public buffer pools:
Small buffers, 104 bytes (total 50, permanent 50):
     49 in free list (20 min, 150 max allowed)
     6802 hits, 0 misses, 0 trims, 0 created
     0 failures (0 no memory)
Middle buffers, 600 bytes (total 25, permanent 25):
     25 in free list (10 min, 150 max allowed)
     2765 hits, 0 misses, 0 trims, 0 created
     0 failures (0 no memory)
Big buffers, 1524 bytes (total 50, permanent 50):
     50 in free list (5 min, 150 max allowed)
     1115 hits, 0 misses, 0 trims, 0 created
     0 failures (0 no memory)
VeryBig buffers, 4520 bytes (total 10, permanent 10):
     10 in free list (0 min, 100 max allowed)
     0 hits, 0 misses, 0 trims, 0 created
     0 failures (0 no memory)
Large buffers, 5024 bytes (total 0, permanent 0):
     0 in free list (0 min, 10 max allowed)
     0 hits, 0 misses, 0 trims, 0 created
     0 failures (0 no memory)
Huge buffers, 18024 bytes (total 0, permanent 0):
     0 in free list (0 min, 4 max allowed)
     0 hits, 0 misses, 0 trims, 0 created
     0 failures (0 no memory)
Interface buffer pools:
Ethernet0 buffers, 1524 bytes (total 32, permanent 32):
     8 in free list (0 min, 32 max allowed)
     24 hits, 0 fallbacks
     8 max cache size, 8 in cache
Serial0 buffers, 1524 bytes (total 32, permanent 32):
     7 in free list (0 min, 32 max allowed)
     705 hits, 0 fallbacks
     8 max cache size, 8 in cache
Serial1 buffers, 1524 bytes (total 32, permanent 32):
     7 in free list (0 min, 32 max allowed)
     25 hits, 0 fallbacks
     8 max cache size, 8 in cache
r2>
```

You *must* know and understand the Cisco IOS to become a CCNP and to give Cisco the information they need to help you. One of the best things to review the previous commands, to assist with your baseline, and to give to TAC is the output of **show tech-support**. It is excellent documentation for you to have the normal output of this command when things are operating the way they should so that you have a comparison when things are not operating so smoothly. The output of **show tech-support** is a little lengthy. I cut most of the output in Example 2-22, but left enough for you to get a feel for the usefulness of the command.

Depending on the hardware and the IOS feature sets, **show tech-support** includes output from the following commands as well as others. The following list shows common shortcuts for some of the full commands displayed in this chapter:

- **sh ver**
- **sh run**
- **sh contr**
- **sh stac**
- **sh int**
- **sh proc mem**
- **sh proc cpu**
- **sh buf**

Example 2-22 **show tech-support** *Output*

```
r2>show tech-support
----------------- show version -----------------
Cisco Internetwork Operating System Software
IOS (tm) 2500 Software (C2500-IS-L), Version 12.0(5), RELEASE SOFTWARE (fc1)
...
32K bytes of non-volatile configuration memory.
16384K bytes of processor board System flash (Read ONLY)
Configuration register is 0x2102
----------------- show running-config -----------------
Building configuration...
Current configuration:
version 12.0
service timestamps debug uptime
service timestamps log uptime
no service password-encryption
hostname r2
...
----------------- show controllers -----------------
LANCE unit 0, idb 0xD9280, ds 0xDAB88, regaddr = 0x2130000, reset_mask 0x2
IB at 0x4006E64: mode=0x0000, mcfilter 0000/0000/0100/0020
station address 0000.0c38.a05d  default station address 0000.0c38.a05d
...
----------------- show stacks -----------------
Minimum process stacks:
```

Example 2-22   **show tech-support** *Output (Continued)*

```
Free/Size   Name
2348/4000   Init
...
Interrupt level stacks:
Level     Called Unused/Size  Name
  3            3  2772/3000   Serial interface state change interrupt
...
------------------ show interfaces ------------------
Ethernet0 is up, line protocol is up
  Hardware is Lance, address is 0000.0c38.a05d (bia 0000.0c38.a05d)
...
Serial0 is up, line protocol is up
...
     DCD=up  DSR=up  DTR=up  RTS=up  CTS=up
Serial1 is administratively down, line protocol is down
...
     DCD=down  DSR=down  DTR=down  RTS=down  CTS=down
------------------ show process memory ------------------
Total: 18260536, Used: 1915584, Free: 16344952
 PID TTY  Allocated      Freed    Holding    Getbufs    Retbufs Process
   0   0      35668       1252    1641800          0          0 *Init*
...                                1914784 Total
------------------ show process cpu ------------------
CPU utilization for five seconds: 21%/14%; one minute: 23%; five minutes: 18%
 PID   Runtime(ms)  Invoked   uSecs    5Sec    1Min    5Min TTY Process
   1          676      6972      96   0.00%   0.00%   0.00%   0 Load Meter
   2         9400       137   68613   7.61%   8.50%   2.59%   0 Exec
...
------------------ show buffers ------------------

Buffer elements:
     500 in free list (500 max allowed)
     19804 hits, 0 misses, 0 created
Public buffer pools:
Small buffers, 104 bytes (total 50, permanent 50):
...
Huge buffers, 18024 bytes (total 0, permanent 0):
Interface buffer pools:
Ethernet0 buffers, 1524 bytes (total 32, permanent 32):
...
Serial0 buffers, 1524 bytes (total 32, permanent 32):
...
Serial1 buffers, 1524 bytes (total 32, permanent 32):
R2>
```

Obviously, this section has not covered all the show commands of the IOS; nor will you ever cover all the show commands because Cisco is constantly improving their IOS. This section has provided an overview of the most useful commands and how to interpret them so that you can use them throughout the exercises in this book. Now that you have examined some of the more common show commands, turn your attention to **ping** to assist with troubleshooting targets up through the Network Layer.

Cisco Ping Commands

Ping is a lifesaver to determine end-to-end connectivity and reachability issues. However, it has the potential to disrupt routers if not handled properly. As with the other tools, it is helpful to baseline and have the normal output of ping commands when the network is working properly to compare against those times when you are troubleshooting. By the way, ping is not just for IP; it is a valuable tool for IP, IPX, and other protocols as well.

NOTE   As previously mentioned, ping may potentially disrupt routers, and this is putting it mildly. Enterprise organizations and Internet service providers (ISPs) generally filter Internet Control Message Protocol (ICMP) packets because they can be used to launch denial-of-service (DoS) and other hack attacks.

I sometimes think of ping as a Ping-Pong game. Ping first sends an ICMP Echo Request packet and awaits an ICMP Echo Reply. Many times ping fails because the Echo Request is successful, but the Echo Reply doesn't have a way to return. Note the basic Cisco ping output in Example 2-23. The success rate of 5/5 is obviously what you want to see compared to the 0/5 (where there is most definitely a problem at Layer 3 or below). If the success rate is less than 5/5, remember to ping again for more accurate results. When the success rate is 4/5 (80 percent) in a Cisco environment, I normally just write it off to ARP performing its duties and ping again if I really must see 5/5 (100 percent). Refer back to Example 2-12 to see the .!!!! (four bangs) and !!!!! (five bangs) with ARP in action. Example 2-23 demonstrates user-mode **ping** across a point-to-point HDLC serial link where ARP is not necessary.

Example 2-23   *User-Mode* **ping**

```
r2>ping 192.168.1.1
Type escape sequence to abort.
Sending 5, 100-byte ICMP Echos to 192.168.1.1, timeout is 2 seconds:
!!!!!
Success rate is 100 percent (5/5), round-trip min/avg/max = 28/30/32 ms
```

From the preceding ping and ARP examples, and in your day-to-day troubleshooting, it is fairly easy to interpret that an exclamation (!) means successful and a period (.) means not successful. The success rate is a percentage of packets echoed back to the router, and anything less than 80 percent is usually problematic. The round-trip time intervals display as minimum, average, and maximum, and are quite helpful to compare against your baseline for how long it takes to receive a reply. Table 2-3 explains ping character output.

Table 2-3   *Cisco Ping-Pong Table*

Output	Description
!	Each bang represents the receipt of a reply.
.	Timeout while waiting for reply.
U	Destination unreachable.
N	Network unreachable.
P	Protocol unreachable.
C	Congestion OCCURRED.
Q	Source quench. Router saying slow down.
M	Maximum transmission unit (MTU) problem. Could not fragment.
A	Administratively prohibited.
I	User-interrupted ping.
?	Unknown packet type.
&	Packet lifetime exceeded.
Ctrl+Shift+6	Abort Cisco ping.
%Unrecognized host or address	Name resolution issue.

The preceding example demonstrates the user-mode ping that can be issued in user or enable mode. Extended ping is available only from enable mode (#). For IP, you can relate these extended options to the fields in the IP packet (after we review the IP header options in Chapter 3, "Shooting Trouble with IP.") Table 2-4 lists the extended ping options.

Table 2-4   *Extended Ping Options*

Field	Description
Protocol[IP]:	Default is IP.
Target IP address:	Destination host name or IP address.
Repeat count[5]:	Number of ping packets. Default is 5 ping packets.
Datagram size [100]:	Size of ping packets. Default size of the ping packet is 100 bytes.
Timeout in seconds[2]:	Default timeout interval is 2 seconds.
Extended commands[n]:	Default is no extended commands, but you can type **Y** to indicate you want a series of additional commands to appear. Some of these commands follow.
Source address or interface:	Set the source address in the ping packet.

continues

Table 2-4   *Extended Ping Options (Continued)*

Type of service [0]:	TOS selection. Default is 0.
Set DF bit in IP header? [no]:	Don't fragment. Drop and send error message instead. Helps determine the smallest MTU in the path. Default is no.
Validate reply data? [no]:	Specify whether to validate the reply data. Default is no.
Data pattern [0xABCD]:	Default is ABCD, but varying to all 1s or 0s can be helpful when debugging channel service units/data service units (CSUs/DSUs) or detecting cable problems such as crosstalk.
Loose, Strict, Record, Timestamp, Verbose[none]:	The default is none. Other header options include the following: **Loose**—List of nodes that must be traversed **Strict**—List of nodes that must be the only nodes traversed **Record**—Path **Timestamp**—Times **Verbose**—Detailed information
Sweep range of sizes[n]:	Vary the size of the echo packets being sent. Useful to determine the minimum MTUs configured from the source to destination. Reduce performance problems related to fragmentation.
!!!!!	Each bang (!) indicates the receipt of a reply, whereas a period (.) indicates a timeout while waiting for a reply.
Success rate is 100 percent	100 percent or 5/5 is obviously what you want to see, not the 0/5, which most definitely indicates a problem at L3 or below. If the success rate is less than 100 percent, remember to ping again for best results. When the success rate is 4/5 (or 80 percent) in a Cisco environment, I normally just write it off to ARP performing its duties.
Round-trip min/avg/max = 1/2/4 ms	Round-trip minimum/average/maximum milliseconds for the reply packet.

Type **ping** and press **Enter** to specify the extended protocol options in Example 2-24.

Example 2-24   *Cisco Extended Ping*

```
r2#ping
Protocol [ip]:
Target IP address: 192.168.4.1
Repeat count [5]:
Datagram size [100]:
Timeout in seconds [2]:
Extended commands [n]: y
Source address or interface: 192.168.3.1
Type of service [0]:
```

Example 2-24 *Cisco Extended Ping (Continued)*

```
Set DF bit in IP header? [no]:
Validate reply data? [no]:
Data pattern [0xABCD]:
Loose, Strict, Record, Timestamp, Verbose[none]:
Sweep range of sizes [n]:
Type escape sequence to abort.
Sending 5, 100-byte ICMP Echos to 192.168.4.1, timeout is 2 seconds:
.....
Success rate is 0 percent (0/5)
r2#
```

Example 2-24 illustrates extended ping in action, but the success rate of 0/5 is not so successful. It is important to note that you must answer **yes** to the extended commands section to get more choices to assist you with troubleshooting.

In the "Cisco Trace Commands" and "Cisco Debug Commands" sections of this chapter, and in Chapter 3, you will explore more troubleshooting using ping. After all, ping is one of the easiest tests you can perform to test all the way through Layer 3.

NOTE Use ping to identify lower-level troubleshooting targets. Ping yourself, ping someone local, ping the default gateway, and ping a remote host. If you are still having problems, trace is a great companion utility to ping. Ping and trace complement one another. Ping shows connectivity and delay up to Layer 3, and trace shows the path from the source to the destination.

Cisco Trace Commands

The **traceroute** command uses a hop-by-hop approach to finding the problem. It is a valuable tool for figuring out how far can you get and finding exactly where the connection fails. Take a look at how the tool works. Three probes are sent to each hop starting with a time-to-live (TTL) of one for the first hop. When the TTL expires, the round-trip time for each probe is sent back to the originator. After every third probe, the TTL is increased by one to make it to the next router. Often, timeouts occur and **traceroute** prints * to the screen. As long as one attempt out of three works, you get hop information, but the exact output depends on such items as the security levels at each hop. Try multiple traces to see whether the same route is taken each time. Table 2-5 describes **traceroute** output. As with Cisco **ping**, **traceroute** offers extended options, too. Just type **trace** or **traceroute** and press Enter to see them.

Table 2-5 **traceroute** *Characters*

Output	Description
nn msec	Round-trip time per probe in milliseconds.
*	The probe timed out.

continues

Table 2-5 **traceroute** *Characters (Continued)*

?	Unknown packet type.
A	Administratively unreachable; check for access list issues.
H	Host unreachable.
N	Network unreachable.
P	Protocol unreachable.
Q	Source quench.
U	Port unreachable. Probe received but discarded because it could not deliver to the application.

Now that I have introduced a few tools, I want you to refer back to the practical examples provided thus far, if necessary, to help troubleshoot a particular problem in Example 2-25. The chapter scenario is pictured in Figure 2-2 for your convenience. I am on r2 trying to ping the far side of r1. This worked in my earlier test when I added RIP, but I can't ping now.

Figure 2-2 *Chapter 2 Scenario and Logging*

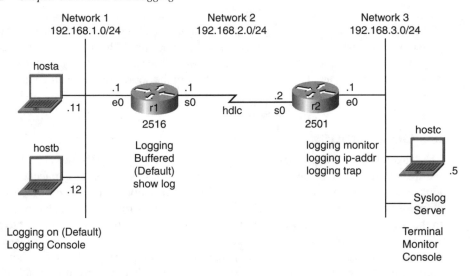

Example 2-25 *Trace Troubleshooting*

```
r2>ping 192.168.1.1
Type escape sequence to abort.
Sending 5, 100-byte ICMP Echos to 192.168.1.1, timeout is 2 seconds:
.....
Success rate is 0 percent (0/5)
r2>trace 192.168.1.1
Type escape sequence to abort.
```

Example 2-25   *Trace Troubleshooting (Continued)*

```
Tracing the route to 192.168.1.1
  1  *   *   *
  2  *   *   *
  3  *   *
r2>show ip route
...
C    192.168.2.0/24 is directly connected, Serial0
C    192.168.3.0/24 is directly connected, Ethernet0
r2>show ip protocols
Routing Protocol is "rip"
  Sending updates every 30 seconds, next due in 23 seconds
...
  Routing for Networks:
    192.168.2.0
    192.168.3.0
...
r2>where
Conn Host                 Address          Byte  Idle Conn Name
*   1 r1                  192.168.2.1         0     2 r1

r1>show ip route
...
C    192.168.1.0/24 is directly connected, Ethernet0
C    192.168.2.0/24 is directly connected, Serial0
r1>show ip protocols
r1>
```

Certainly, we have all had problems where things worked fine yesterday but there seems to be a problem now. Example 2-25 shows the output of my problem. The **ping** command did not work. Because I am trying to ping to a different network and it failed, I thought I would try **traceroute** to see whether there was a particular stopping point. **traceroute** just gave me a bunch of timeouts (*), so I thought I would telnet to r1 to see whether it could reach its own local interface of 192.168.1.1. Instead of letting my screen fill up with asterisks, I pressed the Ctrl+Shift+6 key sequence to abort the **traceroute** command. Then I used the **where** command to see whether I already had a telnet session open. You may be more familiar with the **show sessions** command, but **where** is exactly the same. Because r1 was an active telnet session, I just pressed Enter to return to it. I typed in two commands that output in detail what the problem is. Think about it a little. I will fix the problem in Example 2-26, so you can check to see whether you are right.

NOTE   Just as **where** is an alternative command for **show sessions**, **who** is an alternative command for **show users**.

Example 2-26   *Now I Can Ping*

```
r1(config)#router rip
r1(config-router)#network 192.168.1.0
r1(config-router)#network 192.168.2.0
r1(config-router)#end
r1#write mem
!!!write mem is the same as copy run start
Building configuration...
r1#show ip route
...
C    192.168.1.0/24 is directly connected, Ethernet0
C    192.168.2.0/24 is directly connected, Serial0
R    192.168.3.0/24 [120/1] via 192.168.2.2, 00:00:02, Serial0
r1#exit
[Connection to r1 closed by foreign host]
r2>show ip route
...
R    192.168.1.0/24 [120/1] via 192.168.2.1, 00:00:25, Serial0
C    192.168.2.0/24 is directly connected, Serial0
C    192.168.3.0/24 is directly connected, Ethernet0
r2>ping 192.168.1.1
Type escape sequence to abort.
Sending 5, 100-byte ICMP Echos to 192.168.1.1, timeout is 2 seconds:
!!!!!
Success rate is 100 percent (5/5), round-trip min/avg/max = 32/32/32 ms
r2>trace 192.168.1.1
Type escape sequence to abort.
Tracing the route to 192.168.1.1
  1 r1 (192.168.2.1) 16 msec *  16 msec
r2>
```

NOTE   The moral of this example is that you shouldn't hook your router up to an outlet that is controlled by your light switch and then forget to save your configuration. The more times you do things like that, however, the better support person you will be (because you will certainly remember it the next time). In a practical environment, these devices should be on an uninterruptible power supply (UPS) anyway.

You can thank Van Jacobson for the **traceroute** utility. The Microsoft implementation of trace is **tracert**; the Cisco/UNIX implementation is **traceroute** (or **trace** for short). The Microsoft **tracert** command tests only through Layer 3 because it is based on ICMP packets; whereas the UNIX/Cisco **traceroute** command is UDP-based, so it tests through Layer 4. On a practical note, you better consider this when writing your access lists—many people filter out ICMP by default as a security method for ping scans. Some do, and some do not filter the high-port UDP out. Hence trace results from the same network may deliver different results. The same holds true for traffic engineering giving lower preference to ICMP packets. Example 2-27 shows the output of an extended **traceroute** command.

Example 2-27   *Extended* **traceroute** *Command*

```
r1#trace 192.168.3.5
Type escape sequence to abort.
Tracing the route to HostC (192.168.3.5)
  1 r2 (192.168.2.2) 16 msec 16 msec 16 msec
  2  *
    HostC (192.168.3.5) 20 msec 16 msec
!!!user trace is above
!!!extended trace is below
r1#trace
Protocol [ip]:
Target IP address: 192.168.3.5
Source address:
Numeric display [n]:
Timeout in seconds [3]:
Probe count [3]:
Minimum Time to Live [1]:
Maximum Time to Live [30]:
Port Number [33434]:
Loose, Strict, Record, Timestamp, Verbose[none]:
Type escape sequence to abort.
Tracing the route to HostC (192.168.3.5)
  1 r2 (192.168.2.2) 16 msec 16 msec 16 msec
  2 HostC (192.168.3.5) 16 msec 16 msec 16 msec
r1#
```

Fields unique to the extended **traceroute** command include Source address; Numeric display; Timeout; Probe count; Time to Live; Port number; and Loose, Strict, Record, Timestamp, and Verbose. Numeric display is helpful when DNS is failing. TTL is helpful when you know your network is good but the problem is outside. Suppose, for example, that you are about six hops from the Internet. Just change the minimum TTL to six to start your testing there.

Now that you have **show**, **clear**, **ping**, and **traceroute** in your tool bag, take a look at some other tools innate to the Cisco IOS that are often very helpful for troubleshooting, such as **log** and **debug**.

NOTE   Good documentation techniques—such as adding descriptions on your interfaces, and annotating (! or remark) your configurations—are things you will thank yourself for at a later date. (Refer back to Example 2-27, for instance, where I made a remark about the user and extended trace within the configuration commands.) Another practical example of this is to add a remark when you update an access control list (ACL) with such information as its purpose, the point of contact (POC), and the date.

Cisco Logging Commands

Logging enables you to monitor and view messages that record real-time events, such as errors, warnings, and state transitions. All messages are logged to the console by default, but you can and *should* limit them. Limiting logging is *extremely* important to lessen the impact on performance (and to get your CCNP). Type **show logging**, as in Example 2-28, to see how it is set up.

Example 2-28   **show logging** *Output*

```
r2>show logging
Syslog logging: enabled (0 messages dropped, 0 flushes, 0 overruns)
    Console logging: level debugging, 9 messages logged
    Monitor logging: level debugging, 0 messages logged
    Buffer logging: level debugging, 9 messages logged
    Trap logging: level informational, 13 message lines logged
Log Buffer (4096 bytes):
00:00:42: %LINK-3-UPDOWN: Interface Ethernet0, changed state to up
00:00:42: %LINK-3-UPDOWN: Interface Serial0, changed state to up
```

NOTE   Console logging is harsh. If you must use it, at least go in through the vty (terminal) lines. Logging to a syslog server is even better than telnetting in, and logging to an internal buffer is the best (assuming you increase the buffer size), or least overhead I should say.

Table 2-6 lists levels, keywords, descriptions, and syslog definitions to assist you with minimizing the impact of logging. Error messages are typically structured in the following syntax: *%FACILITY-SEVERITY-MNEMONIC:Message text*, where *FACILITY* examples include two or more capital letters about a hardware device, software module, or protocol. *SEVERITY* is a number from zero to seven, with zero signifying the most serious condition. *MNEMONIC* uniquely identifies the message.

Table 2-6   *Logging Keywords and Levels*

Level	Keyword	Severity Description	Syslog Definition
0	Emergencies	System unusable.	LOG_EMERG
1	Alerts	Immediate action needed.	LOG_ALERT
2	Critical	Critical conditions exist.	LOG_CRIT
3	Errors	Error conditions exist.	LOG_ERR
4	Warnings	Warning conditions exist.	LOG_WARNING
5	Notification	Normal but significant conditions exist.	LOG_NOTICE
6	Informational	Informational messages.	LOG_INFO
7	Debugging	Debugging messages.	LOG_DEBUG

Type **no logging console** or **logging console** [*level*] using one of the levels specified in Table 2-6. Keep in mind that the default level is 7 for debugging, which *includes* levels equal to or less than 7. Example 2-29 illustrates other options for logging; in the example, however, I chose to direct all logging to the console and turn it off to all other supported destinations with **no logging on**.

Example 2-29   **no logging on** *Output*

```
r2(config)#no logging ?
  Hostname or A.B.C.D  IP address of the logging host
  buffered             Set buffered logging parameters
  console              Set console logging level
  facility             Facility parameter for syslog messages
  history              Configure syslog history table
  monitor              Set terminal line (monitor) logging level
  on                   Enable logging to all supported destinations
  source-interface     Specify interface for source address in logging
                       transactions
  trap                 Set syslog server logging level
r2(config)#no logging on
r2(config)#end
01:27:39: %SYS-3-LOGGER_FLUSHING: System pausing to ensure console debugging
output.
%SYS-5-CONFIG_I: Configured from console by consoler2#
r2#show log
Syslog logging: disabled (0 messages dropped, 1 flushes, 0 overruns)
    Console logging: level debugging, 10 messages logged
    Monitor logging: level debugging, 0 messages logged
    Buffer logging: level debugging, 9 messages logged
    Trap logging: level informational, 13 message lines logged
Log Buffer (4096 bytes):
00:00:42: %LINK-3-UPDOWN: Interface Ethernet0, changed state to up
00:00:42: %LINK-3-UPDOWN: Interface Serial0, changed state to up
r2(config)#
```

You *must* configure logging to limit the overhead on your router for logging to the console, logging to other terminals (monitor), and logging to a syslog server. I mentioned the levels in Table 2-6; some of the basic commands are in Table 2-7. Also refer back to Figure 2-2 for a logging illustration of the chapter scenario.

Table 2-7   *Configuring Logging*

Logging Command	Explanation
logging ip address	Log to syslog server.
logging buffered*	Log to internal buffer where the newer logs overwrite the older ones. Show log to see the output.
logging console [*level*]	Log to console according to level specified.
logging monitor [*level*]	Log to vty (terminal) line according to level specified.
logging trap [*level*]	Log to syslog according to level specified. (The four types of syslog messages are listed later in this section.)
no logging on	Logging enabled for console only.

***logging buffered** includes an optional but recommended command to increase the default 4 k memory buffer. Just specify a new buffer size, such as 500, after the command.

Redirecting error message and debug output is critical to router performance. Routers are packet forwarders. Logging and debug are for troubleshooting, *not* for day-to-day routines. The following list re-emphasizes, from highest to lowest, the logging overhead on the router:

- Console
- vty
- Syslog
- Internal buffer logging

The Cisco IOS generates four types of syslog messages:

- Software/hardware malfunctions show at the errors level.
- Interface transitions and system restarts show as notifications.
- Reload requests and stack messages show as informational.
- Debug output shows as debugging.

Logging is quite helpful with troubleshooting and is more than just documentation. You should look up your most common syslog output at Cisco.com so that you can correlate them into your network management program and documentation to help you quickly identify problems. Next look at some common debug commands in the last IOS troubleshooting category covered here.

Cisco Debug Commands

Because of the impact on the processor and memory, only use debug commands for troubleshooting traffic flow or misconfigurations, *not* for normal daily operations. Ideally, debug commands are helpful during periods when there is not much traffic and not many users.

You must be in privileged exec (enable) mode to use it, and debug requires process switching. Some debug commands force you to turn off fast switching entirely to receive debug output. Like logging, debug default system error messages are sent to the console. What this really means is that every character generates a processor interrupt, which in turn is a significant performance hit. As mentioned in the logging section, however, you can issue a **no logging console** command and view the debug output through a telnet session. Use **terminal monitor** (**term mon**) as necessary to view debug over a vty session (**line vty 0 4**). You can even spool the output to a syslog server with the command **logging** [*ip-address*].

The following examples offer some practical suggestions for using debug as a troubleshooting tool. One that I don't plan to capture for you is **debug all**. Do not issue this command in a production environment. The impact of a single debug statement has the potential to bring a router down, so you can imagine the impact of **debug all**. By the way, **u all**, short for **undebug all** or **no debug all**, is how to turn it off—that is, if you haven't rendered the router unusable.

Make use of your history buffer with debug. Type **undebug all**, turn on the required **debug** parameters, for example, and use the Up Arrow key to turn it off. How useful this is really depends on how many commands you input after typing **undebug all**. Whatever the method, make sure you turn debug off after troubleshooting. In addition, if the particular **debug** command forced you to turn off fast switching with the **no ip route-cache** command, I highly recommend you turn it on again.

As you see in Example 2-30, service time stamps are available for logging and debugging. Another tool that makes them a lot more useful is the Network Time Protocol (NTP). It is free, so why not use it. Go to Cisco.com and search for "NTP" to enable and troubleshoot NTP.

Example 2-30 *Practical* **debug** *Using Time Stamps*

```
r1(config)#service timestamps ?
  debug  Timestamp debug messages
  log    Timestamp log messages
  <cr>
r1(config)#service timestamps debug ?
  datetime  Timestamp with date and time
  uptime    Timestamp with system uptime
  <cr>
r1(config)#service timestamps debug datetime ?
  localtime      Use local time zone for timestamps
  msec           Include milliseconds in timestamp
  show-timezone  Add time zone information to timestamp
  <cr>
r1(config)#service timestamps debug uptime ?
  <cr>
```

Knowing and minimizing the impact of troubleshooting tools on device performance should be part of your plan. Good tools require care and feeding, so remember to balance the impact of what you need to capture with device overhead. Debug is a good example. When debugging packets, for instance, use an ACL to limit the output scope. (See Example 2-31.) Caution: *Always* remember to turn the tool off with the command **undebug all**, **no debug all**, or just type **no** in front of the specific **debug** command you want to quit. Always practice safe debug. Cisco helps you out on this one in that debug commands are not saved as part of the NVRAM or startup configuration. You can do anything you want on a test network, but a production network is another story. See the *Debug Command Reference* in Cisco.com documentation for more assistance with debug. You will get very familiar with specific debug output in your own troubleshooting scenarios and as the need arises in the Trouble Tickets to come in this book.

Example 2-31 *Using an ACL with* **debug**

```
r1(config)#ip access-list extended limitdebug
r1(config-ext-nacl)#permit tcp host 192.168.1.11 gt 1023 host 192.168.3.5 eq www
r1(config-ext-nacl)#permit tcp host 192.168.3.5 eq www host 192.168.1.11 gt 1023
r1(config-ext-nacl)#exit
r1(config)#interface s0
r1(config-if)#no ip route-cache
r1(config-if)#end
r1#term mon
r1#debug ip packet limitdebug detail
```

Notice in Example 2-31 that the named ACL limitdebug is created, fast switching is disabled on the interface, and the ACL is applied to only the debug output according to the **permit** statements specified. This not only limits the debug overhead activity on the box, but also limits the extra lines you need to search through to find the problem.

The next couple of examples illustrate some common uses for debug. You will have an opportunity to use debug to debug your own problems in the upcoming Trouble Tickets and in your real-world networks. Example 2-32 captures ICMP traffic.

Example 2-32   debug ip icmp

```
r2#debug ip icmp
ICMP packet debugging is on
r2#ping 192.168.1.1
Type escape sequence to abort.
Sending 5, 100-byte ICMP Echos to 192.168.1.1, timeout is 2 seconds:
!!!!!
Success rate is 100 percent (5/5), round-trip min/avg/max = 32/34/36 ms
r2#
12:53:23: ICMP: echo reply rcvd, src 192.168.1.1, dst 192.168.2.2
12:53:23: ICMP: echo reply rcvd, src 192.168.1.1, dst 192.168.2.2
12:53:23: ICMP: echo reply rcvd, src 192.168.1.1, dst 192.168.2.2
12:53:23: ICMP: echo reply rcvd, src 192.168.1.1, dst 192.168.2.2
12:53:23: ICMP: echo reply rcvd, src 192.168.1.1, dst 192.168.2.2
r2#undebug all
All possible debugging has been turned off
```

Example 2-32 illustrates the five ICMP Echo Replies received from 192.168.1.1, whereas Example 2-33 shows the output of **debug ip packet**. **Packet** *anything* means more detail and stress on the device; therefore, you must weigh the overhead of the command to your troubleshooting needs.

Example 2-33   debug ip packet

```
r2#debug ip packet
IP packet debugging is on
r2#ping 192.168.1.1
Type escape sequence to abort.
Sending 5, 100-byte ICMP Echos to 192.168.1.1, timeout is 2 seconds:
!!!!!
Success rate is 100 percent (5/5), round-trip min/avg/max = 36/36/40 ms
r2#
12:54:13: IP: s=192.168.2.2 (local), d=192.168.1.1 (Serial0), len 100, sending
12:54:13: IP: s=192.168.1.1 (Serial0), d=192.168.2.2 (Serial0), len 100, rcvd 3
12:54:13: IP: s=192.168.2.2 (local), d=192.168.1.1 (Serial0), len 100, sending
12:54:13: IP: s=192.168.1.1 (Serial0), d=192.168.2.2 (Serial0), len 100, rcvd 3
12:54:13: IP: s=192.168.2.2 (local), d=192.168.1.1 (Serial0), len 100, sending
12:54:13: IP: s=192.168.1.1 (Serial0), d=192.168.2.2 (Serial0), len 100, rcvd 3
...
```

Although Example 2-34 is even more stressful, it provides detailed output. First I issue a **show debug** to verify that no debug commands are currently running. Then I issue the **debug ip packet detail** command. Note the shaded area showing the Echo Reply ICMP code as 0 and the Echo ICMP code as 8. Table 2-8 describes the various ICMP codes.

NOTE   Search the Cisco.com for "debug command reference" for more detail.

Example 2-34   **debug ip packet detail**

```
r2#show debug
r2#debug ip packet detail
IP packet debugging is on (detailed)
r2#ping 192.168.1.1
Type escape sequence to abort.
Sending 5, 100-byte ICMP Echos to 192.168.1.1, timeout is 2 seconds:
!!!!!
Success rate is 100 percent (5/5), round-trip min/avg/max = 40/41/44 ms
r2#
03:13:46: IP: s=192.168.2.2 (local), d=192.168.1.1 (Serial0), len 100, sending
03:13:46:      ICMP type=8, code=0
03:13:46: IP: s=192.168.1.1 (Serial0), d=192.168.2.2 (Serial0), len 100, rcvd 3
03:13:46:      ICMP type=0, code=0
03:13:46: IP: s=192.168.2.2 (local), d=192.168.1.1 (Serial0), len 100, sending
03:13:46:      ICMP type=8, code=0
03:13:46: IP: s=192.168.1.1 (Serial0), d=192.168.2.2 (Serial0), len 100, rcvd 3
03:13:46:      ICMP type=0, code=0
...
03:13:52: IP: s=192.168.3.1 (local), d=255.255.255.255 (Ethernet0), len 72,
    sending broad/multicast
03:13:52:      UDP src=520, dst=520
03:13:52: IP: s=192.168.2.2 (local), d=255.255.255.255 (Serial0), len 52,
    sending broad/multicast
03:13:52:      UDP src=520, dst=520
r2#undebug all
```

Table 2-8   *ICMP Type Values and Codes*

Value	Code
0	Echo Reply
3	Destination unreachable
	Code 0 - net unreachable
	Code 1 - host unreachable
	Code 2 - protocol unreachable
	Code 3 - port unreachable
	Code 4 - fragmentation needed and DF set
	Code 5 - source route failed

continues

Table 2-8   *ICMP Type Values and Codes (Continued)*

Value	Code
4	Source Quench
5	Redirect
6	Alternate-address
8	Echo Request
9	Router-advertisement
10	Router-solicitation
11	Time-exceeded Code 0 – TTL exceeded in transit Code 1 – fragment reassembly time exceeded
12	Parameter-problem
13	Timestamp-request
14	Timestamp-reply
15	Information-request
16	Information-reply
17	Mask-request
18	Mask-reply
31	Conversion-error
32	Mobile-redirect

The primary focus of this chapter is on tools innate to the Cisco IOS, such as show, ping, trace, log, and debug. The generic output of each has been covered so far, but I will see that you explore more specifics relating to various protocols and technologies throughout this book. Because other tools are also very valuable in testing and managing the network, the discussion now briefly turns to hardware tools, network monitors, protocol analyzers, network management systems, simulation and modeling tools, desktop tools, and other resources. Sometimes one tool is not enough, or you may have access to one tool and not the other. First, however, I want to make sure you are familiar with CCO.

Cisco Resources

Cisco enables you to be proactive and reactive when it comes to troubleshooting. Some of their resources to prevent problems include Cisco Connection Online (CCO), the Documentation CD-ROM, the Cisco Networking Products Marketplace, and Cisco Technical Assistance Center (TAC).

Cisco Connection Online (CCO)

CCO (www.cisco.com) is a global intranet accessible over the Internet. It contains such links as Solutions for Your Network; Ordering; Training, Events, and Seminars; Corporate News and Information; Products and Technologies; Service and Support; and Partners and Resellers. Products and Technologies is a good place to start for troubleshooting. These pages deliver up-to-date technical information that is continually updated by Cisco TAC engineers. Figure 2-3 shows the CCO home page.

Figure 2-3   *Cisco Connection Online*

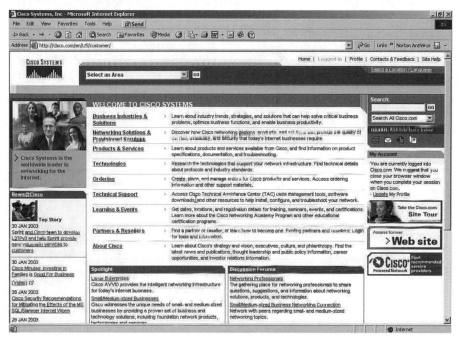

The CCO infrastructure is secured behind a firewall that includes Secure Transport Architecture (STA) providing a secure transaction pipe between the web servers on the public Internet and Cisco's internal systems. CCO is available in English, Chinese, Danish, Dutch, Finnish, French, German, Italian, Japanese, Korean, Norwegian, Portuguese, Russian, Spanish, and Swedish. However, the initial home page is in English; from the home page, you make a selection to view the appropriate translated content.

Cisco provides guest access to company and product information for the general public and registered access for customers that have purchased equipment, support contracts, or who are sponsored by a Cisco-authorized partner. Registration requires a corporate number. Registered users who log in are taken to the main server in San Jose, California. CCO is geographically dispersed for response time. Other servers include Australia, China, France, Hong Kong, Japan, Netherlands, South Korea, and the United Kingdom. Cisco support centers include San Jose, California; Raleigh, North Carolina; Brussels, Belgium; and Sydney, Australia.

NOTE   The book does not differentiate between registered access and guest access; it just assumes you are logged in with your CCO account which you can do from Cisco.com. A registered CCO account is a critical tool for your tool bag.

CCO is in HTML format, which means you can easily return to documents you have looked at before using bookmarks. The history facility enables you to keep track of what you have looked at in the past 60 days. CCO is available on the web or via CD-ROM. It is the best place to get current documentation for technology, products, configuration, commands, and troubleshooting. It includes a search engine (now powered by Google).

Cisco Documentation CD-ROM

The portable version of CCO, the Cisco Documentation CD-ROM (Doc CD), is available to you in many ways, including the following:

- Registered Cisco direct customers can order Cisco product documentation from the Networking Products MarketPlace:

    www.cisco.com/cgi-bin/order/order_root.pl

- Registered cisco.com users can order the Doc CD through the online Subscription Store:

    www.cisco.com/go/subscription

- Nonregistered Cisco.com users can order documentation through a local account representative by calling Cisco corporate headquarters (California, USA) at 408-526-7208 or, elsewhere in North America, by calling 800-553-NETS (6387).

I prefer to go to www.cisco.com/univercd/home/home.htm for the online version that is updated more frequently. The following are some examples of what is contained on the Cisco Doc CD:

- IOS release notes, configuration guides, command references, command summaries

- Debug command reference and system error messages

- Cisco MIB user quick reference and access services

- Quick configuration guide

- Cisco product catalog

- Router and hub installation and configuration guides

- Switch installation and configuration guides and MIB reference guides

- Client/server software installation guides

- Configuration notes for memory upgrades, network interface cards (NICs), rack-mount kits, and other field-upgradeable products

I particularly like the Technology section, which includes selections such as Technology, Design, Installation, Troubleshooting, Case Studies, and a Terms and Acronyms page. The www.cisco.com/univercd/cc/td/doc/cisintwk/itg_v1/index.htm URL is most relevant to support topics; it covers troubleshooting anything. Search for "internetwork troubleshooting guide."

NOTE   Those of you going for a hands-on Cisco test, such as CCIE (Expert) or CCSI (Instructor), must familiarize yourself with the Doc CD. Just like in many real troubleshooting environments, while under great pressure and trying to conserve time, it isn't in your best interest to wait for the search engine to find what you want if you don't even know the categories available.

The Cisco site contains many other helpful web pages with which you should be familiar, from both a practical and test standpoint. Take a look at a few of them here, but I still highly recommend that you go get a CCO account and explore what has happened since this book was published. For example, Cisco considers the Doc CD so important that a link is now available from their main Cisco.com site.

CCO Marketplace

CCO Marketplace is a global e-commerce portal for online ordering and management to give you 24-hour by 7-day online purchasing, 365 days a year. Explore the Networking Products Marketplace at www.cisco.com/go/marketplace, where you can place and manage orders for products and services. Go to the Cisco Merchandise store at Land's End to order shirts, hats, bags, jackets, and other apparel. Land's End is even making use of Cisco technology with their click-to-talk customer-service feature. Shop at the online Gift Store for Cisco merchandise. Check out the Learning Store for educational materials, and the Subscription Store to keep up on sales and marketing materials or to get hard copies of much of what is on the web. Submit orders electronically or fax your orders to Cisco. Marketplace includes status, pricing, configuration, service order, and service parts agents.

The Marketplace Dynamic Configuration Tool is where you can view hardware configurable models by product family. You can buy from anyone, and they will sell you whatever you tell them. However, how do you know you have all the parts and whether they all work together? If you configure it here, you know it works. Check out CCO Ordering information for more details.

Technical Assistance Center (TAC)

The TAC (www.cisco.com/tac) contains a wealth of technical information, tools, and resources to assist you with solving your own problem or properly escalating it to Cisco. Glance through the major sections in Figure 2-4, which include Hardware Support, Software Support, and Technology Support. Explore the Tools & Utilities section, the Software Center, check out What's Hot in TAC, and contact TAC all from the newly remodeled TAC pages.

Figure 2-4 *Cisco TAC*

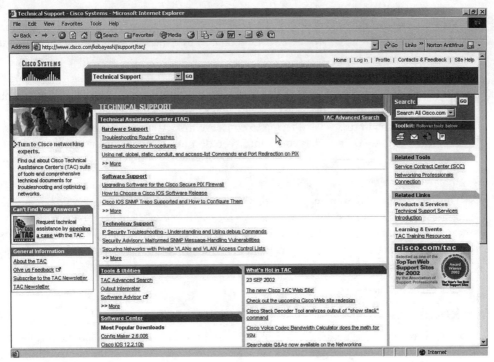

Hardware, Software, and Technology Support

The Hardware Support, Software Support, and Technology Support sections cover routers, switches, and security. Quickly troubleshoot crashes, memory and CPU issues, find specific error messages, and recover from a lost password all from the Hardware Support pages. The Software Support pages offer support for the IOS, CiscoWorks, and CallManager. Get easy access to the Software Center and popular download utilities.

The CCO Software Center conveniently gives you access to products, downloads, utilities, and general information, such as revision levels and major upgrades to the IOS. Get your questions answered about protocol and feature sets. Learn more about naming conventions. For example, a filename has three parts, separated by dashes, such as *xxxx-yyyy-ww*, where

- *xxxx* - Platform

    www.cisco.com/warp/customer/432/platform.html

- *yyyy* - Features

    www.cisco.com/warp/customer/432/features.html

- *ww* - Format (where it executes from if compressed)

    www.cisco.com/warp/customer/432/format.html

Earlier I discussed ED, LD, and GD and how I recommend GD for production deployment and the others for new features not available yet in GD. Try out the IOS Upgrade Planner. It has gone from a simple FTP service to deliver a fix to a customer to a wonderfully organized tool for CCO users. The Hardware-Software Compatibility Matrix, the Software Image Naming Conventions, and the Cisco IOS Roadmap all are worthy of your exploration.

Technology Support offers assistance with routing protocol troubleshooting, virtual private networks (VPNs), ACLs, VLANs, IPSec, and so on.

Tools and Utilities

TAC provides many installation, configuration, assessment, troubleshooting, and case management tools to solve. They are better categorized than ever, as illustrated in Figure 2-5, and you can reach many via their own links.

Figure 2-5 *TAC Tools Link*

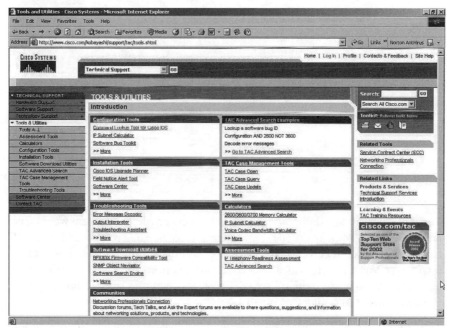

Available installation tools include memory calculators and firmware compatibility tools, an SNMP object navigator, and a discussion forum for networking professionals. An Open Source Initiative Community releases their own tools, scripts, and utilities. You can look up configuration guidelines, create customized command reference documents, sign up to receive automatic product field notices, and request software and hardware upgrades and documentation. Use the IOS Roadmap, Upgrade Planner, Software Advisor, and Software Center to obtain the right software. Attend online TAC seminars and download the Cisco TFTP server. In addition to some of the installation tools, the configuration tools offer an IP subnet calculator.

Assess your network and find out whether it is properly designed for high-availability telephony or search all the TAC knowledgebases for technical issues. The troubleshooting tools are most relevant to this book (see Figure 2-6).

Figure 2-6 *TAC Troubleshooting Tools*

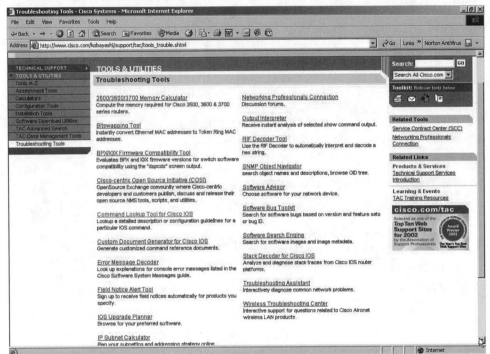

Many of the tools speak for themselves, and others are described here were discussed on previous pages. You can decode error messages, receive bug reports and field notices automatically, and receive instant analysis of command output entered in to the Output Interpreter. You can automatically decode routing information fields (RIFs), stack traces, and interactively diagnose common network problems with the Troubleshooting Assistant and Wireless Troubleshooting Center.

The Troubleshooting Assistant takes the hold-my-hand approach to troubleshooting. It prompts you for questions to help narrow down the problem. You can narrow down problems to protocols, platforms, hardware, configuration, performance, and so on. The Troubleshooting Assistant takes your input and scores the likely solutions. A score of 100 is the highest, so 90 is very likely a solution to the problem (assuming you put in the right criteria).

Explore the Networking Professionals Connection or open discussion forums. This is the Cisco-approved place to ask for advice. You can ask who has done or used what and what weird things they have encountered. You can look for customer experiences in the open forum. CCIEs lurk here (mostly those who work for Cisco). Join in on Tech Talks, Ask the Expert, and sign up for free seminars.

The Advanced Search Tool enables you to search all file types or narrow them down to case studies, configuration examples, field notices, password recovery, Q&A, security advisors, tech notes, white papers, and more.

NOTE   Because websites change daily, this section is very hard to keep current in terms of putting it in print. However, the point is that Cisco does a great job of proactively providing what you need to solve your own problems. It is up to you to use the tools available. Start at Cisco.com, login with your CCO account and go from there.

Contacting TAC

The TAC case management toolkit is available from many pages, including the Cisco home page, and enables you to directly access the TAC. Use it to open, query, or update a case, and have TAC proactively notify you regarding your open cases. Select this and the RMA/Service Order Tools right off the TAC site. Most people rarely pick up the phone to call the TAC unless they have a dead box. On the web, you have a case history and so do they; your communication is not just verbal, and it works rather well.

Gather your facts: your maintenance contract information, the equipment product and serial number, any problem details, and so on. Use the **show tech-support** command on a normal box and then on a problem box. Use the **show tech-support** command on the problem box so that you are ready for anything the Cisco Support Engineer (CSE) may ask. You have to know what works and what normal performance levels are so that you can identify and fix problems.

Open a case at a specific priority level and note the case number. Use the TAC case management toolkit to query and update it. Table 2-9 lists Cisco support priority levels. E-mail is wonderful, but there must be some reason companies give their support people those cell phones. Think about that when you have a high-priority problem. If everyone is down and out, you better place a call.

Table 2-9   *Cisco Support Priority Levels*

Priority	Severity
1	Production network down
2	Production network severely degraded
3	Network performance degraded
4	Information needed on product

NOTE	Take the time to work with the case management toolkit because an online record for each case is a valuable tool for you and the CSE. Contact TAC via phone, fax, e-mail (tac@cisco.com), or via the web (www.cisco.com/tac). Go to TAC and print out the phone numbers for your location so that you have them handy.

I have stressed repeatedly that Cisco wants you to help yourself with the tools they give you (and new and improved tools are coming online all the time). Because no one is perfect and because many commands and tools are undocumented or did not make it in the product in time for release, a valid CCO account will prove very beneficial to you when configuring, monitoring, and debugging your networks.

Project DOTU

What about the undocumented stuff that people tell you about? Where can you get more information on that? For this, there is a Project DOTU: Document the Undocumented at www.boerland.com/dotu (see Figure 2-7). Project DOTU is a viable option; however, I am *not* by any means suggesting that you try all the undocumented commands in a production network. Take a look at the Boerland site and also go to Yahoo! or Google sometime to search for "cisco undocumented."

Figure 2-7 *Project DOTU*

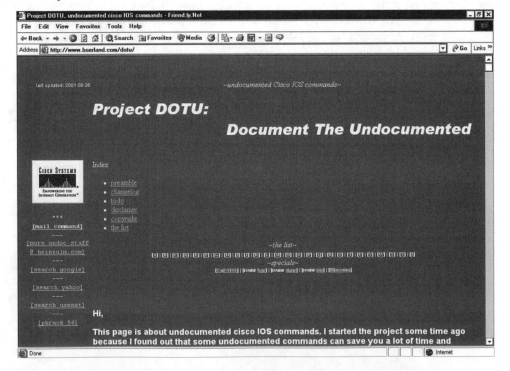

As an example, go to one of your routers and try **sh int switching** to see switching on an interface-by-interface, protocol-by-protocol basis. Example 2-35 shows the output of this on one of my 2500s in the test lab.

Example 2-35   **sh int switching** *Output*

```
r2>sh int switching
Ethernet0 r2 e0 to HostC Win98Dell
          Throttle count         0
     Drops       RP              0         SP           0
 SPD Flushes     Fast            0         SSE          0
 SPD Aggress     Fast            0
 SPD Priority    Inputs          0         Drops        0
     Protocol    Path       Pkts In   Chars In   Pkts Out   Chars Out
        Other    Process         0         0        2296      137760
          Cache misses           0
                 Fast            0         0           0           0
                 Auton/SSE       0         0           0           0
           IP    Process        51     12798         836       73884
          Cache misses           0
                 Fast            0         0           0           0
                 Auton/SSE       0         0           0           0
          ARP    Process         0         0           2         120
          Cache misses           0
                 Fast            0         0           0           0
                 Auton/SSE       0         0           0           0
          CDP    Process         0         0         383      114134
          Cache misses           0
                 Fast            0         0           0           0
                 Auton/SSE       0         0           0           0
Serial0 r2 s0 DCE to r1 s0 DTE
          Throttle count         0
     Drops       RP              0         SP           0
 SPD Flushes     Fast            0         SSE          0
 SPD Aggress     Fast            0
 SPD Priority    Inputs          0         Drops        0
     Protocol    Path       Pkts In   Chars In   Pkts Out   Chars Out
        Other    Process         0         0        2296       50512
          Cache misses           0
                 Fast            0         0           0           0
                 Auton/SSE       0         0           0           0
           IP    Process       886     51823         880       51396
          Cache misses           0
                 Fast            0         0           0           0
                 Auton/SSE       0         0           0           0
          CDP    Process       383    106474         383      106474
          Cache misses           0
                 Fast            0         0           0           0
                 Auton/SSE       0         0           0           0
Interface Serial1 is disabled
```

NOTE   Obviously, some of these commands are probably undocumented for a reason; so if you insist, make sure your job is not on the line. By the way, this is what test labs are for.

The following section moves the focus away from Cisco-specific commands and websites for troubleshooting and looks at network management as a tool.

Network Management

The goals of this section are to introduce you to the International Organization for Standardization (ISO) functional areas of network management and to briefly explore such tools as CiscoWorks and WANDL (Netsys Baseliner).

ISO Functional Areas of Network Management

The ISO has five key functional areas of network management, as follows:

- **Fault management** is very applicable to troubleshooting. A *fault* is defined as any abnormal event. The fault may be indicated by component failures that generate lots of errors. Report faults as they occur. Where did it occur? Can you isolate the problem and minimize the impact on others? Is the fault an abnormal event; is there an excessive number of errors? Should you repair or replace? Must you upgrade hardware, upgrade software (IOS), or configure for performance to fix the problem?

- **Accounting management** measures user, group, or device utilization and regulates resources and quotas appropriately.

- **Configuration and name management** help you account for such items as configuration files, changes in response to performance evaluations, product and IOS upgrades, and fault recovery.

- **Performance management** is about measuring and making sure acceptable levels of throughput, response time, and utilization are maintained.

- **Security management** relates to controlling access according to security standards and policies as to not be sabotaged. It also assists in making sensitive information accessible only to authorized parties.

Network management can be proactive or reactive. As a support person, you must determine a good balance of monitoring devices as to not interfere with the main function of the device. For example, the main purpose of a router is to route packets. Too much monitoring and polling takes precious resources that may not be available. On the other hand, network management programs such as CiscoWorks, Cisco Info Center (CIC), and HP OpenView can simplify configuration, monitoring, and troubleshooting.

CiscoWorks

CiscoWorks, the Cisco network management system (NMS), delivers device monitoring and management products as well as configuration and fault management tools. Products such as HP OpenView and Spectrum are competitor products.

CiscoWorks includes several web-based solutions targeted at configuring, monitoring, and troubleshooting LAN and WAN environments. Go to a search engine such as Google and search for "ciscoworks," which should bring you to Cisco.com to help you understand, monitor, and react to problems.

The LAN Management Solution (LMS) includes the nGenius Real Time Monitor, Campus Manager, Device Fault Manager, Content Flow Monitor, CiscoView, and Resource Manager Essentials. LMS is part of the CiscoWorks family of products for fault and configuration management and troubleshooting of campus LANs and is a follow-on to the CiscoWorks for Switched Internetworks (CWSI) bundle.

nGenius Real Time Monitor is web-enabled and delivers Remote Monitoring (RMON) information from RMON-enabled Catalyst switches, internal modules, and external probes. nGenius includes traffic director and packet analyzer applications. Use it to collect RMON statistics, analyze traffic patterns, and report long-term trend analysis. You can set thresholds on ports for errors, broadcasts, collisions, and so forth; monitor proactive alarms before they affect users. What a way to keep tabs on broadcast traffic! A good rule of thumb is that broadcast traffic should *not* be more than 20 percent of the total traffic per segment. Use nGenius Packet Analyzer to troubleshoot protocol-related issues. The product runs on Microsoft, SunOS, Solaris, HP/UX, and IBM-AIX.

Campus Manager includes Layer 2 tools for configuring, managing, and understanding the infrastructure. Export the maps to Visio, VLAN, LAN Emulation (LANE), and ATM services and assign switch ports. Autodiscovery and topology mapping enable you to get link and device status based on SNMP polling. Diagnostic tools allow automatic location and correlation for user information based on MAC, IP, login name, and physical location. Configure, monitor, and manage VLANs the drag-and-drop way and compile statistics with the VLAN Director. Figure 2-8 shows a list of VLANs.

Figure 2-8 *CiscoWorks VLAN Management with Campus Manager Topology Services*

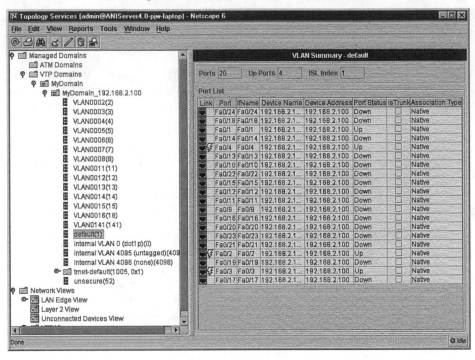

Device Fault Manager (DFM) gives you real-time, problem-focused fault analysis. Intelligent traps are sent to e-mail/pager gateways or displayed in the alarm window.

Content Flow Monitor offers load balancing and performance monitoring.

CiscoView is a GUI for monitoring all Cisco devices, including on-demand access to CCO for new and updated device support (see Figure 2-9). It includes graphical device management, including front and back panel displays; performance management through utilization statistics, frames transmitted and received, errors, and so on; and you can change configurations (for example, routes, VLANs, and duplex settings).

Resource Manager Essentials (RME) streamlines inventory, device configuration, and software updates. It is comprised of applications such as: Inventory Manager, Change Audit, Device Configuration Manager, Software Image Manager, Availability Manager, Syslog Analyzer, and Cisco Management Connection. RME is bundled with CiscoWorks and is also available as a standalone product.

RME integrates with products such as HP OpenView, CIC, IBM NetView, and SunNet Manager to solve fault, configuration, and performance management issues. It even gives you a picture of the device, which is wonderful for basic connectivity status (see Figure 2-10).

Figure 2-9 *CiscoView*

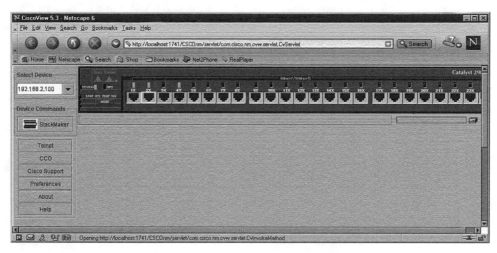

Figure 2-10 *Resource Manager Essentials (RME)*

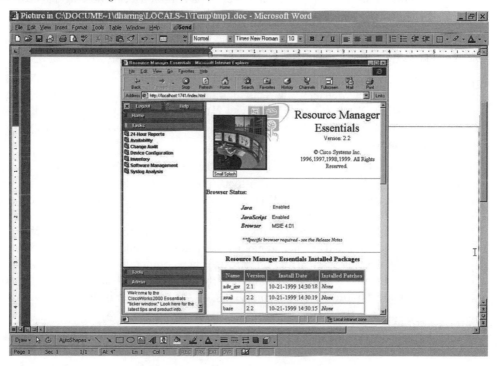

The Software Image Manager goes out to Cisco's website to analyze and run a cron job for when you want to schedule the upgrade. It gives the best match, which obviously speeds up software deployment. This tool provides change control for software and configurations. It actually accounts for that tech who said they did nothing.

NOTE   Campus Bundle for AIX/HP-UX is similar to the LMS available for Windows NT and the Solaris operating systems. It includes Traffic Director, Campus Manager, RME, and CiscoView.

The Routed WAN Management Solution includes nGenius Real Time Monitor, Access Control List Manager, Internetwork Performance Monitor (IPM), CiscoView, and RME. IPM empowers network engineers to proactively troubleshoot response time and availability issues. IPM's server component runs on Sun Solaris and Windows NT/2000.

The Service Management Solution includes Service Level Manager and CiscoView. You can define and monitor service level agreements (SLAs), specifying traffic types and thresholds between enterprise networks or internal or external endpoints. Software agents provide job management and collection.

CiscoWorks QoS Policy Manager (QPM) includes performance protection for voice, video, and data applications through policies and design guide recommendations.

The VPN/Security Management Solution includes a VPN Monitor, RME, CiscoView, and Cisco Secure Policy Manager Lite. This solution is for customers who require remote access and site-to-site VPNs based on IPSec, Layer 2 Tunneling Protocol (L2TP), and Point-to-Point Tunneling Protocol (PPTP) or deployment and management of perimeter security using the Cisco PIX firewall.

CiscoWorks has other advanced applications. The Default Fault Manager (DFM) is part of the LAN solution or an add-on for problem-focused fault analysis. Intelligent traps are sent to e-mail/pager gateways or displayed in the alarm window. The User Registration Tool allows for dynamic assignment of VLANs based on user login. CiscoWorks Voice Manager (CVM) is a voice management and reporting solution. It provides advanced capabilities to configure and provision voice ports and create and modify dial plans for Voice over IP, Frame Relay, and ATM. The ACL Manager is an add-on to RME, but a component of the Routed WAN Management bundle. It offers a web interface to manage access lists. Search for "ciscoworks" at Cisco.com to explore the other applications and the up-to-date bundles.

Netsys Baseliner (Now WANDL)

Cisco acquired Netsys and announced an end-of-life plan in November 2000. Cisco is now partnering with WANDL for the following Netsys platforms: Sun Solaris, HP-UX, AIX, and Windows with the server-side Cisco Netsys-Agent (N-Agent). This opens the product up to other NMSs and operating systems via application programming interfaces (APIs). Search for "wandl" at Cisco.com for more details or go directly to www.wandl.com.

Netsys Baseliner (now WANDL) is a simulation and modeling tool that takes the what-you-see-before-you-get-it (WYSBYGI) approach. It is a what-if tool to test changes and performance issues before you commit to any design changes. It is great for initial network design, analysis for reconfiguration or redesign, and stress-testing situations. The output measures throughput, response times, utilization, packet loss, and so on. Even though Netsys is another company's product now, it is still a great product (and is still covered on the exam).

NOTE   Regardless of the tool you choose, *always* remember to display, debug, and test configurations offline before you put them into your live network. Analyze what-if scenarios to determine what happens prior to implementing changes or to proactively prepare yourself for a failure so that you can react appropriately.

Many times after using IOS commands, CCO, and NMSs, you still need more tools. The following section covers some hardware tools and media testers that may be of help.

Hardware Tools and Media Testers

Network media test equipment is available to install and verify new cabling systems as well as to diagnose and maintain the existing physical infrastructure. At the lower end of the spectrum, there are breakout boxes, cable testers (scanners), volt-ohm meters (VOMs), and digital volt ohm meters (DVOMs). At the higher end of the spectrum, there are time domain reflectometers (TDRs) and optical TDRs (OTDRs). Go to websites such as www.flukenetworks.com, www.blackbox.com, and www.microtest.com for more information.

- **Breakout boxes** check signals and pinouts for RS-232 serial devices.

- **VOMs and DVOMs** test continuity, voltages, current, resistance, and physical connectivity.

- **Cable testers and scanners**, although at the lower end of the troubleshooting spectrum, are good in continuity situations, whether it be installation, maintenance, or support. A cable tester may help you determine whether the port is actually bad on the router or switch, for instance. Many handheld testers today display helpful address and protocol statistics as well. Figure 2-11 shows the Fluke handheld device.

Figure 2-11 *Fluke Handheld Tester*

- **TDRs** are at the higher end of spectrum and are good for cable-break issues. They test for consistency in the impedance over the length of the cable. An electronic pulse is sent to quickly detect shorts, breaks, and throughput issues. You used to really need TDRs for coax cable, but cable scanners work just fine today for twisted-pair cable.

- An **OTDR** is a time domain reflectometer for fiber. It uses optical pulses to check signal loss. A good flashlight, believe it or not, will get you most of the problems. Figure 2-12 shows a fiber tester. TDR products are great, but are normally very expensive. If you are the wiring contractor, however, this is a must for your tool bag.

Figure 2-12 *OmniFiber Tester*

Network Monitors

Network monitors assist with baselining. They include software to look at variations from the normal performance with such items as packet loss, bandwidth, collisions, utilization, cyclical redundancy check (CRC) errors, carrier transitions, host reachability, and so on. Network monitors can continuously track packets at the higher layers using SNMP and keepalive activity. They can collect information from remote sites, send back to headquarters, and warn accordingly. Many include SNMP and RMON capabilities. SNMP bottom line is that it is simple: Get request and get response. If you don't have an easy-to-read interface, however, SNMP is anything but simple.

Protocol Analyzers

Protocol analyzers generate packets and provide real-time data to interactively capture traffic with a layered approach. You will see just how theoretical the OSI model *is not* after using an analyzer. There is a capture and display mode for the individual packet flow. You can generate and edit frames for capacity planning and load testing of devices such as switches, routers, servers, and workstations. Record, interpret, and analyze the life of a packet. Get meaning out of frames. Interpret lots of detail on applications such as Domain Name System (DNS), Dynamic Host Configuration Protocol (DHCP), FTP, and TFTP. Products include Network Associates Sniffer, WildPacket's EtherPeek, Network Monitor from Microsoft, and so on.

NOTE   If you want to compare various protocol analyzer products, check out the interesting article that appeared in the May 21, 2001, edition of *PC Magazine* (www.pcmag.com). *Packet Magazine* (www.cisco.com/go/packet) has many related articles as well. Look for "Tricks of the Trade," for instance.

Many times a protocol analyzer is more advantageous than the innate IOS tools such as debug and log because it is run from a workstation and is less disrupting to the device being monitored. Throughout the scenarios and Trouble Tickets in this book, I use Sniffer Pro to demonstrate concepts; however, you can use any protocol analyzer. Some of these products even have a demo version that enables you to try before you buy; others, such as Ethereal (www.ethereal.com), are free.

This book is not intended to teach you about the Sniffer Pro product. Sniffer Pro is just another tool that enables you to record, display, and analyze various network architectures. Start by getting familiar with the Sniffer Pro interface in Figure 2-13. I am running version 4.5 on a Windows 2000 desktop for my tests.

NOTE   Obtain an evaluation or licensed copy of the protocol analyzer of your choice to work through the rest of the Trouble Tickets throughout this book. A good starting point for more information on protocol analysis is www.nai.com for Sniffer, www.wildpackets.com, www.microsoft.com, or www.ethereal.com. Register on www.sniffer.com to get your *free* protocol poster, and check out some of the other references and tools at WildPackets and Ethereal.

Figure 2-13 *Sniffer Pro Interface*

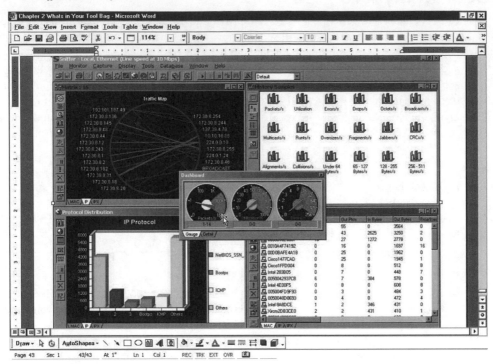

Sniffer Scenario

Take time to get familiar with the basic interface of whichever protocol analyzer you choose to use. If that product is Sniffer/Sniffer Pro, you can choose the **Help > Help Topics > Overview > How To selections** to get yourself started. Although you should take your own self-guided tour, I very briefly describe the windows and how to use the tool so that you can take advantage of it in the Trouble Tickets and in real-world situations. Follow along if you can use Sniffer on your PC or just review the screen shots provided here.

Figure 2-14 displays the physical connectivity for this practical exercise. Use a crossover cable to connect one PC directly to the other PC. Do *not* use a switch (but a hub is fine) to connect the devices; you will work with switches in the chapters to come.

Figure 2-14 *Sniffer Scenario*

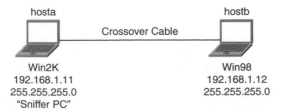

Assign one PC 192.168.1.11 255.255.255.0 and the other one 192.168.1.12 255.255.255.0. Assuming you are using Windows-based PCs, just right-click **Network Neighborhood** or **My Network Places**. Alternatively, choose **Start > Settings > Control Panel > Network** to select your LAN connection. For this scenario, I am using a Windows 2000 Pro notebook for hosta and a Windows 98 notebook for hostb with a crossover cable between them. I assume Windows 95 or higher will work, but in fact the operating system version is not critical for anything you are doing throughout the hands-on exercises. See Figure 2-14 and the address information provided to configure the appropriate IP parameters in the LAN Properties, TCP/IP sheet for both PCs. Name the PCs hosta and hostb.

Use the ipconfig/winipcfg desktop tools to verify your configuration, as in Example 2-36. In addition, ping the other PC to verify connectivity.

Example 2-36   **ipconfig** *on the Desktop*

```
Microsoft Windows 2000 [Version 5.00.2195]
(C) Copyright 1985-2000 Microsoft Corp.
C:\>ipconfig
Windows 2000 IP Configuration
Ethernet adapter {F6BB63C3-5752-480C-96DB-206E49F87839}:
        Connection-specific DNS Suffix  . :
        IP Address. . . . . . . . . . . . : 0.0.0.0
        Subnet Mask . . . . . . . . . . . : 0.0.0.0
        Default Gateway . . . . . . . . . :
Ethernet adapter Local Area Connection:
        Connection-specific DNS Suffix  . :
        Autoconfiguration IP Address. . . : 192.168.1.11
        Subnet Mask . . . . . . . . . . . : 255.255.255.0
        Default Gateway . . . . . . . . . :
C:\>ping 192.168.1.12
Pinging 192.168.1.12 with 32 bytes of data:
Reply from 192.168.1.12: bytes=32 time<10ms TTL=128
Reply from 192.168.1.12: bytes=32 time<10ms TTL=128
Reply from 192.168.1.12: bytes=32 time<10ms TTL=128
Reply from 192.168.1.12: bytes=32 time<10ms TTL=128
Ping statistics for 192.168.1.12:
    Packets: Sent = 4, Received = 4, Lost = 0 (0% loss),
Approximate round trip times in milli-seconds:
    Minimum = 0ms, Maximum =  0ms, Average =  0ms
C:\>
```

Now that you have tested basic configuration and connectivity, turn on Microsoft Networking. Instead of using a third-party program, turn on File and Print Services on hostb by going to the Network Property sheet; thus you can have hostb act as a server. Later you will verify the upper layers using Sniffer. For now, use Sniffer Pro to analyze and extrapolate critical information from your packets.

NOTE   Be patient while the program starts, especially if you are running it on a minimum-memory laptop.

Using Sniffer Pro

Dashboard provides information about packets, utilization, and errors through dials and graphs (see Figure 2-15). It is analogous to the tachometer approach on the dash of your car. Take some time to experiment with the product, but believe me packet analysis is addicting. For now, look at the menus, toolbars, and help system, including the Overview, Basic Capabilities of Sniffer Pro, and How To sections.

Figure 2-15 *Sniffer Dashboard*

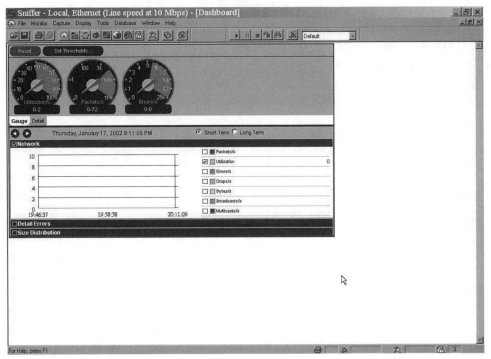

I want you to start right away and capture packets. My capture station is my Windows 2000 PC with an address of 192.168.1.11. You can use the Capture menu to start capturing packets, but I often prefer the toolbar. In Figure 2-15, I clicked the triangle-shaped toolbar button that resembles the button on a CD player.

The icons on the left enable you to view different categories of information loosely based on the OSI layers. The Diagnosis tab displays problems that Sniffer has determined to require your immediate attention, whereas the Symptoms tab specifies potential problems. The Objects tab identifies all the features and network items that Sniffer identified over the entire capture process.

Figure 2-16 shows Sniffer capturing packets, but there is not much activity until you actually do something. Notice the number of packets in the lower-right corner of the expert window and how it increases as you produce traffic. A simple ping from hosta to hostb (192.168.1.12) is enough to change that. Use the IP address for the first ping to eliminate any name resolution for now. Ping again using the host name (hostb), and then stop the Sniffer capture using the toolbar or Capture menu. Example 2-37 shows my command-prompt ping output.

Example 2-37   *Command-Prompt Ping Output*

```
C:\>ping 192.168.1.12
Pinging 192.168.1.12 with 32 bytes of data:
Reply from 192.168.1.12: bytes=32 time<10ms TTL=128
Reply from 192.168.1.12: bytes=32 time<10ms TTL=128
Reply from 192.168.1.12: bytes=32 time<10ms TTL=128
Reply from 192.168.1.12: bytes=32 time<10ms TTL=128
Ping statistics for 192.168.1.12:
    Packets: Sent = 4, Received = 4, Lost = 0 (0% loss),
Approximate round trip times in milli-seconds:
    Minimum = 0ms, Maximum =  0ms, Average =  0ms

C:\>ping hostb
Pinging hostb [192.168.1.12] with 32 bytes of data:
Reply from 192.168.1.12: bytes=32 time<10ms TTL=128
Reply from 192.168.1.12: bytes=32 time<10ms TTL=128
Reply from 192.168.1.12: bytes=32 time<10ms TTL=128
Reply from 192.168.1.12: bytes=32 time<10ms TTL=128
Ping statistics for 192.168.1.12:
    Packets: Sent = 4, Received = 4, Lost = 0 (0% loss),
Approximate round trip times in milli-seconds:
    Minimum = 0ms, Maximum =  0ms, Average =  0ms
C:\>
```

Stop the capture and then view, or do that in one step with the binocular icon. I did the latter in Figure 2-17. Although the current emphasis is on the Decode tab, feel free to take time to explore the other tabs. Click the Decode tab at the bottom and maximize the screen (like I have done in Figure 2-17). Use the File menu to save the capture for later use. Name it *ping pong*.

Notice the three-window display in Figure 2-17 or on your screen. The top pane is a summary pane in which each line is a frame. The middle pane is the detail pane, which is a decode of the frame you are sitting on in the summary pane. The bottom window is the hex pane.

I am sitting on frame 3, which is an Echo Request packet. Earlier my debug output illustrated echo packet types. Here the Sniffer gives you that in the ICMP header in the middle pane. Your goal is to not get wrapped up in the specifics of a protocol analyzer, but to learn the basics and use it as a troubleshooting tool. Speaking of basics, everything goes back to the *not so theoretical* OSI model or TCP/IP suite of protocols discussed in Chapter 1.

Figure 2-16 *Initial Ping Capture*

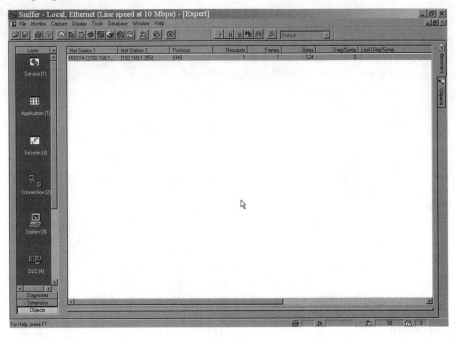

Figure 2-17 *Ping Pong*

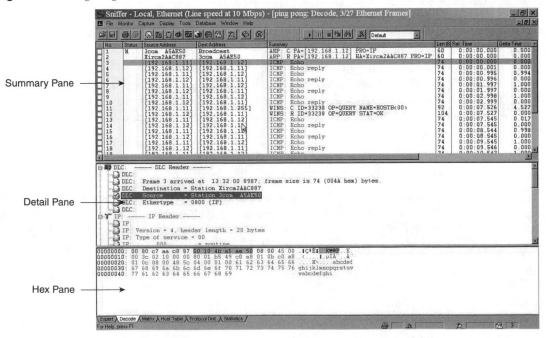

The discussion now turns to the ping activity and the layers involved. Frames 1 and 2 are ARP frames. Because hosta was pinging hostb on the same local segment, ARP broadcasted to find the MAC address for the 192.168.1.12 address in my ping. Take a look at Figure 2-18, where I am sitting on Frame 1, and observe the output in the middle pane. The decode shows the MAC for hosta and the local broadcast for the MAC for hostb. Frame 2 in Figure 2-19 is the local unicast reply from hostb saying, "Hey, that's me, and my MAC is xx-xx-xx-xx-xx."

Figure 2-18 *Frame 1 ARP Request*

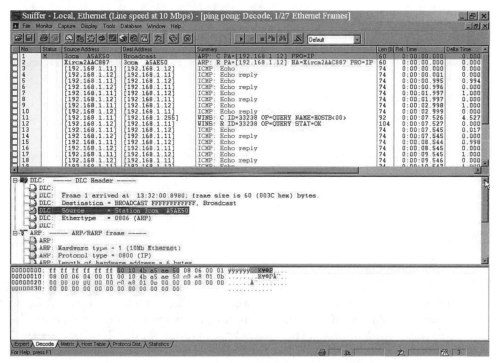

Frames 3, 5, 7, and 9 are Echo Requests, and the even associated frames are the Echo Replies. Remember from Chapter 1 that ICMP is a helper protocol for IP that is responsible for status and error reporting. Here it is in action. You can observe this behavior back in Figure 2-17 as well as see the MAC address in hex because I actually clicked the MAC in the middle pane.

Frames 11 and 12 deal with name resolution and correlate to me typing **ping hostb**. Figure 2-20 illustrates the layers involved with name resolution. By the way, I used the mouse to adjust my window sizes so that I could see more of the decode for this example. For instance, the logical link control (LLC) at Layer 2 uses the EtherType of 0800 to hand off to IP Layer 3. IP uses protocol 17 to hand off to UDP (Layer 4). UDP uses destination port 137 to hand off to NetBIOS name services (upper layers) for name resolution.

Figure 2-19 *Frame 2 ARP Reply*

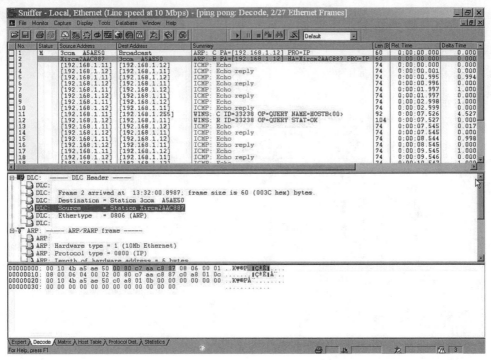

Next move down to Frames 13 through 20 and perform a similar analysis. Earlier I said that ping tests through Layer 3 and uses IP, which has ICMP for a helper. Figure 2-21 clearly demonstrates this fact. Take a look for yourself. If you are not comfortable with this layer-by-layer approach, don't worry; you will continue to review the details in the associated chapters to follow. Understanding the layers just happens to be a required skill for a successful support person.

Protocol analyzers perform some amazing functions. Not only can they capture network traffic, they also can find top bandwidth users, create traffic maps, identify and rank protocols in use, retransmit network traffic, and much more.

NOTE   Again, your goal here is to use a protocol analyzer as a troubleshooting tool, not to learn the details of the product. You will capture and decode various traffic patterns throughout many of the Trouble Tickets in this book to analyze packets in detail.

The last section of this chapter deals with desktop tools, many of which you have already used.

Figure 2-20 *Frame 11 Name Resolution*

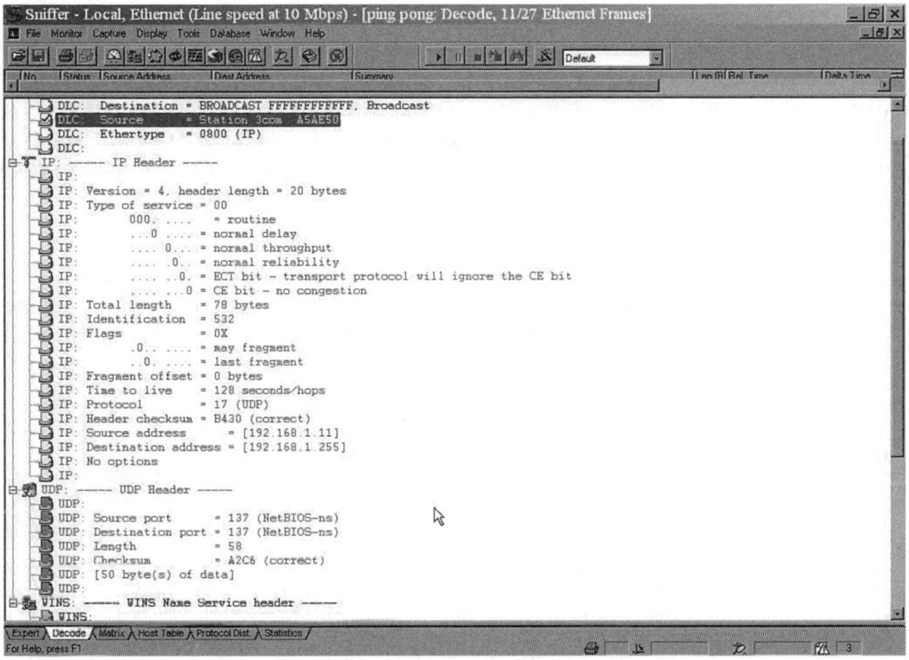

Figure 2-21 *Frames 13–20 Ping Analysis*

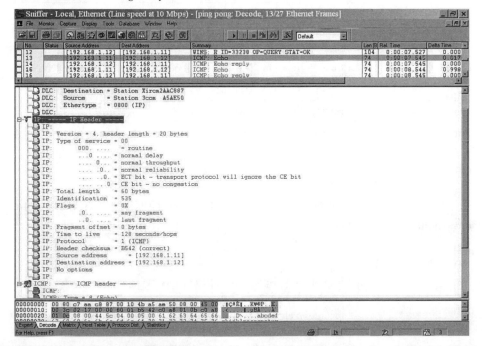

Desktop Tools

Internetworks have become complex for many reasons, including LAN/WAN architecture, media, technologies, and protocols. The progression from host-centric environments to distributed client-server platforms still very much requires a hierarchical network to aid in troubleshooting. So far, I have reviewed various internetworking tools. However, it is impossible to be an expert in everything. If you are a WAN guru, you may lack technical expertise at the desktop. If you are a LAN guru, you may lack technical expertise at the internetwork level. Obviously, because of the added complexities in current LANs and WANs, you need some basic tools to assist.

Refer to the desktop support resources in Table 2-10 and throughout this section to assist with end-to-end troubleshooting. Desktop tools, such as ping and trace, looking at the routing table, logging and monitoring functions, and more are available for your use. Many come with the operating system, and others are supplied by third-party vendors. Use **/?** for command-line help to see the specific options.

Table 2-10   *Desktop Support Resources*

Desktop Tool	Options and Functions
ping	**ping** **ping –t** Continuous ping. **ping –n** Number of echos.
tracert	**tracert** Hop-by-hop test. **tracert –d** Test without DNS lookup **tracert –h** Maximum number of hops to search for target.
pathping	**pathping –n** Test without DNS lookup. **pathping –h** Maximum number of hops to search for target. **pathping** combines **ping** and **tracert** to trace a route and show packet losses for each router in the path (also good for quality of service, QoS).
arp	**arp –a** To view ARP cache.
route	**route print** To view routing table.
netstat	Displays local NetBIOS name table and cache. Displays active TCP and UDP connections and their state.
nbtstat	NetBIOS over TCP statistics. Displays protocol statistics and current TCP connections for NetBIOS over TCP/IP. **nbtstat –RR** to force reinsertion and update of local NetBIOS names.
nslookup	Query DNS servers to check records, services, and operating system information.
ipconfig/winipcfg	**ipconfig** **ipconfig /all** displays more parameters, such as MAC, IP, subnet mask, gateway, WINS, and DNS. **ipconfig /release** **ipconfig /renew**

Try these tools for yourself. For example, ping your favorite website and then trace to it as I do in Figure 2-22 and Figure 2-23.

Figure 2-22 *Ping Cisco Press*

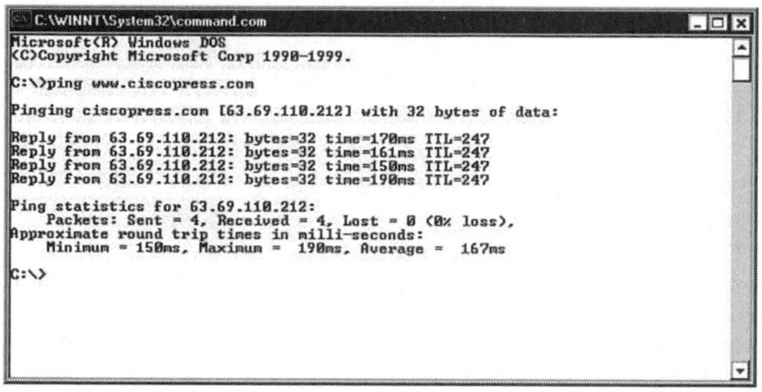

Figure 2-23 *Tracert Cisco Press*

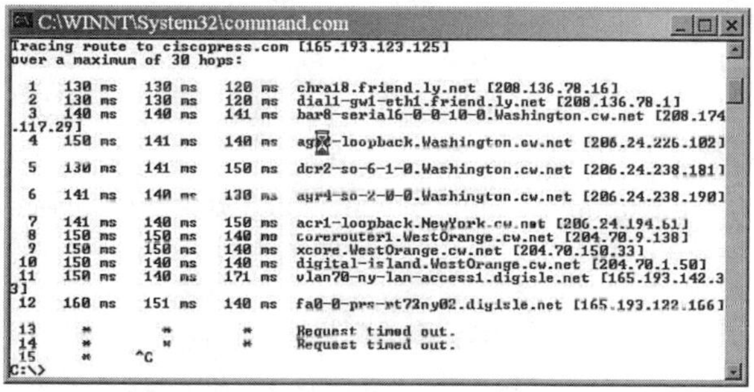

Now turn your attention back to hosta and hostb from the Sniffer capture. First ping from hosta to hostb, tracert, and then look at the ARP cache in Example 2-38.

Example 2-38 *ARP Cache on hosta*

```
C:\>ping hostb
Pinging hostb [192.168.1.12] with 32 bytes of data:
Reply from 192.168.1.12: bytes=32 time<10ms TTL=128
Reply from 192.168.1.12: bytes=32 time<10ms TTL=128
Reply from 192.168.1.12: bytes=32 time<10ms TTL=128
Reply from 192.168.1.12: bytes=32 time<10ms TTL=128
Ping statistics for 192.168.1.12:
    Packets: Sent = 4, Received = 4, Lost = 0 (0% loss),
Approximate round trip times in milli-seconds:
    Minimum = 0ms, Maximum =  0ms, Average =  0ms
C:\>tracert hostb
Tracing route to hostb [192.168.1.12]
over a maximum of 30 hops:
  1    <10 ms   <10 ms   <10 ms  HOSTB [192.168.1.12]
Trace complete.
C:\>arp -a
Interface: 192.168.1.11 on Interface 0x1000005
  Internet Address      Physical Address      Type
  192.168.1.12          00-80-c7-aa-c8-87     dynamic
C:\>
```

The preceding example displays the IP and MAC address for destination hostb in the ARP table, but the entry will stay there for only two minutes unless you use the entry again. Then its life is extended to 10 minutes, total, no matter how many times it is accessed. Next look at the active routes in the routing table on hosta in Example 2-39.

Example 2-39   **route print** *on hosta*

```
C:\>route print
Interface List
0x1 ........................ MS TCP Loopback interface
0x2 ...44 45 53 54 42 00 ...... NOC Extranet Access Adapter
0x4000004 ...00 10 4b a5 ae 50 ...... FE575 Ethernet Adapter
Active Routes:
Network Destination        Netmask          Gateway         Interface  Metric
          127.0.0.0        255.0.0.0        127.0.0.1        127.0.0.1      1
        192.168.1.0    255.255.255.0     192.168.1.11     192.168.1.11      1
       192.168.1.11  255.255.255.255        127.0.0.1        127.0.0.1      1
      192.168.1.255  255.255.255.255     192.168.1.11     192.168.1.11      1
          224.0.0.0        224.0.0.0     192.168.1.11     192.168.1.11      1
    255.255.255.255  255.255.255.255     192.168.1.11                2      1
Persistent Routes:
  None
C:\>
```

Example 2-40 and Example 2-41 display **netstat** and **nbtstat** options. Pick an option and try it out from the command prompt to see the exact display.

Example 2-40   **netstat** *Options*

```
C:\>netstat /?
Displays protocol statistics and current TCP/IP network connections.
NETSTAT [-a] [-e] [-n] [-s] [-p proto] [-r] [interval]
   -a          Displays all connections and listening ports.
   -e          Displays Ethernet statistics. This may be combined with the -s
               option.
   -n          Displays addresses and port numbers in numerical form.
   -p proto    Shows connections for the protocol specified by proto; proto
               may be TCP or UDP.  If used with the -s option to display
               per-protocol statistics, proto may be TCP, UDP, or IP.
   -r          Displays the routing table.
   -s          Displays per-protocol statistics.  By default, statistics are
               shown for TCP, UDP and IP; the -p option may be used to specify
               a subset of the default.
   interval    Redisplays selected statistics, pausing interval seconds
               between each display.  Press CTRL+C to stop redisplaying
               statistics.  If omitted, netstat will print the current
               configuration information once.
C:\>
```

Example 2-41   **nbtstat** *Options*

```
C:\>nbtstat /?
Displays protocol statistics and current TCP/IP connections using NBT
(NetBIOS over TCP/IP).
NBTSTAT [ [-a RemoteName] [-A IP address] [-c] [-n]
```

Example 2-41   nbtstat *Options (Continued)*

```
              [-r] [-R] [-RR] [-s] [-S] [interval] ]
   -a   (adapter status) Lists the remote machine's name table given its name
   -A   (Adapter status) Lists the remote machine's name table given its
                         IP address.
   -c   (cache)          Lists NBT's cache of remote [machine] names and their IP
      addresses
   -n   (names)          Lists local NetBIOS names.
   -r   (resolved)       Lists names resolved by broadcast and via WINS
   -R   (Reload)         Purges and reloads the remote cache name table
   -S   (Sessions)       Lists sessions table with the destination IP addresses
   -s   (sessions)       Lists sessions table converting destination IP
                         addresses to computer NETBIOS names.
   -RR  (ReleaseRefresh) Sends Name Release packets to WINs and then, starts
      Refresh
   RemoteName   Remote host machine name.
   IP address   Dotted decimal representation of the IP address.
   interval     Redisplays selected statistics, pausing interval seconds
                between each display. Press Ctrl+C to stop redisplaying
                statistics.
C:\>
```

Example 2-42 illustrates **ipconfig** with the optional **/all** parameter, which provides more detail (such as the MAC address and name resolution parameters).

Example 2-42   ipconfig /all

```
C:\>ipconfig /all
Windows 2000 IP Configuration
        Host Name . . . . . . . . . . . . : hosta
        Primary DNS Suffix  . . . . . . . :
        Node Type . . . . . . . . . . . . : Hybrid
        IP Routing Enabled. . . . . . . . : No
        WINS Proxy Enabled. . . . . . . . : No
Ethernet adapter {F6BB63C3-5752-480C-96DB-206E49F87839}:
        Connection-specific DNS Suffix  . :
        Description . . . . . . . . . . . : NOC Extranet Access Adapter
        Physical Address. . . . . . . . . : 44-45-53-54-42-00
        DHCP Enabled. . . . . . . . . . . : No
        IP Address. . . . . . . . . . . . : 0.0.0.0
        Subnet Mask . . . . . . . . . . . : 0.0.0.0
        Default Gateway . . . . . . . . . :
        DNS Servers . . . . . . . . . . . :
Ethernet adapter Local Area Connection:
        Connection-specific DNS Suffix  . :
        Description . . . . . . . . . . . : 3Com Megahertz 10/100 LAN CardBus
        PC Card
        Physical Address. . . . . . . . . : 00-10-4B-A5-AE-50
        DHCP Enabled. . . . . . . . . . . : No
        Autoconfiguration IP Address. . . : 192.168.1.11
        Subnet Mask . . . . . . . . . . . : 255.255.255.0
        Default Gateway . . . . . . . . . :
        DNS Servers . . . . . . . . . . . :
C:\>
```

You will continue to use many of these tools in the Trouble Tickets to come. Depending on the operating system, other administrative and troubleshooting tools are available. Other administrative and troubleshooting tools include system configuration utilities, startup menus for safe modes, help troubleshooters, Device Manager, Perfmon, Event Viewer, and Task Manager.

Many third-party tools are worthy of exploring, too. Consider taking a look at TTCP, VMWare, NetOps, and VNC. Microsoft TechNet and Novell Users International (NUI) Technical Resource CD are similar resources to the CCO (but focusing on their proprietary products rather than Cisco products). Explore these tools on your own; some of them are very addicting.

NOTE   If you need more help troubleshooting in this area, I highly recommend CompTIA A+ and Network+ programs or specific operating system resources for more detail. Check out www.comptia.org and individual vendor websites.

After all this information and examination of tools and resources, don't forget the Physical Layer. LEDs are quite helpful in troubleshooting and on a practical note should be your first observation if you have physical access. Try **test led** sometime on a router to make sure that you are actually connected to the box you think you are. Look at the link lights on your NICs and devices. Use multiple tools to administer and manage your internetwork. Pictures and maps are great, but if you can't afford a fancy network management program, do what you can with the IOS and operating system tools and explore other third-party tools.

Use all of these tools in conjunction with sound troubleshooting techniques. Use CDP, draw your own map, know what is normal, know what your configurations look like, annotate them with descriptions and remarks, verify connectivity with ping and trace, log changes, and only use debug to the point that it won't stress out your router. Sometimes a protocol analyzer gives you more detail and is less intrusive on your devices. By now you should be well on your way to a full tool bag that will enable you to work through the more practical portions of the remainder of this book.

NOTE   I used to deliver TCP/IP and CCNP classes for Chesapeake/Mentor Technologies. Recently it was brought to my attention that the old www.ccci.com site is up and running with references to some great tools and resources.

Review Questions

Use this chapter and your practical troubleshooting knowledge and skills to answer the following questions. The answers are located in Appendix A, "Answers to Review Questions."

1 CDP sends and receives neighbor advertisements over multicast address 01-00-0c-cc-cc and uses a proprietary HDLC type value. CDP must run on media that supports what?

2 To match up the following buffer pools with the appropriate sizes (small, middle, big, very big, large, and huge), what IOS command would you use?

    A   104 bytes

    B   600 bytes

    C   1524 bytes

    D   4520 bytes

    E   5024 bytes

    F   18024 bytes

3 Which support tool can monitor up to all seven layers and is the least stressful on the router?

    A   Network monitor

    B   Protocol analyzer

    C   debug

    D   ping

4 List the five categories of network management and give a Cisco example of an NMS.

5 What NMS feature of Cisco's product is a replacement for CWSI? List at least four other features that this product is responsible for.

6 What type of support tool records, displays, and analyzes how a protocol operates and gives a layer-by-layer decode? Give an example.

7 Cable testers (scanners) can be used to test physical connectivity. Many cable testers include TDR functionality. What type of device is used to test signal loss with fiber cable?

8 What support tool is useful for baselining and continuously tracks packets but doesn't decode them?

9 List at least two proactive and two reactive CCO tools?

10 Use the numbers 1–4 to match the priority levels with the following severity level.

___ Information needed on product

___ Production network severely degraded

___ Network performance degraded

___ Production network down

11 Escalation to Cisco support requires certain tasks. The **show tech-support** command is helpful. You need your equipment and service contract information, and you should open a case with specific priority level and case number. What CCO tool enables you to open, query, and update a case with TAC?

12 The Cisco Dynamic Configuration tool enables you to look up the specifics of a WSC1924A you bought off of eBay. You should quickly find that it is a 24-port, 10-MB switch with two 100BASE-TX ports and it is upgradeable to the Enterprise Edition. Under which category would you find this on the website?

Summary

As internetworks grow larger and more complex, a much greater potential exists for problems to disable portions or the entire network. You may also face issues that degrade performance to unacceptable levels. This complexity of additional users, resources, protocols, interfaces, and vendors requires you to have a full tool bag to troubleshoot problems. Scalable networks are not one-size-fits-all. Hardware, software, and the web are constantly changing. The resources innate to the Cisco IOS and various third-party tools covered in this chapter should help you deal with this. These first two chapters are designed to provide you with a foundation for the practical exercises in the remainder of the book. The next two chapters examine IP and IPX in more detail. After that, the focus turns to Layer 2 LAN and WAN technologies to help you continue to build your practical troubleshooting skills.

Supporting IP and IPX

CHAPTER 3

Shooting Trouble with IP

This chapter focuses on a number of objectives falling under the CCNP Troubleshooting guidelines. Understanding basic TCP/IP troubleshooting principles not only applies to the CCNP certification but to all industry certifications. A solid understanding of how IP works is essential for troubleshooting any small, medium, or large network.

This chapter and the remaining chapters assume knowledge of the previous chapters, which deal conceptually with protocol characteristics, models, troubleshooting methods, support tools, and resources. Each chapter starts by introducing a hands-on chapter scenario. To gain practical experience, build the network in the scenario if at all possible and follow along. If that isn't possible, the content and explanations are detailed enough for you to learn from without needing the equipment in front of you. Several integrated walk-through scenarios and Trouble Tickets enable you to benefit from the added learning advantages offered by practical application. After the Shooting Trouble with IP scenario, I explore TCP/IP concepts, symptoms, problems, and action plans.

This chapter covers the following topics:

- Scenario: Shooting Trouble with IP

- Protocols and Packets

- Addressing

- Routing Protocols

- Trouble Tickets

- Trouble Tickets Solutions

Supporting Website Files

You can find files and links to utilities that support this book on the Cisco Press website at www.ciscopress.com/1587200570. Even if you do not have a lab, you can take advantage of the supporting configuration files including the logs to understand device input and output. The files are listed throughout the chapters in italics.

In order to be able to read and work with some of the supporting files offered at www.ciscopress.com/1587200570, you may want to download some of the programs listed in Table I-1 in the Introduction.

Scenario: Shooting Trouble with IP

It is now time to get started with the practical Shooting Trouble with IP scenario. First, add the additional equipment, perform a **write erase** or **erase startup-config** to clear your configurations from previous labs, and rewire according to Figure 3-1.

NOTE   My lab uses the 2514, 2501, 3640, 3620, and 2516 Cisco routers, but yours can include any number of devices that have similar interfaces. See Appendix C, "Equipment Reference," for the hardware used throughout the book.

Figure 3-1   *Shooting Trouble with IP*

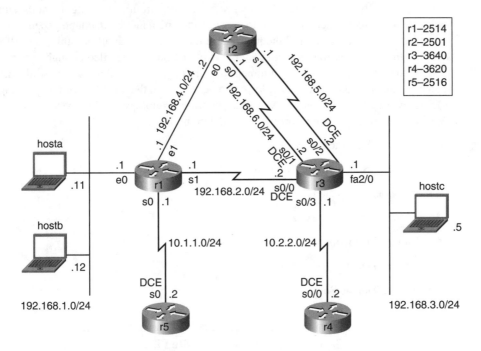

The scenario goal is to put in the basic configurations, and then add Routing Information Protocol (RIP) as the routing protocol to work toward end-to-end connectivity between the hosts. Where appropriate, use best practices such as descriptions on interfaces, hosts tables, and so on. Configure r1 and work your way through r5. As always, test and document along the way and when you finish configuring.

Remember, however, that there is not always one right or wrong way to accomplish the tasks presented. The ability to obtain the end result using good practices is extremely important in any real-world network. My troubleshooting and device configurations start in Example 3-1;

you can compare your work to that and perhaps see a different approach to obtaining the end result. Figure 3-2 shows a picture of my lab before wiring, and Figure 3-3 shows the after-wiring picture. I have physically labeled each of my devices so that I don't have to think about that later. Refer back to Figure 3-1 as you continue to set up and troubleshoot.

Figure 3-2   *Scenario Lab Photo Before Wiring*

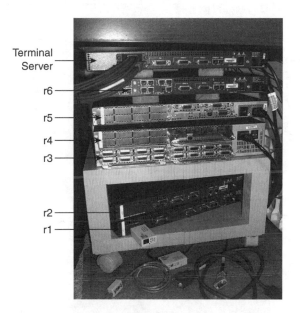

Figure 3-3   *Scenario Lab Photo After Wiring*

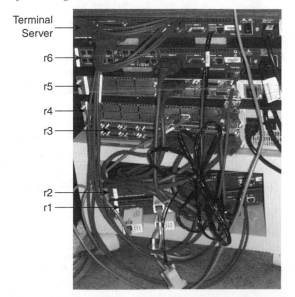

The terminal server at the top of the equipment stack in Figure 3-2 is not a required piece of equipment for the lab, but more a convenience. I am using a Cisco 2511 with the first five terminal leads connected to each of the console ports on my five routers. See Appendix C for more information on how to configure a terminal server and use one for your lab. My 2511 configuration is in Example 3-1 with the significant output shaded.

Example 3-1   *Terminal Server Configuration (2511)*

```
ts#show running-config
...
hostname ts
enable password donna
ip subnet-zero
ip host r1 2001 1.1.1.1
ip host r2 2002 1.1.1.1
ip host r3 2003 1.1.1.1
ip host r4 2004 1.1.1.1
ip host r5 2005 1.1.1.1
interface Loopback0
 ip address 1.1.1.1 255.0.0.0
 no ip directed-broadcast
...
line con 0
 transport input none
line 1 16
 transport input all
 no exec
line aux 0
line vty 0 4
 exec-timeout 30 0
 password donna
 logging synchronous
 login
end
```

Although I give you Figures 3-1 through 3-3, it is really a better practice to draw your own network diagram. Some people prefer columns and rows of this type of data, but I prefer colorful diagrams to assist with troubleshooting later. For example, you might draw your ·devices and media with a blue pen, label the IP parameters with a black pen, label IPX parameters with a red pen, draw a green circle around the Open Shortest Path First (OSPF) areas, and so on. Label which interfaces are DCE or DTE for your lab. Document device names, locations, Layer 2 and Layer 3 addresses, routed and bridged protocols, routing protocols, access control lists (ACLs), configuration files, and verify full connectivity. Perform some simple ping and trace tests (see Table 3-1), run **show tech-support**, and document some more. All of this gives you a starting point for normal *baseline* activity when your network is running well. Keep in mind that I want you to concentrate *only* on IP-related baselining for this chapter.

NOTE	You will adjust your hands-on lab for new equipment, software, protocols, media, services, problems, and so on as you progress through various Trouble Tickets and chapters. Feel free to substitute whatever equipment you have for the hosts, routers, and switches in Figure 3-1. All 2600s and 3600s, or better yet all 6500s, would be nice, but that isn't what I have either.

Table 3-1 gives you a layered yet divide-and-conquer approach to quickly spotting IP issues. It would be wonderful if I could tell you to just start at the first item in the table and work your way through, but you need to think methodically (as Chapter 1, "Shooting Trouble," suggested). It is helpful to divide and conquer along the way in practical application to quickly narrow down the real problem. If you can't communicate with your gateway, for instance, it is a little difficult to communicate with a remote host. If you can't communicate with yourself, it is impossible to communicate with a local host.

Table 3-1   *IP Troubleshooting Checklist*

Isolating Problems	Commands and Symptoms
Check MAC address, IP address, subnet mask, default gateway, and other static or DHCP* parameters.	Windows NT/2000: **ipconfig /all** Windows 95/98: **winipcfg** UNIX: **ifconfig**
Ping your loopback from your workstation to see whether the TCP/IP stack is loaded.	**ping 127.0.0.1**
Ping yourself from your workstation to verify your NIC*.	**ping 192.168.1.11**
Ping a local host from your workstation to verify local communications.	**ping 192.168.1.12**
Ping your default gateway from your workstation to verify you can communicate with your local router interface.	**ping 192.168.1.1**
Are you getting ARPs* from the gateway? If so, the gateway's MAC address should be in the workstation ARP table.	**arp –a**
Ping a remote host and another if it fails from your workstation.	**ping 192.168.3.5**
Perform a trace to the remote host to find hop-by-hop router issues.	Windows: **tracert [-d]** UNIX/Cisco: **traceroute**
Is it a host problem or a router problem?	**show ip interface brief** **show run interface e0** **show ip interface e0** **show interfaces e0** **show ip route** **show ip protocols** **show ip arp** **show ip cache** **show ip access-list**

continues

Table 3-1 *IP Troubleshooting Checklist (Continued)*

Combine ping and trace to look for packet loss in the path.	**pathping 192.168.3.5**
Use an application to test the upper layers. NetBIOS issues Sockets issues	**Start => Run \\192.168.3.5** Find computer **nbtstat –A** *IP_address* **ping 192.168.3.1** **telnet 192.168.3.1** **ftp 192.168.3.1** **tftp 192.168.3.1**

Eliminate any name resolution issues by not using hostnames or NetBIOS names at first.
 	
When other things are working, fix any name resolution issues. Ensure name resolution files are in their required locations and have the appropriate names. Troubleshoot files, DNS*/WINS* servers, and the network issues to and from these devices.
	Name resolution
	
	  DNS, **hosts** file, NIS tables
	
	  WINS, **lmhosts** file (NetBIOS)
	
	     nbtstat –c (view cache)
	
	     nbtstat –R (reload cache)
	
	Microsoft Browser services (NetBIOS issues)
	
	  Start, Run \\computername
	
	  Find computer or **net view**
	
	  nbtstat –A *IP_address*
	
	  Sockets issues
	
	  ping hostc
	
	  telnet hostc

*DHCP = Dynamic Host Configuration Protocol

NICs = Network interface card

ARPs = Address Resolution Protocol

DNS = Domain Name Service

WINS = Windows Internet Naming Service

NOTE   Although the commands I use in this book are in their complete form, using truncated commands is virtually a mandatory practice in the real world. More importantly however, you should know the submode from which the command can be issued. At times I tend to issue global configuration commands in interface submode. This works just fine assuming that you don't need help in the midst of the command. If you are unsure, however, type the command from the appropriate submode and make use of the Tab key and ? for help.

Using the scenario diagram in Figure 3-1, configure r1 similar to what is in Example 3-2. My r1 is a Cisco 2514, but you can use any Cisco router that has two Ethernet interfaces and two serial interfaces for the lab. My passwords are all donna because that is easy to remember for the labs, but that is exactly why they should not all be donna for practical application. Throughout the following examples, I have made a few careless mistakes that you may or may not make. I will troubleshoot them when all my routers are configured per the scenario diagram.

Example 3-2   *r1 Configuration (2514)*

```
Router>enable
Router#configure terminal
Enter configuration commands, one per line.  End with CNTL/Z.
Router(config)#hostname r1
r1(config)#enable password donna
r1(config)#line vty 0 4
r1(config-line)#login
r1(config-line)#password donna
r1(config-line)#exit
r1(config)#interface ethernet 0
r1(config-if)#description e0 to hosta and hostb
r1(config-if)#ip address 192.168.1.1 255.255.255.0
r1(config-if)#no shut
00:10:12: %LINK-3-UPDOWN: Interface Ethernet0, changed state to up
00:10:13: %LINEPROTO-5-UPDOWN: Line protocol on Interface Ethernet0,
    changed state to up
r1(config)#interface ethernet 1
r1(config-if)#description e1 to r2e0
r1(config-if)#ip address 192.168.4.1 255.255.255.0
r1(config-if)#no shut
r1(config-if)#interface serial 0
r1(config-if)#description s0 to r5s0
r1(config-if)#ip address 10.1.1.1 255.255.255.0
r1(config-if)#bandwidth 64
r1(config-if)#no shut
00:13:11: %LINK-3-UPDOWN: Interface Serial0, changed state to down
r1(config-if)#ip host r1 192.168.1.1 192.168.2.1 192.168.4.1 10.1.1.1
r1(config)#ip host r2 192.168.4.2 192.168.5.1 192.168.6.1
r1(config)#$192.168.2.2 192.168.5.2 192.168.6.2 192.168.3.1 10.2.2.1
r1(config)#ip host r4 10.2.2.2
r1(config)#ip host r5 10.1.1.2
r1(config)#router rip
r1(config-router)#network 192.168.1.0
r1(config-router)#network 192.168.2.0
r1(config-router)#network 192.168.4.0
r1(config-router)#network 10.1.1.0
r1(config-router)#end
r1#copy running-config startup-config
```

NOTE   For the first router configuration, I illustrate the **enable** command to take you into enable mode **Router#** and the **configure terminal** command to take you to the global configuration mode **Router(config)#**, where the Cisco output reminds you that you can press Ctrl+Z to return to enable mode from any prompt. Alternatively, you can type **end** to return to the privileged prompt (enable mode) or **exit** to back up one level at a time. I will assume from this point on that you are very comfortable with entering and exiting these modes and therefore I will eliminate the initial **enable** and **configure terminal** commands from my examples.

NOTE   Remember that the dollar sign ($) at the beginning of a line of user input is the Cisco IOS indication that the text was too much for the width of the terminal screen. You can always press Ctrl+A to get to the beginning or Ctrl+E to get to the end of a line.

Now move on to configuring r2 as in Example 3-3. My r2 is a Cisco 2501, but you can use any Cisco router that has at least one Ethernet interface and two serial interfaces for the lab. I copied the hosts table lines from r1 and pasted them into this configuration. In future examples, I plan to just paste the configuration for the hosts table and passwords to save a little typing.

Example 3-3   *r2 Configuration (2501)*

```
Router(config)#hostname r2
r2(config)#enable password donna
r2(config)#line vty 0 4
r2(config-line)#login
r2(config-line)#password donna
r2(config-line)#exit
r2(config)#interface ethernet 0
r2(config-if)#description e0 to r1e1
r2(config-if)#ip address 192.168.4.2 255.255.255.0
r2(config-if)#no shut
r2(config-if)#int
00:41:44: %LINK-3-UPDOWN: Interface Ethernet0, changed state to up
00:41:45: %LINEPROTO-5-UPDOWN: Line protocol on Interface Ethernet0,
    changed state to ups0
r2(config-if)#description s0 to r3s0/1
r2(config-if)#bandwidth 64
r2(config-if)#ip address 192.168.6.1 255.255.255.0
r2(config-if)#no shut
00:42:22: %LINK-3-UPDOWN: Interface Serial0, changed state to down
r2(config-if)#interface serial 1
r2(config-if)#description s1 to r3s0/2
r2(config-if)#bandwidth 64
r2(config-if)#ip address 192.168.5.1 255.255.255.0
r2(config-if)#router rip
r2(config-router)#network 192.168.4.0
r2(config-router)#network 192.168.5.0
```

Example 3-3   *r2 Configuration (2501) (Continued)*

```
r2(config-router)#network 192.168.6.0
r2(config-router)#exit
r2(config)#ip host r1 192.168.1.1 192.168.2.1 192.168.4.1 10.1.1.1
r2(config)#ip host r2 192.168.4.2 192.168.5.1 192.168.6.1
r2(config)#$192.168.2.2 192.168.5.2 192.168.6.2 192.168.3.1 10.2.2.1
r2(config)#ip host r4 10.2.2.2
r2(config)#ip host r5 10.1.1.2
r2(config)#end
r2#copy running-config startup-config
```

NOTE   The shaded output may appear a little confusing in text and is quite annoying in practice. Had I turned on **logging synchronous**, my input would not have been interrupted. You should do this for your configurations.

Configure the rest of your routers now and check your work using the following examples. I copied the text in Example 3-4 to Windows Notepad to easily paste it into r3, r4, and r5.

Example 3-4   *Notepad File Including Passwords and Hosts Table*

```
enable password donna
ip host r1 192.168.1.1 192.168.2.1 192.168.4.1 10.1.1.1
ip host r2 192.168.4.2 192.168.5.1 192.168.6.1
ip host r3 192.168.2.2 192.168.5.2 192.168.6.2 192.168.3.1 10.2.2.1
ip host r4 10.2.2.2
ip host r5 10.1.1.2
line vty 0 4
login
password donna
line console 0
logging synchronous
exit
```

Example 3-5 and Example 3-6 start my r3 configuration. My r3 is a Cisco 3640, but you can use any Cisco router that has at least one Ethernet interface and four serial interfaces for the lab. Although the capabilities are not important in this chapter, having multiple serial interfaces on a router enables you to set up your own Frame Relay switch later in the book. Depending on the capabilities, the Fast Ethernet interface will give you an opportunity to experiment with duplex and speed concepts as well.

Note in Example 3-5 that I attempted to configure the e0 interface when it was really fa2/0 that I needed to configure. A physical inspection of the device confirmed that the Fast Ethernet port was located in Slot 2; because you can't physically see my device, however, I proceeded with the **show interfaces** command.

NOTE   In practical troubleshooting, don't forget the little things. For example, the position of the caret (^) is quite helpful in finding exactly where the syntax error exists within a line.

Wherever you see ... I eliminated some of the output to shorten the length of the configuration.

Example 3-5   *r3 Configuration (3640)*

```
Router(config)#hostname r3
r3(config)#enable password donna
r3(config)#ip host r1 192.168.1.1 192.168.2.1 192.168.4.1 10.1.1.1
r3(config)#ip host r2 192.168.4.2 192.168.5.1 192.168.6.1
r3(config)#$192.168.2.2 192.168.5.2 192.168.6.2 192.168.3.1 10.2.2.1
r3(config)#ip host r4 10.2.2.2
r3(config)#ip host r5 10.1.1.2
r3(config)#line vty 0 4
r3(config-line)#login
r3(config-line)#password donna
r3(config-line)#line console 0
r3(config-line)#logging synchronous
r3(config-line)#exit
r3(config)#int e0
                 ^
% Invalid input detected at '^' marker.
r3(config)#end
r3#show interfaces
Serial0/0 is administratively down, line protocol is down
  Hardware is CD2430 in sync mode
...
FastEthernet2/0 is administratively down, line protocol is down
  Hardware is AmdFE, address is 00b0.6481.e300 (bia 00b0.6481.e300)
  MTU 1500 bytes, BW 100000 Kbit, DLY 100 usec, rely 255/255, load 1/255
  Encapsulation ARPA, loopback not set, keepalive set (10 sec)
  Half-duplex, 100Mb/s, 100BaseTX/FX
  ARP type: ARPA, ARP Timeout 04:00:00
...
r3#configure terminal
Enter configuration commands, one per line.  End with CNTL/Z.
r3(config)#interface fastethernet 2/0
r3(config-if)#ip address 192.168.3.1 255.255.255.0
r3(config-router)#interface serial 0/0
r3(config-if)#desc r3s0/0 to r1s1
r3(config-if)#bandwidth 64
r3(config-if)#clock rate 64000
r3(config-if)#ip address 192.168.2.2 255.255.255.0
r3(config-if)#no shut
r3(config-if)#interface serial 0/1
r3(config-if)#description r3s0/1 to r2s0
r3(config-if)#bandwidth 64
```

Example 3-5 *r3 Configuration (3640) (Continued)*

```
r3(config-if)#clock rate 64000
r3(config-if)#ip address 192.168.6.2 255.255.255.0
r3(config-if)#no shut
r3(config-if)#interface serial 0/2
r3(config-if)#description r3s0/2 to r2s1
r3(config-if)#bandwidth 64
r3(config-if)#clock rate 64000
r3(config-if)#ip address 192.168.5.2 255.255.255.0
r3(config-if)#no shut
```

Finish configuring r3, r4, and r5 and test your configurations.

Now that you have configured your lab, perform some basic lower-layer tests to verify your drawing and your internetwork. Make sure all used interfaces are in a line protocol up state as in Example 3-6; if they are not in a line protocol up state, fix any noticeable problems at this point. Notice how **show ip interface brief** is a very appropriate command to quickly spot lower-level issues.

Example 3-6 *IP Interface Testing*

```
r1>show ip interface brief
Interface          IP-Address      OK? Method Status                Protocol
Ethernet0          192.168.1.1     YES NVRAM  up                    up
Ethernet1          192.168.4.1     YES manual up                    up
Serial0            10.1.1.1        YES NVRAM  up                    up
Serial1            unassigned      YES unset  administratively down down
r2>show ip interface brief
Interface          IP-Address      OK? Method Status                Protocol
Ethernet0          192.168.4.2     YES NVRAM  up                    up
Serial0            192.168.6.1     YES NVRAM  up                    up
Serial1            192.168.5.1     YES NVRAM  administratively down down
r3>show ip interface brief
Interface          IP-Address      OK? Method Status                Protocol
Serial0/0          192.168.2.2     YES unset  down                  down
Serial0/1          192.168.6.2     YES unset  up                    up
Serial0/2          192.168.5.2     YES unset  down                  down
Serial0/3          unassigned      YES unset  down                  down
...
FastEthernet2/0    192.168.3.1     YES manual up                    down
r4>show ip interface brief
Interface          IP-Address      OK? Method Status                Protocol
Ethernet0/0        unassigned      YES unset  administratively down down
Serial0/0          10.2.2.2        YES manual down                  down
Serial0/1          unassigned      YES unset  administratively down down
r5>sh ip int brie
Interface          IP-Address      OK? Method Status                Protocol
BRI0               unassigned      YES unset  administratively down down
BRI0:1             unassigned      YES unset  administratively down down
BRI0:2             unassigned      YES unset  administratively down down
Ethernet0          unassigned      YES unset  administratively down down
Serial0            10.1.1.2        YES manual up                    up
Serial1            unassigned      YES unset  administratively down down
```

NOTE   In the real world of supporting networks, I typically use the shortcut **sh ip int brie** to quickly identify my interface status and addresses. I spell **brief** out to the cheese (**brie**) just in case there are any ISDN Basic Rate Interfaces (BRI).

Think about these line and protocol issues. Target the lower layers to get all the required interfaces to a status of *up/up* before you continue. Check your work using the following examples.

First I spotted, for interface s1, the unassigned IP address and the administratively down status on r1, which I correct in Example 3-7. Because my interface command was interrupted once more, I must have forgotten **logging synchronous** on r1, so I added it and saved the configuration.

Example 3-7   *Correcting Interface Issues on r1*

```
r1(config)#interface serial 1
r1(config-if)#description s1 to r3s0/0
r1(config-if)#bandwidth 64
r1(config-if)#ip address 192.168.2.1 255.255.255.0
r1(config-if)#no shut
05:16:39: %LINK-3-UPDOWN: Interface Serial1, changed state to up
05:16:40: %LINEPROTO-5-UPDOWN: Line protocol on Interface Serial1, changed state
  to up
r1(config-if)#end
r1#sh i
05:16:50: %SYS-5-CONFIG_I: Configured from console by consolep int brief
Interface              IP-Address      OK? Method Status              Protocol
Ethernet0              192.168.1.1     YES NVRAM  up                  up
Ethernet1              192.168.4.1     YES manual up                  up
Serial0                10.1.1.1        YES NVRAM  up                  up
Serial1                192.168.2.1     YES manual up                  up
r1#configure terminal
Enter configuration commands, one per line.  End with CNTL/Z.
r1(config)#line console 0
r1(config-line)#logging synchronous
r1(config-line)#end
r1#copy running-config startup-config
```

The r1s1 interface would have come up fine without the bandwidth statement, but it is optimal for routing protocols to configure the correct bandwidth statement on your interfaces. The **description** is optional as well, but it certainly makes troubleshooting easier when you know exactly what is connected to an interface. Now move along to r2, which has issues with interface s1 being administratively down. Fix these issues now and check your work in Example 3-8.

Example 3-8   *Correcting Interface Issues on r2*

```
r2(config)#interface serial 1
r2(config-if)#no shut
05:20:08: %LINK-3-UPDOWN: Interface Serial1, changed state to up
05:20:09: %LINEPROTO-5-UPDOWN: Line protocol on Interface Serial1,
    changed state to up
r2(config-if)#end
r2#show ip interface brief
Interface            IP-Address      OK? Method Status              Protocol
Ethernet0            192.168.4.2     YES NVRAM  up                  up
Serial0              192.168.6.1     YES NVRAM  up                  up
Serial1              192.168.5.1     YES NVRAM  up                  up
r2#copy running-config startup-config
```

r3 requires you to look at your drawing more closely so that you can concentrate on just the interfaces being used. Configure any missing IP addresses and issue a **no shut** command on any used interfaces that are showing as *administratively down*. Check the status of the interfaces in Example 3-9.

Example 3-9   *Correcting Interface Issues on r3*

```
r3#show ip interface brief
Interface            IP-Address      OK? Method Status              Protocol
Serial0/0            192.168.2.2     YES manual up                  up
Serial0/1            192.168.6.2     YES manual up                  up
Serial0/2            192.168.5.2     YES manual up                  up
Serial0/3            unassigned      YES manual down                down
...
FastEthernet2/0      192.168.3.1     YES manual up                  down
```

Example 3-9 indicates that a problem still exists with s0/3 and fa2/0. The other end (host) is not running for my Ethernet hostc connection, but you need to examine further the cause of the down/down status for s0/3. Think about what's in your tool bag from the preceding chapter to assist you further in spotting lower-layer problems. Check your thoughts against Example 3-10.

Example 3-10   *Correcting Physical Issues on r3*

```
r3#show controllers serial 0/3
CD2430 Slot 0, Port 3, Controller 0, Channel 3, Revision 15
Channel mode is synchronous serial
idb 0x6129A1A0, buffer size 1524, V.35 DTE cable
...
```

Everything looks normal on the r3 end of things from a physical point of view, so now investigate the other end of the connection as in Example 3-11.

Example 3-11 *Investigate r4 serial 0/0 Connection*

```
r4#show controllers serial 0/0
Interface Serial0/0
Hardware is Quicc 68360
No serial cable attached
idb at 0x60AC9A40, driver data structure at 0x60ACEE10
...
```

I have an advantage in that I can physically inspect my devices; I hope you can do the same if you are following along in your own lab. If you look very closely in the picture of my equipment, you may be able to detect the error, but I won't assume that for now. The **show controllers** commands certainly display the problem here. Although I did not specifically illustrate the output of **show controllers s0/1**, the output of s0/0 is quite helpful. I had the cable plugged into s0/1 rather than s0/0 on r4. On the 3640, s0/0 is closest to the power switch, which is typical. This mistake affected the serial connection between r3 and r4. Example 3-12 shows the output **show ip interface brief** after the physical correction and assigning the appropriate address to s0/3.

Example 3-12 *After the Physical Cable Swap from serial 0/1 to serial 0/0*

```
r3#show ip interface brief
Interface            IP-Address       OK? Method Status          Protocol
Serial0/0            192.168.2.2      YES manual up              up
Serial0/1            192.168.6.2      YES manual up              up
Serial0/2            192.168.5.2      YES manual up              up
Serial0/3            10.2.2.1         YES manual up              up
...
FastEthernet2/0      192.168.3.1      YES manual up              down
r3#copy running-config startup-config
```

After you bring your hosts back online, the Fast Ethernet 2/0 status should change from *up/down* to *up/up*. I give that a test in Example 3-13. My Fast Ethernet interface did not come up when I brought the host online, so follow along to determine the issue.

The first thing I noted was that the network card dongle did not light up for 10 or 100 Mbps. Next, look at Figure 3-1 and label what type of cable you need if you have the PC connected directly into the Fast Ethernet port. Category 5 crossover is correct. I fixed the problem by replacing my original straight-through cable with a crossover Category 5 in-line coupler so that I could use two short straight-through cables to make my connection. Figure 3-4 shows a picture of the coupler. In practical application, this is where using colored cables would help you to very quickly spot the issue. For example, use the normal gray cable for straight-through and use red for crossovers. Things appear to be working for now in Example 3-13.

Figure 3-4   *Crossover Category 5 In-line Coupler*

Example 3-13   *Fast Ethernet 2/0 Status*

```
r3#show run interface fastethernet 2/0
interface FastEthernet2/0
 ip address 192.168.3.1 255.255.255.0
 no ip directed-broadcast
end
...
07:22:02: %LINEPROTO-5-UPDOWN: Line protocol on Interface FastEthernet2/0,
    changed state to up
r3#show ip interface brief
Interface           IP-Address      OK? Method Status              Protocol
Serial0/0           192.168.2.2     YES manual up                  up
Serial0/1           192.168.6.2     YES manual up                  up
Serial0/2           192.168.5.2     YES manual up                  up
Serial0/3           10.2.2.1        YES manual up                  up
...
FastEthernet2/0     192.168.3.1     YES manual up                  up
```

Make sure you have made all corrections, including those that you need for your lab, so that you can continue the tests in Example 3-14 for some simple router ping tests. Recall from the preceding chapters that ping tests up through Layer 3.

Example 3-14 *Testing the Scenario with Ping*

```
r1>ping r2
Type escape sequence to abort.
Sending 5, 100-byte ICMP Echos to 192.168.4.2, timeout is 2 seconds:
.!!!!
Success rate is 80 percent (4/5), round-trip min/avg/max = 4/4/4 ms
r1>ping r3
Type escape sequence to abort.
Sending 5, 100-byte ICMP Echos to 192.168.2.2, timeout is 2 seconds:
!!!!!
Success rate is 100 percent (5/5), round-trip min/avg/max = 28/30/32 ms
r1>ping r4
Type escape sequence to abort.
Sending 5, 100-byte ICMP Echos to 10.2.2.2, timeout is 2 seconds:
.....
Success rate is 0 percent (0/5)
r1>ping r5
Type escape sequence to abort.
Sending 5, 100-byte ICMP Echos to 10.1.1.2, timeout is 2 seconds:
!!!!!
Success rate is 100 percent (5/5), round-trip min/avg/max = 28/30/32 ms
```

Next check the routing tables and routing protocols as in Example 3-15 to make sure r1 has a route to get to r4.

Example 3-15 *r1 Routing Table*

```
r1>show ip route
Codes: C - connected, S - static, I - IGRP, R - RIP, M - mobile, B - BGP
       D - EIGRP, EX - EIGRP external, O - OSPF, IA - OSPF inter area
       N1 - OSPF NSSA external type 1, N2 - OSPF NSSA external type 2
       E1 - OSPF external type 1, E2 - OSPF external type 2, E - EGP
       i - IS-IS, L1 - IS-IS level-1, L2 - IS-IS level-2, * - candidate default
       U - per-user static route, o - ODR
Gateway of last resort is not set…
C    192.168.4.0/24 is directly connected, Ethernet1
R    192.168.5.0/24 [120/1] via 192.168.2.2, 00:00:02, Serial1
     10.0.0.0/24 is subnetted, 1 subnets
C       10.1.1.0 is directly connected, Serial0
R    192.168.6.0/24 [120/1] via 192.168.2.2, 00:00:02, Serial1
C    192.168.1.0/24 is directly connected, Ethernet0
C    192.168.2.0/24 is directly connected, Serial1
R    192.168.3.0/24 [120/1] via 192.168.2.2, 00:00:02, Serial1
r1>show ip protocols
Routing Protocol is "rip"
  Sending updates every 30 seconds, next due in 3 seconds
  Invalid after 180 seconds, hold down 180, flushed after 240
  Outgoing update filter list for all interfaces is not set
  Incoming update filter list for all interfaces is not set
  Redistributing: rip
  Default version control: send version 1, receive any version
    Interface        Send   Recv   Key-chain
    Ethernet0         1      1 2
    Ethernet1         1      1 2
    Serial0           1      1 2
```

Example 3-15 *r1 Routing Table (Continued)*

```
      Serial1           1       1 2
   Routing for Networks:
     10.0.0.0
     192.168.1.0
     192.168.2.0
     192.168.4.0
   Routing Information Sources:
     Gateway          Distance      Last Update
     192.168.2.2          120       00:00:02
   Distance: (default is 120)
```

Continue to think about the issue here; the output contains some pretty useful information (particularly the shaded areas). However, you should analyze any problems that I specifically mentioned and fix them now. Check your configurations against mine so that you can return and continue to test out end-to-end host connectivity. I made a few other minor changes, which I highlight in the next few examples. Examples 3-16 through 3-21 include the running configurations for all my routers at this time.

NOTE   Checking the running and startup configurations is not the most efficient way to troubleshoot, but this is a good check to make sure that your configurations are as close to mine as possible with your lab environment. For those of you who are relying on me for your lab, this gives you an opportunity to analyze the configurations for existing and future issues.

Example 3-16 *r1 (2514) Configuration*

```
r1#show running-config
...
hostname r1
enable password donna
ip subnet-zero
ip host r1 192.168.1.1 192.168.2.1 192.168.4.1 10.1.1.1
ip host r2 192.168.4.2 192.168.5.1 192.168.6.1
ip host r3 192.168.2.2 192.168.5.2 192.168.6.2 192.168.3.1 10.2.2.1
ip host r4 10.2.2.2
ip host r5 10.1.1.2
!
interface Ethernet0
 description e0 to hosta and hostb
 ip address 192.168.1.1 255.255.255.0
 no ip directed-broadcast
interface Ethernet1
 description e1 to r2e0
 ip address 192.168.4.1 255.255.255.0
 no ip directed-broadcast
interface Serial0
 description s0 to r5s0
 bandwidth 64
```

continues

Example 3-16 *r1 (2514) Configuration (Continued)*

```
 ip address 10.1.1.1 255.255.255.0
 no ip directed-broadcast
 no ip mroute-cache
 no fair-queue
interface Serial1
 description s1 to r3s0/0
 bandwidth 64
 ip address 192.168.2.1 255.255.255.0
 no ip directed-broadcast
router rip
 network 10.0.0.0
 network 192.168.1.0
 network 192.168.2.0
 network 192.168.4.0
ip classless
line con 0
 logging synchronous
 transport input none
line aux 0
line vty 0 4
 password donna
 login
end
r1#
```

Next look at r2's configuration in Example 3-17.

Example 3-17 *r2 (2501) Configuration*

```
r2#show running-config
...
hostname r2
enable password donna
ip subnet-zero
ip host r1 192.168.1.1 192.168.2.1 192.168.4.1 10.1.1.1
ip host r2 192.168.4.2 192.168.5.1 192.168.6.1
ip host r3 192.168.2.2 192.168.5.2 192.168.6.2 192.168.3.1 10.2.2.1
ip host r4 10.2.2.2
ip host r5 10.1.1.2
interface Ethernet0
 description e0 to r1e1
 ip address 192.168.4.2 255.255.255.0
 no ip directed-broadcast
interface Serial0
 description s0 to r3s0/1
 bandwidth 64
 ip address 192.168.6.1 255.255.255.0
 no ip directed-broadcast
 no ip mroute-cache
 no fair-queue
interface Serial1
 description s1 to r3s0/2
 bandwidth 64
 ip address 192.168.5.1 255.255.255.0
```

Example 3-17 *r2 (2501) Configuration*

```
 no ip directed-broadcast
router rip
 network 192.168.4.0
 network 192.168.5.0
 network 192.168.6.0
ip classless
line con 0
 logging synchronous
 transport input none
line aux 0
line vty 0 4
 password donna
 login
end
r2#
```

Make any adjustments to your r2, and then analyze the r3 configuration in Example 3-18.

Example 3-18 *r3 (3640) Configuration*

```
r3#show running-config
...
hostname r3
enable password donna
ip subnet-zero
ip host r1 192.168.1.1 192.168.2.1 192.168.4.1 10.1.1.1
ip host r2 192.168.4.2 192.168.5.1 192.168.6.1
ip host r3 192.168.2.2 192.168.5.2 192.168.6.2 192.168.3.1 10.2.2.1
ip host r4 10.2.2.2
ip host r5 10.1.1.2
interface Serial0/0
 description s0/0 to r1s1
 bandwidth 64
 ip address 192.168.2.2 255.255.255.0
 no ip directed-broadcast
 no ip mroute-cache
 clockrate 64000
interface Serial0/1
 description s0/1 to r2s0
 bandwidth 64
 ip address 192.168.6.2 255.255.255.0
 no ip directed-broadcast
 clockrate 64000
interface Serial0/2
 description s0/2 to r2s1
 bandwidth 64
 ip address 192.168.5.2 255.255.255.0
 no ip directed-broadcast
 clockrate 64000
...
interface FastEthernet2/0
 description fa2/0 to hostc
 ip address 192.168.3.1 255.255.255.0
 no ip directed-broadcast
```

continues

Example 3-18 *r3 (3640) Configuration*

```
router rip
 network 10.0.0.0
 network 192.168.2.0
 network 192.168.3.0
 network 192.168.5.0
 network 192.168.6.0
ip classless
line con 0
 logging synchronous
 transport input none
line aux 0
line vty 0 4
 password donna
 login
end
r3#
```

Descriptions are the only modifications I found necessary and this may seem a little mundane, but documentation is extremely helpful for troubleshooting. Next analyze the r4 configuration in Example 3-19.

Example 3-19 *r4 (3620) Configuration*

```
r4#show running-config
...
hostname r4
enable password donna
ip host r1 192.168.1.1 192.168.2.1 192.168.4.1 10.1.1.1
ip host r2 192.168.4.2 192.168.5.1 192.168.6.1
ip host r3 192.168.2.2 192.168.5.2 192.168.6.2 192.168.3.1 10.2.2.1
ip host r4 10.2.2.2
ip host r5 10.1.1.2
interface Ethernet0/0
 no ip address
 shutdown
interface Serial0/0
 description s0/0 to r3s0/3
 ip address 10.2.2.2 255.255.255.0
 no ip mroute-cache
 bandwidth 64
 clockrate 64000
interface Serial0/1
 no ip address
 shutdown
router rip
 network 10.0.0.0
ip classless
line con 0
 logging synchronous
line aux 0
line vty 0 4
 password donna
 login
end
r4#
```

Last but not least, compare your r5 configuration to Example 3-20.

Example 3-20   *3-20 r5 (2516) Configuration*

```
r5#show running-config
...
hostname r5
enable password donna
ip subnet-zero
ip host r1 192.168.1.1 192.168.2.1 192.168.4.1 10.1.1.1
ip host r2 192.168.4.2 192.168.5.1 192.168.6.1
ip host r3 192.168.2.2 192.168.5.2 192.168.6.2 192.168.3.1 10.2.2.1
ip host r4 10.2.2.2
ip host r5 10.1.1.2
hub ether 0 1
 link-test
 auto-polarity
...
interface Serial0
 description s0 to r1s0
 bandwidth 64
 ip address 10.1.1.2 255.255.255.0
 no ip directed-broadcast
 no ip mroute-cache
 no fair-queue
 clockrate 64000
...
router rip
 network 10.0.0.0
ip classless
line con 0
 logging synchronous
 transport input none
line aux 0
line vty 0 4
 password donna
 login
end
r5#
```

Although you have tested many things, there is still a problem with the routing table display (as you witnessed in Example 3-15). There are many ways to fix this problem, and by now I predict that you thoroughly looked through the configurations and researched your network diagram (refer to Figure 3-1) to spot the issue of *discontiguous subnets*.

NOTE   This is probably an opportune time to review IP classless, because it automatically showed up in your configurations. It is the default for IOS 12.0 and it very much affects how the router does a lookup and whether it makes use of a default route even if one exists. Believe it or not, the **ip classless** command changes the classful lookup to classless even for classful routing protocols. At times the router might receive packets destined for a subnet of a network that has no network default route. To have the Cisco IOS software forward such packets to the best supernet route possible, use the **ip classless** global configuration command. To disable this feature, use the no form of this command: **no ip classless**. I'll have you experiment with this in the Trouble Tickets.

The Routing Information Protocol (RIP) *does not* support discontiguous subnets, or at least RIPv1 does not support this. However, what would be the result of changing the routing protocol to RIPv2? Example 3-21 displays the steps necessary to change the existing RIPv1 to RIPv2 on r1; repeat these steps on r2 through r5 as well.

Example 3-21   *Configuring RIPv2*

```
r1(config)#router rip
r1(config-router)#version ?
  <1-2>   version
r1(config-router)#version 2
r1(config-router)#end
r1#copy running-config startup-config
```

Test and analyze the results of your configuration. First look at the output of **show ip route** and **show ip protocols** as in Example 3-22 and test with ping as in Example 3-23. Display the routing table, the IP routing protocols, and ensure that r1 can ping all other routers before you continue. Compare the results to Figure 3-1 to determine if anything is missing.

NOTE   I assume you are familiar with the routing table legend that tells you that *R* is for RIP and *C* is for directly connected routes, so I have eliminated that part of the routing table display in many examples. Refer back to Example 3-15 if you need to review it again.

Example 3-22   *Testing and Analyzing r1 RIPv2 Routes and Protocols*

```
r1#show ip route
...
C    192.168.4.0/24 is directly connected, Ethernet1
R    192.168.5.0/24 [120/1] via 192.168.2.2, 00:00:13, Serial1
     10.0.0.0/8 is variably subnetted, 2 subnets, 2 masks
R       10.0.0.0/8 [120/1] via 192.168.2.2, 00:00:13, Serial1
C       10.1.1.0/24 is directly connected, Serial0
R    192.168.6.0/24 [120/1] via 192.168.2.2, 00:00:13, Serial1
```

Example 3-22 *Testing and Analyzing r1 RIPv2 Routes and Protocols (Continued)*

```
C     192.168.1.0/24 is directly connected, Ethernet0
C     192.168.2.0/24 is directly connected, Serial1
R     192.168.3.0/24 [120/1] via 192.168.2.2, 00:00:13, Serial1
r1#show ip protocols
Routing Protocol is "rip"
  Sending updates every 30 seconds, next due in 1 seconds
  Invalid after 180 seconds, hold down 180, flushed after 240
  Outgoing update filter list for all interfaces is not set
  Incoming update filter list for all interfaces is not set
  Redistributing: rip
  Default version control: send version 2, receive version 2
    Interface         Send  Recv   Key-chain
    Ethernet0         2     2
    Ethernet1         2     2
    Serial0           2     2
    Serial1           2     2
  Routing for Networks:
    10.0.0.0
    192.168.1.0
    192.168.2.0
    192.168.4.0
  Routing Information Sources:
    Gateway         Distance       Last Update
    192.168.2.2         120        00:00:05
  Distance: (default is 120)
r2#show ip route
Codes: C - connected, S - static, I - IGRP, R - RIP, M - mobile, B - BGP
       D - EIGRP, EX - EIGRP external, O - OSPF, IA - OSPF inter area
       N1 - OSPF NSSA external type 1, N2 - OSPF NSSA external type 2
       E1 - OSPF external type 1, E2 - OSPF external type 2, E - EGP
       i - IS-IS, L1 - IS-IS level-1, L2 - IS-IS level-2, * - candidate default
       U - per-user static route, o - ODR
Gateway of last resort is not set
C     192.168.4.0/24 is directly connected, Ethernet0
C     192.168.5.0/24 is directly connected, Serial1
R     10.0.0.0/8 [120/1] via 192.168.4.1, 00:00:05, Ethernet0
                 [120/1] via 192.168.6.2, 00:00:16, Serial0
                 [120/1] via 192.168.5.2, 00:00:16, Serial1
C     192.168.6.0/24 is directly connected, Serial0
R     192.168.1.0/24 [120/1] via 192.168.4.1, 00:00:05, Ethernet0
R     192.168.2.0/24 [120/1] via 192.168.4.1, 00:00:05, Ethernet0
                     [120/1] via 192.168.6.2, 00:00:16, Serial0
                     [120/1] via 192.168.5.2, 00:00:16, Serial1
R     192.168.3.0/24 [120/1] via 192.168.6.2, 00:00:16, Serial0
                     [120/1] via 192.168.5.2, 00:00:16, Serial1
```

Perform your ping tests if you like, but you may not be any more successful than you were with RIPv1 from r2's standpoint. Even if you were, for a hint as to the real issue here, the same thing would occur if I told you to use Enhanced Interior Gateway Routing Protocol (EIGRP) instead of RIPv2. The fix is in Example 3-23, so check your thoughts against it and make any necessary changes to your configurations.

Example 3-23   *Turning Off Automatic Summarization and Reviewing the Routing Table*

```
r1(config)#router rip
r1(config-router)#no auto-summary
r1(config-router)#end
r1#copy running-config startup-config

r3(config)#router rip
r3(config-router)#no auto-summary
r3(config-router)#end
r3#copy running-config startup-config

r2#show ip route
Codes: C - connected, S - static, I - IGRP, R - RIP, M - mobile, B - BGP
       D - EIGRP, EX - EIGRP external, O - OSPF, IA - OSPF inter area
       N1 - OSPF NSSA external type 1, N2 - OSPF NSSA external type 2
       E1 - OSPF external type 1, E2 - OSPF external type 2, E - EGP
       i - IS-IS, L1 - IS-IS level-1, L2 - IS-IS level-2, * - candidate default
       U - per-user static route, o - ODR
Gateway of last resort is not set
C    192.168.4.0/24 is directly connected, Ethernet0
C    192.168.5.0/24 is directly connected, Serial1
     10.0.0.0/24 is subnetted, 2 subnets
R       10.2.2.0 [120/1] via 192.168.6.2, 00:00:00, Serial0
                 [120/1] via 192.168.5.2, 00:00:00, Serial1
R       10.1.1.0 [120/1] via 192.168.4.1, 00:00:20, Ethernet0
C    192.168.6.0/24 is directly connected, Serial0
R    192.168.1.0/24 [120/1] via 192.168.4.1, 00:00:20, Ethernet0
R    192.168.2.0/24 [120/1] via 192.168.6.2, 00:00:00, Serial0
                    [120/1] via 192.168.5.2, 00:00:00, Serial1
                    [120/1] via 192.168.4.1, 00:00:20, Ethernet0
R    192.168.3.0/24 [120/1] via 192.168.6.2, 00:00:01, Serial0
                    [120/1] via 192.168.5.2, 00:00:01, Serial1
```

As a result of the **no auto-summary** command on r1 and r3, Example 3-23 clearly illustrates that r2 is less confused about where to send the packets destined for network 10.0.0.0.

RIPv2 is classless and RIPv1 is classful. Classless routing protocols—such as RIPv2, EIGRP, OSPF, and Intermediate System-to-Intermediate System (IS-IS)—support variable-length subnet masking (VLSM) and summarization. All routing protocols support summarization, but the classful ones do that in a fixed manner, at the class boundary. Hence in this example, the routers could not differentiate between 10.1.1.0/24 and 10.2.2.0/24 because a completely different network separated them. This is what is meant by discontiguous subnets. The "Routing Protocol" and "Summarization" sections of this chapter provide a little more detail. You can count on gaining more practical experience with this issue in the Trouble Tickets.

NOTE	Just remember that pinging by hostname tries only the first IP in the hosts table. However, the other addresses in the hosts table (**show hosts**) are reachable via other commands, such as **telnet**. Other interfaces could be down or unreachable and you wouldn't know about it if you just pinged by hostname. So the **show ip interface brief** command complements this. Be wary, however, of the one-way link on Ethernet. This just means that you may be transmitting (Tx) but not receiving packets (Rx) or vice versa. Keep in mind that you transmit over one pair and receive over the other, so the Physical Layer is never exempt from problems even though you know you connected everything properly.

After you verify router connectivity, move on to verify host-to-host connectivity as in Example 3-24. You may find Table 3-1 to be a helpful guide here. This is a good time to check the interfaces and routing tables on all your other routers, too. Although I didn't display the output, all of my routers can ping all my other routers using the configured hosts table.

Example 3-24 displays the host-to-host testing from hosta to hostc. I assume you took time to configure the appropriate default gateways for your hosts; if not, do that now.

Example 3-24 *Testing and Analyzing Host-to-Host Connectivity from hosta to hostc*

```
C:\>ipconfig
Windows 2000 IP Configuration
Ethernet adapter Local Area Connection:
        Connection-specific DNS Suffix  . :
        IP Address. . . . . . . . . . . : 192.168.1.11
        Subnet Mask . . . . . . . . . . : 255.255.255.0
        Default Gateway . . . . . . . . : 192.168.1.1
!!!hosta can ping itself
C:\>ping 192.168.1.11
Pinging 192.168.1.11 with 32 bytes of data:
Reply from 192.168.1.11: bytes=32 time<10ms TTL=128
Reply from 192.168.1.11: bytes=32 time<10ms TTL=128
Reply from 192.168.1.11: bytes=32 time<10ms TTL=128
Reply from 192.168.1.11: bytes=32 time<10ms TTL=128
Ping statistics for 192.168.1.11:
    Packets: Sent = 4, Received = 4, Lost = 0 (0% loss),
Approximate round trip times in milli-seconds:
    Minimum = 0ms, Maximum =  0ms, Average =  0ms
!!!hosta can ping its gateway
C:\>ping 192.168.1.1
Pinging 192.168.1.1 with 32 bytes of data:
Reply from 192.168.1.1: bytes=32 time<10ms TTL=255
Reply from 192.168.1.1: bytes=32 time<10ms TTL=255
Reply from 192.168.1.1: bytes=32 time<10ms TTL=255
Reply from 192.168.1.1: bytes=32 time<10ms TTL=255
Ping statistics for 192.168.1.1:
    Packets: Sent = 4, Received = 4, Lost = 0 (0% loss),
Approximate round trip times in milli-seconds:
    Minimum = 0ms, Maximum =  0ms, Average =  0ms
!!!hosta can ping hostc
```

continues

Example 3-24   *Testing and Analyzing Host-to-Host Connectivity from hosta to hostc (Continued)*

```
C:\>ping 192.168.3.5
Pinging 192.168.3.5 with 32 bytes of data:
Request timed out.
Reply from 192.168.3.5: bytes=32 time=20ms TTL=126
Reply from 192.168.3.5: bytes=32 time=10ms TTL=126
Reply from 192.168.3.5: bytes=32 time=10ms TTL=126
Ping statistics for 192.168.3.5:
    Packets: Sent = 4, Received = 3, Lost = 1 (25% loss),
Approximate round trip times in milli-seconds:
    Minimum = 10ms, Maximum =  20ms, Average =  10ms
C:\>
```

Just in case you have any issues, you might find it helpful to display the host routing tables as in Example 3-25. Hosta has a default gateway of its local router interface 192.168.1.1. Hostc has a default gateway of 192.168.3.1, which you can verify by issuing the **route print** or **ipconfig/winipcfg** commands on the host.

Example 3-25   *Testing and Analyzing Host-to-Host Connectivity from hosta Continued*

```
C:\>route print
Interface List
0x1 ......................... MS TCP Loopback interface
0x2 ...44 45 53 54 42 00 ...... NOC Extranet Access Adapter
0x1000004 ...00 10 4b a5 ae 50 ...... FE575 Ethernet Adapter
Active Routes:
Network Destination        Netmask          Gateway       Interface  Metric
        0.0.0.0          0.0.0.0      192.168.1.1    192.168.1.11       1
      127.0.0.0        255.0.0.0        127.0.0.1      127.0.0.1       1
    192.168.1.0    255.255.255.0    192.168.1.11    192.168.1.11       1
   192.168.1.11  255.255.255.255        127.0.0.1      127.0.0.1       1
  192.168.1.255  255.255.255.255    192.168.1.11    192.168.1.11       1
      224.0.0.0        224.0.0.0    192.168.1.11    192.168.1.11       1
255.255.255.255  255.255.255.255    192.168.1.11              2       1
Default Gateway:        192.168.1.1
Persistent Routes:
  None
```

Now that you have a working IP scenario, it's time to investigate some of the underlying components of the TCP/IP suite.

Protocols and Packets

This section covers some of the protocols, applications, and utilities at each layer of the TCP/IP suite that may assist you with supporting day-to-day internetworks. First the Internet Layer is discussed, then the Transport Layer, and finally the Application Layers. Each layered subsection contains protocol analysis and packet captures, including a review of the packet headers, to help you better understand the packet traces and prepare you for troubleshooting on your own.

Table 3-2 and the following subsections provide a layered perspective of many of the TCP/IP-related protocols, applications, and utilities.

NOTE   The asterisk (*) next to the protocols in Table 3-2 is just to draw your attention to the fact that protocols and applications are written to perform functions. The * denotes that these particular protocols, applications, and utilities are generally classified at Layer 3 (as discussed in the previous chapters). Although I hesitate to bring it up because it is such a point of contention, OSPF and EIGRP are not transports; they are routing protocol (applications). They run as independent processes/applications. As with all applications, the developer can decide to use Transport Control Protocol (TCP) or User Datagram Protocol (UDP) or to create his/her own. The latter was done for both of these. ARP is similar in this regard; it is not a Network Layer protocol. It is an application that bolts directly onto the Data Link Layer. Therefore, it would be more accurate to say that the intervening layers are skipped. A whole different way to characterize these message types is as control plane, management plane, and data plane. This is why I suggested you read the RFCs in the first chapter. However, my objective here is to briefly review the protocols, applications, and utilities and use a protocol analyzer to analyze the layers for troubleshooting purposes.

Table 3-2   *TCP/IP Protocols, Applications, and Utilities*

Layer	ISO's OSI Model	DoD TCP/IP Suite	Protocols, Applications, and Utilities
7	Application	Application	Telnet, NFS, FTP, TFTP, HTTP, DNS, X.500, *RIP, *BGP, *DHCP, ASCII, EBCDIC, JPEG, GIF, NetBIOS, SOCKETS
6	Presentation		
5	Session		
4	Transport	Transport Host-to-Host	TCP, UDP, *OSPF, *EIGRP
3	Network	Internet	IP, ICMP, ARP/RARP
2	Data Link	Data Link	Ethernet, Token Ring, FDDI, Frame Relay, ATM, ISDN, HDLC, over various media types
1	Physical	Physical	

Frame Types

Encapsulation, frame format, frame type—they all mean the same thing, which is packaging the upper-layer data, voice, or video into an Layer 2 frame. See Chapter 4, "Shooting Trouble with Novell IPX," and the detailed Layer 2 LAN and WAN chapters for frame type information. Part III of this book covers supporting Ethernet, switches, and virtual LANs (VLANs) and Part IV is about supporting the WAN.

Internet Layer Protocols, Applications, and Utilities

Internet protocols such as those listed in the Table 3-2 are well suited for LAN and WAN heterogeneous communications. The Internet suite of protocols includes not only TCP and IP but also many upper-layer applications and utilities for file, print, messaging, database, and other common practical services.

Ensure that your lab is up and running properly so that you spend your efforts on what happens behind the scenes when hosta pings hostc from an IP standpoint. In this section, you turn on your Sniffer on segment 1 and at least capture a ping from hosta to hostc so that you can walk through the fields in the IP header.

Example 3-26 lists in bold the recommended steps to perform from hosta while capturing the packets with Sniffer Pro or the protocol analyzer you are using for your lab.

Example 3-26 *Steps Performed on hosta While Capturing the Packets with Sniffer Pro*

```
C:\>ping 192.168.3.5
Pinging 192.168.3.5 with 32 bytes of data:
Request timed out.
Reply from 192.168.3.5: bytes=32 time=20ms TTL=126
Reply from 192.168.3.5: bytes=32 time=10ms TTL=126
Reply from 192.168.3.5: bytes=32 time=10ms TTL=126
Ping statistics for 192.168.3.5:
    Packets: Sent = 4, Received = 3, Lost = 1 (25% loss),
Approximate round trip times in milli-seconds:
    Minimum = 10ms, Maximum =  20ms, Average =  10ms
C:\>ping 192.168.3.5
Pinging 192.168.3.5 with 32 bytes of data:
Reply from 192.168.3.5: bytes=32 time=10ms TTL=126
Reply from 192.168.3.5: bytes=32 time=10ms TTL=126
Reply from 192.168.3.5: bytes=32 time=10ms TTL=126
Reply from 192.168.3.5: bytes=32 time=20ms TTL=126
Ping statistics for 192.168.3.5:
    Packets: Sent = 4, Received = 4, Lost = 0 (0% loss),
Approximate round trip times in milli-seconds:
    Minimum = 10ms, Maximum =  20ms, Average =  12ms
C:\>tracert 192.168.3.5
Tracing route to HOSTC [192.168.3.5]
over a maximum of 30 hops:
  1    10 ms   <10 ms   <10 ms  192.168.1.1
  2    20 ms    20 ms    20 ms  192.168.2.2
  3    20 ms    30 ms    30 ms  HOSTC [192.168.3.5]
Trace complete.
C:\>pathping 192.168.3.5
```

Example 3-26 *Steps Performed on hosta While Capturing the Packets with Sniffer Pro (Continued)*

```
Tracing route to HOSTC [192.168.3.5]
over a maximum of 30 hops:
  0  HOSTA [192.168.1.11]
  1  192.168.1.1
  2  192.168.2.2
  3  HOSTC [192.168.3.5]
Computing statistics for 75 seconds...
              Source to Here   This Node/Link
Hop   RTT     Lost/Sent = Pct  Lost/Sent = Pct  Address
  0                                              HOSTA [192.168.1.11]
                               0/ 100 =  0%    |
  1    0ms    0/ 100 =  0%     0/ 100 =  0%    192.168.1.1
                               0/ 100 =  0%    |
  2    20ms   0/ 100 =  0%     0/ 100 =  0%    192.168.2.2
                               0/ 100 =  0%    |
  3    20ms   0/ 100 =  0%     0/ 100 =  0%    HOSTC [192.168.3.5]
Trace complete.
C:\>arp -a
Interface: 192.168.1.11 on Interface 0x1000005
  Internet Address      Physical Address      Type
  192.168.1.1           00-00-0c-8d-67-05     dynamic
C:\>
```

Table 3-3 lists the fields of the IP header (packet or datagram), and Figure 3-5 shows the first significant ping lines of the Sniffer packet capture of hosta pinging hostc. Refer to the file *chapter 3 ping from hosta to hostc sniffer capture*.

NOTE The practical studies lab-based nature of the rest of the material in this book assumes some basic knowledge of shooting trouble and working with tools. As necessary, refer back to the Chapter 1 encapsulation topic to review the way data is *packaged* in an IP packet. For a review of the Sniffer Pro interface and how to use the tool, refer back to Chapter 2, "What's in Your Tool Bag?"

Table 3-3 *The IP Header (Packet or Datagram)*

Fields	Bits	Description
Version	4	Version of IP.
Header length	4	Length in 32-bit words (HLEN).
Priority and TOS	8 (more detail)	Datagram handling for the upper-layer protocol (delay, throughput, reliability, and cost).
Total length	16	Maximum length of datagram is 65535 bytes (data and header).

continues

Table 3-3 *The IP Header (Packet or Datagram) (Continued)*

Fields	Bits	Description
Identification	16	Identifies smaller fragments that need to be re-assembled back into the same packet.
Flags	3	Specify whether packet can be fragmented and whether there are any more fragments.
Fragment offset	13	The order (byte count) of the fragment in the big packet for re-assembly purposes.
TTL	8	Time-to-live for the packet. When it decrements to 0, the packet is discarded. Keeps packets from looping forever.
Protocol	8	Pointer to the upper-layer protocol.
Header checksum	16	For header integrity.
Source IP address		32-bit sending node.
Destination IP address	32	32-bit receiving node.
Options	0–32	Allows IP to support such options as security, testing, or debugging.
Data	Varies	The actual data and upper-layer information.

Figure 3-5 *Hosta ARPs the Router*

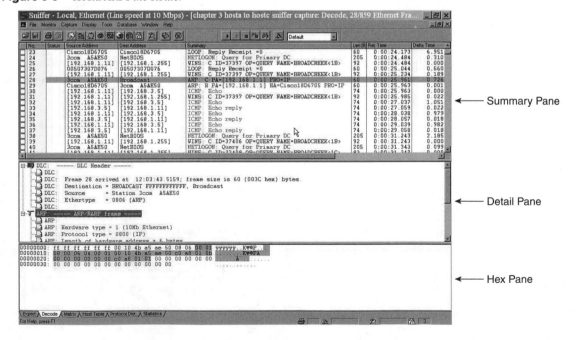

View the summary pane to be aware of the general packet flow when hosta initiated a ping to hostc in Figure 3-5. Hosta is on network 192.168.1.0/24, and hostc is on network 192.168.3.0/24, so hosta relied on its default gateway (local router interface) in which to hand the packets. Line 28 shows the local ARP request as a broadcast command, and line 29 shows the unicast ARP response from 192.168.1.1 (default gateway). Compare this to the **arp –a** output on hosta back in Example 3-26. Lines 30 to 37 illustrate the ICMP Echo Requests and Echo Replies. Normally, Microsoft hosts issue four requests and four replies, whereas Cisco routers give you five by default. However, there are not four replies here. Look back at Example 3-26 to analyze why.

Move along to the Echo Request packet on line 32 in Figure 3-6. Notice how I sized my windows to see more of the detailed IP header. These are the same fields that are in Table 3-3. Compare them one-by-one until you are comfortable with the IP packet structure (although this will not be your last chance to do this). Also note the differences between the Echo Request and the Echo Reply packet. Figure 3-7 displays the output of an Echo Reply.

Figure 3-6   *Analyzing the IP Header of an Echo Request Packet*

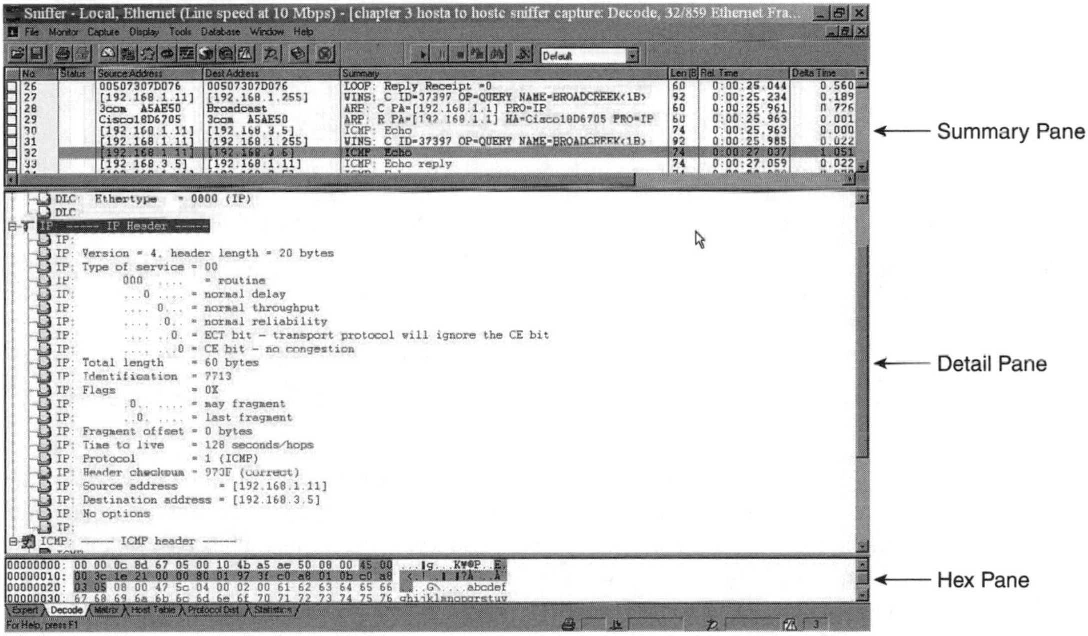

Figure 3-7 *Analyzing the IP Header of an Echo Reply Packet*

The main differences you should have noted in the Sniffer traces include the following:

- The source and destination MAC addresses are reversed per the Data Link Control (DLC) header.

- The source and destination IP addresses are reversed per the IP header.

- The Internet Control Message Protocol (ICMP) type is 8 for the Echo Request and 0 for the Echo Reply per the ICMP header.

Real-world packet analysis should make you a little more comfortable with how IP works, but I'll certainly test that out in the upcoming Trouble Tickets. IP is the main protocol at the Internet Layer that has helpers such as ARP and ICMP to assist it with its duties. ARP is for resolving an IP address to a MAC address, whereas Reverse Address Resolution Protocol (RARP) is for resolving a MAC address to an IP address. ICMP is for status and error reporting. Look back at Example 3-26 to see the status lines, such as Reply from..., and the error reporting, such as Request timed out. Obviously, this is why you didn't have four successful replies in the protocol analyzer capture. Also note in the Example that 192.168.3.5 is nowhere to be found in the ARP cache; instead, the default gateway IP and MAC address is there. Example 3-27 displays the e0 interface on r1 so that you can compare this information. Also note that r1 has hosta 192.168.1.11 in its IP and ARP cache.

Example 3-27 *r1 Ethernet 0 IP and MAC Addresses*

```
r1#show interfaces ethernet 0
Ethernet0 is up, line protocol is up
  Hardware is Lance, address is 0000.0c8d.6705 (bia 0000.0c8d.6705)
  Description: e0 to hosta and hostb
  Internet address is 192.168.1.1/24
  MTU 1500 bytes, BW 10000 Kbit, DLY 1000 usec, rely 255/255, load 1/255
  Encapsulation ARPA, loopback not set, keepalive set (10 sec)
  ARP type: ARPA, ARP Timeout 04:00:00
  Last input 00:00:00, output 00:00:09, output hang never
  Last clearing of "show interface" counters never
Queueing strategy: fifo
  Output queue 0/40, 0 drops; input queue 1/75, 0 drops
  5 minute input rate 0 bits/sec, 0 packets/sec
  5 minute output rate 0 bits/sec, 0 packets/sec
     2358 packets input, 361385 bytes, 0 no buffer
     Received 1949 broadcasts, 0 runts, 0 giants, 0 throttles
     0 input errors, 0 CRC, 0 frame, 0 overrun, 0 ignored, 0 abort
     0 input packets with dribble condition detected
     2889 packets output, 320787 bytes, 0 underruns
     0 output errors, 11 collisions, 2 interface resets
     0 babbles, 0 late collision, 15 deferred
     0 lost carrier, 0 no carrier
     0 output buffer failures, 0 output buffers swapped out
r1#show ip cache
IP routing cache 1 entry, 172 bytes
   5 adds, 4 invalidates, 0 refcounts
Minimum invalidation interval 2 seconds, maximum interval 5 seconds,
   quiet interval 3 seconds, threshold 0 requests
Invalidation rate 0 in last second, 0 in last 3 seconds
Prefix/Length           Age        Interface         Next Hop
192.168.1.11/32         03:02:54   Ethernet0         192.168.1.11
r1#show arp
Protocol  Address         Age (min)  Hardware Addr   Type    Interface
Internet  192.168.1.11          34   0010.4ba5.ae50  ARPA    Ethernet0
Internet  192.168.1.1            -   0000.0c8d.6705  ARPA    Ethernet0
Internet  192.168.4.1            -   0000.0c8d.6706  ARPA    Ethernet1
Internet  192.168.4.2           42   0000.0c38.a05d  ARPA    Ethernet1
r1#
```

NOTE   ARP is dynamic in nature, but once in a while in troubleshooting you may need to manually clear an entry or two. On a router, **clear arp-cache** does not truly clear the table; instead, it refreshes the entire table, and depending on the number of entries this could be more of an impact than you intend. Use **shut / no shut** to remove the entries associated with a given interface. On a Windows-based machine, the command is **arp -d** *ip address* to remove a particular address.

I want to continue the layered approach to discussing TCP/IP, so next the discussion moves up the stack to the Transport Layer. After I discuss the Transport and Application Layers, I spend a bit more time on addressing and protocols before venturing into the Trouble Tickets.

Transport (Host-to-Host) Layer Protocols, Applications, and Utilities

Recall from the OSI model in Chapter 1, the Transport Layer is all about host-to-host delivery. TCP and UDP are the Transport Layer twins. TCP is connection-oriented (logical connection) and reliable (ACKs).

UDP, like IP at the Internet Layer, is connectionless and unreliable; therefore it relies on the upper layers for reliability. TCP is like the certified mail protocol, whereas UDP is like the regular mail (or better yet, bulk mail) protocol.

UDP is *connectionless*, which means it does not require an established connection before communications can occur. It is unreliable at the Transport Layer, which means that its reliability is left up to the application. Compare the TCP and UDP packet formats in Tables 3-4 and 3-5.

NOTE   Perhaps the word *unreliable* is a bit harsh for UDP. What I mean is that UDP is not reliable because it has no built-in mechanism to detect and overcome errors, so it must hand off to an upper-layer protocol to perform that task.

Table 3-4   *The TCP Segment*

Fields	Bits	Description
Source Port	16	Sending port.
Destination Port	16	Receiving port.
Sequence Number	32	Tracks byte transfer.
Acknowledgment Number	32	Confirms byte transfer. Forward referenced and expectational in that it contains the sequence number of the next byte expected.
Data Offset	4	Number of 32-bit words in the header.
Reserved	6	For future use.
Flags	6 flags of TCP	Synchronization (SYN) Acknowledgement (ACK) Finish (FIN) Push (PSH) Urgent (URG) Reset (RST)
Window Size	16	How many bytes are sent per segment. Size of sender's receive window. Incoming buffer space. (How many pizzas can you put in the warming bag if you are the delivery person?)

Table 3-4   *The TCP Segment (Continued)*

Fields	Bits	Description
Checksum		Sender generates and receiver verifies to see whether the header was damaged in transit.
Urgent Pointer		Points to first urgent data byte, such as Ctrl+Z to end urgent data.
Options	32	Various options must end on a 32-bit boundary, and padding guarantees this.
Data	Varies	Upper-layer information.

Table 3-5   *The UDP Datagram*

Fields	Bits	Description
Source Port	16	Sending port
Destination Port	16	Receiving port
UDP Length	16	Data and header
Checksum	16	Optional
Data	Varies	Upper-layer information

The 20-byte TCP header is a lot more sophisticated than the 8-byte UDP header, as you will again confirm with Sniffer. First, open the previous Sniffer Pro trace where you issued the ping and tracert commands in Example 3-26. I named my file *chapter 3 ping from hosta to hostc sniffer capture*. Use this file to analyze the layers or refer to Figure 3-8, in which I emphasize the layers of a RIP packet.

Although the focus in this subsection is the Transport Layer, remember that each layer depends on the functionality of another layer to carry out communications. The Sniffer trace certainly illustrates that. For example, the RIP packet at the Data Link Layer is a good example of multicast communications. RIPv2 works via multicast address 01005E000009 at Layer 2, whereas RIPv1 works via broadcast, which would be shown as all Fs at Layer 2. The EtherType is 0800, which tells the Data Link Layer to hand off to IP at the Internet Layer for further processing.

Review the IP header fields—Version, Header length, TOS, Total length, Identification, Flags, Fragment offset, TTL, Protocol, Checksum, Addresses, and Options. The IP header contains the Protocol field to hand off to at the next layer in the stack. In Figure 3-8, for example, the protocol number is 17, which means to hand up to UDP. The source address is the Ethernet 0 interface on r1, and the destination is again the reserved multicast address of 224.0.0.9 for RIPv2, but this time at the Internet Layer.

IANA has reserved addresses from 224.0.0.0 through 224.0.0.255, such as those in Table 3-6, for local multicasts.

Figure 3-8 *Analyzing the RIP Packet at Layers 2, 3, and 4*

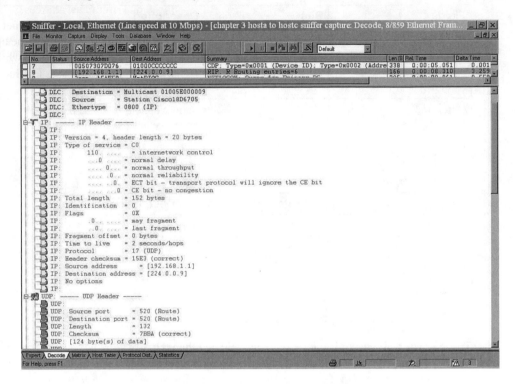

Table 3-6 *Local Multicast Addresses*

Multicast Address	Description
224.0.0.1	All systems on this subnet
224.0.0.2	All routers on this subnet
224.0.0.5	OSPF routers
224.0.0.6	OSPF designated routers
224.0.0.9	RIPv2

Globally scoped addresses from 224.0.1.0 through 238.255.255.255 can be used to *multicast* data between organizations and across the Internet. An example of an IANA reserved address is 224.0.1.1 for Network Time Protocol (NTP).

NOTE   Refer to www.iana.org/assignments/multicast-addresses for more information and examples.

In addition, IANA owns a block of Ethernet MAC addresses that start with 01:00:5E, where half of the block (0100.5e00.0000 through 0100.5e7f.ffff) is allocated for multicast addresses. In the Ethernet address, 23 bits correspond to the IP multicast group address. Search for "ethernet mac multicast" at Cisco.com to get a detailed explanation and pictures. With this mapping, the upper 5 bits of the IP multicast address are dropped and the resulting address is not unique, which results in different multicast group IDs that all map to the same Ethernet address. The Internet Group Management Protocol (IGMP) dynamically registers individual hosts in a multicast group. The hosts send IGMP messages to their router. The routers listen and periodically send out queries to discover which groups are active or inactive on a particular subnet.

The Transport Layer contains the fields listed Table 3-5 for the UDP datagram. RIP works via UDP port 520, which is clearly revealed here. UDP port 520 is how the Transport Layer hands off to the Application Layer for RIP communications (as discussed in more detail later). For now, look at the details of TCP.

TCP provides end-to-end full-duplex delivery, flow control through windowing, and error-detection and -correction services. Data moves in a continuous byte stream, in which bytes are identified by sequence numbers. TCP hides lower-layer intricacies from the upper layers on the receiving host. It segments and re-assembles data for upper-layer applications based on various port numbers. Unlike UDP, however, a 3-way handshake must occur before communications can begin. This establishes the virtual connection between the two communicating parties (see Figure 3-9).

Figure 3-9 *The TCP 3-Way Handshake Sequence*

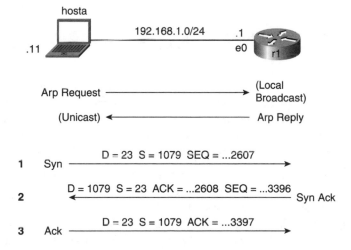

A good example of an application that uses TCP is telnet. Try it out and telnet from hosta (at the command prompt) to r1. Capture your results with Sniffer (see Figure 3-10). Save the Sniffer file as *chapter 3 telnet from hosta to r1 sniffer capture* so that you can refer back to it

later. Analyze your own capture or look at my Sniffer trace. It may prove helpful to use the
Sniffer output to label the 3-way handshake in Figure 3-9, including flags, ports, sequence, and
acknowledgement numbers.

Figure 3-10 *Analyzing Telnet and the 3-Way Handshake*

In the preceding example, hosta was configured with the local router IP address as its default
gateway. Because of this, hosta sent an ARP request packet to its default gateway to learn the
MAC address of the Ethernet 0 interface on r1. The command **arp –a** on the host would have
shown this, whereas **show ip arp** is the command on the router. ARP frames are not part of the
3-way handshake or TCP session, but are certainly required for hosta to transmit data.

Study TCP in the Sniffer capture and drawing. It is often referred to as the 3-way handshake.
Step 1 of the 3-way handshake (SYN) is like me introducing myself to you and giving you my
basic communication parameters so that we can talk. Step 2 is like you saying, "Okay (ACK),
Donna, I want to talk, too; here are my communication parameters (SYN)." Step 3 is my okay
(ACK) to you. After a 3-way handshake, the two communicating parties are virtually connected
and TCP communications can then occur. Some applications require multiple handshakes. A
bona fide example is anything involving the World Wide Web (WWW). Every time you click a
link on a web page, another TCP session starts. Another example is a phone call. The
connection is set up and you talk; then the logical connection is torn down and is available for
someone else.

Next look a little closer at the exact packets in the Sniffer capture for the 3-way handshake. You can glean a lot from the summary pane on this one, but the detail pane is shown as well. The shaded line 7 starts the handshake described in Figure 3-9. It shows the SYN from hosta (192.168.1.11) to the router (192.168.1.1). The source port (S) is random (ephemeral) port number 1079, but the destination port is the well-known port number 23 for telnet.

Ports are places to leave stuff for applications to pick up, as you will continue to see throughout this book. A client typically establishes a port within first 4 bytes of the Transport Layer header. Notice how the ports reverse depending on who is doing the talking, hosta or the router. Line 8 shows the router responding back to hosta with ACK number ...2608, which if you look close is one more than the previous SEQ number of ...2607. The SEQ of Step 2 of the handshake is ...3396. Step 3 of the handshake in line 9 ACKs the previous SEQ number with ...3397. When the TCP session has been established, the numbers increment by the actual number of bytes transferred.

Instead of analyzing the telnet details, I want you to pay attention to the TCP session tear down next. Open your Sniffer capture and refer to the very end of the file as I illustrate in Figure 3-11.

Figure 3-11 *TCP Session Disconnect*

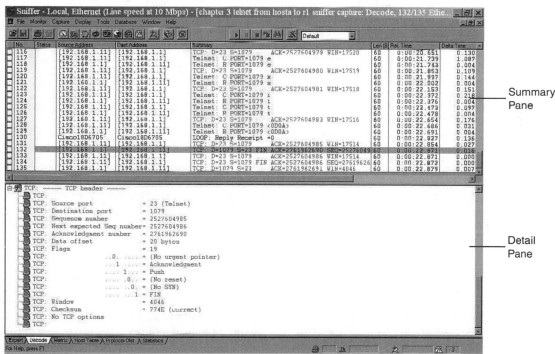

Frame 132 starts the TCP disconnect with the FIN flag from the router. Hosta ACKs in frame 133 and says, "Hey, I am also finished," in frame 134 (FIN). The router gives the final ACK in the last frame. A 4-way disconnect like this is common.

Next I want you to think outside the box a little. What would have happened if the default gateway was not configured on the host or if the router was not local in the preceding testing? You can give me the number one phrase that most support people give, which is, *it depends*; as usual, however, I'll cringe at that answer. In many cases, however, that is the best answer. Actually, the packets may still get to their destination assuming *proxy ARP* is enabled on the router and that hosta will ARP for nonlocal destinations.

Proxy ARP helps hosts reach remote subnets without configuring routing or a default gateway. Configuring the host with a smaller subnet mask *would* make the host ARP for everything and thus send all packets via the router. The router just replies to the host with its MAC address assuming that it is configured to accept and respond to proxy ARP. Obviously, there are security and overhead disadvantages to proxy ARP. The Cisco IOS interface command **no ip proxy-arp** turns this off and is shown in Example 3-28.

Example 3-28 *Proxy ARP*

```
r1#show run interface ethernet 0
interface Ethernet0
 description e0 to hosta and hostb
 ip address 192.168.1.1 255.255.255.0
 no ip directed-broadcast
end
r1#configure terminal
r1(config)#interface ethernet 0
r1(config-if)#no ip proxy-arp
r1(config-if)#end
r1#show run interface ethernet 0
interface Ethernet0
 description e0 to hosta and hostb
 ip address 192.168.1.1 255.255.255.0
 no ip directed-broadcast
 no ip proxy-arp
end
r1#configure terminal
r1(config)#interface e0
r1(config-if)#ip proxy-arp
r1(config-if)#end
```

Prior to the thinking outside the box exercise, you were working with telnet, which is an application based on TCP port 23. TCP port 23 is the pointer from the Transport Layer to the Application Layer, just as the IP packet contains a protocol number such as 6 to link to the Transport Layer TCP protocol for further processing. Figure 3-12 shows this layer linkage for the UDP and TCP applications you previously examined. You can always compare this to your saved Sniffer traces to validate the theory from the lower layers to the upper layers.

Figure 3-12 *Protocols, Applications, and Utilities*

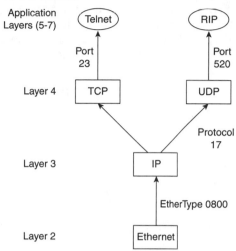

Many applications have well-known port numbers assigned. Ports greater than 1024 are referred to as ephemeral, random, short-lived, or temporary, whereas numbers below 1024 are considered well-known ports.

Figure 3-13, www.iana.org, and RFC 1700 provide you with more detail. Ports are often categorized as follows:

- 0–1023 Well-known

- 1024–49151 Registered

- 49152–65535 Dynamic (private)

Figure 3-13 *Application Port Numbers*

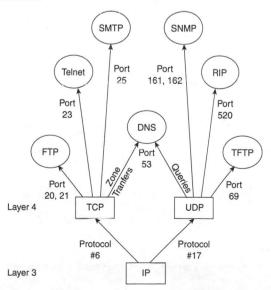

As you have seen in the previous subsections, after you have eliminated Physical Layer issues, protocol connections are troubleshooting targets that must be considered. After the protocol connections have been confirmed as operational, it is time to move up to the Application Layers. I could not begin to cover the vast variety of upper-layer applications in use today, but I will introduce some of the major Application Layer protocols of the TCP/IP suite.

Upper-Layer Protocols, Applications, and Utilities

This subsection covers applications such as telnet, FTP, TFTP, SMTP, POP3, DNS, SNMP, RIP, HTTP, HTTPS, and DHCP. Obviously, these are not the only applications you will need to troubleshoot, but they are very common.

First look at the terminal emulation protocol telnet from an application perspective. Review Figures 3-9 and 3-10 and your Sniffer capture file (*chapter 3 telnet from hosta to r1 sniffer capture*). Figure 3-14 illustrates the telnet session from hosta on port 1079 to r1 on port 23. Line 10 starts the telnet session, which was dependent on the TCP 3-way handshake in lines 7, 8, and 9. Notice the echo, window size, and terminal negotiation in lines 10 to 15. Frame 12 is waiting for the login that eventually appears in lines 17 to 25 one character at a time. In addition, notice how that after the user-level password I typed the necessary command and password to get into enable mode. Although I do not show all this in the screen capture of Figure 3-14, if you have your own file you can see the rest of the commands that were typed on the router, letter for letter. It is pretty obvious here that the standard telnet programs do not encrypt the login information, and I doubt that this is what you want people to see when you telnet to your devices to configure them. In the real-world application of telnet where security is more of a concern, many people use secure telnet programs (Secure Shell [SSH] port 22). Examples include SecureCRT, CommNet, and PuTTY.SSH.

Figure 3-14 *Telnet from an Application Perspective*

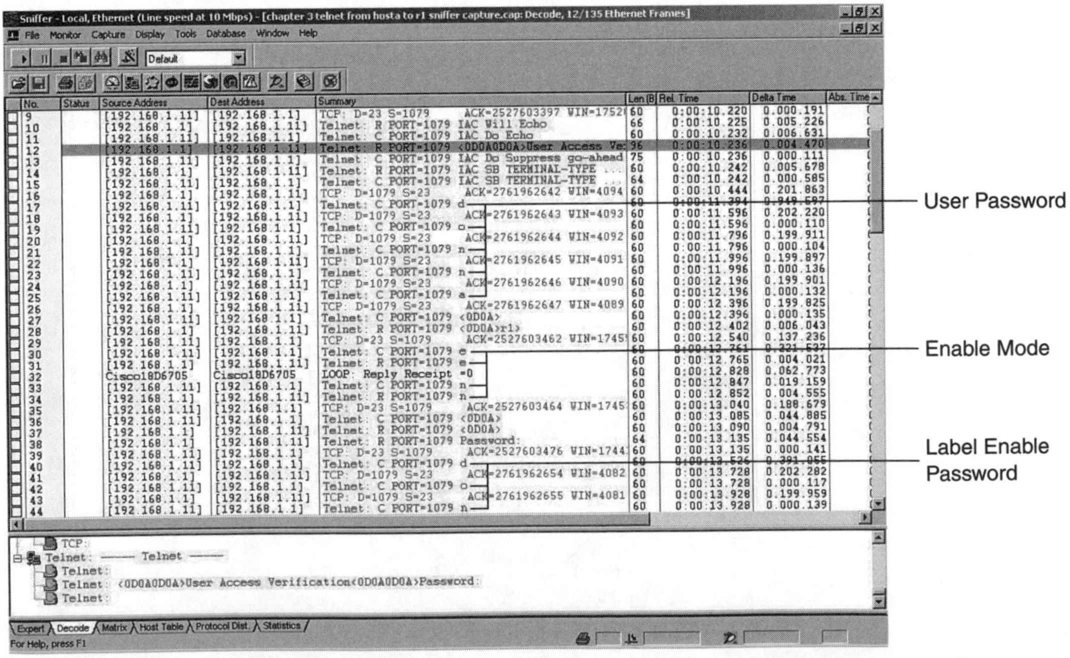

Next look at TFTP and FTP. As I illustrated in Figure 3-13, TFTP typically operates over UDP port 69, and FTP typically operates over TCP port 21 for control and 20 for data. When I say *typically*, I really mean that this is entirely up to the developer. FTP and TFTP are very useful applications in the support environment. For instance, what happens if you lose the configuration on one of your routers? Hopefully, you have an automated way to restore it instead of having to type in the configuration line-for-line.

To test TFTP, I am using a freeware program called PumpKin in Figure 3-15. You can download PumpKin, set up another router as a TFTP server, or use any TFTP application you like. I started and configured PumpKin to *put and get* all files, started a new Sniffer capture, and proceeded to copy my r1 configuration file to the TFTP server for this test. You should even go a few steps further to wipe your configuration with the **erase startup-config** or **write erase** command to ensure this really works. After all, this is the type of thing you should do in a lab environment many times so that you are prepared for the unexpected. Use Example 3-29 as a guide for this exercise.

NOTE   The shaded output in Example 3-29 is *not* required for the TFTP exercise. It is meant to review that the effect of copying anything to the running configuration is a *merge* rather than a *replace* to the existing configuration.

Save the Sniffer file as *chapter 3 tftp from r1 to hosta and back sniffer capture* for further review.

NOTE   Just as I am in the habit of typing **write mem** (**wr**) to save my running configuration to the startup configuration, I typically type **write erase** (**wr er**) to erase the startup. However, **write mem** and **write erase** are the old way; **copy running-config startup-config** and **erase startup-config** are the newer (10.3+) commands. I thought I would point this out in case you see the old commands in some of my examples or Sniffer traces.

Figure 3-15 *Using PumpKin for a TFTP Server*

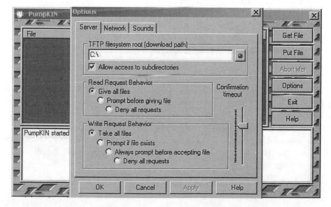

Example 3-29 *Copying r1 Configuration to a TFTP Server*

```
r1#copy running-config tftp
Address or name of remote host []? 192.168.1.11
Destination filename [running-config]? hosta-config
!!
1093 bytes copied in 5.888 secs (218 bytes/sec)
r1#erase startup-config
Erasing the nvram filesystem will remove all files! Continue? [confirm]
[OK]
Erase of nvram: complete
!!!The next 2 shaded commands are not necessary for the tftp exercise
!!!However, it is a good time to review when files are replaced or
!!!just modified.
r1#copy startup-config running-config
Destination filename [running-config]?
r1#show running-config
Building configuration...
Current configuration:
version 12.0
service timestamps debug uptime
service timestamps log uptime
no service password-encryption
hostname r1
enable password donna
ip subnet-zero
ip host r1 192.168.1.1 192.168.2.1 192.168.4.1 10.1.1.1
ip host r2 192.168.4.2 192.168.5.1 192.168.6.1
ip host r3 192.168.2.2 192.168.5.2 192.168.6.2 192.168.3.1 10.2.2.1
ip host r4 10.2.2.2
ip host r5 10.1.1.2
...!
```

Next reload the router as in Example 3-30.

Example 3-30 *Reloading the Router*

```
r1#reload
Proceed with reload? [confirm]
02:21:13: %SYS-5-RELOAD: Reload requested
System Bootstrap, Version 5.2(8a), RELEASE SOFTWARE
Copyright  1986-1995 by cisco Systems
2500 processor with 2048 Kbytes of main memory
F3: 7464832+102636+503004 at 0x3000060
                Restricted Rights Legend
...
Cisco Internetwork Operating System Software
IOS (tm) 2500 Software (C2500-IS-L), Version 12.0(5), RELEASE SOFTWARE (fc1)
Copyright  1986-1999 by cisco Systems, Inc.
Compiled Tue 15-Jun-99 19:57 by phanguye
Image text-base: 0x0303D744, data-base: 0x00001000
cisco 2500 (68030) processor (revision L) with 2048K/2048K bytes of memory.
Processor board ID 03074719, with hardware revision 00000000
Bridging software.
X.25 software, Version 3.0.0.
```

Example 3-30 *Reloading the Router (Continued)*

```
2 Ethernet/IEEE 802.3 interface(s)
2 Serial network interface(s)
32K bytes of non-volatile configuration memory.
8192K bytes of processor board System flash (Read ONLY)
%Error opening tftp://255.255.255.255/network-confg (Timed out)
%Error opening tftp://255.255.255.255/cisconet.cfg (Timed out)
SETUP: new interface Ethernet0 placed in "shutdown" state
SETUP: new interface Ethernet1 placed in "shutdown" state
%Error opening tftp://255.255.255.255/network-confg (Timed out)
%Error opening tftp://255.255.255.255/cisconet.cfg (Timed out)
%Error opening tftp://255.255.255.255/router-confg (Timed out)
%Error opening tftp://255.255.255.255/ciscortr.cfg (Timed out)
Press RETURN to get started!
...
00:03:45: %SYS-5-RESTART: System restarted --
Cisco Internetwork Operating System Software
IOS (tm) 2500 Software (C2500-IS-L), Version 12.0(5), RELEASE SOFTWARE (fc1)
Copyright  1986-1999 by cisc
Router>o Systems, Inc.
Compiled Tue 15-Jun-99 19:57 by phanguye
Router>enable
Router#configure terminal
Enter configuration commands, one per line.  End with CNTL/Z.
Router(config)#interface ethernet 0
Router(config-if)#ip address 192.168.1.1 255.255.255.0
Router(config-if)#no shut
...
Router(config-if)#end
```

Now copy the file from the TFTP to r1 as in Example 3-31. By the way, a router with no configuration is often referred to as a router out of the box (ROTB).

Example 3-31 *Copying the Configuration from the TFTP Server*

```
Router#copy tftp running-config
Address or name of remote host []? 192.168.1.11
Source filename []? hosta-config
Destination filename [running-config]?
Accessing tftp://192.168.1.11/hosta-config...
Loading hosta-config from 192.168.1.11 (via Ethernet0): !
[OK - 1093/2048 bytes]
1093 bytes copied in 5.124 secs (218 bytes/sec)
r1#copy running-config startup-config
Destination filename [startup-config]?
Building configuration...
```

NOTE   Remember to stop and save the Sniffer file as *chapter 3 tftp from r1 to hosta and back sniffer capture*.

In the preceding example, I copied my file to a TFTP server and made sure it was really there. Then I performed an **erase start** on the router to erase the startup configuration. When I tried to overwrite the running configuration with the startup configuration, however, it acted as a *merge*, which is what you should expect. To really get rid of the running configuration, you must **reload** the router; so I did. When the router came back up, it had no configuration, but it was certainly looking for one (as you can see from the shaded output in Example 3-30). Next I configured the IP address on the Ethernet 0 interface and issued a **no shut**. If the TFTP server were not local, a default gateway would be required as well. Now that I had TCP/IP communications, I continued and copied the configuration file from the TFTP server back to the router and saved the configuration.

TFTP and FTP can assist you with saving configurations and IOS images depending on your IOS version. To explore the differences, save the TFTP capture or refer to my Sniffer files to later compare it to FTP. Make a list of the major differences as you observe the two applications.

Before you experiment with FTP, take a few minutes to decode the TFTP Sniffer capture. The shaded line in Figure 3-16 highlights a TFTP write request, which Sniffer portrays as opcode 2 in the detail pane. Lines 63 to 69 include the actual file transfer. Line 64 is an opcode 3 and is the first data packet transfer. Notice that the first block, or 512 bytes, of data was transferred and line 65 is the application acknowledgement to the first data packet with an opcode 4. Table 3-7 lists the common opcodes.

NOTE   My TFTP Sniffer captures have an error in them because of an old Sniffer bug. In Figures 3-16 and 3-17, for example, frame 60 must actually follow frames 61 and 62. I prefer not to doctor my Sniffer capture but rather tell you that it's not possible for it to behave as shown.

Table 3-7   *OpCodes*

OpCode Text	OpCode Number
Read request	1
Write request	2
Data	3
Ack	4
Error	5

Figure 3-16 *TFTP Write Request*

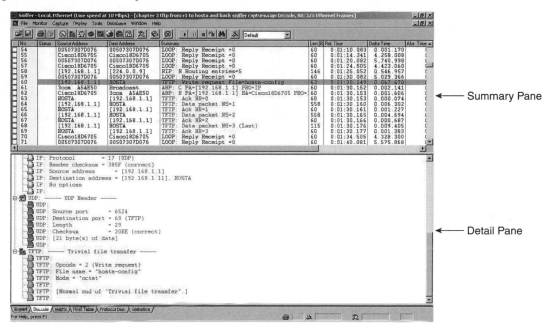

Also note that the Sniffer trace does not in any way hide the configuration while it is transferring. Figure 3-17 shows the ending configuration, including passwords. Notice how you can read the entire configuration file when you open each data packet individually.

Using the Sniffer capture, take a few minutes to draw a simple picture of what happens when you transfer a file using TFTP. Include communications between r1 and hosta, including line numbers, ports, and opcodes, as I did in Figure 3-18.

Many UDP-based applications such as some implementations of TFTP and DNS use a fixed data length (such as 512 bytes) to operate, but the maximum per segment is 65535 bytes.

NOTE   In the Cisco environment, you may need to use FTP to update large IOS images (over 16 MB) or transfer larger files. A more likely reason to use FTP over TFTP is that the latter operates in a ping-pong, request/response fashion with no windowing, which greatly impacts throughput in high-latency paths. In addition, the retransmit timers are fixed, so they do not adapt to the round-trip time as does TCP.

Figure 3-17 *TFTP Clear Text*

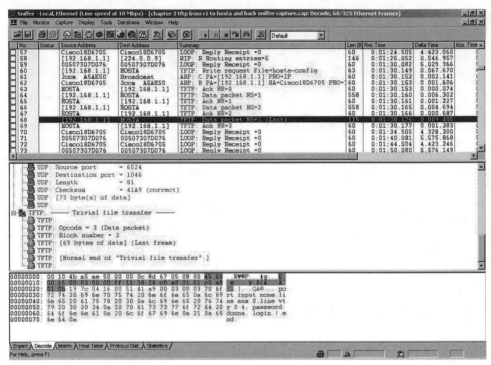

Figure 3-18 *TFTP Communications*

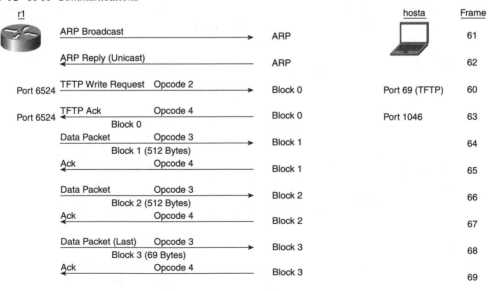

As you verified in the previous figures, TFTP transfers text in the clear. Use FTP to perform the same file transfer as in the TFTP exercise. Actually, I transferred the configuration from r1 and r2 to the FTP server in my test. Any FTP application is appropriate. I am using 3CDaemon in Figure 3-19, a freeware program I downloaded from support.3com.com/infodeli/swlib/utilities_for_windows_32_bit.htm for the lab in Example 3-32. Use Sniffer to capture the results, analyze your findings, list or draw a picture of what happens when you transfer a file using FTP, and, last but not least, compare the two IP-based applications.

Figure 3-19 *FTP Server Software*

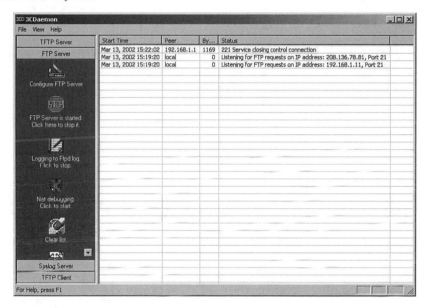

Example 3-32 *Copying r1 and r2 Configuration to an FTP Server*

```
r1(config)#ip ftp username anonymous
r1(config)#ip ftp password donna@shoretraining.com
r1(config)#end
r1#copy running-config startup-config
r1#copy running-config ftp
Address or name of remote host []? 192.168.1.11
Destination filename [running-config]? r1-config
Writing r1-config !
1169 bytes copied in 8.836 secs (146 bytes/sec)
...
```

I did not take the time to erase my configuration and test this out as I did with the TFTP example. If you need more practice, you can do just that. My *chapter 3 ftp from r1 and r2 to hosta sniffer capture* file displays in Figure 3-20. Follow the TCP sessions and data transfer, including the sequence and acknowledgement numbers for a review.

Figure 3-20 *FTP Write Request*

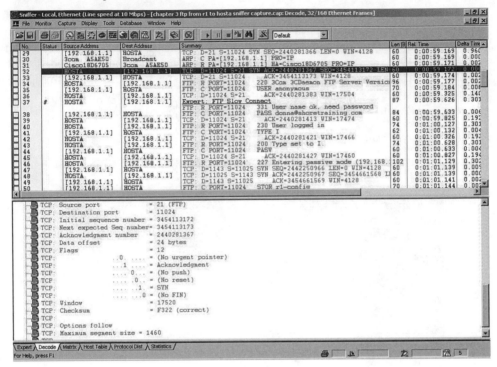

Feel free to draw a more specific picture with line numbers, ports, and sequence and acknowledgement numbers. However, the following gives a general picture of how FTP works:

- ARP and TCP 3-way handshake (FTP control port 21)

- FTP user login (anonymous) and password (donna@shoretraining.com)

- TCP 3-way handshake (FTP data transfer port 20)

- FTP data transfer (clear text)

- Session tear down (data port 20)

- Session tear down (control port 21)

The main difference is that the program I used for the test does not use an individual port 20 for each data transfer, but instead uses a separate ephemeral port.

NOTE	Actually my FTP client specified a PASV (passive) transfer mode, and the 3CDaemon server supported it. This makes FTP a little confusing because, as I just illustrated, the data port is not always port 20. In passive-mode FTP, the client initiates both the control and data connection to the server. Obviously this can be good or bad depending on server and firewall configurations. Research FTP modes for more detail.

You should have notes similar to the following to compare TFTP and FTP communications:

- The client uses an ephemeral port to initiate communications to TFTP server port 69 and the server picks an ephemeral port to respond to the client. FTP uses port 21 for control and a separate port 20 for file transfer, and the server port doesn't need to change for multiple clients because of the TCP session.

- No login, username, or password is used for TFTP. FTP requires login and can allow anonymous login with the e-mail address for the password.

- TFTP transfers a minimum of 512 bytes of data per datagram, and the application ACKs each one individually because UDP has no reliability mechanism; FTP, on the other hand, uses a TCP session for each file transfer.

- TFTP and FTP use clear-text data transmission. FTP secure implementations are available.

In addition, TFTP and FTP are very helpful in the Cisco environment to copy not only configurations but also Cisco Operating System images. Many times I set up my router as a TFTP server so that I can copy the IOS to another location. Appendix B provides more detail on such topics.

As you can see, it is helpful to understand the basics of how applications work to more easily troubleshoot them. Next take a look at the Simple Mail Transfer Protocol (SMTP) and Post Office Protocol (POP3) in Figure 3-21.

Figure 3-21 *SMTP and POP3*

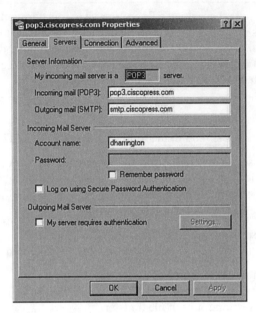

SMTP is like the mail truck delivering from post office to post office. If you work for Cisco Press and you want to set up your mail client to send your mail, for example, you may set up smtp.ciscopress.com, which by default occurs on TCP port 25.

POP3 is more of a server to the client mail delivery protocol that operates by default on TCP port 110. Therefore if you work for Cisco Press and want to set up your mail client, you may set up pop3.ciscopress.com to receive your mail.

Assume user@ciscopress.com wants to send an e-mail to donna@shoretraining.com. That user clicks Send and SMTP is used to transfer the e-mail from the user to his mail server using SMTP TCP port 25. The mail server delivers the mail to the shoretraining.com domain over port 25. When I check my mail on shoretraining, my e-mail program establishes a connection to my mail server over POP3 port 110.

Knowing the overall SMTP/POP3 delivery process may assist you with troubleshooting your e-mail one day. For example, I have been in situations where I could send e-mail but not receive, which turned out to be a POP3 issue. Perhaps a particular port or address was blocked by an access list. I have also been in situations where the opposite occurs. For example, many times you may have the luxury of using a higher-speed network connection but your ISP may not allow you to "relay" through another system. However, troubleshooting e-mail issues happens to be another book in itself (as are most applications).

NOTE	Like telnet, SMTP and POP3 are clear-text protocols for all e-mail and password information. You can add security with better alternatives. Secure POP (SPOP, port 995) uses Secure Sockets Layer (SSL). SMTP (still port 25) can use SSL as well. Internet Message Access Protocol (IMAP, port 143) is inherently more secure than POP3 is. Previously in this chapter, I compared SSH (port 22) to telnet (port 23).

DNS is another application that it is quite helpful to understand in the support world. I would much rather type www.cisco.com than its IP address every time I want to look up something on Cisco.com. DNS maps an IP address to a hostname so that humans can relate to it a little better.

Hostname resolution once was a flat hosts file, but who would have enough memory to open such a thing today? Hosts files are still available for use, however. You have them on each of your routers now. Type **show hosts** with me on r1 as in Example 3-33.

Example 3-33 *Cisco Hosts File*

```
r1>show hosts
Default domain is not set
Name/address lookup uses domain service
Name servers are 255.255.255.255
Host                 Flags         Age Type    Address(es)
r1                   (perm, OK) 23     IP      192.168.1.1   192.168.2.1
                                               192.168.4.1   10.1.1.1
r2                   (perm, OK) 23     IP      192.168.4.2   192.168.5.1
                                               192.168.6.1
r3                   (perm, OK) 23     IP      192.168.2.2   192.168.5.2
                                               192.168.6.2   192.168.3.1
                                               10.2.2.1
r4                   (perm, OK) 23     IP      10.2.2.2
r5                   (perm, OK) 23     IP      10.1.1.2
```

Hosts files on PCs are typically found in locations such as \Windows, \Etc, \Winnt\System32\Drivers\Etc and are named hosts. Reference Figure 3-22 for a sample Windows 2000 hosts file.

Figure 3-22 *Windows 2000 Hosts File*

The other files listed in Figure 3-22 can be quite helpful, too. Lmhosts is for NetBIOS name resolution. The other files contain common network, protocol, and port numbers. At the upper layers, I often ask myself whether a hostname or a NetBIOS issue exists. Figure 3-23 provides some examples, as does Table 3-1 earlier in this chapter.

Figure 3-23 *Name and Address Resolution*

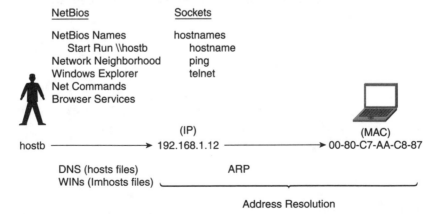

DNS is hierarchical in nature; therefore, fully qualified domain names (FQDN) must be unique. Upper-level domain names include such domain names as com, edu, net, and gov. Second-level domain names must be registered. For example, ciscopress.com and shoretraining.com are both part of the top-level com domain. Cisco Press has authority over what they do under ciscopress.com, and I have control over what I do under shoretraining.com. Obviously, these second-level domains must be registered through Internet service providers (ISPs) or companies such as VeriSign.

NOTE	Some implementations of DNS do not allow hostnames with underscores (_).

The name space contains domains, subdomains, and hosts. The servers contain zones, which are database files with various record types. Common record types include alias (canonical name) or mail (MX) records.

Why do you care? Name resolution is certainly something to check for in the upper layers. If you can ping the IP address but not the hostname, for example, chances are you have a hostname resolution issue. If you can issue a **Start > Run \\192.168.1.12** but not a **Start > Run \\hostb**, the problem is probably NetBIOS name resolution. These could in turn be DNS or WINS issues, *depending* on the applications and settings in your environment.

If you were capturing DNS information with Sniffer, you would see that queries typically are done over UDP port 53, whereas zone transfers are completed over TCP port 53. Next take a look at SNMP, which is everything but simple.

SNMP was originally for remote management of network hardware devices, but today is used for lots more. A management console sends a request to an agent (managed device) over UDP port 161, and the agent generates a trap on port 162 to a specific address. An agent really can't initiate anything on its own, but it can notify the manager of events, such as a link up or down or a software mail problem. The requests are part of a database referred to as a Management Information Base (MIB) in the SNMP world. Communities are groups that talk to one another to assist with security, and public is the default community. CiscoWorks, Cisco Info Center (CIC), and HP OpenView are examples of network management platforms that support SNMP-based management.

Next I review the RIP application. RIP is the routing protocol you set up earlier in the chapter so that one end system could get to another end system. RIP is an application that operates over UDP port 520. RIPv2 still operates over UDP port 520, but it uses 224.0.0.9 as a destination IP multicast address. Although each of the prefix entries includes a mask, RIPv2 is more considerate of the hosts, which are not interested in its messages, because their NICs will filter the frames at Layer 2. Figure 3-24 enables you to analyze the RIP header. Does my capture display RIPv1 or RIPv2?

Figure 3-24 *RIP*

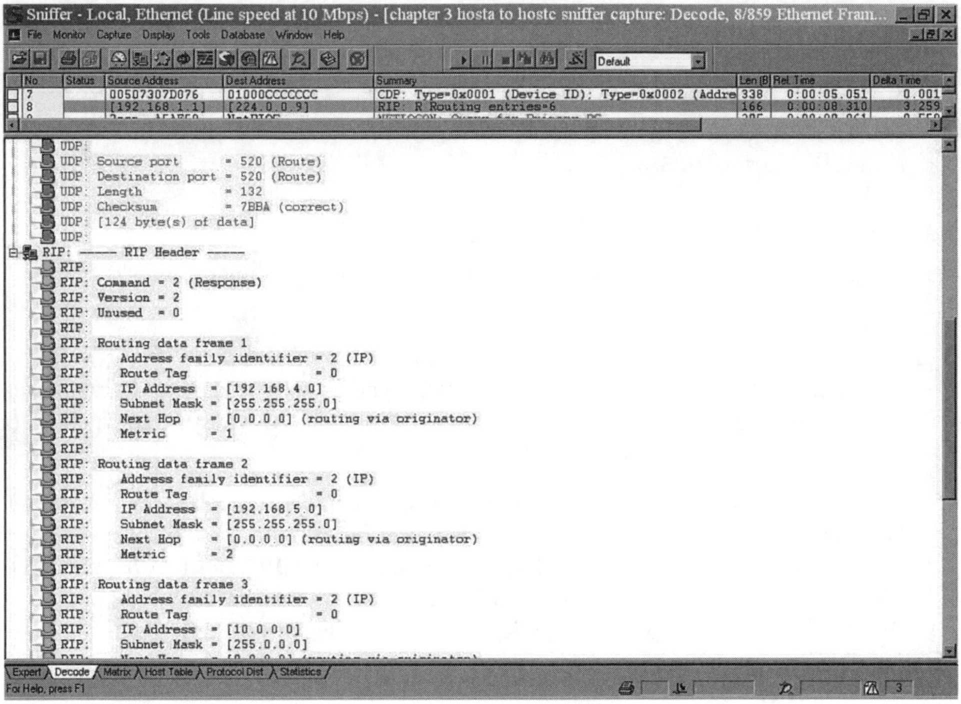

You are correct if you said Figure 3-24 displays RIPv2 because the destination is the multicast 224.0.0.9 address rather than a local broadcast.

Now look at another application that is common in a day-to-day environment; Hypertext Transport Protocol (HTTP) uses TCP port 80 to provide web services. It also uses clear-text data transmission. Obviously this is a very big issue with purchasing items over the Internet. E-commerce applications make use of more secure protocols such as HTTPS over TCP port 443. If you compare a Sniffer trace of HTTP and HTTPS traffic, the HTTPS data is encrypted. Figure 3-25 shows you what people can sniff when you use HTTP to access a switch. I had to turn port monitoring on for this to work. Those details are covered more depth in the switch chapters, Chapter 6, "Shooting Trouble with CatOS and IOS," and Chapter 7, "Shooting Trouble with VLANs on Routers and Switches." For now, analyze the layered approach to HTTP as you have done with the other applications.

Figure 3-25 *HTTP to a 1900 Switch*

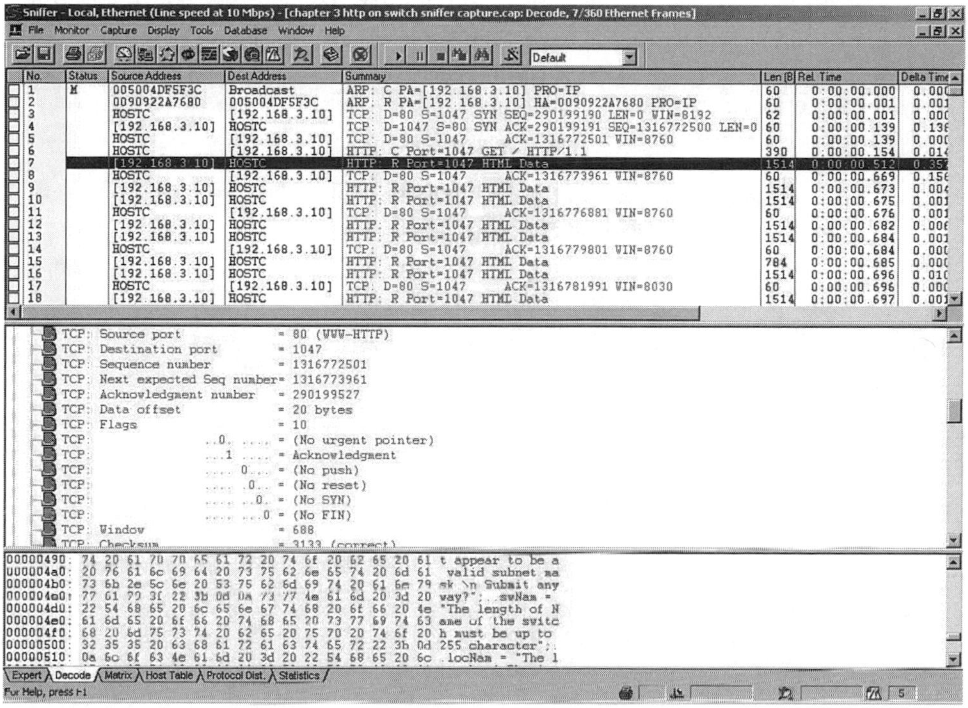

NOTE   HTTP 1.0 opens a new TCP connection for each item, but HTTP 1.1 does not, as you can verify at www.w3.org/Protocols/Activity.html. In addition, this Sniffer decode offers a good opportunity to point out the default behavior of most TCPs, to acknowledge every other packet.

Now that I have touched on all the layers of the TCP/IP suite to lead into the addressing section, I will discuss DHCP. First there was RARP, then BOOTP, and now DHCP. The basic concept is the same. Take RARP, for example. It is used to resolve MAC addresses to IP addresses. It is the opposite of ARP, with which I know you have become pretty comfortable by now. The Bootstrap Protocol (BOOTP) was developed to allow diskless workstations to obtain IP information upon bootup. BOOTP spawned DHCP, which is widely used today.

DHCP is not fully automatic because someone must configure the server with a range of IP addresses (scope) and other optional parameters such as the mask, gateway, DNS server, WINS server, and so on. Clients request DHCP parameters via Layer 2 and Layer 3 broadcasts to UDP port 67. The server sends messages to the client on UDP port 68. However, it would defeat the purpose of a router if it were allowed to forward all broadcasts. On the other hand, it is possible for you to open up certain ports for routers to forward via the **ip helper-address** [*ipaddress*] command. Request forwarding is also possible via DHCP proxy agents. Figure 3-26 provides examples of the **ip helper** command. Helpers in effect change the local broadcast destination to a unicast or directed broadcast to reach the DHCP server. Table 3-8 shows DHCP frames that you should capture sometime with a protocol analyzer.

Figure 3-26   *IP Helper*

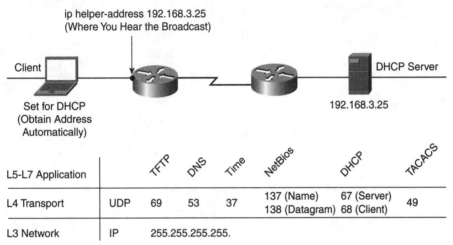

L5-L7 Application	TFTP	DNS	Time	NetBios	DHCP	TACACS
L4 Transport	UDP	69	53	37	137 (Name) 138 (Datagram)	67 (Server) 68 (Client)	49
L3 Network	IP	255.255.255.255.				

NOTE   To forward fewer than the eight default ports that IP helper opens up, you can use the **ip forward-protocol udp** *port* command for the ports you want to forward followed by the **no ip forward-protocol udp** *port* for the ports you do not want to forward.

Table 3-8   *DHCP Frames*

DHCP Frame	Description
Discover	Client is looking for DHCP server (broadcast).
Offers	DHCP servers respond (broadcast).
Request	Client asks for first server that offered (broadcast).
Ack	DHCP server sends.
ARP	Client sends an ARP to check for duplicate addresses.

Addressing

Whether you use DHCP or static IP addressing, understanding addressing is a very important skill. As a CCNP Support candidate, assumed skills include basic things such as addressing, subnetting, summarizing, and routing. In this section I take the time to review because too many problems occur because of lack of planning with IP addressing. Proper planning prevents poor performance in all circumstances. Besides, you will need these skills in the Trouble Tickets, but more importantly in the real world.

Chapter 1 covered the basics of IP addressing, discussing the 4.2 billion (2^{32}), 32-bit, dotted-decimal format. Table 3-9 reviews classes and masks.

Table 3-9   *IP Address Classes and Masks*

	Class and Range	Decimal Mask	Bitwise Mask
0	A 1–127[*]	255.0.0.0	/8
10	B 128–191	255.255.0.0	/16
110	C 192–223	255.255.255.0	/24

*Loopback

Public addresses are registered through your ISP or at www.arin.net. ARIN is one of the three regional Internet registries (and is the authority in the United States). RIPE NCC is the authority for Europe, the Middle East, North Africa, and parts of Asia. APNIC is the Asia Pacific Network Information Centre (and is the authority for parts of Asia not under the authority of RIPE NCC). I registered my domain name information with VeriSign and my local ISP hosts the ShoreTraining.com website for me. Take a few minutes and go out to ARIN's website, use their whois tool to do a lookup of any public address you like. An example of a public address is 216.239.51.100, which happens to be one of my favorite search engines. This address falls within the network block of 216.239.32.0 to 216.239.63.255. However, I do not like to pick on public sites, so I will stay with private addresses for the practical studies. Private addresses should not be routed on the Internet, and they fall within the following ranges:

- 10.0.0.0/8 (10.0.0.0 to 10.255.255.255)
- 172.16.0.0/12 (172.16.0.0 to 172.31.255.255)
- 192.168.0.0/16 (192.168.0.0 to 192.168.255.255)

Notice that no matter whether you are using a public or private address, you still need a subnet mask to divide the network and host portion. I am certain you have heard many analogies on this by now, but the most common is probably the street being the network and your house number being a host on the network. Alternatively, look at the address and use your "network tape measure" to measure off the network bits from left to right, or just think of a painter masking off what he does not want to paint.

Look back at Figure 3-1 to review your streets (networks) and houses (hosts). Quickly make a list or table of your networks and hosts as in Table 3-10, because you will soon be changing your IP addressing scheme. Notice how I also included the router interfaces, because they need an address to operate with IP (unless, of course, you are using something like IP unnumbered).

Table 3-10   *Current IP Addressing*

Network	Address	Interface
192.168.1.0/24	192.168.1.1/24	r1e0
	192.168.1.11/24	hosta
	192.168.1.12/24	hostb
192.168.2.0/24	192.168.2.1/24	r1s1
	192.168.2.2/24	r3s0/0
192.168.3.0/24	192.168.3.1/24	r3fa2/0
	192.168.3.5/24	hostc
192.168.4.0/24	192.168.4.1/24	r1e1
	192.168.4.2/24	r2e0
192.168.5.0/24	192.168.5.1/24	r2s1
	192.168.5.2/24	r3s0/2
192.168.6.0/24	192.168.6.1/24	r2S0
	192.168.6.2/24	r3s0/1
10.1.1.0/24	10.1.1.1/24	r1s0
	10.1.1.2/24	r5s0
10.2.2.0/24	10.2.2.1/24	r3s0/3
	10.2.2.2/24	r4s0/0

What a waste of address space, you should be thinking to yourself right about now, and if you were using public addresses, that would be more of a waste. Although the problem may not be apparent with a list of networks and hosts, many problems show up later. Keep your table handy; you will continue to examine this. First, however, I want to review subnetting in a little more detail.

Subnetting

From my back yard I can see the Chesapeake Bay Bridge and the eastbound and westbound cars. From Memorial Day to Labor Day is prime beach time. Every Friday night people head for the beach and return home on Sunday. Cars are almost at a standstill on the bridge at those times. Needless to say, this is one huge collision and broadcast domain. Sometimes the Mass Transit Authority (MTA) subnets, and I bet they don't even know it. They borrow temporarily less-congested lanes from the westbound side to send more people down the eastbound side. They also implemented EZPass to let the commuters have their own lanes (like queuing). That is all subnetting is. Now not as many cars (hosts) can travel the westbound side, because MTA borrowed them to make more lanes (subnets) for eastbound traffic. Subnetting is all about borrowing from the host bits to get more networks. Routers handle multiple subnets by partitioning collision and broadcast domains to avoid congestion.

Feel free to review the subnetting examples from Chapter 1, but you may as well put this to practice in your lab. Look at your routing tables to see how they display the networks you are using. Refer to Example 3-34 for mine.

Example 3-34 *Chapter 3 Networks*

```
r1#show ip route
Codes: C - connected, S - static, I - IGRP, R - RIP, M - mobile, B - BGP
       D - EIGRP, EX - EIGRP external, O - OSPF, IA - OSPF inter area
       N1 - OSPF NSSA external type 1, N2 - OSPF NSSA external type 2
       E1 - OSPF external type 1, E2 - OSPF external type 2, E - EGP
       i - IS-IS, L1 - IS-IS level-1, L2 - IS-IS level-2, * - candidate default
       U - per-user static route, o - ODR
Gateway of last resort is not set
C    192.168.4.0/24 is directly connected, Ethernet1
R    192.168.5.0/24 [120/1] via 192.168.4.2, 00:00:23, Ethernet1
                     [120/1] via 192.168.2.2, 00:00:18, Serial1
     10.0.0.0/8 is variably subnetted, 3 subnets, 2 masks
R       10.0.0.0/8 [120/2] via 192.168.4.2, 00:00:24, Ethernet1
R       10.2.2.0/24 [120/1] via 192.168.2.2, 00:00:18, Serial1
C       10.1.1.0/24 is directly connected, Serial0
R    192.168.6.0/24 [120/1] via 192.168.4.2, 00:00:24, Ethernet1
                     [120/1] via 192.168.2.2, 00:00:18, Serial1
C    192.168.1.0/24 is directly connected, Ethernet0
C    192.168.2.0/24 is directly connected, Serial1
R    192.168.3.0/24 [120/1] via 192.168.2.2, 00:00:18, Serial1
r2>show ip route
…
C    192.168.4.0/24 is directly connected, Ethernet0
C    192.168.5.0/24 is directly connected, Serial1
     10.0.0.0/24 is subnetted, 2 subnets
R       10.1.1.0 [120/1] via 192.168.4.1, 00:00:08, Ethernet0
R       10.2.2.0 [120/1] via 192.168.6.2, 00:00:23, Serial0
                  [120/1] via 192.168.5.2, 00:00:23, Serial1
C    192.168.6.0/24 is directly connected, Serial0
R    192.168.1.0/24 [120/1] via 192.168.4.1, 00:00:08, Ethernet0
R    192.168.2.0/24 [120/1] via 192.168.4.1, 00:00:08, Ethernet0
                     [120/1] via 192.168.6.2, 00:00:23, Serial0
                     [120/1] via 192.168.5.2, 00:00:23, Serial1
R    192.168.3.0/24 [120/1] via 192.168.6.2, 00:00:23, Serial0
                     [120/1] via 192.168.5.2, 00:00:23, Serial1
r3>show ip route
…
R    192.168.4.0/24 [120/1] via 192.168.2.1, 00:00:17, Serial0/0
                     [120/1] via 192.168.6.1, 00:00:11, Serial0/1
                     [120/1] via 192.168.5.1, 00:00:11, Serial0/2
```

continues

Example 3-34 *Chapter 3 Networks (Continued)*

```
C    192.168.5.0/24 is directly connected, Serial0/2
     10.0.0.0/8 is variably subnetted, 3 subnets, 2 masks
R       10.1.1.0/24 [120/1] via 192.168.2.1, 00:00:17, Serial0/0
R       10.0.0.0/8 [120/2] via 192.168.6.1, 00:00:11, Serial0/1
                       [120/2] via 192.168.5.1, 00:00:11, Serial0/2
C       10.2.2.0/24 is directly connected, Serial0/3
C    192.168.6.0/24 is directly connected, Serial0/1
R    192.168.1.0/24 [120/1] via 192.168.2.1, 00:00:18, Serial0/0
C    192.168.2.0/24 is directly connected, Serial0/0
C    192.168.3.0/24 is directly connected, FastEthernet2/0
r4>show ip route
…
R    192.168.4.0/24 [120/2] via 10.2.2.1, 00:00:13, Serial0/0
R    192.168.5.0/24 [120/1] via 10.2.2.1, 00:00:14, Serial0/0
     10.0.0.0/8 is variably subnetted, 3 subnets, 2 masks
R       10.1.1.0/24 [120/2] via 10.2.2.1, 00:00:14, Serial0/0
R       10.0.0.0/8 [120/3] via 10.2.2.1, 00:00:14, Serial0/0
C       10.2.2.0/24 is directly connected, Serial0/0
R    192.168.6.0/24 [120/1] via 10.2.2.1, 00:00:14, Serial0/0
R    192.168.1.0/24 [120/2] via 10.2.2.1, 00:00:14, Serial0/0
R    192.168.2.0/24 [120/1] via 10.2.2.1, 00:00:14, Serial0/0
R    192.168.3.0/24 [120/1] via 10.2.2.1, 00:00:14, Serial0/0
r5>show ip route
…
R    192.168.4.0/24 [120/1] via 10.1.1.1, 00:00:05, Serial0
R    192.168.5.0/24 [120/2] via 10.1.1.1, 00:00:06, Serial0
     10.0.0.0/8 is variably subnetted, 3 subnets, 2 masks
R       10.2.2.0/24 [120/2] via 10.1.1.1, 00:00:06, Serial0
R       10.0.0.0/8 [120/3] via 10.1.1.1, 00:00:06, Serial0
C       10.1.1.0/24 is directly connected, Serial0
R    192.168.6.0/24 [120/2] via 10.1.1.1, 00:00:06, Serial0
R    192.168.1.0/24 [120/1] via 10.1.1.1, 00:00:06, Serial0
R    192.168.2.0/24 [120/1] via 10.1.1.1, 00:00:06, Serial0
R    192.168.3.0/24 [120/2] via 10.1.1.1, 00:00:06, Serial0
r5>
```

You can apply the shaded output in the preceding example to the other routers, but on r1 I am illustrating that there are multiple paths to subnet 192.168.5.0 and 192.168.6.0. Note how the routing table output shows 10.0.0.0/8, which is the classful mask, with the subnets 10.1.1.0/24 and 10.2.2.0/24 beneath it.

To prepare for the chapter Trouble Tickets, I want you to plan your new addressing scheme using 192.168.5.0/24 as a starting point. You know how many networks and hosts you have, but plan on adding a few more for growth. Do not assume that you can use subnet 0 (the first subnet), the last subnet, or VLSM for now. Write out your calculations as I do in Figure 3-27, but save the actual configuration for the chapter Trouble Tickets. Feel free to expand the binary to truly help you master the subnetting concepts.

Figure 3-27 *Subnetting*

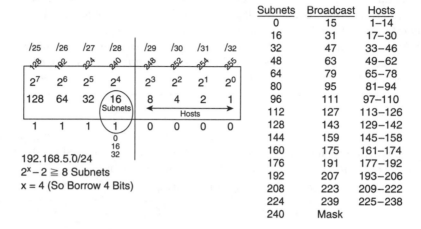

Subnets	Broadcast	Hosts
0	15	1–14
16	31	17–30
32	47	33–46
48	63	49–62
64	79	65–78
80	95	81–94
96	111	97–110
112	127	113–126
128	143	129–142
144	159	145–158
160	175	161–174
176	191	177–192
192	207	193–206
208	223	209–222
224	239	225–238
240	Mask	

NOTE   For more practice, go to www.learntosubnet.com or return to Chapter 1. When you have mastered these concepts, you can check your work against the subnet calculator at Cisco.com.

You certainly should plan your addresses carefully, and this is more than just compiling an Excel spreadsheet and checking off what you have handed out to everyone. However, what could you do if I told you that I want to take one of the subnets and subdivide it to maximize the number of subnets I can possibly get from it? I tend to reserve subnet 0 for this purpose, so take 192.168.5.0/28 and further subnet it according to the information provided. Figure 3-28 shows my VLSM calculations.

Figure 3-28 *VLSM*

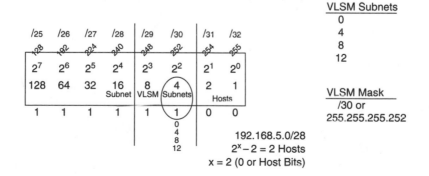

VLSM Subnets
0
4
8
12

VLSM Mask
/30 or
255.255.255.252

NOTE   Subnetting and VLSM are all about moving the network mask bit boundary to the right. For every host bit borrowed, the available subnets double and similarly the hosts exponentially decrease, too. When I make a cake for desert and plan on 8 people eating, for example, I would probably cut it into 10 or 12 pieces to make sure I have enough cake (subnets) for all. If I cut the cake into exactly eight pieces, however, and each guest brings a friend, I guess I could perform VLSM on the pieces of cake.

I took the VLSM example from a different approach in that I knew I never needed more than two hosts. So I used the $2^x - 2$ formula to calculate hosts and placed the 0s in the chart first. Tables are helpful to organize such data, as I demonstrate in Table 3-11.

Table 3-11   *Subnets, Broadcast Addresses, Hosts, and VLSM Subnets*

Subnets	0	16	32	48	64	80	96	...	224
Broadcast	15	31	47	63	79	95	111	...	239
Hosts	1–14	17–33	33–46	49–62	65–78	81–94	97–110	...	225–238
VLSM subnets (hosts)	0 (1–2) 4 (5–6) 8 (9–10) 12 (13–14)								

Some general suggestions I can recommend for VLSM include the following:

Step 1   Start with your host requirements.

Step 2   Next calculate for the LAN segments.

Step 3   Then subnet a LAN to get your WANs.

Step 4   More than three levels can get a little too confusing.

Real-world solutions include topics such as proxy servers and Network Address Translation (NAT), which are covered in a little more detail in the *Practical Studies Remote Access Guide*. A proxy server, for example, has one NIC to the outside world and one to inside network. Requests made by the inside hosts are made to the proxy server to relay the requests and responses. NAT doesn't use a proxy service. Instead, a router running NAT can replace the inside addresses with outside addresses. Finally, both of these techniques can be combined.

Ultimately, besides being neat about things and saving addresses, you want to plan your address scheme so that it is not so stressful on your routing tables. It would be a perfect world if everyone really understood the importance of this. After all, there is more to life than just sharing your cake; you must eat it too. Figure 3-29 offers a hierarchical view of the subnetting and VLSM math you did previously, which will in turn make summarizing a breeze.

Figure 3-29 *Summarization*

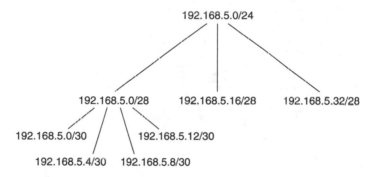

Summarization

Summarization is the real reason you want to pay attention to your addressing scheme. Besides only having a finite number of addresses, routing table growth has just exploded over the years. There are more than 100,000 Internet routes to date. See for yourself in Figures 3-30 and 3-31 or go to a similar site for a more current report. Summarizing enables you to have a single IP address range represent a collection of smaller ranges when deployed hierarchically. Collapsing the routing table is an obvious advantage to summarization, but think about the impact on my network if my routing tables are affected every time a link goes down on your network.

NOTE	Summarization increases stability in that if one of your links flap up and down, my routing tables are not flapping reachable and unreachable. If I have network 192.168.5.0/24 and you have 192.168.7.0/24, for example, I really don't have the need to know about your 192.168.7.4/30. All I care about is to get to 192.168.7. *anything* I send to you.

Summarization limits the number of routers that need to recalculate routing tables. To determine a summary route, a router determines the high-order (1) bits that match for all addresses. Sometimes this is done on the classful boundary automatically and other times you and I may need to include the appropriate summary statement, depending on the routing protocol.

Figure 3-30 *Route Server*

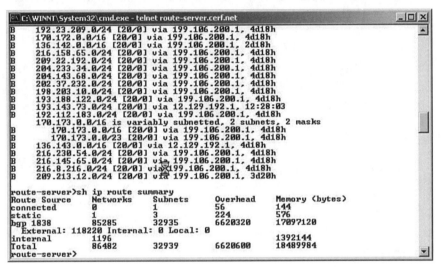

```
C:\WINNT\System32\cmd.exe - telnet route-server.cerf.net                    _ _ X
B     192.23.209.0/24 [20/0] via 199.106.200.1, 4d18h
B     170.172.0.0/16 [20/0] via 199.106.200.1, 4d18h
B     136.142.0.0/16 [20/0] via 199.106.200.1, 2d18h
B     216.158.65.0/24 [20/0] via 199.106.200.1, 4d18h
B     209.22.192.0/24 [20/0] via 199.106.200.1, 4d18h
B     204.233.34.0/24 [20/0] via 199.106.200.1, 4d18h
B     204.143.68.0/24 [20/0] via 199.106.200.1, 4d18h
B     202.37.232.0/24 [20/0] via 199.106.200.1, 4d18h
B     198.203.10.0/24 [20/0] via 199.106.200.1, 4d18h
B     193.188.122.0/24 [20/0] via 199.106.200.1, 4d18h
B     193.143.73.0/24 [20/0] via 12.129.192.1, 12:28:03
B     192.112.183.0/24 [20/0] via 199.106.200.1, 4d18h
      170.173.0.0/16 is variably subnetted, 2 subnets, 2 masks
B        170.173.0.0/16 [20/0] via 199.106.200.1, 4d18h
B        170.173.0.0/23 [20/0] via 199.106.200.1, 4d18h
B     136.143.0.0/16 [20/0] via 12.129.192.1, 4d18h
B     216.230.54.0/24 [20/0] via 199.106.200.1, 4d18h
B     216.145.65.0/24 [20/0] via 199.106.200.1, 4d18h
B     216.8.216.0/24 [20/0] via 199.106.200.1, 4d18h
B     209.213.12.0/24 [20/0] via 199.106.200.1, 3d20h

route-server>sh ip route summary
Route Source    Networks    Subnets    Overhead    Memory (bytes)
connected       0           1          56          144
static          1           3          224         576
bgp 1838        85285       32935      6620320     17097120
   External: 118220 Internal: 0 Local: 0
internal        1196                               1392144
Total           86482       32939      6620600     18489984
route-server>
```

Figure 3-31 *Classless Interdomain Routing (CIDR) Report*

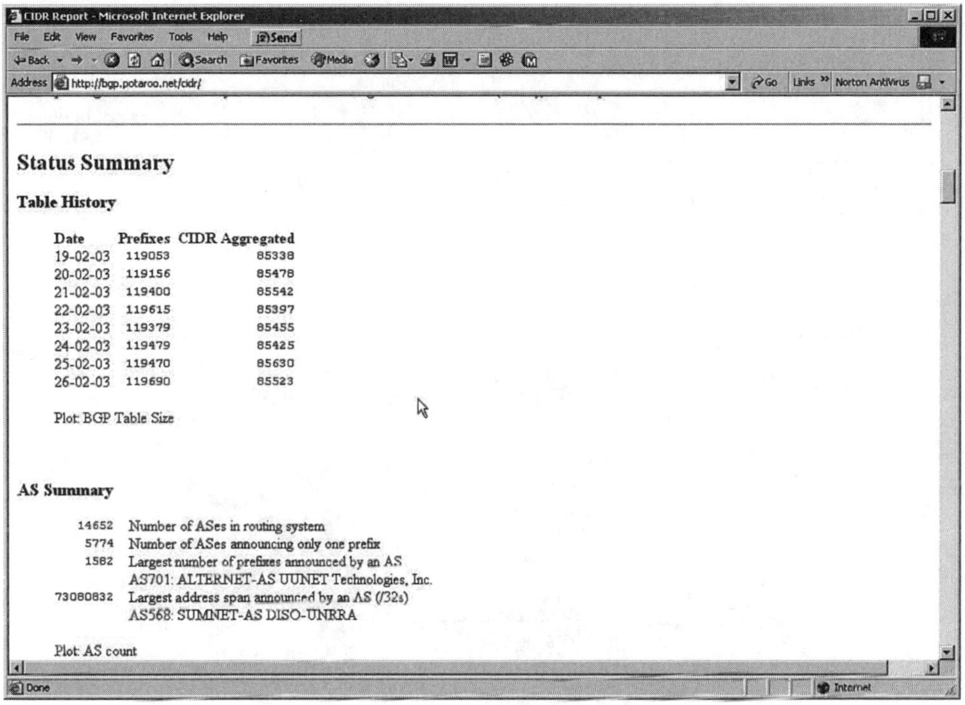

Subnetting, VLSM, summarization, aggregation, supernetting, and CIDR are all about matching bits. Subnetting and VLSM move the network bit boundary to the right, whereas summarization, aggregation, supernetting, and CIDR move the network bit boundary to the left. In Figure 3-32, HQ starts with 192.168.5.0/24 and breaks it down into subnet 192.168.5.32/27 for the Northern Region, 192.168.5.64/27 for the Western Region, 192.168.5.96/27 for the Southern Region, and 192.168.5.128/27 for the Eastern Region. In turn, each of the regions uses VLSM to subnet their Ethernets to a /28 and their serials to a /30. Yet each region can summarize the /27 back to HQ Core.

Figure 3-32 *Network Bit Boundaries*

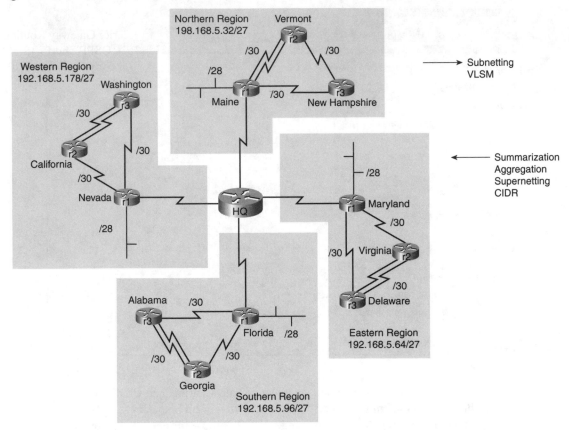

The practical addressing examples certainly bring out the mathematics involved, but decreasing the impact on networks attached to the routers and ultimately the hosts connected to various switches is the goal. I address that topic a bit more in Part III, "Supporting Ethernet, Switches, and VLANs." Now I want to quickly review routing protocols so that you can shoot their troubles throughout the book.

Routing Protocols

Routing protocols have their own unique characteristics, and various Layer 2 encapsulation types have a big impact on them. Understanding how they work will certainly assist you in troubleshooting them now and later. Most of the statistics listed for each can be found with IOS commands such as **show ip protocols**, **show ip route**, and **show ip** *routing-protocol* **?**. Logging, debug, and protocol analyzers all with various levels of impact on the working environment are certainly valuable tools to see more detail when troubleshooting, too.

However, I want you to reserve them for later chapters. After all, many of these protocols are not just IP-specific.

First I discuss the following Interior Gateway Protocols (IGPs): RIP, Interior Gateway Routing Protocol (IGRP)/Enhanced Interior Gateway Routing Protocol (EIGRP), OSPF, and IS-IS. Then I review Border Gateway Protocol (BGP), which is an Exterior Gateway Protocol (EGP).

RIP

Routing Information Protocol (RIP) was originally designed for Xerox PARC Universal Protocol (PUP), and in many ways is still for "pups." It was called GWINFO in the Xerox Network Systems (XNS) protocol suite in 1981, and defined in RFC 1058 in 1988. It is easy to configure, and it works very well in small networks. In larger networks, however, it can be less effective; as I say to myself, "It can RIP you apart." There are alternatives to RIP for larger environments.

Everyone knows RIP because it has been widely adopted by PC, UNIX, and router makers alike. RIP has disadvantages in that it operates over UDP port 520 and the maximum hop count is 15. RIPv2 assists with the broadcast nature in that it operates via multicast over 224.0.0.9. Both RIPv1 and RIPv2 are distance vector routing protocols, which are often referred to as *routing by rumor* protocols.

Examine the following list of RIP characteristics and refer back to the examples throughout the chapter, for you have already experimented with RIPv1 and RIPv2. I hope your practical exercises, with RIPv1 not supporting discontiguous subnets and RIPv2 supporting them, will stay with you for a long time.

The following are RIP characteristics:

- Open protocol, widely used, stable.
- Good for small networks in that it is very easy to configure.
- There are RIP-like distance vector routing protocols for Novell and AppleTalk.
- Distance vector routing protocol.
- IGP.
- IP RIP updates are sent every 30 seconds via broadcast (224.0.0.9 for RIPv2).
- UDP port 520
- Administrative distance is 120.
- Single metric is hop count. (The limit is 15 to assist with count-to-infinity.)
- Timers help regulate performance:

— **Update timer**—Frequency of routing updates. Every 30 seconds IP RIP sends a complete copy of its routing table, subject to split horizon. (IPX RIP does this every 60 seconds.)

— **Invalid timer**—Absence of refreshed content in a routing update. RIP waits 180 seconds to mark a route as invalid and immediately puts it into holddown.

— **Hold-down timers and triggered updates**—Assist with stability of routes in the Cisco environment. Holddowns ensure that regular update messages do not inappropriately cause a routing loop. The router doesn't act on nonsuperior new information for a certain period of time. RIP's hold-down time is 180 seconds.

— **Flush timer**—RIP waits an additional 240 seconds after holddown before it actually removes the route from the table.

- Other stability features to assist with routing loops include the following:

— **Split horizon**—Not useful to send information about a route back in the direction from which it came.

— **Poison reverse**—Updates that are sent to invalidate a route and place it in holddown.

- Bellman-Ford algorithm.

- RIPv2 supports VLSM and summarization. (RIPv1 doesn't.) RIPv2 always autosummarizes at the class boundary.

RIP maintains only the best route in its routing table, as you can verify in examples throughout the chapter. In Example 3-2, for example, I configured RIPv1 on r1 and continued to configure the other routers. In Example 3-15, while troubleshooting I looked at the routing tables and IP routing protocols. Then I configured RIPv2 in Example 3-21. Example 3-22 displays the routing tables and output of **show ip protocols** with RIPv2 configured. Look back at these examples to review such things as the update characteristics, timers, and administrative distance associated with RIP.

Example 3-35 illustrates routes in holddown. First I turn on service time stamps and set the clock so that you can see the actual timing of events. Then I turn on **debug ip rip events**, remove the cable from router 2 Serial 1, plug it back in, watch the routing updates, and view the appropriate routing tables.

NOTE   As always, in a practical environment be very careful with running debug commands due to their excessive memory requirements and stressful nature on the devices. Notice my in-line comments where I unplugged and plugged the cable back in.

Example 3-35 *Debug Output for RIPv2 Packets*

```
r1(config)#service timestamps debug datetime localtime
r1(config)#end
r1#clock set 3:22:00 11 October 2002
r1#copy running-config startup-config
Destination filename [startup-config]?
Building configuration...
[OK]
r1#debug ip rip events
RIP event debugging is on
Oct 11 03:22:52: RIP: sending v2 update to 224.0.0.9 via Ethernet0 (192.168.1.1)
Oct 11 03:22:52: RIP: Update contains 8 routes
Oct 11 03:22:52: RIP: Update queued
Oct 11 03:22:52: RIP: sending v2 update to 224.0.0.9 via Ethernet1 (192.168.4.1)
Oct 11 03:22:52: RIP: Update sent via Ethernet0
Oct 11 03:22:52: RIP: Update contains 5 routes
Oct 11 03:22:52: RIP: Update queued
Oct 11 03:22:52: RIP: sending v2 update to 224.0.0.9 via Serial0 (10.1.1.1)
Oct 11 03:22:52: RIP: Update sent via Ethernet1
Oct 11 03:22:52: RIP: Update contains 8 routes!
Oct 11 03:22:52: RIP: Update queued
Oct 11 03:22:52: RIP: sending v2 update to 224.0.0.9 via Serial1 (192.168.2.1)
Oct 11 03:22:52: RIP: Update sent via Serial0
Oct 11 03:22:52: RIP: Update contains 4 routes
Oct 11 03:22:52: RIP: Update queued
Oct 11 03:22:52: RIP: Update sent via Serial1
Oct 11 03:22:59: RIP: received v2 update from 192.168.2.2 on Serial1
Oct 11 03:22:59: RIP: Update contains 5 routes
Oct 11 03:23:02: RIP: received v2 update from 192.168.4.2 on Ethernet1
Oct 11 03:23:02: RIP: Update contains 4 routes
r1#!!!now I will unplug the r2s1 cable
r1#
Oct 11 03:23:14: RIP: received v2 update from 192.168.2.2 on Serial1
Oct 11 03:23:14: RIP: Update contains 5 routes
Oct 11 03:23:14: RIP: received v2 update from 192.168.4.2 on Ethernet1
Oct 11 03:23:14: RIP: Update contains 4 routes
Oct 11 03:23:14: RIP: sending v2 update to 224.0.0.9 via Ethernet0 (192.168.1.1)
Oct 11 03:23:14: RIP: Update contains 8 routes
Oct 11 03:23:14: RIP: Update queued
...
r1#show ip route
...
C    192.168.4.0/24 is directly connected, Ethernet1
R    192.168.5.0/24 is possibly down, routing via 192.168.4.2, Ethernet1
     10.0.0.0/8 is variably subnetted, 3 subnets, 2 masks
R       10.2.2.0/24 [120/1] via 192.168.2.2, 00:00:10, Serial1
R       10.0.0.0/8 [120/2] via 192.168.4.2, 00:00:07, Ethernet1
C       10.1.1.0/24 is directly connected, Serial0
R    192.168.6.0/24 [120/1] via 192.168.4.2, 00:00:07, Ethernet1
                    [120/1] via 192.168.2.2, 00:00:11, Serial1
C    192.168.1.0/24 is directly connected, Ethernet0
C    192.168.2.0/24 is directly connected, Serial1
R    192.168.3.0/24 [120/1] via 192.168.2.2, 00:00:11, Serial1
```

Plug the cable back in, continue to review the results, and turn off all debug activity, as in Example 3-36.

Example 3-36 *Plug the Cable Back In and Observe the Results*

```
r1#!!!now I will plug the cable back in
...
r1#show ip route
C    192.168.4.0/24 is directly connected, Ethernet1
R    192.168.5.0/24 is possibly down, routing via 192.168.4.2, Ethernet1
     10.0.0.0/8 is variably subnetted, 3 subnets, 2 masks
R       10.2.2.0/24 [120/1] via 192.168.2.2, 00:00:13, Serial1
...
Oct 11 03:26:16: RIP: received v2 update from 192.168.4.2 on Ethernet1
Oct 11 03:26:16: RIP: Update contains 4 routes
Oct 11 03:26:16: RIP: sending v2 update to 224.0.0.9 via Ethernet0 (192.168.1.1)
Oct 11 03:26:16: RIP: Update contains 8 routes
Oct 11 03:26:16: RIP: Update queued
Oct 11 03:26:16: RIP: sending v2 update to 224.0.0.9 via Ethernet1 (192.168.4.1)
Oct 11 03:26:16: RIP: Update sent via Ethernet0
Oct 11 03:26:16: RIP: Update contains 5 routes
Oct 11 03:26:16: RIP: Update queued
…
r1#show ip route
...
C    192.168.4.0/24 is directly connected, Ethernet1
R    192.168.5.0/24 [120/1] via 192.168.4.2, 00:00:04, Ethernet1
     10.0.0.0/8 is variably subnetted, 3 subnets, 2 masks
R       10.2.2.0/24 [120/1] via 192.168.2.2, 00:00:07, Serial1
R       10.0.0.0/8 [120/2] via 192.168.4.2, 00:00:04, Ethernet1
C       10.1.1.0/24 is directly connected, Serial0
R    192.168.6.0/24 [120/1] via 192.168.4.2, 00:00:04, Ethernet1
                    [120/1] via 192.168.2.2, 00:00:07, Serial1
C    192.168.1.0/24 is directly connected, Ethernet0
C    192.168.2.0/24 is directly connected, Serial1
R    192.168.3.0/24 [120/1] via 192.168.2.2, 00:00:07, Serial1
r1#undebug all
```

Fix any issues before you continue. If you cannot see the debug output when you telnet in, you may need to turn on **terminal monitor** (**term mon**). In this example, I did not show the output of the interface status on r2, but that is pretty important in troubleshooting such issues. Repeat the example as necessary or log it for future reference.

See Figure 3-24 or look at one of your Sniffer traces to analyze the RIP packet format. Up to 25 destinations can be listed in a single packet. Next I discuss the Cisco proprietary routing protocols IGRP and EIGRP.

IGRP/EIGRP

Interior Gateway Routing Protocol (IGRP) was developed in the mid-1980s as a *Cisco proprietary* protocol to help overcome some of limitations of RIP, such as the single metric of hop count. It has stability features similar to RIP—hold-down timers, split horizon, poison reverse, and triggered updates. The timers are as follows: invalid 270 seconds, holddown 280 seconds, and flush 630 seconds. It also contains mechanisms to influence route selection and unequal load sharing. I use the phrase **B**ig **D**ogs **R**eally **L**ike **M**eat to remember the metrics for IGRP and EIGRP:

- **B**andwidth
- **D**elay
- **R**eliability
- **L**oad
- **M**TU

IGRP is an IGP, a distance vector routing protocol based on the Bellman-Ford algorithm that broadcasts routing updates every 90 seconds over IP protocol number 9. It is fine for small and medium-size networks, but Cisco enhanced it greatly and added VLSM support to its replacement, EIGRP.

Cisco developed Enhanced IGRP (EIGRP) in the early 1990s to overcome limitations of RIP and its own IGRP. Cisco says IGRP is going to be removed from IOS. EIGRP is suitable for large networks today and supports multiple routed protocols. It consumes significantly less bandwidth because of its partial, bounded updates, and can be one of the fastest converging routing protocols there is.

The following are EIGRP characteristics:

- Cisco proprietary protocol.
- Good for small to large networks.
- Very easy to configure. Uses autonomous system (AS) number.
- Supports multiple Layer 3 routed protocol stacks, such as IP, Novell IPX, and AppleTalk.
- Advanced distance vector routing protocol. Often called a hybrid due to its incremental updates and rapid convergence capabilities.
- IGP.
- Multicast triggered updates over 224.0.0.10, not periodic.
- IP protocol number 88.
- Internal administrative distance is 90; external is 170.
- Metrics are bandwidth, delay, reliability, load, and MTU.
- Supports equal- and unequal-cost load sharing.
- Other stability features to assist with routing loops:

— **Split horizon**—Not useful to send information about a route back in the direction from which it came

— **Poison reverse**—Updates that are sent to remove a route and place it in holddown

- Uses Diffusing Update algorithm (DUAL) to select loop-free paths and give it very fast convergence.

- Supports VLSM and manual summarization (classless).

- Automatic classful boundary summarization.

- Manual summarization on update sent out each interface.

- Automatic redistribution with IGRP if same AS number.

- Route tagging for policy-based routing.

EIGRP gets its reliability from the Reliable Transport Protocol (RTP). It maintains not only a routing table, but also a neighbor and topology table. EIGRP maintains alternate routes referred to as successors (routing table) and feasible successors (topology table) to quickly converge. The following packet types are used for neighbor communications: hellos (multicast) and acks (unicast), update (multicast or unicast), query (multicast), reply (unicast), and request (multicast or unicast). Packets are held in a queue for retransmission, and there are separate neighbor tables (and entirely separate processes) for each protocol.

Cisco has some wonderful white papers on EIGRP that you should download and review to assist you with troubleshooting. Other popular references include the book *EIGRP Network Design Solutions* (Cisco Press). Just remember when troubleshooting EIGRP, active *ain't* good, but passive is. Active means that you are actively looking for something that you don't have. Pay particular attention to summarization when you are experiencing stuck-in-active situations. Besides the basic IOS commands in your repertoire, you should add **show ip eigrp ?** and **debug ip eigrp ?** for your EIGRP IP troubleshooting assistance. Next I very briefly review OSPF, IS-IS, and BGP. You will continue to configure, analyze, and troubleshoot the convergence of these protocols over various Layer 2 technologies throughout the rest of this book.

OSPF

Open Shortest Path First (OSPF) overcomes the disadvantages of RIP and is not proprietary in nature, but its openness supports only the IP routed protocol. The protocol is a link-state IGP based on the Dijkstra algorithm developed by the Internet Engineering Task Force (IETF) to support large heterogeneous networks. Lots of research was completed from 1987 until the current OSPFv2 specification in 1991. Link-state advertisements are sent to all, which causes an initial flood on the router; after that, however, OSPF is very efficient in operation. It uses three different databases (tables) for the neighbors, link states, and routes.

The following are OSPF characteristics:

- Open protocol.

- Good for small to large networks.

- Not as easy to design and configure as other protocols.

- Supports only the IP Layer 3 routed protocol stack.

- Link-state routing protocol (doesn't just send to neighbors like distance vector).

- IGP.

- Multicast link-state advertisement (LSA) updates over 224.0.0.5 and 224.0.0.6.

- IP protocol number 89.

- Administrative distance is 110.

- Metric is a cumulative cost (inversely proportional to bandwidth).

- Supports only equal-cost load sharing, but some implementations can take advantage of type of service (TOS) requests.

- Requires a routing hierarchy in that every area must touch the backbone area (otherwise temporary fixes such as virtual links are used). Various router types, LSA types, area types, and states, depending on your design and Layer 2 topology.

- Uses Dijkstra algorithm to select loop-free paths and give it fast convergence. This uses LSAs and is based on the Shortest Path First (SPF) algorithm, where the protocol got its name.

- Supports VLSM and summarization (classless).

- Supports manual summarization only; this is not automatic like EIGRP. Must be performed on an ABR (area range) or ASBR (summary address) only.

- Route tagging for policy-based routing.

Besides the basic IOS commands in your repertoire, you should add **show ip ospf ?** and **debug ip ospf ?** for your OSPF troubleshooting assistance.

OSPF references include the books *OSPF Network Design Solutions* (Cisco Press) and *OSPF: Anatomy of an Internet Routing Protocol* (Addison-Wesley). John Moy is the author of the latter, and if you truly want the RFC detail, this is the book to read. Next take a look at IS-IS.

IS-IS

The ISO was working on Intermediate System-to-Intermediate System (IS-IS) about the same time the IAB was working on OSPF. The late 1980s and early 1990s, a time in our history when everyone thought the OSI suite would overtake TCP/IP, was when Integrated IS-IS was proposed. Although originally designed for OSI routing, IS-IS was developed by ISO to support

CLNS/CLNP. Integrated IS-IS, which supports IP, was a later development. The purpose was to provide a single routing protocol that could route Connectionless Network Protocol (CLNS) and IP. IS-IS is in use by ISPs today. OSPF and IS-IS have many common features.

The following are IS-IS characteristics:

- Open protocol.
- Good for medium to very large networks.
- ISO link-state routing protocol similar to OSPF.
- IGP.
- IS-IS Layer 2 PDUs rather than IP packets.
- Uses Layer 2 multicast.
- Administrative distance is 115.
- Very limited metric dynamic range (0–63).
- Equal-cost load sharing.
- Two-level hierarchical topology.
- Uses Dijkstra/SPF algorithm.
- Supports VLSM and summarization.
- Manual summarization.
- Route tagging for policy-based routing.

Besides the basic IOS commands in your repertoire, you should add **show is-is ?**, **show clns ?**, and **debug is-is ?** for your IS-IS troubleshooting assistance.

Jeff Doyle's *Routing TCP/IP*, Volume I does a good job of explaining many topics, including IS-IS. Volume II is great for BGP, as is Sam Halabi's *Internet Routing Architecture*s.

BGP

Border Gateway Protocol (BGP) is an EGP that pretty much replaces the legacy EGP protocol itself. BGP performs routing between autonomous systems and is the standard routing protocol on the Internet. This is referred to as External BGP (EBGP), whereas when BGP is used to route within an AS it is referred to as Interior (IBGP). BGP is not a routing protocol for the fainthearted. It requires all manual configurations for a very good reason; you are not only affecting you, but you are also affecting me. For troubleshooting BGP, if routes are not in the BGP table, there is no way they will be in the routing table. Always make sure your neighbors are talking to you. One of the most useful commands in troubleshooting BGP is **show ip bgp summary**.

The following are BGP characteristics:

- Open protocol.

- Good for very large internetworks.

- Not as easy to design and configure as other protocols. Everything is manual, including neighbors (peers).

- Advanced distance vector or path vector routing protocol.

- EGP.

- TCP port 179.

- Internal administrative distance is 200; external is 20.

- Metrics include many attributes such as MED, Origin, AS-Path, Next-hop, and Community.

- Does not demand a particular routing hierarchy; roll your own.

- Automatic and manual summarization features.

- Route tagging for policy-based routing.

Besides the basic IOS commands in your repertoire, you should add **show ip bgp ?** and **debug ip bgp ?** for your BGP troubleshooting assistance. Remember that BGP is an EGP and that what you do affects others. ISPs often turn on dampening to account for those who really don't know what they are doing with BGP configuration or to compensate for link flaps. Too many changes within a certain period of time may mean that you don't get to communicate at all.

Individual routing protocols are books in themselves. However, I have quickly summarized the common routing protocols for you. The routing table is a good place to start troubleshooting, but if routes are missing, ultimately they may depend on Physical Layer or Data Link Layer issues, neighbor relationships, and topology or link-state tables. Cisco does a great job at categorizing more specific IP routing issues for you (see Figure 3-33).

Figure 3-33 *IP Routing Top Issues*

NOTE   Refer back to Chapter 1, Table 1-3, for a quick comparison of routing protocols.

Now it is time for the Trouble Tickets. The plan here is to give you several things to do, let you make mistakes and fix some things on your own, and to introduce other problems that you should have some experience with as a support person. Shooting trouble with IP can easily be a multiple-volume set of books in itself. Because it is a big part of troubleshooting today, I also integrate more IP-related issues into the other chapters.

NOTE   Do *not* **write erase** your routers and start from scratch. Whether it is now or later, you will learn from your own mistakes. In the real world, many times I find it easier to just start from scratch if things differ that much. In many cases, you do not have that luxury—for what you change on a router affects not just one person, but many others, and change control is a definite must.

Trouble Tickets

Complete the following Trouble Tickets in order. Use the tools from this and the preceding chapters to analyze, test, and document as you go. Feel free to create your own Physical Layer problems if you need more practice there. Sample solutions are provided after this section.

Trouble Ticket 1

Quickly review your existing configurations and copy them to a TFTP server as r1-rip2, r2-rip2, r3-rip2, r4-rip2, and r5-rip2 so that you can use them again later.

Trouble Ticket 2

Draw a new Chapter 3 scenario diagram and label the address ranges and interfaces per your calculations in Figure 3-27. Leave the links to r4 and r5 numbered as they are.

Trouble Ticket 3

Re-address the network using your new diagram. Remove RIP and save your configurations.

Trouble Ticket 4

Change the routing protocol from RIP to EIGRP using an AS number of choice. Verify routing processes, protocols, and that you have the correct information in each routing table. Disconnect and reconnect the r1s1 cable and experiment a bit.

Trouble Ticket 5

Ping and trace from hosta to hostc and capture the results. Save all configurations and verify everything before you continue. Quickly review your configurations and copy them to a TFTP server as r1-eigrp, r2-eigrp, r3-eigrp, r4-eigrp, and r5-eigrp so that you can use them again later.

Trouble Ticket 6 (Optional)

Set up an access list to allow only hosta to telnet to r1. The other hosts should not be able to telnet, but should be able to ping or trace. Apply and test the ACL. Leave the ACL configuration, but remove the application of it from the interface after you verify that it works.

Trouble Ticket 7 (Optional)

Set up one of your clients for DHCP to capture and analyze the Discover, Offers, Request, and Acknowledgement frames.

NOTE   Trouble Tickets 6 and 7 are optional bonus exercises because there will be plenty of opportunity to perform similar tests later in the book. Trouble Tickets 6 and 7 are for you to work through on your own and do not have a solution provided.

Trouble Tickets Solutions

These solutions are not always the only way to perform these tasks. However, the upcoming chapter scenarios are based on these solutions.

Trouble Ticket 1 Solution

I reviewed and copied my existing configurations to my TFTP server as rx-rip2, where I replaced *x* for each router number. In Example 3-37, I performed a simple ping first to make sure I had connectivity to the TFTP server, and then copied the files. You may want to tweak the configuration of your TFTP server to place the files in the location you prefer for easy access later. You should also get familiar with how your particular TFTP server handles files that already exist. For example, you may want to have it prompt you as to what to do if the files already exist. The answer shows the output for r1 only, but this was performed from each router.

Example 3-37 *Copying Existing Configurations to a TFTP Server*

```
r1#ping 192.168.1.11
Type escape sequence to abort.
Sending 5, 100-byte ICMP Echos to 192.168.1.11, timeout is 2 seconds:
.!!!!
Success rate is 80 percent (4/5), round-trip min/avg/max = 1/3/4 ms
r1#copy running-config tftp
Address or name of remote host []? 192.168.1.11
Destination filename [running-config]? r1-rip2
!!
1169 bytes copied in 5.680 secs (233 bytes/sec)
r1#
```

Trouble Ticket 2 Solution

Figure 3-34 displays the new addressing scheme that I used as a guide for configurations in the examples to follow.

Figure 3-34 *Trouble Tickets Scenario*

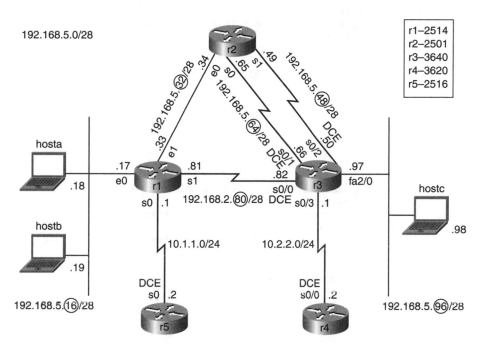

Trouble Ticket 3 Solution

I used Figure 3-34 as a guide to re-address the network. Example 3-38 shows a few problems I had when re-addressing the interfaces. I could have typed **no ip address** on each interface to remove the old one before I started, but then you may not have realized the overlapping problems. While on each router, I also issued **no router rip** to quickly remove the RIP routing protocol commands. A quick test after the configuration is to perform **show ip interface brief** to verify the configuration against the drawing.

NOTE   Although I did not shut my interfaces down before and after configuring them, that is certainly the best practice to do so.

Example 3-38 *Re-Addressing and Removing RIP*

```
r1(config)#interface e0
r1(config-if)#ip address 192.168.5.17 255.255.255.240
r1(config-if)#interface e1
r1(config-if)#ip address 192.168.5.33 255.255.255.240
r1(config-if)#interface s1
r1(config-if)#ip add 192.168.5.81 255.255.255.240
r1(config-if)#no router rip
r1(config)#end
r1#copy running-config startup-config

r2(config)#interface e0
r2(config-if)#ip address 192.168.5.34 255.255.255.240
192.168.5.32 overlaps with Serial1
r2(config-if)#interface s1
r2(config-if)#ip address 192.168.5.49 255.255.255.240
r2(config-if)#interface e0
r2(config-if)#ip address 192.168.5.34 255.255.255.240
r2(config-if)#interface s0
r2(config-if)#ip address 192.168.5.65 255.255.255.240
r2(config-if)#no router rip
r2(config)#end
r2#copy running-config startup-config

r3(config)#interface s0/0
r3(config-if)#ip address 192.168.5.82 255.255.255.240
192.168.5.80 overlaps with Serial0/2
r3(config-if)#interface s0/2
r3(config-if)#ip address 192.168.5.50 255.255.255.0
r3(config-if)#interface s0/0
r3(config-if)#ip address 192.168.5.82 255.255.255.240
192.168.5.80 overlaps with Serial0/2
r3(config-if)#interface s0/2
r3(config-if)#ip address 192.168.5.50 255.255.255.240
r3(config-if)#interface s0/0
r3(config-if)#ip address 192.168.5.82 255.255.255.240
r3(config-if)#interface s0/1
r3(config-if)#ip address 192.168.5.66 255.255.255.240
r3(config-if)#interface fa2/0
r3(config-if)#ip address 192.168.5.97 255.255.255.240
r3(config-if)#no router rip
r3(config)#end
r3#copy running-config startup-config
r4(config)#no router rip
r4(config)#end
r4#copy running-config startup-config
r5(config)#no router rip
r5(config)#end
r5#copy running-config startup-config

r1#show ip interface brief
Interface          IP-Address      OK? Method Status              Protocol
Ethernet0          192.168.5.17    YES manual up                  up
Ethernet1          192.168.5.33    YES manual up                  up
Serial0            10.1.1.1        YES NVRAM  up                  up
Serial1            192.168.5.81    YES manual up                  up
```

Example 3-38 *Re-Addressing and Removing RIP (Continued)*

```
r2#show ip interface brief
Interface              IP-Address       OK? Method Status          Protocol
Ethernet0              192.168.5.34     YES manual up              up
Serial0                192.168.5.65     YES manual up              up
Serial1                192.168.5.49     YES manual up              up
r3#show ip interface brief
Interface              IP-Address       OK? Method Status          Protocol
Serial0/0              192.168.5.82     YES manual up              up
Serial0/1              192.168.5.66     YES manual up              up
Serial0/2              192.168.5.50     YES manual up              up
Serial0/3              10.2.2.1         YES NVRAM  up              up
...
FastEthernet2/0        192.168.5.97     YES manual up              up
```

Trouble Ticket 4 Solution

Example 3-39 starts the EIGRP configuration and testing. I used AS number 500 for my test and saved my configurations as I went along. Notice in Example 3-39 how I configured 10.1.1.0 and 10.2.2.0. **show running-config** shows 10.0.0.0. EIGRP is relatively easy to configure, but remember that it is proprietary.

Example 3-39 *EIGRP Configuration*

```
r1(config)#router eigrp 500
r1(config-router)#network 192.168.5.0
r1(config-router)#network 10.1.1.0
r1(config-router)#end
r1#copy running-config startup-config
r2(config)#router eigrp 500
r2(config-router)#network 192.168.5.0
r2(config-router)#end
r2#copy running-config startup-config
r3(config)#router eigrp 500
r3(config-router)#network 192.168.5.0
r3(config-router)#network 10.2.2.0
r3(config-router)#end
r3#copy running-config startup-config
r4(config)#router eigrp 500
r4(config-router)#network 10.2.2.0
r4(config-router)#end
r4#copy running-config startup-config
r5(config)#router eigrp 500
r5(config-router)#network 10.1.1.0
r5(config-router)#end
r5#copy running-config startup-config
r5#show running-config
...
router eigrp 500
 network 10.0.0.0
!
ip classless
!
...
end
```

Example 3-40 illustrates **show ip protocols** and **show ip route** to verify EIGRP parameters and routes. You should verify every router; I have listed only the first one. The EIGRP learned routes are shown with a *D*, whereas RIP represented them with an *R*. It is important to note how EIGRP automatically summarizes on the classful boundary.

Example 3-40 *EIGRP Testing with* **show ip protocols** *and* **show ip route**

```
r1>show ip protocols
Routing Protocol is "eigrp 500"
  Outgoing update filter list for all interfaces is not set
  Incoming update filter list for all interfaces is not set
  Default networks flagged in outgoing updates
  Default networks accepted from incoming updates
  EIGRP metric weight K1=1, K2=0, K3=1, K4=0, K5=0
  EIGRP maximum hopcount 100
  EIGRP maximum metric variance 1
  Redistributing: eigrp 500
  Automatic network summarization is in effect
  Automatic address summarization:
    10.0.0.0/8 for Ethernet0, Ethernet1, Serial1
      Summarizing with metric 40512000
    192.168.5.0/24 for Serial0
      Summarizing with metric 281600
  Routing for Networks:
    10.0.0.0
    192.168.5.0
  Routing Information Sources:
    Gateway         Distance      Last Update
    (this router)          5      00:16:31
    10.1.1.2              90      00:15:44
    192.168.5.82          90      00:16:31
    Gateway         Distance      Last Update
    192.168.5.34          90      00:16:32
  Distance: internal 90 external 170
r1>show ip route
Codes: C - connected, S - static, I - IGRP, R - RIP, M - mobile, B - BGP
       D - EIGRP, EX - EIGRP external, O - OSPF, IA - OSPF inter area
       N1 - OSPF NSSA external type 1, N2 - OSPF NSSA external type 2
       E1 - OSPF external type 1, E2 - OSPF external type 2, E - EGP
       i - IS-IS, L1 - IS-IS level-1, L2 - IS-IS level-2, * - candidate default
       U - per-user static route, o - ODR
Gateway of last resort is not set
     192.168.5.0/24 is variably subnetted, 7 subnets, 2 masks
D       192.168.5.96/28 [90/40514560] via 192.168.5.82, 00:16:37, Serial1
D       192.168.5.64/28 [90/40537600] via 192.168.5.34, 00:16:37, Ethernet1
C       192.168.5.80/28 is directly connected, Serial1
C       192.168.5.32/28 is directly connected, Ethernet1
D       192.168.5.48/28 [90/40537600] via 192.168.5.34, 00:16:37, Ethernet1
D       192.168.5.0/24 is a summary, 00:18:11, Null0
C       192.168.5.16/28 is directly connected, Ethernet0
     10.0.0.0/8 is variably subnetted, 2 subnets, 2 masks
D       10.0.0.0/8 is a summary, 00:16:37, Null0
C       10.1.1.0/24 is directly connected, Serial0
```

NOTE   Think about the routing table issues as you work through some common EIGRP troubleshooting commands.

Example 3-41 further explores EIGRP with some EIGRP-specific IOS debug commands. I disconnected the r1S1 cable after turning on a pretty explicit command for you to see the EIGRP packet and update process. After looking at the routing table, I plugged the cable back in and explored some of the EIGRP show and logging commands that are quite helpful in troubleshooting in Example 3-42.

Example 3-41   *Experimenting with EIGRP Troubleshooting Tools*

```
r1#debug eigrp ?
  fsm        EIGRP Dual Finite State Machine events/actions
  neighbors  EIGRP neighbors
  packets    EIGRP packets
  transmit   EIGRP transmission events
r1#debug eigrp transmit
EIGRP Transmission Events debugging is on
    (ACK, PACKETIZE, STARTUP, PEERDOWN, LINK, BUILD, STRANGE, DETAIL)
01:21:06: %LINK-3-UPDOWN: Interface Serial1, changed state to down
01:21:06: DNDB QUERY 192.168.5.80/28, serno 3 to 16, refcount 3
01:21:06:   Anchoring Serial0, starting Serial0 timer
01:21:06:   Anchoring Ethernet1, starting Ethernet1 timer
01:21:06:   Anchoring Serial1, starting Serial1 timer
01:21:06: Peer 192.168.5.82 going down
01:21:06: DNDB QUERY 192.168.5.96/28, serno 15 to 17, refcount 3
01:21:06: Last peer deleted from Serial1
01:21:06:   Dropping refcount on 192.168.5.80/28, refcount now 2
01:21:06:   Dropping refcount on 192.168.5.96/28, refcount now 2
01:21:06: Packetizing timer expired on Serial0
01:21:06: Packets pending on Serial0
01:21:06: Intf Serial0 packetized QUERY 16-17
01:21:06:   Interface is now quiescent
01:21:06: Building multicast QUERY packet for Serial0, serno 16-17
01:21:06:   Items:  U16 U17
01:21:06: Packetizing timer expired on Ethernet1
01:21:06: Packets pending on Ethernet1
01:21:06: Intf Ethernet1 packetized QUERY 16-17
01:21:06:   Interface is now quiescent
01:21:06: Building multicast QUERY packet for Ethernet1, serno 16-17
01:21:06:   Items:  16 17
01:21:06: Packetizing timer expired on Serial1
01:21:06: Packet acked from 192.168.5.34 (Ethernet1), serno 16-17
01:21:06: Flow blocking cleared on Ethernet1
01:21:06: Multicast acked from Ethernet1, serno 16-17
01:21:06:   Found serno 16, refcount now 1
01:21:06:   Found serno 17, refcount now 1
01:21:06: Packet acked from 10.1.1.2 (Serial0), serno 16-17
01:21:06: Flow blocking cleared on Serial0
...
```

continues

Example 3-41 *Experimenting with EIGRP Troubleshooting Tools (Continued)*

```
01:21:07: %LINEPROTO-5-UPDOWN: Line protocol on Interface Serial1,
       changed state to down
r1#show ip route
...
     192.168.5.0/24 is variably subnetted, 6 subnets, 2 masks
D       192.168.5.96/28 [90/40540160] via 192.168.5.34, 00:00:12, Ethernet1
D       192.168.5.64/28 [90/40537600] via 192.168.5.34, 00:32:10, Ethernet1
C       192.168.5.32/28 is directly connected, Ethernet1
D       192.168.5.48/28 [90/40537600] via 192.168.5.34, 00:32:10, Ethernet1
D       192.168.5.0/24 is a summary, 00:33:44, Null0
C       192.168.5.16/28 is directly connected, Ethernet0
     10.0.0.0/8 is variably subnetted, 2 subnets, 2 masks
D       10.0.0.0/8 is a summary, 00:32:11, Null0
C       10.1.1.0/24 is directly connected, Serial0
01:21:38: %LINK-3-UPDOWN: Interface Serial1, changed state to up
01:21:38: DNDB UPDATE 192.168.5.80/28, serno 0 to 20, refcount 2
01:21:38:    Anchoring Serial0, starting Serial0 timer
01:21:38:    Anchoring Ethernet1, starting Ethernet1 timer
01:21:38: Packetizing timer expired on Serial0
01:21:38: Packets pending on Serial0
01:21:38: Intf Serial0 packetized UPDATE 20-20
01:21:38:    Interface is now quiescent
01:21:38: Building multicast UPDATE packet for Serial0, serno 20-20
01:21:38:    Items:  S20
01:21:38:    Suppressed.
...
01:21:38: Building startup packet for 192.168.5.82, serno 1-20
01:21:38:    Items:  1 2 S4 S5 6 7 8 19 S20
01:21:39: %LINEPROTO-5-UPDOWN: Line protocol on Interface Serial1,
       changed state to up
01:21:40: Building startup packet for 192.168.5.82, serno 1-20
01:21:40:    Items:  1 2 S4 S5 6 7 8 19 S20
01:21:42: DNDB UPDATE 192.168.5.96/28, serno 19 to 21, refcount 3
01:21:42:    Anchoring Serial1, starting Serial1 timer
01:21:42:    Anchoring Ethernet1, starting Ethernet1 timer
01:21:42:    Anchoring Serial0, starting Serial0 timer
01:21:42: Packetizing timer expired on Serial1
01:21:42: Packets pending on Serial1
01:21:42: Intf Serial1 packetized UPDATE 21-21
r1#show ip route
...
     192.168.5.0/24 is variably subnetted, 7 subnets, 2 masks
D       192.168.5.96/28 [90/40514560] via 192.168.5.82, 00:00:04, Serial1
D       192.168.5.64/28 [90/40537600] via 192.168.5.34, 00:00:04, Ethernet1
C       192.168.5.80/28 is directly connected, Serial1
C       192.168.5.32/28 is directly connected, Ethernet1
D       192.168.5.48/28 [90/40537600] via 192.168.5.34, 00:00:04, Ethernet1
D       192.168.5.0/24 is a summary, 00:34:12, Null0
C       192.168.5.16/28 is directly connected, Ethernet0
     10.0.0.0/8 is variably subnetted, 2 subnets, 2 masks
D       10.0.0.0/8 is a summary, 00:00:04, Null0
C       10.1.1.0/24 is directly connected, Serial0
r1#undebug all
```

Example 3-42   *Troubleshooting Using EIGRP Show Commands*

```
r1#show ip eigrp ?
  interfaces  IP-EIGRP interfaces
  neighbors   IP-EIGRP neighbors
  topology    IP-EIGRP Topology Table
  traffic     IP-EIGRP Traffic Statistics
r1#show ip eigrp neighbors
IP-EIGRP neighbors for process 500
H   Address                 Interface    Hold Uptime   SRTT   RTO  Q  Seq
                                         (sec)         (ms)       Cnt Num
1   192.168.5.82            Se1          12 00:01:15   24   2280  0  38
2   10.1.1.2                Se0          14 00:33:05   44   2280  0  3
0   192.168.5.34            Et1          10 00:34:23   25    200  0  35
r1#show ip eigrp interfaces
IP-EIGRP interfaces for process 500
                   Xmit Queue   Mean   Pacing Time   Multicast    Pending
Interface   Peers  Un/Reliable  SRTT   Un/Reliable   Flow Timer   Routes
Et0         0      0/0          0      0/10          0            0
Et1         1      0/0          25     0/10          108          0
Se1         1      0/0          24     10/380        380          0
Se0         1      0/0          44     10/380        556          0
r1#show ip eigrp topology ?
  <1-65535>        AS Number
  A.B.C.D          Network to display information about
  active           Show only active entries
  all-links        Show all links in topology table
  pending          Show only entries pending transmission
  summary          Show a summary of the topology table
  zero-successors  Show only zero successor entries
  <cr>
r1#show ip eigrp topology active
IP-EIGRP Topology Table for process 500
```

The next two commands are very useful for EIGRP troubleshooting. Turn them on and note the output (as I do in Example 3-43). To force some changes, I issued a **no shut** on r1s1 to see a neighbor change. I brought that interface back up, turned off the neighbor changes, and turned on the neighbor warnings. Then I went to r2 to bounce (**shut/no shut**) the Ethernet 0 interface to observe the results.

Example 3-43   *EIGRP Logging*

```
r1(config)#router eigrp 500
r1(config-router)#eigrp ?
  log-neighbor-changes   Enable/Disable IP-EIGRP neighbor logging
  log-neighbor-warnings  Enable/Disable IP-EIGRP neighbor warnings
r1(config-router)#eigrp log-neighbor-changes
r1(config-router)#end
...
r1(config)#interface s1
r1(config-if)#shut
01:42:34: %DUAL-5-NBRCHANGE: IP-EIGRP 500: Neighbor 192.168.5.82 (Serial1) is
    down: interface down
```

continues

Example 3-43   *EIGRP Logging (Continued)*

```
01:42:36: %LINK-5-CHANGED: Interface Serial1, changed state to
    administratively down
01:42:37: %LINEPROTO-5-UPDOWN: Line protocol on Interface Serial1,
    changed state to down
r1(config-if)#no shut
01:42:54: %LINK-3-UPDOWN: Interface Serial1, changed state to up
01:42:55: %LINEPROTO-5-UPDOWN: Line protocol on Interface Serial1,
    changed state to up
01:42:56: %DUAL-5-NBRCHANGE: IP-EIGRP 500: Neighbor 192.168.5.82 (Serial1) is
    up: new adjacency
r1(config-if)#exit
r1(config)#router eigrp 500
r1(config-router)#no eigrp log-neighbor-changes
r1(config-router)#eigrp log-neighbor-warnings
r1(config-router)#exit
r1(config)#interface s1
r1(config-if)#shut
01:43:33: %DUAL-5-NBRCHANGE: IP-EIGRP 500: Neighbor 192.168.5.82 (Serial1) is
    down: interface down
01:43:35: %LINK-5-CHANGED: Interface Serial1, changed state to
    administratively down
01:43:36: %LINEPROTO-5-UPDOWN: Line protocol on Interface Serial1,
    changed state to down
r1(config-if)#no shut
r2(config)#interface e0
r2(config-if)#shut
r1 01:44:30: %DUAL-5-NBRCHANGE: IP-EIGRP 500: Neighbor 192.168.5.34 (Ethernet1) is
    down: holding time expired
r2(config-if)#no shut
r1 01:44:55: %DUAL-5-NBRCHANGE: IP-EIGRP 500: Neighbor 192.168.5.34 (Ethernet1) is
    up: new adjacency
```

Look back through the examples and compare the output of some of the commands to your drawing. There are still issues with EIGRP. Can you spot them? Fix them and continue on to the next Trouble Ticket.

A simple ping test or looking at the routing tables for network 10.0.0.0 should have told you that EIGRP automatically summarizes on the classful boundary. On r1 and r5, for example, you could see 10.1.1.0 but not 10.2.2.0. r3 and r4 displayed 10.2.2.0, but not 10.1.1.0. The fix is in Example 3-44, and the commands are required on r1 and on r3 since they cross network boundaries. Test by displaying the routing table on r2 and ping testing from router to router, although a better test would be from hosta to 10.2.2.2.

Example 3-44   *EIGRP no auto-summary Fix*

```
r2#show ip route
     192.168.5.0/28 is subnetted, 6 subnets
D        192.168.5.96 [90/40514560] via 192.168.5.66, 00:03:35, Serial0
                      [90/40514560] via 192.168.5.50, 00:03:35, Serial1
C        192.168.5.64 is directly connected, Serial0
D        192.168.5.80 [90/40537600] via 192.168.5.33, 00:03:36, Ethernet0
```

Example 3-44 *EIGRP* **no auto-summary** *Fix (Continued)*

```
C        192.168.5.32 is directly connected, Ethernet0
C        192.168.5.48 is directly connected, Serial1
D        192.168.5.16 [90/307200] via 192.168.5.33, 00:03:36, Ethernet0
D     10.0.0.0/8 [90/40537600] via 192.168.5.33, 00:03:36, Ethernet0

r1(config)#router eigrp 500
r1(config-router)#no auto-summary
r1(config-router)#end
r1#copy running-config startup-config
r3(config)#router eigrp 500
r3(config-router)#no auto-summary
r3(config-router)#end
r3#copy running-config startup-config

r2>show ip route
Codes: C - connected, S - static, I - IGRP, R - RIP, M - mobile, B - BGP
       D - EIGRP, EX - EIGRP external, O - OSPF, IA - OSPF inter area
       N1 - OSPF NSSA external type 1, N2 - OSPF NSSA external type 2
       E1 - OSPF external type 1, E2 - OSPF external type 2, E - EGP
       i - IS-IS, L1 - IS-IS level-1, L2 - IS-IS level-2, * - candidate default
       U - per-user static route, o - ODR
Gateway of last resort is not set
     192.168.5.0/28 is subnetted, 6 subnets
D        192.168.5.96 [90/40514560] via 192.168.5.66, 00:00:50, Serial0
                      [90/40514560] via 192.168.5.50, 00:00:50, Serial1
C        192.168.5.64 is directly connected, Serial0
D        192.168.5.80 [90/40537600] via 192.168.5.33, 00:00:50, Ethernet0
C        192.168.5.32 is directly connected, Ethernet0
C        192.168.5.48 is directly connected, Serial1
D        192.168.5.16 [90/307200] via 192.168.5.33, 00:00:50, Ethernet0
     10.0.0.0/24 is subnetted, 2 subnets
D        10.2.2.0 [90/41024000] via 192.168.5.66, 00:00:50, Serial0
                  [90/41024000] via 192.168.5.50, 00:00:50, Serial1
D        10.1.1.0 [90/40537600] via 192.168.5.33, 00:00:51, Ethernet0
r2>
```

Notice how the 10.1.1.0 and 10.2.2.0 subnets now display in the routing table with a *D* in front. Just as with the previous RIPv2 examples, the **no auto-summary** command is critical in a situation such as this in order for EIGRP to support discontiguous subnets. EIGRP enables you to summarize manually on any boundary and interface you so choose.

Trouble Ticket 5 Solution

You should now be able to successfully ping and trace between all your routers. That is great, but the real goal is host-to-host, end-to-end connectivity. See whether you can ping and tracert from hosta to hostc and capture the results. Of course, if you are like me, you may have forgotten to change the IP address information on your hosts. Obviously that is a prerequisite to the rest of this. Table 3-12 shows my host parameters. If you need more help with addresses, masks, and gateways, experiment a little more here by changing one at the time and observing the results. Practice does make perfect! Compare your results to my output in Example 3-45 and Figure 3-35. Also take time to examine how Sniffer displays EIGRP. Remember to save all your configuration files to the TFTP server with the rx-eigrp name format.

Table 3-12 *Trouble Ticket Host Configuration*

	IP Address	Subnet Mask	Gateway
hosta	192.168.5.18	255.255.255.240	192.168.5.17
hostb	192.168.5.19	255.255.255.240	192.168.5.17
hostc	192.168.5.98	255.255.255.240	192.168.5.97

Example 3-45 *Trouble Ticket 5 Ping and Trace Output*

```
C:\>ping 192.168.5.98
Pinging 192.168.5.98 with 32 bytes of data:
Request timed out.
Reply from 192.168.5.98: bytes=32 time=20ms TTL=126
Reply from 192.168.5.98: bytes=32 time=10ms TTL=126
Reply from 192.168.5.98: bytes=32 time=10ms TTL=126
Ping statistics for 192.168.5.98:
    Packets: Sent = 4, Received = 3, Lost = 1 (25% loss),
Approximate round trip times in milli-seconds:
    Minimum = 10ms, Maximum =  20ms, Average =  10ms
C:\>tracert 192.168.5.98
Tracing route to HOSTC [192.168.5.98]
over a maximum of 30 hops:
  1    <10 ms    10 ms    <10 ms   192.168.5.17
  2     20 ms    20 ms     20 ms   192.168.5.82
  3     20 ms    30 ms     30 ms   HOSTC [192.168.5.98]
Trace complete.
```

I captured my file just after I made the change to the hostb IP changes. I started Sniffer upon bootup to capture the Windows 98 client bootup for later review. The file is *chapter 3 eigrp and client initialization traffic sniffer capture*.

The first couple of hundred lines of the Sniffer capture include hostb booting up to the Windows 98 operating system. Starting in line 221, I issued a **ping** and then a **tracert** from hosta to hostc as the output in Example 3-45 depicts. See the EIGRP multicast 224.0.0.10 hello address and IP handing off to EIGRP over protocol number 88.

You have completed the chapter Trouble Tickets when you feel comfortable with the tasks assigned and the various scenarios throughout the chapter. I saved my configurations to the TFTP server and also logged the output of **show running-config** to a file. I did not bother with changing the hosts files, but you certainly can if you so desire. However, I will have you **write erase** in the next chapter anyway.

Figure 3-35 *EIGRP and Client Initialization Traffic*

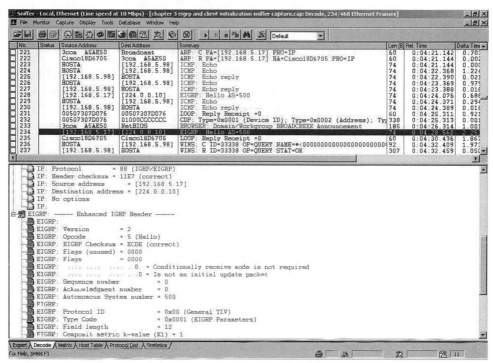

Review or experiment in the areas where you need more help. Understanding and troubleshooting in a simple environment is certainly the foundation for understanding and troubleshooting complex protocols and technologies. Check your understanding with the chapter review questions.

Review Questions

Use this chapter and your practical troubleshooting knowledge and skills to answer the following questions. The answers are located in Appendix A, "Answers to Review Questions."

1 In the RIP scenario, why were you successful with using RIPv2 rather than RIPv1?

2 A Cisco router maintains ARP entries much longer than most PCs. How can you remove all entries from the ARP cache on a Cisco router? It would be less detrimental to all to just remove an entry associated with a given interface. Can you do that on a router? On a Windows-based PC?

3 Draw a table comparing TCP/IP layers, protocols, applications, and utilities to the OSI model.

4   On a Cisco router, **show ip route** displays the routing table. What are the numbers in brackets []?

5   Subnetting, aggregation, VLSM, CIDR, supernetting, and summarization are all about moving bit boundaries. Which one(s) move the network mask bit boundary to the right?

6   Assume you moved into apartment 172.16.3.10 (host address) located at 172.16 Broad Creek Drive (network address). Other floors in the apartment building are numbered 172.16.1.0, 172.16.2.0, and 172.16.4.0. What floor (subnet) are you on? What are all the available hosts on that subnet? What is the directed broadcast address of your subnet?

7   Compare the protocol and port numbers for telnet, RIP, FTP, and TFTP.

8   You can ping by the IP address but not by the hostname. What is a very likely problem?

9   You need to forward DHCP requests to another subnet, but you do not want to forward NetBIOS communications. Is this possible?

10   What IOS command enables you to verify that RIP sends broadcast routing updates? To what address are broadcast updates sent?

11   Using 192.168.5.0/24, address the network according to the following requirements: three LAN segments—one with 125 hosts, one with 50 hosts, and one with 25 hosts—and at least two and maybe more WAN segments.

12   You are having a problem with three subnets connected via two Cisco routers. Each router can ping its own interfaces but can't get to the far side of the other router. So you decide to put in the appropriate default route statement, but things still are not operational. You are not running routing protocols because default routes serve this scenario well. Can you spot the issue?

Summary

Shooting trouble with IP is not just crossing the bridge to get to the beach. As more and more companies are adopting IP-based networks, network engineers and analysts must continue to ensure the internetworks are available, reliable, redundant, responsive, accessible, and secure. Every one of you must understand TCP/IP end-to-end issues and know where to find the right tools and use the proper methods to make the IP world happy. This chapter reviewed IP protocols and packets, addressing, and routing protocol topics to get you started with IP troubleshooting. The next chapter examines IPX and *many other hidden troubleshooting issues*. Then the focus turns to Layer 2 LAN and WAN technologies to continue to build your practical troubleshooting skills.

CHAPTER 4

Shooting Trouble with Novell IPX

Much great networking matter came from Xerox Palo Alto Research Center (PARC). Novell NetWare is no exception; it was derived from Xerox Network Systems (XNS) in the early 1980s. It is a client-server network operating system (NOS) well known for its file and print services.

Cisco routers are found in Novell networks because they offer features not available in Novell's own product implementations. This chapter focuses on common issues in supporting Novell clients, servers, and Cisco routers in a day-to-day practical environment. This chapter assumes knowledge of the previous chapters, which dealt with protocol characteristics, models, troubleshooting methods, support tools, resources, and TCP/IP communications.

Throughout the chapter, you will apply a layered troubleshooting methodology to analyze real-world Novell IPX network issues, such as encapsulation, addressing, protocols, client initialization, and server login including routing and Service Advertisement Protocol (SAP) traffic. You will also identify targets and document the results using IPX ping, show, clear, debug, monitor, config, inetcfg, and other troubleshooting utilities; explore precaptured NetWare-related protocol analyzer files and sniff the network on your own to spot the issues. Analyze, break, fix, and learn from doing is what troubleshooting is all about. Supporting Novell is no different.

This chapter covers the following topics:

- Scenario: Shooting Trouble with IPX
- Protocols and Packets
- Addressing
- Routing Protocols
- Trouble Tickets
- Trouble Tickets Solutions

Supporting Website Files

You can find files and links to utilities that support this book on the Cisco Press website at www.ciscopress.com/1587200570. Even if you do not have a lab, you can take advantage of the supporting configuration files including the logs to understand device input and output. The files are listed throughout the chapters in italics.

In order to be able to read and work with some of the supporting files offered at www.ciscopress.com/1587200570, you may want to download some of the programs listed in Table I-1 in the Introduction.

Scenario: Shooting Trouble with IPX

This chapter starts with the same hands-on scenario you left off with at the Trouble Tickets at the end of the Chapter 3, "Shooting Trouble with IP." Now is a good time to erase your configurations from previous labs and configure the Cisco router portion according to Figure 4-1. Rewiring is not necessary unless you want the practice.

NOTE   Like the preceding chapter, my lab uses the 2514, 2501, 3640, 3620, and 2516 Cisco routers; but yours can include any number of devices that have similar interfaces. See Appendix C, "Equipment Reference," for the hardware used throughout the book.

Figure 4-1 *Shooting Trouble with IPX*

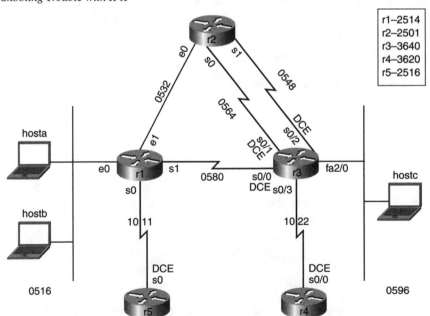

The scenario goal is to configure the routers, servers, and clients using Internetwork Packet Exchange (IPX) as the *routed protocol* and IPX Routing Information Protocol (RIP) as the *routing protocol* to ensure end-to-end connectivity. More importantly, you need to document your steps and *any* problems along the way. Configure the routers starting with r1 first and work your way through r5.

Remember, however, that there is not always one right or wrong way to accomplish the tasks presented. The ability to obtain the end result using good practices is extremely important in any real-world network. Starting in Example 4-1, my troubleshooting and device configurations enable you to compare your work and perhaps see a different approach to obtaining the end result. Refer to Figure 4-1 as you continue to set up and troubleshoot.

Although I give you Figure 4-1, it is really a better practice to draw your own network diagram. Alternatively, use different-colored pens or pencils and add to the IP scenario from the preceding chapter. Label interfaces DCE or DTE and document device names, locations, Layer 2 and Layer 3 addresses, encapsulation types, routed and bridged protocols, access control lists (ACLs), and configuration files. Then verify full connectivity. Perform some simple **ping ipx** tests (as shown in Table 4-1), run **show tech-support**, and document everything. All of this gives you a starting point for normal *baseline* activity when your network is running well. Keep in mind that although NetWare 5.x and 6.x are native IP environments, I want you to concentrate on IPX-related baselining for this chapter.

Table 4-1   *IPX Troubleshooting Checklist*

Isolating Problems	Commands and Symptoms
On the Novell client: Physical cable and NIC Drivers, encapsulation, IPX address, other protocols Client software	**ipxroute config** **ipconfig /all** (if also running IP) **slist** **rconsole** **net config workstation** **net config server** Use protocol analyzer to get addresses Network Neighborhood properties
On the Novell server: Physical cable and NIC Drivers, encapsulation, IPX address, other protocols Server software	**config** **display servers** **display networks** **load monitor** **load inetcfg** **load startup.ncf** **load autoexec.ncf**

continues

Table 4-1   *IPX Troubleshooting Checklist (Continued)*

On the Cisco router: Ping Show Trace Debug Note: *externalipx* is the network number for the wire like an IP subnet number. *internalipx* is the network number internal to the Novell server.	**ipx ping-default ?** **ping ipx** *externalipx.mac-address* **ping ipx** *internalipx*.**0.0.1** **show ipx interface brief** **show run interface e0** **show ipx interface e0** **show interfaces e0** **show ipx servers** **show ipx route** **show protocols** **show ipx cache** **show ipx access-list** **show ipx traffic** **debug ipx routing ?** **debug ipx sap ?** **show tech-support**
NetBIOS, sockets, and name resolution issues	See the IP checklist in Chapter 3

Table 4-1 gives you a layered yet divide-and-conquer approach to quickly spotting IPX client, server, or router issues. Just as with troubleshooting IP, understanding the problem is most of the battle. You may find problems such as workgroup/domain issues, client issues, file and print services issues, protocol issues, primary network login issues, browser service issues, license issues, Directory services issues, socket issues, NetWare Loadable Module (NLM) issues, version issues, application issues, and so on. If you can't communicate with your local router interface, however, it is a little difficult to communicate with a remote host. If you can communicate with one remote host but not another, check the configuration on the other remote host. With NetWare, the client configuration is intentionally very simple. If the client gets the frame type (encapsulation) correct, it will likely work.

NOTE   When shooting Novell trouble, remember to check the following websites for help: Cisco (www.cisco.com/tac), Novell (support.novell.com), Microsoft (www.microsoft.com/technet), and other hardware and software vendors.

Using the Figure 4-1 scenario diagram, configure r1 similar to what is in Example 4-1. Throughout the following examples, I have made a few careless mistakes that you may or may not make. I will troubleshoot them as required or when all my routers are configured. I am using the same terminal server configuration from Example 3-1 in Chapter 3.

NOTE   It is of extreme importance that you know the mode from which the command can be issued. At times I tend to issue global configuration commands in interface mode. This works just fine so long as you don't need help in the midst of the command. If you are unsure, however, type the command from the appropriate mode and make use of the Tab key and ? for help.

Example 4-1   *r1 Configuration (2514)*

```
Router>enable
Router#configure terminal
Router(config)#hostname r1
r1(config)#enable password donna
r1(config)#line vty 0 4
r1(config-line)#login
r1(config-line)#password donna
r1(config-line)#interface serial 0
r1(config-if)#bandwidth 64
r1(config-if)#exit
r1(config)#ipx ?
% Unrecognized command
r1(config)#end
r1#show version
Cisco Internetwork Operating System Software
IOS (tm) 2500 Software (C2500-IS-L), Version 12.0(5), RELEASE SOFTWARE (fc1)
...
System image file is "flash:c2500-i
00:03:53: %SYS-5-CONFIG_I: Configured from console by consoles-1.120-5.bin"
cisco 2500 (68030) processor (revision L) with 2048K/2048K bytes of memory.
...
8192K bytes of processor board System flash (Read ONLY)
Configuration register is 0x2102
```

NOTE   The system file image name ended up with text in the middle of it. This can be quite annoying in practice. Had I turned on **logging synchronous**, things like this would not have been interrupted. You should turn this command on for your configurations.

Obviously, there are some IPX issues with r1. Review the output and in particular the shaded areas. You may or may not have the same types of issues I am having. Hence you may be able to go a little further with your configuration. For now, if you are experiencing difficulty, you should continue on to configure r2 through r5. Actually, I am having similar issues with r2 recognizing IPX, so I moved on to r3 in Example 4-2.

Example 4-2 *r3 Configuration (3640)*

```
Router(config)#hostname r3
r3(config)#enable password donna
r3(config-line)#line vty 0 4
r3(config-line)#login
r3(config-line)#password donna
r3(config-line)#interface serial 0/0
r3(config-if)#bandwidth 64
r3(config-if)#clock rate 64000
r3(config-if)#no shut
r3(config-if)#ipx ?
  access-group      Apply an access list to inbound or outbound packets
  accounting        Enable IPX accounting on this interface
...
  rip-multiplier    Multiple of RIP update interval for aging of RIP routes
rip-response-delay   Delay in answering RIP on this interface
```

Example 4-2 clearly shows that IPX is available and has many options on r3, whereas r1 and r2 both did not recognize IPX commands at all. You could have verified this at either the interface or global configuration mode. Continue to configure IPX on r3 as in Example 4-3 and Figure 4-1.

Example 4-3 *r3 Configuration (3640)*

```
r3(config-if)#ipx network ?
  <1-FFFFFFFD>  IPX network number (default route enabled)
r3(config-if)#ipx network 0580
%Must give "ipx routing" command first
r3(config-if)#exit
r3(config)#ipx routing
r3(config)#interface serial 0/0
r3(config-if)#ipx network 0580
r3(config-if)#no shut
r3(config-if)#interface serial 0/1
r3(config-if)#bandwidth 64
r3(config-if)#clock rate 64000
r3(config-if)#ipx network 0564
r3(config-if)#no shut
r3(config-if)#interface serial 0/2
r3(config-if)#bandwidth 64
r3(config-if)#clock rate 64000
r3(config-if)#ipx network 0548
r3(config-if)#no shut
r3(config-if)#interface fastethernet 2/0
r3(config-if)#ipx network 0596
r3(config-if)#no shut
r3(config-if)#interface serial 0/3
r3(config-if)#bandwidth 64
r3(config-if)#ipx network 1022
r3(config-if)#end
r3#copy running-config startup-config
```

Prior to configuring r4 and r5, take time to quickly review the shaded output in Example 4-3 emphasizing the IPX configuration on r3. The IP routing process is enabled by default, but IPX routing is not. In a practical environment, it is best practice to manually specify a node number for the serial interfaces to enable you to ping the serial interface using a known, predefined IPX node number. This is possible with the command ipx routing [node], where node could be something easy to remember such as 3.3.3 for your serial interfaces. Enabling IPX routing enables IPX RIP by default, as you will verify later with the **show ipx route** command. Quickly view the IPX network numbers, default encapsulation, and link status for r3 in Example 4-4.

Example 4-4   *r3 Configuration (3640)*

```
r3#show ipx interface brief
Interface        IPX Network Encapsulation Status              IPX State
Serial0/0        580         HDLC          down                [up]
Serial0/1        564         HDLC          down                [up]
Serial0/2        548         HDLC          down                [up]
Serial0/3        1022        HDLC          administratively down [up]
Serial0/4        unassigned  not config'd  administratively down n/a
...
Serial1/7        unassigned  not config'd  administratively down n/a
FastEthernet2/0  596         NOVELL-ETHER  up                  [up]
```

Do not be concerned with the down status in Example 4-4 at this point for you really have only configured one router for IPX. Example 4-4 certainly illustrates that Cisco serial links default to High-Level Data Link Control (HDLC) encapsulation and that Ethernet defaults to Novell-Ether encapsulation (802.3).

NOTE   Frame types are potential lower-level IPX troubleshooting target areas in any Novell network where Cisco routers are involved. See the "Protocols and Packets" section for more detail.

Continue configuring your routers as in Example 4-5.

Example 4-5   *r4 Configuration (3620)*

```
Router(config)#hostname r4
r4(config)#enable password donna
r4(config)#line vty 0 4
r4(config-line)#login
r4(config-line)#password donna
r4(config-line)#exit
r4(config)#ipx routing
r4(config)#interface serial 0/0
r4(config-if)#bandwidth 64
r4(config-if)#clock rate 64000
r4(config-if)#ipx network 1022
r4(config-if)#end
r4#copy running-config startup-config
r4#show ipx interface brief
Interface        IPX Network Encapsulation Status              IPX State
Ethernet0/0      unassigned  not config'd  administratively down n/a
Serial0/0        1022        HDLC          administratively down [up]
Serial0/1        unassigned  not config'd  administratively down n/a
```

The display for r5 in my lab is similar to r1 and r2, so I did not bother to display it at this point. Configure your r5, analyze any problems, fix them, and document the particulars. Depending on your exact lab setup, you may or may not have these same issues, and you may have different ones.

Example 4-6 gives you some hints as to the real problem. Use some of the tools you learned about in Chapter 2, "What's in Your Tool Bag?" and in other experiences to determine the issues and resolve the problems.

Example 4-6   *Current IOS Versions in Flash*

```
r5#show flash
System flash directory:
File  Length    Name/status
  1   7567500   c2500-is-l.120-5.bin
[7567564 bytes used, 9209652 available, 16777216 total]
16384K bytes of processor board System flash (Read ONLY)
r4#show flash
System flash directory:
File  Length    Name/status
  1   3971288   c3620-d-mz.113-9.T
[3971352 bytes used, 12805864 available, 16777216 total]
16384K bytes of processor board System flash (Read/Write)
r3#show flash
System flash directory:
File  Length    Name/status
  1   6786288   c3640-js-mz.120-13.bin
[6786352 bytes used, 9990864 available, 16777216 total]
16384K bytes of processor board System flash (Read/Write)
r2#show flash
System flash directory:
File  Length    Name/status
  1   7567500   c2500-is-l.120-5.bin
[7567564 bytes used, 9209652 available, 16777216 total]
16384K bytes of processor board System flash (Read ONLY)
r1#show flash
System flash directory:
File  Length    Name/status
  1   7567500   c2500-is-l.120-5.bin
[7567564 bytes used, 821044 available, 8388608 total]
8192K bytes of processor board System flash (Read ONLY)
```

Now that you determined that the problem routers are all 2500 series and that the installed IOS supports only IP, you need to determine your next step. Another critical component is how much RAM and Flash you have on each of the problem routers. Table 4-2 displays my findings.

Table 4-2   *Router Memory*

Router	RAM in MB (show version)	Flash in MB (show flash)
r1 – 2514	2/2	8
r2 – 2501	16/2	16
r5 – 2516	14/2	16

r1 does not have much RAM. I had some RAM and Flash memory that I swapped over from a spare router so that r1 can run the same IOS as r2 and r5. Refer to Figure 4-2 or check out Cisco.com for any RAM/Flash upgrades and upgrade your lab as necessary. For the r1 IOS upgrade, upgrade the r1 Flash memory from 8 MB to 16 MB and download the required IOS file from the Cisco.com Software Center to the TFTP server directory.

NOTE   For the RAM/Flash upgrade, remove the slotted screw between the two pry slots on the router. Use a large flat-blade screwdriver to twist open the two-pry slots and remove the cover. I recommend you use a wrist strap to assist with static issues. Remove the old RAM/Flash, if required, and insert the new. My old RAM memory was 2 MB/2 MB, but my new RAM is 14 MB/2 MB, similar to what I have on r5 (as you can verify with a before and after **show version**). My old Flash memory was 8 MB, but my new one is 16 MB, which you can verify with a before and after **show flash** command.

The Flash is somewhat like a hard drive on a PC. Partition the Flash into one partition to hold a new IOS larger than 8 MB and verify the Flash memory upgrade on r1 as in Example 4-7. Figure 4-2 illustrates the actual hardware upgrade. Refer to Cisco.com and Appendix B, "Troubleshooting Resources," for more information on Cisco hardware and software upgrades.

Figure 4-2   *r1 RAM and Flash Upgrade*

Example 4-7 *Partition Flash on r1*

```
r1(config)#partition flash ?
  <1-8>  Number of partitions in device
r1(config)#partition flash 1
...
r1>show version
Cisco Internetwork Operating System Software
IOS (tm) 2500 Software (C2500-IS-L), Version 12.0(5), RELEASE SOFTWARE (fc1)
...
System restarted by power-on
System image file is "flash:c2500-is-1.120-5.bin"
cisco 2500 (68030) processor (revision L) with 14336K/2048K bytes of memory.
...
16384K bytes of processor board System flash (Read ONLY)
Configuration register is 0x2102
r1>show flash
System flash directory:
File  Length    Name/status
  1   7567500   c2500-is-1.120-5.bin
[7567564 bytes used, 9209652 available, 16777216 total]
16384K bytes of processor board System flash (Read ONLY)
```

NOTE   In Example 4-7, I first partitioned the Flash into one partition. I exited completely out of enable mode just to illustrate that many commands are available from user mode. For example, **show version** shows not only the IOS version, but also the amount of RAM memory right from user mode. Likewise, **show flash** displays that 16 MB of Flash memory is available with about 9 MB free from user mode.

The IOS Upgrade Planner is a very useful tool here. Select the Software Center from Cisco.com to locate the IOS Upgrade Planner in the Tools section. Unless I can't find the feature I need, my preference is to work with General Deployment (GD) code. 12.2 is not GD at the time of this writing; however, 12.1 and 12.0 are. You need something to support your hardware using at least IP and IPX as well as to enable you to experiment with other things in the scenarios and Trouble Tickets to come. For testing purposes in this book, use Enterprise Plus, if possible, to include more features. Although in a practical environment, you should standardize the code you use; it is fine to use different versions in the lab scenarios and Trouble Tickets in case there are more issues related to the versions you are using. Determine the best requirements for your own lab and upgrade the hardware and software as required.

NOTE   The Feature Navigator is very helpful in determining whether a given feature set or release level supports a given feature. Search by feature or release. Go to www.cisco.com/cgi-bin/Support/FeatureNav/FN.pl or search for "feature navigator" on Cisco.com to explore this tool.

Figure 4-3 displays the IOS Upgrade Planner. It displays the RAM and Flash memory requirements prior to download. Many times it gives you a link to critical issues (such as this one does with the Must Read link to Simple Network Management Protocol [SNMP] vulnerability information).

Figure 4-3 *IOS Upgrade Planner*

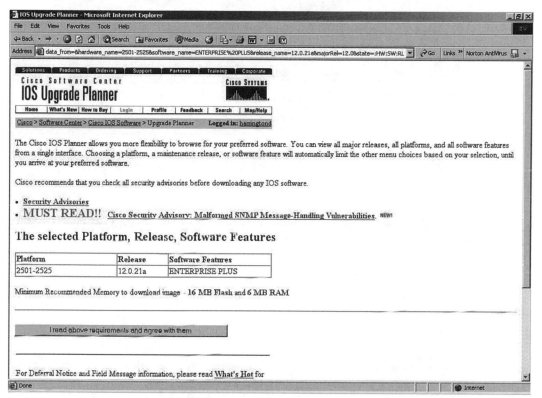

12.021a Enterprise Plus is GD. It requires a minimum of 6 MB RAM and 16 MB Flash as Figure 4-3 shows. Assuming you are logged in with your CCO account and have proper authorization, download the IOS now for use on r1, r2, and r5.

Next you should use a PC-based TFTP server for your r1 IOS and configuration backup. I used PumpKin (see Figure 4-4), but any TFTP server is fine. Although not necessary, this step is highly recommended and is a good practice. Certainly, this would be an easier task if your routers were still configured from the end of the IP chapter, but it is best you know how to do this starting from no configuration at all. Follow along in Example 4-8 to set up the necessary connectivity and IP address parameters to perform the backup.

Figure 4-4 *r1 IOS and Configuration Backup to TFTP*

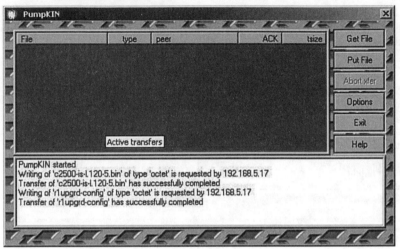

NOTE   If you prefer, you can use just an Ethernet crossover and console cable from the TFTP PC to the router you are configuring at the time. Remember to save your software changes so they are still in effect when you reload the router.

Example 4-8 *r1 IOS and Configuration Backup to TFTP*

```
r1#show flash
System flash directory:
File  Length    Name/status
  1   7567500   c2500-is-l.120-5.bin
[7567564 bytes used, 821044 available, 8388608 total]
8192K bytes of processor board System flash (Read ONLY)
r1#configure terminal
r1(config)#interface ethernet 0
r1(config-if)#ip address 192.168.5.17 255.255.255.240
r1(config-if)#no shut
r1(config-if)#end
r1#copy running-config startup-config
r1#ping 192.168.5.18
Type escape sequence to abort.
Sending 5, 100-byte ICMP Echos to 192.168.5.18, timeout is 2 seconds:
.!!!!
Success rate is 80 percent (4/5), round-trip min/avg/max = 1/3/4 ms
!!!first copy the old IOS to the tftp server
r1#copy flash tftp
Source filename []? c2500-is-l.120-5.bin
Address or name of remote host []? 192.168.5.18
Destination filename [c2500-is-l.120-5.bin]?
```

Example 4-8 *r1 IOS and Configuration Backup to TFTP (Continued)*

```
!!!!!!!!!!!!!!!!!!!!!!!!!!!!!!!!!!!!!!!!!!!!!!!!!!!!!!!!!!!!!!!!!!!!!!!!!!
...
7567500 bytes copied in 94.196 secs (80505 bytes/sec)
!!!next copy the configuration file to the tftp server
r1#copy running-config tftp
Address or name of remote host []? 192.168.5.18
Destination filename [running-config]? r1upgrd-config
!!
645 bytes copied in 5.544 secs (129 bytes/sec)
```

Now that you have prepared the hardware and made your backups, upgrade the IOS using the **copy tftp flash** command similar to Example 4-9. Follow the generic steps in Appendix B to upgrade the IOS or use Cisco.com to research your exact requirements. Remember that the Flash is read-only on a 2500 series router because it is in fact a run-from-flash device. Use the **config-register** command to change to the boot helper mode (rxboot mode) so that you can change the Flash to read/write so that the router is ready to accept the new IOS. Remember that rxboot mode is an IP host implementation and will not work without the **ip default-gateway** statement unless the TFTP server is directly attached.

NOTE Although I did not show the exact commands, my first couple of attempts to upgrade r1 failed. After I replaced the bad Flash memory, Example 4-9 worked fine. Obviously, this is an issue you may not have, but perhaps you can learn from my troubles. Look up any specific error messages you run into on Cisco.com to get more comfortable with the tools Cisco offers.

Example 4-9 *r1 IOS Upgrade from TFTP Server*

```
r1(config)#config-register 0x2101
r1(config)#end
...
r1#reload
Proceed with reload? [confirm]
00:18:07: %SYS-5-RELOAD: Reload requested
...
r1(boot)#copy tftp flash
System flash directory:
File  Length   Name/status
  1   5726508  c2500-i-l.120-9
[5726572 bytes used, 11050644 available, 16777216 total]
Address or name of remote host [255.255.255.255]? 192.168.5.18
Source file name? c2500-js-l.120-21a.bin
Destination file name [c2500-js-l.120-21a.bin]?
Accessing file 'c2500-js-l.120-21a.bin' on 192.168.5.18...
Loading c2500-js-l.120-21a.bin from 192.168.5.18 (via Ethernet0): ! [OK]
Erase flash device before writing? [confirm]
Flash contains files. Are you sure you want to erase? [confirm]
Copy 'c2500-js-l.120-21a.bin' from server
```

continues

Example 4-9 *r1 IOS Upgrade from TFTP Server (Continued)*

```
      as 'c2500-js-l.120-21a.bin' into Flash WITH erase? [yes/no]y
Erasing device... eeeeeeeeeeeeeeeeeeeeeeeeeeeeeeeeeeeeeeeeeeeeeeeeeeeeeeeeeeeee
      eeeee ...erased
Loading c2500-js-l.120-21a.bin from 192.168.5.18 (via Ethernet0):
!!!!!!!!!!!!!!!!!!!!!!!!!!!!!!!!!!!!!!!!!!!!!!!!!!!!!!!!!!!!!!!!!!!!!!!
...
[OK - 10253564/16777216 bytes]
Verifying checksum... OK (0xFA32)
Flash copy took 0:05:55 [hh:mm:ss]
r1(boot)#show flash
System flash directory:
File  Length   Name/status
  1   10253564  c2500-js-l.120-21a.bin
[10253628 bytes used, 6523588 available, 16777216 total]
16384K bytes of processor board System flash (Read/Write)
r1(boot)#configure terminal
r1(boot)(config)#config-register 0x2102
r1(boot)(config)#end
r1(boot)#reload
...
Proceed with reload? [confirm]
```

CAUTION   Be careful when you come out of config mode from changing the configuration register and issue the **reload** command. In boot helper (rxboot) mode, it is important *not* to save the configuration. If you save at this point, some commands may be lost because the bootstrap software does not support the full command set.

Note how you were made to confirm more than once that you really wanted to erase Flash. Whether you need to erase depends on the amount of Flash installed and how much the IOS file or any configuration files use. A checksum is performed at the end of the copy to verify the upgrade.

Using a PC-based TFTP server is not the only method available for this task. So to get familiar with another method, you should set up r1 as a TFTP server serving the IOS image for r2 and r5 as in Example 4-10.

Example 4-10 *Set Up r1 as a TFTP Server*

```
r1(config)#tftp-server flash:c2500-js-l.120-21a.bin
r1(config)#interface ethernet 1
r1(config-if)#ip address 192.168.5.33 255.255.255.240
r1(config-if)#no shut
r1(config-if)#end
r1#copy running-config startup-config
```

Now that r1 is configured to serve up the IOS image, upgrade r2 using r1 over the common Ethernet link as in Example 4-11. Verify that the IOS is in Flash.

Example 4-11 *r2 IOS Upgrade from r1 as a TFTP Server*

```
r2(config)#interface ethernet 0
r2(config-if)#ip address 192.168.5.34 255.255.255.240
r2(config-if)#no shut
r2(config-if)#end
...
r2#copy running-config startup-config
...
r2#copy tftp flash
                         ****  NOTICE  ****
Flash load helper v1.0
This process will accept the copy options and then terminate
the current system image to use the ROM based image for the copy.
Routing functionality will not be available during that time.
If you are logged in via telnet, this connection will terminate.
Users with console access can see the results of the copy operation.
                    ---- ******** ----
Proceed? [confirm]
Address or name of remote host []? 192.168.5.33
Source filename []? c2500-js-l.120-21a.bin
Destination filename [c2500-js-l.120-21a.bin]?
Accessing tftp://192.168.5.33/c2500-js-l.120-21a.bin...
Erase flash: before copying? [confirm]
01:10:07: %SYS-5-RELOAD: Reload requested
%SYS-4-CONFIG_NEWER: Configurations from version 12.0 may not be correctly
    understood.
%FLH: c2500-js-l.120-21a.bin from 192.168.5.33 to flash ...
System flash directory:
File  Length   Name/status
  1   7567500  c2500-is-l.120-5.bin
[7567564 bytes used, 9209652 available, 16777216 total]
Accessing file 'c2500-js-l.120-21a.bin' on 192.168.5.33...
Loading c2500-js-l.120-21a.bin from 192.168.5.33 (via Ethernet0): ! [OK]
Erasing device... eeeeeeeeeeeeeeeeeeeeeeeeeeeeeeeeeeeeeeeeeeeeeeeeeeeeeeee
    eeeeeeeeeee ...erased
Loading c2500-js-l.120-21a.bin from 192.168.5.33 (via Ethernet0):
!!!!!!!!!!!!!!!!!!!!!!!!!!!!!!!!!!!!!!!!!!!!!!!!!!!!!!!!!!!!!!!!!!!!!!!!!
...
[OK - 10253564/16777216 bytes]
Verifying checksum...  OK (0xFA32)
Flash copy took 0:05:03 [hh:mm:ss]
%FLH: Re-booting system after download
F3: 10029384+224148+563164 at 0x3000060
              Restricted Rights Legend
Use, duplication, or disclosure by the Government is
...
Cisco Internetwork Operating System Software
IOS (tm) 2500 Software (C2500-JS-L), Version 12.0(21a), RELEASE SOFTWARE (fc1)
...
cisco 2500 (68030) processor (revision D) with 16384K/2048K bytes of memory.
...
```

continues

Example 4-11 *r2 IOS Upgrade from r1 as a TFTP Server (Continued)*

```
16384K bytes of processor board System flash (Read ONLY)
…
r2>show flash
System flash directory:
File  Length   Name/status
   1   10253564  /c2500-js-l.120-21a.bin
[10253628 bytes used, 6523588 available, 16777216 total]
16384K bytes of processor board System flash (Read ONLY)
```

Example 4-11 shows how Flash load helper was invoked to copy the image, which included the appropriate configuration register and reboot requirements. The new IOS file is now in Flash. Appendix B offers more information on router bootup and configuration register parameters.

Prepare r5 for IPX by upgrading the IOS using r1 as a TFTP server over the 64 kbps serial link as in Example 4-12. Perform the upgrade from boot helper (rxboot) mode.

Example 4-12 *Preparing r1 and r5 for the Upgrade*

```
r1(config)#interface serial 0
r1(config-if)#ip address 10.1.1.1 255.255.255.0
r1(config-if)#no shut
r1(config-if)#end
r1#copy running-config startup-config
r5(config)#interface serial 0
r5(config-if)#clock rate 64000
r5(config-if)#ip address 10.1.1.2 255.255.255.0
r5(config-if)#no shut
r5(config-if)#exit
r5(config)#config-register 0x2101
r5(config)#exit
r5#reload
System configuration has been modified. Save? [yes/no]: y
...
16384K bytes of processor board System flash (Read/Write)
```

The shaded output in Example 4-12 illustrates how to change r5 to rxboot mode so that the Flash is read/write. Now you can copy the new IOS from r1 to r5 as in Example 4-13.

Example 4-13 *r5 IOS Upgrade from r1 as a TFTP Server*

```
r5(boot)>enable
r5(boot)#copy tftp flash
System flash directory:
File  Length   Name/status
   1   7567500  c2500-is-l.120-5.bin
[7567564 bytes used, 9209652 available, 16777216 total]
Address or name of remote host [255.255.255.255]?10.1.1.1
Source file name? c2500-js-l.120-21a.bin
Destination file name [c2500-js-l.120-21a.bin]?
Accessing file 'c2500-js-l.120-21a.bin' on 10.1.1.1...
Loading c2500-js-l.120-21a.bin from 10.1.1.1 (via Serial0): ! [OK]
```

Example 4-13 *r5 IOS Upgrade from r1 as a TFTP Server (Continued)*

```
Erase flash device before writing? [confirm]
Flash contains files. Are you sure you want to erase? [confirm]
Copy 'c2500-js-l.120-21a.bin' from server
  as 'c2500-js-l.120-21a.bin' into Flash WITH erase? [yes/no]y
Erasing device... eeeeeeeeeeeeeeeeeeeeeeeeeeeeeeeeeeeeeeeeeeeeeeeeeeeeeeeeeee
    eeeeeeee ...erased
Loading c2500-js-l.120-21a.bin from 10.1.1.1 (via Serial0):
    !!!!!!!!!!!!!!!!!!!!!!!!!!!!!!!!!!!!!!!!!!!!!!!!!!!!!!!!!!!!!!!!!!!!!!!!!!!
...
[OK - 10253564/16777216 bytes]
Verifying checksum... OK (0xFA32)
Flash copy took 0:28:32 [hh:mm:ss]
r5(boot)#configure terminal
r5(boot)(config)#config-register 0x2102
r5(boot)(config)#end
r5(boot)#reload
System configuration has been modified. Save? [yes/no]: n
Warning: Attempting to overwrite an NVRAM configuration written
by a full system image. This bootstrap software does not support
the full configuration command set. If you write memory now, some
configuration commands may be lost.
...
Cisco Internetwork Operating System Software
IOS (tm) 2500 Software (C2500 JS-L), Version 12.0(21a), RELEASE SOFTWARE (fc1)
...
cisco 2516 (68030) processor (revision J) with 14336K/2048K bytes of memory.
Processor board ID 02959130, with hardware revision 00000000
...
16384K bytes of processor board System flash (Read ONLY)
Press RETURN to get started!
```

The r5 IOS Flash copy took 28 minutes 32 seconds to complete, which is quite a bit of time difference between this 64k link and the 10-MB Ethernet from the previous example. As with anything else, more is normally better. The faster bandwidth is the better download method if in fact you have a choice. Note the shaded message about the NVRAM overwrite that I previously warned you about if you save while in rxboot mode.

NOTE   I had you use different methods to upgrade the IOS on your routers just so you would become familiar with the different methods. However, all of my methods involved the TFTP server being local to the device you were copying to. If the TFTP server is not directly connected, you need to configure the **ip default-gateway** statement on your routers.

Now that all your routers are IPX-capable and more, configure the rest. Remove any IP configuration on the routers and configure IPX; **enable password**, **enable secret**, and telnet passwords on all routers as in Example 4-14.

NOTE   Proper planning would certainly have eliminated the IOS upgrade in the midst of trying to configure IPX. This goes back to methodology and knowing your requirements up front. It is critical for you to keep that in mind for practical application.

Example 4-14 *r1 IPX Configuration*

```
r1(config)#line console 0
r1(config-line)#logging synchronous
r1(config-line)#exit
r1(config)#enable password donna
r1(config)#enable secret donna
The enable secret you have chosen is the same as your enable password.
This is not recommended.  Re-enter the enable secret.
r1(config)#line vty 0 4
r1(config-line)#login
r1(config-line)#password donna
r1(config-line)#exit
r1(config)#ipx routing
r1(config)#interface ethernet 0
r1(config-if)#description r1e0 to hosta and hostb
r1(config-if)#ipx network 0516
r1(config-if)#no ip address
r1(config-if)#no shut
r1(config-if)#interface ethernet 1
r1(config-if)#description r1e1 to r2e0
r1(config-if)#ipx network 532
r1(config-if)#no ip address
r1(config-if)#no shut
r1(config-if)#interface serial 1
r1(config-if)#description r1s1 to r3s0/0
r1(config-if)#ipx network 580
r1(config-if)#no ip address
r1(config-if)#bandwidth 64
r1(config-if)#no shut
r1(config-if)#interface serial 0
r1(config-if)#description r1s0 to r5s0
r1(config-if)#ipx network 1011
r1(config-if)#bandwidth 64
r1(config-if)#no ip address
r1(config-if)#no shut
r1(config-if)#end
r1#copy running-config startup-config
```

On r1, I put in the **enable password** and **enable secret** password. The IOS recommended I didn't make them the same password because of security, but it took the password anyway. The **show running-config** command in Example 4-15 shows the enable password in clear text, so it is pretty easy to guess the enable secret in this example. Verify this and the other IPX-specific parameters as in Example 4-15. Notice how the IOS puts a 5 before the enable secret password for the MD5-type of encryption.

NOTE	Most people insist on typing **enable secret password** when the command is actually just **enable secret**. A good guess for the **enable secret password** is spacebar *password* or spacebar *password* spacebar or some combination of that followed by the word the person thinks is the password. If you are not such a good guesser, Cisco has great documentation on password recovery at www.cisco.com/warp/public/474/index.shtml. Check out this website, Cisco.com, and Appendix B for more detail.

Example 4-15 *r1 Running Configuration*

```
r1#show running-config
Building configuration...
Current configuration:
version 12.0
service timestamps debug uptime
service timestamps log uptime
no service password-encryption
hostname r1
enable secret 5 $1$m0s2$Pq/6.NpOCSzhbQlNy.cnG/
enable password donna
ip subnet-zero
ipx routing 0000.0c8d.6705
interface Ethernet0
 description r1e0 to hosta and hostb
 no ip address
 no ip directed-broadcast
 no ip route-cache
 no ip mroute-cache
 ipx network 516
interface Ethernet1
 description r1e1 to r2e0
 no ip address
 no ip directed-broadcast
 no ip route-cache
 no ip mroute-cache
 ipx network 532
interface Serial0
 description r1s0 to r5s0
 bandwidth 64
 no ip address
 no ip directed-broadcast
 no ip route-cache
 no ip mroute-cache
 ipx network 1011
interface Serial1
 description r1s1 to r3s0/0
 bandwidth 64
 no ip address
 no ip directed-broadcast
 no ip route-cache
 no ip mroute-cache
 ipx network 580
```

continues

Example 4-15 *r1 Running Configuration (Continued)*

```
ip classless
tftp-server flash:c2500-js-l.120-21a.bin
line con 0
 logging synchronous
 transport input none
line aux 0
 transport input all
line vty 0 4
 password donna
 login
end
```

Notice that both the **enable password** and **enable secret** passwords are in the configuration. When the **enable** and **enable secret** passwords are configured, the **enable secret** always takes precedence. Feel free to make the **enable** and **enable secret** passwords different sometime to prove that theory. In a practical sense, just use **enable secret**.

Look at the shaded IPX routing line. There is a number after it that you did not configure. If you were to issue the **show ipx interface ethernet 0** command, you would see the IPX address as 516.0000.0c8d.6705. Because you did not specify the optional node parameter when you configured IPX routing, the router configured it for you. It borrowed the first available Ethernet MAC address for this purpose. Duplication is not a problem here because the external network number (wire number) differs for each link. Because Novell uses a MAC address for the node, you must either configure it or accept the default for your serial interfaces. Although you may not see the relevance of configuring your own node address for the serial links now, it is best practice to do so (as you will experiment with in the Trouble Tickets). Compare the IPX network numbers in the configuration against Figure 4-1 to see that the leading 0s are suppressed. Notice also that r1 is still configured as a TFTP server for the IOS image. Now configure r2 per Figure 4-1 as in Example 4-16.

NOTE   Because you are familiar with hostnames, passwords, logging synchronous, and such, I am only showing the IPX global and interface configurations for the rest of the routers. Assume a bandwidth of 64 kbps and clock rate of 64000 unless specifically mentioned to be something else.

Example 4-16 *r2 IPX Configuration*

```
r2(config)#ipx routing
r2(config)#interface ethernet 0
r2(config-if)#description r2e0 to r1e1
r2(config-if)#ipx network 532
r2(config-if)#no ip address
r2(config-if)#no shut
r2(config-if)#interface serial 1
```

Example 4-16 *r2 IPX Configuration (Continued)*

```
r2(config-if)#description r2s1 to r3s0/2
r2(config-if)#ipx network 548
r2(config-if)#no ip address
r2(config-if)#bandwidth 64
r2(config-if)#no shut
r2(config-if)#interface serial 0
r2(config-if)#description r2s0 to r3s0/1
r2(config-if)#ipx network 564
r2(config-if)#no ip address
r2(config-if)#bandwidth 64
r2(config-if)#no shut
r2(config-if)#end
r2#copy running-config startup-config
```

Now configure r3 per Figure 4-1 as in Example 4-17.

Example 4-17 *r3 IPX Configuration*

```
r3(config-line)#ipx routing
r3(config)#interface serial 0/0
r3(config-if)#description r3s0/0 to r1s1
r3(config-if)#ipx network 580
r3(config-if)#no ip address
r3(config-if)#bandwidth 64
r3(config-if)#clock rate 64000
r3(config-if)#no shut
r3(config-if)#interface serial 0/1
r3(config-if)#description r3s0/1 to r2s0
r3(config-if)#bandwidth 64
r3(config-if)#clock rate 64000
r3(config-if)#ipx network 564
r3(config-if)#no ip address
r3(config-if)#no shut
r3(config-if)#interface serial 0/2
r3(config-if)#description r3s0/2 to r2s1
r3(config-if)#bandwidth 64
r3(config-if)#clock rate 64000
r3(config-if)#ipx network 548
r3(config-if)#no ip address
r3(config-if)#no shut
r3(config-if)#interface serial 0/3
r3(config-if)#description r3s0/3 to r4s0/0
r3(config-if)#bandwidth 64
r3(config-if)#ipx network 1022
r3(config-if)#no ip address
r3(config-if)#no shut
r3(config-if)#interface fastethernet 2/0
r3(config-if)#description r3fa2/0 to hostc
r3(config-if)#ipx network 596
r3(config-if)#no ip address
r3(config-if)#no shut
r3(config-if)#end
r3#copy running-config startup-config
```

Now configure r4 per Figure 4-1 as in Example 4-18.

Example 4-18 *r4 IPX Configuration*

```
r4(config)#ipx routing
r4(config)#interface serial 0/0
r4(config-if)#description r4s0/0 to r3s0/3
r4(config-if)#ipx network 1022
r4(config-if)#no ip address
r4(config-if)#bandwidth 64
r4(config-if)#clock rate 64000
r4(config-if)#no shut
r4(config-if)#end
r4#copy running-config startup-config
```

Now configure r5 per Figure 4-1 as in Example 4-19.

Example 4-19 *r5 IPX Configuration*

```
r5(config)#ipx routing
r5(config)#interface serial 0
r5(config-if)#description r5s0 to r1s0
r5(config-if)#bandwidth 64
r5(config-if)#clock rate 64000
r5(config-if)#ipx network 1011
r5(config-if)#no ip address
r5(config-if)#no shut
r5(config-if)#end
r5#copy running-config startup-config
```

Now that IPX is configured on the routers in your lab, use Example 4-20 as a guide to test routers 1 through 5. Compare the output to your IPX scenario drawing to spot any issues and to document the network.

Example 4-20 *r1 Testing*

```
r1>show ipx interface brief
Interface          IPX Network Encapsulation Status          IPX State
Ethernet0          516         NOVELL-ETHER  up              [up]
Ethernet1          532         NOVELL-ETHER  up              [up]
Serial0            1011        HDLC          up              [up]
Serial1            580         HDLC          up              [up]
r1#show ipx route
Codes: C - Connected primary network,    c - Connected secondary network
       S - Static, F - Floating static, L - Local (internal), W - IPXWAN
       R - RIP, E - EIGRP, N - NLSP, X - External, A - Aggregate
       s - seconds, u - uses, U - Per-user static
7 Total IPX routes. Up to 1 parallel paths and 16 hops allowed.
No default route known.
C        516 (NOVELL-ETHER),   Et0
C        532 (NOVELL-ETHER),   Et1
C        580 (HDLC),           Se1
C       1011 (HDLC),           Se0
R        548 [02/01] via       532.0000.0c38.a05d,    45s, Et1
```

Example 4-20   *r1 Testing (Continued)*

```
R        564 [02/01] via      532.0000.0c38.a05d,   45s, Et1
R       1022 [07/01] via      580.00b0.6481.e300,   45s, Se1
r1#show ipx servers
r1#show protocols
Global values:
  Internet Protocol routing is enabled
  IPX routing is enabled
Ethernet0 is up, line protocol is up
  IPX address is 516.0000.0c8d.6705
Ethernet1 is up, line protocol is up
  IPX address is 532.0000.0c8d.6706
Serial0 is up, line protocol is up
  IPX address is 1011.0000.0c8d.6705
Serial1 is up, line protocol is up
  IPX address is 580.0000.0c8d.6705
```

The IOS commands used in Example 4-20 prove quite helpful for spotting Novell issues. You
have been using **show ipx interface brief** throughout this chapter to get a basic idea of the
networks, encapsulation types, and status thereof. The next command, **show ipx route**, is
extremely helpful. For instance, count the wires on your Figure 4-1 diagram. I count eight
wires, but only see seven networks on the router display. Looking at the **show ipx route** display
and my drawing helps me to determine that the missing network is 596. Router 2 is a little closer
to the destination network. Investigate whether it can see network 596 (as in Example 4-21). No
IPX servers are listed yet, and the output of **show protocols** is extremely helpful to inform you
that IPX routing is in fact on, but better yet, all your node addresses are in one place.

Example 4-21   *r2 Testing*

```
r2#show ipx route
...
7 Total IPX routes. Up to 1 parallel paths and 16 hops allowed.
No default route known.
C        532 (NOVELL-ETHER),  Et0
C        548 (HDLC),          Se1
C        564 (HDLC),          Se0
R        516 [02/01] via      532.0000.0c8d.6706,   0s, Et0
R        580 [02/01] via      532.0000.0c8d.6706,   0s, Et0
R       1011 [02/01] via      532.0000.0c8d.6706,   0s, Et0
R       1022 [07/01] via      564.00b0.6481.e300,  45s, Se0
```

The problem still exists, for r2 does not see any more networks than r1 does. Because the
missing network is off of r3, move your testing closer to the problem (as I do in Example 4-22).
A layered troubleshooting approach is critical here, because the real problem in my lab is a
loose cable on r3 fa2/0, which completely isolates network 596. Pull your cable or completely
power off hostc to simulate the issue. Assuming you don't have a lot of network activity, you
might also find it helpful to turn on **debug ipx routing events** to watch what is happening with
the routing updates.

Example 4-22 *r3 Testing*

```
r3#show interfaces fastethernet 2/0
FastEthernet2/0 is up, line protocol is down
  Hardware is AmdFE, address is 00b0.6481.e300 (bia 00b0.6481.e300)
...
r3#debug ipx routing ?
  activity  IPX RIP routing activity
  events    IPX RIP routing events
r3#debug ipx routing events
IPX routing events debugging is on
r3#!!!plug in the cable and/or turn hostc on
03:48:35: IPXRIP: 548 FFFFFFFF not added, entry in table is static/
    connected/internal
03:48:35: IPXRIP: 564 FFFFFFFF not added, entry in table is static/
    connected/internal
03:48:36: IPXRIP: positing full update to 580.ffff.ffff.ffff via
    Serial0/0 (broadcast)
03:48:47: %LINEPROTO-5-UPDOWN: Line protocol on Interface FastEthernet2/0,
    changed state to up
03:48:47: IPXRIP: Marking network 596 FFFFFFFF for Flash Update
03:48:47: IPXRIP: General Query src=596.00b0.6481.e300, dst=596.ffff.ffff.ffff,
    packet sent (via FastEthernet2/0)
03:48:47: IPXRIP: positing flash update to 580.ffff.ffff.ffff via
    Serial0/0 (broadcast)
03:48:47: IPXRIP: positing flash update to 564.ffff.ffff.ffff via
    Serial0/1 (broadcast)
03:48:47: IPXRIP: positing flash update to 548.ffff.ffff.ffff via
    Serial0/2 (broadcast)
03:48:47: IPXRIP: positing flash update to 1022.ffff.ffff.ffff via
    Serial0/3 (broadcast)
03:48:47: IPXRIP: positing flash update to 596.ffff.ffff.ffff via
    FastEthernet2/0 (broadcast)
03:48:47: IPXRIP: positing full update to 596.ffff.ffff.ffff via
    FastEthernet2/0 (broadcast)
03:48:47: IPXRIP: suppressing null update to 596.ffff.ffff.ffff
    (FastEthernet2/0)
03:48:47: IPXRIP: 596 FFFFFFFF not added, entry in table is static/
    connected/internal
...
r3#undebug all
All possible debugging has been turned off
r3#show ipx route
...
8 Total IPX routes. Up to 1 parallel paths and 16 hops allowed.
No default route known.
C       548 (HDLC),        Se0/2
C       564 (HDLC),        Se0/1
C       580 (HDLC),        Se0/0
C       596 (NOVELL-ETHER), Fa2/0
C      1022 (HDLC),        Se0/3
R       516 [07/01] via    580.0000.0c8d.6705,    25s, Se0/0
R       532 [07/01] via    564.0000.0c38.a05d,    56s, Se0/1
R      1011 [07/01] via    580.0000.0c8d.6705,    25s, Se0/0
r3#
```

When you fixed the issue, a Flash update was immediately sent to update the routing tables. Network 596 now displays, so continue testing and troubleshooting r4 and r5.

All eight networks are present in r1 through r5, but when did you turn on RIP? Actually you never turned on IPX RIP; it comes automatic with IPX. This was definitely not the case in the Chapter 3 with IP RIP.

This is a great time to further document your scenario drawing. As you can tell from the previous examples, **show protocols** is great for address documentation. I often log this type of data to a log file with SecureCRT. I just choose Log Session from the File menu, turn it off when I have captured the appropriate data, and rename the SecureCRT session file. Alternatively, you can use the HyperTerm Transfer menu to capture text. For more IPX-related commands and information, familiarize yourself with **show tech-support** in an IPX environment (as I do in Example 4-23). Because you are familiar with many of the individual commands, much of the output is omitted.

Example 4-23 *show tech-support in an IPX Environment*

```
r1#show tech-support
----------------- show version -----------------
----------------- show running-config -----------------
----------------- show controllers -----------------
----------------- show stacks -----------------
----------------- show interfaces -----------------
----------------- show region -----------------
----------------- show process memory -----------------
----------------- show process cpu -----------------
----------------- show buffers -----------------
```

Now that this chapter's IPX lab scenario is configured from the router point of view, turn your attention to the following section, "Protocols and Packets." It starts with a layered approach to the Novell NOS to review IPX concepts, symptoms, problems, and action plans. There are more walk-through scenarios and practical Trouble Tickets for you to explore, because, after all, you learn more by doing; besides you need to configure your Novell server and clients. For those who do not have equipment handy or the desire to work with Novell anymore, I will continue to include many relevant figures and examples so that you, too, can shoot trouble with IPX. However, you will find that I am a firm believer in letting **routers route** and **servers serve**.

Protocols and Packets

Applying what you have learned to real-world troubleshooting is important for the successful support person. Starting with Table 4-3, I compare some of the protocols, applications, and utilities at each layer of Novell's IPX/SPX stack to the TCP/IP suite to assist you with supporting day-to-day internetworks.

Table 4-3   *Novell Protocols, Applications, and Utilities*

Layer	ISO's OSI Model	DoD TCP/IP Suite	Novell IPX/SPX Stack
7	Application	Application	Applications
6	Presentation		NetBIOS
			NCP*
			SAP*
			RIP
			NLSP*
5	Session		
4	Transport	Transport Host-to-Host	SPX
3	Network	Internet	IPX
2	Data Link	Data Link	Various LAN/WAN technologies such as Ethernet, Token Ring, FDDI, Frame Relay, HDLC, PPP
1	Physical	Physical	

*NCP = NetWare Core Protocol

SAP = Service Advertisement Protocol

NLSP = NetWare Link State (Services) Protocol

Networks today are predominantly IP, but IPX still exists. NetWare 5 and 6 run native IP, but earlier Novell networks used Novell's own flavor of IP. Internetwork Packet Exchange (IPX), like IP, is a connectionless datagram delivery routed protocol that encompasses the upper five layers of the OSI model. IPX relies on its counterpart Sequenced Packet Exchange (SPX) for reliability like IP relies on TCP or an upper-layer application. At Layer 2, IPX supports media such as Ethernet, Token Ring, FDDI, Frame Relay, HDLC, and PPP. However, the *main* IPX troubleshooting target at Layer 2 is encapsulation.

NOTE   With NetWare, the client configuration is intentionally very simple. If the client gets the frame type (encapsulation) correct, it will likely work.

Frame Types

Encapsulation, frame format, frame type—they all mean the same thing, which is packaging the upper-layer data, voice, or video into a Layer 2 frame. Compare the IPX and IP framing examples in Figure 4-5.

Figure 4-5   *IP/IPX Encapsulation*

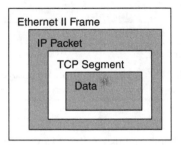 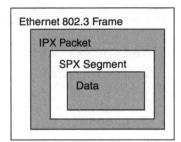

Frame types are not just another table to memorize to take a Cisco test. They are real troubleshooting targets regardless of the upper-layer protocols. For instance, machines running only Ethernet_II cannot see machines running only Ethernet_802.3 and vice versa. On the Cisco side, subinterfaces and secondary addresses support multiple frame types, and on the Novell server side you can bind multiple frame types to the NIC or use multiple NICs. Be aware, however, that running multiple frame types affects network speed and performance. Routers assist with multiple frame types by stripping the Layer 2 package and repackaging it according to the destination network address.

Although frame formats are covered more thoroughly in Chapter 5, "Shooting Trouble with Ethernet," they are covered briefly here because you must at least be familiar with them to support the Novell environment. Review them in Table 4-4.

Table 4-4   *Frame Formats*

802.3 RAW (Novell) Frame Format			
802.3		IPX	
• 802.3 RAW is Novell's 802.3 for IPX over Ethernet.			
• Uses 802.3 length field but not 802.2 LLC (SAPs)			
• First 2 bytes in data field are set to FFFF.			
802.3 (IEEE) Frame Format with an 802.2 (LLC) SAP Header			
802.3	802.2 LLC	IPX	
• 802.2 is IEEE's 802.3 for IPX over Ethernet (and other Layer 2 technologies).			
• IPX uses DSAP and SSAP of e0. (SAP is the Layer 2 pointer to the Layer 3 protocol.)			
• Uses length field.			
802.3 (IEEE) Frame Format with a 802.2 (LLC) SAP/SNAP Header			
802.3	802.2 LLC	SNAP	IPX
• SNAP has 802.3, 802.2 SAP, and SNAP headers.			
• Uses length field.			
• DSAP and SSAP are AA in the LLC header.			

Table 4-4   *Frame Formats (Continued)*

Ethernet II (DIX) Frame Format	
Ethernet II	IPX

- Ethernet II is Digital Intel Xerox (DIX) Ethernet.
- IPX uses an EtherType field of 8137/8138. (EtherType is the pointer from Layer 2 to the Layer 3 protocol.)

NOTE   Unfortunately many acronyms are re-used in the industry. 802.2 LLC SAPs are service access points or pointers to the Layer 3 protocol. They have nothing to do with the Novell Service Advertisement Protocol (SAP).

The default frame type on Novell servers varies from NetWare version to NetWare version. In the next chapter, you will use your protocol analyzer to analyze the frame types in more detail, but for now use the following NetWare version list as a guide:

- Ethernet_II is the default for NetWare 5.x and 6.x for Ethernet links.
- HDLC is the default for serial links.
- Ethernet_802.3 is the default for NetWare 3.11 and prior for Ethernet links.
- Ethernet_802.2 is the default to NetWare 3.12 through 4.x for Ethernet links.
- SNAP is the default for Token Ring and FDDI.

NOTE   In a TCP/IP Ethernet environment, Cisco defaults to ARPA, whereas in a Novell IPX network, Cisco defaults to Novell-Ether. In either case, serial links default to HDLC encapsulation. However, Cisco has never changed their default IPX frame type. If NetWare is using IP, there is no IPX, so there is no issue with IPX frame types. Hence, there is some validity to drop the X in IPX and things work just fine.

Table 4-5 illustrates the Cisco names and Novell names for the various frame types. This is not only critical CCNA/CCNP material but information you need to configure IPX on Cisco routers in the real world.

Table 4-5   *Cisco Encapsulation/Novell Frame Type Examples*

Cisco Encapsulation	Novell Frame Type	Description	Novell Version Default
ARPA (Default for IP Ethernet)	Ethernet_II	EtherType pointer to Layer 3	NetWare 6.x NetWare 5.x
SAP	Ethernet_802.2	Length field 802.2 LLC SAP pointer to Layer 3	NetWare 3.12 through NetWare 4.x
Novell-Ether (Default for IPX Ethernet)	Ethernet_802.3	Length field	NetWare 3.11 and below
SNAP	Ethernet_SNAP	Length field 802.2 LLC SAP SNAP header	SNAP default for Token Ring and FDDI
HDLC	HDLC	Serial links	All versions for serial links

Now is a good time to bring a Novell server online or to investigate my scenario so that you can witness a practical example of framing issues. My Novell server is a 4.11 box that is also serving as a GroupWise mail server. However, my Novell server, named gwise is beeping pretty loud and quite often right now. Example 4-24 displays the server output that is occurring about every 60 seconds.

Example 4-24   *Bringing the Novell NetWare 4.11 Box Online*

```
#4-01-02    6:26:36pm:    IPXRTR-6.50-2
RIP router configuration error detected.
Node 00000C8D6705 claims network address 8DA0A850 should be 00000516.
```

What is wrong? You can press Ctrl+Esc to see the current screens on the Novell server and type **help** at the NetWare console (GWISE: server prompt) for hints and help with Novell commands.

From the server console, I issued the **load monitor** command to look at the Available Options menu and found the LAN/WAN information to be quite useful. Example 4-25 displays the information I gleaned from the Novell monitor.

Example 4-25   **load monitor** *Displays the Bindings*

```
#NE2000_1_E82 [NE2000 port=300 int=A frame=ETHERNET_802.2]
NE2000_1_E83 [NE2000 port=300 int=A frame=ETHERNET_802.3]
NE2000_1_EII [NE2000 port=300 int=A frame=ETHERNET_II]
```

Pressing Enter on each of the bindings in the preceding example yields the following information:

- 802.2 binding:

    Node address 008029E85C6B

    IPX network address 8A4A85A5

- 802.3 binding:

    Node address 008029E85C6B

    IPX network address 8DA0A850

- Ethernet II binding:

    Node address 008029E85C6B

    Address Resolution Protocol (ARP) and IP protocols

The NetWare **display networks** command shows the following networks: 346648E2, 8A4A85A5, and 8DA0A850. 346648E2 is the *IPX internal network number* for the server, which always has a node address of 000000000001. The others are IPX external numbers that are bound to the NIC. 8A4A85A5 is for frame type 802.2, and 8DA0A850 is for frame type 802.3. Look back at the original problem and note that the server is saying that 8DA0A850, the 802.3 network, should be 516. Refer back to Figure 4-1 to confirm the whereabouts of IPX network 516 to determine the issue.

NOTE   The exact error message is often helpful when trying to find the problem. This one happens to be: "RIP router configuration error detected. Node 00000C8D6705 claims network address 8DA0A850 should be 00000516."

Next I typed **load edit** to bring up the Novell autoexec.ncf file, but my parameters were transferred to a netinfo.cfg file by the inetcfg NLM. So I typed **load inetcfg** to configure the correct network for frame type 802.3. *Remember* the default frame type for NetWare 4.x is Novell 802.2 or Cisco SAP, which is the issue here. From the inetcfg menu, I picked Internetworking Configuration and then the Bindings submenu to change the 8DA0A850 network to 516. For the commands to take effect, I had to type the **reinitialize system** command.

You can do the same thing in multiple ways. For example, instead of using the menus as I did, you could do everything from the Novell server console prompt, where you would have to issue the **unbind** command first and then **bind**. In addition, instead of downing and exiting the console, you certainly could issue the **down** command and then **restart server**, or **down**, then **exit**, and then **server**. Example 4-26 illustrates loading drivers and binding IPX to the NIC at the console.

Example 4-26 *Loading Drivers and Binding IPX to the NIC at the Console*

```
LOAD NE2000 NAME=NE2000_1_E83 FRAME=ETHERNET_802.3 INT=A PORT=300
BIND IPX NE2000_1_E83 NET=516
...
```

NOTE   Whether from the command line or inetcfg, these commands prove quite helpful in a Cisco/
Novell support environment; after all, incorrect frame types are a common issue between
Novell and Cisco devices. Multiple frame types are supported in Novell and Cisco, although
not a best practice. On Cisco devices, the preferred method is to configure subinterfaces, but
secondary addresses still work too.

That did it. You fixed the beep and can see the following networks, including the tick/hop count
with **display networks** at the server console:

- 516 0/1

- 532 1/2

- 548 2/3

- 564 2/3

- 580 2/3

- 596 2/8

- 1011 1/2

- 1022 2/8

- 346648E2 0/1 (internal IPX number)

- 8A4A85A5 0/1

NOTE   Ticks/hops and the network numbers are explained in the section "Internet Layer Protocols,
Applications, and Utilities" later in this chapter.

NOTE   The Cisco equivalent command to Novell's **display networks** is **show ipx route**. Remember
that as with other protocols, all routes can be cleared to force convergence with **clear ipx route ***,
but clearing an individual route is preferable and therefore not as much of a career-limiting
move (CLM) in the practical environment.

The Novell **config** console command is great for getting a quick display of the hardware settings, node address, frame type, board name, and bindings for documentation or for setting up filters. Use it to check your work on the server (see Figure 4-6).

NOTE   I am recommending you update your drawing at this point. However, I am assuming that you have realized the importance of documentation and have been doing so all along. I will continue without too many reminders in this area.

Figure 4-6   *Novell Config*

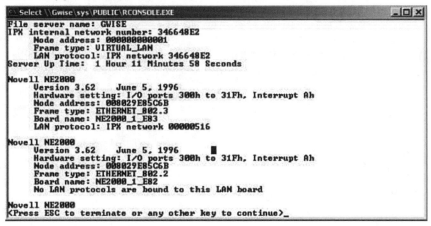

NOTE   It is a good practice to always specify encapsulation when you configure Novell interfaces on Cisco routers. Whether the default or not, this will make you conscious of the correct encapsulation type. Besides, this is a good item to document.

Next you should configure at least one IPX host to prepare for the rest of the chapter. Using the Network Properties sheet, configure hostb for IPX as the default protocol using the Microsoft Client for NetWare as the primary logon with auto frame-type detection. Follow these steps for the Windows 98 hostb client. Other Microsoft client configurations are very similar. If you prefer to use the Novell clients, go to Novell's website for specific instructions.

Step 1   Go to **Start > Settings > Control Panel** and choose Network or just right-click Network Neighborhood to get to Properties.

Step 2   Add the Microsoft Client for NetWare and select it as the Primary Network Logon.

Step 3   Add the Microsoft protocol IPX/SPX (or NWLink). Enable NetBIOS support in the Properties sheet and review the other tabs. On the Advanced tab, locate where you adjust the frame type so that you are familiar with it. Also put a check in the box for IPX to be the default protocol. It is not necessary to run TCP/IP on the client at all for this chapter.

Step 4   Make sure the Novell server is up and running before you reboot the client. Reboot the client and log in with the Administrator account and password for your Novell server.

Step 5   Right-click Network Neighborhood and edit the Microsoft Client for NetWare. Choose the preferred server name for your lab from the drop-down list. For example, mine is gwise.

NOTE   Many workstations send out Get Nearest Server (GNS) requests in a specific order, such as 802.3, 802.2, Ethernet_II, and SNAP. To stop a workstation from attaching itself to a server with the wrong frame type, manually set the correct frame type under the IPX properties. Depending on the client, you can check this information using **ipxroute config** at the command prompt.

Internet Layer Protocols, Applications, and Utilities

The Novell IPX suite of protocols includes not only IPX and SPX but also many upper-layer applications and utilities for file, print, messaging, database, and other common practical services. You confirmed this when you enabled IPX routing, because it automatically enabled IPX RIP as the routing protocol by default.

IPX uses RIP and SAP broadcasts to build a table of routes and a table of services. Just as with an IP packet, routing decisions must be made for an IPX packet based on the destination network.

Your first task in this subsection is to turn on **debug ipx packet** and ping the Novell server *internal IPX number* from r1 using the address from the Novell console **config** command (as in Example 4-27). Next ping a few router interfaces. Why can you ping the router interfaces but not the Novell server? Capture this activity to a Sniffer file and save it as *chapter 4 ping fails from r1 to novell server sniffer capture*.

Example 4-27   *Ping IPX Fails from R1 to Novell Server*

```
r1#debug ipx packet
IPX packet debugging is on
r1#ping
Protocol [ip]: ipx
Target IPX address: 346648e2.0000.0000.0001
Repeat count [5]:
Datagram size [100]:
Timeout in seconds [2]:
Verbose [n]:
Type escape sequence to abort.
Sending 5, 100-byte IPXcisco Echoes to 346648E2.0000.0000.0001,
```

continues

Example 4-27   *Ping IPX Fails from R1 to Novell Server (Continued)*

```
       timeout is 2 seconds:
01:28:39: IPX: local:516.0000.0c8d.6705->346648E2.0000.0000.0001
    ln=100 tc=00 pt=01 ds=0002 ss=0002, gw=Et0:516.0080.29e8.5c6b.
01:28:41: IPX: local:516.0000.0c8d.6705->346648E2.0000.0000.0001
    ln=100 tc=00 pt=01 ds=0002 ss=0002, gw=Et0:516.0080.29e8.5c6b.
01:28:43: IPX: local:516.0000.0c8d.6705->346648E2.0000.0000.0001
    ln=100 tc=00 pt=01 ds=0002 ss=0002, gw=Et0:516.0080.29e8.5c6b.
01:28:45: IPX: local:516.0000.0c8d.6705->346648E2.0000.0000.0001
    ln=100 tc=00 pt=01 ds=0002 ss=0002, gw=Et0:516.0080.29e8.5c6b.
01:28:47: IPX: local:516.0000.0c8d.6705->346648E2.0000.0000.0001
    ln=100 tc=00 pt=01 ds=0002 ss=0002, gw=Et0:516.0080.29e8.5c6b
01:28:47: IPX: Se1:580.00b0.6481.e300->580.ffff.ffff.ffff ln= 72
    tc=00 pt=01 ds=0453 ss=0453, rcvd
01:28:47: IPX: Se1:580.00b0.6481.e300->580.ffff.ffff.ffff ln= 72
    tc=00 pt=01 ds=0453 ss=0453, local.
Success rate is 0 percent (0/5)
...
r1#show ipx interface ethernet 1
Ethernet1 is up, line protocol is up
  IPX address is 532.0000.0c8d.6706, NOVELL-ETHER [up]
  Delay of this IPX network, in ticks is 1 throughput 0 link delay 0
...
r1#ping ipx 532.0000.0c8d.6706
01:29:20: IPX: Et0:516.0080.29e8.5c6b->516.ffff.ffff.ffff ln= 40 tc=00
    pt=01 ds=0453 ss=0453, rcvd
01:29:20: IPX: Et0:516.0080.29e8.5c6b->516.ffff.ffff.ffff ln= 40 tc=00
    pt=01 ds=0453 ss=0453, local0c38.a05d
Type escape sequence to abort.
Sending 5, 100-byte IPXcisco Echoes to 532.0000.0c38.a05d, timeout is 2 seconds:
!!!!!
Success rate is 100 percent (5/5), round-trip min/avg/max = 16/16/16 ms
r1#
01:29:26: IPX: local:532.0000.0c8d.6706->532.0000.0c38.a05d ln=100 tc=00
    pt=01 ds=0002 ss=0002, gw=Et1:532.0000.0c38.a05d
01:29:26: IPX: Et1:532.0000.0c38.a05d->532.0000.0c8d.6706 ln=100 tc=00
    pt=02 ds=0002 ss=0002, rcvd
01:29:26: IPX: Et1:532.0000.0c38.a05d->532.0000.0c8d.6706 ln=100 tc=00
    pt=02 ds=0002 ss=0002, local
01:29:26: IPX: local:532.0000.0c8d.6706->532.0000.0c38.a05d ln=100 tc=00
    pt=01 ds=0002 ss=0002, gw=Et1:532.0000.0c38.a05d
01:29:26: IPX: Et1:532.0000.0c38.a05d->532.0000.0c8d.6706 ln=100 tc=00
    pt=02 ds=0002 ss=0002, rcvd
...
r2#show ipx interface serial 0
Serial0 is up, line protocol is up
  IPX address is 564.0000.0c38.a05d [up]
r2#ping ipx 564.0000.0c38.a05d
type escape sequence to abort.
Sending 5, 100-byte IPXcisco Echoes to 564.0000.0c38.a05d, timeout is 2 seconds:
!!!!!
Success rate is 100 percent (5/5), round-trip min/avg/max = 60/60/64 ms
r1#undebug all
All possible debugging has been turned off
```

NOTE   In the previous examples you looked at the interfaces to gather the IPX address to ping. Don't forget that **show cdp neighbors detail** gives that information for remote devices too. Just like with IP it is helpful to test local and remote communications. Use the CDP method to locate the r2e0 address to ping test it.

A simple ping is the most basic testing tool with IPX, too, for checking whether packets make it to the destination. In IPX, however, the address is a little more difficult to type because you need the network number followed by the node address (MAC address). The default ping is a Cisco ping, which uses *IPX protocol number 2* (as you can verify in the shaded output of the preceding example). The IPX official ping uses *socket number 0x9086*. Cisco ping works fine for your Cisco devices, but your IPX devices do not understand its proprietary nature. It is good practice to change the IPX ping type using the **ipx ping-default novell global** configuration command on your routers. Fix the IPX ping problem and verify as in Example 4-28. Change the ping type to Novell on r1 through r5 and save your configurations. Capture the results with a protocol analyzer to a file named *chapter 4 ping fix from r1 to novell server sniffer capture*.

Example 4-28 *Ping IPX Fix from r1 to Novell Server*

```
r1(config)#ipx ping-default ?
  cisco       use cisco echoes for IPX ping
  diagnostic  use Diagnostic Request/Response for IPX ping
  novell      use Novell Standard echoes for IPX ping
r1(config)#ipx ping-default novell
r1(config)#end
r1#copy running-config startup-config
...
r1#ping ipx 346648e2.0.0.1
Type escape sequence to abort.
Sending 5, 100-byte IPX Novell Echoes to 346648E2.0000.0000.0001,
    timeout is 2 seconds:
!!!!!
Success rate is 100 percent (5/5), round-trip min/avg/max = 4/4/4 ms
r1#debug ipx packet
IPX packet debugging is on
01:42:05: IPX: Et1:532.0000.0c38.a05d->532.ffff.ffff.ffff ln= 64 tc=00
    pt=01 ds=0453 ss=0453, rcvd
01:42:05: IPX: Et1:532.0000.0c38.a05d->532.ffff.ffff.ffff ln= 64 tc=00
...
r1#ping ipx 346648e2.0.0.1
Type escape sequence to abort.
Sending 5, 100-byte IPX Novell Echoes to 346648E2.0000.0000.0001,
    timeout is 2 seconds:
!!!!!
Success rate is 100 percent (5/5), round-trip min/avg/max = 16/16/20 ms
r1#
01:42:16: IPX: local:516.0000.0c8d.6705->346648E2.0000.0000.0001 ln=100
    tc=00 pt=04 ds=9086 ss=9086, gw=Et0:516.0080.29e8.5c6b
01:42:16: IPX: Et0:346648E2.0000.0000.0001->516.0000.0c8d.6705 ln=100
```

continues

Example 4-28 *Ping IPX Fix from r1 to Novell Server (Continued)*

```
     tc=01 pt=04 ds=9086 ss=9086, rcvd
01:42:16: IPX: Et0:346648E2.0000.0000.0001->516.0000.0c8d.6705 ln=100
     tc=01 pt=04 ds=9086 ss=9086, local
01:42:16: IPX: local:516.0000.0c8d.6705->346648E2.0000.0000.0001 ln=100
     tc=00 pt=04 ds=9086 ss=9086, gw=Et0:516.0080.29e8.5c6b
...
r1#undebug all
All possible debugging has been turned off
```

The Cisco **debug ipx packet** command is quite helpful in this instance. Notice that when you change the ping type to Novell, socket 0x9086 is used, whereas previously it was protocol number 2. The 452s and 453s shown are for SAP and RIP sockets. Later you may notice 455 for NetBIOS. Also compare the Example 4-28 Novell IPX echos to the Example 4-27 Cisco IPX echos. You can also **load ipxping** at the Novell server console and test things from that direction if you desire.

Figure 4-7 *Cisco Ping and IPX Protocol 2*

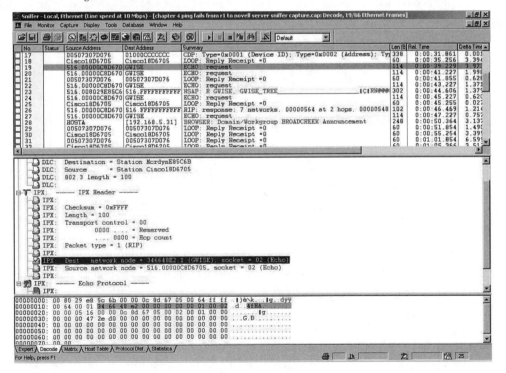

NOTE   The **debug ipx packet** command was helpful in finding the source of this problem, but **debug packet** *anything* is *not* the best choice in a production environment. Actually, not all Novell hosts respond to a ping, and in the real world you might have to resort to pinging a router interface and using other upper-layer testing methods for the host. Problems such as these are mind teasers at times and often frustrating. If all else fails with your structured layered methodology, remember to ask someone for help or get a good night's sleep on it.

Compare the output of the debug and Sniffer captures for the ping portion only. Figure 4-7 and Figure 4-8 help you locate the protocol and socket information in Sniffer.

Figure 4-8   *IPX Ping and Socket 0x9086*

Table 4-6 lists the fields of the IPX header (packet or datagram). Use the Sniffer capture of the IPX ping file from the preceding example to view the fields as in Figure 4-9.

Table 4-6 *The IPX Header (Packet or Datagram)*

Field	Bits	Description
Checksum	16 bits	Not used when set to all 1s (FFFF).
Packet Length	16 bits	Number of bytes up to the MTU* size. No fragmentation.
Transport Control	8 bits	Shows routers the packet has transited. The limit is 16.
Packet Type	8 bits	Link to next layer (like IP protocol number). Examples include 0-unknown, 1-RIP, 5-SPX, and 17-NCP.
Destination Network	32 bits	External (wire) network number.
Destination Node	48 bits	MAC address.
Destination Socket	16 bits	See source socket.
Source Network	32 bits	External (wire) network.
Source Node	48 bits	MAC address.
Source Socket	16 bits	Pointer to upper layers (like a TCP/UDP port number). Examples include 0451-NCP, 0452-SAP, 0453-RIP, 0455-NetBIOS, and 0456-Diagnostics. 4000–6000 are ephemeral sockets for server and network communications.
Upper Layer Data	Varies	Information for upper-layer processes.

*MTU = Maximum Transmission Unit

NOTE The first 2 bytes of the IPX header are a 2-byte checksum. It is calculated in 1's complement binary, not 2's complement, so FFFF = minus 0 has the reserved meaning of "no checksum performed."

Figure 4-9   *Analyzing the IPX Header*

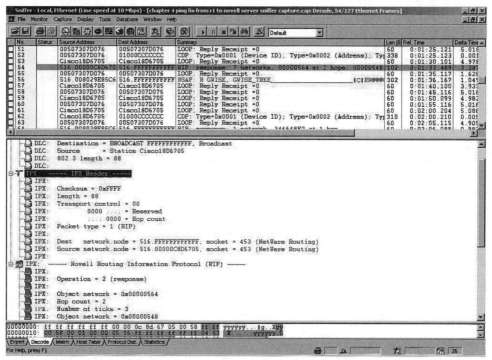

The checksum is not used when set to all FFFFs. The length of the selected packet is 88 bytes; remember IPX does not fragment packets like IP. The transport control shows that 0 routers have been transited. Note that IPX time-to-live (TTL) counts up to a maximum of 16. In the IP header, TTL is initialized to a maximum of 255 and decremented to 0. The packet type is 1, which is how IPX links to the next layer. Sniffer is friendly enough to display packet type 1 as RIP rather than make you look up the data. Other sample protocol numbers you can expect to see here include the following:

- **SPX**—5

- **NCP**—17

- **SAP**—4

- **IPX RIP**—1

- **NetBIOS**—20

- **Any**—0

The destination network.node is 516.FFFFFFFFFFFF, which is the directed broadcast for network 516. The source network.node is 516.00000c8d6705 for r1, which is the same as the source MAC from the Data Link Layer. The source and destination socket numbers are 453, which is the socket for RIP to link to the RIP header. Now review the IPX RIP packet in the Sniffer output in Figure 4-10. Compare it to Table 4-7.

Figure 4-10 *Analyzing the IPX RIP Header*

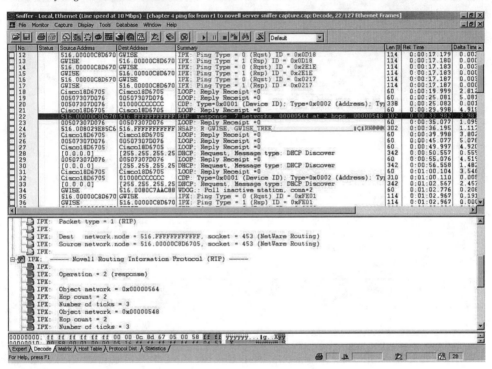

Table 4-7   *The IPX RIP Packet*

Field	Description
Operation	1 RIP request
	2 RIP response
Network number	Specified external IPX number
Number of hops	Routers passed through
Number of ticks	Time to reach network (about 1/18 of a second)
	1 tick for LAN
	6 ticks for WAN
SAP packet	See Table 4-8

Figure 4-10 illustrates Frame 22 of the previous ping file. The RIP header displays operation 2, which is a RIP response about various IPX external network numbers (wire IDs), including 548. The hop count is 2, which means passing through two routers, and the tick count is 3, which is how long it took, which in this case was about 3/18 of a second. Review Table 4-8 and Figure 4-11 to get more familiar with the IPX RIP SAP packet.

Table 4-8   *The IPX RIP SAP Packet**

Field	Description
Operation	1 General service request
	2 General service reply
	3 Nearest service request
	4 Nearest service reply
Service type	4 File server
	7 Print server
	47 Advertising print server
	112 HP print server
	26B Time synchronization
	278 NDS server
Server name	48 bytes
Network address	32-bit network, 48-bit node
Node address	48-bit MAC address
Socket address	16-bit socket number
Hops to server	Routers passed through

*Refer to IANA's Novell SAP Table for a list of SAPs from various sources (www.iana.org/assignments/novell-sap-numbers).

The first occurrence of any SAP activity in Figure 4-11 and my previous ping Sniffer capture is Frame 24. The operation is a general service response for the following services:

- 0004 File Server
- 026B Time Synchronization
- 0278 NetWare Directory Server
- 0107 RSPX

Figure 4-11 *Analyzing the IPX RIP SAP Header*

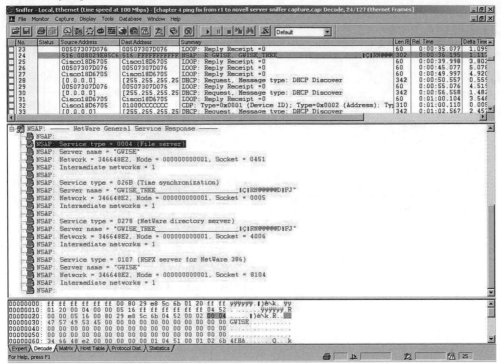

The network.node information for each of these services is 346648e2.0000.0000.0001, which is the internal IPX number for my gwise server. The socket information is as follows:

- 0451 NCP

- 0005 Time Synchronization

- 4006 Ephemeral

- 8104 RConsole

<table>
<tr><td>**NOTE**</td><td>IPX sockets 4000 to 6000 are temporary sockets used for interaction with NetWare servers and other network communications.</td></tr>
</table>

You might find it interesting to go to your protocol analyzer with this capture open to check the SAP interval. Select the first SAP frame, use the Display menu to mark it, go down to the next SAP frame and view the relative or delta, which is roughly 1 minute. Obviously this can cause problems, especially over dial-on-demand routing (DDR) links. However, the Cisco IOS can spoof this traffic. NetWare 5 and above replace SAP with Service Location Protocol (SLP) so that service and directory agents interact to locate network services. See Novell's website for more information.

SAPs remind me of commercials on television. They just keep reminding you of things to eat or buy. This extra traffic is definitely not advantageous on the WAN. SAP tables can get rather large, and at a minimum you should limit SAP traffic on the WAN using SAP filters. Alternatively, you can adjust the SAP interval on the WAN interfaces or just don't configure IPX on the interface at all. Otherwise, you will severely impact the bandwidth available to users. Printers are a good example. They are typically local to your facility, so why advertise them to the rest of the world? SAP filters are from 1000 to 1099.

Consider this example. Assume that print servers are configured on the chapter scenario network 516. hosta and hostb need all IPX services on network 516. However, the other routers and hostc need only to be made aware of IPX file servers. Think about how to configure this and check your thoughts against Example 4-29.

Example 4-29 *SAP Filter to Allow Only IPX File Servers*

```
r1(config)#access-list 1005 permit ?
  -1           Any IPX net
  <0-FFFFFFFF>  Source net
  N.H.H.H       Source net.host address
r1(config)#access-list 1005 permit -1 ?
  <0-FFFF>  Service type-code (0 matches all services)
  N.H.H.H   Source net.host mask
  <cr>
r1(config)#access-list 1005 permit -1 4
r1(config)#interface ethernet 1
r1(config-if)#ipx output-sap-filter 1005
r1(config)#interface serial 0
r1(config-if)#ipx output-sap-filter 1005
r1(config)#interface serial 1
r1(config-if)#ipx output-sap-filter 1005
r1(config-if)#end
r1#copy running-config startup-config
```

The problem with Example 4-29 is that it blocks services other than print services. Remove the preceding filter if you actually configured this on your router. Apply a SAP filter to permit everything except print services, as in Example 4-30. Whether you need all the **no** statements is IOS version-dependent.

Example 4-30 *SAP Filter to Deny All IPX Print Servers*

```
r1(config)#no access-list 1005
r1(config)#interface ethernet 1
r1(config-if)#no ipx output-sap-filter 1005
r1(config)#interface s0
r1(config-if)#no ipx output-sap-filter 1005
r1(config)#interface s1
r1(config-if)#no ipx output-sap-filter 1005
r1(config-if)#exit
r1(config)#access-list 1005 deny -1 7
r1(config)#access-list 1005 deny -1 47
r1(config)#access-list 1005 permit -1
r1(config)#interface e1
r1(config-if)#ipx output-sap-filter 1005
```

continues

Example 4-30 *SAP Filter to Deny All IPX Print Servers (Continued)*

```
r1(config)#interface s0
r1(config-if)#ipx output-sap-filter 1005
r1(config)#interface s1
r1(config-if)#ipx output-sap-filter 1005
r1(config-if)#end
r1#copy running-config startup-config
```

NOTE   Input and output SAP filters are very effective. In general you should block Novell SAPs as close to the source as possible. Any network is permitted or denied by using **-1,** whereas any service is permitted or denied using **0.** A combination of IPX standard access lists and SAP filters can accomplish quite a bit on the IPX scene. SAP filters are popular and useful, but be aware of how Novell print services works (because the printer SAP entry must be known to the file server).

Static SAPs can be created to simulate services that would show up with the **show ipx servers** command. The syntax is as follows:

```
router(config)#ipx sap service-type name network.node socket hop-count
```

The network must be in the router's IPX routing table. Take a look at a SAP table for many common SAP numbers and their descriptions. One way to do this in a lab environment is to enter **ipx network** commands on loopback interfaces. Then point the static SAPs to them. Remember that both IPX RIP and SAP obey split horizon.

Setting up your routers, the Novell server, and the clients; working with various commands; and performing the packet analysis in your lab should have made you a little more comfortable with how IPX works. I'll certainly test that out in the upcoming Trouble Tickets. IPX is the main protocol at the Internet Layer for the IPX/SPX stack. Helpers such as ARP and Reverse Address Resolution Protocol (RARP) are not used with IPX because the MAC address is the node address.

Before you venture into the Trouble Tickets, I'll spend a bit more time discussing addressing and routing protocols as I cover the Transport and Application Layers.

Transport (Host-to-Host) Layer Protocols, Applications, and Utilities

As you recall from the OSI model in Chapter 1, "Shooting Trouble," the Transport Layer is all about host-to-host delivery. IPX is a Layer 3 unreliable connectionless datagram delivery protocol; its Layer 4 counterpart, reliable connection-oriented SPX, is for things such as remote console and printing. SPX II is compatible with SPX and in addition provides features such as sliding windows, end-to-end large data packets, and an orderly release of a connection. Check out www.novell.com for more details. Figure 4-12 displays Sniffer's view of the SPX header format when I issued the RConsole command from my client. Feel free to capture your own

RConsole session, open the Sniffer file (*chapter 4 remote console and spx sniffer capture*) or just view the output from Figure 4-12.

Figure 4-12 *Analyzing the RConsole SPX Packet*

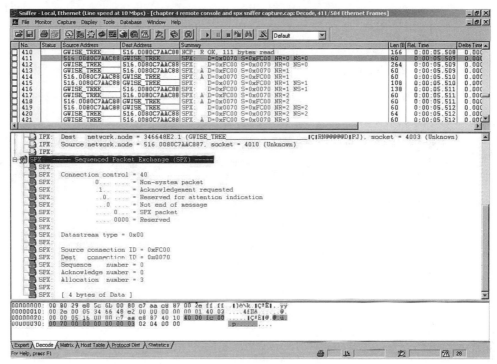

As you have seen in the previous layered subsections, after you have eliminated Physical Layer issues, protocol connections are troubleshooting targets that must be considered. After the protocol connections have been confirmed as operational, it is time to move up to the Application Layers. I could not begin to cover the vast variety of upper-layer applications in use today, but I will introduce some more of the major Application Layer protocols of the IPX/SPX suite.

Prepare for the next section by performing the following:

- Use Sniffer to capture the Novell server starting up; use a **config** command on the Novell box and a **ping** to the Novell server from r1. Save the file as *chapter 4 startup 8023 server config and ping sniffer capture.*

- Use Sniffer to capture a client startup on an 802.3 network. Browse Network Neighborhood and look at the sys volume on the Novell server. Next select **Start > Run \\gwise\vol1**, choose **Software** and then **Client**. Optionally, select **Whoami** by right-clicking Network Neighborhood. Save the file as *chapter 4 client startup on 8023 browse net neigh and sys sniffer capture.*

Upper-Layer Protocols, Applications, and Utilities

At the upper layers of the IPX/SPX protocol stack, the Novell NetWare Core Protocol (NCP) is used by file servers and clients alike for server routines and file and print management. Novell clients make a GNS request, and Novell servers or Cisco routers can respond. This is possible because Cisco routers maintain a RIP and SAP table. However, the Cisco device is polite in that it lets a Novell server of the requested type respond if one exists in the direction from where the request was heard. When the client finds a server, it broadcasts a RIP request to locate a route to the server. Finally, the Novell client can send NCP requests to log on and use the file system.

Analyze the Sniffer client startup file that you captured earlier as I do in Figure 4-13 and Figure 4-14.

Figure 4-13 *Analyzing the IPX Client Startup*

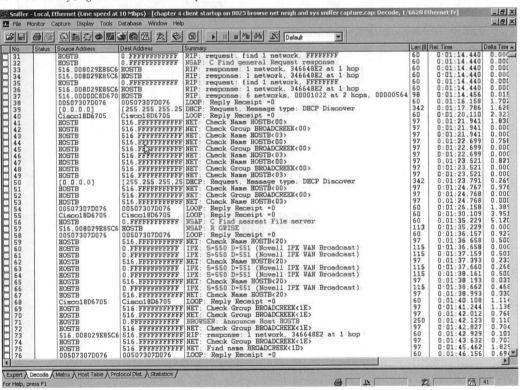

The IPX header in frame 26 shows the RIP request where the source address is 0.*hostbmac* and the destination is broadcast. The client does not actually learn its IPX network address until after the RIP response, as you can see in frame 33. Follow the overall sequence of messages in the Sniffer summary pane for GNS, the IPX RIP request, the NCP connection and negotiation, including the volume mounting. The IPX header in frame 32 displays the source and destination address as 0, which means this wire and the all FFFFFFFFFFFFs indicate a broadcast on this wire.

Figure 4-14 *Analyzing the IPX Client Startup*

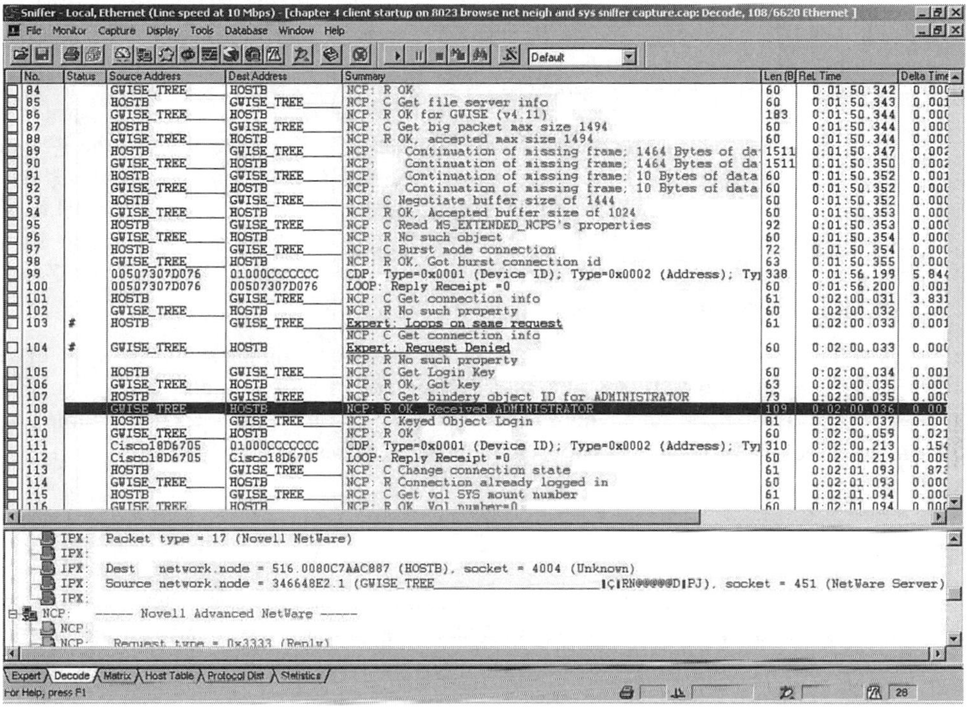

The NCP connection and negotiation occurs in lines 83 to 114. Frame 87 mentions the *negotiation of get big packet max size* where it is negotiating the path MTU size. IPX uses path MTU discovery rather than fragmentation. I think of this portion of NCP as like Microsoft's Server Message Block (SMB) protocol. Frames 89 to 92 sends two full MTU-size echos to port 0x4002 for testing. ACK packets take up space and burst mode is there for windowing, which can improve throughput for file transfers. NetWare increases and decreases the gap between packets for windowing. Login starts in f4rame 105, where Sniffer shows the bindery object information for Administrator. NCP continues the mounting of the sys volume and volume 1 as well as the Administrator login.

NOTE   The *bindery* is a flat database on each server, whereas Novell Directory Services (NDS) is a hierarchical database of all objects in directory trees and organizational units. Although you can use just bindery services today, most Novell shops take advantage of the NDS capabilities for single-login purposes to use and manage network resources.

Another example of upper-layer services is Network Basic Input/Output System (NetBIOS). You enable NetBIOS support on the client. It is a Session Layer interface for IBM and Microsoft. Practical applications of NetBIOS include browsing Network Neighborhood and using many of the command-line net commands. Type **net /?** at the client command prompt to see the available network commands.

For example, I can type **net view \\GWISE** to see the sys volume and volume 1 on my server or type **net use** to map a drive. The **net use g: \\gwise\sys** command maps the G: drive to my NetWare sys volume, so I can get to it as easily as I can to my C: drive. Type **net config** to see client and server information. These commands and others are very helpful troubleshooting commands for Windows-based clients, whether they are running the Microsoft Client for Novell Networks or for Microsoft Networks.

As with any protocol suite, you can spend a lifetime learning the specifics of the upper layers. For IPX in particular, you might want to spend more time researching NDS, ZenWorks, the NLMs, and other add-on modules for Novell and third-party services responsible for management, file, print, message, and database services.

Addressing

Regardless of what is happening at the upper layers, the IPX addressing scheme is an integral part of routing. NetWare is a software router. The routing table consists of unique internal (server) and external (wire) IPX numbers. The internal network number is internal to the file server and always ends in 0000.0000.0001. It is a logical network that routes packets to the physical networks to which a server is attached. Think of it like a loopback interface on a Cisco router. The external network number is the wire ID analogous to a subnet in IP. Periodic broadcasts are sent out on the wire, and the network and encapsulation numbers must match (as you saw in the chapter scenario).

You viewed the router routing table with **show ipx route** and the services table with **show ipx servers**. You can even see the server list from the client with **slist/nlist**. You viewed the Novell routing table on the server with **display networks** and the Novell SAP table with **display servers**.

NetWare addresses consist of an 80-bit *network.host* hex number. The network number is 32 bits—an 8-digit hex number where the leading 0s are suppressed. The host (node) number is 48 bits, or a 6-digit hex number. Because the MAC address is the node address, there is no need for ARP in an IPX environment. Hexadecimal is Base16, where the digits 0 to 9 and the letters A to F are available. The following Cisco commands are quite helpful for addressing:

- **show ipx interface brief**
- **show ipx interface** *interface*
- **show protocols**

NOTE   Novell offers the Novell Network Registry, which is a service to assign and track IPX network addresses and organization names. The Registry assigns a contiguous block of addresses unique to your organization. This way when companies merge or want to interconnect, the numbers are ensured to be unique. Send an e-mail to registry@novell.com or call 408 577-7506 to receive a copy of the Novell Network Registry if you are still using IPX.

How do you determine the network number? You could ask someone, use Cisco Discovery Protocol (CDP), or use the NetWare **config** command at the file server console.

You have certainly witnessed practical examples of where you need to know addressing. Another example is an access list. Unlike IP, IPX standard access lists (800 to 899) include both source and destination addresses. Therefore, many things can be accomplished with either a standard ACL or a SAP filter (1000 to 1099). If you need extended protocol or socket capabilities, extended IPX ACLs (900 to 999) provide that.

Routing Protocols

As mentioned in the preceding chapter, routing protocols have their own unique characteristics, and various Layer 2 encapsulation types have a big impact on them. Understanding how they work will certainly assist you in troubleshooting them now and later. Most of the statistics listed for each can be found with IOS commands, such as **show protocols** and **show ipx route**. Logging, debugging, and Sniffer are certainly valuable tools to see more detail when troubleshooting, too.

The following subsections briefly examine the RIP, NLSP, and EIGRP IPX routing protocols. This discussion assumes you understand the basic background and theory of each of these routing protocols and therefore focuses on practical application.

IPX RIP

IPX RIP is the default distance vector routing protocol for IPX. It is enabled automatically when you enable IPX routing. The IPX RIP metrics are ticks (1/18 of a second) and then hops. When you previously issued the **display networks** command on the Novell server, the ticks/hops followed the network number. The WAN interface default ticks is 6. The LAN interface default ticks is 1. To change the ticks value on an interface, use the following interface configuration command:

```
ipx delay [0-65535]
```

Novell added the Service Advertisement Protocol (SAP) (not to be confused with IEEE 802.2 LLC service access points) to its RIP implementation. This is how servers broadcast (advertise) the services and addresses they have available. Cisco routers do not forward individual SAPs;

instead, they build SAP tables just as they do routing tables. These tables are broadcast every 60 seconds in an IPX RIP environment.

Configuring IPX RIP is as simple as turning on IPX routing. If you can't use the **show ipx route** command, you may not have IPX routing turned on; if you can't turn that on, you may need a different IOS feature set image. Then you must worry about having enough memory to support the new IOS with the appropriate feature set.

NOTE   To save you a little frustration, the global configuration command to turn off IPX RIP is **no router ipx rip**.

NLSP and EIGRP are viable alternatives for IPX RIP. NLSP is Novell's link-state routing protocol, and EIGRP is a Cisco proprietary routing protocol that supports multiple routed protocols (including IPX).

NLSP

NetWare Link Services (State) Protocol (NLSP) has several advantages over IPX RIP. It is more scalable and stores a complete map of the network rather than just next-hop information. It was designed to replace RIP and SAP on large global networks with less overhead. As its name describes, NLSP is a link-state routing protocol that transmits route and service changes, not periodic updates. Reliability is increased and routing is improved especially on the WAN through IPX header compression and multicast addressing to all NLSP routers.

Search at Cisco.com for "configure nlsp" for help with this routing protocol. The following site is very helpful for other IPX-related routing protocols and sample configurations, too:

> www.cisco.com/univercd/cc/td/doc/product/software/ios121/121cgcr/atipx_c/ipx/
> 2cdipxex.htm#xtocid1085930

EIGRP

Novell servers do not understand the Enhanced IGRP (EIGRP) routing protocol. However, EIGRP is a viable solution for IPX on the LAN and EIGRP on the WAN. Table 4-9 illustrates some IPX EIGRP configuration and troubleshooting commands. Redistribution occurs automatically between IPX and EIGRP unless you turn this feature off with **no redistribute**. Other reasons for IPX on the LAN and EIGRP on the WAN include the increased network width and incremental SAP updates.

Table 4-9   *IPX EIGRP Configuration and Troubleshooting Commands*

Task	IPX EIGRP Command
Enable the routing process using an AS number	r1(config)#**ipx router eigrp 100**
Configure the directly connected networks	r1(config-ipx-router)#**network 516**
	r1(config-ipx-router)#**network 532**
	r1(config-ipx-router)#**network 580**
	r1(config-ipx-router)#**network 1011**
	r1(config-ipx-router)#**end**
Miscellaneous parameters	r1(config-ipx-router)#**no redistribute ?**
	r1(config-ipx-router)#**ipx hello-interval eigrp ?**
	r1(config-ipx-router)#**ipx hold-time eigrp ?**
	r1(config-ipx-router)#**no ipx split-horizon eigrp ?**
	r1(config-ipx-router)#**ipx sap-incremental eigrp** *ASnumber* **?**
	r1(config-ipx-router)#**distribute-list** *ASnumber* **?**
	r1(config)#**ipx backup-server-query-interval ?**
Monitor IPX EIGRP	r1#**show ipx eigrp ?**
	r1#**show ipx eigrp neighbors ?**
	r1#**show ipx eigrp topology ?**
	r1#**show ipx eigrp route ?**
	r1#**show ipx eigrp traffic ?**

As mentioned in Chapter 3, individual routing protocols are books in themselves. The routing table is a good place to start troubleshooting; if routes are missing, however, ultimately that may depend on Physical or Data Link issues, neighbor relationships, and/or topology tables. Cisco does a great job at assisting you with IP and IPX troubleshooting, as you can see in Figure 4-15.

If you are still using Novell's IPX in your environment, look up some of the case studies displayed in Figure 4-15. Other troubleshooting issues include timers. They must match between routers (and servers) on a given data link; otherwise routes/services appear to come and go, resulting in intermittent connections.

Now it is time for the chapter Trouble Tickets. The plan here is to give you several things to do, let you make mistakes and fix some things on your own, and to introduce other problems that you should have some experience with as a support person. Shooting trouble with IPX can be as easy as dropping the X, which may in fact be appropriate on the WAN. However, that solution is not a viable one for the Trouble Tickets. The IPX Trouble Tickets start where the chapter leaves off for the client, server, and router configurations.

Figure 4-15 *Troubleshooting Novell IP and IPX Issues*

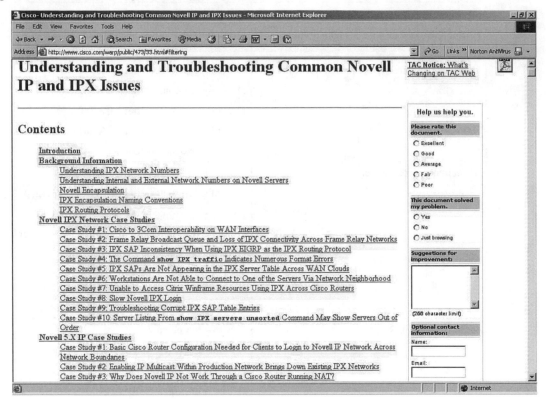

Trouble Tickets

Complete the following Trouble Tickets in order. Use the tools from this and the previous chapters to analyze, test, and document as you go. Feel free to create your own physical layer problems if you need more practice there. Sample solutions are provided after this section.

Trouble Ticket 1

Set up each router so that when you ping a serial interface you are pinging the *wire number.router number*. Use numbers such as all 1s for r1, all 2s for r2, and so on. Display the router and interface configuration for all routers as I do for r1 in the solution. Ping a serial interface on another router to verify connectivity. Document within the configuration right before you ping the other router's serial interface.

Trouble Ticket 2

Change the frame type for network 516 to 802.2. Ping from r1 to the Novell server to verify connectivity. Issue an extended trace, too.

Trouble Ticket 3

Change the routing protocols so that you are using RIP on the Novell LAN and EIGRP for everything else with an AS number of 100. Configure the WAN links between r2 and r3 to load balance if possible. View the routing table and use debug to watch the routing and SAP updates. Save the data to a log file for later review. Make sure there are no filters or ACLs blocking anything.

Trouble Ticket 4

Use Sniffer to capture the Novell server startup. Ping it when it is up from r1.

Trouble Ticket 5

Use Sniffer to capture the hostb client startup on 802.2. Verify connectivity through all layers. Set the client set to the wrong frame type. What happens?

Trouble Ticket 6

Use tools such as CDP to assist you in updating your chapter scenario diagram. Label things such as device types, IOS versions, node addresses, wire addresses, cable specs, routed/routing protocols, and so on.

Trouble Tickets Solutions

These solutions are not always the only way to perform these tasks. However, the upcoming chapter scenarios are based on these solutions.

Trouble Ticket 1 Solution

Example 4-31 and Example 4-32 illustrate the **ipx routing** command on each of the routers. I used 1111.1111.1111 for r1, but 1.1.1 would also work just fine. This optional node command makes troubleshooting serial interfaces easier because you are not just having them automatically use the MAC address from an available Ethernet, Token Ring, or FDDI interface but rather one you are familiar with for all serial interfaces on the router. The **show ipx interface** serial 0 command is a quick way to see that the serial 0 interface is utilizing the IPX routing node you configured.

Example 4-31 *IPX Trouble Ticket 1*

```
r1(config)#ipx routing ?
  H.H.H  IPX address of this router
  <cr>
r1(config)#ipx routing 1111.1111.1111
r1(config)#end
r1#show ipx interface serial 0
Serial0 is up, line protocol is up
  IPX address is 1011.1111.1111.1111 [up]
  Delay of this IPX network, in ticks is 6 throughput 0 link delay 0
  IPXWAN processing not enabled on this interface.
  IPX SAP update interval is 60 seconds
...
r1#show running-config
Building configuration...
Current configuration:
version 12.0
service timestamps debug uptime
service timestamps log uptime
no service password-encryption
hostname r1
enable secret 5 $1$m0s2$Pq/6.NpOCSzhbQlNy.cnG/
enable password donna
ip subnet-zero
ipx routing 1111.1111.1111
ipx ping-default novell
interface Ethernet0
...
r1#copy running-config startup-config
```

Example 4-32 shows IPX routing commands on r2 through r5. My test shows a ping to r2s0.
Remember to save all the configurations.

Example 4-32 *Configuring IPX Routing on r2 Through r5*

```
r2(config)#ipx routing 2222.2222.2222
r3(config)#ipx routing 3333.3333.3333
r4(config)#ipx routing 4444.4444.4444
r5(config)#ipx routing 5555.5555.5555
r2#show ipx interface serial 0
Serial0 is up, line protocol is up
  IPX address is 564.2222.2222.2222 [up]
...
r2#ping ipx 564.2222.2222.2222
...
Sending 5, 100-byte IPX Novell Echoes to 564.2222.2222.2222, timeout is
   2 seconds:
!!!!!
Success rate is 100 percent (5/5), round-trip min/avg/max = 60/60/60 ms
r1#!!!now pinging r2s0 from r1
r1#ping ipx 564.2222.2222.2222
Type escape sequence to abort.
Sending 5, 100-byte IPX Novell Echoes to 564.2222.2222.2222,
   timeout is 2 seconds:
!!!!!
Success rate is 100 percent(5/5), round-trip min/avg/max = 4/4/8 ms
r1#
```

Trouble Ticket 2 Solution

Configure the Novell server with the **unbind** and **bind** commands or the inetcfg bindings menu (**load inetcfg**) as well as the r1 interface connected to wire 516. The commands for r1 are in Example 4-33.

Example 4-33   *IPX Trouble Ticket 2*

```
r1(config)#interface ethernet 0
r1(config-if)#ipx encapsulation ?
  arpa         IPX Ethernet_II
  hdlc         HDLC on serial links
  novell-ether IPX Ethernet_802.3
  sap          IEEE 802.2 on Ethernet, Token Ring, and FDDI
  snap         IEEE 802.2 SNAP on Ethernet, Token Ring, and FDDI
r1(config-if)#ipx encapsulation sap
r1(config-if)#end
r1#show ipx servers
Codes: S - Static, P - Periodic, E - EIGRP, N - NLSP, H - Holddown, + = detail
U - Per-user static
4 Total IPX Servers
Table ordering is based on routing and server info
    Type Name                      Net      Address    Port    Route Hops Itf
P    4 GWISE                   346648E2.0000.0000.0001:0451    2/01   1  Et0
P  107 GWISE                   346648E2.0000.0000.0001:8104    2/01   1  Et0
P  26B GWISE_TREE_____  ___  346648F2.0000.0000.0001:0005    2/01   1  Et0
P  278 GWISE_TREE_____    346648E2.0000.0000.0001:4006    2/01   1  Et0
r1#show ipx interface brief
Interface         IPX Network Encapsulation Status           IPX State
Ethernet0         516         SAP          up                [up]
Ethernet1         532         NOVELL-ETHER up                [up]
Serial0           1011        HDLC         up                [up]
Serial1           580         HDLC         up                [up]
r1#ping ipx 346648e2.0.0.1
Sending 5, 100-byte IPX Novell Echoes to 346648E2.0000.0000.0001, timeout is
    2 seconds:
!!!!!
Success rate is 100 percent (5/5), round-trip min/avg/max = 1/1/1 ms
r1#trace
Protocol [ip]: ipx
Target IPX address: 346648e2.0.0.1
Numeric display [n]:
Timeout in seconds [3]:
Probe count [3]:
Minimum Time to Live [0]:
Maximum Time to Live [1]:
Verbose [n]:
Type escape sequence to abort.
Tracing the route to 346648E2.0000.0000.0001
  0  *  *  *
  1  *  *  *
... tracing the route using Diagnostic Requests
  2 346648E2.0000.0000.0001 (GWISE) 0 msec 8 msec 8 msec
```

NOTE	Novell echoes are being sent in the ping packets because the **ipx ping-default novell** command was previously issued in the chapter. Look at your r1 configuration to verify this. If it is not there, the default is to send Cisco Echoes, which the Novell server would not understand.

Trouble Ticket 3 Solution

Example 4-34 illustrates the EIGRP configuration on the routers. As far as the log file, I used a SecureCRT session, but you could have used the HyperTerm, Transfer menu, Capture Text method, or options from other terminal emulator programs.

Example 4-34 *IPX Trouble Ticket 3*

```
r1(config)#ipx router eigrp 100
r1(config-ipx-router)#network 580
r1(config-ipx-router)#network 1011
r1(config-ipx-router)#end
r1#copy running-config startup-config
r2(config)#ipx router eigrp 100
r2(config-ipx-router)#network 548
r2(config-ipx-router)#network 564
r2(config-ipx-router)#exit
r2(config)#ipx maximum-paths 2
r2(config)#end
r2#copy running-config startup-config
r3(config)#ipx router eigrp 100
r3(config-ipx-router)#network 548
r3(config-ipx-router)#network 564
r3(config-ipx-router)#network 580
r3(config-ipx-router)#exit
r3(config)#ipx maximum-paths 2
r3(config)#end
r3#copy running-config startup-config
r4(config)#ipx router eigrp 100
r4(config-ipx-router)#network 1022
r4(config-ipx-router)#end
r4#copy running-config startup-config
r5(config)#ipx router eigrp 100
r5(config-ipx-router)#network 1011
r5(config-ipx-router)#end
r5#copy running-config startup-config
```

One major thing is missing from the preceding example as a result of you already having IPX configured on the routers. Issue **debug ipx routing** events and **debug ipx sap events** to give you some hints and fix the issues as I do in Example 4-35.

Example 4-35 *Turning Off IPX RIP*

```
r1(config)#no ipx router rip
r1(config)#ipx router rip
r1(config-ipx-router)#network 516
r1(config-ipx-router)#network 532
```

Example 4-35 *Turning Off IPX RIP (Continued)*

```
r1(config-ipx-router)#end
r1#copy running-config startup-config

r2(config)#no ipx router rip
r2(config)#ipx router rip
r2(config-ipx-router)#network 532
r2(config)#end
r2#copy running-config startup-config

r3(config)#no ipx router rip
r3(config)#ipx router rip
r3(config-ipx-router)#network 596
r3(config-ipx-router)#end
r3#copy running-config startup-config

r4(config)#no ipx router rip
r4(config)#end
r4#copy running-config startup-config

r5(config)#no ipx router rip
r5(config)#end
r5#copy running-config startup-config
```

Example 4-36 displays the IPX routing table. Notice the EIGRP-learned routes and the multiple paths to get to your destination. IPX load balancing is not enabled by default. By default the IOS splits traffic on a per-packet basis; NetWare NCP does not handle out-of-order packets within a burst gracefully. It uses per-host load balancing.

Example 4-36 *IPX Load Sharing*

```
r2#show ipx route
Codes: C - Connected primary network,    c - Connected secondary network
       S - Static, F - Floating static, L - Local (internal), W - IPXWAN
       R - RIP, E - EIGRP, N - NLSP, X - External, A - Aggregate
       s - seconds, u - uses, U - Per-user static
9 Total IPX routes. Up to 2 parallel paths and 16 hops allowed.
No default route known.
C        532 (NOVELL-ETHER),  Et0
C        548 (HDLC),          Se1
C        564 (HDLC),          Se0
E        516 [41049600/1] via  564.3333.3333.3333, age 00:43:45,u, Se0
                          via  548.3333.3333.3333, age 00:43:45, 0u, Se1
E        580 [41024000/0] via  564.3333.3333.3333, age 00:44:10, 1u, Se0
                          via  548.3333.3333.3333, age 00:44:10, 0u, Se1
E        596 [40514560/1] via  564.3333.3333.3333, age 00:44:10, 1u, Se0
                          via  548.3333.3333.3333, age 00:44:10, 0u, Se1
E       1011 [41536000/0] via  564.3333.3333.3333, age 00:43:50,1u, Se0
                          via  548.3333.3333.3333, age 00:43:50, 0u, Se1
E       1022 [41024000/0] via  548.3333.3333.3333, age 00:44:15, 1u, Se1
                          via  564.3333.3333.3333, age 00:44:15, 0u, Se0
E   346648E2 [270336000/2] via 564.3333.3333.3333, age 00:22:02,93u, Se0
                          via  548.3333.3333.3333, age 00:22:02,0u, Se1
r2#
```

Trouble Ticket 4 Solution

I performed the protocol analyzer capture and saved it as *chapter 4 startup 8022 server config and ping sniffer capture*. Look at Figure 4-16 or your Sniffer capture to examine the differences between IPX over 802.3 and 802.2 frames.

Figure 4-16   *802.2 Server*

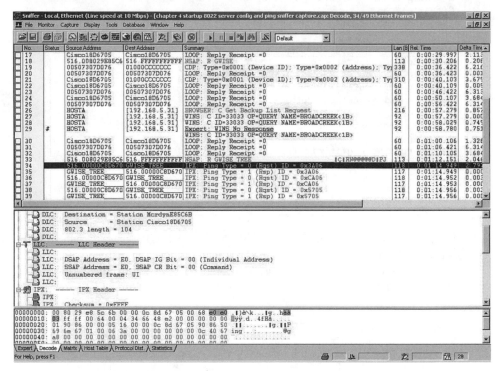

Trouble Ticket 5 Solution

I performed the protocol analyzer capture and saved it as *chapter 4 bring up auto client on 802.2 server sniffer capture*. Look at Figure 4-17 or your Sniffer capture to analyze the layers and the incorrect frame type.

Network Neighborhood is one way to verify all the layers. If you have problems with that, try the Find Computer selection or the **net view** command and capture the results in the protocol analyzer.

When you set the client to the wrong frame type, the Novell Primary Network Login does not display, but the Client for Microsoft does. Other symptoms include Network Neighborhood showing the Entire Network icon only. You can't browse it, but the Microsoft client does point you to the Network Troubleshooter. That should give you another tool for your bag, but more importantly lead you to the issue of an incorrect frame type.

Figure 4-17 *802.2 Client*

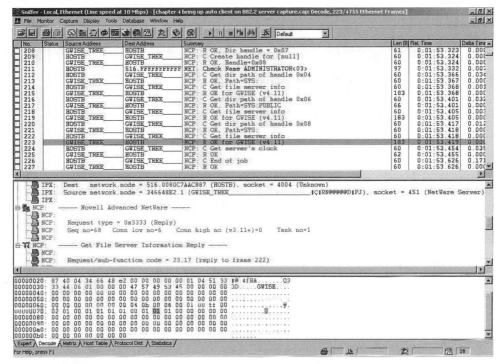

Trouble Ticket 6 Solution

I have highlighted some of the helpful output of CDP in Example 4-37 to assist you with updating your chapter scenario diagram. Check your work against Figure 4-1.

Example 4-37 *IPX Trouble Ticket 6*

```
r1#show cdp neighbors detail
Device ID: r2
Entry address(es):
  Novell address: 532.0000.0c38.a05d
Platform: cisco 2500,  Capabilities: Router
Interface: Ethernet1,  Port ID (outgoing port): Ethernet0
Holdtime : 124 sec
     Version :
Cisco Internetwork Operating System Software
IOS (tm) 2500 Software (C2500-JS-L), Version 12.0(21a), RELEASE SOFTWARE (fc1)
Copyright  1986-2002 by cisco Systems, Inc.
Compiled Sat 02-Feb-02 02:08 by nmasa
--------------------------
Device ID: r3
Entry address(es):
  Novell address: 580.3333.3333.3333
Platform: cisco 3640,  Capabilities: Router
Interface: Serial1,  Port ID (outgoing port): Serial0/0
```

continues

Example 4-37 *IPX Trouble Ticket 6 (Continued)*

```
Holdtime : 138 sec
Version :
Cisco Internetwork Operating System Software
IOS (tm) 3600 Software (C3640-JS-M), Version 12.0(13), RELEASE SOFTWARE (fc1)
Copyright  1986-2000 by cisco Systems, Inc.
Compiled Tue 05-Sep-00 21:39 by linda
-------------------------
Device ID: r5
Entry address(es):
  Novell address: 1011.5555.5555.5555
Platform: cisco 2516,  Capabilities: Router
Interface: Serial0,  Port ID (outgoing port): Serial0
Holdtime : 163 sec
Version :
Cisco Internetwork Operating System Software
IOS (tm) 2500 Software (C2500-JS-L), Version 12.0(21a), RELEASE SOFTWARE (fc1)
Copyright  1986-2002 by cisco Systems, Inc.
Compiled Sat 02-Feb-02 02:08 by nmasa
```

Example 4-37 illustrates that r1's directly connected neighbors are r2, r3, and r5. Compare this output to Figure 4-1 and add notes such as r2 is connected to r1 via the r1e1 r2e0 Ethernet link with an external IPX network number of 532. The r2 IOS is 12.0(21a). CDP assists you with MAC addresses, too. For example, look at r3 and r5 where the MAC addresses match the node you specified to use for serial interfaces in the first Trouble Ticket. The r1 device connects to r3 via its s1 interface and to r5 via its s0 interface. At a minimum, also document the frame types where IPX is concerned; **show ipx interface brief** can help with that. Other helpful documentation commands include **show ipx route**, **show protocols**, and so on, which you should perform on all your routers to get comfortable with your environment. Example 4-38 displays CDP information for r2.

Example 4-38 *CDP on r2*

```
r2>show cdp neigh detail
Device ID: r3
Entry address(es):
  Novell address: 548.3333.3333.3333
Platform: cisco 3640,  Capabilities: Router
Interface: Serial1,  Port ID (outgoing port): Serial0/2
Holdtime : 126 sec
Version :
Cisco Internetwork Operating System Software
IOS (tm) 3600 Software (C3640-JS-M), Version 12.0(13), RELEASE SOFTWARE (fc1)
Copyright  1986-2000 by cisco Systems, Inc.
Compiled Tue 05-Sep-00 21:39 by linda
-------------------------
Device ID: r3
Entry address(es):
  Novell address: 564.3333.3333.3333
Platform: cisco 3640,  Capabilities: Router
Interface: Serial0,  Port ID (outgoing port): Serial0/1
Holdtime : 125 sec
Version :
```

Example 4-38 *CDP on r2 (Continued)*

```
Cisco Internetwork Operating System Software
IOS (tm) 3600 Software (C3640-JS-M), Version 12.0(13), RELEASE SOFTWARE (fc1)
Copyright  1986-2000 by cisco Systems, Inc.
Compiled Tue 05-Sep-00 21:39 by linda
-----------------------
Device ID: r1
Entry address(es):
  Novell address: 532.0000.0c8d.6706
Platform: cisco 2500,  Capabilities: Router
Interface: Ethernet0,  Port ID (outgoing port): Ethernet1
Holdtime : 131 sec
Version :
Cisco Internetwork Operating System Software
IOS (tm) 2500 Software (C2500-JS-L), Version 12.0(21a), RELEASE SOFTWARE (fc1)
Copyright  1986-2002 by cisco Systems, Inc.
Compiled Sat 02-Feb-02 02:08 by nmasa
```

Review Questions

Use this chapter and your practical troubleshooting knowledge and skills to answer the following questions. The answers are located in Appendix A, "Answers to Review Questions."

1 What IOS command assists in determining detailed information if the router is propagating RIP updates?

2 What IOS command assists in determining detailed information if the router is propagating SAP updates?

3 What is the difference between the Novell internal IPX number and the Novell external IPX number?

4 Fill in the following table with the missing Cisco and Novell encapsulation names.

Cisco Encapsulation	Novell Frame Type	Description	Novell Version Default
ARPA	Ethernet_II	EtherType pointer to Layer 3	NetWare 6.x NetWare 5.x
SAP		Length field 802.2 LLC SAP pointer to Layer 3	NetWare 3.12 through NetWare 4.x
Novell-Ether		Length field	≤ NetWare 3.11
	Ethernet_SNAP	Length field 802.2 LLC SAP SNAP header	SNAP default for Token Ring and FDDI
		Serial links	All versions for serial links

5 What type of packet does Figure 4-18 display? What form of Cisco encapsulation is used?

Figure 4-18 *Review Question 5*

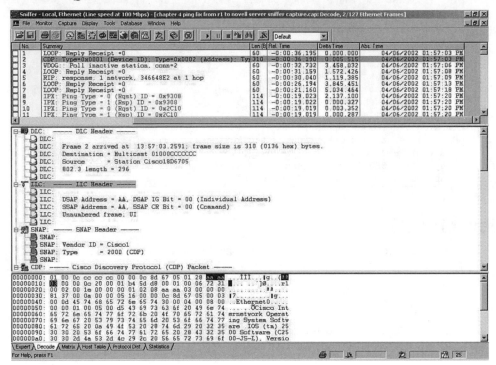

6 Explain the difference between Cisco ping and IPX ping. Which one is the default? Why would you change the default? How do you change the default?

7 MTU is negotiated by NCP. It is 1500 for a local Ethernet segment and 576 bytes for the internetwork. How can you verify this?

8 The **route print** command displays the routing table on a PC. How can you see this information on a router running IPX RIP? How about on a Novell server?

9 How do you configure IPX RIP on a Cisco router?

10 Why doesn't IPX need ARP?

11 Explain the following address:

12345678.0000.0000.0001:0451

12 How does IPX RIP find the best path to another network? How does this differ from IP RIP?

13 In the chapter scenario, hosta is a Windows 2000 box. What command gives you the display in Figure 4-19?

Figure 4-19 *Review Question 13*

```
NWLink IPX Routing and Source Routing Control Program v2.00

Num  Name                      Network    Node          Frame
=======================================================================
1.   IpxLoopbackAdapter        00000516   00104ba5ae50  [802.2]
2.   Local Area Connection     00000516   00104ba5ae50  [802.2]
3.   NDISWANIPX                00000000   e0fc20524153  [EthII] -
```

Summary

More and more companies are adopting IP-based networks, so shooting trouble with IPX may or may not be among your worries. To enhance your overall troubleshooting skills, you should gain an understanding of IPX end-to-end issues and know where to find the right tools and how to use the proper methods to ensure internetwork connectivity, availability, redundancy, responsiveness, and security. This chapter reviewed IPX protocols and packets, addressing, and routing protocol topics to prepare you for IPX troubleshooting. The focus now turns to Layer 2 LAN and WAN technologies to continue to build your practical troubleshooting skills.

PART III

Supporting Ethernet, Switches, and VLANs

CHAPTER 5

Shooting Trouble with Ethernet

A solid understanding of Ethernet is as essential as supporting TCP/IP today. Many people have been using Ethernet since they started networking. Others have used it since the "frozen yellow garden hose" days of 10BASE5. You have used it in all the scenarios and Trouble Tickets thus far and will continue to use it throughout the book and in the real world. Understanding and supporting Ethernet not only applies to the CCNP certification but to all industry certifications. This chapter assumes your understanding of the information from the previous chapters, including protocols, models, troubleshooting methods, support tools, and resources.

In this chapter you combine some of the tasks from the preceding two chapters to build this chapter's scenario. Following the scenario is a review of Ethernet concepts, symptoms, problems, and action plans. To help you gain practical experience, this chapter contains several walk-through scenarios and practical Trouble Tickets for you explore. For those of you who do not have equipment handy, there are many relevant figures, examples, and explanations so that you, too, can shoot trouble with Ethernet.

This chapter covers the following topics:

- Scenario: Shooting Trouble with Ethernet
- A Brief Summary of Ethernet
- Ethernet Frames
- Ethernet Addressing
- Ethernet at the Physical Layer
- Shooting Trouble with Ethernet
- Trouble Tickets
- Trouble Tickets Solutions

Supporting Website Files

You can find files and links to utilities that support this book on the Cisco Press website at www.ciscopress.com/1587200570. Even if you do not have a lab, you can take advantage of the supporting configuration files including the logs to understand device input and output. The files are listed throughout the chapters in italics.

In order to be able to read and work with some of the supporting files offered at www.ciscopress.com/1587200570, you may want to download some of the programs listed in Table I-1 in the Introduction.

Scenario: Shooting Trouble with Ethernet

This chapter starts with the IPX hands-on scenario you left off with at the end of the Trouble Tickets in Chapter 4, "Shooting Trouble with Novell IPX." The goals of the Shooting Trouble with Ethernet scenario are for you to modify your routers according to Figure 5-1 and verify end-to-end connectivity. Hostb requires use of an IPX application on the gwise server, but it should also be able to communicate via IP to the other hosts. The rest of the scenario suggests IP as the routed protocol and Enhanced Interior Gateway Routing Protocol (EIGRP) as the routing protocol using autonomous system (AS) 500. The IP subnets are the circled numbers on the wires. There should be end-to-end IP connectivity between hosta and hostc. Run IPX RIP on network number 516. The rest of the chapter deploys this scenario, so be sure to save your configurations before, during, and after you configure your devices.

NOTE   My lab uses the 2514, 2501, 3640, 3620, and 2516 Cisco routers, but yours can include any number of devices that have similar interfaces. Connect the hosts off of r1e0 by way of a hub. See Appendix C, "Equipment Reference," for the hardware used throughout this book.

Figure 5-1 *Shooting Trouble with Ethernet*

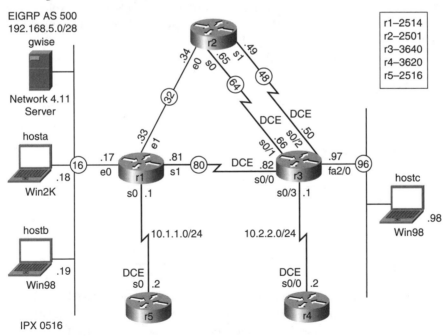

Document your steps and *any* problems along the way. Save your work and don't forget to test things out. Remember, however, that there is not always one right or wrong way to accomplish the task or tasks presented. The ability to obtain the end result using good practices is extremely important in any real-world network. My ending configurations are printed starting in Example 5-1 through Example 5-5 so that you can compare your work. Use the previous troubleshooting checklists, your step-by-step troubleshooting methodology, and the Ethernet checklist in Table 5-1 to assist in testing. Refresh your memory by looking back at Table 3-1 (IP Checklist) and Table 4-1 (IPX Checklist) now.

NOTE   A very quick way to eliminate all IPX commands on r2 through r5 is by using the global command **no ipx routing**.

Table 5-1   *Ethernet Layer 1 and 2 Quick Troubleshooting Checklist*

Isolating Problems	Commands and Symptoms

Cable, NIC, hub, switch
   Physical inspection
   Protocol analyzer
   TDR/OTDR
NIC software configuration
Segmentation
Concentrate on interfaces and controllers for lower-level targets
	See IP and IPX Checklists for ping, trace, and other relevant router/desktop tools.
	show ip interface brief
	show ipx interface brief
	show controllers
	show interfaces [*interface*]
	show ip interface [*interface*]
	show ipx interface [*interface*]

Drivers	www.winfiles.com www.driverguide.com
Encapsulation Know your frame types	**show interfaces** [*interface*] **show ipx interface brief** NIC diagnostics/properties
Autonegotiation Speed issues cause connectivity problems Duplex issues cause performance problems	**show interface** [*interface*] Collisions on a full-duplex link, for example.
One-way link You can receive but can't transmit or vice versa	Check the cable.

Example 5-1   *r1 Configuration (2514)*

```
r1#show running-config
Building configuration...
Current configuration:
version 12.0
service timestamps debug uptime
service timestamps log uptime
no service password-encryption
hostname r1
```

continues

Example 5-1   *r1 Configuration (2514) (Continued)*

```
enable secret 5 $1$m0s2$Pq/6.NpOCSzhbQlNy.cnG/
enable password donna
ip subnet-zero
ipx routing 1111.1111.1111
ipx ping-default novell
interface Ethernet0
 description r1e0 to hosta and hostb
 ip address 192.168.5.17 255.255.255.240
 no ip directed-broadcast
 ipx encapsulation SAP
 ipx network 516
interface Ethernet1
 description r1e1 to r2e0
 ip address 192.168.5.33 255.255.255.240
 no ip directed-broadcast
interface Serial0
 description r1s0 to r5s0
 bandwidth 64
 ip address 10.1.1.1 255.255.255.0
 no ip directed-broadcast
 no ip mroute-cache
 no fair-queue
interface Serial1
 description r1s1 to r3s0/0
 bandwidth 64
 ip address 192.168.5.81 255.255.255.240
 no ip directed-broadcast
router eigrp 500
 network 10.0.0.0
 network 192.168.5.0
 no auto-summary
ip classless
tftp-server flash:c2500-js-l.120-21a.bin
line con 0
 logging synchronous
 transport input none
line aux 0
line vty 0 4
 password donna
 login
end
```

Example 5-2   *r2 Configuration (2501)*

```
r2#show running-config
Building configuration...
Current configuration:
version 12.0
service timestamps debug uptime
service timestamps log uptime
no service password-encryption
hostname r2
enable secret 5 $1$5FjB$OHtAhTOCisLWIa5qzy3RJ1
enable password donna
```

Example 5-2 *r2 Configuration (2501) (Continued)*

```
ip subnet-zero
interface Ethernet0
 description r2e0 to r1e1
 ip address 192.168.5.34 255.255.255.240
 no ip directed-broadcast
interface Serial0
 description r2s0 to r3s0/1
 bandwidth 64
 ip address 192.168.5.65 255.255.255.240
 no ip directed-broadcast
 no ip mroute-cache
 no fair-queue
interface Serial1
 description r2s1 to r3s0/2
 bandwidth 64
 ip address 192.168.5.49 255.255.255.240
 no ip directed-broadcast
router eigrp 500
 network 192.168.5.0
ip classless
line con 0
 logging synchronous
 transport input none
line aux 0
line vty 0 4
 password donna
 login
end
```

Example 5-3 *r3 Configuration (3640)*

```
r3#show running-config
Building configuration...
Current configuration:
version 12.0
service timestamps debug uptime
service timestamps log uptime
no service password-encryption
hostname r3
enable secret 5 $1$VA..$TqTkW/PwrI4bRPF1zjZCu1
enable password donna
ip subnet-zero
interface Serial0/0
 description r3s0/0 to r1s1
 bandwidth 64
 ip address 192.168.5.82 255.255.255.240
 no ip directed-broadcast
 no ip mroute-cache
 no fair-queue
 clockrate 64000
interface Serial0/1
 description r3s0/1 to r2s0
 bandwidth 64
 ip address 192.168.5.66 255.255.255.240
```

continues

Example 5-3 *r3 Configuration (3640) (Continued)*

```
 no ip directed-broadcast
 clockrate 64000
interface Serial0/2
 description r3s0/2 to r2s1
 bandwidth 64
 ip address 192.168.5.50 255.255.255.240
 no ip directed-broadcast
 clockrate 64000
interface Serial0/3
 description r3s0/3 to r4s0/0
 bandwidth 64
 ip address 10.2.2.1 255.255.255.0
 no ip directed-broadcast
...
interface FastEthernet2/0
 description r3fa2/0 to hostc
 ip address 192.168.5.97 255.255.255.240
 no ip directed-broadcast
router eigrp 500
 network 10.0.0.0
 network 192.168.5.0
 no auto-summary
ip classless
line con 0
 logging synchronous
 transport input none
line aux 0
line vty 0 4
 password donna
 login
end
```

Example 5-4 *r4 Configuration (3620)*

```
r4#show running-config
Building configuration...
Current configuration:
version 11.3
service timestamps debug uptime
service timestamps log uptime
no service password-encryption
hostname r4
enable secret 5 $1$C0Dd$kkBg8CqXD2ZVjcHq8uvxB/
enable password donna
interface Ethernet0/0
 no ip address
 shutdown
interface Serial0/0
 description r4s0/0 to r3s0/3
 ip address 10.2.2.2 255.255.255.0
 no ip mroute-cache
 bandwidth 64
 no fair-queue
```

Example 5-4 *r4 Configuration (3620)*

```
 clockrate 64000
interface Serial0/1
 no ip address
 shutdown
router eigrp 500
 network 10.0.0.0
 no auto-summary
ip classless
line con 0
 logging synchronous
line aux 0
line vty 0 4
 password donna
 login
end
```

Example 5-5 *r5 Configuration (2516)*

```
r5#show running-config
Building configuration...
Current configuration:
version 12.0
service timestamps debug uptime
service timestamps log uptime
no service password-encryption
hostname r5
enable secret 5 $1$eozM$NyPHA2CFPGE4V4xV806YS0
enable password donna
ip subnet-zero
...
interface Ethernet0
 no ip address
 no ip directed-broadcast
 shutdown
interface Serial0
 description r5s0 to r1s0
 bandwidth 64
 ip address 10.1.1.2 255.255.255.0
 no ip directed-broadcast
 no ip mroute-cache
 no fair-queue
 clockrate 64000
interface Serial1
 no ip address
 no ip directed-broadcast
 shutdown
interface BRI0
 no ip address
 no ip directed-broadcast
 shutdown
router eigrp 500
 network 10.0.0.0
```

continues

Example 5-5   *r5 Configuration (2516) (Continued)*

```
 no auto-summary
ip classless
line con 0
 logging synchronous
 transport input none
line aux 0
line vty 0 4
 password donna
 login
end
```

Next you should double-check your host configurations. Physically hosta, hostb, and the gwise server should be connected to r1e0 via a hub. Internetwork Packet Exchange (IPX) should be running on at least hostb, and IP should be running on all hosts. (See Table 5-2.)

Table 5-2   *IP Host Configuration*

	IP Address	Subnet Mask	Gateway
hosta	192.168.5.18	255.255.255.240	192.168.5.17
hostb	192.168.5.19	255.255.255.240	192.168.5.17
hostc	192.168.5.98	255.255.255.240	192.168.5.97

Now that the routers and the hosts are configured for interoperability, test things out starting with r1 in Example 5-6. I started with **show ip route** because, most of the time, I don't assume that there is something wrong. If things are missing from the routing table, you need to investigate why.

Example 5-6   *Verifying IP Routes on r1*

```
r1#show ip route
Codes: C - connected, S - static, I - IGRP, R - RIP, M - mobile, B - BGP
       D - EIGRP, EX - EIGRP external, O - OSPF, IA - OSPF inter area
       N1 - OSPF NSSA external type 1, N2 - OSPF NSSA external type 2
       E1 - OSPF external type 1, E2 - OSPF external type 2, E - EGP
       i - IS-IS, L1 - IS-IS level-1, L2 - IS-IS level-2, * - candidate default
       U - per-user static route, o - ODR
Gateway of last resort is not set
     192.168.5.0/28 is subnetted, 6 subnets
D       192.168.5.96 [90/40514560] via 192.168.5.82, 00:39:19, Serial1
D       192.168.5.64 [90/40537600] via 192.168.5.34, 00:39:19, Ethernet1
C       192.168.5.80 is directly connected, Serial1
C       192.168.5.32 is directly connected, Ethernet1
D       192.168.5.48 [90/40537600] via 192.168.5.34, 00:39:19, Ethernet1
C       192.168.5.16 is directly connected, Ethernet0
     10.0.0.0/24 is subnetted, 2 subnets
D       10.2.2.0 [90/41024000] via 192.168.5.82, 00:39:19, Serial1
C       10.1.1.0 is directly connected, Serial0
r1#
```

Compare the output of Example 5-6 to Figure 5-1. Ensure that all of your directly connected routes are listed in your routing table as well as the EIGRP-learned routes. At a quick glance, the shaded output indicates six subnets under 192.168.5.0/28 and two subnets under 10.0.0.0/24. If any subnets are missing, investigate why.

Looking at the routing table is a quick way to troubleshoot many issues. If you are looking for a particular network, however, it is less confusing to just list the address after the **show ip route** command as in Example 5-7.

Example 5-7   *Finding a Particular Route on r1*

```
r1#show ip route 10.2.2.0
Routing entry for 10.2.2.0/24
  Known via "eigrp 500", distance 90, metric 41024000, type internal
  Redistributing via eigrp 500
  Last update from 192.168.5.82 on Serial1, 00:51:39 ago
  Routing Descriptor Blocks:
  * 192.168.5.82, from 192.168.5.82, 00:51:39 ago, via Serial1
      Route metric is 41024000, traffic share count is 1
      Total delay is 40000 microseconds, minimum bandwidth is 64 Kbit
      Reliability 255/255, minimum MTU 1500 bytes
      Loading 1/255, Hops 1
r1#
```

If your routing table looks like the one in Example 5-8 rather than the one in Example 5-6, refer back to Chapter 3, "Shooting Trouble with IP," or research discontiguous subnets and EIGRP on Cisco.com for help.

Example 5-8   *Missing Network 10.2.2.0*

```
r1#show ip route
...
     192.168.5.0/24 is variably subnetted, 7 subnets, 2 masks
D       192.168.5.96/28 [90/2172416] via 192.168.5.82, 00:05:10, Serial1
D       192.168.5.64/28 [90/40537600] via 192.168.5.34, 00:15:18, Ethernet1
C       192.168.5.80/28 is directly connected, Serial1
C       192.168.5.32/28 is directly connected, Ethernet1
D       192.168.5.48/28 [90/40537600] via 192.168.5.34, 00:15:18, Ethernet1
D       192.168.5.0/24 is a summary, 00:23:00, Null0
C       192.168.5.16/28 is directly connected, Ethernet0
     10.0.0.0/8 is variably subnetted, 2 subnets, 2 masks
C       10.1.1.0/24 is directly connected, Serial0
D       10.0.0.0/8 is a summary, 00:11:38, Null0
r1#
```

From your research, you should have found that EIGRP handles discontiguous subnets just like RIPv2 does. For this to work properly, you must use the **no auto-summary** command in the router configuration mode. Your routing table hint should have been the automatic classful summarization of 192.168.5.0/24 and 10.0.0.0/8 with a summary route to null0. A quick ping test from hosta to hostc would have illustrated end-to-end host connectivity, but would not have brought out any network 10.0.0.0 issues. However, r2 would have been pretty confused as to which way to direct the packets for network 10.0.0.0.

Next verify that IPX and RIP are running on r1e0 with me in Example 5-9.

Example 5-9 *Verify IPX on r1*

```
r1#show ipx route
Codes: C - Connected primary network,    c - Connected secondary network
       S - Static, F - Floating static, L - Local (internal), W - IPXWAN
       R - RIP, E - EIGRP, N - NLSP, X - External, A - Aggregate
       s - seconds, u - uses, U - Per-user static
2 Total IPX routes. Up to 1 parallel paths and 16 hops allowed.
No default route known.
C        516 (SAP),          Et0
R    346648E2 [02/01] via    516.0080.29e8.5c6b,    56s, Et0
r1#show ipx interface ethernet 0
Ethernet0 is up, line protocol is up
  IPX address is 516.0000.0c8d.6705, SAP [up]
  Delay of this IPX network, in ticks is 1 throughput 0 link delay 0
...
  RIP packets received 119, RIP packets sent 3977
  SAP packets received 117, SAP packets sent 1
r1#show ipx servers
Codes: S - Static, P - Periodic, E - EIGRP, N - NLSP, H - Holddown, + = detail
U - Per-user static
4 Total IPX Servers
Table ordering is based on routing and server info
    Type Name                     Net     Address     Port    Route Hops Itf
P      4 GWISE               346648E2.0000.0000.0001:0451     2/01   1  Et0
P    107 GWISE               346648E2.0000.0000.0001:8104     2/01   1  Et0
P    26B GWISE_TREE_____346648E2.0000.0000.0001:0005     2/01   1  Et0
P    278 GWISE_TREE_____346648E2.0000.0000.0001:4006     2/01   1  Et0
r1#ping ipx 346648e2.0.0.1
Type escape sequence to abort.
Sending 5, 100-byte IPX Novell Echoes to 346648E2.0000.0000.0001, timeout is 2
seconds:
!!!!!
Success rate is 100 percent (5/5), round-trip min/avg/max = 4/4/4 ms
r1#
```

Although not shown in these examples, the rest of the routers have the correct information in their routing tables. Verify yours now. Perform some ping tests from every router (like I do with r2 in Example 5-10).

Example 5-10 *r2 Ping Testing*

```
r2>ping 192.168.5.17
Type escape sequence to abort.
Sending 5, 100-byte ICMP Echos to 192.168.5.17, timeout is 2 seconds:
!!!!!
Success rate is 100 percent (5/5), round-trip min/avg/max = 4/4/4 ms
r2>ping 192.168.5.82
Type escape sequence to abort.
Sending 5, 100-byte ICMP Echos to 192.168.5.82, timeout is 2 seconds:
!!!!!
Success rate is 100 percent (5/5), round-trip min/avg/max = 28/31/32 ms
```

Example 5-10 *r2 Ping Testing (Continued)*

```
r2>ping 192.168.5.97
Type escape sequence to abort.
Sending 5, 100-byte ICMP Echos to 192.168.5.97, timeout is 2 seconds:
!!!!!
Success rate is 100 percent (5/5), round-trip min/avg/max = 28/29/32 ms
r2>ping 10.2.2.2
Type escape sequence to abort.
Sending 5, 100-byte ICMP Echos to 10.2.2.2, timeout is 2 seconds:
!!!!!
Success rate is 100 percent (5/5), round-trip min/avg/max = 60/61/68 ms
r2>
```

Finally, analyze the host routing tables and ping from hosta and hostb to hostc to test end-to-end host connectivity as in Example 5-11. To test the higher layers, feel free to run an application such as Telnet, TFTP, or FTP. If you can copy all of your configuration files to the same TFTP server, for example, that would test from the Physical to the Application Layers. Alternatively, if you can Telnet to every router from every host, that is another good test of all the layers.

Example 5-11 *Testing End-to-End Connectivity from hosta to hostc*

```
C:\>route print
===========================================================================
Interface List
0x1 ........................... MS TCP Loopback interface
0x2 ...44 45 53 54 42 00 ...... NOC Extranet Access Adapter
0x1000004 ...00 10 4b a5 ae 50 ...... FE575 Ethernet Adapter
===========================================================================
Active Routes:
Network Destination        Netmask          Gateway       Interface  Metric
          0.0.0.0          0.0.0.0    192.168.5.17    192.168.5.18       1
        127.0.0.0        255.0.0.0       127.0.0.1       127.0.0.1       1
     192.168.5.16  255.255.255.240    192.168.5.18    192.168.5.18       1
     192.168.5.18  255.255.255.255       127.0.0.1       127.0.0.1       1
    192.168.5.255  255.255.255.255    192.168.5.18    192.168.5.18       1
        224.0.0.0        224.0.0.0    192.168.5.18    192.168.5.18       1
  255.255.255.255  255.255.255.255    192.168.5.18               2       1
Default Gateway:       192.168.5.17
===========================================================================
Persistent Routes:
  None
C:\>ping 192.168.5.98
Pinging 192.168.5.98 with 32 bytes of data:
Reply from 192.168.5.98: bytes=32 time=20ms TTL=126
Reply from 192.168.5.98: bytes=32 time=10ms TTL=126
Reply from 192.168.5.98: bytes=32 time=10ms TTL=126
Reply from 192.168.5.98: bytes=32 time=10ms TTL=126
Ping statistics for 192.168.5.98:
    Packets: Sent = 4, Received = 4, Lost = 0 (0% loss),
Approximate round trip times in milli-seconds:
    Minimum = 10ms, Maximum = 20ms, Average = 12ms
```

continues

Example 5-11 *Testing End-to-End Connectivity from hosta to hostc (Continued)*

```
C:\>arp -a
Interface: 192.168.5.18 on Interface 0x1000004
  Internet Address      Physical Address      Type
  192.168.5.17          00-00-0c-8d-67-05     dynamic
C:\>tracert 192.168.5.98
Tracing route to HOSTC [192.168.5.98]
over a maximum of 30 hops:
  1    <10 ms    10 ms    <10 ms   192.168.5.17
  2     20 ms    20 ms     20 ms   192.168.5.82
  3     20 ms    30 ms     30 ms   HOSTC [192.168.5.98]
Trace complete.
C:\>
```

NOTE   If you are seeing other routes in your routing table, you may be connected to the Internet via your Internet service provider (ISP). Disconnect to alleviate the confusion, for the labs in this book assume you are connected only to what is in the scenario drawings.

These tools are the same tools you have been using throughout this book and are the same tools you will continue to use in supporting day-to-day networks. If Layer 3 is working, so are Layer 2 and Layer 1). The ping from hosta to hostc verifies that you can communicate to a remote network unless an access list or something is blocking a particular address, network, or application port. Don't forget to verify the same tests from hostb to hostc. Compare the Address Resolution Protocol (ARP) tables on the hosts to the ARP table on r1 as in Example 5-12. At first my ARP table on r1 did not display an entry for hostb, but later I found that I had an incorrect IP address configured for hostb. When I fixed that, the ARP table was correct.

Example 5-12 *r1 ARP Table*

```
r1>show ip arp
Protocol  Address          Age (min)  Hardware Addr   Type   Interface
Internet  192.168.5.33         -      0000.0c8d.6706  ARPA   Ethernet1
Internet  192.168.5.34        157     0000.0c38.a05d  ARPA   Ethernet1
Internet  192.168.5.17         -      0000.0c8d.6705  ARPA   Ethernet0
Internet  192.168.5.18         2      0010.4ba5.ae50  ARPA   Ethernet0
!!!fixed ip address on hostb here
r1>show ip arp
Protocol  Address          Age (min)  Hardware Addr   Type   Interface
Internet  192.168.5.33         -      0000.0c8d.6706  ARPA   Ethernet1
Internet  192.168.5.34        174     0000.0c38.a05d  ARPA   Ethernet1
Internet  192.168.5.17         -      0000.0c8d.6705  ARPA   Ethernet0
Internet  192.168.5.19         0      0080.c7aa.c887  ARPA   Ethernet0
Internet  192.168.5.18        18      0010.4ba5.ae50  ARPA   Ethernet0
r1>
```

For a change, everything is successful for this chapter scenario. However, you must be familiar with the right tools to help you find and narrow the problem down into its components. Besides ping, trace, ARP, and routing tables, Cisco Discovery Protocol (CDP) is quite helpful in initial troubleshooting steps as well.

Ethernet operates at Layer 1 and Layer 2 and lower layer targets in general are interfaces and controllers. A quick test for host or router communications is to ping from end-to-end as you did in the previous examples. However, what if the end-to-end ping fails? The **tracert** command in Example 5-11 illustrates the exact path the packets took from hosta to hostc. The hop-by-hop display can assist with finding where the pings are failing. The ping and trace tools most definitely complement one another and should be used together.

NOTE	As emphasized in Chapter 2, "What's in Your Tool Bag?" you should use ping to identify lower-level troubleshooting targets. Ping the loopback address (127.0.0.1), ping yourself (your IP address), ping someone local, ping the default gateway, and ping a remote host. I must tell you, however, that many times I skip the local activity and just try my gateway first; then I can work from there. If you are still having problems, trace is a great companion utility to ping. The ping and trace tools complement one another. Ping shows connectivity and delay up to Layer 3, and trace shows the path from the source to the destination. Don't forget about the extended versions of both of them from the enable mode. For example, perhaps the issue is your gateway and you can source the ping from another interface.

Continue to use a layered methodology yet divide and conquer to fix any problems at this time. Refer back to the previous chapters' quick troubleshooting checklists for hints.

Next I want to focus a little more on lower-layer targets. It is vital to look at interfaces and controllers to assist with Ethernet troubleshooting at the Data Link Layer. Documentation such as charts and drawings make this much easier. In addition, the ping statistics prove quite useful to see whether a link is down or there is some type of congestion. If a problem exists between the source and the destination, trace is useful to narrow down where to start your troubleshooting.

Use the commands in Table 5-3 to prepare a page of documentation for each one of your routers. Appendix B, "Troubleshooting Resources," includes this as a router documentation template for your use.

Table 5-3   *Commands to Help You Document Your Routers*

Command	Information Provided
show version	IOS, RAM, Flash, and configuration register
show cdp neighbors *detail*	IP, device, and IOS version, and the connected interfaces
show ip interface brief	Status and IP
show ipx interface brief	Network, encapsulation, IPX status and state
show interfaces [*interface*]	MAC, IP, Bandwidth (BW), encapsulation, keepalive, duplex, and speed
show ip interface [*interface*]	IP statistics
show ipx interface [*interface*]	IPX statistics
show protocols	IP and IPX routing process and addresses
show ip protocols	Routing protocol and details, including summarization and redistribution
show access-lists **show ip access-lists** [*access-list*] **show ipx access-lists** [*access-list*]	Access Lists (ACLs) and hits

Figure 5-2   *r1 Documentation*

, IP EIGRP

Hostname: r1   **Model:** 2514
IOS: 12.0(21a)   **Filename:** c2500-js-l.120-21a.bin
RAM: 14336K/2048K   **Flash:** 16384K   **Config register:** 0x2102
Routing protocols: IPX RIP
Redistribution:
Bridging:
Other notes:
hosta: Win2K WinBook (192.168.5.18/28) (3Com PCMCIA NIC 00104BA5AE50) IP-arpa/IPX-sap 10Mbps/half Client for Microsoft and NetWare Networks
hostb: Win98 Toshiba (192.168.5.19/28) (Xircom CE-IIps NIC 0080C7AAC887) IP-arpa/IPX-sap 10 Mbps/half Client for Microsoft and NetWare Networks File and Printer Sharing for Microsoft
gwise: NetWare 4.11 Server(NE2000Plus NIC 008029E85C6B) Frame type 802.2 IRQ10/1O300 administrator:password

Interface	MAC Address	IP Address	IP Encap	IPX Address	IPX Encap	Serial Encap
e0 10M/half	0000.0c8d.6705	192.168.5.17/28	ARPA	516.mac	novell-ether	
e1 10M/half	0000.0c8d.6706	192.168.5.33/28	ARPA			
s0 64K/DTE		10.1.1.1/24				HDLC
s1 1544K/DTE		192.168.5.81/28				HDLC

The commands on r1 appear in Example 5-13 through Example 5-20. You will thank yourself not only during the Trouble Tickets but also in the real world if you take the time to do this up front. Alternatively, you can get a very large sheet of paper and increase the size of your scenario drawing so that you have room for all the minute details that may assist you in troubleshooting later. Many network management programs capture these statistics automatically for you today. However, people like you and I still need to know where to start to get things back to normal when lights and alerts go off. It helps to have a drawing and the detailed data if someone comes to you with a real Trouble Ticket to solve.

Example 5-13 *r1* **show version**

```
r1#show version
Cisco Internetwork Operating System Software
IOS (tm) 2500 Software (C2500-JS-L), Version 12.0(21a), RELEASE SOFTWARE (fc1)
Copyright  1986-2002 by cisco Systems, Inc.
Compiled Sat 02-Feb-02 02:08 by nmasa
Image text-base: 0x030520E0, data-base: 0x00001000
ROM: System Bootstrap, Version 5.2(8a), RELEASE SOFTWARE
BOOTFLASH: 3000 Bootstrap Software (IGS-RXBOOT), Version 10.2(8a), RELEASE
SOFTWARE (fc1)
r1 uptime is 3 days, 21 hours, 24 minutes
System restarted by power-on
System image file is "flash:c2500-js-l.120-21a.bin"
cisco 2500 (68030) processor (revision L) with 14336K/2048K bytes of memory.
Processor board ID 03074719, with hardware revision 00000000
Bridging software.
X.25 software, Version 3.0.0.
SuperLAT software (copyright 1990 by Meridian Technology Corp).
TN3270 Emulation software.
2 Ethernet/IEEE 802.3 interface(s)
2 Serial network interface(s)
32K bytes of non-volatile configuration memory.
16384K bytes of processor board System flash (Read ONLY)
Configuration register is 0x2102
```

Example 5-14 *r1 Neighbors*

```
r1#show cdp neighbors
Capability Codes: R - Router, T - Trans Bridge, B - Source Route Bridge
                 S - Switch, H - Host, I - IGMP, r - Repeater
Device ID      Local Intrfce     Holdtme    Capability  Platform  Port ID
r2             Eth 1             157         R           2500      Eth 0
r3             Ser 1             174         R           3640      Ser 0/0
r5             Ser 0             132         R           2516      Ser 0
r1#show cdp neighbors detail
-------------------------
Device ID: r2
Entry address(es):
  IP address: 192.168.5.34
Platform: cisco 2500,  Capabilities: Router
Interface: Ethernet1,  Port ID (outgoing port): Ethernet0
Holdtime : 149 sec
Version :
```

Example 5-14 *r1 Neighbors (Continued)*

```
Cisco Internetwork Operating System Software
IOS (tm) 2500 Software (C2500-JS-L), Version 12.0(21a), RELEASE SOFTWARE (fc1)
Copyright  1986-2002 by cisco Systems, Inc.
Compiled Sat 02-Feb-02 02:08 by nmasa
-------------------------
Device ID: r3
Entry address(es):
  IP address: 192.168.5.82
Platform: cisco 3640,  Capabilities: Router
Interface: Serial1,  Port ID (outgoing port): Serial0/0
Holdtime : 164 sec
Version :
Cisco Internetwork Operating System Software
IOS (tm) 3600 Software (C3640-JS-M), Version 12.0(13), RELEASE SOFTWARE (fc1)
Copyright  1986-2000 by cisco Systems, Inc.
Compiled Tue 05-Sep-00 21:39 by linda
-------------------------
Device ID: r5
Entry address(es):
  IP address: 10.1.1.2
Platform: cisco 2516,  Capabilities: Router
Interface: Serial0,  Port ID (outgoing port): Serial0
Holdtime : 121 sec
Version :
Cisco Internetwork Operating System Software
IOS (tm) 2500 Software (C2500-JS-L), Version 12.0(21a), RELEASE SOFTWARE (fc1)
Copyright  1986-2002 by cisco Systems, Inc.
Compiled Sat 02-Feb-02 02:08 by nmasa
```

Example 5-15 *r1 Brief Interface Statistics*

```
r1#show ip interface brief
Interface            IP-Address      OK? Method Status            Protocol
Ethernet0            192.168.5.17    YES manual up                up
Ethernet1            192.168.5.33    YES manual up                up
Serial0              10.1.1.1        YES manual up                up
Serial1              192.168.5.81    YES manual up                up
r1#show ipx interface brief
Interface   IPX Network Encapsulation Status            IPX State
Ethernet0   516         SAP           up                [up]
Ethernet1   unassigned  not config'd  up                n/a
Serial0     unassigned  not config'd  up                n/a
Serial1     unassigned  not config'd  up                n/a
```

Example 5-16 *r1 Interface Statistics*

```
r1#show interfaces
Ethernet0 is up, line protocol is up
  Hardware is Lance, address is 0000.0c8d.6705 (bia 0000.0c8d.6705)
  Description: r1e0 to hosta and hostb
  Internet address is 192.168.5.17/28
  MTU 1500 bytes, BW 10000 Kbit, DLY 1000 usec, rely 255/255, load 1/255
```

continues

Example 5-16 *r1 Interface Statistics (Continued)*

```
   Encapsulation ARPA, loopback not set, keepalive set (10 sec)
  ARP type: ARPA, ARP Timeout 04:00:00
  Last input 00:00:10, output 00:00:01, output hang never
  Last clearing of "show interface" counters 1d03h
Queueing strategy: fifo
  Output queue 0/40, 0 drops; input queue 0/75, 0 drops
  5 minute input rate 0 bits/sec, 0 packets/sec
  5 minute output rate 0 bits/sec, 0 packets/sec
     8201 packets input, 1586890 bytes, 0 no buffer
     Received 7778 broadcasts, 0 runts, 0 giants, 0 throttles
     0 input errors, 0 CRC, 0 frame, 0 overrun, 0 ignored, 0 abort
     0 input packets with dribble condition detected
     33932 packets output, 2793718 bytes, 0 underruns
     0 output errors, 0 collisions, 1 interface resets
     0 babbles, 0 late collision, 0 deferred
     0 lost carrier, 0 no carrier
     0 output buffer failures, 0 output buffers swapped out
Ethernet1 is up, line protocol is up
  Hardware is Lance, address is 0000.0c8d.6706 (bia 0000.0c8d.6706)
  Description: r1e1 to r2e0
  Internet address is 192.168.5.33/28
  MTU 1500 bytes, BW 10000 Kbit, DLY 1000 usec, rely 255/255, load 1/255
  Encapsulation ARPA, loopback not set, keepalive set (10 sec)
  ARP type: ARPA, ARP Timeout 04:00:00
  Last input 00:00:00, output 00:00:04, output hang never
  Last clearing of "show interface" counters 1d03h
  Queueing strategy: fifo
  Output queue 0/40, 0 drops; input queue 0/75, 0 drops
  5 minute input rate 0 bits/sec, 0 packets/sec
  5 minute output rate 0 bits/sec, 0 packets/sec
     23310 packets input, 2098244 bytes, 0 no buffer
     Received 23260 broadcasts, 0 runts, 0 giants, 0 throttles
     0 input errors, 0 CRC, 0 frame, 0 overrun, 0 ignored, 0 abort
     0 input packets with dribble condition detected
     33572 packets output, 2717907 bytes, 0 underruns
     0 output errors, 0 collisions, 3 interface resets
     0 babbles, 0 late collision, 1 deferred
     0 lost carrier, 0 no carrier
     0 output buffer failures, 0 output buffers swapped out
Serial0 is up, line protocol is up
  Hardware is HD64570
  Description: r1s0 to r5s0
  Internet address is 10.1.1.1/24
  MTU 1500 bytes, BW 64 Kbit, DLY 20000 usec, rely 255/255, load 1/255
  Encapsulation HDLC, loopback not set, keepalive set (10 sec)
  Last input 00:00:03, output 00:00:00, output hang never
  Last clearing of "show interface" counters 1d03h
  Queueing strategy: fifo
  Output queue 0/40, 0 drops; input queue 0/75, 0 drops
  5 minute input rate 0 bits/sec, 0 packets/sec
  5 minute output rate 0 bits/sec, 0 packets/sec
     33112 packets input, 2054389 bytes, 0 no buffer
     Received 11686 broadcasts, 0 runts, 0 giants, 0 throttles
```

Example 5-16 *r1 Interface Statistics (Continued)*

```
        0 input errors, 0 CRC, 0 frame, 0 overrun, 0 ignored, 0 abort
        33165 packets output, 2058532 bytes, 0 underruns
        0 output errors, 0 collisions, 0 interface resets
        0 output buffer failures, 0 output buffers swapped out
        0 carrier transitions
        DCD=up  DSR=up  DTR=up  RTS=up  CTS=up
Serial1 is up, line protocol is up
  Hardware is HD64570
  Description: r1s1 to r3s0/0
  Internet address is 192.168.5.81/28
  MTU 1500 bytes, BW 64 Kbit, DLY 20000 usec, rely 255/255, load 1/255
  Encapsulation HDLC, loopback not set, keepalive set (10 sec)
  Last input 00:00:03, output 00:00:03, output hang never
  Last clearing of "show interface" counters 1d03h
  Input queue: 0/75/0 (size/max/drops); Total output drops: 0
  Queueing strategy: weighted fair
  Output queue: 0/1000/64/0 (size/max total/threshold/drops)
     Conversations  0/2/256 (active/max active/max total)
     Reserved Conversations 0/0 (allocated/max allocated)
  5 minute input rate 0 bits/sec, 0 packets/sec
  5 minute output rate 0 bits/sec, 0 packets/sec
     33646 packets input, 2123261 bytes, 0 no buffer
     Received 11701 broadcasts, 0 runts, 0 giants, 0 throttles
     0 input errors, 0 CRC, 0 frame, 0 overrun, 0 ignored, 0 abort
     33764 packets output, 2105641 bytes, 0 underruns
     0 output errors, 0 collisions, 0 interface resets
     0 output buffer failures, 0 output buffers swapped out
     0 carrier transitions
     DCD=up  DSR=up  DTR=up  RTS=up  CTS=up
```

Example 5-17 *IP Interface Defaults and Settings*

```
r1#show ip interface
Ethernet0 is up, line protocol is up
  Internet address is 192.168.5.17/28
  Broadcast address is 255.255.255.255
  Address determined by setup command
  MTU is 1500 bytes
  Helper address is not set
  Directed broadcast forwarding is disabled
  Multicast reserved groups joined: 224.0.0.10
  Outgoing access list is not set
  Inbound  access list is not set
  Proxy ARP is enabled
  Security level is default
  Split horizon is enabled
  ICMP redirects are always sent
  ICMP unreachables are always sent
  ICMP mask replies are never sent
  IP fast switching is enabled
  IP fast switching on the same interface is disabled
  IP Fast switching turbo vector
```

continues

Example 5-17 *IP Interface Defaults and Settings (Continued)*

```
        IP multicast fast switching is enabled
        IP multicast distributed fast switching is disabled
        IP route-cache flags are Fast
        Router Discovery is disabled
        IP output packet accounting is disabled
        IP access violation accounting is disabled
        TCP/IP header compression is disabled
        RTP/IP header compression is disabled
        Probe proxy name replies are disabled
        Policy routing is disabled
        Network address translation is disabled
        Web Cache Redirect is disabled
        BGP Policy Mapping is disabled
Ethernet1 is up, line protocol is up
        Internet address is 192.168.5.33/28
        Broadcast address is 255.255.255.255
        Address determined by setup command
        MTU is 1500 bytes
        Helper address is not set
        Directed broadcast forwarding is disabled
        Multicast reserved groups joined: 224.0.0.10
        Outgoing access list is not set
        Inbound  access list is not set
        Proxy ARP is enabled
        Security level is default
        Split horizon is enabled
        ICMP redirects are always sent
        ICMP unreachables are always sent
        ICMP mask replies are never sent
        IP fast switching is enabled
        IP fast switching on the same interface is disabled
        IP Fast switching turbo vector
        IP multicast fast switching is enabled
        IP multicast distributed fast switching is disabled
        IP route-cache flags are Fast
        Router Discovery is disabled
        IP output packet accounting is disabled
        IP access violation accounting is disabled
        TCP/IP header compression is disabled
        RTP/IP header compression is disabled
        Probe proxy name replies are disabled
        Policy routing is disabled
        Network address translation is disabled
        Web Cache Redirect is disabled
        BGP Policy Mapping is disabled
Serial0 is up, line protocol is up
        Internet address is 10.1.1.1/24
        Broadcast address is 255.255.255.255
        Address determined by setup command
        MTU is 1500 bytes
        Helper address is not set
        Directed broadcast forwarding is disabled
        Multicast reserved groups joined: 224.0.0.10
        Outgoing access list is not set
```

Example 5-17 *IP Interface Defaults and Settings (Continued)*

```
        Inbound  access list is not set
        Proxy ARP is enabled
        Security level is default
        Split horizon is enabled
        ICMP redirects are always sent
        ICMP unreachables are always sent
        ICMP mask replies are never sent
        IP fast switching is enabled
        IP fast switching on the same interface is enabled
        IP Fast switching turbo vector
        IP multicast fast switching is disabled
        IP multicast distributed fast switching is disabled
        IP route-cache flags are Fast
        Router Discovery is disabled
        IP output packet accounting is disabled
        IP access violation accounting is disabled
        TCP/IP header compression is disabled
        RTP/IP header compression is disabled
        Probe proxy name replies are disabled
        Policy routing is disabled
        Network address translation is disabled
        Web Cache Redirect is disabled
        BGP Policy Mapping is disabled
Serial1 is up, line protocol is up
        Internet address is 192.168.5.81/28
        Broadcast address is 255.255.255.255
        Address determined by setup command
        MTU is 1500 bytes
        Helper address is not set
        Directed broadcast forwarding is disabled
        Multicast reserved groups joined: 224.0.0.10
        Outgoing access list is not set
        Inbound  access list is not set
        Proxy ARP is enabled
        Security level is default
        Split horizon is enabled
        ICMP redirects are always sent
        ICMP unreachables are always sent
        ICMP mask replies are never sent
        IP fast switching is enabled
        IP fast switching on the same interface is enabled
        IP Fast switching turbo vector
        IP multicast fast switching is enabled
        IP multicast distributed fast switching is disabled
        IP route-cache flags are Fast
        Router Discovery is disabled
        IP output packet accounting is disabled
        IP access violation accounting is disabled
        TCP/IP header compression is disabled
        RTP/IP header compression is disabled
        Probe proxy name replies are disabled
        Policy routing is disabled
        Network address translation is disabled
        Web Cache Redirect is disabled
        BGP Policy Mapping is disabled
```

Example 5-18 *IPX Interface Ethernet 0 Statistics*

```
r1#show ipx interface ethernet 0
Ethernet0 is up, line protocol is up
  IPX address is 516.0000.0c8d.6705, SAP [up]
  Delay of this IPX network, in ticks is 1 throughput 0 link delay 0
  IPXWAN processing not enabled on this interface.
  IPX SAP update interval is 60 seconds
  IPX type 20 propagation packet forwarding is disabled
  Incoming access list is not set
  Outgoing access list is not set
  IPX helper access list is not set
  SAP GNS processing enabled, delay 0 ms, output filter list is not set
  SAP Input filter list is not set
  SAP Output filter list is not set
  SAP Router filter list is not set
  Input filter list is not set
  Output filter list is not set
  Router filter list is not set
Netbios Input host access list is not set
  Netbios Input bytes access list is not set
  Netbios Output host access list is not set
  Netbios Output bytes access list is not set
  Updates each 60 seconds aging multiples RIP: 3 SAP: 3
  SAP interpacket delay is 55 ms, maximum size is 480 bytes
  RIP interpacket delay is 55 ms, maximum size is 432 bytes
  RIP response delay is not set
  IPX accounting is disabled
  IPX fast switching is configured (enabled)
  RIP packets received 1659, RIP packets sent 3977
  SAP packets received 1653, SAP packets sent 1
```

Example 5-19 *r1 Protocol Commands*

```
r1#show protocols
Global values:
  Internet Protocol routing is enabled
  IPX routing is enabled
Ethernet0 is up, line protocol is up
  Internet address is 192.168.5.17/28
  IPX address is 516.0000.0c8d.6705
Ethernet1 is up, line protocol is up
  Internet address is 192.168.5.33/28
Serial0 is up, line protocol is up
  Internet address is 10.1.1.1/24
Serial1 is up, line protocol is up
  Internet address is 192.168.5.81/28
r1#show ip protocols
Routing Protocol is "eigrp 500"
  Outgoing update filter list for all interfaces is not set
  Incoming update filter list for all interfaces is not set
  Default networks flagged in outgoing updates
  Default networks accepted from incoming updates
  EIGRP metric weight K1=1, K2=0, K3=1, K4=0, K5=0
```

Example 5-19 *r1 Protocol Commands (Continued)*

```
EIGRP maximum hopcount 100
  EIGRP maximum metric variance 1
  Redistributing: eigrp 500
  Automatic network summarization is not in effect
  Routing for Networks:
    10.0.0.0
    192.168.5.0
  Routing Information Sources:
    Gateway         Distance      Last Update
    (this router)          5      1d03h
    10.1.1.2              90       05:21:22
    192.168.5.82         90       05:21:24
    192.168.5.34         90       05:21:23
  Distance: internal 90 external 170
```

Example 5-20 *Access Lists*

```
r1#show access-lists
r1#show ip access-lists
r1#show ipx access-lists
r1#
```

As you can see, the commands presented in Table 5-3 are helpful to compile the documentation presented in Figure 5-2. You should be feeling much better about the importance of documentation. Pictures and tables help capture lots of useful information that saves you a great deal of time when it comes to troubleshooting. This makes it easy to spot any inconsistencies. In the practical environment, I would much rather do more work up front rather than when people are waiting for me to fix something.

NOTE   Although I have provided documentation only for r1, you should now repeat this for every device in your lab. Use the r1 worksheet in Figure 5-2 as a template. If you are using higher end routers/switches for your lab, add modules and slots to your documentation. I cover that more in Chapter 6, "Shooting Trouble with CatOS and IOS," and Chapter 7, "Shooting Trouble with VLANs on Routers and Switches."

Now that the existing Ethernet scenario is documented, I briefly discuss Ethernet and then cover Ethernet Data Link and Physical Layer troubleshooting targets in more detail.

A Brief Summary of Ethernet

Ethernet dates back to the late 1960s, when Norman Abramson designed the University of Hawaii's Aloha radio network. It connected the IBM mainframe on the island of Oahu to the other islands and ships at sea.

Bob Metcalfe was working for Xerox Corporation's Palo Alto Research Center (PARC) in the early 1970s. He stumbled across the earlier work of Abramson during his task to connect the ALTO (first PC with a graphical user interface) to ARPANET. The *Alto Aloha Network* first ran in 1973, and Bob Metcalfe talked about the physical medium as *ether*. The original Ethernet bandwidth was 2.94 Mbps.

NOTE   View the first Ethernet drawing and investigate more extensive details about Ethernet at www.ethermanage.com/ethernet/ethernet.html.

Today, Ethernet works over various speeds (10, 100, 1000, and 10,000 Mbps) and over a multitude of media types such as coax, twisted pair, fiber, and wireless.

10-Mbps Ethernet

The 2.94-Mbps Xerox Ethernet set the stage for Institute of Electrical and Electronic Engineers (IEEE) and Digital Intel Xerox (DIX) Ethernet. In 1980 Xerox along with Digital and Intel published DIX Ethernet version 1. This same consortium published DIX version 2 (Ethernet II) around 1982. Before the final standards were in place, Metcalfe was off in another entrepreneurial venture helping 3Com productize Ethernet with Ethernet NICs and other devices.

About the same time the DIX specs were published, the IEEE 802 project formed. According to grouper.ieee.org/groups/802/overview2000.pdf, the first meeting of the IEEE local network standards committee was in February 1980. This is certainly an easy way to remember the 802 standards (1980, February). The IEEE 802.3 CSMA/CD Ethernet standard was first published in 1985. By the late 1980s, Ethernet gained international recognition by the ISO through standard IS88023.

NOTE   The IEEE 802 standards are available for free download at standards.ieee.org/getieee802/.

The 10-Mbps Ethernet standards are categorized as follows:

- 10BASE5
- 10BASE2

- 10BASE-T
- 10BASE-FL
- 10BASE-FB
- 10BASE-FP

The majority of Ethernet networks use *baseband* signaling as in 10*BASE*5, which means that all stations share the same frequency channel. A *broadband* network is more like cable TV where different services communicate across different channels (frequencies). Think of *band* as a range of frequencies. In sharing the band, one can take turns using the entire band (baseband/time-division multiplexing [TDM]) or divide the band into multiple frequency channels (broadband/frequency-division multiplexing [FDM]). With baseband, for instance, there are time slots for data, voice, and video. With broadband, however, data, voice, and video are more simultaneous. Each one runs at a different frequency, which means that all stations utilize a shared limited frequency range.

NOTE   Beginning in 1983, Novell developed its own proprietary Ethernet frame type to run over thick and thin coax; they completed its development in 1985. This was prior to the IEEE 802.3 specification.

Both DIX Ethernet and IEEE Ethernet are broadcast-based *logical bus* networks that use carrier sense multiple access with collision detection (CSMA/CD) as a method of taking turns on the wire. The CSMA/CD access method says that Ethernet is a *shared media* access method where all stations see all frames and take turns using the media. Even Token Ring and FDDI are shared media access methods, but the method for taking turns is not contention-based.

- CSMA/CD is like taking turns talking on a conference call or at a meeting. Take a look at the following list. Everyone is listening (CS), but no one is talking. Now multiple people talk at once (MA). However, you really can't understand each other (CD), so you wait a random amount of time and try again:
- **Carrier sense (CS)**—Listen before your talk.
- **Multiple access (MA)**—If there are simultaneous transmissions, a collision occurs.
- **Collision detection (CD)**—Both stations must back off and wait a random period of time.

The Data Link Layer combines bits into bytes and bytes into frames. Ethernet is canonical on the wire. The preamble is sent out to indicate that Ethernet is coming. Although not all protocol analyzers display it for you, the preamble is the first 8 bytes, which end in two consecutive ones, of the frame. A collision occurs only after the preamble has been sent. The first host to detect the additional voltage on the wire that indicates multiple hosts attempting simultaneous communication issues a *jam signal*. All hosts on the collision domain now know that a collision has occurred. Retransmission randomly occurs up to 15 times per the CSMA/CD specifications. After 30 percent to 40 percent utilization, collisions *rise* exponentially with shared Ethernet. The more people taking turns to use the same wire, the more contention and competition, and therefore collisions occur more often. The "Ethernet Frames" section provides more detail.

NOTE   Distance matters with collisions. It takes an electrical signal 51.2 microseconds to be carried from one end of a cable segment to the other using the maximum distance for the medium (100 meters [m] on twisted pair, 185 m on coax, 500 m on thick Ethernet). During that same time period, the sending station will have put up to 64 bytes of information on the line before the first bit reaches the other end. That's why collisions can be up to 64 bytes and still be okay, and that's why distance matters, and that's where you'll get late collisions in longer (out-of-specification) cable runs.

Although Ethernet has no flex time, you can scale it across 10-Mbps, 100-Mbps, and 1000-Mbps architectures, especially if you understand the bottlenecks. You must deal with three elements: the physical medium, the access method, and the frame type. For example, is the problem a too busy server, a shared-medium hub, an ill-performing NIC, or are there just too many users or too much broadcast-based traffic on a segment?

Ethernet is scalable. You can segment it while preserving the existing infrastructure. It includes multivendor support, and the old and the new work well together. Bridges and switches have drastically increased its life span, probably much longer than Metcalfe ever dreamed.

Bridges started as two-port devices to interconnect LANs. Switches are a marketing term for bridges as a way to boost LAN performance. Switches (or even crossover cables) allow for full-duplex communications over 10/100/1000/10,000-Mbps Ethernet where a device can transmit and receive simultaneously. *No* collisions occur in full-duplex Ethernet. Conversely, to be full-duplex, you *must* be a point-to-point link. For more details on switches and duplex communications, refer to Chapter 6; the entire chapter is dedicated to Ethernet switches. Regardless of the Ethernet speed, for specific trouble targets see the section "Shooting Trouble with Ethernet" later in this chapter. For now, look at 100-Mbps Ethernet, which has been and is still gaining more popularity at Cisco's Access Layer (where the users are).

100-Mbps Ethernet

Originally two approaches were presented when the IEEE first began work on Fast Ethernet standards. 100BASE-X (Fast Ethernet) was first proposed by Grand Junction Networks to the IEEE in 1992. In 1993, the first full-duplex EtherSwitch came to market from Kalpana. Crescendo Communications presented switching hubs with high-speed FDDI and Ethernet ports. HP and AT&T approached IEEE 802.3 with an entirely new medium access control mechanism where priority was built in to the hubs first for Ethernet and later for Token Ring, too. Because of the two approaches, 100-Mbps standards wars began occurring in the early 1990s. Therefore, a group of cooperative vendors agreeing to keep a technical focus formed the Fast Ethernet Alliance group to alleviate the standards wars.

HP and AT&T's joint venture, 100VG-AnyLAN, ended up as IEEE 802.12 Demand Priority Access Method, which was abandoned in 1994. In October 1993, 100BASE-, known today as 100BASE-TX, was published. March 1995 marked the approval of IEEE 802.3u, and the alliance group disbanded.

Fast Ethernet brought about the quick adoption of dual-speed 10/100 NICs for easy migration paths. 100BASE-T is really just a generic name for the early 100-Mbps standards; however, it is probably the most often used term when people (including myself) really mean 100BASE-TX. 100BASE-X is a generic name that uses X as a variable for 100-Mbps using 4B/5B encoding (for instance, the existing FDDI standard). The 100-Mbps standards are categorized as follows:

- 100BASE-TX

- 100BASE-FX

- 100BASE-T4

- 100BASE-T2

FDDI was already in full swing when 100-Mbps Ethernet was developed. The benefits gained included a variation of the existing nonreturn to zero, invert on one (NRZI) transmission method. 100BASE-TX uses NRZI-3 or multiple level transition (MLT-3), in which bits are encoded as transitions (as in NRZI and the Ethernet Manchester encoding scheme).

100-Mbps Ethernet is 10-Mbps Ethernet times 10 with a few exceptions. It retains the same 10-Mbps Ethernet MAC header except for the interframe gap (IFG), which goes from 9.6 microseconds to .96 microseconds. The round-trip propagation delay in 1 collision domain must not exceed 5.12 microseconds, which is the time it takes a sender to transmit 512 bits on 100-Mbps Ethernet. Distance limitations and shared devices are among the differences. In particular, two types of repeaters are defined in the 100BASE-T specifications:

- Class I repeaters allow only one repeater hop and have a latency of .7 microseconds or less.

- Class II repeaters allow one or two repeater hops and have a latency of .46 microseconds or less.

Repeater hops have varied somewhat over the years according to the manufacturer, but you can relate any variation back to the 10-Mbps 5-4-3 rule of 5 segments connected by 4 repeaters; where 3 segments are populated with nodes, 2 segments act as inter-repeater links (IRLs), but there is still only 1 collision/broadcast domain.

Ethernet continues to evolve to assist with bottlenecks not only at the Access and Distribution Layers but also into the Core. Next in the evolution is 1000-Mbps Ethernet, which is more often referred to as *Gigabit Ethernet*.

1000-Mbps Ethernet

Gigabit Ethernet significantly leverages off of some of the existing key components from IEEE 802.3 Ethernet and ANSI X3T11 FibreChannel. Cisco helped to lead the Gigabit Alliance Group since its inception in March 1996. A big enhancement includes a change to the MAC layer standards to support higher-speed networks. The frame size was *not* changed, but a carrier extension was added to the Gigabit Ethernet chipset so that the sender sends for a longer period of time to support a larger topology. So with 10, 100, and 1000-Mbps Ethernet, the minimum frame size is equal to the network maximum round-trip propagation delay, which is 512 bits (64 bytes). This is equal to the slot time in 10 and 100-Mbps networks, but the slot time now increases to 4096 bit times or *512 bytes*. Short frames are automatically extended to one slot time in length. This may not sound so delightful from a troubleshooting standpoint, but the IEEE 802.3z standards let a user send multiple frames without contending again for use of the bandwidth. A good example of this new bursting feature is Voice over IP (VoIP).

Cisco supports 10/100/1000/10,000 Ethernet in its vast array of products, including the 2900s, 3500s, 4000s, and 6500s. Even though you may have taken advantage of 100-Mbps Ethernet technology down to the desktop, you may still have bottlenecks at the wiring closet. This is where Gigabit Ethernet can assist. Cisco uses the 1000BASE-T Gigabit Interface Converter (GBIC) to provide full-duplex Gigabit Ethernet connectivity to high-end workstations and between wiring closets over existing copper infrastructures for their 2900 and 3500 XL customers. For more information, review the Cisco online seminar with Bruce Tolley on "Scaling Bandwidth with 10 Gigabit Ethernet" or point your browser to www.cisco.com/warp/customer/cc/techno/media/lan/gig/tech/gigbt_tc.htm.

10,000-Mbps Ethernet

Cisco is also part of the 10 Gigabit Ethernet Alliance, leading the initiative to accelerate 10 Gigabit Ethernet to the networking community. For example, there are 10 Gigabit Ethernet modules available for the 6500 series. Refer to www.cisco.com/warp/public/cc/techno/media/lan/gig/tech/10gig_sd.htm for more 10 Gigabit Ethernet details.

10 Gigabit Ethernet provides high bandwidth, scalability, and very high-speed connections between buildings and their Point of Presence (POP). It aggregates multiple gigabit segments for links between switches and servers or clusters thereof over fiber.

NOTE   Dark fiber is unlit fiber that is not currently carrying any traffic.

The 10 Gigabit Ethernet High Speed Study Group (HSSG) began its initial research in March 1999, which led to the IEEE forming the 802.3ae 10 Gigabit Ethernet Task Force in March 2000. The standard was formally ratified in 2002. For more information go to www.10gea.org.

Wireless Ethernet

Cisco, among others, is working hard to future-proof wireless communications. They are combining wireless and IP technology to create anytime, anywhere connections to the Internet and enterprise networks. Whether in a campus environment or distant mobile location, Cisco's high-speed, secure wireless technology enables users to be constantly connected. See newsroom.cisco.com/dlls/hd_041702.html for a quick glimpse of Cisco's position on wireless technology.

There are various IEEE wireless standards, including 802.11a and 802.11b. However, the world is concerned with the security of wireless Ethernet. Interesting websites on the topic include "The Unofficial 802.11 Security Web Page" at www.drizzle.com/~aboba/IEEE/ and "Offsite Wireless," at www.offsitewireless.com.

NOTE   Wireless LANs do not equal Ethernet. They run a completely different data-link scheme, and definitely a different Physical Layer scheme.

Summary of IEEE 802.3 Ethernet Evolution

Ethernet is not limited to the wired LAN today, for it is found in wireless LANs as well as in long-haul optical Ethernet WAN communications. Refer to the IEEE standards for complete details. Table 5-4 summarizes the information about the evolution of Ethernet presented in this section.

Table 5-4   *IEEE 802.3 Ethernet Evolution*

Standard	IEEE	Year	Stations per Segment	Segment Length in Meters	Medium
10BASE-5	802.3	1983	100	500	50ohm coax thicknet
10BASE-2	802.3a	1985	30	185	50ohm coax thinnet
10Broad-36	802.3b	1985	100	1800	75ohm coax 3 channels each direction
FOIRL	802.3d	1987	2 hubs	1000	Fiber
1BASE-5	802.3e	1987	12/hub	250	2 pair Category 3 StarLAN

continues

Table 5-4 *IEEE 802.3 Ethernet Evolution (Continued)*

Standard	IEEE	Year	Stations per Segment	Segment Length in Meters	Medium
10BASE-X Ethernet					
10BASE-T	802.3i	1990	12/hub	100	2 pair Category 3 or better UTP*
10BASE-F	802.3j	1993	2 hubs	400 MMF* half-duplex 2000 MMF full-duplex 10k SMF*	2 strands MMF SMF
100BASE-X Fast Ethernet					
100BASE-TX	802.3u	1995	1024	100	2 pair Category 5
100BASE-FX	802.3u	1995		2000	2 strands MMF
100BASE-T4	802.3u	1995	1024	100	4 pair Category 3 or better
100BASE-X T2	802.3x	1997	1024	100	2 pair Category 3 or better
1000BASE-X Gigabit Ethernet					
1000BASE-CX	802.3z	1998		25	2 pair STP*
1000BASE-SX	802.3z	1998		550	2 strands MMF
1000BASE-LX	802.3z	1998		550 MMF 10k SMF	2 strands MMF SMF
1000BASE-T	802.3ab	1999		100	4 pair Category 5
10GE	802.3ae	2002		300 40+k	MMF SMF

*UTP = Unshielded twisted-pair

MMF = Multimode fiber

SMF = Single-mode fiber

STP = Shielded twisted-pair

As you can see, Ethernet is everywhere. Refer to the Cisco.com Products and Technologies pages, IEEE sites, and Charles Spurgeon's website for the constantly updated detailed explanations of Ethernet from Aloha to today, including known problems, steps to help you correct them, and tools to assist. Now that you have experienced the Ethernet evolution, the next section covers Ethernet frame formats in more detail.

Ethernet Frames

In Chapter 1, "Shooting Trouble," you learned that the protocol data unit (PDU) for Layer 2 is frames. Frames refer to the entire message from Layer 2 to Layer 7. Control bits mark the beginning and end of frames just as picture frames mark the edges of a picture. Because you are already familiar with how Layer 2 allows different devices to take turns on the media (media access control), and how the network works (logical topologies), now I want you to look at how Ethernet data is actually packaged at Layer 2. In particular, compare DIX Ethernet to IEEE Ethernet, including the various Layer 2 headers in Figure 5-3.

Figure 5-3   *Ethernet Frame Formats*

Ethernet II (DIX Ethernet)					
PRE	DA	SA	Ether Type	DATA	FCS
IEEE 802.3 RAW (Novell 802.3)					
PRE	DA	SA	Length	DATA	FCS
IEEE 802.3 Ethernet with 802.2 (LLC) SAP Header					
PRE	DA	SA	Length	DATA LLC Header	FCS
IEEE 802.3 Ethernet with SNAP Header					
PRE	DA	SA	Length	DATA SNAP Header LLC Header	FCS

Use Figure 5-3 and the Figure 5-4 flowchart as a guide to walk through the Ethernet frames and their headers in the following subsections. Verify the Ethernet frame format details and how the data links change but the upper-layer data remains the same from end to end.

Figure 5-4   *Ethernet Frames*

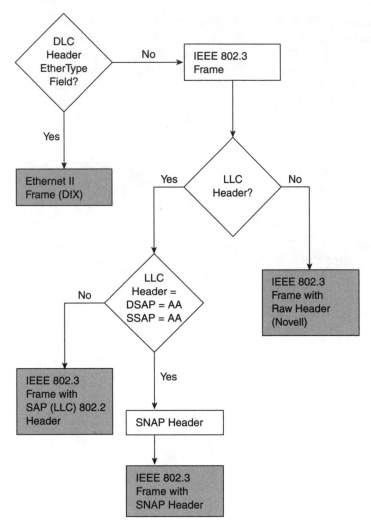

Ethernet II (DIX Ethernet) Frame Format

Figure 5-5 displays Ethernet II (DIX Ethernet) details.

Figure 5-5   *Ethernet II (DIX Ethernet)*

Ethernet II (DIX Ethernet) Frame Format					
8 Bytes	6 Bytes	6 Bytes	2 Bytes	46-1500 Bytes	4 Bytes
PRE	DA	SA	Ether Type (See Figure 5-7)	DATA	FCS

Figure 5-5 shows the following fields:

- **Preamble (PRE)**—Indicates the start of an Ethernet frame, but really not counted as part of the 14-byte frame header.

- **Destination address (DA)**—Unicast, multicast, or broadcast.

- **Source address (SA)**—Always unicast.

- **EtherType**—Identifies the encapsulated Layer 3 (see Figure 5-7).

- **Data**—Varies. A 14-byte header + 4-byte trailer cyclical redundancy check (CRC) = 18 bytes. The 46 data bytes + 18 header bytes = 64 bytes. IEEE 802.3 specification includes requirement to pad the data to the 46-byte requirement, but the Ethernet specification really doesn't.

- **Frame check sequence (FCS)**—A 4-byte *error detection* CRC created by the sender and recalculated by the receiver to check for transit damage. The 1500 data bytes + 14 header bytes = 1514 bytes, or with the FCS (CRC) 1518 bytes.

NOTE   Anything below the minimum of 64 bytes is considered a *runt*. Anything above the maximum of 1518 is considered a *giant*. See the "Shooting Trouble with Ethernet" section for more on runts and giants.

Figure 5-6 displays a protocol analyzer trace of an Ethernet II ARP frame. Frame 221 in the Summary pane clearly displays the source address, destination address, summary, and timing summary. The DLC header displays the destination address as broadcast or all FFFFs, the source address as the MAC address of hosta (unicast), and the EtherType of 0x0806, which Sniffer informs you is ARP. Follow through the ARP/Reverse Address Resolution Protocol

(RARP) frame to see that an IP Layer 3 address is contained in the message as indicated by protocol type 0x0800. Refer to the Ethernet Frame Types helper chart in Figure 5-4 to help identify the frame as an Ethernet II/DIX frame format just because an EtherType is present. Actually the 0x0800 and 0x0806 EtherType values are both greater than 0x05dc or 1500 bytes decimal, which is the allowed length for an 802.3 frame. Use your scientific calculator to perform the math.

Figure 5-6   *Ethernet II ARP Frame*

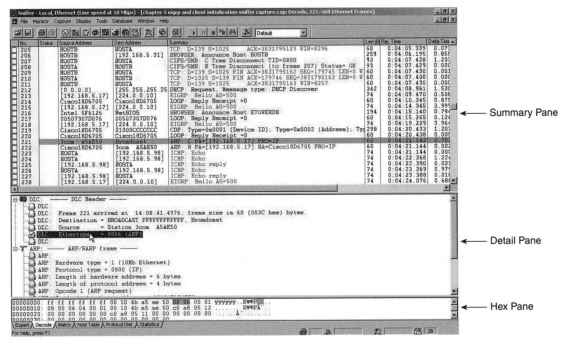

Figure 5-7 displays another example of Ethernet II that displays the EtherType for IP. This is how the Data Link Layer hands off to the next-layer protocol.

In both Figure 5-6 and Figure 5-7, you identify the frame type by looking at the 2-byte EtherType field in the DLC header. The value of the EtherType indicates the next-layer protocol to hand off to. Look up www.cavebear.com/CaveBear/Ethernet/type.html as in Figure 5-8 or http://standards.ieee.org/regauth/ethertype/type-pub.html for more EtherTypes. Cavebear also has a fairly comprehensive list of Ethernet vendor codes and multicast addresses (which are discussed in more detail in the "Ethernet Addressing" section later in this chapter).

Figure 5-7 *Ethernet II IP Frame*

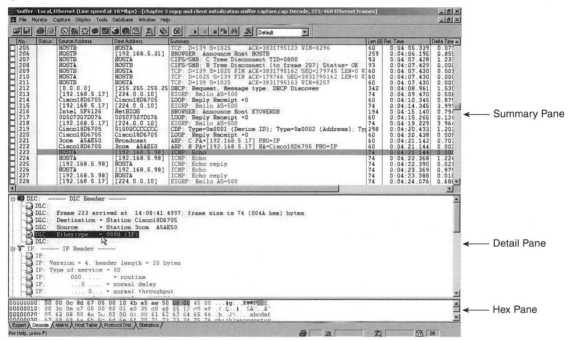

Summary Pane

Detail Pane

Hex Pane

Figure 5-8 *EtherTypes*

NOTE   The maximum packet length for Ethernet is 1500 bytes. If the length field is less than or equal to 1500 (0x5dc, where 0x designates hex) bytes, the frame format is IEEE 802.3 Ethernet. If the length field is not a valid length (greater than 1500), a type field is used and the frame type is Ethernet II. The value of the type field further defines the Layer 3 protocol, such as 0x800 for IP or 0x8137/0x8138 for IPX. Excluding the preamble bytes, 13 and 14 are the determining bytes.

IEEE 802.3 Ethernet Frame Format with Raw (Novell 802.3) Header

Now look at the detailed Sniffer frame format for IEEE 802.3 Raw in Figure 5-9. Remember that IEEE 802.3 Ethernet uses a valid length field (<= 1500 bytes) rather than the EtherType field.

Figure 5-9   *IEEE 802.3 RAW (Novell 802.3)*

IEEE 802.3 RAW (Novell 802.3)					
8 Bytes	6 Bytes	6 Bytes	2 Bytes	46-1500	4 Bytes
PRE	DA	SA	Length	DATA	FCS

Identify the following fields in a protocol analyzer trace such as the one in Figure 5-10:

- **Preamble**—Indicates the start of an Ethernet frame, but really not counted as part of the 14-byte frame header.

- **Destination address**—Unicast, multicast, or broadcast.

- **Source address**—Always unicast.

- **Length**—Valid length field (<= 1500 bytes or 0x05dc).

- **Data**—Varies. A 14-byte header + 4 byte trailer (CRC) = 18 bytes. The 46 data bytes + 18 byte header = 64 bytes. IEEE 802.3 specification includes requirement to pad the data to the 46-byte requirement, but the Ethernet specification really doesn't.

- **Frame check sequence**—A 4-byte *error detection* CRC created by the sender and recalculated by the receiver to check for transit damage. The 1500 data bytes + 14 bytes = 1514 bytes, or with the FCS 1518 bytes.

Figure 5-10 displays an example of an IEEE 802.3 Ethernet frame. Frame 65 that is highlighted in the Summary pane clearly displays the source address, destination address, summary, and timing summary for an IPX ping packet. It is equivalent to the details in the DLC header of the Detail pane. The destination and source addresses are both unicast, as you can verify in the Hex pane at the bottom. Follow through the IPX header to see that the checksum is 0xFFFF, which means that it is not used; this is what you should expect for the Ethernet RAW format. Refer to the Ethernet Frame Types helper chart in Figure 5-3 to see that an EtherType is not present, and the frame does not have an LLC header; you can identify it as IEEE 802.3 RAW.

Figure 5-10 *IEEE 802.3 RAW (Novell 802.3)*

IEEE 802.3 Ethernet Frame Format with 802.2 SAP Header

Other header types used with the IEEE 802.3 frame format include SAP and SNAP. Figure 5-11 illustrates the IEEE 802.3 Frame Format with an 802.2 (Logical Link Control, LLC) SAP header.

Figure 5-11 *IEEE 802.3 Ethernet with 802.2 SAP header*

IEEE 802.3 Ethernet with 802.2 (LLC) SAP Header					
8 Bytes	6 Bytes	6 Bytes	2 Bytes	46-1500 Bytes	4 Bytes
PRE	DA	SA	Length	DATA LLC Header	FCS

Refer to the preceding subsection for an explanation of the individual fields in the header. The only difference here is that part of the data field is borrowed for the LLC header, which uses Service Access Points (SAPs) to point up to the Layer 3 protocols (see Figure 5-12).

NOTE   Remember that IEEE SAPs differ from the Novell SAPs discussed in the preceding chapter. IEEE 802.3 with a SAP header uses 802.2 LLC SAPs to point to the Layer 3 protocol.

Figure 5-12 illustrates a protocol analyzer trace of an IPX ping using Novell's 802.2 frame type (Cisco's SAP encapsulation), whereas the preceding example used Novell's 802.3 (Cisco's Novell-Ether encapsulation) frame format. The DSAP and SSAP of e0 in the LLC header point to IPX at Layer 3. If they were 06 instead of e0, they would link to IP (see Figure 5-13). For more DSAP (destination) and SSAP (source) values, go to www.cisco.com/warp/public/473/111_12.html.

Figure 5-12 *IEEE 802.3 Ethernet with 802.2 SAP Header*

Figure 5-13 *IEEE SAPS*

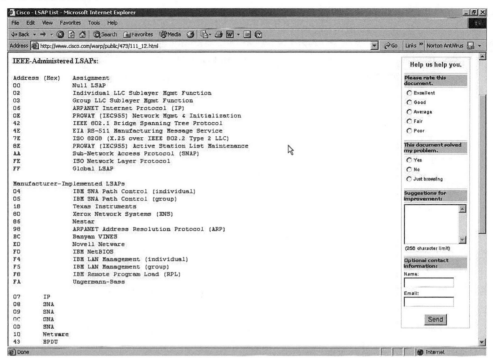

IEEE 802.3 Ethernet Frame Format with SNAP Header

The final Ethernet frame in Figure 5-14 is an IEEE 802.3 frame with a SNAP header. In addition to the 802.3 Data Link header and the 802.2 LLC header, it contains a SNAP header.

Figure 5-14 *IEEE 802.3 Ethernet with SNAP header*

IEEE 802.3 Ethernet with SNAP Header					
8 Bytes	6 Bytes	6 Bytes	2 Bytes	46-1500 Bytes	4 Bytes
PRE	DA	SA	Length	DATA SNAP Header LLC Header	FCS

Figure 5-15 illustrates a protocol analyzer trace of CDP as an example of the IEEE 802.3 frame with a SNAP header. Marked frame number 1 illustrates DLC, LLC, SNAP, and CDP headers.

The DLC destination address is multicast address 01000ccccccc, which is reserved for CDP. The DSAP and SSAP of the LLC header are both AA, which indicates that a SNAP header follows as shown. Note the vendor ID of Cisco1 and the SNAP Type of 2000 for CDP. (In the Hex/ASCII window at the bottom, locate the corresponding bytes.) SNAP is like putting the type field back in for various vendors! In point of fact, additional data bytes are borrowed to give more room for proprietary protocols.

NOTE Because 00000C is an Organizationally Unique Identifier (OUI) reserved to Cisco, 01000Cxxxxxx is the range of multicast addresses also reserved to Cisco. Just as each vendor is responsible for suballocating the lower 3 bytes for unicast source addresses, vendors can do as they want with proprietary multicast MACs.

Figure 5-15 *IEEE 802.3 Ethernet with SNAP Header*

To summarize, the Ethernet frame format rules concentrate on the 2-byte type/length field (byte 13 and 14 excluding the preamble). If these 2 bytes are >= 0x05dc, it is Ethernet II (DIX). If they are <= 0x05dc and FF FF with no LLC header, it is Novell's 802.3 RAW. If they are <= 0x05dc and AA AA, it is IEEE 802.3 with SAP (LLC) 802.2 and SNAP headers. If they are <= 0x05dc but not AA AA or FF FF, it is IEEE 802.3 frame with a SAP (LLC) 802.2 header.

Encapsulation (frame format) is a likely troubleshooting target on your data links regardless of whether you are using Ethernet, Token Ring, FDDI, High-Level Data Link Control (HDLC), PPP, Frame Relay, ATM, or something else. Although this section has primarily discussed Ethernet frame formats, you can find the other formats at Cisco.com or you can purchase detailed protocol reference guides from sites such as www.hollisterassociates.com/protocol_reference_guides.htm. Another important Layer 2 troubleshooting topic is addressing.

Ethernet Addressing

At the Data Link Layer, Ethernet, Token Ring and FDDI all share the same addressing format of 48 bits. This, as many other things in networking, came from Xerox PARC, but is now administered by the IEEE. Think of this like a social security number and a name. I am certain there is another Donna Harrington in the world, but we do not share the same social security number. I don't think I'll capture my social security number for you in Sniffer just in case.

Figure 5-16 illustrates some examples of vendor codes. It is not my intent to make any snide vendor remarks in the case of duplicate addresses because even the well-known manufacturers have made mistakes. Take a look at Example 5-21 or one of your previous **show interfaces** command outputs to see that there is room for duplication on your part, too.

Figure 5-16 *Ethernet Vendor Codes*

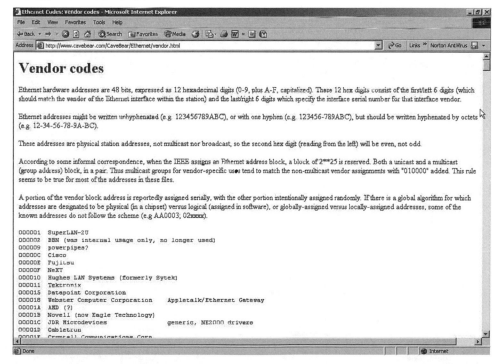

Example 5-21   *Burned in Address (BIA)*

```
r1#show interfaces ethernet 0
Ethernet0 is up, line protocol is up
  Hardware is Lance, address is 0000.0c8d.6705 (bia 0000.0c8d.6705)
  Description: r1e0 to hosta and hostb
  Internet address is 192.168.5.17/28
```

Example 5-21 shows the address and burned-in-address (BIA) to be one and the same. However, someone can use the **mac-address** [*new mac address*] command to change this on the interface. Obviously, this should be done with care because interfaces on the same LAN sharing the same MAC will not function properly. Perhaps you will get an opportunity to experience that sooner than you think. The format for the new MAC address is xxxx.xxxx.xxxx. However, MAC addresses are commonly displayed with dashes, spaces, or dots for readability, as follows:

- xx-xx-xx-xx-xx-xx

- xx xx xx xx xx xx

- xxxx.xxxx.xxxx

Certain addresses are reserved for multicast purposes. Notice that the last bit of the first byte is set to 1 for the examples presented in Figure 5-17. This is actually the first bit of the 48-bit address as it is serially transmitted onto the medium. The bytes are sent left-to-right, but within each byte the bits are sent right-to-left. This is referred to as canonical order, as illustrated back in Chapter 1, "Shooting Trouble."

Figure 5-17   *Multicast Addresses*

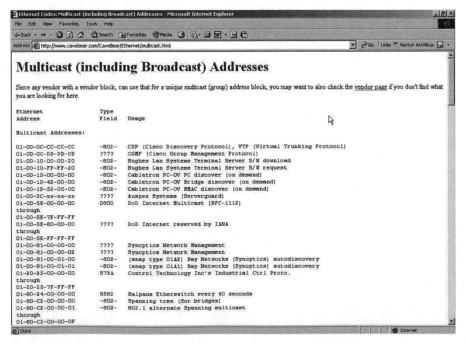

Ethernet at the Physical Layer

Keep in mind that troubleshooting Ethernet may be a Data Link Layer issue, a Physical Layer issue, or both. IEEE 802.3 Ethernet specifies various media types including coax, twisted pair, and fiber. From a troubleshooting viewpoint, it is critical to be aware of the specifications for the Ethernet media you are deploying. Refer back to Table 5-4 to review the various Ethernet media types. For pinout information, refer to Chapter 1, cable vendor sites, and Cisco.com.

Although not as common anymore, you may have the need to configure the media type on your router as in Example 5-22.

Example 5-22 *Media Type Command*

```
r1(config)#interface ethernet 0
r1(config-if)#media-type ?
10BaseT  Use RJ45 connector
  AUI      Use AUI connector
r1(config-if)#end
```

Today, media type is primarily autosensed. In the past, you used to have to decide whether you wanted to use the AUI or RJ-45 connector and hard code the media type appropriately. Decisions like these are also required with 100-Mbps standards. For example, you may need to choose between 100BASE-TX for RJ-45 or *medium-independent interface* (MII). The MII is a 40-pin, high-density D-connector that carries various signals to support 10/100-Mbps transceivers that use different encoding schemes. The Gigabit MII (GMII) leverages off of the design of the MII to allow a gigabit controller to connect 1000BASE-X and 1000BASE-T transceivers. The MII enables you to substitute the Layer 1 of your choice.

Shooting Trouble with Ethernet

Shooting trouble with Ethernet primarily requires you to deal with the Physical and Data Link Layers of the OSI model. I will not change the methodology on you here. Layer 2 depends on Layer 1. You will have an opportunity to prove it yourself if you haven't already.

There are lots of things to check to assist you with narrowing down the possible causes of a problem. Suppose, for example, that you can ping a local host but not a remote one. This could be a routing or routed protocol issue, but it may in fact be a link problem. Next you could ping from a different host or source the ping from a different interface on the router. Perhaps the route is fine, the local router is okay, and the links to the destination are fine, too. You can verify all that with trace. This may lead you to the segment where the destination host is located. Check the interface status to lead you to a Physical Layer or Data Link Layer issue. Perhaps the issue is not with the remote router or switch the PC is plugged into at all, but with the host itself. You can certainly test this theory by pinging other devices on the segment. Do you have link lights on the NIC? Work your way back up the layers on the destination host as it pulls the bits off the wire. Network property sheets and the software tools that come with your NIC can help you find lower-layer issues such as drivers, media types, speed and duplex settings, MAC addresses, frame types, clients, protocols, and so on. Review the quick troubleshooting checklists at the beginning of each chapter and use a layered, yet divide-and-conquer approach to assist you with checking possible causes of the problem.

More than half of the battle with supporting users is recognizing what they see compared to what you actually need to target. After you have narrowed down the scope of the problem, use tools from NIC vendors, troubleshooters from client operating system vendors, Cisco.com, and others to search for specifics. For example, www.networkcomputing.com offers an interactive site for various main Ethernet symptoms. Perhaps you are the WAN nerd and can pass this off to the LAN nerd, but you must admit that you need to be cross-trained enough to know whether it is a WAN problem, LAN problem, host problem, or other.

NOTE   Don't be insulted by *nerd*. Remember nerd in this book stands for network emergency repair dude (or dudette).

Speaking of the specifics, use Table 5-5 and Table 5-6 to assist you with spotting Ethernet interface issues in the Trouble Tickets and in the practical environment. Keep in mind that collisions are normal and expected in a half-duplex shared Ethernet world, but not so expected in a point-to-point, full-duplex environment. However, repeated collisions may mean traffic issues in a shared environment or that you have duplex issues in a point-to-point environment. To know whether you have problems, it helps to understand terms such as the following to get started:

- **Wire speed**—Actual speed along the cable measured in Mbps.

- **Capacity**—Capacity or bandwidth is the maximum possible rate of transmission. For Ethernet, it is quantified in bits per second (bps) and in frames per second. The former is determined by the clock rate and encoding scheme; the latter is due to the 64-byte minimum frame size. Cisco displays bandwidth in Kbps. Delay is inversely proportional to bandwidth. Observe the round-trip delay of ping, for example.

- **Utilization**—Number of bps successfully transmitted divided by the capacity of the medium in bps. Cisco displays utilization in the interface statistics as *load*, as you can see in Table 5-5.

- **Throughput**—The rate at which data is transmitted, measured in Mbps. Throughput is impacted by the number of devices that attempt to transmit and how often they do so, because this will increase the likelihood of collisions, necessitating backoff and retransmission. Lots of test equipment gives you average and peak throughput levels. Throughput excludes the IFG, jam signals, and bad frames. If your 10-Mbps Ethernet device successfully transmits half the time, for instance, your utilization is 50 percent and your throughput is 5 Mbps.

- **Reliability**—Stability of an interface. Cisco uses *rely* to display reliability as a fraction of 255, where 255/255 is 100 percent reliable. With low reliability and not much other activity, expect a hardware issue with the cable, connection, or NIC. If rely is low and collisions are high, however, expect duplex mismatches or you may in fact need to segment your network.

Network management programs and performance monitoring tools are great to measure these statistics over time and report abnormalities through alerts. However, the Cisco IOS enables you to target Data Link Layer and Physical Layer issues in general by viewing your interfaces and controllers. Table 5-5 displays interface targets.

Table 5-5   *Interface Targets*

Output	Description
MTU	The maximum transmission unit of the interface without the frame encapsulation overhead.
BW	The interface bandwidth in kilobits per second.
DLY	Interface delay in microseconds.
Rely	Interface reliability. 255/255 is 100 percent reliable calculated as an exponential average over 5 minutes.
Load (utilization)	The interface load as a fraction of 255 as an exponential average over 5 minutes. 255 is saturated.
Keepalive	Shows whether keepalives are set. You send to your own MAC on the LAN, whereas on the WAN you send to the partner router.
Last Input	Lets you know how long since the last packet was received by the interface.
Last Output	Lets you know how long since the last packet was transmitted by the interface.
Last Clearing	Shows when counters were reset to 0.
Output Q and Input Q Drops	Show maximum Q size, followed by packets dropped due to a full Q.
Packets Input	Shows good packets received.
Bytes Input	Shows good bytes received, including data and MAC encapsulation.
No Buffers	Shows discarded packets as a result of no system buffers. Compare with ignored and check for broadcast storms.
Received Broadcasts	Shows broadcast and multicast packets received. Should be less than 20 percent of the total number of input packets unless total input is small.
Runts	Smaller than the medium's minimum packet size. In Ethernet this is 64 bytes and is normally caused by collisions. Investigate more than one runt per million bytes received.
Giants	Exceed the maximum packet size. In Ethernet this is 1518 bytes.

continues

Table 5-5 *Interface Targets*

Output	Description
CRC Errors	Generated when the CRC generated by the sender does not match the CRC on the data received. High number may be due to collisions or bad data transmission. Investigate more than one per million packets received on a LAN and more than one per thousand packets received on a WAN.
Frame	Shows number of packets received with CRC error and noninteger number of octets. Investigate collision problems, bad NIC, or physical medium for frame and alignment errors.
Overrun	Indicates how many times the receiver hardware was unable to store into a packet buffer because of an oversubscribed data bus within the router. Check hardware configuration.
Ignored	Shows received packets ignored because interface ran out of internal buffers. Broadcast storms and noise cause this.
Collisions	Shows retransmissions due to Ethernet collisions. Router knows only about collisions on its interface—only the ones it participates in. Excessive collisions may mean bad NIC, faulty cabling, or repeater problem. Divide the number of collisions by the number of output packets; the result should be less than 0.1 percent.
Interface Resets	Indicates how many times an interface has been completely reset. May happen if packets queued could not be sent because of lack of carrier or clocking, unplugged cable, and so on.
Restarts	Indicates how many times a Type2 Ethernet controller was restarted due to errors. Compare with **show controllers**, line restarts.

Use Table 5-5 and Example 5-23 to help you review these interface statistics. When monitoring an interface over a particular period of time, clear the interface counters before your test.

NOTE   Clearing the interface counters before your test is *very* important. If the counters have accumulated for weeks or months, it's quite difficult to tell whether an apparent symptom is still occurring or whether it happened a long time ago.

Example 5-23   show interfaces [*interface*]

```
r3#show interface fastethernet 2/0
FastEthernet2/0 is up, line protocol is up
  Hardware is AmdFE, address is 00b0.6481.e300 (bia 00b0.6481.e300)
  Description: r3fa2/0 to hostc
  Internet address is 192.168.5.97/28
  MTU 1500 bytes, BW 10000 Kbit, DLY 1000 usec, rely 220/255, load 1/255
  Encapsulation ARPA, loopback not set, keepalive set (10 sec)
```

Example 5-23   **show interfaces** [*interface*] *(Continued)*

```
Full-duplex, 100Mb/s, 100BaseTX/FX
  ARP type: ARPA, ARP Timeout 04:00:00
  Last input 00:03:53, output 00:00:01, output hang never
  Last clearing of "show interface" counters never
Queueing strategy: fifo
  Output queue 0/40, 0 drops; input queue 0/75, 0 drops
  5 minute input rate 0 bits/sec, 0 packets/sec
  5 minute output rate 0 bits/sec, 0 packets/sec
     374 packets input, 55460 bytes
     Received 374 broadcasts, 0 runts, 0 giants, 0 throttles
     0 input errors, 0 CRC, 0 frame, 0 overrun, 0 ignored, 0 abort
     0 watchdog, 0 multicast
     0 input packets with dribble condition detected
     6405 packets output, 525206 bytes, 0 underruns
     22 output errors, 0 collisions, 7 interface resets
     0 babbles, 0 late collision, 0 deferred
     22 lost carrier, 0 no carrier
     0 output buffer failures, 0 output buffers swapped out
```

The shaded output in Example 5-23 clearly demonstrates that at some point in time a Layer 1 link was missing and therefore an inability to transmit. The 220/255 rely is your first indication to look further. Notice the 22 output errors and 22 lost carriers, but no collisions. The load is very low too, so at some point in time you had a hardware issue. Because these problems are not occurring now, you should clear the counters and look at the interface statistics again as in Example 5-24.

Example 5-24   *Interface Counters*

```
r3#clear counters
Clear "show interface" counters on all interfaces [confirm]
r3#
05:21:49: %CLEAR-5-COUNTERS: Clear counter on all interfaces by console
r3#show interface fastethernet 2/0
FastEthernet2/0 is up, line protocol is up
  Hardware is AmdFE, address is 00b0.6481.e300 (bia 00b0.6481.e300)
  Description: r3fa2/0 to hostc
  Internet address is 192.168.5.97/28
  MTU 1500 bytes, BW 10000 Kbit, DLY 1000 usec, rely 227/255, load 1/255
  Encapsulation ARPA, loopback not set, keepalive set (10 sec)
Full-duplex, 100Mb/s, 100BaseTX/FX
  ARP type: ARPA, ARP Timeout 04:00:00
  Last input 00:04:28, output 00:00:01, output hang never
  Last clearing of "show interface" counters 00:00:13
  Queueing strategy: fifo
  Output queue 0/40, 0 drops; input queue 0/75, 0 drops
  5 minute input rate 0 bits/sec, 0 packets/sec
  5 minute output rate 0 bits/sec, 0 packets/sec
     0 packets input, 0 bytes
     Received 0 broadcasts, 0 runts, 0 giants, 0 throttles
     0 input errors, 0 CRC, 0 frame, 0 overrun, 0 ignored, 0 abort
     0 watchdog, 0 multicast
```

continues

Example 5-24 *Interface Counters (Continued)*

```
        0 input packets with dribble condition detected
        4 packets output, 282 bytes, 0 underruns
        0 output errors, 0 collisions, 0 interface resets
        0 babbles, 0 late collision, 0 deferred
        0 lost carrier, 0 no carrier
        0 output buffer failures, 0 output buffers swapped out
r3#
```

Instead of clearing all the counters, you can individually clear the counters for a particular interface. At least now you can troubleshoot them from this point forward. Clear the counters on all your routers and save your configurations to prepare for the upcoming Trouble Tickets.

Although collisions are not an issue in the example, an absolute number of collisions is not the best threshold to determine how many are too many. Setting a collision rate by percentage is a better way. For example, collisions should not exceed 1 percent of total packets output. Also keep in mind that a router knows only about the collisions in which it participates. Calculate the collision rate by dividing collisions by the output packets.

Most collisions occur in the preamble, and depending on your protocol analyzer you may witness the damaged frame by seeing repeating bytes of 0xAA or 0x55. Frames shorter than 64 bytes are generally caused by collisions (runts). Frames longer than 1518 (giants) normally indicate a bad NIC. Giants may also indicate an encapsulation mismatch because Inter-Switch Link (ISL) and 802.1q will produce baby giants for full MTU payloads. Repeaters forward them; switches drop them.

Excessive collisions should never occur. It indicates that the NIC attempted to transmit a frame 16 times without success, getting a collision every time. Check the cabling and the NIC. If there are excessive CRC errors but not many collisions, check the cable. Dirty or unstable connectors or a bad NIC tend to cause lots of CRC errors.

Late collisions occur after the initial 64 bytes and are commonly a result of duplex mismatches. Another harder-to-troubleshoot reason for late collisions is a cable run longer than the specification. Physical Layer troubleshooting is often overlooked.

There have been interesting issues over the years with autonegotiation, especially with proprietary NICs, hubs, and switches. My preference is still to set speed and duplex manually where at all possible. Because 10BASE-T and 100BASE-TX are electrically incompatible, the autonegotiation hierarchy is built in to the IEEE 802.3u specifications. The specification controls the order of negotiation from top to bottom (see Table 5-6).

Table 5-6 *IEEE 802.3u Autonegotiation Specifications*

Autonegotiation Level	Mode of Operation	Maximum Total Transfer Rate
9	1000BASE-T full-duplex	2000
8	1000BASE-T half-duplex	1000
7	100BASE-T2 full-duplex	200

Table 5-6   *IEEE 802.3u Autonegotiation Specifications*

Autonegotiation Level	Mode of Operation	Maximum Total Transfer Rate
6	100BASE-TX full-duplex	200
5	100BASE-T2 half-duplex	100
4	100BASE-T4 half-duplex	100
3	100BASE-TX half-duplex	100
2	10BASE-T full-duplex	20
1	10BASE-T half-duplex	10

NOTE   Although performance usually suffers, communication normally occurs with duplex mismatches. On the other hand, communications will not occur if there are speed mismatches; the symptoms are just like having the wrong cable connected. Check your LEDs if you can physically inspect the device; check your **show interfaces** display if you can't physically inspect the device if customer impact is in fact a concern.

Pick a normal activity time for a baseline to do your interface and controller monitoring. Compare the same activity at different times of the day, week, month, and year and capture the details in a spreadsheet or database for performance management and long-term planning. You must document and update your findings to succeed in troubleshooting.

Once again it is time for the chapter Trouble Tickets. The plan here is to give you several things to do, let you make mistakes and fix some things on your own, and to introduce other problems that you should have some experience with as a support person. Shooting trouble with Ethernet is critical to the support person because Ethernet primarily dominates the market today.

NOTE   *Do not* **write erase** your routers and start from scratch. Whether it is now or later, you will learn from your own mistakes. In the real world, many times I find it easier to just start from scratch if things are that different. In many cases you do not have that luxury, for what you change on a router affects not just one person, but many others, and change control is a definite must.

Trouble Tickets

Complete the following Trouble Tickets in order. They assume you have followed along with the Shooting Trouble with Ethernet chapter scenario thus far. Use the chapter scenario drawings and tools from the previous chapters to analyze, test, and document as you go. Do not expect all troubles to be limited to just Ethernet issues. Feel free to create your own Physical Layer or other problems if you need more practice in that area. Sample solutions are provided.

Trouble Ticket 1

A new administrator is at the r5 location performing some simple tests. She tells you she can't ping to the other side of the network over on r4. You have her issue a **show arp** command on her router and nothing displays. You are at the r1 location and you can't get to network 10.2.2.0 either, but in your earlier testing you know you were able to get to the other end of the network because you issued a **ping** from hosta to hostc. Example 5-25 displays the r1 routing table. Can you spot the issue(s)? Fix the problem(s). You may or may not have this particular issue in your lab right now, but you should help the new administrator troubleshoot the problem.

Example 5-25 *Trouble Ticket 1 IP Testing*

```
r5>ping 10.2.2.2
Type escape sequence to abort.
Sending 5, 100-byte ICMP Echos to 10.2.2.2, timeout is 2 seconds:
.....
Success rate is 0 percent (0/5)
r5>show arp
r5>!!nothing is here
r1>show ip route
     192.168.5.0/24 is variably subnetted, 7 subnets, 2 masks
D       192.168.5.96/28 [90/2172416] via 192.168.5.82, 01:12:02, Serial1
D       192.168.5.64/28 [90/40537600] via 192.168.5.34, 01:12:03, Ethernet1
C       192.168.5.80/28 is directly connected, Serial1
C       192.168.5.32/28 is directly connected, Ethernet1
D       192.168.5.48/28 [90/40537600] via 192.168.5.34, 01:12:03, Ethernet1
D       192.168.5.0/24 is a summary, 01:12:08, Null0
C       192.168.5.16/28 is directly connected, Ethernet0
     10.0.0.0/8 is variably subnetted, 2 subnets, 2 masks
D       10.0.0.0/8 is a summary, 01:12:03, Null0
C       10.1.1.0/24 is directly connected, Serial0
r1#end
```

Trouble Ticket 2

You completed Trouble Ticket 1 as far as IP is concerned, but what about IPX? IPX should be running only on the LAN that hosta is on, including the server, hosts, and router interface. Note and fix any issues. The Novell server **display networks** command shows 516 0/1 and 346648E2 0/1, and the router display is in Example 5-26. You may or may not have this particular issue in your lab right now, but you should troubleshoot the problem as it exists here.

Example 5-26 *Trouble Ticket 2 IPX Testing*

```
r1#show ipx interface brief
Interface          IPX Network Encapsulation Status        IPX State
Ethernet0          516         NOVELL-ETHER  up            [up]
Ethernet1          unassigned  not config'd  up            n/a
Serial0            unassigned  not config'd  up            n/a
Serial1            unassigned  not config'd  up            n/a
r1#show ipx interface ethernet 0
Ethernet0 is up, line protocol is up
  IPX address is 516.0000.0c8d.6705, NOVELL-ETHER [up]
```

Example 5-26 *Trouble Ticket 2 IPX Testing (Continued)*

```
   Delay of this IPX network, in ticks is 1 throughput 0 link delay 0
...
r1#show ipx route
1 Total IPX routes. Up to 1 parallel paths and 16 hops allowed.
No default route known.
C        516 (NOVELL-ETHER),  Et0
r1#end
```

Trouble Ticket 3

Change the frame type for network 516 to Ethernet II only. Ping from r1 to the Novell server to verify connectivity.

Trouble Ticket 4

Configure the MAC address of r1e0 to be identical to hostb's MAC address. What happens? Turn on **debug arp**. Ping the r1e0 interface from the hostb command prompt. What happens? Ping hostb from r1. Fix the duplicate MAC issue. Although not shown in the answer output, it might be a good time to check your other hosts on the same Ethernet segment to verify that you gave them IP addresses. Clean up the clients so that they are running TCP/IP and the Microsoft Client. Put the Novell server to rest for the remainder of the labs.

Trouble Ticket 5

What is the effect of duplicate IP addresses? Change hosta to the same address as r1e0. Observe the results and change the address after the fact.

Trouble Ticket 6

It is helpful to be aware of *housekeeping-type traffic* on your network so that you can easily spot issues. Log all activity to a file (such as I do with SecureCRT for the answer). Debug CDP events and analyze the packet capturing. Optionally, turn on debugs for EIGRP, too. Use Sniffer to capture the activity for about 3 or 4 minutes to a file and save the file as *chapter 5 background traffic sniffer capture*.

Trouble Ticket 7

Clear the interface counters for r1e0. Turn on **debug arp**. Start a continuous ping from hosta to hostb using **ping -t**. Make sure you can see both your command-prompt window and your connection to r1 on your screen at the same time. Disconnect the cable from the Ethernet dongle on hosta. Show the interface a couple of times while you wait about 20 seconds. Plug the cable back in and observe the results. Ctrl+C stops the continuous ping. Log all activity to a file using a terminal-emulation application such as HyperTerm or SecureCRT.

Trouble Ticket 8

Configure all routers to send their syslog output to hosta, and set up hosta as a syslog server. To test this out, you can download the 3CDaemon product for free from support.3com.com/infodeli/swlib/utilities_for_windows_32_bit.htm. What is the default speed and duplex setting for r3's fast Ethernet interface? Clear the interface statistics for r3fa2/0. Turn on **debug arp**. Start a continuous ping from hostc to hostb using **ping -t**. Disconnect the cable from the Ethernet dongle on hostc. Show the interface a couple of times while you wait about 20 seconds. Plug the cable back in and observe the results. Ctrl+C stops the continuous ping.

Trouble Tickets Solutions

These solutions are not always the only way to perform these tasks. However, the upcoming chapter scenarios are based on these solutions.

Trouble Ticket 1 Solution

There are a couple of issues in Trouble Ticket 1. First, you do not have a route to the 10.2.2.0 network in the r1 routing table, much less the r5 routing table. This is because EIGRP automatically summarizes IP at the classful boundary. Actually, you had this problem back in the IP chapter, and in this chapter's scenario. The **no auto-summary** command is a good command to remember for classless protocols such as EIGRP and RIPv2 that automatically summarize at the classful boundary. Look back at the routing table display in Trouble Ticket 1 to see the null 0 routes for the classful boundary of 192.168.5.0/24 and 10.0.0.0/8. Fix the issue as in Example 5-27 so that you can see both 10.1.1.0 and 10.2.2.0 from any router. This issue is referred to as *discontiguous subnets*. EIGRP is a classless routing protocol and certainly supports them, but not with the default automatic classful summarization. If you actually had this issue, perhaps you did not save your **running-config** to your **startup-config** when you fixed the problem earlier in the chapter. Therefore when the device rebooted because of a power problem, it read the contents of NVRAM. Turning off summarization is not best practice either. Summarize the 192.168.5.0 network using a 255.255.255.0 mask so that you minimize the impact of changes made in the internetwork.

Example 5-27 *Summarizing EIGRP*

```
r1(config)#router eigrp 500
r1(config-router)#no auto-summary
r1(config-router)#interface serial 0
r1(config-if)#ip summary-address eigrp 500 192.168.5.0 ?
  A.B.C.D  IP network mask
r1(config-if)#ip summary-address eigrp 500 192.168.5.0 255.255.255.0

r3(config)#router eigrp 500
r3(config-router)#no auto-summary
r3(config-router)#interface serial 0/3
r3(config-if)#ip summary-address eigrp 500 192.168.5.0 255.255.255.0
```

Example 5-27 *Summarizing EIGRP (Continued)*

```
r3(config-if)#end
r3#show ip route
     192.168.5.0/24 is variably subnetted, 7 subnets, 2 masks
C       192.168.5.96/28 is directly connected, FastEthernet2/0
C       192.168.5.64/28 is directly connected, Serial0/1
C       192.168.5.80/28 is directly connected, Serial0/0
D       192.168.5.32/28 [90/40537600] via 192.168.5.81, 00:00:40, Serial0/0
                        [90/40537600] via 192.168.5.49, 00:00:40, Serial0/2
                        [90/40537600] via 192.168.5.65, 00:00:40, Serial0/1
C       192.168.5.48/28 is directly connected, Serial0/2
D       192.168.5.0/24 is a summary, 00:00:14, Null0
D       192.168.5.16/28 [90/40537600] via 192.168.5.81, 00:00:40, Serial0/0
     10.0.0.0/24 is subnetted, 2 subnets
D       10.1.1.0 [90/41024000] via 192.168.5.81, 00:00:40, Serial0/0
C       10.2.2.0 is directly connected, Serial0/3
r4#show ip route
D    192.168.5.0/24 [90/40514560] via 10.2.2.1, 00:00:31, Serial0/0
     10.0.0.0/24 is subnetted, 2 subnets
D       10.1.1.0 [90/41536000] via 10.2.2.1, 00:00:32, Serial0/0
C       10.2.2.0 is directly connected, Serial0/0
r5#show ip route
D    192.168.5.0/24 [90/40537600] via 10.1.1.1, 00:00:04, Serial0
     10.0.0.0/24 is subnetted, 2 subnets
D       10.2.2.0 [90/41536000] via 10.1.1.1, 00:00:04, Serial0
C       10.1.1.0 is directly connected, Serial0
r5#ping 10.2.2.2
Type escape sequence to abort.
Sending 5, 100-byte ICMP Echos to 10.2.2.2, timeout is 2 seconds:
!!!!!
Success rate is 100 percent (5/5), round-trip min/avg/max = 84/88/92 ms
```

EIGRP enables you to summarize on any interface you choose and requires you to turn off classful summarization for discontiguous subnets to work. Draw yourself a picture if you need to. Draw subnet 10.1.1.0/24 on the left, 192.168.5.0/24 in the middle, and 10.2.2.0/24 on the right. Then it will be clear that you have two network 10.0.0.0 subnets separated by the 192.168.5.0 network. The **no auto-summary** was not necessary on r2, r4, r5, but required on r1 and r3. A good test is to go to r2 and make sure it has a route for 10.1.1.0/24 and a route for 10.2.2.0/24. However, the ping from r5 to 10.2.2.2 works just fine, too.

R1 and r3 have interfaces in multiple networks. By summarizing the 192.168.5.0 routes to r5 and r4, you significantly reduce the routing table size as well as localize the impact of changes. Note also the multiple paths to 192.168.5.32 as shaded in the r3 routing table.

Remember to save all your configurations to **startup-config** (NVRAM). Compare them to my SecureCRT log if you need something to compare them to. Although not specified in the Trouble Ticket, it is assumed knowledge to also copy the configurations to another location for backup (to a TFTP server, for instance).

Trouble Ticket 2 Solution

Looks like someone forgot the encapsulation on r1e0. Example 5-28 shows the fix.

Example 5-28 *SAP Encapsulation*

```
r1(config)#interface ethernet 0
r1(config-if)#encap sap
r1(config-if)#!!!better try again
r1(config-if)#ipx encap sap
r1(config-if)#end
r1#show ipx interface brief
Interface           IPX Network Encapsulation Status        IPX State
Ethernet0           516         SAP           up            [up]
Ethernet1           unassigned  not config'd  up            n/a
Serial0             unassigned  not config'd  up            n/a
Serial1             unassigned  not config'd  up            n/a
r1#show ipx route
2 Total IPX routes. Up to 1 parallel paths and 16 hops allowed.
No default route known.
C        516 (SAP),           Et0
R     346648E2 [02/01] via    516.0080.29e8.5c6b,    5s, Et0
r1#debug ipx sap activity
IPX service debugging is on
r1#
02:10:21: IPXSAP: Response (in) type 0x2 len 288 src:516.0080.29e8.5c6b
    dest:516.ffff.ffff.ffff(452)
02:10:21:   type 0x4, "GWISE", 346648E2.0000.0000.0001(451), 1 hops
02:10:21:   type 0x26B, "GWISE_TREE_____GRN@@@@@DPJ",
    346648E2.0000.0000.0001(5), 1 hops
02:10:21:   type 0x278, "GWISE_TREE_____GRN@@@@@DPJ",
    346648E2.0000.0000.0001(4006), 1 hops
02:10:21:   type 0x107, "GWISE", 346648E2.0000.0000.0001(8104), 1 hops
02:10:46: IPXSAP: positing update to 516.ffff.ffff.ffff via Ethernet0
    (broadcast) (full)
02:10:46: IPXSAP: suppressing null update to 516.ffff.ffff.ffff
r1#undebug all
All possible debugging has been turned off
r1#copy running-config startup-config
```

It is always a good practice to show your interfaces as in the original Trouble Ticket for troubleshooting. If you were to issue the **show ipx interface brief** command, for instance, you would quickly see the encapsulation and status IPX network 516, whereas **show ipx interface e0** would show the node address, too. Copy all configurations to a TFTP server for backup.

Trouble Ticket 3 Solution

This requires commands on the server and on the router. Use a utility such as inetcfg or the command line on the server to change the frame type to bind an appropriate IP address to the NIC. I used 192.168.5.20/28. You can unbind any other frame types for now. Remember to issue the **reinitialize system** command at the Novell command prompt and verify with **config**. Change the encapsulation on r1e0 to ARPA for Ethernet II to match the server as in Example 5-29.

Example 5-29 *ARPA Encapsulation*

```
r1(config-if)#ipx encap arpa
r1(config-if)#end
r1#show ipx route
C        516 (ARPA),          Et0
r1#ping 192.168.5.20
Type escape sequence to abort.
Sending 5, 100-byte ICMP Echos to 192.168.5.20, timeout is 2 seconds:
!!!!!
Success rate is 100 percent (5/5), round-trip min/avg/max = 1/2/4 ms
r1#copy running-config startup-config
```

It is always a good practice to show your interfaces as in the original Trouble Ticket for troubleshooting. If you were to issue the **show ipx interface brief** command, for instance, you would quickly see the encapsulation and status IPX network 516 (whereas **show ipx interface e0** would show the node address, too).

Trouble Ticket 4 Solution

With duplicate MAC addresses involving a router, the router address takes priority and wins out over the host. (See Example 5-30.) Although there is really no message that comes right out and tells you there is a problem until you go to use the address, the output of **debug arp** is quite helpful. Remember to change the MAC address back after you experiment.

Example 5-30 *Duplicate MACs (Router and hostb)*

```
r1(config)#interface ethernet 0
r1(config-if)#mac-address ?
  H.H.H  MAC address
r1(config-if)#mac-address 0080.c7aa.c887
r1(config-if)#end
r1#show interface ethernet 0
Ethernet0 is up, line protocol is up
  Hardware is Lance, address is 0080.c7aa.c887 (bia 0000.0c8d.6705)
  Description: r1e0 to hosta hostb and gwise
  Internet address is 192.168.5.17/28
  MTU 1500 bytes, BW 10000 Kbit, DLY 1000 usec, rely 255/255, load 1/255
  Encapsulation ARPA, loopback not set, keepalive set (10 sec)
  ARP type: ARPA, ARP Timeout 04:00:00
...
r1#debug arp
ARP packet debugging is on
03:19:16: IP ARP req filtered src 192.168.5.19 0080.c7aa.c887, dst 192.168.5.17
     0000.0000.0000 it's our address
03:19:18: IP ARP req filtered src 192.168.5.19 0080.c7aa.c887, dst 192.168.5.17
     0000.0000.0000 it's our address
03:19:19: IP ARP req filtered src 192.168.5.19 0080.c7aa.c887, dst 192.168.5.17
     0000.0000.0000 it's our address
03:19:20: IP ARP req filtered src 192.168.5.19 0080.c7aa.c887, dst 192.168.5.17
```

continues

Example 5-30 *Duplicate MACs (Router and hostb) (Continued)*

```
     0000.0000.0000 it's our address
r1#ping 192.168.5.19
Type escape sequence to abort.
Sending 5, 100-byte ICMP Echos to 192.168.5.19, timeout is 2 seconds:
03:20:11: IP ARP: creating incomplete entry for IP address: 192.168.5.19
03:20:12: IP ARP: sent req src 192.168.5.17 0080.c7aa.c887,
             dst 192.168.5.19 0000.0000.0000 Ethernet0.
03:20:13: IP ARP: sent req src 192.168.5.17 0080.c7aa.c887,
             dst 192.168.5.19 0000.0000.0000 Ethernet0.
….
Success rate is 0 percent (0/5)
r1#show arp
Protocol  Address          Age (min)  Hardware Addr   Type   Interface
Internet  192.168.5.33        -       0000.0c8d.6706  ARPA   Ethernet1
Internet  192.168.5.34        3       0000.0c38.a05d  ARPA   Ethernet1
Internet  192.168.5.20        3       0080.29e8.5c6b  ARPA   Ethernet0
Internet  192.168.5.17        -       0080.c7aa.c887  ARPA   Ethernet0
Internet  192.168.5.19        0       Incomplete      ARPA
r1#undebug all
All possible debugging has been turned off
```

Because you didn't have CiscoWorks Campus Manager in your environment to help you run a report for duplicate MAC or IP addresses, your IOS show, logging, and debug commands can help you pinpoint the issue. Notice the incomplete ARP entry when you attempted to ping a host with the same MAC address as r1e0. Prior to that, note the output of **debug arp** where the router complains about the address. Fix the issue as in Example 5-31 and verify your ping.

Example 5-31 *Resetting the MAC address Back to the Original*

```
r1(config)#interface ethernet 0
r1(config-if)#no mac-address
r1(config-if)#end
r1#show interface ethernet 0
Ethernet0 is up, line protocol is up
  Hardware is Lance, address is 0000.0c8d.6705 (bia 0000.0c8d.6705)
…
r1#show arp
Protocol  Address          Age (min)  Hardware Addr   Type   Interface
Internet  192.168.5.33        -       0000.0c8d.6706  ARPA   Ethernet1
Internet  192.168.5.34        2       0000.0c38.a05d  ARPA   Ethernet1
Internet  192.168.5.20        2       0080.29e8.5c6b  ARPA   Ethernet0
Internet  192.168.5.17        -       0000.0c8d.6705  ARPA   Ethernet0
r1#ping 192.168.5.19
Type escape sequence to abort.
Sending 5, 100-byte ICMP Echos to 192.168.5.19, timeout is 2 seconds:
.!!!!
Success rate is 80 percent (4/5), round-trip min/avg/max = 1/1/4 ms
r1#ping 192.168.5.19
Type escape sequence to abort.
Sending 5, 100-byte ICMP Echos to 192.168.5.19, timeout is 2 seconds:
!!!!!
Success rate is 100 percent (5/5), round-trip min/avg/max = 1/1/1 ms
r1#copy running-config startup-config
```

If issues remain, you may need to clear the ARP table using the **clear arp-cache** command because the entries are kept there for a 4-hour time period in Cisco devices. Because you really can't just clear one entry, it is better practice to bounce (**shut/no shut**) the affected interface first. If necessary, an ARP packet is broadcast (local broadcast) to resolve the destination IP address (Layer 3) to its equivalent MAC address (Layer 2). If the destination host is on the same subnet, the MAC is the destination host's address. If the destination host is on a different subnet, however, the resulting resolution is generally the default gateway (local router interface) MAC address. Because ARP is dynamic, any leftover issues eventually fix themselves. If you do need to fix them immediately, however, remember to **shut/no shut** the interface first and **clear arp** if necessary.

Trouble Ticket 5 Solution

Figure 5-18 shows the duplicate IP on hosta (a Windows 2000 box) after I configured it with the same IP as r1e0.

Figure 5-18 *Duplicate IP on hosta (Windows 2000)*

The router displayed the following:

```
1w4d: %IP-4-DUPADDR: Duplicate address 192.168.5.17 on Ethernet0,
    sourced by 0010.4ba5.ae50
```

IP devices detect a duplicate because they hear an ARP broadcast with a source IP that matches their own. This message immediately shows up on the console of the router and would show up with **show logging history,** too.

Trouble Ticket 6 Solution

Open Sniffer and observe the housekeeping traffic as I do in Figure 5-19, Figure 5-20, and Example 5-32. A quick glimpse shows that EIGRP, loop reply receipt, and CDP are running without you or me sending any data at all.

If you are opening your own Sniffer file, right-click to mark the first loop reply receipt and click the next occurrence with the same address. Scroll if needed to see the relative time column to record that they occur every 10 seconds. These are Layer 2 keepalives. Notice in particular how on Ethernet the interface talks to itself quite frequently. When an interface misses three consecutive keepalives, the line protocol goes down. By talks to itself, I mean sends to its own MAC. In the Sniffer decode, when one is determining the period by locating each occurrence, one must ignore keepalives sent by other Cisco devices (with a different source MAC).

It's important to note that the Ethernet keepalive provides a limited confidence test. On full-duplex media (UTP, fiber), for instance, the sender of the keepalive will *not* receive its own transmission. So the only assurance from the keepalive is that it can successfully transmit out the NIC. The receipt of the link pulses provides the only confidence in the other direction. It is quite possible to have one-way link, if the medium works only in one direction. One device will report that "line protocol is up" whereas the partner shows it as down.

In addition, loss of link (Layer 1) causes the interface status to change to down within 1 second rather than in 30 seconds (Layer 2 keepalive). This also applies to the HDLC keepalive dependence on Layer 1 (DCD, CTS, Rx clock) for serial links on the WAN.

Figure 5-19 *Ethernet Keepalives*

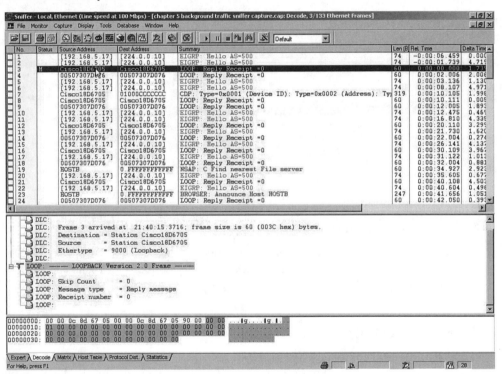

Example 5-32 *CDP Traffic*

```
r1#debug cdp events
CDP events debugging is on
r1#debug cdp packets
CDP packet info debugging is on
04:08:42: CDP-PA: Packet received from r3 on interface Serial1
04:08:42: **Entry  found in cache**
04:08:55: CDP-PA: Packet received from r2 on interface Ethernet1
```

Example 5-32 *CDP Traffic (Continued)*

```
04:08:55: **Entry  found in cache**
04:09:02: CDP-PA: Packet received from 804_rtr on interface Ethernet0
04:09:02: **Entry  found in cache**
04:09:24: CDP-PA: Packet received from r5 on interface Serial0
04:09:24: **Entry  found in cache**
04:09:30: CDP-PA: Packet sent out on Ethernet0
04:09:30: CDP-PA: Packet sent out on Ethernet1
04:09:30: CDP-PA: Packet sent out on Serial0
04:09:30: CDP-PA: Packet sent out on Serial1
04:09:42: CDP-PA: Packet received from r3 on interface Serial1
04:09:42: **Entry  found in cache**
…
r1#show cdp
Global CDP information:
        Sending CDP packets every 60 seconds
        Sending a holdtime value of 180 seconds
r1#undebug all
```

Because you captured CDP packets, take time to analyze them in the protocol analyzer trace in Figure 5-20. If you are curious about the 804 router in my display, it is just being used as hub to connect some devices together. Confirm that CDP messages occur every 60 seconds and that they use the destination multicast address of 01000ccccccc as in line 7 of Figure 5-20. Also note the EIGRP AS 500 multicast hellos over 224.0.0.10.

Figure 5-20 *CDP Packets*

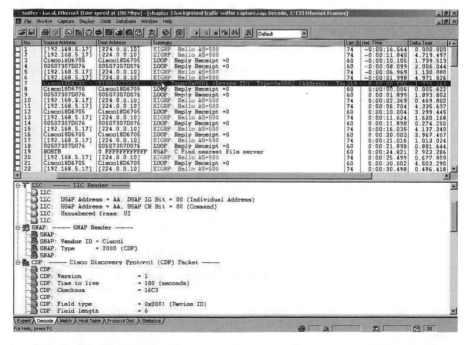

NOTE   If you are not seeing the housekeeping output mentioned, you may have a switch in your lab
scenario and special commands are required to monitor the same activity. You will become
familiar with that in the next chapter. Of course, CDP could be turned off as well.

Trouble Ticket 7 Solution

The **clear counters ethernet 0** command clears just the counters for the e0 interface rather than
all the counters that show up when you type **show interfaces** at the router enable prompt. When
disconnecting the cable from the Windows 2000 box, the host very quickly flashes "hardware
error, the request timed out," and then repeated a "destination host unreachable" message.
When you plug the cable back in, things just pick up where they left off with the continuous
ping on the host. The router receives the ARP broadcast, but the interface *does not* go down
because it and the hosts on subnet 192.168.5.16/28 are plugged into a hub (see Example 5-33).

Example 5-33   *hosta Cable Disconnect SecureCRT Output*

```
r1#clear counters ethernet 0
Clear "show interface" counters on this interface [confirm]
00:25:45: %CLEAR-5-COUNTERS: Clear counter on interface Ethernet0 by console
r1#debug arp
ARP packet debugging is on
00:26:07: IP ARP: rcvd req src 192.168.5.18 0010.4ba5.ae50,
    dst 192.168.5.19 Ethernet0
r1#show interface ethernet 0
Ethernet0 is up, line protocol is up
  Hardware is Lance, address is 0000.0c8d.6705 (bia 0000.0c8d.6705)
  Description: r1e0 to hosta hostb and gwise
  Internet address is 192.168.5.17/28
  …
r1#!!!this is when I plugged the cable back in
r1#show interface ethernet 0
Ethernet0 is up, line protocol is up
  Hardware is Lance, address is 0000.0c8d.6705 (bia 0000.0c8d.6705)
  Description: r1e0 to hosta hostb and gwise
  Internet address is 192.168.5.17/28
  MTU 1500 bytes, BW 10000 Kbit, DLY 1000 usec, rely 255/255, load 1/255
  Encapsulation ARPA, loopback not set, keepalive set (10 sec)
  ARP type: ARPA, ARP Timeout 04:00:00
  Last input 00:00:00, output 00:00:02, output hang never
  Last clearing of "show interface" counters 00:01:33
  Queueing strategy: fifo
00:27:17: IP ARP: rcvd req src 192.168.5.18 0010.4ba5.ae50,
    dst 192.168.5.18 Ethernet0
00:27:17: IP ARP: rcvd req src 192.168.5.18 0010.4ba5.ae50,  .
    dst 192.168.5.19 Ethernet0
00:27:17: IP ARP: rcvd req src 192.168.5.18 0010.4ba5.ae50,
    dst 192.168.5.18 Ethernet0
...
00:27:18: IP ARP: rcvd req src 192.168.5.18 0010.4ba5.ae50,
    dst 192.168.5.18 Ethernet0
r1#
```

If you analyzed the ARP table on the host with **arp –a**, you should have the MAC addresses and IP addresses for hosta and hostb.

Trouble Ticket 8 Solution

Configuring all routers for syslog is no more than just adding the global **logging 192.168.5.18** command to each router. This assumes that you are running the syslog on hosta. The default setting for r3 fa2/0 is 100-Mbps, full-duplex (see Example 5-34). To verify or change the setting on the host, you need the software that comes with the NIC (see Figure 5-21).

Figure 5-21   *3Com NIC Diagnostics*

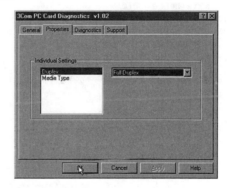

Example 5-34   *hostc Cable Disconnect*

```
r3#show interface fastethernet 2/0
FastEthernet2/0 is up, line protocol is up
  Hardware is AmdFE, address is 00b0.6481.e300 (bia 00b0.6481.e300)
  Description: r3fa2/0 to hostc
  Internet address is 192.168.5.97/28
  MTU 1500 bytes, BW 100000 Kbit, DLY 100 usec, rely 255/255, load 1/255
  Encapsulation ARPA, loopback not set, keepalive set (10 sec)
  Full-duplex, 100Mb/s, 100BaseTX/FX
  ARP type: ARPA, ARP Timeout 04:00:00
...
r3#show running-config interface fastethernet2/0
Current configuration:
interface FastEthernet2/0
 description r3fa2/0 to hostc
 ip address 192.168.5.97 255.255.255.240
 no ip directed-broadcast
end
r3#clear counters fastethernet 2/0
Clear "show interface" counters on this interface [confirm]
r3#debug arp
00:58:53: %CLEAR-5-COUNTERS: Clear counter on interface
    FastEthernet2/0 by console
ARP packet debugging is on
```

continues

Example 5-34   *hostc Cable Disconnect (Continued)*

```
r3#
00:59:37: IP ARP: rcvd req src 192.168.5.98 0050.04df.5f3c,
    dst 192.168.5.97 FastEthernet2/0
00:59:37: IP ARP: creating entry for IP address: 192.168.5.98, hw: 0050.04df.5f3c
00:59:37: IP ARP: sent rep src 192.168.5.97 00b0.6481.e300,
                    dst 192.168.5.98 0050.04df.5f3c FastEthernet2/0
01:00:06: %LINEPROTO-5-UPDOWN: Line protocol on Interface FastEthernet2/0,
    changed state to down
01:00:06: IP ARP: sent req src 192.168.5.97 00b0.6481.e300,
                    dst 192.168.5.98 0050.04df.5f3c FastEthernet2/0
01:00:06: IP ARP: sent rep src 192.168.5.97 00b0.6481.e300,
                    dst 192.168.5.97 ffff.ffff.ffff FastEthernet2/0
r3#show interface fastethernet 2/0
FastEthernet2/0 is up, line protocol is down
  Hardware is AmdFE, address is 00b0.6481.e300 (bia 00b0.6481.e300)
  Description: r3fa2/0 to hostc
  Internet address is 192.168.5.97/28
  MTU 1500 bytes, BW 100000 Kbit, DLY 100 usec, rely 255/255, load 1/255
  Encapsulation ARPA, loopback not set, keepalive set (10 sec)
Full-duplex, 100Mb/s, 100BaseTX/FX
  ARP type: ARPA, ARP Timeout 04:00:00
  Last input 00:00:58, output 00:00:01, output hang never
  Last clearing of "show interface" counters 00:01:42
```

Trouble Ticket 8 has a point-to-point connection, whereas Trouble Ticket 7 had a shared hub connection. Line protocol goes down when the host misses three consecutive keepalives in a shared environment, but here the line protocol goes down upon loss of link. In Example 5-35, notice how because of autonegotiation the duplex setting ended up as half-duplex. This is the frequent cause of errors and bizarre problems. Although autonegotiation has certainly matured over the years, in most cases I still recommend that the settings be specified on both ends. You can hard code the duplex to full using the interface **full-duplex** command. Syslog should have indicated the clearing of the counters and the interface changes such as in Example 5-36.

Example 5-35   *Plug the Cable Back In*

```
01:00:56: %LINEPROTO-5-UPDOWN: Line protocol on Interface FastEthernet2/0,
    changed state to up
01:00:59: IP ARP: creating incomplete entry for IP address: 192.168.5.98
01:00:59: IP ARP: sent req src 192.168.5.97 00b0.6481.e300,
                    dst 192.168.5.98 0000.0000.0000 FastEthernet2/0
01:00:59: IP ARP: rcvd rep src 192.168.5.98 0050.04df.5f3c,
    dst 192.168.5.97 FastEthernet2/0
r3#show interface fastethernet 2/0
FastEthernet2/0 is up, line protocol is up
  Hardware is AmdFE, address is 00b0.6481.e300 (bia 00b0.6481.e300)
  Description: r3fa2/0 to hostc
  Internet address is 192.168.5.97/28
  MTU 1500 bytes, BW 100000 Kbit, DLY 100 usec, rely 255/255, load 1/255
  Encapsulation ARPA, loopback not set, keepalive set (10 sec)
Half-duplex, 100Mb/s, 100BaseTX/FX
  ARP type: ARPA, ARP Timeout 04:00:00
```

Example 5-36 *Syslog Output*

```
Nov 11 19:04:02 192.168.5.82 82: 1w5d: %CLEAR-5-COUNTERS:
    Clear counter on interface FastEthernet2/0 by console
Nov 11 19:06:21 192.168.5.82 83: 1w5d: %LINEPROTO-5-UPDOWN:
    Line protocol on Interface FastEthernet2/0, changed state to down
Nov 11 19:07:42 192.168.5.82 84: 1w5d: %LINEPROTO-5-UPDOWN:
    Line protocol on Interface FastEthernet2/0, changed state to up
```

You have completed the chapter Trouble Tickets when you feel comfortable with the tasks assigned and the various scenarios throughout the chapter. Review or experiment in the areas where you need more help. Understanding and troubleshooting in a simple environment is certainly the foundation for understanding and troubleshooting more complex protocols and technologies. Check your understanding with the chapter review questions.

Review Questions

Use the chapter and your practical troubleshooting knowledge and skills to answer the following questions. The answers are located in Appendix A, "Answers to Review Questions."

1 How would a user complain to you about an incorrect frame type issue?

2 What is the EtherType and SAP for Novell IPX? How does the receiving station recognize an 802.3 Novell-Ether frame?

3 How do you know when an Ethernet network needs to be upgraded?

4 What does the following error message indicate: "%CDP-4-DUPLEXMISMATCH:Full/ half duplex mismatch detected"?

5 Will communications occur if the port on one side of the link is set to full-duplex and the other side is set to half-duplex? How about if there is a speed mismatch?

6 True or false: Fast Ethernet can carry more than 1500 bytes of data in the payload.

7 What types of housekeeping traffic would you expect on the wire with Ethernet in a network similar to the chapter scenario? (Refer back to Figure 5-1.)

8 When should you clear the counters on an Ethernet interface? How do you clear the counters for interface e0?

9 Compare DIX Ethernet to IEEE Ethernet

10 What frame type carries CDP packets? How do you know?

11 What command shows you the Layer 2 address for Ethernet on a Microsoft client? On a Cisco router?

12 Are collisions an issue in full-duplex Ethernet? Why or why not?

Summary

Despite its historical contending nature, it still continues to grow. Ethernet is everywhere. If only Bob Metcalfe would have known the future when he decided on the name. Understanding it and leveraging off of the existing Ethernet makes it easier to configure and troubleshoot. Ethernet has always been appropriate for sporadic, occasionally heavy traffic at high-peak data rates, but Ethernet switching is really what has kept Ethernet alive. The full-duplex capabilities take the collisions out of Ethernet and can really drive up the throughput.

This chapter reviewed the evolution of Ethernet, including standards and detailed information at the Data Link and Physical Layers, to assist you with shooting Ethernet troubles. The next two chapters continue your Ethernet experience with Ethernet switching and VLANs.

CHAPTER 6

Shooting Trouble with CatOS and IOS

Cisco started its internetworking revolution with routers, but soon found out with the help of those they acquired that switches are quite beneficial, too. A solid understanding of switches and routers is crucial for supporting networks as well as obtaining your CCNP and other industry certifications. This chapter assumes knowledge of the previous chapters, but in particular Chapter 5, "Shooting Trouble with Ethernet," and Chapter 3, "Shooting Trouble with IP."

In this chapter you eliminate any hubs and connect your hosts to Cisco switches to build the scenario. Then you review Ethernet switching concepts, symptoms, problems, and action plans. Throughout the chapter there are several walk-through scenarios and practical Trouble Tickets for you to explore. For those of you who do not have equipment handy, the rest of this book contains many relevant figures, examples, and explanations so that you too can follow along to gain practical experience.

This chapter covers the following topics:

- Scenario: Shooting Trouble with CatOS and IOS
- Segmentation Review
- Spanning Tree Protocol (STP)
- The Cisco Command-Line Interface (CLI)
- Cat5000/Cat6000 Architecture
- Shooting Trouble with Switches
- Trouble Tickets
- Trouble Tickets Solutions

Supporting Website Files

You can find files and links to utilities that support this book on the Cisco Press website at www.ciscopress.com/1587200570. Even if you do not have a lab, you can take advantage of the supporting configuration files including the logs to understand device input and output. The files are listed throughout the chapters in italics.

In order to be able to read and work with some of the supporting files offered at www.ciscopress.com/1587200570, you may want to download some of the programs listed in Table I-1 in the Introduction.

Scenario: Shooting Trouble with CatOS and IOS

This chapter requires changes to your physical topology. You configure the Cisco routers and switches as shown Figure 6-1. The rest of the chapter deploys this scenario, so be sure to save your configurations before, during, and after. For example, I saved my Chapter 5 configurations to a file called *Chapter 5 Ending Configs*.

Ideally, you should have at least one *CatOS-based switch* and one *IOS-based switch*. The CatOS uses the **set**, **show**, **clear** syntax, whereas the IOS is more like using the command-line interface (CLI) of a router. I picked three different switches for the scenario so that you get a feel for using HTTP and menus on a 1900, IOS on a 3512XL, and CatOS on a 2900. The 2900 CatOS box has many similarities to the 4000/5000/6000 family of Cisco switches. Although the 2900 in my lab has been discontinued for several years, it's basically a fixed configuration 5002, limited to a Supervisor I. By all means, if you have access to newer devices (such as 6509s), use them instead. My point of using the older ones is to illustrate the fact that you don't need to spend a lot of money on new devices to learn how to troubleshoot.

NOTE   What this chapter is not is a device manual for all of Cisco's switches. If you want that, go to Cisco.com, search for "cisco product quick reference guide" to view it online or order your own subscription. The quick reference guide includes product overviews, photos, technical specifications, and more.

I will briefly review such topics as segmentation, switching modes, speed and duplex settings, the switched port analyzer (SPAN) for port monitoring, and the Spanning Tree Protocol (STP) to assist you with supporting switched Ethernet environments. As in the other practical study support topics, it is essential for you to continue to identify targets and document the results using such commands as **ping**, **trace**, **set**, **show**, **clear**, and other troubleshooting utilities.

The scenario goal is to analyze real-world Catalyst switch issues including physical, data-link, and configuration errors. Document your steps and *any* problems along the way. For this chapter keep everything on subnet 192.168.5.96/28 and assume no VLANs other than the default. Ensure that you can telnet to each switch to configure it. Optionally attach the switches to the terminal server for convenience. Configure the switches starting with the 1900 first, then the 3512XL IOS-based switch, and finally the 2900 CatOS switch as shown in Figure 6-1. On the router, advertise loopback 10 (192.168.6.100/28) in RIP to simulate an external network. Save your work, and don't forget to test things out. All hosts should be able to communicate with the servers you choose to set up on your server farm off of the 2900 as well as to the outside world.

There is not always one right or wrong way to accomplish the tasks presented. The ability to obtain the end result using good practices is extremely important in any real-world network. Where specific parameters are not given, feel free to make the necessary choices to work through the scenario. Troubleshooting and device configurations are included so that you can compare your work and perhaps see a different approach to obtaining the end result. Use the previous IP (Table 3-1) and Ethernet (Table 5-1) quick checklists, your step-by-step troubleshooting methodology and intuition, and the switch quick checklist in Table 6-1 to assist in testing.

Figure 6-1   *Shooting Trouble with CatOS and IOS*

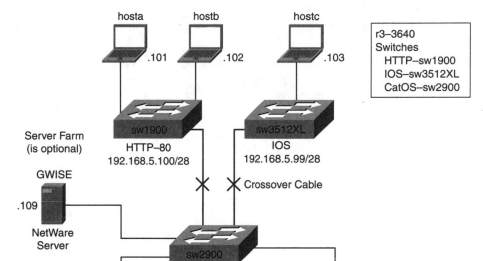

The switch troubleshooting checklist in Table 6-1 assumes that you are familiar with the Ethernet and IP quick troubleshooting checklists from the previous chapters, so those commands are not repeated here. Instead, Table 6-1 displays how to quickly spot issues with modules and ports because they are the main targets for switch troubleshooting. A more complete table of CatOS and IOS commands is provided in the section "The Cisco Command-Line Interface (CLI)."

Table 6-1   *Switch Quick Troubleshooting Checklist*

CatOS Syntax	IOS Syntax
show cdp neighbors	>show cdp neighbors
show module	>show module
show version	>show version
show config/write terminal	#show config/show startup-config
show arp	>show arp
show cam dynamic	#show mac-address-table
show port	#show interface status
set trace	#debug

This chapter scenario's switch, router, and host configurations are displayed starting in Example 6-1. The 1900 switch is not running the Enterprise Edition of the software, so the CLI is not available. Instead of upgrading the software, reset the switch to its factory defaults using the menus as in Example 6-1.

Example 6-1   *Resetting the 1900 to the Factory Defaults Using the Menu Interface*

```
Catalyst 1900 Management Console
Copyright (c)  Cisco Systems, Inc.  1993-1998
All rights reserved.
Standard Edition Software
Ethernet Address:      00-90-92-2A-76-80
PCA Number:            73-2239-05
PCA Serial Number:     FAA02291854
Model Number:          WS-C1924-A
System Serial Number:  FAA0227W0U1
-------------------------------------------------
1 user(s) now active on Management Console.
        User Interface Menu
     [M] Menus
     [I] IP Configuration
Enter Selection:  M
        Catalyst 1900 - System Configuration
        System Revision:  1   Address Capacity:  1024
        System UpTime:    0day(s) 00hour(s) 00minute(s) 45second(s)
    --------------------- Settings --------------------------------------
    [N] Name of system                          sw1900
    [C] Contact name                            donna l harrington
    [L] Location                                broad creek
    [S] Switching mode                          Store-and-Forward
    [U] Use of store-and-forward for multicast  Disabled
    [A] Action upon address violation           Disable
    [G] Generate alert on address violation     Disabled
    [I] Address aging time                      300 second(s)
    [P] Network port                            None
    [H] Half duplex back pressure   (10-mbps ports) Disabled
    [E] Enhanced congestion control (10-mbps ports) Adaptive
    --------------------- Actions --------------------------------------
    [R] Reset system                       [F] Reset to factory defaults
    --------------------- Related Menus --------------------------------
    [B] Broadcast storm control            [X] Exit to Main Menu
Enter Selection:  F
This command resets the switch with factory defaults.  All system
parameters will revert to their default factory settings.  All static
and dynamic addresses will be removed.
Reset system with factory defaults, [Y]es or [N]o?  Yes
```

Next configure the IP parameters and make sure HTTP is operational on port 80 as in Examples 6-2 and 6-3.

Example 6-2   *Setting the IP Parameters on the 1900 (HTTP Port 80)*

```
Catalyst 1900 - Main Menu
    [C] Console Settings
    [S] System
    [N] Network Management
    [P] Port Configuration
...
    [H] Help
    [X] Exit Management Console
Enter Selection:  N


        Catalyst 1900 - Network Management
    [I] IP Configuration
    [S] SNMP Management
    [B] Bridge - Spanning Tree
    [C] Cisco Discovery Protocol
    [G] Cisco Group Management Protocol
    [H] HTTP Server Configuration
    [X] Exit to Main Menu
Enter Selection:  H

   Catalyst 1900 - HTTP Server Configuration
   --------------------- Settings ------------------------------------
    [H] HTTP                              Enabled
    [P] HTTP Port                         80
    [X] Exit to previous menu
Enter Selection:  X
```

The shaded output indicates that HTTP port 80 is the default on the 1900. HTTP and menus are generally available on Cisco switches, but not always configured as the default for security reasons. For example, the global command **ip http server** enables this on my IOS switch, although most people want to know how to disable such features. Type **no ip http server** to disable it afterward if you want to experiment with the web-based Visual Switch Manager on the 3512XL.

Next, set the IP address on the 1900 as in Example 6-3 so that you can manage the device remotely.

Example 6-3   *Setting the IP Parameters on the 1900 (Address)*

```
        Catalyst 1900 - Network Management
    [I] IP Configuration
    [S] SNMP Management
    [B] Bridge - Spanning Tree
    [C] Cisco Discovery Protocol
    [G] Cisco Group Management Protocol
    [H] HTTP Server Configuration
    [X] Exit to Main Menu
Enter Selection:  I

        Catalyst 1900 - IP Configuration
        Ethernet Address:  00-90-92-2A-76-80
```

continues

Example 6-3 *Setting the IP Parameters on the 1900 (Address) (Continued)*

```
--------------------- Settings ---------------------------------------
    [I] IP address                           0.0.0.0
    [S] Subnet mask                          0.0.0.0
    [G] Default gateway                      0.0.0.0
    [M] IP address of DNS server 1           0.0.0.0
    [N] IP address of DNS server 2           0.0.0.0
    [D] Domain name
    [R] Use Routing Information Protocol     Enabled
--------------------- Actions ----------------------------------------
    [P] Ping
    [X] Exit to previous menu
Enter Selection:  I
This command assigns an administrative IP address to this switch.
The new address will take effect immediately.
If no IP address is assigned (or if the IP address is removed by setting
it to 0.0.0.0), and the switch is connected to a DHCP server, the DHCP
server may automatically assign an address to the switch.
Enter administrative IP address in dotted quad format (nnn.nnn.nnn.nnn):
Current setting ===>   0.  0.  0.  0
    New setting ===> 192.168.5.100
```

Configure the subnet mask as in Example 6-4.

Example 6-4 *Setting the IP Parameters on the 1900 (Subnet Mask)*

```
        Catalyst 1900 - IP Configuration
          Ethernet Address:  00-90-92-2A-76-80
--------------------- Settings ---------------------------------------
    [I] IP address                           192.168.5.100
    [S] Subnet mask                          0.0.0.0
    [G] Default gateway                      0.0.0.0
    [M] IP address of DNS server 1           0.0.0.0
    [N] IP address of DNS server 2           0.0.0.0
    [D] Domain name
    [R] Use Routing Information Protocol     Enabled
--------------------- Actions ----------------------------------------
    [P] Ping
    [X] Exit to previous menu
Enter Selection:  S
This command defines the subnet mask for the IP address set by the
[I] IP Address command.
Enter IP subnet mask in dotted quad format (nnn.nnn.nnn.nnn):
Current setting ===>   0.  0.  0.  0
    New setting ===> 255.255.255.240
        Catalyst 1900 - IP Configuration
          Ethernet Address:  00-90-92-2A-76-80
```

Although not required for the chapter labs, configure the default gateway as in Example 6-5 and note when it is used in the menu output.

Example 6-5   *Setting the IP Parameters on the 1900 (Default Gateway)*

```
---------------------- Settings ---------------------------------------
      [I] IP address                            192.168.5.100
      [S] Subnet mask                           255.255.255.240
      [G] Default gateway                       0.0.0.0
      [M] IP address of DNS server 1            0.0.0.0
      [N] IP address of DNS server 2            0.0.0.0
      [D] Domain name
      [R] Use Routing Information Protocol      Enabled
---------------------- Actions ---------------------------------------
      [P] Ping
      [X] Exit to previous menu
Enter Selection:  G
The default gateway IP address is the address of the next hop
router the switch uses to reach a non-local IP host when the switch
does not know the return route.  During a normal management protocol
exchange with an IP client host, the switch simply sends its response
onto the same route from which the request was received.  The default
gateway route is only used when the switch itself initiates an exchange,
e.g., a TFTP upgrade, with the client.
Type the address in dotted quad format (nnn.nnn.nnn.nnn):
Current setting ===>   0.  0.  0.  0
    New setting -==> 192.168.5.97
        Catalyst 1900 - IP Configuration
        Ethernet Address:  00-90-92-2A-76-80
---------------------- Settings ---------------------------------------
      [I] IP address                            192.168.5.100
      [S] Subnet mask                           255.255.255.240
      [G] Default gateway                       192.168.5.97
      [M] IP address of DNS server 1            0.0.0.0
      [N] IP address of DNS server 2            0.0.0.0
      [D] Domain name
      [R] Use Routing Information Protocol      Enabled
---------------------- Actions ---------------------------------------
      [P] Ping
      [X] Exit to previous menu
Enter Selection:  X
```

NOTE   The management IP address is configured in global configuration mode rather than on an interface for a Layer 2 device. The interfaces are Layer 2 ports and do not understand IP, which is Layer 3.

The Enterprise Edition on the 1900 would have enabled you to reset the switch to the factory defaults and set the IP parameters using the commands in Example 6-6. Remember that the

1900 automatically writes the configuration to NVRAM like the Cat5000 series switches and the older 2900 I am using for my lab.

Example 6-6   *Configuring the 1900 with the Enterprise Edition CLI*

```
switch>enable
switch#delete nvram
switch#reload...
switch#configure terminal
switch(config)#hostname sw1900
sw1900(config)#ip address 192.168.5.100 255.255.255.240
sw1900(config)#ip default-gateway 192.168.5.97
```

NOTE   Although Example 6-6 illustrates the **hostname** command to give the switch a name, you have not configured that yet using the menus. You can do this from the main menu by selecting **System** and then **Name of System**. However, I will have you assign this later using the HTTP interface.

Configure hosta and hostb as in Table 6-2 to test your IP connectivity to the switch. Compare your results against Example 6-7.

Table 6-2   *Scenario Host Configuration*

Host	IP Address	Subnet Mask	Gateway
hosta	192.168.5.101	255.255.255.240	192.168.5.97
hostb	192.168.5.102	255.255.255.240	192.168.5.97
hostc	192.168.5.103	255.255.255.240	192.168.5.97

Example 6-7   *Ping Test from hosta to the 1900*

```
C:\>ping 192.168.5.100
Pinging 192.168.5.100 with 32 bytes of data:
Request timed out.
Request timed out.
Request timed out.
Request timed out.
Ping statistics for 192.168.5.100:
    Packets: Sent = 4, Received = 0, Lost = 4 (100% loss),
```

As you can see, the ping from hosta to the 1900 switch failed. Software configuration is one thing, but you better have the physical means of getting the packets from the host to the switch. That means you need a cable and a *straight-through cable* at that; so plug it in and troubleshoot further until your pings are successful. While you are at it, verify all physical connectivity against the chapter scenario in Figure 6-1.

Next validate communications up through the Application Layer by using your web browser (Internet Explorer or Netscape) on hosta to manage the switch as in Figure 6-2.

Figure 6-2   *Accessing 1900 Through a Web Browser*

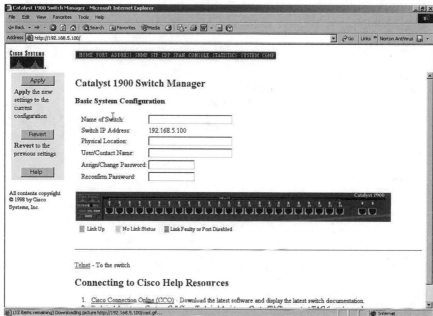

Name the switch **sw1900**, apply your changes, and experiment with the HTTP interface a bit, including moving the cable from one port to another. Now that you confirmed operations from the Physical through the Application Layers on the 1900, proceed to the 3512XL configuration as in Example 6-8. Clear any previous configuration and set up the IP address and subnet mask.

Example 6-8   *Clearing the Existing Configuration on the sw3512XL Using the Cisco IOS*

```
c3512xl#write erase
c3512xl#reload
...
The system is not configured to boot automatically.  The
following command will finish loading the operating system
software:
    boot
switch: boot
Loading "flash:c3500XL-c3h2s-mz-112.8.2-SA6.bin"...#####
    #####################################################################
File "flash:c3500XL-c3h2s-mz-112.8.2-SA6.bin" uncompressed and installed, entry
point: 0x3000
executing...
                Restricted Rights Legend
...
Cisco Internetwork Operating System Software
IOS (tm) C3500XL Software (C3500XL-C3H2S-M), Version 11.2(8.2)SA6,
    MAINTENANCE INTERIM SOFTWARE
...
```

My switch has some interesting issues in that it does not boot up automatically. Look up the message on Cisco's website so that you can fix the boot issue if a similar type of thing happens to you.

Now that you have cleared the contents of NVRAM, configure the hostname and IP parameters as in Example 6-9. View the configuration in RAM.

Example 6-9 *Configuring the 3512XL Using the Cisco IOS*

```
Switch>enable
Switch#configure terminal
Switch(config)#hostname sw3512XL
SW3512XL(config)#ip address 192.168.5.99 255.255.255.240
                       ^
% Invalid input detected at '^' marker.
SW3512XL(config)#end
SW3512XL#show running-config
...
hostname SW3512XL
interface VLAN1
 no ip route-cache
interface FastEthernet0/1
interface FastEthernet0/2
...
SW3512XL#configure terminal
SW3512XL(config)#interface vlan1
SW3512XL(config-if)#ip address 192.158.5.99 255.255.255.240
SW3512XL(config-if)#no shut
SW3512XL(config-if)#end
SW3512XL#copy running-config startup-config
SW3512XL#show running-config
...
hostname SW3512XL
interface VLAN1
 ip address 192.158.5.99 255.255.255.240
 no ip route-cache
...
```

NOTE   Note how you needed to assign the IP address to a logical interface such as interface vlan1 for telnet and management purposes in Example 6-9. This is common for Layer 2-based IOS switches.

Example 6-10 *Fix the 3512XL Manual Boot Issue*

```
SW3512XL>enable
SW3512XL#show boot
BOOT path-list:        flash:c3500XL-c3h2s-mz-112.8.2-SA6.bin
Config file:           flash:config.text
Enable Break:          1
Manual Boot:           yes
HELPER path-list:
```

Example 6-10 *Fix the 3512XL Manual Boot Issue (Continued)*

```
NVRAM/Config file
      buffer size:   32768
SW3512XL#configure terminal
SW3512XL(config)#no boot manual
SW3512XL(config)#end
SW3512XL#copy running-config startup-config
…
SW3512XL#reload
Proceed with reload? [confirm]
%SYS-5-RELOAD: Reload requested
C3500XL Boot Loader (C3500-HBOOT-M) Version 11.2(8.1)SA6, MAINTENANCE INTERIM
SOFTWARE
Compiled Fri 14-May-99 17:59 by jchristy
 starting...
Base ethernet MAC Address: 00:d0:79:68:84:80
...
C3500XL INIT: Complete
SW3512XL>enable
SW3512XL#show boot
BOOT path-list:        flash:c3500XL-c3h2s-mz-112.8.2-SA6.bin
Config file:           flash:config.text
Enable Break:          1
Manual Boot:           no
HELPER path-list:
NVRAM/Config file
      buffer size:   32768
```

Set up hostc as in Table 6-2. Ensure connectivity between hostc and the 3512XL with me in Example 6-11.

Example 6-11 *Ping Test from sw3512XL to hostc*

```
SW3512XL>ping 192.168.5.103
Sending 5, 100-byte ICMP Echos to 192.168.5.103, timeout is 2 seconds:
.....
Success rate is 0 percent (0/5)
SW3512XL>show ip interface brief
Interface              IP-Address        OK? Method Status               Protocol
VLAN1                  192.168.5.99      YES NVRAM  up                   up
FastEthernet0/1        unassigned        YES unset  down                 down
...
FastEthernet0/12       unassigned        YES unset  down                 down
GigabitEthernet0/1     unassigned        YES unset  down                 down
GigabitEthernet0/2     unassigned        YES unset  down                 down
SW3512XL>enable
SW3512XL#configure terminal
SW3512XL(config)#interface vlan1
SW3512XL(config-if)#ip address 192.168.5.99 255.255.255.240
SW3512XL(config-if)#end
SW3512XL#copy running-config startup-config
SW3512XL#show ip interface brief
```

Example 6-11 *Ping Test from sw3512XL to hostc (Continued)*

```
Interface                IP-Address      OK? Method Status        Protocol
VLAN1                    192.168.5.99    YES manual up            up
FastEthernet0/1          unassigned      YES unset  down          down
...
FastEthernet0/11         unassigned      YES unset  up            up
SW3512XL#ping 192.168.5.103
Sending 5, 100-byte ICMP Echos to 192.168.5.103, timeout is 2 seconds:
!!!!!
Success rate is 100 percent (5/5), round-trip min/avg/max = 1/202/1004 ms
```

As you can confirm from the shaded output, I typed incorrectly when I put in the IP address. My first intuition, however, might have been that there is a cable problem.

Move along to the 2900 CatOS-based switch. Clear the configuration and configure the switch as in Example 6-12.

Example 6-12 *Clearing and Configuring the 2900 Using CatOS*

```
Cat2900> (enable) clear config all
This command will clear all configuration in NVRAM.
This command will cause ifIndex to be reassigned on the next system startup.
Do you want to continue (y/n) [n]? y
........
System configuration cleared.
Console> (enable) set system name sw2900
System name set.
sw2900> (enable) set interface sc0 1 192.168.5.98 255.255.255.240
Interface sc0 vlan set, IP address and netmask set.
sw2900> (enable) set interface sc0 up
Interface sc0 administratively up.
sw2900> (enable) show config
...
```

If you have one, set the Windows NT Server with 192.168.5.110/28 and a gateway of 192.168.5.97. Perform a ping test from the Windows NT Server to sw2900. Don't be concerned if you don't have a Novell Server or a Windows NT Server on your server farm. The advantage to having a server is you can turn on a routing protocol for the server to learn the routes out of the network if you have multiple ways out. Because this lab really only has one way out, a default gateway serves the purpose just fine. After you set up the 2900 and the router, use the router to test connectivity as in Example 6-14.

When you cleared the CatOS box, the default name was console. You gave it a system name and could have configured a prompt to override the system name. The next part of the configuration is the sc0 port, which stands for Supervisor Console 0. It is the in-band IP management port for the box (so you can telnet to it, for example). This is equivalent to the **interface vlan #** command in Example 6-9 for the IOS box. The results of **show config** have been omitted here for brevity. However, **show config** in CatOS gives you about the same as the **show startup-config** command you are familiar with on the router in IOS. You will have an opportunity to look at it later.

All three of these switches portray the types of commands you need to support different Cisco switch devices. The 1900 is kind of an overlay of the Cisco IOS. The 3500 series switches use the Cisco IOS, which is the same IOS you are used to on the routers. The older 2900s are often thought of as part of the 5000 series family because they use the **set**, **show**, and **clear** commands referred to as CatOS. This also is similar to the CatOS on the 6000/6500 switches used in many practical environments today. The section on IOS and CatOS should help you support both operating systems over a variety of hardware platforms.

Next, compare your physical topology to Figure 6-3, where I have provided a little more detail. Although you may have experienced a little vagueness, the point of not telling you where to plug in the cables thus far was to emphasize that it really doesn't matter on a Layer 2 device (as long as the speeds are compatible). However, it will be easier for you to follow along if you rearrange your physical connections to match the new diagram and update your documentation appropriately.

Figure 6-3   *New Scenario Diagram*

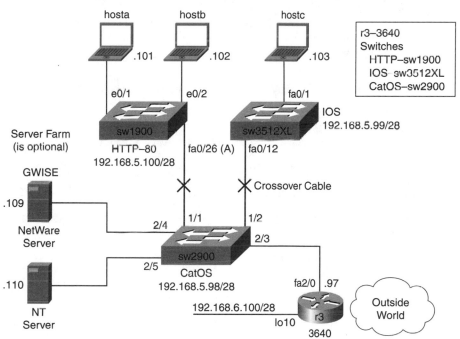

The next task is to prepare the router you have been using for r3 per Figure 6-3. Erase the configuration using **write erase** or **erase start** and configure the router as in Example 6-13.

Example 6-13 *Configuring the Router*

```
Router(config)#hostname r3
r3(config)#enable secret donna
r3(config)#line vty 0 4
r3(config-line)#login
r3(config-line)#password donna
r3(config-line)#line console 0
r3(config-line)#logging synchronous
r3(config-line)#exit
r3(config)#interface fastEthernet 2/0
r3(config-if)#description r3fa2/0 to CatOS sw2900 2/3
r3(config-if)#ip address 192.168.5.97 255.255.255.240
r3(config-if)#no shut
r3(config-if)#exit
r3(oonfig)#interface loopback 10
r3(config-if)#ip address 192.168.6.100 255.255.255.240
r3(config-if)#no shut
r3(config-if)#exit
r3(config)#router rip
r3(config-router)#network 192.168.5.0
r3(config-router)#network 192.168.6.0
r3(config-router)#end
r3#copy running-config startup-config
```

Now test to make sure the router can communicate with the hosts as in Example 6-14.

Example 6-14 *Ping Tests from the Router*

```
r3#ping 192.168.5.101
Sending 5, 100-byte ICMP Echos to 192.168.5.101, timeout is 2 seconds:
.....
Success rate is 0 percent (0/5)
r3#ping 192.168.5.102
Sending 5, 100-byte ICMP Echos to 192.168.5.102, timeout is 2 seconds:
.....
Success rate is 0 percent (0/5)
r3#ping 192.168.5.103
Type escape sequence to abort.
Sending 5, 100-byte ICMP Echos to 192.168.5.103, timeout is 2 seconds:
.!!!!
Success rate is 80 percent (4/5), round-trip min/avg/max = 1/1/4 ms
```

Example 6-14 clearly illustrates that r3 can ping hostc, (well at least four out of five times) but not hosta or hostb. Look at your current drawing to help you determine where to start troubleshooting. If r3 can't ping hostc, check end-to-end physical connectivity between the router and the host as well as addressing.

You should have gleaned that the first ping from r3 to hostc was missed due to Address Resolution Protocol (ARP) and that the right half of the network is working but the left half is broken. Work your way out from the router to hosta and hostb to find the issues. Example 6-15 shows the port status of port 1/1 on the 2900.

Example 6-15 *Testing the 2900*

```
sw2900> (enable) show port 1/1
Port  Name              Status      Vlan       Level  Duplex Speed Type
----- ----------------- ----------- ---------- ------ ------ ----- ------------
 1/1                    connected   1          normal half   100   100BaseTX
```

Review the port status on the 1900 in Example 6-16.

Example 6-16 *Testing the 1900*

```
        Catalyst 1900 - Usage Summaries
    [P] Port Status Report
    [A] Port Addressing Report
    [E] Exception Statistics Report
    [U] Utilization Statistics Report
    [B] Bandwidth Usage Report
    [X] Exit to Main Menu
Enter Selection:  P
        Catalyst 1900 - Port Status Report
 1  : Enabled                   13 : Suspended-no-linkbeat
 2  : Enabled                   14 : Suspended-no-linkbeat
...
        Catalyst 1900 - Main Menu
    [C] Console Settings
    [S] System
    [N] Network Management
    [P] Port Configuration
    [A] Port Addressing
...
    [H] Help
    [X] Exit Management Console
Enter Selection:  P
Identify Port:  1 to 24[1-24], [AUI], [A], [B]:
Select [1 - 24, AUI, A, B]:  A
        Catalyst 1900 - Port A Configuration
        Built-in 100Base-TX
        802.1d STP State:  Forwarding      Forward Transitions:  1
        Auto-negotiation status:  Half duplex
```

NOTE   The main menu and other output have been eliminated from the display where you see ... in several instances.

The 2900 can get to the 1900 but not to the hosts, so continue to troubleshoot. Although not shown, the 1900 can't communicate with hosta or hostb either.

My PCs were used for other purposes and when I last configured hosta, for some reason it didn't take the address. I had to set it for Dynamic Host Configuration Protocol (DHCP) and then manually configure an address to clear the problem. Hostb, on the other hand, did not shut down properly after the new address was configured, so it still had an old address on another subnet. The **ipconfig/winipcfg** tools are quite helpful in illustrating these types of issues on the hosts. Learning through an experience such as this one is what troubleshooting is all about.

After fixing the host addresses, ping from the 2900 to the hosts and analyze the MAC address table as in Example 6-17.

Example 6-17 *Pinging the Hosts from the 2900*

```
sw2900> (enable) ping 192.168.5.101
192.168.5.101 is alive
sw2900> (enable) ping 192.168.5.102
192.168.5.102 is alive
sw2900> (enable) show cam dynamic
* = Static Entry. + = Permanent Entry. # = System Entry. R = Router Entry. X = Port
Security Entry
VLAN  Dest MAC/Route Des  Destination Ports or VCs / [Protocol Type]
----  ------------------  ------------------------------------------------
1     00-90-92-2a-76-9a   1/1 [ALL]
1     00-80-c7-aa-c8-87   1/1 [ALL]
1     00-50-04-df-5f-3c   1/2 [ALL]
1     00-10-4b-a5-ae-50   1/1 [ALL]
1     00-d0-79-68-84-8d   1/2 [ALL]
Total Matching CAM Entries Displayed = 5
```

According to the 2900, the hosts are alive and there are entries in the content addressable memory (CAM) for hosta, hostb, and hostc.

NOTE It is often helpful to monitor the learned MAC addresses in the switch, to differentiate that Layer 2 is working, yet Layer 3 is not. On a CatOS switch, the command is **show cam dynamic**, and on an IOS switch the command is **show mac-address-table**.

Now for the true end-to-end test, make sure the hosts can ping each other and the loopback on the router. First, view the IP configuration on hosta as in Example 6-18. Then perform the ping tests in Example 6-19.

Example 6-18 *hosta IP Configuration*

```
C:\>ipconfig
Windows 2000 IP Configuration
Ethernet adapter Local Area Connection:
        Connection-specific DNS Suffix  . :
        IP Address. . . . . . . . . . . : 192.168.5.101
        Subnet Mask . . . . . . . . . . : 255.255.255.240
        Default Gateway . . . . . . . . : 192.168.5.97
```

Example 6-19 *hosta ping Tests*

```
C:\>remark hosta pings itself
C:\>ping 192.168.5.101
Pinging 192.168.5.101 with 32 bytes of data:
Reply from 192.168.5.101: bytes=32 time<10ms TTL=128
Reply from 192.168.5.101: bytes=32 time<10ms TTL=128
Reply from 192.168.5.101: bytes=32 time<10ms TTL=128
Reply from 192.168.5.101: bytes=32 time<10ms TTL=128
Ping statistics for 192.168.5.101:
    Packets: Sent = 4, Received = 4, Lost = 0 (0% loss),
Approximate round trip times in milli-seconds:
    Minimum = 0ms, Maximum =  0ms, Average =  0ms
C:\>remark hosta pings sw1900
C:\>ping 192.168.5.100
Pinging 192.168.5.100 with 32 bytes of data:
Reply from 192.168.5.100: bytes=32 time<10ms TTL=255
Reply from 192.168.5.100: bytes=32 time<10ms TTL=255
Reply from 192.168.5.100: bytes=32 time<10ms TTL=255
Reply from 192.168.5.100: bytes=32 time<10ms TTL=255
Ping statistics for 192.168.5.100:
    Packets: Sent = 4, Received = 4, Lost = 0 (0% loss),
Approximate round trip times in milli-seconds:
    Minimum = 0ms, Maximum =  0ms, Average =  0ms
C:\>remark hosta pings sw2900
C:\>ping 192.168.5.98
Pinging 192.168.5.98 with 32 bytes of data:
Reply from 192.168.5.98: bytes=32 time<10ms TTL=60
Reply from 192.168.5.98: bytes=32 time<10ms TTL=60
Reply from 192.168.5.98: bytes=32 time<10ms TTL=60
Reply from 192.168.5.98: bytes=32 time<10ms TTL=60
Ping statistics for 192.168.5.98:
    Packets: Sent = 4, Received = 4, Lost = 0 (0% loss),
Approximate round trip times in milli-seconds:
    Minimum = 0ms, Maximum =  0ms, Average =  0ms
C:\>remark hosta pings the r3 loopback
C:\>ping 192.168.6.100
Pinging 192.168.6.100 with 32 bytes of data:
Reply from 192.168.6.100: bytes=32 time<10ms TTL=255
Reply from 192.168.6.100: bytes=32 time<10ms TTL=255
Reply from 192.168.6.100: bytes=32 time<10ms TTL=255
Reply from 192.168.6.100: bytes=32 time<10ms TTL=255
Ping statistics for 192.168.6.100:
    Packets: Sent = 4, Received = 4, Lost = 0 (0% loss),
Approximate round trip times in milli-seconds:
    Minimum = 0ms, Maximum =  0ms, Average =  0ms
C:\>remark hosta pings sw3512xl
C:\>ping 192.168.5.99
Pinging 192.168.5.99 with 32 bytes of data:
Request timed out.
Reply from 192.168.5.99: bytes=32 time=10ms TTL=255
Reply from 192.168.5.99: bytes=32 time<10ms TTL=255
Reply from 192.168.5.99: bytes=32 time<10ms TTL=255
Ping statistics for 192.168.5.99:
    Packets: Sent = 4, Received = 3, Lost = 1 (25% loss),
```

Example 6-19 *hosta ping Tests (Continued)*

```
Approximate round trip times in milli-seconds:
    Minimum = 0ms, Maximum =  10ms, Average =  2ms
C:\>remark hosta pings hostc
C:\>ping 192.168.5.103
Pinging 192.168.5.103 with 32 bytes of data:
Reply from 192.168.5.103: bytes=32 time<10ms TTL=128
Reply from 192.168.5.103: bytes=32 time<10ms TTL=128
Reply from 192.168.5.103: bytes=32 time<10ms TTL=128
Reply from 192.168.5.103: bytes=32 time<10ms TTL=128
Ping statistics for 192.168.5.103:
    Packets: Sent = 4, Received = 4, Lost = 0 (0% loss),
Approximate round trip times in milli-seconds:
    Minimum = 0ms, Maximum =  0ms, Average =  0ms
C:\>remark what a success
```

Whether you do it now or later (or had to already do it), set the passwords so that you can telnet to the devices. The steps for changing the passwords start in Example 6-20 and go through Example 6-22. The router was set back in Example 6-13. I set/changed them all to donna for lab purposes. You should spend some time researching passwords because there are lots of levels of control that you can take advantage of in the practical environment.

Example 6-20 *1900 Passwords*

```
          Catalyst 1900 - Main Menu
     [C] Console Settings
     [S] System
     [N] Network Management
     [P] Port Configuration
...
     [H] Help
     [X] Exit Management Console
Enter Selection:  C
        Catalyst 1900 - Console Settings
--------------------- Settings ----------------------------------
     [P] Password intrusion threshold          3 attempt(s)
     [S] Silent time upon intrusion detection  None
     [T] Management Console inactivity timeout  None
     [D] Default mode of status LED            Port Status
--------------------- Actions -----------------------------------
     [M] Modify password
     [X] Exit to Main Menu
Enter Selection:  M
The Management Console password can help prevent unauthorized accesses.
When specifying a password, use a minimum of 4 characters and
maximum of 8 characters.  The password is case insensitive and
can contain any character with a legal keyboard representation.
For the user's protection, the password must be entered the same
way twice before it will be accepted.
        Enter current password:   *****
           Enter new password:    *****
Reenter to verify new password:   *****
Password modified
Press any key to continue.
```

Example 6-21 *2900 Passwords (CatOS)*

```
sw2900> (enable) set password
Enter old password:
Enter new password:
Retype new password:
Password changed.
sw2900> (enable) set enablepass
Enter old password:
Enter new password:
Retype new password:
Password changed.
```

Example 6-22 *3512XL Passwords*

```
sw3512XL#configure terminal
sw3512XL(config)#enable secret donna
sw3512XL(config)#line vty 0 4
sw3512XL(config-line)#password donna
sw3512XL(config-line)#end
sw3512XL#copy running-config startup-config
```

Unless you have already done so, issue the commands in Example 6-23 from the hosta prompt to test telnet access to all your switches. In the practical environment, DNS or host files would enable you to telnet to a hostname rather than an IP address. Troubleshoot as necessary.

Example 6-23 *telnet Testing from hosta to the Switches*

```
C:>telnet 192.168.5.100
C:>telnet 192.168.5.99
C:>telnet 192.168.5.98
```

You should still do many other little things to the Chapter 6 scenario, such as descriptions, speed and duplex settings, logging synchronous, add some redundancy, and so on. Do it now, during my review topics, or during the Trouble Tickets.

NOTE   Documentation and consistency are two things you can't do too much of in the support environment.

For now, save any configurations that you haven't already and take some time to review the sections on segmentation, spanning tree, and the Cisco CLI to assist you in your day-to-day troubleshooting and prepare you for the Trouble Tickets.

Segmentation Review

Many times the network engineer is the referee between the users wanting more bandwidth and management wanting to put more people on the network. These issues may be political or real. A practical number of users on any one LAN segment depends a lot on the applications being used as well as the number of devices, distance constraints, traffic volume, and so on.

Any way you look at it, networking is all about taking turns. Obviously, the more people you have to take turns, the more chaotic things can get.

Hubs and repeaters really don't do a lot to assist with nodes taking turns; they are first rate for extending networks or collision domains, however. Other devices facilitate segmentation to assist with such constraints as distance and bandwidth limitations. The following subsections on repeaters (hubs), bridges, switches, and routers are meant as a quick review to assist you with supporting different devices.

Repeaters (Hubs)

Repeaters or hubs are Layer 1 devices that extend distance limitations, which in turn extends collision and broadcast domains. All stations on all segments (wires) see *everything*, good and bad; there is no filtering. Layer 1 devices are at the lower end of the OSI model and thus are not too intelligent. Take Ethernet, for instance; even though there are separate physical ports on a hub effectively shaped like a physical star, logically Ethernet behaves as a bus.

On a shared device such as a hub, you can estimate user bandwidth by dividing total bandwidth by the number of transmitting stations. No priority is given to one station over another. However, average and peak numbers are quite helpful for upgrading and replacement purposes. Layer 2 devices are more commonly used to connect users to the LAN today.

NOTE   In my discussion of repeaters and hubs, I am strictly referring to Layer 1 devices (although there are hubs that work all the way up the OSI stack).

Repeaters/hubs accept all bit streams and repeat them, whereas bridges/switches actively look at each frame and make a more intelligent decision. Look at them next.

Bridges

Bridges are Layer 2 devices that promiscuously listen to each and every frame. Bridges connect collision domains while keeping them independent. If 10 users are sharing 1 segment (1 Mbps each), for example, with a bridge you can get 2 (or maybe 3) segments with better access to bandwidth but still less than dedicated bandwidth.

NOTE   A bridge receives a frame on one segment (collision domain) and must decide whether to forward it to another segment (collision domain). I use the terms *bridge* and *switch* interchangeably throughout this book.

As Figure 6-4 depicts, Ethernet uses *transparent bridging* to forward traffic and the STP to avoid loops, whereas Token Ring typically uses *source route bridging*. Source-route translational bridging (SR/TLB) or routers offer Ethernet-to-Token Ring protocol translation. I highly recommend *Interconnections: Bridges, Routers, Switches, and Internetworking Protocols*, Second Edition (Addison-Wesley), by Radia Perlman, who developed STP while she was working at DEC. She also reviewed the STP material in *Cisco LAN Switching* (Cisco Press), by Kennedy Clark and Kevin Hamilton, which belongs on everyone's shelf.

Figure 6-4   *802.1D Ethernet Transparent Bridging Flow*

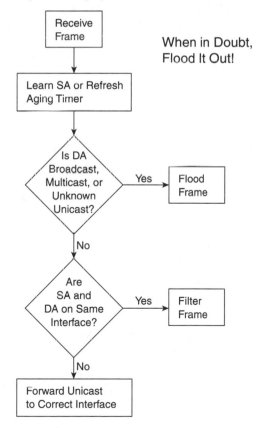

Decisions to forward, filter, or flood are based on the destination MAC address. It is the motto of a bridge *when in doubt to flood it out*. However, all segments still belong to the same broadcast domain. Layer 2 and Layer 3 addresses are not changed during transmission.

NOTE   The traditional 80/20 segmentation rule says that 80 percent of the traffic should be local and 20 percent remote. However, the exact opposite 20/80 rule is the typical today with high-speed backbones to support it.

Layer 3 addresses in general on bridges/switches are for remote management capabilities. For example, you added an IP address to each of the Layer 2 switches in the chapter scenario to be able to ping, telnet, or web into the devices because each port was not capable of its own IP address.

NOTE   Bridges/switches learn based on *source address* (SA) and filter or forward based on *destination address* (DA). A bridge/switch really doesn't care whether the SA and DA are on the same interface or port. It only cares about having learned the location of the DA. Even if the SA is unknown until this frame, forwarding may be accomplished by the DA.

Switches

Switches are more or less a marketing term for fast bridges. They are desktop connectivity devices capable of multiple broadcast domains through VLANs, the topic of the next chapter. Each wire segment has dedicated bandwidth assuming no hubs are attached. If 10 users are attached to a 10-Mbps hub, for example, that is about 1 Mbps each. Replace the hub with a switch to get a dedicated 10 Mbps each or 20 Mbps for full duplex.

NOTE   Most 10/100 hubs are actually mini hub-switch combinations. The 10 ports are shared (hub), the 100 ports are shared (hub), but there is a 2-port switch talking between the 2 hubs.

Advantages of switches include the following:

- Application-specific integrated circuits (ASICs) to perform operations in hardware.
- More ports.
- Dedicated per-port bandwidth; simultaneous conversation support.
- Low latency.
- Aggregate bandwidth.
- VLAN capabilities to segment broadcast domains.

- Some level of security just by plugging users into a switch. (Consider what you don't see by default with a protocol analyzer.) Can extend this with port security features.

Bridges/switches have a number of inputs just like our telephone system. If there are too many at one time, you get a busy signal—unless of course the switch has a nonblocking design with sufficient capacity. Line cards or port expansion modules are inserted into the backplane of the switch. Different cards communicate with each other by going through a high-speed switching fabric or they may have their own ASICs. Quality of service (QoS) provides congestion management within the switch to solve queuing issues.

There are various switch forwarding types (modes) and frame sizes that obviously play an important role in transporting frames from one device to another that you should recognize in Figure 6-5 and Table 6-3.

Figure 6-5   *Switch Forwarding Types (Modes)*

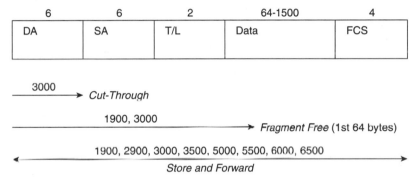

Refer back to previous examples and figures to examine the switch forwarding types (modes) used in your lab. The default varies according to hardware model and software version.

Table 6-3   *Frame Sizes*

LAN/MAN Technologies	Minimum Frame Size in Bytes	Maximum Frame Size in Bytes
Ethernet	64	1518
Token Ring (4 Mbps)	21	4511
Token Ring (16 Mbps)	21	17839
FDDI	28	4500

Assuming no VLANs, bridges/switches assist with collision domains but *not* broadcast domains. That is where routers or Layer 3 devices come in handy.

Routers

In addition to extending the network-like bridges and switches, breaking up the collision domains, and containing errors, routers also segment broadcast domains. Layer 3 devices filter on Layer 3 addresses (such as IP), whereas Layer 2 devices filter on MAC addresses. Table 6-4 portrays the layered devices with the associated number of broadcast and collision domains.

NOTE   If you need a good example of how routers work, go back to Chapter 3 to review ARP and how it works via a local broadcast. The Layer 3 addresses stay the same from end to end, but Layer 2 addresses change.

Table 6-4   *Collision and Broadcast Domains*

Device	Broadcast domains	Collision domains
Hub	1	1
Bridge	1	1 per wire
Switch	1 per VLAN	1 per wire
Router	1 per wire	1 per wire

While on the topic of routers, you should view the fa2/0 interface and hard code the speed and duplex as in Example 6-24. Although autonegotiation is present, I find it less problematic to hard code this on switches and routers. Assuming your hosts do not move around, you can hard code it there, too. If you are not sure where people will be connecting into the network and whether it is 10 or 100 Mbps, however, autonegotiation was designed for such activity.

Example 6-24   *Hard Code Speed and Duplex on the Router*

```
r3#show interfaces fastethernet 2/0
FastEthernet2/0 is up, line protocol is up
  Hardware is AmdFE, address is 00b0.6481.e300 (bia 00b0.6481.e300)
  Description:  r3fa2/0 to CatOS sw2900 2/3
  Internet address is 192.168.5.97/28
  MTU 1500 bytes, BW 100000 Kbit, DLY 100 usec, rely 255/255, load 1/255
  Encapsulation ARPA, loopback not set, keepalive set (10 sec)
  Half-duplex, 100Mb/s, 100BaseTX/FX
...
r3#configure terminal
r3(config)#interface fastethernet 2/0
r3(config-if)#speed 100
r3(config-if)#full-duplex
r3(config-if)#end
r3#show interfaces fastethernet 2/0
FastEthernet2/0 is up, line protocol is up
...
  Full-duplex, 100Mb/s, 100BaseTX/FX
```

When the speed and duplex are hard coded, they show up in the configuration as you can see in Example 6-25.

Example 6-25 *Speed and Duplex in the Config File*

```
r3#show run interface fastethernet 2/0
interface FastEthernet2/0
 description  r3fa2/0 to CatOS sw2900 2/3
 ip address 192.168.5.97 255.255.255.240
 no ip directed-broadcast
 speed 100
 full-duplex
end
```

NOTE   Speed is actually more problematic than duplex, for connectivity does not happen with mismatched speeds. Mismatched duplex settings cause performance-type issues but normally not connectivity issues.

After you hard code speed, autonegotiation is off. Make sure you know exactly what your device is doing. If you reset speed back to auto, for instance, you may be setting duplex back to auto as well.

Configuration and proper segmentation are both critical to maintaining day-to-day operations and long-term optimization. Now I want to briefly chat about STP, (the LAN treatment, not the oil treatment), because it accounts for a significant amount of Layer 2 troubleshooting.

STP

Lots of things in networking are based on trees, branches, and leaves. STP is no exception. My intent is not to give you a book or chapter that tells you everything you need to know about STP, but rather to review the critical components and analyze it from the practical perspective.

You, like many other network engineers, might consider STP to be one of those theory things that you never have to worry with in the practical world. However, the truth is STP accounts for more than half of the issues with configuring, maintaining, and supporting campus networks.

STP is so critical because it is a dynamic loop prevention protocol for Layer 2. Time to live (TTL) does not exist at Layer 2; STP is what prevents frames from looping endlessly around the network. I know you would never intentionally create a bridge loop at Layer 2, but redundancy is a good thing to build in to your environment to eliminate single points of failure. Redundancy may lead to bridge loops and bridge loops may lead to broadcast storms. This is not to say redundancy is bad, but a mechanism such as STP keeps it under control.

Broadcast storms are feedback loops that occur in both directions. Want to see one? Just create a physical loop in your topology and turn off STP with a command such as **set spantree disable** [*vlan#*]. Do *not* do this in a production environment.

NOTE   In many places throughout this chapter I may give the IOS command or the OS command (**set**, **show**, **clear**). This is one thing that makes supporting Cisco switches a little challenging. In the section "The Cisco Command-Line Interface (CLI)," you will find some helpful comparison sheets of the major commands you need for troubleshooting.

There is a DEC version and IEEE version of STP that, although similar, are not compatible. This chapter focuses on only the IEEE version because that is what many of the Layer 2 Catalyst switches support. However, Cisco routers and Layer 3 switches support multiple versions. For example, the following command output shows you how to change this parameter on an IOS-based switch if required to do so:

```
sw3512XL(config)#spanning-tree protocol ?
  dec   Digital spanning-tree protocol
  ibm   IBM spanning-tree protocol
  ieee  IEEE Ethernet spanning-tree protocol
```

Bridges dynamically form a tree of the physical topology by exchanging bridge protocol data units (BPDUs). At first all ports send BPDUs out every two seconds to build the tree. The best ports are *forwarding* and the alternate ports are *blocking* as to not form bridge loops. See the STP decision criteria in the following section. STP convergence requires the election of a root bridge, root ports, and designated ports.

STP Decision Criteria

Many decisions are made in STP:

- **Who is the root bridge?**—Lowest BID. (I bet many of you can relate to that terminology.)

- **How far away is the root bridge?**—Lowest path cost (highest bandwidth) to root bridge.

- **Who sent this BPDU?**—Lowest sender BID.

- **What port did this BPDU come from?**—Lowest port ID.

It is helpful to think of the *root bridge* as a wagon wheel with spokes going out to the other switches. Just like many other things in life, the lowest BID wins again. BID in the sense of STP is a concatenation of the bridge priority and the 6-byte MAC address. By default the 2-byte priority field is 32,768 decimal or 8000 hex, so the MAC address is really the tiebreaker.

Every *non-root bridge* must select a *root port*, which is the port closest to the root bridge. This closeness is measured by the *root path cost*, which is the cumulative cost of all links leading to the root bridge. The STP costs are incremented as BPDUs are *received* on a port.

Costs are associated with various LAN segments. The original IEEE 802.1D specification didn't really take into consideration Gigabit Ethernet, ATM, and 10 Gigabit Ethernet technologies. The original specification was a linear value derived from the formula 1000 Mbps divided by the bandwidth of a segment. An example for FDDI or Fast Ethernet is as follows: 1000/100 = 10. Table 6-5 illustrates the latest IEEE path costs.

Table 6-5   *Latest IEEE STP Nonlinear Path Costs**

Bandwidth	Path Cost
4 Mbps	250
10 Mbps	100
16 Mbps	62
45 Mbps	39
100 Mbps	19
155 Mbps	14
622 Mbps	6
1 Gbps	4
10 Gbps	2

*Changes in bandwidth dictate software changes. This only ever happened once to go from a linear to a nonlinear scale to account for the old and new schemes to interoperate.

NOTE   Path cost and root path cost are not one in the same. *Path cost* is a value assigned to each port. *Root path cost* is the cumulative cost to the root bridge.

Every segment elects a designated port based on the lowest cumulative root path cost (best) to the root bridge. Now that I have discussed root bridge, non-root bridge, root port, and designated port, I want to mention nondesignated ports or ports that are in a blocking state. Blocking is not truly blocking because the port must still listen for BPDUs unless of course you take advantage of the new improved Rapid Spanning Tree Protocol (RSTP). Figure 6-6 displays the five STP states and associated timers.

All ports start out in either a *blocking* or a *disabled* state and work their way to a *forwarding* state. The disabled state is the one most people forget; it is when the port is administratively shut down. Ports are listening for BPDUs while they are in the blocking state in case there is a change in topology. The port transitions to a *listening* state where it is sending and receiving

BPDUs to determine the current active topology. By default, a 15-second forward delay timer is associated with the listening state. The designated and root ports then progress to the *learning* state. There is then another 15-second forward delay time when tables are being built but still no user data has passed. Next the port transitions to the most wanted forwarding state, where it actually sends and receives user data. All ports that are not in a forwarding state at this point are in a blocking state. This entire process might sound slow and bad and make you want to turn STP off. Do *not* do it! (However, there are ways to tweak STP that I mention at the end of the section.) From a troubleshooting perspective, the issues are whether anything breaks STP and causes a forwarding loop, and the impact of the delays on user traffic. Techniques such as RSTP, portfast, uplinkfast, and so on improve on the 20-year-old approach. See the practical STP and RSTP sections.

Figure 6-6   *STP Port States and Timers*

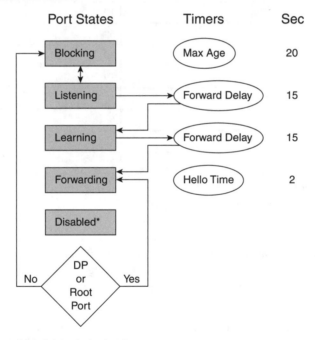

*Administratively shutdown

As you have seen in previous chapters, tools such as Sniffer Pro are quite helpful to understand the interworkings of things. However, switches are not quite as free flow as hubs are when it comes to monitoring ports with protocol analyzers. Port monitoring, therefore, is a topic of necessary discussion.

Port Monitoring

Unlike hubs flooding to all ports, switches learn Layer 2 addresses so that they can filter and send only unicast traffic to the correct recipient. From a Sniffer standpoint, you will capture the broadcast-type frames but miss a lot of unicast frames unless you intentionally monitor the right ports. Essentially you must select a port to receive or mirror the traffic you want to capture. This is called the SPAN port and has nothing to do with STP. The source SPAN port(s) or ingress ports are where traffic enters the switch, and the destination SPAN port or egress port is where the network analyzer is connected.

Configuring port monitoring on an IOS-based switch is as simple as going to the destination interface where the Sniffer is located and getting into interface configuration mode. Turn on port monitoring for each individual port you want to act as a source. If you just issue the **port monitor** command, all ports in the same VLAN are monitored. Use **show port monitor** to see the results.

On a CatOS-based switch, you need to turn on SPAN, the Catalyst switched port analyzer. It enables you to mirror the data from one port, trunk, or VLAN to another port so that you can monitor it. This command turns STP off *on the mirrored port*. Use **set span help** for assistance. For example, **set span 1/1 2/1 both** takes the transmit (Tx) and receive (Rx) traffic source of port 1/1 and mirrors it to port 2/1 for monitoring. The *inpkts* option determines whether frames emitted by the SPAN collector are processed or ignored. Use **show span** to see the results. Use commas and dashes to specify multiple ports.

NOTE   Cisco has a great tech note on configuring the catalyst SPAN feature at www.cisco.com/warp/public/473/41.html (if you need more details).

Port monitoring and SPAN are one and the same. It just depends whether you are on an IOS-based switch or a CatOS-based switch. Look at the Figure 6-3 and contemplate how you can monitor the traffic using a tool such as Sniffer Pro. Although I wanted to briefly mention port monitoring, the real goal at this point in time is to analyze BPDUs.

Analyzing BPDUs

Analyze the configuration BPDU Sniffer capture in Figure 6-7. You will capture your own data in the Trouble Tickets.

Configuration BPDUs flow from the root bridge to others. A BPDU is an IEEE 802.3 frame with 802.2 LLC SAP header. The Type is 0 because it is a configuration BPDU rather than a topology change BPDU. The root bridge at the time of this capture was the CatOS sw2900 that has a MAC that ends in 1400. The default priority is 8000 hex. The root path cost is 10. The sending BID is from the sw1900 that has a MAC that ends in 7680. The max age is 20 seconds, the hellos are every 2 seconds, and the forward delay is 15 seconds as discussed earlier. Compare Figure 6-7 to the following headers:

- 802.3 header:

    — Source MAC is the Catalyst port that sent the BPDU.

    — Destination MAC is the IEEE 802.1D STP multicast address 0180c2000000.

Figure 6-7 *Configuration BPDU*

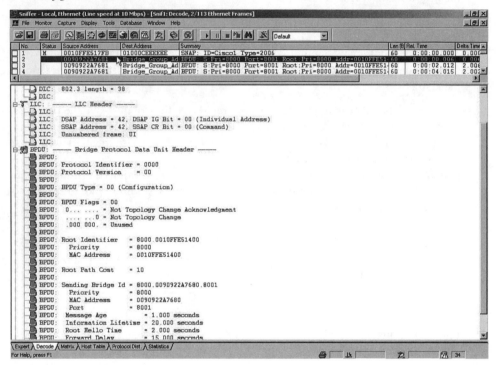

- LLC header:

    — DSAP and SSAP are both 0x42 for STP.

- The configuration BPDU:

    — Protocol ID   Always 0.

    — Version   Always 0.

    — Type   0 for configuration BPDU; 0x80 for topology change notification (TCN BPDU).

    — Flags   Topology change or acknowledgement.

— Root BID   Concatenation of priority and MAC to form the bridge ID for the root bridge.

— Root Path Cost   Cumulative cost of links toward the root bridge.

— Sender BID   Bridge ID of the sender of the BPDU.

— Port ID   Unique value for port that sent the BPDU.

— Message Age   Time since the root bridge first created this BPDU. This is not max age. Think of it like a reverse TTL where 1 is added at every bridge hop.

— Max Age   Time period to save BPDU information.

— Hello Time   Time interval between BPDUs.

— Forward Delay   For listening and learning states.

STP convergence time is 20 max age + 30 for the two 15-second forward delays, for a total of 50 seconds. Tools such as Sniffer Pro and the CatOS or IOS spanning-tree commands in Table 6-7 or even more automated tools such as the CiscoWorks Campus Manager can lend a hand in drawing a very informative Layer 2 STP diagram to assist you in supporting STP issues.

TCN BPDUs are one way to speed up this convergence. They flow from the *spoke* bridges to the *center of the wheel* root bridge to let the root bridge know that the topology has changed. You analyze TCNs in more detail in the Trouble Tickets.

Tuning STP in a Practical Environment

As you can see, STP is quite complex, but necessary to avoid Layer 2 broadcast storms. Think of it as the Layer 2 "TTL." The following items and commands are suggestions for tuning STP in a practical environment:

- Create a design hierarchy including Layer 3 switches rather than a flat network.

- Understand how STP works, particularly on your network. Draw pictures of what you have and what you will have after a failure. Use tools such as the Campus Manager CWSI STP mapping tool to get a good Layer 2 picture.

- Plan root bridge placement. Centrally locate them close to heavy traffic destinations and don't choose your lowest caliber switch. The **set spantree priority** *priority* [*vlan*] command enables you to adjust the priority of a switch on a VLAN basis, and with Cisco there is one instance of STP per VLAN. Alternatively, **set spantree root** is a macro that places its results in the configuration file.

- Set more than one root bridge in case of failure. The backup acts like a hot standby until needed. For example, type **set spantree priority 100 1** on one switch to make it the primary. Use **set spantree priority 200 1** on another switch to configure it as the backup root bridge. VLAN 1 is the default, and therefore is really not necessary in this example. However, you must specify the VLAN if different from VLAN 1.

- Do not use **set spantree portvlanpri** for back-to-back switch load balancing. Use Fast or Gigabit EtherChannel instead.

- Use port/VLAN cost load balancing in situations where you can't use the root bridge form of load balancing. For example: **set spantree portvlancost 2/1 cost 2000 10** assigns a path cost of 2000 to port 2/1 for VLAN 10 on the trunk.

- Turn on portfast and disable Port Aggregation Protocol (PAgP) for hosts. Some PCs boot faster than the time it takes STP to go through its blocking, listening, learning, and forwarding states. However, you can't turn off STP for an individual port. Portfast essentially skips the steps prior to the forwarding and immediately starts the port in a forwarding state when it first initializes. Practical places to implement portfast include Microsoft hosts looking for a domain controller or DHCP server or Novell clients that never seem to find the login screen upon boot up. In most cases it is not necessary to enable portfast on servers because they rarely reboot. The **set spantree portfast 2/1-12 enable** command sets portfast on for ports 1 through 12 on module 2. If port 1 connects this switch to another, however, you do not want portfast on for that port, so you can disable it with **set spantree portfast 2/1 disable**. Use **show spantree 1** to see the results (assuming this is VLAN 1).

CAUTION   Use portfast only when connecting a single host to an access port, otherwise you are asking for a network loop.

- BPDUguard assists with helping you find invalid configurations of portfast. In a valid configuration, the portfast ports do not receive BPDUs. In an invalid configuration, they do and STP places the port in a blocking state. Enable BPDUguard with **set spantree portfast bpdu-guard enable** so that STP automatically shuts the portfast port down if it receives a BPDU to recalculate STP.

- Enable uplinkfast on wiring closet switches (STP leaves) but not in the core for root port optimization for directly connected failed links. Uplinkfast is for dual-homed access layer switches or any similar topology. *Don't* do this on root bridges or transit switches. Enable uplinkfast with **set spantree uplinkfast enable** and view your changes with **show spantree uplinkfast**.

- Enable backbonefast using **set spantree backbone fast enable** on *every switch* in your network to assist with indirect failures and optimize max age.

- Verify such features as BPDUguard, uplinkfast, and backbonefast with **show spantree summary**.

- With EtherChannel it is normally best practice to set the ports to desirable. The following command sets port 2/1 to desirable: **set port channel 2/1 desirable**.

- Take advantage of the IEEE RSTP/Multiple STP (MSTP) where possible. See the "Rapid STP (RSTP)" section.

The commands for tuning STP in a practical environment are all given in the CatOS syntax. However, you can compare the IOS equivalent commands in Table 6-7.

Rapid STP (RSTP)

Although VLANs and trunking are the topic of the next chapter, they are certainly a relative topic when it comes to STP. Cisco enhanced the original IEEE 802.1Q standard with features such as portfast, uplinkfast, and backbonefast, per VLAN STP (PVST+), and Multiple Instance STP (MISTP), but they are proprietary. Although not a standard yet as of this writing, RSTP IEEE 802.1w is available in newer versions of the IOS and is backward compatible with 802.1D STP. It was first implemented in CatOS 7.1 and IOS 12.1(11)EX as Multiple STP (MSTP). CatOS 7.5 and IOS 12.1(13)E offer RSTP where the switch runs an RSTP instance on each VLAN, like the Cisco PVST. Compare the 802.1D and 802.1w port states in Table 6-6.

Table 6-6   *Compare STP 802.1D and 802.1w Port States*

IEEE 802.1D STP	IEEE 802.1w RSTP
Disabled (administratively shut down)	Discarding
Blocking	Discarding
Listening	Discarding
Learning	Learning
Forwarding	Forwarding

The end result is the same for STP or RSTP, but the overall STP convergence is much improved with the latter (50 seconds to 1 second). The main reason is the way topology changes are detected and propagated. The initiator of the topology change directly forwards the change throughout the network instead of waiting for the root bridge to do so. Although the inherent fast convergence benefits are lost when your network includes legacy bridges, STP and RSTP are compatible.

MSTP IEEE 802.1s uses RSTP to provide very fast convergence, as well as to group VLANs into an instance of STP to provide multiple forwarding paths and load balancing. A big advantage is that a failure in one instance doesn't affect another STP instance. Although not a standard yet as of this writing, MSTP was released in CatOS version 7.1 via the following command: **set spantree mode MST**. By default, all VLANs are in instance 0 unless you use the **set spantree MST 20 vlan 1-6,12** command. This puts ports 1 through 6 and 12 in MST instance 20. To commit the changes, use **set spantree MST config commit**. In IOS there is a separate mode for MSTP configuration. When you are in global config mode, enter MSTP config with **spanning-tree mst configuration,** where you enter the instance ID and VLAN range.

NOTE	For an excellent white paper explaining how RSTP works and the command set, see http://cco-rtp-1.cisco.com/en/US/tech/tk389/tk689/technologies_white_paper09186a0080094cfa.shtml.

Cisco switches have certainly evolved over the years. They are easy to configure, maintain, and support when you maintain a good balance of hierarchical routing and switching, not flat networks. As discussed in the "STP" and "Rapid STP (RSTP)" sections, Cisco has their own improvements to the current STP standards, and IEEE has a few in the works. You should also consider the idea of using point-to-point links as Layer 3 networks for fast failover rather than the 50-second STP convergence.

As mentioned in the early chapters of this book, the Core, Distribution, and Access Layers describe Cisco's three-layer tiered hierarchy in which switches and routers are both important components. Many times you will see the following acronyms in use for the layers:

- **IDF**—Intermediate distribution frame (Access Layer)

- **MDF**—Main distribution frame (Distribution Layer)

- **MDF to MDF**—Core Layer

The layered hierarchy is more of a design focus, and obviously a good design helps things run well and lessens support issues. However, next I want to focus more on the evolution of the software on Cisco switches to assist you with analyzing common issues.

The Cisco CLI

Cisco's IOS maintains the same look and feel across the entire router family of products. Unfortunately, I can't say the same for the entire switch family of products. However, it is a Cisco goal for that to occur one day. The reason for the two main command sets of the switches is basically evolutionary, partly Cisco and partly their acquisition of products with a good installed base. Some of these products are listed here:

- Grand Junction 1900 and 2800 switches use a main menu display where you select a letter.

- Kalpana 3000 series switches have you move through menus by highlighting an option using the arrow keys and pressing Enter rather than a letter (like the Grand Junction products).

- Crescendo 2900 and 5000 series introduced the CatOS.

- Cisco developed switches such as the 2900XL and 8500 families that use the Cisco IOS.

- The 5000 and 6000 use a slightly different CLI from others.

As you can see, switches are very much a multivendor experience. Instead of discussing history and vendors, I want to spend some time comparing the CatOS and IOS for support purposes.

NOTE   Besides being familiar with the software, it is a good idea to have the right console connector and cable in your tool bag. Always carry a 9-pin and 25-pin console connector with plenty of reliable cables. Be prepared for straight-through, crossover, and rollover situations. Generally IOS devices need a rolled console cable (1 to 8, 2 to 7, 3 to 6, and 4 to 5), and COS devices need a straight cable.

CatOS-Based Switches

Now if you don't like all the modes and separate histories with the routers, you might actually enjoy the CatOS. The normal mode is like user mode on the router, and the privileged exec (enable) mode is the configuration mode. Set, show, and clear commands are issued from the enable mode. It annoys me that you can't enter show commands while in configuration mode in IOS. Although you don't need to be as concerned with modes, with CatOS it is very easy to prematurely enter something you don't mean to when all you want is help. Just remember to type the question mark (?) so that you don't fall into that trap. CatOS examples include: 2900, 4000, 5000, and 6000.

NOTE   See the Technical Assistance Center (TAC) for common CatOS/IOS error messages on Cisco Catalyst switches for your particular switch.

Set commands are used to configure or overwrite. Show commands are used to view, and clear commands are used to either reset or delete. For example, **clear config all** through a telnet session is a career-limiting move (CLM) because you clear not only the VLANs, STP, and Supervisor module back to its defaults, but you also wipe out the management IP address. Just in case you don't follow my logic here, you no longer have a telnet session to the box. The same type of situation can occur with making changes to the IP, mask, or VLAN associated with sc0.

NOTE   The **clear config all** does not clear ATM LAN emulation (LANE) module or Route Switch Module (RSM) configurations. Go to these modules with the **session** *mod#* command, which is like an internal telnet, so that you can make module changes. Use **show module** to view the cards installed on the box. These modules use the IOS commands rather than the CatOS. On the 6000/6500, the same holds true for a Multilayer Switch Feature Card (MSFC).

Like the 1900, the Catalyst 5000 automatically stores your configuration changes to NVRAM, whereas the IOS requires a **write mem** or **copy run start**. Obviously there is good and bad to this. Depending on your environment, you can reload if you haven't saved your running configuration to the startup configuration and all changes will be gone with IOS-based devices. CatOS devices maintain the configuration changes even through a reload. As a little tip, you can copy your configuration to Notepad. Use **set length 0** to inhibit pagination. Issue **show config** to capture the current configuration. Now if you goof on your changes, you can **clear config all** and use the current configuration you captured.

NOTE	On a CatOS device, **show config all** displays the defaults, too.

From a support standpoint, it is important to understand show commands, system commands, configuration and operating system commands, spanning-tree commands, logging and monitoring commands, network management commands, and others. It is critical to know how to get into the box locally and remotely. Table 6-7 contains some helpful examples of commands.

Table 6-7 *Catalyst OS and IOS Commands*

CatOS – 2900/4000/5000/6000	IOS – 2900XL/3500XL
Show commands	
show cdp neighbors	**>show cdp neighbors**
show module	**>show module**
show version	**>show version**
show config/write terminal	**#show config/show start**
show arp	**>show arp**
show cam dynamic	**#show mac-address-table**
show port	**#show interfaces**
	#show interface status
System commands	
Enable	**>enable**
show system	
show test	**#show diag**
set password	(config)#**line console 0**
	(config-line)#**password** *donna*
set enablepass	(config)#**enable password** *donna*
set system name *sw2900*	(config)#**hostname** *sw3512xl*
set prompt *sw2900*	
set time *monday 11/25/02 07:00:00*	**#clock set** *07:00:00 25 nov 02*
set interface sc0 *1 192.168.5.98 255.255.255.240*	(config)#**interface** *vlan1*
	(config-if)#**ip address** *192.168.5.99 255.255.255.240*
show interface	**#show interface** *vlan1*

Table 6-7   *Catalyst OS and IOS Commands (Continued)*

CatOS – 2900/4000/5000/6000	IOS – 2900XL/3500XL
Port configuration commands	
set port name *1/1 hosta*	(config)#**interface** *fa0/1*
	(config-if)#**description** fa0/1 to 2900
set port speed *2/4-5 10*	(config)#**interface range** fa0/4 – 5
set port speed *2/3 100*	(config-if)#**speed** *10*
	(config-if)#**speed** *100*
set port duplex *1/1 full*	(config-if)#**duplex** *full*
set port disable 1/1	(config-if)#**shut**
set port enable 1/1	(config-if)#**no shut**
show port	#**show interfaces**
show port status	#**show interface status**
	#**show ip interface brief**
set module enable *2*	
set module disable *2*	
show module	#**show module**
set trunk *1/1-2 on*	(config)#**interface fa0/12**
show trunk	(config-if)#**switchport mode** *trunk*
	#**show interface fa0/12 switchport**
Port security	
	(config)#**interface fa0/1**
	(config-if)**switchport mode access**
	(config-if)**switchport port-security mac-address** *mac-addr*
set port security *mod#/port#* **enable** *mac-addr*	(config-if)**switchport port-security**
	(config-if)**switchport port-security maximum** *value*
set port security *mod#/port#* **maximum** *value*	
set port security *mod#/port#* **violation ?**	(config-if)**switchport port-security violation ?**
	(config-if)**end**
show port security	#**show port-security ?**
clear port security *mod#/port#* **?**	(config-if)**no switchport port-security**

Table 6-7 *Catalyst OS and IOS Commands (Continued)*

CatOS – 2900/4000/5000/6000	IOS – 2900XL/3500XL
Spanning tree	
set spantree portfast *2/4-5 enable* **show spantree** *1* **show port spantree** *2/4*	(config)#**interface fa0/1** (config-if)#**spanning-tree portfast** #**show spanning-tree** *vlan 1* #**show spanning-tree** *interface fa0/1* #**show spanning-tree**
set spantree portfast bpdu-guard enable **show spantree summary**	(config)#**spanning-tree portfast bpduguard** #**show spanning-tree summary totals**
set spantree priority *100 1* (primary) **set spantree priority** *200 1* (backup) **set spantree root** (macro)	(config)#**spanning-tree priority** *100* (config)#**spanning-tree priority** *200*
Logging and management commands	
set logging timestamp enable	(config)#**service timestamps log ?** (config)#**service timestamps debug ?**
set logging console di*sable*	(config)#**no logging console**
set logging server 192.168.5.17	(config)#**logging 192.168.5.17**
set logging level *all 7* (facility severity default)	(config)#**logging ?**
show logging ?	>**show logging ?**
set trace ? **show trace**	#**debug** #**show debug**
show history	>**history**
set span *1/1 2/5 both inpkts* **show span**	(config)#**interface fa0/12** (config-if)#**port monitor** (monitors all ports to fa0/12) (config-if)#**port monitor** *fa0/2* (monitors port 2 to port 12) #**show port monitor** #**show monitor**

Table 6-7   *Catalyst OS and IOS Commands (Continued)*

CatOS – 2900/4000/5000/6000	IOS – 2900XL/3500XL
SNMP* and RMON**	
set system contact *donna harrington 410-123-4567*	(config)#**snmp-server contact** *donna harrington 410-123-4567*
set system location bldg rm rack loc	(config)#**snmp-server location** bldg rm rack loc
set snmp community *read-only public*	(config)#**snmp-server community** *public ro*
set snmp trap *192.168.5.101 public*	(config)#**snmp-server host** *192.168.5.101 public*
set snmp trap *enable*	(config)#**snmp enable traps** *snmp*
show snmp	#**show snmp**
set snmp rmon *enable*	(config)#**rmon ?** >**show rmon statistics**
IP host commands	
set ip route default *192.168.5.97* **show ip route**	(config)#**ip default-gateway** *192.168.5.97* >**show ip route**
Configuration management	
Automatic	#**copy run start/write mem** (save config)
write *192.168.5.101 catos.cfg*	#**copy run tftp/write net** (copy config to tftp)
configure *192.168.5.101 catos.cfg*	#**copy tftp run/configure net** (copy config from tftp)
Operating system management	
copy flash tftp **upload** *192.168.5.101 catos.bin*	#**copy flash:catios.bin tftp:**
copy tftp flash **download** *192.168.5.101 catos.bin*	#**copy tftp://<*ip*>/catios.bin flash:newios.bin**
reset system	#**reload**
VLANs and VTP†	
set vtp domain *donna* **set vtp mode** *transparent* **vlan 2 name** *eng* **type** *ethernet* **show vlan** **clear vlan 2** **show vtp domain**	#**vlan database** (vlan)#**vtp domain donna** (vlan)#**vtp transparent** (vlan)#**vlan 2 name** *eng* **media** *ethernet* (vlan)#**show** (vlan)#**no vlan 2 name** *eng* **media** *ethernet* (vlan)#**exit** #**show vtp status**

*SNMP = Simple Network Management Protocol   **RMON = Remote Monitoring

†VTP = VLAN Trunking Protocol

NOTE   Check out the newer methods for configuring VLANs at www.cisco.com/univercd/cc/td/doc/
product/lan/cat2950/12111ea1/scg/swvlan.htm#xtocid7. This is preferable because the VLAN
information is part of the textual configuration rather than in a separate vlan.dat file.

IOS-Based Switches

The IOS-based switches use basically the same IOS as Cisco routers. Examples include
2900XL, 3500XL, 6000, and 3550. A practical example today is the 6500 running in native
mode. Switch troubleshooting tools such as CiscoWorks, RMON, LED indicators, ping, telnet,
Cisco Discovery Protocol (CDP), SPAN, various show commands, and debug are quite helpful
if in fact you understand what you are looking at. Debug is not available on the CatOS like it is
on the IOS switches.

The next section provides a quick overview of the terminology associated with the Cat5000/Cat6000
architecture. For more details on this topic, refer to the other Cisco Press titles and Cisco.com.

Cat5000/Cat6000 Architecture

Besides the ports, several other components make up the overall architecture of a switch. The
switching engine makes decisions, and the switch memory buffers frames from port to port. The
switching fabric connects all the components together. For example, devices such as the
Catalyst 2900XL, 3500XL, and 4000 deploy a shared memory fabric where all ports share the
same memory pool. The Cat5000 and Cat6000 are store-and-forward switches that use a
switching bus architecture arbitration method where a central bus arbiter works with an arbiter
on each line card to control queuing for each port. The 6500 with a fabric module installed
deploys a crossbar fabric whereby hardware-based ASICs provide many switching paths; this
is also known as a nonblocking architecture. Nonblocking in a nutshell means that the switch
has more bandwidth than all the ports together. The 6500 can also deploy a local switching
fabric so local ports do not have to go through the switching fabric. Modular switches dedicate
slot 1 for the Supervisor Engine that monitors system components as well as the switching
functions within the switch. This list contains some common terminology and functionality of
the 5000:

- Ethernet ports use a custom ASIC called Synergy Advanced Interface and Network
  Termination (SAINT).

- Other ports use a custom ASIC called Synergy Advanced Gate-Array Engine (SAGE).

- Encoded Address Recognition Logic (EARL) is an ASIC that works with bus arbitration
  for packet transfers.

- The Network Management Processor/Master Control Processor (NMP/MCP) aggregates data
  from processes such as SNMP and RMON and includes information from STP, CDP, and VTP.

- Built-in Gate Array (BIGA) connects the NMP to the 1.2-Gbps bus.

- Line-module Communication Processor (LCP)

- A typical Catalyst power-up self-test includes such things as an LED check, memory test, and address recognition logic such as ROM, RAM, EARL, and BootROM. Figure 6-8 gives you a visual of one of the higher-end modular Catalyst 6000 family devices in case you don't have anything like this in your lab.

Figure 6-8   *Catalyst 6509 Series Switches*

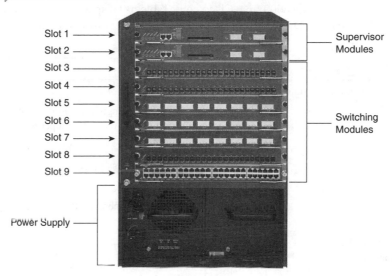

With its drastic increase in capacity and throughput, the Cat6000 is a very powerful big brother/ sister to the 5000 series. If you are familiar with the 4000 or 5000, you are well on your way to supporting the 6000s. CatOS and the native IOS modes are both available, although not all features are supported in both. The following list contains some common terminology and functionality of the 6000:

- The Catalyst switch processor (SP) controls system operation, port management, and services such as STP, VLANs, VTP, Internet Group Management Protocol (IGMP), DDSN Transfer Protocol (DTP), and provides the physical console connection during the initial boot.

- The MSFC is the route processor (RP) that provides Layer 3 functionality and controls the CEF table so that all routing takes place in hardware. It controls services such as CDP and PagP and provides the physical console connection after the system is up and running.

- The MSFC may have a policy feature card (PFC) as a daughter card. This provides QOS capabilities and security features such as virtual access control lists (VACLs).

- Hybrid mode. CatOS on the Supervisor for Layer 2 forwarding and IOS on the MSFC (which is optional) for Layer 3 forwarding. CatOS is the default for this mode.

- Native mode. Integrated single IOS image on the Supervisor with only a bootloader image on the MSFC. Operates as a Layer 3 router by default.

- Use the **show version** command to see which mode you are using. If you see *MSFC* in the image name, you know you are in the hybrid mode; whereas if you just have an image with *sup* for supervisor, you are operating in integrated IOS or native mode.

Regardless of the device, pay particular attention to the LED status and ports to assist you in narrowing down switch problems. Table 6-8 displays the LED part of the technical specifications for the 6000 from Cisco.com. Table 6-9 displays the fields associated with **show port**. Physical and Data Link targets such as these are key to supporting switched environments.

Table 6-8 *Catalyst 6000 LEDs*

LED	Status
Supervisor Engine status LED	**Orange** Module is booting; running diagnostics; minor temperature threshold exceeded; standby mode with redundant supervisors. **Green** All diagnostics pass; module is operational. **Red** Failed diagnostics; major temperature threshold exceeded; module not operational.
System LED displays chassis environmental status	**Green** All chassis environmental monitors okay. **Orange** Power-supply failure; incompatible power supplies installed; power-supply fan failure; minor backplane temperature threshold exceeded; redundant backplane clock failure. **Red** Supervisor Engine over temperature condition; major backplane temperature threshold exceeded.
Supervisor Active LED	**Green** Operational and active. **Orange** Standby mode.
PWR MGMT (Power Management) LED	**Green** Sufficient power for all modules. **Orange** Insufficient power for all modules.

Table 6-8   *Catalyst 6000 LEDs (Continued)*

LED	Status
PCMCIA LED	Lights when the PCMCIA device is accessed.
LINK LEDs for Gigabit Ethernet ports on the Supervisor Engine	**Green** Port is operational. **Orange** Software disabled (solid); disabled due to hardware failure (flashing).

Table 6-9   **show port** *Command Output Fields*

Field	Description
Port	Module and port number.
Name	Name of port if configured (description).
Status	Status of the port such as connected, notconnected, faulty, remfault, disable, remdisable, configerr, remcfgerr, or disagree.
Vlan	VLANs to which the port belongs.
Duplex	auto, full, fdx, half, hdx, a-half, a-hdx, a-full, or a-fdx.
Speed	auto, 10, 100, 155, a-10, a-100, 4, 16, a-14, or a-16.
Type	Port type (for example, 100BASE-FX MM, 100BASE-FX SM, 10/100BASE-TX, or RSM.
Security	Port security status.
Secure-Src-Addr	Secure MAC address for the security enabled port.
Last-Src-Addr	Source MAC address of the last packet received by the port.
Shutdown	Status of whether the port was shut down because of security.
Trap	Status of whether port trap is enabled or disabled.
IfIndex	Number of the ifIndex.
Broadcast-Limit	Broadcast threshold configured for the port.
Broadcast-Drop	Number of broadcast/multicast packets dropped because the broadcast limit for the port was exceeded.
Send admin	Flow-control administration. Possible settings: On indicates the local port sends flow control to the far end; off indicates the local port does not send flow control to the far end; desired indicates the local end sends flow control to the far end if the far end supports it.
FlowControl oper	Flow-control operation. Possible setting: Disagree indicates the two ports could not agree on a link protocol.
Receive admin	Flow-control administration. Possible settings: On indicates the local port requires the far end to send flow control; off indicates the local port does not allow the far end to send flow control; desired indicates the local end allows the far end to send flow control.

Table 6-9   **show port** *Command Output Fields (Continued)*

Field	Description
FlowControl oper	Flow-control operation. Possible setting: Disagree indicates the two ports could not agree on a link protocol.
RxPause	Number of pause frames received.
TxPause	Number of pause frames transmitted.
Unsupported Opcodes	Number of unsupported operating codes.
Align-Err	Number of frames with alignment errors (frames that do not end with an even number of octets and have a bad CRC*) received on the port.
FCS-Err	The number of valid size frames with FCS** error but no framing errors.
Xmit-Err	Number of transmit errors that occurred on the port (indicating that the internal transmit buffer is full).
Rcv-Err	Number of receive errors that occurred on the port (indicating that the internal receive buffer is full).
UnderSize	Number of received frames less than 64 bytes long (but are otherwise well-formed).
Single-Coll	Number of times one collision occurred before the port transmitted a frame to the media successfully.
Multi-Coll	Number of times multiple collisions occurred before the port transmitted a frame to the media successfully.
Late-Coll	Number of late collisions (collisions detected beyond 64 bytes).
Excess-Col	Number of excessive collisions that occurred on the port (indicating that a frame encountered 16 collisions and was discarded).
Carri-Sen	Number of times the port sensed a carrier (to determine whether the cable is currently being used).
Runts	Number of received runt frames (frames that are smaller than the minimum IEEE 802.3 frame size of 64 bytes) on the port.
Giants	Number of received giant frames (frames that exceed the maximum IEEE 802.3 frame size) on the port.
Last-Time-Cleared	Last time the port counters were cleared.
Auto-Part	The number of times the port entered the autopartition state due to excessive consecutive collisions.
Data-rate mismatch	The number of valid size frames experienced overrun or underrun.
Src-addr change	The number of times the last source address changed.
Good-bytes	The total number of octets in frames with no error.
Short-event	The number of times activity with a duration less than the ShortEventMax Time (74–82 bit times) is detected.

*CRC = Cyclical redundancy check

**FCS = Frame check sequence

Shooting Trouble with Switches

Shooting trouble with switches requires that you understand Physical and Data Link Layer targets and well as normal switch operations. A physical and logical map is not just something nice to have but a necessity in real-world operations. It is not easy to create if you don't understand how things work, in particular STP for Layer 2 devices. You must continue to follow a consistent methodology such as those suggested in the first part of the book to assist you in isolating fault domains.

It is probably not a bad idea to go back and review the Ethernet and switch beginning checklists and ending sections on shooting trouble. All of them allude to the fact that interfaces (ports) are the main Data Link Layer target. It is up to you to use known-good switches, modules, ports, cables, connectors, and transceivers for connectivity and performance purposes. Hardware issues could be a bad or loose cable, a faulty module or port; and they may be intermittent, in which case electrostatic discharge (ESD) may have originally caused the problem. Always reseat connections and modules, before you call for help. If the Supervisor module is not in slot 1, for example, the system doesn't boot up. In general, disconnect and reconnect; try a different port; try a different known-good cable.

Link lights (LEDs) are good but not always a 100-percent test. An 80-percent to 100-percent switch load may indicate a broadcast storm. On the other line card modules, the LEDs should flash orange (amber) or green during startup, and turn green to indicate successful initialization. Red indicates failure (reseat the module), and flashing orange could be a problem on some modules, although an instance of redundancy on others. As far as the port link integrity, LED issues can be anything from the port, to the cable, to the network interface card (NIC), or the negotiation for speed/duplex. Utilize your tools. Test with a reliable cable as well as a time domain reflectometer/optical time domain reflectometer (TDR/OTDR) to find cable length and impedance issues. Use protocol analyzers for protocol information; cable testers for cable issues; and network monitors to continuously monitor network traffic. There still could be a cable problem with lots of packet loss. On the other hand, things may work fine and the LED may just be burned out.

Other types of connection issues include using fiber where negotiation is not an issue but connectivity is. A common problem here is to plug Tx to Tx and Rx to Rx, but if you want things to work you need to connect Tx to Rx.

Pay attention not only to your LED lights but also to your logs for configuration issues. If you see a solid orange light, for instance, this may just indicate a shutdown port. A user or internal process could have shut it down but might not have automatically brought it back up. Perhaps there are speed/duplex issues. The best practice is to hard code fixed devices so that there is no negotiation. Perhaps STP has the port in a blocking state because it would cause a loop.

When things are working normally, you want to make them optimal. Performance commands include **set port host**, which is a macro that combines **set spantree portfast**, **set port channel mode off**, and **set trunk off**. Experiment with timing issues with and without portfast. Change the logging level for the session to **set logging level spantree 7** and observe the time-stamped log messages to see how long the port stays in each state. You can accomplish this on an IOS box with the **spanning-tree portfast** interface command; the following global commands: **service timestamps debug datetime localtime msec**, and **service timestamps log datetime**

localtime msec; and the following privileged exec command: **debug spantree events**. You can shut down a port and bring it back up to see a topology change and the associated activity. Don't forget that turning on portfast for a port really doesn't change the topology; instead it allows the switch to not send a TCN when a port becomes active.

Traffic issues may lead to segmentation of some sort or to upgrading the devices themselves. Use **show port**, **show mac**, and network management programs to monitor the average and peak utilization carefully.

NOTE   If **reset system**, the **reload** command, or rebooting seems to clear the issue and it continues to happen, perceptibly the reboot is more of a short-term fix than a permanent solution.

Obviously, you may have a software or hardware bottleneck. Know the limitations of your transport and your devices. For example, you still have collisions if Gigabit pipes are feeding 10-Mbps shared users. Use Cisco.com to assist with corrupted IOS issues; reload the operating system; and upgrade to the appropriate feature set. Again, all of this systematic troubleshooting relates back to the OSI model. Do you have power? Are the power supply and fans running? Are devices turned on? Do they have link lights? Work your way up the layers. (Refer to Table 1-2 in Chapter 1, "Shooting Trouble," for a review of the OSI layers.)

Once again it is time for the chapter Trouble Tickets. The plan here is to give you several things to do, let you make mistakes and fix some things on your own, and to introduce other problems that you should have some experience with as a support person. Routing and switching issues are unstated knowledge for the Cisco support person today.

Trouble Tickets

Complete the following Trouble Tickets in order. Use the information and tools from this chapter and the previous chapters to analyze, test, and document. Create your own Physical Layer or other problems if you need more practice in that area. Sample solutions are provided at the end of the section.

Trouble Ticket 1

Start a terminal session and new log on the 2900. Move hosta from the sw1900 to an open port on the sw2900 CatOS box. Configure hosta or the 2900 so that it will monitor the activity of ports 1/1, 1/2, and 2/3 (or other ports you are using). Be sure to save your configuration if not using a CatOS box.

Trouble Ticket 2

Power down all devices in the network including routers, switches, and hosts except hosta. (It gets pretty quiet, doesn't it?) Power up the 3512 IOS box and hostc and observe the LED activity. Analyze, test, and fix any issues.

Trouble Ticket 3

Power up the 1900 and observe the LED activity. Power on hostb. Analyze, test, and fix any issues.

Trouble Ticket 4

Power up the 2900 IOS-based switch and observe the LED activity. Analyze, test, and fix any issues.

Trouble Ticket 5

Hard code the switches to the highest available speed and duplex settings and configure portfast where appropriate.

Trouble Ticket 6

Physically add another cable between the 1900 and the 3512XL for redundancy and observe the new STP topology. Set the 3512XL to log spanning-tree debug events, and ensure the time stamps are accurate to the date and time (down to the millisecond). Break the Layer 2 loop by disconnecting the cable on the 3512XL port fa0/12. Watch the STP states.

Trouble Ticket 7

Make sure the spanning-tree debug is still running from the preceding Trouble Ticket. Hard code the 3512XL to be the root bridge by adjusting the priority field. Using the most useful menus, CatOS and IOS commands, draw a Layer 2 map including the new spanning tree. Check your work against the examples and Figure 6-9 in the solution.

Trouble Ticket 8

Start a continuous ping from hosta to hostc. Unplug portA or B on the 1900 to force a topology change. Capture all of this with Sniffer Pro on hosta, but do not stop the capture until the pings stop and then automatically start again. Stop and analyze the Sniffer Pro capture of a TCN BPDU as in Figure 6-10 in the solution. Plug the cable back in and save all of the chapter device configurations to a file.

Trouble Tickets Solutions

The following are the solutions to the Trouble Tickets.

Trouble Ticket 1 Solution

I am assuming that Sniffer Pro or similar software and drivers are loaded on hosta so that you can later use it to monitor the Layer 2 environment. The SPAN commands are in Example 6-26 for your review.

Example 6-26   *Setting Up Port 2/1 on the 2900 to Monitor*

```
sw2900> (enable) !!!I plugged hosta into port 2/1 and enabled port monitoring
sw2900> (enable) set span 1/1-2 2/1 both
Enabled monitoring of Port 1/1-2,2/3 transmit/receive traffic by Port 2/1
sw2900> (enable) show port capabilities 1/1
Model                    WS-X2900
Port                     1/1
Type                     100BaseTX
Speed                    100
Duplex                   half,full
Trunk encap type         ISL
Trunk mode               on,off,desirable,auto,nonegotiate
Channel                  no
Broadcast suppression    no
Flow control             no
Security                 yes
Membership               static,dynamic
Fast start               yes
Rewrite                  no
sw2900> (enable) !!!notice how the next command shows STP rather than port
    monitoring information
sw2900> (enable) show port span
Port      Vlan  Port-State      Cost   Priority  Fast-Start  Group-Method
--------  ----  ------------    -----  --------  ----------  ------------
 1/1       1    forwarding       19        32    disabled
 1/2       1    forwarding       19        32    disabled
 2/2       1    not-connected   100        32    disabled
 2/3       1    forwarding       19        32    disabled
 2/4       1    not-connected   100        32    disabled
...
sw2900> (enable) !!!look at the mod#/port# to see the port monitoring status
sw2900> (enable) show port 2/1
Port  Name              Status      Vlan      Level  Duplex Speed Type
----- ----------------- ---------- ---------- ------ ------ ----- ------------
 2/1                    monitor    1                 normal a-full a-100 10/100BaseTX
sw2900> (enable) show span
Status         : enabled
Admin Source   : Port 1/1-2
Oper Source    : Port 1/2
Destination    : Port 2/1
Direction      : transmit/receive
Incoming Packets: disabled
sw2900> (enable)
```

You will further take advantage of this port monitoring configuration in Trouble Ticket 8, in which you use a protocol analyzer to capture packets in a switched environment.

Trouble Ticket 2 Solution

The flashing orange and green LEDs should go away. The System and Status LEDs should turn solid green. Feel free to experiment with the mode button to look at things such as utilization, duplex, and speed. Port 1 (fa0/1) should be green for the host, although amber while going through the STP states. Telnet from the host to the switch to verify connectivity and test the layers from the bottom to the top.

Trouble Ticket 3 Solution

All LEDs start out as green, and then there is some other testing including the individual ports. All green lights go out except for the System status. The 1900 also has a mode button to toggle between *stat*, *utl*, and *fdup*. When you power on hostb, the associated port LED comes on the switch for port 2 (e0/2). Once again, telnet would be a better test from the host to the switch than ping because it tests all the layers.

Trouble Ticket 4 Solution

You notice quick flashes of orange, then red, then green, then red, then orange. Finally the multiple colors turn to a happy green for the System and the Console comes alive. Several flashing orange and green tests occur before the System, Status, Fan, Power Supply, and both Fast Ethernet ports turn solid green. The bottom 10/100 Fast Ethernet module 2 goes through the red and orange tests, too. I would expect the System LED to stay green, and port 2/1 and 2/3 should eventually light up for hosta and the router. However mine does not, and the console states the following:

```
%SYS-5-MOD_OK:Module 1 is online
%SYS-5-MOD_OK:Module 2 is online
%SYS-3-MOD_FAIL:Module 2 failed to come online
%SYS-3-MOD_FAIL:Module 2 failed to come online
```

I see orange lights but not green lights on the bottom card. Diagnose and fix the problem.

I issued the command **show module 2** on the 2900 and received a *faulty status*, as you can see in Example 6-27. Faulty could indicate a hardware issue, but I will not believe that until I have exhausted other possibilities such as resetting, reseating, or rebooting the module. I resorted to disabling the module through the software and enabling it once again. In practice it would be best to do this first before a hard reset. Both modules appear to now be online and in working condition, but for how long may be another issue. This is one of those indicators you should obviously keep track of in case of future issues. Helpful commands include **show module**, **show log**, and **show system**.

Example 6-27   *Faulty Module 2 on the 2900*

```
sw2900> (enable) show module 2
Mod Module-Name          Ports Module-Type           Model       Serial-Num Status
--- ------------------   ----- --------------------- ----------- ---------- -------
2                         12    10/100BaseTX Ethernet WS-X2901    008675483 faulty
Mod MAC-Address(es)                              Hw    Fw         Sw
--- -------------------------------------------- ----- ---------- ------------------
2    00-10-7b-53-4b-9c to 00-10-7b-53-4b-a7 1.4   3.1(1)     4.4(1)
sw2900> (enable) set module disable 1
Cannot disable Supervisor module.
sw2900> (enable) set module disable 2
Module 2 disabled.
sw2900> (enable) set module enable 2
Module 2 enabled.
sw2900> (enable) %SYS-5-MOD_OK:Module 2 is online
```

All lights are green that I would expect at this point. On port 1/3, the Speed LED is green but the Link LED is not lit. If you trace the cable over to the router, however, you will find it to be one of those "Layer 0" issues. "Layer 0" is really not part of the OSI model, but perhaps it should be. Power on the router to take care of that little issue.

Things appear to be working and you probably didn't have this issue (or could you duplicate it for that matter). At least you can remind yourself to do things such as reset ports or modules, move modules if possible, power things down and bring them back up before you give up on yourself or think you have a dead box. Obviously this may be the beginning of a hardware failure, but this is why accurate logs and documentation are so critical in the long run.

Trouble Ticket 5 Solution

Example 6-28 shows the commands to set the speed to 100 Mbps and the duplex to full on port 2/1 and 2/3. I discovered that ports 1/1 and 1/2 are fixed 100BASE-TX ports with the **show port capabilities** command. Telnet is a quick test of all the layers.

Example 6-28   *Setting Speed and Duplex on the 2900 CatOS Box*

```
sw2900> (enable) set port speed 1/1-2,2/1,2/3 100
Ports 2/1,2/3 transmission speed set to 100Mbps.
sw2900> (enable) set port speed 1/1-2 100
Failed to set transmission speed for ports 1/1-2.
sw2900> (enable) show port capabilities 1/1
Model                   WS-X2900
Port                    1/1
Type                    100BaseTX
Speed                   100
Duplex                  half,full
...
sw2900> (enable) set port duplex 1/1-2,2/1,2/3 full
Ports 1/1-2,2/1,2/3 set to full-duplex.
sw2900> (enable) telnet 192.168.5.100
```

Example 6-29 illustrates the menu commands to configure speed and duplex for e0/2 on the 1900. The commands for fa0/26(port A) and fa0/27(port B) are the same but are not shown in the output. Telnet tests things out through all the layers.

Example 6-29 *Setting Speed and Duplex on the 1900 Using the Menus*

```
 -------------------------------------------------
        Catalyst 1900 - Main Menu
     [C] Console Settings
     [S] System
     [N] Network Management
     [P] Port Configuration
  ...
     [H] Help
     [X] Exit Management Console
Enter Selection:  P
Identify Port:  1 to 24[1-24], [AUI], [A], [B]:
Select [1 - 24, AUI, A, B]:  2
        Catalyst 1900 - Port 1 Configuration
        Built-in 10Base-T
        802.1d STP State:  Blocking      Forward Transitions:  0
 --------------------- Settings --------------------------------------
     [D] Description/name of port
     [S] Status of port                         Suspended-no-linkbeat
     [F] Full duplex                            Disabled
     [I] Port priority (spanning tree)          128 (80 hex)
     [C] Path cost (spanning tree)              100
     [H] Port fast mode (spanning tree)         Enabled
  ...
Enter Selection:  F
Full duplex can double a port bandwidth by allowing it to simultaneously
transmit and receive.
Full duplex may be [E]nabled or [D]isabled:
Current setting ===> Disabled
   New setting ===> Enabled
  ...
sw2900> (enable) telnet 192.168.5.99
```

NOTE   You should have surmised on the 1900 that port e/02 is 10-Mbps/half-duplex by default with portfast enabled. However, fa0/26 and fa0/27, ports A and B are 100-Mbps/auto-duplex with portfast disabled by default. Because the display clearly illustrates that descriptions were missed earlier, if this were a practical environment I would recommend you configure them.

Example 6-30 shows the fa0/1 speed and duplex configuration on the 3512XL IOS box. Interface fa0/12 is configured exactly the same.

Example 6-30 *Setting Speed and Duplex on the 3512XL IOS Box*

```
3512XL(config)#interface fastethernet 0/1
3512XL(config-if)#speed 100
3512XL(config-if)#duplex full
3512XL(config-if)#end
3512XL#show interfaces fastethernet 0/1
FastEthernet0/1 is up, line protocol is up
  Hardware is Fast Ethernet, address is 00d0.7968.8481 (bia 00d0.7968.8481)
  MTU 1500 bytes, BW 100000 Kbit, DLY 100 usec, rely 255/255, load 1/255
  Encapsulation ARPA, loopback not set, keepalive not set
  Full-duplex, 100Mb/s, 100BaseTX/FX
```

Portfast should be implemented only on the three switch ports that connect to the hosts. It was on by default for e/02 on the 1900, but needs to be set on the 3512 and 2900. First look at STP in Example 6-31.

Example 6-31 *STP on the 3512XL IOS Box*

```
3512XL#show spantree
Spanning tree 1 is executing the IEEE compatible Spanning Tree protocol
  Bridge Identifier has priority 32768, address 00d0.7968.8480
  Configured hello time 2, max age 20, forward delay 15
  Current root has priority 32768, address 0010.ffe5.1400
  Root port is 25, cost of root path is 19
  Topology change flag set, detected flag not set, changes 9
  Times:  hold 1, topology change 35, notification 2
          hello 2, max age 20, forward delay 15
  Timers: hello 0, topology change 0, notification 0

Interface Fa0/1 (port 13) in Spanning tree 1 is FORWARDING
  Port path cost 19, Port priority 128
  Designated root has priority 32768, address 0010.ffe5.1400
  Designated bridge has priority 32768, address 00d0.7968.8480
  Designated port is 13, path cost 19
  Timers: message age 0, forward delay 0, hold 0
  BPDU: sent 1064, received 0

Interface Fa0/2 (port 14) in Spanning tree 1 is down
  Port path cost 100, Port priority 128
  Designated root has priority 32768, address 0010.ffe5.1400
  Designated bridge has priority 32768, address 00d0.7968.8480
  Designated port is 14, path cost 19
  Timers: message age 0, forward delay 0, hold 0
  BPDU: sent 0, received 0
...
Interface Fa0/12 (port 25) in Spanning tree 1 is FORWARDING
  Port path cost 19, Port priority 128
  Designated root has priority 32768, address 0010.ffe5.1400
  Designated bridge has priority 32768, address 0010.ffe5.1400
  Designated port is 1, path cost 0
  Timers: message age 1, forward delay 0, hold 0
  BPDU: sent 12, received 998
```

Only a few interfaces are shown in the shaded output, but remember the first interface is the actual interface on the box and the port number in parentheses () is the way the interface was logically calculated for STP purposes.

Now configure portfast on fa0/1 where hostc connects as in Example 6-32.

Example 6-32 *Configuring STP Portfast on the 3512XL Host Connections*

```
3512XL(config)#interface fastethernet 0/1
3512XL(config-if)#spanning-tree portfast
3512XL(config-if)#end
3512XL#copy running-config startup-config
```

Show STP statistics on port 2/1 on the 2900 CatOS box to see that portfast is referred to as fast-start. Turn it on for the connection to hosta as in Example 6-33.

Example 6-33 *Configuring STP Portfast on the 2900 Host Connection*

```
sw2900> show spantree 2/1
Port        Vlan  Port-State     Cost   Priority  Fast-Start  Group-Method
---------   ----  -------------  -----  --------  ----------  ------------
sw2900> (enable) set spantree portfast 2/1 enable
Warning: Spantree port fast start should only be enabled on ports connected
to a single host.  Connecting hubs, concentrators, switches, bridges, etc. to
a fast start port can cause temporary spanning tree loops.  Use with caution.
Spantree port 2/1 fast start enabled.
```

Trouble Ticket 6 Solution

Connect a crossover cable between port B on the 1900 and fa0/11 on the 3512XL. The orange port turns green on 1900, but stays orange on the 3512XL because of STP. Fa0/11 is in the blocking state. If you pull the fa0/12 cable, obviously that would change because you would take away the Layer 2 loop. STP is just doing its job here and if you had a picture of your environment in front of you this would be very easy to see; don't worry if you don't because that is part of the next Trouble Ticket. Example 6-34 illustrates some helpful debug and logging setups to help you analyze STP. Remember that you may need to turn on **terminal monitor** to see your debug output remotely.

Example 6-34 *Testing STP on the 3512*

```
sw3512XL#show clock
sw3512XL#clock set 8:00:00 25 Nov 2002
sw3512XL#configure terminal
sw3512XL(config)#service timestamps debug datetime msec localtime
sw3512XL(config)#service timestamps log datetime msec localtime
sw3512XL(config)#end
sw3512XL#copy running-config startup-config
sw3512XL#debug spantree events
```

Unplug the connection to fa0/11 on the 3512XL and wait for the line and protocol to go down. Plug the cable back in and watch the debug output that displays as in Example 6-35.

Example 6-35 *Testing STP on the 3512*

```
Nov 25 08:15:36.580: %LINK-3-UPDOWN: Interface FastEthernet0/11, changed state to
down
Nov 25 08:15:37.204: %LINEPROTO-5-UPDOWN: Line protocol on Interface
FastEthernet0/11, changed state to down
sw3512XL#!!!now plug the cable back in
Nov 25 08:15:57.229: ST: FastEthernet0/11 -> listening
Nov 25 08:15:57.234: %LINK-3-UPDOWN: Interface FastEthernet0/11, changed state to up
Nov 25 08:15:57.242: %LINEPROTO-5-UPDOWN: Line protocol on Interface
FastEthernet0/11, changed state to up
Nov 25 08:15:57.994: ST: FastEthernet0/11 -> blocking
sw3512XL#show spantree
Spanning tree 1 is executing the IEEE compatible Spanning Tree protocol
  Bridge Identifier has priority 32768, address 00d0.7968.8480
  Configured hello time 2, max age 20, forward delay 15
  Current root has priority 32768, address 0010.ffe5.1400
  Root port is 25, cost of root path is 19
  Topology change flag not set, detected flag not set, changes 11
  Times:  hold 1, topology change 35, notification 2
          hello 2, max age 20, forward delay 15
  Timers: hello 0, topology change 0, notification 0
Interface Fa0/1 (port 13) in Spanning tree 1 is FORWARDING
   Port path cost 19, Port priority 128
   Designated root has priority 32768, address 0010.ffe5.1400
   Designated bridge has priority 32768, address 00d0.7968.8480
   Designated port is 13, path cost 19
   Timers: message age 0, forward delay 0, hold 0
   BPDU: sent 4238, received 0
Interface Fa0/11 (port 24) in Spanning tree 1 is BLOCKING
   Port path cost 19, Port priority 128
   Designated root has priority 32768, address 0010.ffe5.1400
   Designated bridge has priority 32768, address 0090.922a.7680
   Designated port is 27, path cost 10
   Timers: message age 3, forward delay 0, hold 0
   BPDU: sent 2, received 693
Interface Fa0/12 (port 25) in Spanning tree 1 is FORWARDING
   Port path cost 19, Port priority 128
   Designated root has priority 32768, address 0010.ffe5.1400
   Designated bridge has priority 32768, address 0010.ffe5.1400
   Designated port is 2, path cost 0
   Timers: message age 4, forward delay 0, hold 0
   BPDU: sent 5, received 3484
```

The time and date stamps at the millisecond intervals are quite helpful here because you can see that the calculations occurred rather quickly. Ports 1 and 12 are in a forwarding state. Port 11 is in a blocking state but is still processing BPDUs in case of a topology change. Disconnect the cable on fa0/12 to verify this and observe the debug activity in Example 6-36. Note that it takes about 30 seconds from the time the link goes down until the redundant link takes over automatically.

Example 6-36 *Watching a Topology Change and the STP States*

```
Nov 25 08:30:12.869: %LINK-3-UPDOWN: Interface FastEthernet0/12, changed state to
down
Nov 25 08:30:12.869: ST: sent Topology Change Notice on FastEthernet0/12
Nov 25 08:30:12.875: ST: FastEthernet0/12 -> blocking
Nov 25 08:30:12.880: ST: FastEthernet0/11 -> listening
Nov 25 08:30:13.129: %LINEPROTO-5-UPDOWN: Line protocol on Interface
FastEthernet0/12, changed state to down
Nov 25 08:30:14.869: ST: sent Topology Change Notice on FastEthernet0/11
Nov 25 08:30:27.882: ST: FastEthernet0/11 -> learning
Nov 25 08:30:42.890: ST: sent Topology Change Notice on FastEthernet0/11
Nov 25 08:30:42.890: ST: FastEthernet0/11 -> forwarding
sw3512XL#
```

CAUTION   Debug output is quite helpful in a lab situation to understand exactly what is happening. Be very cautious in the production environment. Always use the question mark (?) to find the right command to help you limit the amount of debug activity when troubleshooting and remember to turn debug off when you are done. CatOS does not offer debug, but the **set trace ?** command gives you similar output.

Reconnect the cable on port fa0/12 of the 3512XL switch and allow STP to converge before beginning the next trouble ticket.

Trouble Ticket 7 Solution

Example 6-37 illustrates that STP debugging is still on and is the command to hard code the root bridge.

Example 6-37 *Configuring the Root Bridge*

```
3512XL#show debug
General spanning tree:
  Spanning Tree event debugging is on
3512XL#configure terminal
3512XL(config)#spanning-tree ?
  forward-time  Set a Spanning Tree FORWARD Interval
  hello-time    Set a Spanning Tree HELLO Interval
  max-age       Set a Spanning Tree MAX AGE Interval
  priority      Set a Spanning Tree Priority
  protocol      Spanning tree protocol type
  uplinkfast    Enable UplinkFast Feature
  vlan          VLAN Switch Spanning Trees
  <cr>
```

Example 6-37 *Configuring the Root Bridge (Continued)*

```
3512XL(config)#spanning-tree priority ?
  <0-65535>  Set a Spanning Tree Priority
3512XL(config)#!!!lowest BID wins
3512XL(config)#spanning-tree priority 100
Nov 25 08:40:00.178: ST: FastEthernet0/11 -> listening
Nov 25 08:40:00.199: ST: Topology Change rcvd on FastEthernet0/12
Nov 25 08:40:15.178: ST: FastEthernet0/11 -> learning
Nov 25 08:40:30.204: ST: FastEthernet0/11 -> forwarding
3512XL(config)#exit
3512XL#copy running-config startup-config
```

Show the spanning tree to verify that the 3512 is in fact now the root bridge. The shaded output in Example 6-38 certainly helps you out with that.

Example 6-38 *We Are the Root of the Spanning Tree*

```
3512XL#show spanning-tree
Spanning tree 1 is executing the IEEE compatible Spanning Tree protocol
  Bridge Identifier has priority 100, address 00d0.7968.8480
  Configured hello time 2, max age 20, forward delay 15
  We are the root of the spanning tree
  Topology change flag not set, detected flag not set, changes 9
  Times:  hold 1, topology change 35, notification 2
          hello 2, max age 20, forward delay 15
  Timers: hello 1, topology change 0, notification 0
Interface Fa0/1 (port 13) in Spanning tree 1 is FORWARDING
  Port path cost 19, Port priority 128
  Designated root has priority 100, address 00d0.7968.8480
  Designated bridge has priority 100, address 00d0.7968.8480
  Designated port is 13, path cost 0
  Timers: message age 0, forward delay 0, hold 0
  BPDU: sent 56902, received 0
  The port is in the portfast mode
...
Interface Fa0/11 (port 24) in Spanning tree 1 is FORWARDING
  Port path cost 19, Port priority 128
  Designated root has priority 100, address 00d0.7968.8480
  Designated bridge has priority 100, address 00d0.7968.8480
  Designated port is 24, path cost 0
  Timers: message age 0, forward delay 0, hold 0
  BPDU: sent 56006, received 5
Interface Fa0/12 (port 25) in Spanning tree 1 is FORWARDING
  Port path cost 19, Port priority 128
  Designated root has priority 100, address 00d0.7968.8480
  Designated bridge has priority 100, address 00d0.7968.8480
  Designated port is 25, path cost 0
  Timers: message age 0, forward delay 0, hold 0
  BPDU: sent 3844, received 4
```

Lowering the priority forced the 3512 to become the root bridge, and all the ports are designated or in a forwarding state. Show STP on the 2900 as in Example 6-39 to help you gather the statistics for your Layer 2 drawing.

Example 6-39 *The STP Topology on the 2900*

```
sw2900> (enable) show spantree
VLAN 1
Spanning tree enabled
Spanning tree type          ieee
!!! global parameters are above
!!! root bridge parameters are below followed by local switch and port
Designated Root             00-d0-79-68-84-80
Designated Root Priority    100
Designated Root Cost        19
Designated Root Port        1/2
Root Max Age   20 sec    Hello Time 2  sec   Forward Delay 15 sec
Bridge ID MAC ADDR          00-10-ff-e5-14-00
Bridge ID Priority          32768
Bridge Max Age 20 sec    Hello Time 2  sec   Forward Delay 15 sec
Port      Vlan  Port-State    Cost   Priority Fast-Start  Group-Method
--------- ----  ------------- -----  -------- ----------  ------------
 1/1       1    blocking        19       32    disabled
 1/2       1    forwarding      19       32    disabled
 2/2       1    not-connected  100       32    disabled
 2/3       1    forwarding      19       32    disabled
 2/4       1    not-connected  100       32    disabled
```

The designated root port is the path by which the 2900 gets to the root bridge. By definition all ports on the root bridge must be in a forwarding state. However, STP takes care of the Layer 2 loop by blocking port 1/1 on the 2900. Analyze the 1900 to complete your drawing. (See Example 6-40.)

Example 6-40 *The STP Topology on the 1900*

```
         Catalyst 1900 - Main Menu
    [C] Console Settings
    [S] System
    [N] Network Management
    [P] Port Configuration
...
Enter Selection:  P
Identify Port:  1 to 24[1-24], [AUI], [A], [B]:
Select [1 - 24, AUI, A, B]:  A
       Catalyst 1900 - Port A Configuration
       Built-in 100Base-TX
       802.1d STP State:  Forwarding    Forward Transitions:  1
    --------------------- Settings ----------------------------------
    [D] Description/name of port
    [S] Status of port                      Enabled
    [I] Port priority (spanning tree)        128 (80 hex)
    [C] Path cost (spanning tree)            10
    [H] Port fast mode (spanning tree)       Disabled
    [E] Enhanced congestion control          Disabled
    [F] Full duplex / Flow control           Full duplex
    --------------------- Related Menus -----------------------------
    [A] Port addressing          [V] View port statistics
    [N] Next port                [G] Goto port
```

Example 6-40 *The STP Topology on the 1900 (Continued)*

```
     [P] Previous port              [X] Exit to Main Menu
Enter Selection:  N
         Catalyst 1900 - Port B Configuration
         Built-in 100Base-TX
         802.1d STP State:  Forwarding    Forward Transitions:  1
    --------------------- Settings ----------------------------------------
     [D] Description/name of port
     [S] Status of port                       Enabled
     [I] Port priority (spanning tree)         128 (80 hex)
     [C] Path cost (spanning tree)             10
     [H] Port fast mode (spanning tree)        Disabled
     [E] Enhanced congestion control           Disabled
     [F] Full duplex / Flow control            Full duplex
    --------------------- Related Menus -----------------------------------
     [A] Port addressing           [V] View port statistics
     [N] Next port                 [G] Goto port
     [P] Previous port             [X] Exit to Main Menu
Enter Selection:  G
Identify Port:  1 to 24[1-24], [AUI], [A], [B]:
Select [1 - 24, AUI, A, B]:  2
         Catalyst 1900 - Port 2 Configuration
         Built-in 10Base-T
         802.1d STP State:  Forwarding     Forward Transitions:  87
...
```

The 1900 is forwarding on all used ports and is running portfast to the hostb connection. Port A is the designated port for the segment between the 1900 and the 2900, and Port B is the root port, which is the 1900's path to the root bridge.

If necessary, rerun the **show spanning-tree** command on any IOS device, run **show spantree** on any CatOS device, or use HTTP or menus to complete a Layer 2 STP drawing (see Figure 6-9). Feel free to add the costs to your drawing for an additional level of detail.

Figure 6-9   *Layer 2 STP Drawing*

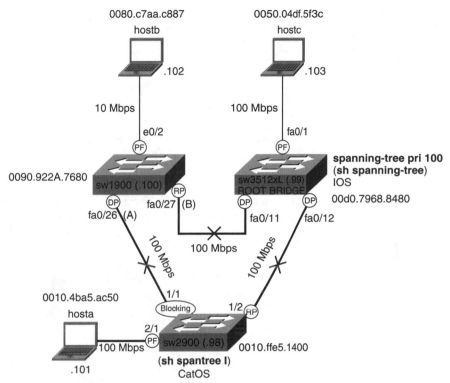

Note: All Designated Ports (DP) and Root Ports (RP) are in
a Forwarding (F) state as are the host parts configured with
Port Fast (PF).

Trouble Ticket 8 Solution

Example 6-41 starts the continuous ping from hosta so that you can analyze STP in action.
When you disconnect the cable connected to port A on the 1900, the ping times out and because
of STP it automatically starts working again.

Example 6-41   *STP in Action*

```
Microsoft Windows 2000 [Version 5.00.2195]
 Copyright 1985-2000 Microsoft Corp.
C:\>ping 192.168.5.103 -t
Pinging 192.168.5.103 with 32 bytes of data:
Reply from 192.168.5.103: bytes=32 time<10ms TTL=128
Reply from 192.168.5.103: bytes=32 time<10ms TTL=128
Reply from 192.168.5.103: bytes=32 time<10ms TTL=128
```

Example 6-41 *STP in Action (Continued) (Continued)*

```
Reply from 192.168.5.103: bytes=32 time<10ms TTL=128
Reply from 192.168.5.103: bytes=32 time<10ms TTL=128
Request timed out.
Request timed out.
Request timed out.
Request timed out.
Reply from 192.168.5.103: bytes=32 time<10ms TTL=128
Reply from 192.168.5.103: bytes=32 time<10ms TTL=128
Reply from 192.168.5.103: bytes=32 time<10ms TTL=128
Ping statistics for 192.168.5.103:
    Packets: Sent = 54, Received = 24, Lost = 30 (55% loss),
Approximate round trip times in milli-seconds:
    Minimum = 0ms, Maximum =  0ms, Average =  0ms
```

Figure 6-10 illustrates the ping and the TCN BPDU. The TCN doesn't have as many fields as the configuration BPDU because TCNs are topology changes that are sent to the root bridge. The significance of a TCN is that the learned addresses get aged-out very quickly.

Figure 6-10 *Trouble Ticket 8 TCN BPDU*

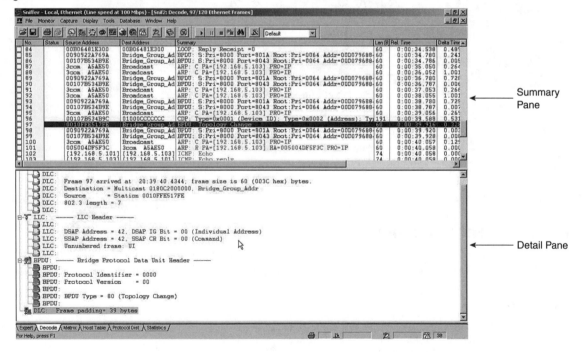

Remember to plug the cable back in and save your chapter configurations to a file called *Chapter 6 Ending Configs*. You have completed the chapter Trouble Tickets when you feel comfortable with the tasks assigned and the various scenarios throughout the chapter. Review or experiment in the areas where you need more help. Understanding and troubleshooting in a simple environment is certainly the foundation for understanding and troubleshooting more complex protocols and technologies. Check your understanding with the chapter review questions.

Review Questions

Use the information in this chapter to answer the following questions. The answers are located in Appendix A, "Answers to Review Questions."

1 On the 1900, portfast is enabled on the 10-Mbps ports and disabled on the uplink ports. Can you change this? If so, how? Give a practical example of using portfast.

2 What command outputs the following on a 2900 CatOS:

```
* = Static Entry. + = Permanent Entry. # = System Entry. R = Router Entry.
  X = Port Security Entry
VLAN  Dest MAC/Route Des  Destination Ports or VCs / [Protocol Type]
----  ------------------  ------------------------------------------------
1       00-90-92-2a-76-9a   1/1 [ALL]
1       00-80-c7-aa-c8-87   1/2 [ALL]
1       00-50-04-df-5f-3c   1/2 [ALL]
1       00-d0-79-68-84-8d   1/2 [ALL]
1       00-b0-64-81-e3-00   2/3 [ALL]
```

3 What command outputs the following on an IOS-based switch:

```
Dynamic Address Count:                 7
Secure Address (User-defined) Count:   0
Static Address (User-defined) Count:   0
System Self Address Count:             37
Total MAC addresses:                   44
Maximum MAC addresses:                 8192
Non-static Address Table:
Destination Address  Address Type  VLAN  Destination Port
-------------------  ------------  ----  ------------------
0010.4ba5.ae50       Dynamic         1   FastEthernet0/12
0010.ffe5.17fd       Dynamic         1   FastEthernet0/12
0010.ffe5.17ff       Dynamic         1   FastEthernet0/12
0050.04df.5f3c       Dynamic         1   FastEthernet0/1
0080.c7aa.c887       Dynamic         1   FastEthernet0/11
0090.922a.769b       Dynamic         1   FastEthernet0/11
00b0.6481.e300       Dynamic         1   FastEthernet0/12
```

4 Is a port receiving traffic if it is in the STP blocking state?

5 What are the STP state transitions?

6 How do you view the speed and duplex settings on a router or IOS-based switch? On a CatOS-based switch?

7 It is common practice to use loopbacks for testing. Can you be sure that a loopback address is always up?

8 I issued the following **show interface** command on the 2900 CatOS box to view the management IP address and its parameters. What is the 192.168.5.111 address?

```
sw2900> (enable) show interface
sl0: flags=51<UP,POINTOPOINT,RUNNING>
        slip 0.0.0.0 dest 0.0.0.0
sc0: flags=63<UP,BROADCAST,RUNNING>
        vlan 1 inet 192.168.5.98 netmask 255.255.255.240 broadcast 192.168.5.111
```

9 Encoded Address Recognition Logic (EARL) is an ASIC that works with the bus arbitration for packet transfers in a Catalyst 5000. Ethernet ports use a custom ASIC called _____. Other ports use a custom ASIC called _____.

10 You are at a host and attempt to telnet to a switch. The following message appears:

```
Password required, but none set
Connection to host lost.
```

What's the issue?

11 Assume your environment to be what it is now for the chapter scenario. On hosta you type the command **tracert 192.168.5.103**. How many hops to the destination?

Summary

Shooting trouble with the CatOS and IOS is a necessity today. Many things that used to be performed on routers are now performed on switches with router capability. Although many switches are usable the minute you take them out of the box, they are more optimal if configured for the environment. Supporting Layer 2 and Layer 3 devices not only requires a good basis of switching and routing, but an understanding of the devices and operating systems, too. LEDs, SPAN, and various show commands are excellent Layer 2 tools if you use them. Like it or not, full-duplex switching has allowed Ethernet to be reborn again. So until the next big architecture comes along, you can continue to leverage off of what you know about legacy Ethernet to assist you in supporting today's switched Ethernet environments.

This chapter reviewed segmentation, STP, 5000/6000 architecture, and the evolution of Cisco switches, including examples of the devices and the operating systems. The next chapter continues your Ethernet, IP, and switching experience with supporting VLANs.

CHAPTER 7

Shooting Trouble with VLANs on Routers and Switches

This chapter continues the practical switching focus and includes a number of objectives falling under the CCNP troubleshooting guidelines. Understanding and supporting Ethernet switches, routers, and virtual LANs (VLANs) applies to all of Cisco's current certifications. A solid understanding of VLANs and the role of routers and switches in the internetwork is essential in your practical studies. This chapter assumes knowledge of the previous chapters, but in particular of Chapter 3, "Shooting Trouble with IP," Chapter 5, "Shooting Trouble with Ethernet," and Chapter 6, "Shooting Trouble with CatOS and IOS."

You build the chapter scenario to assist you in supporting routing and switching using VLANs. The chapter reviews VLAN concepts, symptoms, problems, and action plans while you configure your VLANs. As you are used to by now, throughout the chapter there are several walk-through scenarios and practical Trouble Tickets for you to explore. For those of you who do not have equipment handy, I include many relevant figures and examples so that you too can shoot trouble with VLANs.

This chapter covers the following topics:

- Scenario: Shooting Trouble with VLANs on Routers and Switches
- Why VLANs?
- Trunking
- Managing VLANs
- Inter-VLAN Routing
- Route Switch Technologies
- Shooting Trouble with VLANs
- Trouble Tickets
- Trouble Tickets Solutions

Supporting Website Files

You can find files and links to utilities that support this book on the Cisco Press website at www.ciscopress.com/1587200570. Even if you do not have a lab, you can take advantage of the supporting configuration files including the logs to understand device input and output. The files are listed throughout the chapters in italics.

In order to be able to read and work with some of the supporting files offered at www.ciscopress.com/1587200570, you may want to download some of the programs listed in Table I-1 in the Introduction.

Scenario: Shooting Trouble with VLANs on Routers and Switches

The chapter scenario uses some of the same routers and switches you have configured for the other scenarios. You modify your lab according to Figure 7-1 and start with everything in VLAN1.

Figure 7-1 *Chapter 7 Scenario Physical Layout*

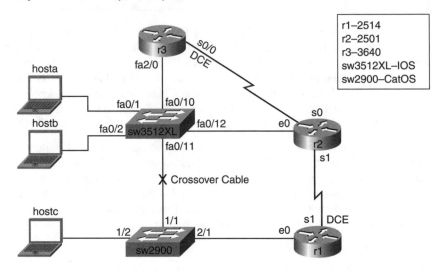

Document your steps and *any* problems along the way. Remember, however, that there is not always one right way to accomplish the tasks presented. The ability to obtain the end result using good practices is extremely important in any real-world network. My troubleshooting and device configurations are presented starting in Example 7-1 so that you can compare your work and perhaps see a different approach to obtaining the end result. Use the previous troubleshooting checklists, your step-by-step troubleshooting methodology, and the VLAN checklist in Table 7-1 to assist in testing.

Table 7-1 *VLAN Quick Troubleshooting Checklist*

CatOS	IOS
set vtp domain donna	**#vlan database** (vlan)#**vtp domain donna**
set vtp mode transparent	(vlan)#**vtp transparent**
vlan 2 name eng type ethernet	(vlan)#**vlan 2 name eng media ethernet**
show vlan **show spantree** *vlan#*	(vlan)#**show** #**show spanning-tree** *vlan#*

Table 7-1   *VLAN Quick Troubleshooting Checklist (Continued)*

CatOS	IOS
clear vlan 2	(vlan)#**no vlan 2 name eng media ethernet** (vlan)#**exit**
show vtp domain	#**show vtp status**
set trunk 1/1-2 on	(config)#**interface fa0/12** (config-if)#**switchport mode trunk**
show trunk	#**show interface fa0/12 switchport**
show spantree ? **show port spantree 2/4**	#**show spanning-tree ?** #**show spannting-tree interface fa0/1**

See also www.cisco.com/univercd/cc/td/doc/product/lan/cat2950/12111ea1/scg/swvlan.htm#xtocid7.

As I discuss real-world VLAN-to-VLAN communication—including issues such as addressing the broadcast domains, default gateways, VLAN Trunking Protocol (VTP) mode tuning, trunking issues, routing issues, vanishing VLANs, and so on—continue to identify targets and document the results using **ping**, **trace**, **set**, **show**, **clear**, Cisco Discovery Protocol (CDP), **debug,** protocol analyzers, and other troubleshooting tools.

First you should physically disconnect all serial and Ethernet cables and wire your lab according to Figure 7-1. My terminal server is a 2511 (not pictured in the diagram), r1 is a 2514, r2 is a 2501, r3 is a 3640, the IOS-based switch is a 3512XL, and the CatOS-based switch is a 2900. The 1900 used in the preceding chapter is *not* being used here. I am assuming you have a Fast Ethernet connection from r3 to the 3512XL switch as well as between the switches. My connections between r1/r2 and their respective switches are only 10 Mbps, but 10 or 100 is fine. Assuming you have the correct number and type of interfaces, other equipment is suitable, too. Configure the terminal server (optional) and clear the configurations. The **write erase** or **erase startup-config** command followed by the **reload** command works fine for the routers and the IOS-based switch. Use **clear config all** for the CatOS box.

Inspect the LEDs for all devices and prepare for console or terminal server connectivity to each device. Globally configure such items as hostnames and passwords. Configure what is appropriate for the router interfaces, including descriptions, speed and duplex settings, bandwidth, and clock rate. Remember to issue a **no shut** on the interfaces and turn on **logging synchronous** for the console. Use the default encapsulations but do *not* configure the IP parameters as of yet. Example 7-1 displays the r1 configuration.

Example 7-1   *r1 Configuration*

```
Router>enable
Router#configure terminal
Router(config)#hostname r1
r1(config)#enable secret donna
r1(config)#line vty 0 4
```

continues

Example 7-1 *r1 Configuration (Continued)*

```
r1(config-line)#login
r1(config-line)#password donna
r1(config-line)#interface ethernet 0
r1(config-if)#description r1e0 to sw2900 2/1
r1(config-if)#speed 10
r1(config-if)#duplex half
r1(config-if)#no shut
r1(config-if)#interface serial 1
r1(config-if)#description r1s1 to r2s1
r1(config-if)#bandwidth 64
r1(config-if)#clock rate 64000
r1(config-if)#no shut
r1(config-if)#exit
r1(config)#line console 0
r1(config-line)#logging synchronous
r1(config-line)#end
r1#copy running-config startup-config
```

Speed and duplex settings may or may not be available depending upon your hardware and software.

Next configure r2 as in Example 7-2.

Example 7-2 *r2 Configuration*

```
Router(config)#hostname r2
r2(config)#enable secret donna
r2(config)#line vty 0 4
r2(config-line)#login
r2(config-line)#password donna
r2(config-line)#interface ethernet 0
r2(config-if)#description r2e0 to sw3512xl fa0/12
r2(config-if)#speed 10
r2(config-if)#duplex half
r2(config-if)#no shut
r2(config-if)#interface serial 0
r2(config-if)#description r2s0 to r3s0/0
r2(config-if)#bandwidth 64
r2(config-if)#no shut
r2(config-if)#interface serial 1
r2(config-if)#description r2s1 to r1s1
r2(config-if)#bandwidth 64
r2(config-if)#no shut
r2(config-if)#exit
r2(config)#line console 0
r2(config-line)#logging synchronous
r2(config-line)#end
r2#show ip interface brief
Interface              IP-Address      OK? Method Status              Protocol
Ethernet0              unassigned      YES unset  up                  up
Serial0                unassigned      YES unset  down                down
Serial1                unassigned      YES unset  up                  up
r2# copy running-config startup-config
```

Now that Layer 1 and Layer 2 are up for r1 and r2, move along to configure r3 as in Example 7-3.

Example 7-3   *r3 Configuration*

```
Router(config)#hostname r3
r3(config)#enable secret donna
r3(config)#line vty 0 4
r3(config-line)#login
r3(config-line)#password donna
r3(config-line)#interface fastethernet 2/0
r3(config-if)#description r3 fa2/0 to sw3512xl fa0/10
r3(config-if)#speed 100
r3(config-if)#full-duplex
r3(config-if)#no shut
r3(config)#interface serial 0/0
r3(config-if)#description r3s0/0 to r2s0
r3(config-if)#bandwidth 64
r3(config-if)#clock rate 64000
r3(config-if)#no shut
r3(config-if)#exit
r3(config)#line console 0
r3(config-line)#logging synchronous
r3(config-line)#end
r3#show ip interface brief
Interface             IP-Address      OK? Method Status         Protocol
Serial0/0             unassigned      YES unset  up             up
...
FastEthernet2/0       unassigned      YES unset  up             up
r3#copy running-config startup-config
```

Now that the basic router configurations are in place, configure the switches as in Examples 7-4, 7-5, and 7-6 (including the hostnames, passwords, and most appropriate duplex, speed, and portfast settings). Verify CDP communications from both switches as a quick physical test as in Example 7-7.

Example 7-4   *sw3512XL IOS Switch Configuration*

```
Switch(config)#hostname sw3512xl
sw3512xl(config)#enable secret donna
sw3512xl(config)#line vty 0 4
sw3512xl(config-line)#login
sw3512xl(config-line)#password donnna
sw3512xl(config-line)#!!!better to fix this now than later
sw3512xl(config-line)#password donna
sw3512xl(config-line)#interface fastethernet 0/1
sw3512xl(config-if)#description sw3512xl fa0/1 to hosta
sw3512xl(config-if)#speed 100
sw3512xl(config-if)#duplex full
sw3512xl(config-if)#spanning-tree portfast
sw3512xl(config-if)#no shut
sw3512xl(config-if)#interface fastethernet 0/2
sw3512xl(config-if)#description sw3512xl fa0/2 to hostb
sw3512xl(config-if)#speed 10
sw3512xl(config-if)#duplex half
```

continues

Example 7-4   *sw3512XL IOS Switch Configuration (Continued)*

```
sw3512xl(config-if)#spanning-tree portfast
sw3512xl(config-if)#no shut
sw3512xl(config-if)#interface fastethernet 0/10
sw3512xl(config-if)#description sw3512xl fa0/10 to r3 fa2/0
sw3512xl(config-if)#speed 100
sw3512xl(config-if)#duplex full
sw3512xl(config-if)#no shut
sw3512xl(config-if)#interface fastethernet 0/11
sw3512xl(config-if)#description sw3512xl fa0/11 to sw2900 1/1
sw3512xl(config-if)#speed 100
sw3512xl(config-if)#duplex full
sw3512xl(config-if)#no shut
sw3512xl(config-if)#interface fastethernet 0/12
sw3512xl(config-if)#description sw3512xl fa0/12 to r2e0
sw3512xl(config-if)#speed 10
sw3512xl(config-if)#duplex half
sw3512xl(config-if)#no shut
sw3512xl(config-if)#exit
sw3512xl(config)#line console 0
sw3512xl(config-line)#logging synchronous
sw3512xl(config-line)#end
sw3512xl#copy running-config startup-config
```

The shaded output illustrates where I incorrectly typed the password. Because I realized it right away, I just quickly repeated the line (using the up arrow key) with the correct password. These self-inflicted errors always make troubleshooting a challenge.

Continue your configuration with the 2900. Example 7-5 illustrates clearing the existing configuration. Keep in mind this wouldn't be a best practice over a telnet connection because you lose all configuration, which includes your management interface, too. Example 7-6 displays the 2900 scenario configuration.

Example 7-5   *Clearing the sw2900 CatOS Switch Configuration*

```
sw2900 (enable) clear config all
This command will clear all configuration in NVRAM.
This command will cause ifIndex to be reassigned on the next system startup.
Do you want to continue (y/n) [n]? y
.duplicate IP address 0.0.0.0 sent from MAC address: 00-d0-79-68-84-80
.......
................
System configuration cleared.
```

Example 7-6   *sw2900 CatOS Switch Configuration*

```
Console> (enable) set system name sw2900
System name set.
sw2900> (enable) set enablepass
Enter old password:
Enter new password:
Retype new password:
```

Example 7-6   *sw2900 CatOS Switch Configuration (Continued)*

```
Password changed.
sw2900> (enable) set port name ?
Usage: set port name <mod_num/port_num> [port_name]
sw2900> (enable) set port name 1/1 sw2900 1/1 to sw3512xl fa0/11
Name string must be less than 21 characters.
sw2900> (enable) set port name 1/1 to sw3512xl fa0/11
Port 1/1 name set.
sw2900> (enable) set port speed 100
Usage: set port speed <mod_num/port_num> <4 ¦ 10 ¦ 16 ¦ 100 ¦ auto>
sw2900> (enable) set port speed 1/1 100
Feature not supported on Module 1.
sw2900> (enable) set port duplex 1/1 full
Port(s) 1/1 set to full-duplex.
sw2900> (enable) set port enable 1/1
Port 1/1 enabled.
sw2900> (enable) set port name 1/2 to hostc
Port 1/2 name set.
sw2900> (enable) set port speed 1/2 100
Feature not supported on Module 1.
sw2900> (enable) set port duplex 1/2 full
Port(s) 1/2 set to full-duplex.
sw2900> (enable) set port enable 1/2
Port 1/2 enabled.
sw?900> (enable) set port name 2/1 to r1e0
Port 2/1 name set.
sw2900> (enable) set port speed 2/1 10
Port(s) 2/1 speed set to 10Mbps.
sw2900> (enable) set port duplex 2/1 half
Port(s) 2/1 set to full-duplex.
Sw2900>!!!alternately could have set all the ports to full duplex as follows
sw2900> (enable) set port duplex 1/1-2,2/1 full
Ports 1/1-2,2/1 set to full-duplex.
```

Now that the switches are configured, verify the neighboring devices from the perspective of both switches as in Example 7-7.

Example 7-7   *CDP Testing*

```
sw3512xl>show cdp neighbors
Capability Codes: R - Router, T - Trans Bridge, B - Source Route Bridge
                  S - Switch, H - Host, I - IGMP, r - Repeater
Device ID          Local Intrfce     Holdtme    Capability  Platform  Port ID
005352782(sw2900)Fas 0/11            172            T S       WS-C2900  1/1
r2                 Fas 0/12           176            R         2500      Eth 0
r3                 Fas 0/10           162            R         3640      Fas 2/0
sw2900> (enable) show cdp neighbors
Capability Codes: R - Router, T - Trans Bridge, B - Source Route Bridge
                  S - Switch, H - Host, I - IGMP, r - Repeater
Port     Device-ID            Port-ID         Platform           Capability
-------- -------------------- --------------- ------------------ ----------
 1/1     sw3512xl             FastEthernet0/11 cisco WS-C3512-XL  S
 2/1     r1                   Ethernet0        cisco 2500         R
```

Because the Physical and Data Link Layers are up and running, take a closer look at the chapter scenario. Using the same physical layout, you will assign IP addresses as required and control broadcast traffic using VLANs. I want to review a few things about VLANs before you configure them.

Why VLANs?

Many people will tell you VLANs are so darn *virtual* that you tend to lose them for no apparent reason. I'll save that discussion for the "Shooting Trouble with VLANs" section and the Trouble Tickets. To get a handle on VLANs, I want you to think about the function of a router. Physically each interface or wire is a broadcast domain, but it is more often referred to as a subnet. Traffic from one router can pass from one local interface to another because the router knows about its directly connected networks. Interrouter communications occur because of not only physical components but also because of routed and routing protocols.

Switch broadcast domains are called VLANs. By default all ports on a switch belong to VLAN1, as you can verify in Example 7-8. Other VLANs can be configured to facilitate smaller broadcast domains and smaller spanning trees. However, traffic from one VLAN cannot pass directly to another VLAN, whether within a switch or between switches, without a router of some sort.

Example 7-8   *By Default All Ports Are in VLAN1 (1 Broadcast Domain)*

```
sw3512xl#show vlan
VLAN Name                             Status    Ports
---- -------------------------------- --------- -------------------------------
1    default                          active    Fa0/1, Fa0/2, Fa0/3, Fa0/4,
                                                Fa0/5, Fa0/6, Fa0/7, Fa0/8,
                                                Fa0/9, Fa0/10, Fa0/11, Fa0/12,
                                                Gi0/1, Gi0/2
1002 fddi-default                     active
1003 token-ring-default               active
1004 fddinet-default                  active
1005 trnet-default                    active
!!!these are the default or reserved vlans
VLAN Type  SAID    MTU   Parent RingNo BridgeNo Stp  BrdgMode Trans1 Trans2
---- ----- ------- ----- ------ ------ -------- ---- -------- ------ ------
1    enet  100001  1500  -      -      -        -    -        1002   1003
1002 fddi  101002  1500  -      -      -        -    -        1      1003
1003 tr    101003  1500  1005   0      -        -    srb      1      1002
1004 fdnet 101004  1500  -      -      1        ibm  -        0      0
1005 trnet 101005  1500  -      -      1        ibm  -        0      0

sw2900> (enable) show vlan
VLAN Name                             Status    IfIndex Mod/Ports, Vlans
---- -------------------------------- --------- ------- -------------------------
1    default                          active    28      1/1-2
                                                        2/1-12
1002 fddi-default                     active    29
1003 token-ring-default               active    32
1004 fddinet-default                  active    30
1005 trnet-default                    active    31
```

Example 7-8 displays a couple of sections. The first section is a quick status of the VLANs and the associated ports on the 3512XL. The second section displays the default VLANs, including the maximum transmission unit (MTU) size and other Token Ring and FDDI parameters. The second section is not shown for the CatOS 2900, but all ports are in VLAN 1 by default. 1002 FDDI and 1003 TRCRF are reserved for FDDI and Token Ring transparent bridging; whereas 1004 FDNET and 1005 TRBRF are reserved for Token Ring and source route bridging. Although the default reserved VLANs can't be removed, they can be modified (as you can prove by trying to clear one of the defaults). If I were to type **clear vlan 1002** on the 2900 right now, for example, it would tell me that the VLAN needs to be within the range of 2 to 1000.

Understanding what VLANs are and how they work is half the battle of supporting them. Think of a physical switch or switches that are divided up into logical bridges to assist with broadcasts. Logical bridges or broadcast domains, more often referred to as VLANs, are possible within or between switches, as you can see in Figure 7-2.

NOTE   If you have more VLANs in your lab scenario, at this point you may need to clear them or delete *flash:vlan.dat* to completely remove them. My devices are in the out-of-the-box default VLAN Trunking Protocol (VTP) server mode and default to Inter-Switch Link (ISL) encapsulation. (Your equipment may vary.) You might need to change your boxes to server mode or change the encapsulation to follow along and understand.

Figure 7-2   *VLANs Are Logical Bridges*

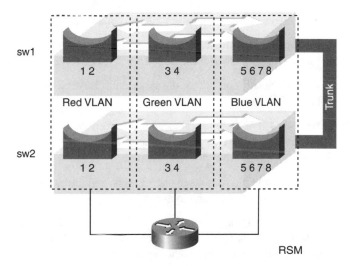

Figure 7-2 illustrates two switches where ports are logically grouped into three different VLANs: RED, GREEN, and BLUE. The RED VLAN members are able to talk to others within the same VLAN (subnet). The GREEN VLAN members are able to talk to others within the same VLAN (subnet). The BLUE VLAN members are able to talk to others within the same VLAN (subnet). Although the VLANs are isolated from one another, intra-VLAN communications can occur. Intra-VLAN traffic can occur within or between the switches because the trunk carries RED, GREEN, and BLUE VLAN traffic. However, inter-VLAN communications such as RED to GREEN, RED to BLUE, GREEN to BLUE, and so on are not possible without some Layer 3 decisions because each VLAN is a separate subnet. The Route Switch Module/Multilayer Switch Feature Card (RSM/MSFC) (router blade) in Figure 7-2 is one way of supporting VLAN-to-VLAN communications. It uses a separate physical or logical interface for each VLAN to support the inter-VLAN routing function. By logically grouping the ports on a switch or among different switches, you can virtually create separate bridges within a switch and have a router route the packets between them. Next, I want to look into some of the practical advantages to using VLANs.

VLAN Advantages

The following are some advantages of VLANs:

- **Security**—VLANs enable you to isolate groups of users. Can you imagine a student adjusting a teacher's salary because they are physically on the same network? How about health records? Police records?

- **Segment broadcasts**—If you are only talking about one particular box causing the majority of broadcast traffic, you should probably look at just isolating that box. If broadcasts come from various stations, VLANs can assist.

- **Better utilization of bandwidth**—You can separate management and control traffic from that of the end user. Smaller spanning trees help with Layer 2 convergence.

- **Reduced latency**—Smaller broadcast domains using Layer 2 devices to minimize the number of Layer 3 devices.

- **Easy to move users**—For example, a user moves from the Sales department to the Engineering department. Just associate the appropriate port with the appropriate VLAN instead of making wiring closet physical changes.

As you can see, there are multiple reasons to use VLANs, and understanding them a little better will certainly help you keep a more stable network.

Trial and error has proven that flat networks and end-to-end VLANs do not scale. Modern implementations use Layer 2 switches for the access layer and Layer 3 switches in the distribution and core layers. Regardless of the equipment, it is up to you and me to make sure end-to-end communications occur and that everyone is happy.

NOTE   Catalyst VLANs are very port-centric, and proper planning is critical to ease the maintenance thereof. For example, it is not a good VLAN design to mix control and management traffic with end-user traffic. You should analyze the various types of VLAN traffic so that you can at a minimum separate the management and control traffic from the user traffic.

VLAN Traffic Types

Types of VLAN traffic include the following:

- **Control**—Protocol traffic such as Spanning Tree Protocol (STP), CDP, Dynamic Trunking Protocol (DTP), VTP, and Port Aggregation Protocol (PAgP) typically use VLAN1.

- **End-user**—VLANs create isolation. If one workstation goes berserk, the impact is limited to the user VLAN.

- **Management**—Services such as telnet, Simple Network Management Protocol (SNMP), VLAN Membership Policy Server (VMPS), and Syslog normally use whatever VLAN that is assigned to the Supervisor Console (sc0) port.

Configuring VLANs

Planning is the most important part of VLANs. VLANs are subnets and thus are part of the IP addressing design. Often it is helpful to have a recognizable pattern. Perhaps you might use something like 10.*bldg.vlan.node*/24 with .1, .2, and .3 reserved for Hot Standby Router Protocol (HSRP) and .4 through .20 for router interfaces, servers, and printers.

NOTE   If you attach a hub to a port assigned to a VLAN, all ports on the hub are part of the VLAN.

Other things the support person should be familiar with include the fact that all ports start out in VLAN1. If you associate a port with a different VLAN and then delete that VLAN with **clear vlan #**, however, all ports associated with that VLAN will be in an *inactive* state. You can fix that by creating the VLANs again, which is much easier if you previously saved the configuration to a file. As you configure the chapter scenario, you will experience these and other VLAN advantages and disadvantages.

Start your planning and configuring using the chapter scenario VLANs in Figure 7-3. Each VLAN has a number and an associated network (such as IP or IPX). VLANs are Layer 2; however, inter-VLAN connectivity is through routers (Layer 3). Use subnet 192.168.5.16/28 for VLAN1, 192.168.5.32/28 for VLAN10, 192.168.5.48/28 for VLAN20, and subnet 192.168.5.0/30 for the serial links. Create the VLANs, associate ports, and assign IP addresses using Figure 7-3 as a guide. Assign host default gateways using the last address (not the broadcast) for each subnet. Use Table 7-2 if you need more host detail. Do *not* configure the VLAN-to-VLAN routing or trunking yet.

NOTE   Refer to Tables 7-1 and 6-7 for assistance with IOS compared to CatOS VLAN commands.

Figure 7-3   *Chapter Scenario VLANs*

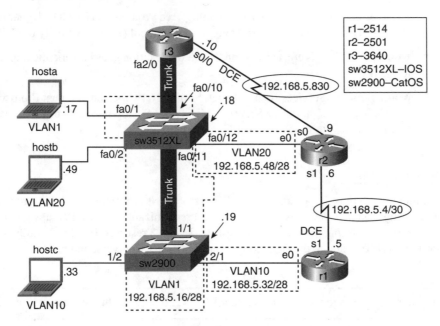

Table 7-2   *Host Configuration*

Host	IP Address	Subnet Mask	Gateway
hosta (VLAN1)	192.168.5.17	255.255.255.240	192.168.5.30
hostb (VLAN20)	192.168.5.49	255.255.255.240	192.168.5.62
hostc (VLAN10)	192.168.5.33	255.255.255.240	192.168.5.46

After your host configuration, create VLAN20 using the VLAN database mode as in Example 7-9. Pay *particular attention* that this is not performed from global configuration mode. The command to exit and apply the changes is **exit**.

Example 7-9 *Creating VLAN20 on the 3512XL (IOS)*

```
sw3512xl#vlan database
sw3512xl(vlan)#vlan 20 name vlan20
VLAN 20 added:
   Name: vlan20
sw3512xl(vlan)#?
VLAN database editing buffer manipulation commands:
  abort  Exit mode without applying the changes
  apply  Apply current changes and bump revision number
  exit   Apply changes, bump revision number, and exit mode
  no     Negate a command or set its defaults
  reset  Abandon current changes and reread current database
  show   Show database information
  vlan   Add, delete, or modify values associated with a single VLAN
  vtp    Perform VTP administrative functions.
sw3512xl(vlan)#exit
APPLY completed.
Exiting....
```

Example 7-10 continues the configuration by associating interface fa0/2 and fa0/12 with VLAN20.

Example 7-10 *Associating fa0/2 and fa0/12 with VLAN20 on the 3512XL (IOS)*

```
sw3512xl(config)#interface fastethernet 0/2
sw3512xl(config-if)#switchport ?
  access  Set access mode characteristics of the interface
  mode    Set trunking mode of the interface
  multi   Set characteristics when in multi-VLAN mode
  trunk   Set trunking characteristics of the interface
sw3512xl(config-if)#switchport access vlan 20
sw3512xl(config-if)#interface fastethernet 0/12
sw3512xl(config-if)#switchport access vlan 20
sw3512xl(config-if)#end
```

Next, verify that the ports were in fact added to VLAN20 as in Example 7-11.

Example 7-11 *Verifying the VLAN Configuration*

```
sw3512xl#show vlan
VLAN Name                             Status    Ports
---- -------------------------------- --------- -------------------------------
1    default                          active    Fa0/1, Fa0/3, Fa0/4,
                                                Fa0/5, Fa0/6, Fa0/7, Fa0/8,
                                                Fa0/9, Fa0/10, Fa0/11, Gi0/1,
                                                Gi0/2
20   vlan20                           active    Fa0/2, Fa0/12
1002 fddi-default                     active
1003 token-ring-default               active
1004 fddinet-default                  active
1005 trnet-default                    active
...
```

Don't forget to configure and verify the VLAN1 IP parameters for management purposes so that you can telnet to the device (see Example 7-12). In such a small lab scenario, VLAN 1 is fine. However, it is a better practice to use another VLAN for management purposes.

Example 7-12 *In-band Management for the 3512XL (IOS)*

```
sw3512xl(config)#interface vlan1
sw3512xl(config-if)#ip address 192.168.5.18 255.255.255.240
sw3512xl(config-if)#no shut
sw3512xl(config-if)#end
sw3512xl#copy running-config startup-config
sw3512xl#show interface vlan1
VLAN1 is up, line protocol is up
  Hardware is CPU Interface, address is 00d0.7968.8480 (bia 00d0.7968.8480)
  Internet address is 192.168.5.18/28
...
```

IOS offers Layer 3 interfaces and Layer 2 ports or switchports. To convert the interface from a routed interface to a switched port, you use the interface command **switchport mode access**. This sets the port as an access port rather than a trunk port. On many devices, the **interface range** command enables you to do this to lots of ports simultaneously **interface range 6/1-24, 7/1-12**. The command enables you to configure ports 1 through 24 on module 6 and ports 1 through 12 on module 7 all at once. These switchports default to VLAN1, but the **switchport access vlan** *vlan#* command enables you to assign the port to a particular VLAN. Because these ports are technically Layer 2 now, you can't assign an IP address to them directly. Instead, you need a separate interface to act as a routed interface for both of them. This calls for a switched virtual interface (SVI), which you created in Example 7-12 using the **interface vlan1** command. You assigned it an IP address and verified it using the **show interface vlan1** command.

Next, create VLAN10 and associate the ports as in Figure 7-3 on the CatOS-based 2900 switch as in Example 7-13.

Example 7-13 *Creating VLAN10 and Associating the Ports on the 2900 (CatOS)*

```
sw2900> (enable) set vlan 10 name vlan10
Cannot add/modify VLANs on a VTP server without a domain name.
sw2900> (enable) set vtp ?
Usage: set vtp [domain <name>] [mode <mode>] [passwd <passwd>]
               [pruning <enable ¦ disable>] [v2 <enable ¦  disable>
       (mode = client ¦  server ¦  transparent
        Use passwd '0' to clear vtp password)
Usage: set vtp pruneeligible <vlans>
       (vlans = 2..1000
        An example of vlans is 2-10,1000)
sw2900> (enable) set vtp domain donna
VTP domain donna modified
sw2900> (enable) set vlan 10 name vlan10
Vlan 10 configuration successful
sw2900> (enable) set vlan 10 1/2,2/1
VLAN 10 modified.
VLAN 1 modified.
VLAN  Mod/Ports
```

Example 7-13 *Creating VLAN10 and Associating the Ports on the 2900 (CatOS) (Continued)*

```
---- ---------------------
10    1/1-2
      2/1
sw2900> (enable) show vlan
VLAN Name                             Status    IfIndex Mod/Ports, Vlans
---- -------------------------------- --------- ------- ------------------------
1    default                          active    5       2/2-12
10   vlan10                           active    10      1/2
                                                        2/1
...
```

Notice how Example 7-13 insisted you create a VTP domain name before you could create any VLANs or associate the ports. VTP is the VLAN Trunking Protocol (discussed in more detail in the section "Managing VLANs"). Next, set up the 2900 IP parameters to allow telnet to the box. Example 7-14 illustrates how to configure the Supervisor Console.

Example 7-14 *In-band Management for the 2900 (CatOS)*

```
sw2900> (enable) set interface sc0 1 192.168.5.19 255.255.255.240
Interface sc0 vlan set, IP address and netmask set.
sw2900> (enable) set interface sc0 up
Interface sc0 administratively up.
```

After the VLAN was created, I noticed some error messages on the port in my example. However, the counters had never been cleared, so I cleared them and didn't notice any more errors. The sc0 port was used to assign the IP address to the CatOS-based switch like the SVI for the IOS-based switch. In practical application use another VLAN other than VLAN1.

As you can verify in the previous examples, making VLANs work is a multistep process. However, you only created VLANs on two switches. What if you had 500?

VLAN Membership Policy Server (VMPS)

An alternative to manual VLAN association is the dynamic VMPS. However, it is still lots of work to build the initial database, which is why many choose to just go with static VLANs. The VMPS database is a text file residing on a TFTP server. The VMPS server reads the text file and remembers the data. Dynamic VLANs then look to the VMPS server for MAC lookup when it attaches to a port. Other Catalysts are configured as VMPS clients that communicate with the server over UDP port 1589 for port-to-VLAN authorization. You then use commands such as **show vmps** and **show port** to display the dynamic ports. Two optional Cisco tools for building the database include the User Registration Tool (URT) and CiscoWorks for Switched Networks (CWSI). URT is based on NetBIOS login information and managed with CWSI. The User Tracker for CWSI keeps track of individual stations on the network and automatically populates the VMPS server. See Cisco.com or *Cisco LAN Switching* (Cisco Press) by Kennedy Clark and Kevin Hamilton for more detail on configuring dynamic VLANs. In practical application of VLANs, static VLANs are by far the most common.

The GARP Registration Protocol (GVRP) provides dynamic VLAN creation for IEEE 802.1Q-compliant VLANs. GARP stands for Generic Attribute Registration Protocol. GVRP(802.1P) is also used for standards-based VLAN pruning.

Thus far, you have worked with access links. Because they are designed for one VLAN only, they do not scale. Next, you will learn about trunking so that you see how VLANs on one switch can communicate with others in the same VLAN on another switch via a trunk port.

Trunking

Routing provides *inter-VLAN* connectivity, whereas *trunking* provides *intra-VLAN* connectivity. Trunks, whether between switches, from a router to a switch, or from a switch to a file server, minimize the number of interfaces and cables to transport multi-VLAN traffic.

There are various methods of multiplexing VLANs in trunking:

- Cisco

    — Ethernet–ISL or 802.1Q

    — FDDI–802.10

    — ATM–LAN Emulation (LANE) or multiprotocol over ATM (MPOA)

- Mixed-vendor environment

    — 802.1Q

    — LANE or MPOA

Cisco uses its own proprietary ISL and the standards-based IEEE 802.1Q for trunking. (See Figure 7-4.) However, Cisco has started to favor 802.1Q over ISL. Some newer switches such as the 2950 support only 802.1Q.

Figure 7-4   *Trunking*

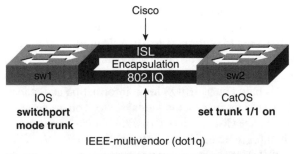

Trunking is running multiple VLANs over one connection

Go ahead and configure ISL trunking from the 3512XL to the 2900 using Example 7-15 and Figure 7-3 as guides.

Example 7-15 *Configuring Cisco ISL Trunking Between the 2900 and 3512*

```
sw3512xl(config)#interface fastethernet 0/11
sw3512xl(config-if)#switchport mode trunk
sw3512xl(config-if)#end
sw3512xl#show interfaces fastethernet 0/11 switchport
Name: Fa0/11
Switchport: Enabled
Administrative mode: trunk
Operational Mode: trunk
Administrative Trunking Encapsulation: isl
Operational Trunking Encapsulation: isl
Negotiation of Trunking: Disabled
Access Mode VLAN: 0 ((Inactive))
Trunking Native Mode VLAN: 1 (default)
Trunking VLANs Enabled: ALL
Trunking VLANs Active: 1,20
Pruning VLANs Enabled: NONE
sw3512xl#copy running-config startup-config
```

ISL is the default trunking encapsulation here, but always check the port capabilities on your particular switch to see what is actually available. Next, configure the other end of the trunk on the 2900 CatOS box as in Example 7-16.

Example 7-16 *Trunking on the 2900 CatOS*

```
sw2900> (enable)set trunk 1/1 on
Port(s) 1/1 trunk mode set to on.
sw2900> (enable) %DTP-5-TRUNKPORTON:Port 1/1 has become isl trunk
sw2900> (enable)show trunk
Port      Mode         Encapsulation  Status        Native vlan
--------  -----------  -------------  ------------  -----------
1/1       on           isl            trunking      1
Port      Vlans allowed on trunk
--------  ----------------------------------------------------------------
1/1       1-1005
Port      Vlans allowed and active in management domain
--------  ----------------------------------------------------------------
1/1       1,10
Port      Vlans in spanning tree forwarding state and not pruned
--------  ----------------------------------------------------------------
1/1
sw2900>show port capabilities 1/1
Model                     WS-X2900
Port                      1/1
Type                      100BaseTX
Speed                     100
Duplex                    half,full
Trunk encap type          ISL
Trunk mode                on,off,desirable,auto,nonegotiate
Channel                   no
```

continues

Example 7-16 *Trunking on the 2900 CatOS (Continued)*

```
Broadcast suppression    no
Flow control             no
Security                 yes
Membership               static,dynamic
Fast start               yes
Rewrite                  no
sw2900> (enable)
```

The **switchport mode trunk** IOS command turned the fa0/11 port into a trunk, which you
verified with **show interfaces fastethernet 0/11 switchport**. Besides trunking, the preceding
show command displayed encapsulation and active VLANs, too. All VLANs are allowed by
default, but you can remove VLANs with the **switchport trunk allowed vlan remove** *11-1000*
command; the numbers at the end are the VLANs you want to remove. The commands were
different for the CatOS 2900, but the effect was the same. The **show port capabilities**
command is quite helpful to know what the port is capable of in terms of speed, duplex,
encapsulation, and trunking.

NOTE   Notice the shaded output about DTP, which is a trunk negotiation protocol. The XL switches
do not yet support DTP, so the switch on the other end of the trunk link must be manually set
to trunk.

Save your configurations and then experiment for a moment. Bounce (**shut/no shut**) fa0/11 on
the 3512. Verify your VTP status on both switches as in Example 7-17. Look at your VLANs
again in Example 7-18.

Example 7-17 *The Result of Bouncing an Interface*

```
sw3512xl#copy running-config startup-config
sw3512xl(config)#interface fastethernet 0/11
sw3512xl(config-if)#shut
sw3512xl(config-if)#no shut
sw3512xl(config-if)#end
sw3512xl#show vtp status
VTP Version                     : 2
Configuration Revision          : 1
Maximum VLANs supported locally : 254
Number of existing VLANs        : 6
VTP Operating Mode              : Server
VTP Domain Name                 : donna
VTP Pruning Mode                : Disabled
VTP V2 Mode                     : Disabled
VTP Traps Generation            : Disabled
MD5 digest                      : 0x1F 0xAF 0x58 0x06 0x31 0x48 0x80 0xD9
Configuration last modified by 0.0.0.0 at 5-26-02 12:34:06
sw3512xl#!!!the vtp domain name is donna yet you only set it on the 2900
```

Example 7-17 *The Result of Bouncing an Interface (Continued)*

```
sw2900> (enable)show vtp domain
Domain Name                            Domain Index VTP Version Local Mode  Password
------------------------------------- ------------ ----------- ----------- ----------
donna                                  1            2           server      -
...
```

Example 7-18 *Verifying VLANs*

```
sw2900> (enable)show vlan
VLAN Name                             Status    IfIndex Mod/Ports, Vlans
---- ------------------------------- --------- ------- ------------------------
1    default                         active    28      2/2-12
10   vlan10                          active    10      1/2
                                                       2/1
...
sw3512xl#show vlan
VLAN Name                             Status    Ports
--- -------------------------------- --------- -------------------------------
1    default                         active    Fa0/1, Fa0/2, Fa0/3, Fa0/4,
                                               Fa0/5, Fa0/6, Fa0/7, Fa0/8,
                                               Fa0/9, Fa0/10, Gi0/1, Gi0/2
10   vlan10                          active
1002 fddi-default                    active
1003 token-ring-default              active
1004 fddinet-default                 active
1005 trnet-default                   active
```

You are not imagining things. Some of your VLANs disappeared. VLAN10 is on both switches, but VLAN20 totally disappeared. Both switches are in the VTP server mode and use revision numbers to track changes; thus the highest revision number wins. Certainly what happened here is not what you want to happen in a practical environment. It is recommended to have all transparent or a series of client/server boxes in your network. The penalty for using transparent mode is that you need to manually create your VLANs on all your switches. The section "Managing VLANs" discusses VTP in more detail.

Change the 3512XL to *transparent* mode, configure VLAN20 once again, and verify your configuration as in Example 7-19.

Example 7-19 *Changing the 3512 to Transparent Mode*

```
sw3512xl#vlan database
sw3512xl(vlan)#vtp transparent
Setting device to VTP TRANSPARENT mode.
sw3512xl(vlan)#exit
APPLY completed.
Exiting....
sw3512xl(vlan)#vtp transparent
Device mode already VTP TRANSPARENT.
sw3512xl(vlan)#vlan 20 name vlan20
VLAN 20 added:
```

continues

Example 7-19 *Changing the 3512 to Transparent Mode (Continued)*

```
     Name: vlan20
sw3512xl(vlan)#exit
APPLY completed.
Exiting....
sw3512xl#show vlan
VLAN Name                             Status    Ports
---- -------------------------------- --------- -------------------------------
1    default                          active    Fa0/1, Fa0/3, Fa0/4, Fa0/5, Fa0/6,
                                                 Fa0/7, Fa0/8, Fa0/9, Gi0/1, Gi0/2
10   vlan10                           active
20   vlan20                           active    Fa0/2, Fa0/12
...
sw3512xl#copy running-config startup-config
```

Note that fa0/2 and fa0/12 are the active ports for VLAN20. The port association was automatic because it was there before. Now view the VLANs on the 2900 in Example 7-20.

Example 7-20 *Viewing the VLANs on the 2900*

```
sw2900> (enable)show vlan
VLAN Name                             Status    IfIndex Mod/Ports, Vlans
---- -------------------------------- --------- ------- ------------------------
1    default                          active    28      2/2-12
10   vlan10                           active    33      1/2,2/1
...
```

Perform a **shut/no shut** on interface fa0/11 once again and verify your VLANs as in Example 7-21.

Example 7-21 *Verifying VLANs*

```
sw3512xl(config)#interface fastethernet 0/11
sw3512xl(config-if)#shut
sw3512xl(config-if)#no shut
sw3512xl(config-if)#end
sw3512xl#show vlan
VLAN Name                             Status    Ports
---- -------------------------------- --------- -------------------------------
1    default                          active    Fa0/1, Fa0/3, Fa0/4,
                                                 Fa0/5, Fa0/6, Fa0/7, Fa0/8,
                                                 Fa0/9, Fa0/10, Gi0/1, Gi0/2
10   vlan10                           active
20   vlan20                           active    Fa0/2, Fa0/12
...
sw2900> (enable)show vlan
VLAN Name                             Status    IfIndex Mod/Ports, Vlans
---- -------------------------------- --------- ------- ------------------------
1    default                          active    28      2/2-12
10   vlan10                           active    10      1/2
                                                         2/1
...
```

It is correct that the 3512XL shows both VLANs because it previously learned about VLAN10 via VTP from the 2900, when it was in server mode. It is also correct that the 2900 only displays VLAN10 because VLAN20 was created in the 3512XL while it was in transparent mode (so VLAN20 did not get propagated throughout the VTP domain).

Now that your switches are in a more stable state, the VLANs are configured, and the ISL trunking is passing VTP information, I want to continue discussing other trunking methods.

NOTE   You *cannot* route from VLAN to VLAN for a couple of reasons at this point, but I will revisit that issue and more VTP management details soon.

Inter-Switch Link (ISL)

ISL is a Cisco proprietary VLAN tagging method that is used only for point-to-point connections on equipment that supports ISL trunking. For that matter, *any* trunk must be point-to-point. Although 100 Mbps or better is recommended, the specifications support 10 Mbps, too. You set your trunks to ISL encapsulation. (Actually, that was the default for the lab scenario switches.)

When a frame goes out an ISL trunk, it gets encapsulated by tagging it with a 26-byte ISL header and another 4-byte cyclical redundancy check (CRC) trailer. Therefore it is possible for an ISL frame to be $1518 + 30 = 1548$ bytes, also known as a "baby giant." ISL trunks can carry not only Ethernet traffic, but also Token Ring and FDDI due to the *reserved field* in the ISL header.

Previously, you had to manually configure ISL on both ends, but DTP allows the switch to negotiate trunking. Frames are sent out every 30 seconds through the same multicast MAC as CDP but with a different Subnetwork Access Protocol (SNAP) value. The trunk modes for use with the **set trunk** *mod#/port# mode* command are on, off, desirable, auto, and nonegotiate. Do you recall the DTP message when you set the trunk on the 2900. Look back at Example 7-16 to review it now. DTP enhances the older Dynamic Inter-Switch Link (DISL) functionality in that it negotiates trunking for not only ISL, but also IEEE 802.1Q.

Because negotiation is in progress, there is room for negotiation not to occur. Things are fine when the results are on/on because both ends are trunking. If the result is off/off, you probably are looking at an access link and not a trunk. It is when you end up with on/off or off/on that you need to investigate the settings. Normally, desirable or auto on one side with the other side of the trunk set to on works just fine. Consider hard coding your critical links.

Whether negotiated or hard coded, by default all VLANs can use the trunk. Create another VLAN on the 2900 and set some trunk restrictions as in Example 7-22.

Example 7-22 *Trunk Restrictions*

```
sw2900> (enable)set vlan 100
Vlan 100 configuration successful
sw2900> (enable)show trunk
Port      Mode          Encapsulation Status        Native vlan
--------  ------------  ------------  ------------  -----------
 1/1      on            isl           trunking      1
Port      Vlans allowed on trunk
--------  -------------------------------------------------------------
 1/1      1-1005
Port      Vlans allowed and active in management domain
--------  -------------------------------------------------------------
 1/1      1,10,100
Port      Vlans in spanning tree forwarding state and not pruned
--------  -------------------------------------------------------------
 1/1      1,10
sw2900> (enable)clear trunk ?
Usage: clear trunk <mod/ports...> [vlans...]
       (An example of mod/ports is 1/1,2/1-12,3/1-2,4/1-12
       vlans = 2..1005
       An example of vlans is 2-10,1005)
sw2900> (enable)clear trunk 1/1 100
Removing Vlan(s) 100 from allowed list.
Port 1/1 allowed vlans modified to 1-99,101-1005.
```

Another method of controlling which VLANS are allowed is the **set trunk** *mod#/port#* **?**
command. Available options include the following:

```
Usage: set trunk <mod_num/port_num> [on | off | desirable | auto | nonegotiate] [vlans]
                  [trunk_type]
     (vlans = 1..1005
      An example of vlans is 2-10,1005)
     (trunk_type = isl,dot1q,dot10,lane,negotiate)
```

Example 7-23 illustrates first using CatOS and then using IOS for trunk restrictions.

Example 7-23 *Trunk Restrictions*

```
sw2900> (enable)!!!CatOS Example
sw2900> (enable)set trunk 1/1 on ?
Usage: set trunk <mod_num/port_num> [on ¦ off ¦ desirable ¦ auto ¦ nonegotiate]
[vlans]
                                     [trunk_type]
       (vlans = 1..1005
        An example of vlans is 2-10,1005)
       (trunk_type = isl,dot1q,dot10,lane,negotiate)
sw2900> (enable)
sw3512xl#!!!IOS Example
sw3512xl(config-if)#switchport trunk allowed vlan ?
  WORD    VLAN IDs of the allowed VLANs when this port is in trunking mode
  add     add VLANs to the current list
  all     all VLANs
  except  all VLANs except the following
  remove  remove VLANs from the current list
```

Because the chapter scenario equipment you are using is all Cisco and uses ISL, that has been the focus thus far. However, dot1Q provides multivendor support.

IEEE 802.1Q (dot1Q)

Unlike ISL, IEEE 802.1Q offers multivendor support. As shown in Figure 7-5, ISL is more of an encapsulation (external tagging) method, whereas 802.1Q is an internal frame tagging method of VLAN identification.

Figure 7-5 *ISL Encapsulation and 802.1Q Frame Tagging*

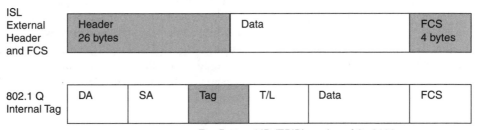

802.1Q also allows prioritization of traffic using the Priority field within the 802.1Q tag. ISL has three COS bits as well; they automatically map to the IP TOS field. 802.3ac extends Ethernet's frame size to 1522 bytes to allow for the internal tag. Obviously, equipment that doesn't understand these so-called baby giant frames complains.

802.1Q allows VLAN values up to 4095, but the Catalyst may only allow up to 1005, so in a mixed environment it is best practice to not go above 1005.

Configuring 802.1Q on the Catalyst is as easy as using the following command:

```
set trunk mod#/port# [on | desirable | auto | nonegotiate] dot1q
```

Using the commands from the ISL section, check your hardware and IOS version to see whether your environment supports ISL, 802.1Q, or both. Although my lab switches default to ISL, there are many switches that default to the dot1Q standard.

EtherChannel is another method of combining multiple segments into one that I briefly mention in the next subsection. Normally if you have multiple parallel connections between the same two switches, you would pass traffic on only one of them. (STP would put the others into blocking state, and they would provide redundancy but no performance advantage.) With EtherChannel, STP treats the aggregate bundle of connections as one logical connection and the individual ports are in forwarding state.

EtherChannel

EtherChannel combines multiple Fast or Gigabit segments where the speeds match into groups of two, four, or eight. However, some switches and cards are less restrictive than others with the way bandwidth is aggregated. On the Cat6000 family, for instance, you can load share traffic on a source/destination IP address basis, in addition to the regular source and destination MAC method. Use the **show module** command to see whether your switch supports EtherChannel frame distribution so that you can decide whether MAC or IP load sharing is best for your environment.

The EtherChannel group is known by one MAC address: that of the primary link. The primary link is the link with the lowest MAC address, and it is used for control messages and monitoring. Recovery is very important. If the primary link dies, what happens? In the past, the whole group would die. Now, in 4 kbps, 5 kbps, and 6 kbps switches, the link with the next lowest MAC address takes over. In XL-based switches, the link with the lowest utilization at that moment takes over. In the 1900s, you can only have two links in an EtherChannel, so the one left is alone. The bundles can be configured as an EtherChannel trunk. Then when you configure any port in the channel, it applies to all ports. Cisco created the PAgP for channel negotiation with auto and desirable modes.

- If two ports are desirable, they trunk in EtherChannel.
- Auto and desirable trunk in EtherChannel.
- Auto and auto do not trunk because they never negotiate.

You might run across the terms Fast EtherChannel (FEC) and Gigabit EtherChannel (BEC), which are faster Ethernet technologies leveraging off of the link aggregation provided via EtherChannel.

Table 7-3 provides the basic commands to configure EtherChannel. For a more exhaustive list that pertains to additional devices, refer to Cisco.com.

Table 7-3 *Configuring EtherChannel*

CatOS	IOS

set port channel *mod#/ports* [*admin group*]
 	
 set port channel *mod#/port#* **mode**
 [**on|off|desirable|auto**] [**silent|non-silent**]
	interface fa0/1
	   port group 1
	 interface fa0/2
	   port group 1

On MSFC:
 interface vlan1
   ip address 10.10.1.252 255.255.255.0
	interface vlan 1
	   ip address 10.10.1.253 255.255.255.0

set port channel all distribution
   {**ip|mac**}[**source|destination|both**]
	interface fa0/1
	   port group 1 distribution ?

show channel group **show channel cost** **show channel**	**show etherchannel** [**summary**] **show interfaces etherchannel**

If you want to set it up, you could certainly connect the 1900 up to the 2900 or 3512XL to experiment in your lab. However, be careful with switches, such as the XL series, that do not support PAgP. It is recommended to disable the ports on both ends and create the port channel on the XL switch first. Next, create the port channel and set the mode on the CatOS box; then you can re-enable the ports. (The rest of this chapter and the Trouble Tickets do not assume that EtherChannel is configured, however.)

Other Trunking

Other trunking methods are beyond the scope of the book, but are important to you if you are using FDDI or ATM. To enable multiple VLANs to use an FDDI ring, 802.10 encapsulation is available. On the router, the encapsulation type is sde. On the Catalyst, set the VLAN type to FDDI as you create your VLAN, as follows:

set vlan *vlan#* **type fddi**

When you create an FDDI VLAN, the switch adds 100,000 to your VLAN number to arrive at a security association identifier (SAID). Verify the SAID with the **show vlan** command. Catalyst switches also support LANE and MPOA for ATM trunking.

Obviously VLANs are great in that they assist with broadcast domains to help localize traffic. Also, VLANs enable you to use more switches and fewer routers. If not set up and managed properly, however, VLANs result in broken networks. Common issues may include incorrect VTP modes (vanishing VLANs), addressing, access or trunk ports, encapsulation, and STP.

Managing VLANs

This section further discusses topics such as STP and VTP and how they affect your VLANs. For example, it wasn't too inspiring to lose your VLANs earlier, but it's better to have this happen in a lab than in a practical environment. Understanding VTP is critical to your success in supporting VLANs. Using the default of every switch being in the VTP server mode is chaotic to say the least. At most, only a few switches should be in the VTP server mode with many clients. Alternatively, configure them all as transparent mode. You previously learned how to control which VLANs are allowed on a trunk. Now you will optimize and control VLANs with pruning.

NOTE   An excellent tech note at Cisco.com is www.cisco.com/warp/public/473/103.html. It is titled "Best Practices for Catalyst 4000, 5000, and 6000 Series Switch Configuration and Management," and that it is.

STP and VLANs

The Spanning Tree Protocol was a topic in Chapter 6. However, now that you have looked at VLANs, you must go back and revisit how STP works with VLANs in place. The initial release of IEEE 802.1Q only specified a single instance of STP. However, Cisco's PVST stands for Per VLAN STP, which means just what it says: small spanning trees. With PVST+, Cisco allows PVST and Mono Spanning Tree (MST) regions to interoperate. Between PVST and PVST+, the mapping of spanning trees is one-to-one. Between MST and PVST+, the MST spanning tree maps to one only PVST in the PVST+ region. The default mapping for the Common Spanning Tree (CST) is the PVST of VLAN1, which is the native VLAN. MST is actually IEEE 802.1s, which is a form of IEEE 802.1w (RSTP) that some Catalysts support via the **set spantree mode mst** and **set spantree mst ?** commands.

Helpful CatOS spanning tree commands include the following:

- **show spantree ?**
- **show spantree** *mod#/port#*
- **show spantree** *vlan#* [**active**]
- **show spantree summary**
- **show spantree blockedports**
- **show spantree statistics**

Review the IOS spanning-tree show commands with **show spanning-tree ?**. Example 7-24 reviews the shortcut commands for viewing STP on the CatOS. When you do not specify a VLAN, the native VLAN1 is assumed.

Example 7-24 *Cisco's PVST*

```
sw2900> show spant
VLAN 1
Spanning tree enabled
Spanning tree type           ieee
Designated Root              00-10-ff-e5-14-00
Designated Root Priority     32768
Designated Root Cost         0
Designated Root Port         1/0
Root Max Age   20 sec    Hello Time 2  sec   Forward Delay 15 sec
Bridge ID MAC ADDR           00-10-ff-e5-14-00
Bridge ID Priority           32768
Bridge Max Age 20 sec    Hello Time 2  sec   Forward Delay 15 sec
Port      Vlan  Port-State    Cost   Priority  Fast-Start  Group-Method
--------- ----  ------------  -----  --------  ----------  ------------
  1/1      1    forwarding       19        32  disabled
  2/2      1    not-connected   100        32  disabled
  2/3      1    not-connected   100        32  disabled
  2/4      1    not-connected   100        32  disabled
  2/5      1    not-connected   100        32  disabled
  2/6      1    not-connected   100        32  disabled
  2/7      1    not-connected   100        32  disabled
```

Example 7-24 *Cisco's PVST (Continued)*

```
2/8      1     not-connected   100      32   disabled
2/9      1     not-connected   100      32   disabled
2/10     1     not-connected   100      32   disabled
2/11     1     not-connected   100      32   disabled
2/12     1     not-connected   100      32   disabled

sw2900>  show spant 10
VLAN 10
Spanning tree enabled
Spanning tree type          ieee
Designated Root             00-10-ff-e5-14-09
Designated Root Priority    32768
Designated Root Cost        0
Designated Root Port        1/0
Root Max Age   20 sec    Hello Time 2  sec   Forward Delay 15 sec
Bridge ID MAC ADDR          00-10-ff-e5-14-09
Bridge ID Priority          32768
Bridge Max Age 20 sec    Hello Time 2  sec   Forward Delay 15 sec
Port     Vlan Port-State    Cost   Priority Fast-Start Group-Method
-------- ---- ------------- ----- -------- ---------- ------------
1/1      10   forwarding       19       32   disabled
1/2      10   forwarding       19       32   disabled
2/1      10   forwarding      100       32   disabled
sw2900>  show spant 20
VLAN 20 does not exist.
```

Example 7-25 illustrates the shortcut commands for viewing STP on the IOS. Note again that VLAN1 is the default if not specified. Only a few ports are shown in the output, but remember that the interface is the actual interface on the box and the port number in parentheses is the way the interface was logically calculated for STP purposes.

Example 7-25 *Cisco's PVST*

```
sw3512xl#show span
Spanning tree 1 is executing the IEEE compatible Spanning Tree protocol
  Bridge Identifier has priority 32768, address 00d0.7968.8480
  Configured hello time 2, max age 20, forward delay 15
  Current root has priority 32768, address 0010.ffe5.1400
  Root port is 24, cost of root path is 19
  Topology change flag not set, detected flag not set, changes 25
  Times:  hold 1, topology change 35, notification 2
          hello 2, max age 20, forward delay 15
  Timers: hello 0, topology change 0, notification 0

Interface Fa0/1 (port 13) in Spanning tree 1 is FORWARDING
  Port path cost 19, Port priority 128
  Designated root has priority 32768, address 0010.ffe5.1400
  Designated bridge has priority 32768, address 00d0.7968.8480
  Designated port is 13, path cost 19
  Timers: message age 0, forward delay 0, hold 0
  BPDU: sent 26610, received 0
  The port is in the portfast mode
```

continues

Example 7-25   *Cisco's PVST (Continued)*

```
sw3512xl#show spanning-tree vlan 10
Spanning tree 10 is executing the IEEE compatible Spanning Tree protocol
  Bridge Identifier has priority 32768, address 00d0.7968.8481
  Configured hello time 2, max age 20, forward delay 15
  Current root has priority 32768, address 0010.ffe5.1409
  Root port is 24, cost of root path is 19
  Topology change flag not set, detected flag not set, changes 15
  Times:  hold 1, topology change 35, notification 2
          hello 2, max age 20, forward delay 15
  Timers: hello 0, topology change 0, notification 0

Interface Fa0/10 (port 23) in Spanning tree 10 is FORWARDING
   Port path cost 19, Port priority 128
   Designated root has priority 32768, address 0010.ffe5.1409
   Designated bridge has priority 32768, address 00d0.7968.8481
   Designated port is 23, path cost 19
   Timers: message age 0, forward delay 0, hold 0
   BPDU: sent 186213, received 0

sw3512xl#show spanning-tree vlan 20
Spanning tree 20 is executing the IEEE compatible Spanning Tree protocol
  Bridge Identifier has priority 32768, address 00d0.7968.8482
  Configured hello time 2, max age 20, forward delay 15
  We are the root of the spanning tree
  Topology change flag not set, detected flag not set, changes 9
  Times:  hold 1, topology change 35, notification 2
          hello 2, max age 20, forward delay 15
  Timers: hello 0, topology change 0, notification 0
```

Show the spanning tree for each VLAN on each switch in your lab to get comfortable with STP and VLANs. Look back at Example 6-36 in the preceding chapter to review the STP port states in action, and be sure to review the best practices section. Feel free also to repeat any of the STP exercises from the preceding chapter with your current configuration.

It is a common practice to distribute your VLAN traffic across redundant trunk links, and there are many ways to accomplish that. Ideally you should plan your root bridges where you can using the CatOS **set spantree priority** *pri#* [*vlan#*] command or the IOS **spanning-tree priority** *vlan#* command and take advantage of Fast or Gigabit EtherChannel. Other STP tuning methods include STP path cost (**set spantree portvlancost**), which works with trunks from the same or a different switch and STP port priority (**set spantree portvlanpri**), which only works with both trunks on the same switch. Higher priority is given to lower values, such that a port priority of 20 would carry the VLANs over a particular trunk because it is less than the default of 128. To configure VLAN 100, 102, and 104 to use the fa0/1 trunk under the trunk interface, use the following command:

```
spanning-tree vlan 100 102 104 port-priority 20
```

Whereas the following command would allow the fa0/2 trunk to carry VLAN 101, 103, and 105:

```
spanning-tree vlan 101 103 105 port-priority 20
```

With the port cost method, the commands are as follows:

```
spanning-tree vlan 100 102 104 cost 30
spanning-tree vlan 101 103 105 cost 30
```

On one trunk, for example, you could set this command for all your even VLANs and on another trunk, you could set this for all your odd VLANs to help share the load between the trunks. This increases throughput capacity and offers fault tolerance for it; if one of the trunks fails, the other handles all the traffic.

Certainly, by now you are comfortable with CatOS and IOS differences, such as the fact that anything that starts with **spanning-tree** is IOS, whereas the CatOS equivalent is **set spantree**. If not, use the help (**?**) on both platforms and all the CatOS/IOS command tables in Part III of this book, "Supporting Ethernet, Switches, and VLANs," to work your way through anything.

VLAN Trunking Protocol (VTP)

VTP is a Cisco proprietary Layer 2 multicast messaging protocol that can make VLAN administration easy or put you in a state of misery depending on how you look at it. You got a taste of that in the chapter scenario with both switches being in the server mode. VTP enables you to create a VLAN and have it propagate to other switches within the same domain. VTP transmits messages according to the VTP mode. From a practical sense, VTP is what saves you and me from going to each and every switch to create VLANs. See Table 7-4 for VTP operating modes.

NOTE	VTP has nothing to do with encapsulation or trunking; it is a communications protocol to distribute VLAN information across a common management domain. VTP messages are encapsulated inside of a trunking protocol frame such as ISL or 802.1Q.

Table 7-4   *VTP Modes*

VTP Mode	Description	Storage
Server*	Just as it sounds, it sources and listens for VTP messages. Create, modify, and delete VLANs within a management domain.	NVRAM.
Transparent	Does not source or listen for VTP messages but does propagate those of neighbor switches. Create, modify, and delete VLANs, but they are locally significant to the switch.	NVRAM.
Client*	Processes and listens for VTP messages. Cannot create, modify, or delete VLANs.	Information is not stored in NVRAM.

*When VTP clients or servers receive a message with the VTP multicast address of 01000cccccccc and a SNAP value of hex 2003, they process it according to revision numbers.

Assign a CatOS-based switch to a VTP domain using the following command: **set vtp domain** *vtpname*. (It is cAsE sEnSiTiVe). This can help divide a large network into smaller management domains. The command on an IOS-based switch is **vtp domain** *vtpname* in the VLAN database mode.

NOTE   If you change the domain name on one of the switches to something different and create VLAN30 on each switch, VLAN30 is VLAN30 regardless of the VTP name. This is true because the VTP domain name is not in the frame, only the number. Remember the type of frame here is Ethernet, and the protocols are IP and VTP.

Now you might be saying to yourself, "I have VLANs but I am not using VTP." Well, I guess that is your decision to run around and create the same VLAN on every switch or do everything in the transparent mode because you worry about losing your VLANs. For small networks, that actually is a pretty good approach. On the other hand, the larger your network, the more rational you have to be with automating VLAN propagation by using VTP. This gets into a design issue, questioning how far VLANs should sprawl across the topology. Cisco now concurs that flatter is not necessarily better, so a given VLAN should not need to exist in very many switches. In this chapter, I hope you are experiencing the things that many people tend to experience first on live networks. Obviously, that is not the best time to learn VTP.

NOTE   Routers do not participate in VTP, so they ignore VTP messages and discard them at the router interface. Only trunk-enabled adjacent switches in the server or client mode actually pay attention to VTP messages.

VTP advantages are as follows:

- VLAN consistency throughout a management domain
- Less manual configuration for creating and deleting VLANs, but you still need to associate the ports at each device
- More control and security through a VTP domain name and passwords
- Limits the extent of VTP message propagation

Take a few minutes and compare the VTP header in Figure 7-6 to Table 7-5.

Table 7-5   *VTP Header*

ISL	802.3	LLC AAAA03	SNAP 00000C VTP 2003	CRC
26 bytes	14	3	5	4

Figure 7-6 *Sniffing VTP*

Sniffer clearly displays the Data Link Control (DLC), Logical Link Control (LLC), SNAP, and VTP headers. If you want to capture this on your own, remember to turn port monitoring on for the trunk and output the data to hosta, where the protocol analyzer is running. Make sure that VTP debug events are on and wait for the next VTP log message to appear on the console before you stop Sniffer as in Example 7-26. It is also helpful to make sure that you have the correct time and that logging and debug time stamps are turned on.

Example 7-26 *Monitoring VTP Messages*

```
sw3512XL(config)#service timestamps debug datetime localtime msec
sw3512XL(config)#service timestamps log datetime localtime msec
sw3512XL(config)#end
sw3512XL#clear counters
sw3512XL#clear log
sw3512xl#debug sw-vlan vtp events
vtp events debugging is on
sw3512xl#configure terminal
sw3512xl(config)#interface fastethernet 0/1
sw3512xl(config-if)#port monitor fastethernet 0/11
sw3512xl(config-if)#end
sw3512xl#show port monitor
Monitor Port            Port Being Monitored
--------------------    --------------------
FastEthernet0/1         FastEthernet0/11
sw3512xl#show log
Syslog logging: enabled (0 messages dropped, 0 flushes, 0 overruns)
    Console logging: level debugging, 332 messages logged
```

continues

Example 7-26 *Monitoring VTP Messages (Continued)*

```
        Monitor logging: level debugging, 0 messages logged
        Trap logging: level informational, 67 message lines logged
        File logging: disabled
        Buffer logging: level debugging, 332 messages logged
Log Buffer (4096 bytes):
ARENT MODE (nc = false)
VTP LOG RUNTIME: Relaying packet received on trunk Fa0/11 -
    in TRANSPARENT MODE (nc = false)

...
sw3512xl#show vlan brief
VLAN Name                             Status    Ports
---- -------------------------------- --------- -------------------------------
1    default                          active    Fa0/1, Fa0/3, Fa0/4,
                                                Fa0/5, Fa0/6, Fa0/7, Fa0/8,
                                                Fa0/9, Fa0/10, Gi0/1, Gi0/2

10   vlan10                           active
20   vlan20                           active    Fa0/12, Fa0/12
1002 fddi-default                     active
1003 token-ring-default               active
1004 fddinet-default                  active
1005 trnet-default                    active
```

VTP messages always travel over the default VLAN. Figure 7-6 is an example of a VTP summary advertisement. Refer to Table 7-5 for VTP header information and Table 7-6 for VTP message types.

The Summary Pane and DLC header of Figure 7-6 show the destination MAC address of 01000CCCCCCC. LLC uses AA to indicate that the SNAP header follows. The SNAP header includes Cisco as a vendor/OUI with a type of 2003 for VTP. The VTP header includes such fields as the protocol version, a message type of 0x01 for the summary advertisement, the management domain size and name, any padding, the configuration revision number, the updater identity IP address, a time stamp, and an MD5 digest hash value.

Table 7-6 *VTP Message Types*

Message	Description
Summary advertisements	Issued by servers and clients every 5 minutes.
	If higher revision number, the receiving switch issues an advertisement request for the new VLAN information.
	Fields include version, type, number of subnet advertisement messages, domain name length, managed domain name, configuration revision number, updater identity, update time stamp, and MD5 digest.
Subset advertisements	Issued due to changes such as creating, suspending, activating, renaming, or changing the MTU of a VLAN.
	One or more advertisements depending on how many VLANs.
Advertisement requests	When device hears of higher revision number, it asks for it.
VTP join messages	For pruning.

The command **show vtp statistics** is used to track VTP activity, as you can verify in Example 7-27. You can compare the statistics to the VTP message types in Table 7-6 to see how many of each message type have been sent. Keep an eye on the "Number of config digest errors"; unless you have other transmit-type errors, it is a good indication that someone is trying to hack in and corrupt things.

Revision numbers are critical in the VTP server mode, but *not* used in the transparent mode. They range from 0 to 2,147,483,648. The **set vtp domain name** command is a quick way to reset the counter to 0 without having to make too many changes. *Remember this* when you are adding new switches into your environment.

The same version of VTP is needed throughout the management domain. VTP version 2 includes such functionality as Token Ring and various consistency checks. You can turn on version 2 with the **set vtp v2 enable** command and verify it with **show vtp domain**.

Example 7-27 *VTP Statistics on IOS*

```
sw3512xl>show vtp ?
  counters   VTP statistics
  status     VTP domain status
VTP LOG RUNTIME: Relaying packet received on trunk Fa0/11 -
    in TRANSPARENT MODE (nc = false)
sw3512xl>show vtp counters
VTP statistics:
Summary advertisements received   : 8
Subset advertisements received    : 1
Request advertisements received   : 0
Summary advertisements transmitted : 1
Subset advertisements transmitted  : 1
Request advertisements transmitted : 0
Number of config revision errors  : 0
Number of config digest errors    : 0
Number of V1 summary errors       : 0
VTP pruning statistics:
Trunk           Join Transmitted Join Received    Summary advts received from
                                                  non-pruning-capable device
--------------- ---------------- ---------------- ---------------------------
Fa0/11                1                0                0

sw3512xl>show vtp status
VTP Version                   : 2
Configuration Revision        : 0
Maximum VLANs supported locally : 254
Number of existing VLANs      : 7
VTP Operating Mode            : Transparent
VTP Domain Name               : donna
VTP Pruning Mode              : Disabled
VTP V2 Mode                   : Disabled
VTP Traps Generation          : Disabled
MD5 digest                    : 0x5F 0xFF 0xAC 0x3D 0xF9 0x1B 0x60 0x4B
Configuration last modified by 192.168.5.18 at 12-5-02 03:25:47
```

Example 7-27 displays the IOS VTP commands, and Example 7-28 illustrates the same for CatOS.

Example 7-28 *VTP Statistics on CatOS*

```
sw2900> show vtp ?
Show vtp commands:
----------------------------------------------------------------------------
show vtp domain          Show VTP domain information
show vtp help            Show this message
show vtp statistics      Show VTP statistics

sw2900> show vtp domain
Domain Name                          Domain Index VTP Version Local Mode  Password
------------------------------------ ------------ ----------- ----------- ----------
donna                                1            2           server      -
Vlan-count Max-vlan-storage Config Revision Notifications
---------- ---------------- --------------- -------------
6          1023             1               disabled
Last Updater    V2 Mode  Pruning  PruneEligible on Vlans
--------------- -------- -------- ------------------------
0.0.0.0         disabled disabled 2-1000

sw2900> show vtp statistics
VTP statistics:
summary advts received          0
subset  advts received          0
request advts received          0
summary advts transmitted       255
subset  advts transmitted       1
request advts transmitted       0
No of config revision errors    0
No of config digest errors      0
VTP pruning statistics:
Trunk     Join Transmitted  Join Received  Summary advts received from
                                           non-pruning-capable device
--------  ----------------- -------------- --------------------------
 1/1      0                 0              0
```

The Example 7-28 output ends with displaying that the 2900 in the lab is a non-pruning-capable device. Just like you need to prune your plants as they grow, you should prune your VLANs, too.

VTP Pruning

Bridges and switches are inherently designed to flood multicast or broadcast frames as well as frames that they don't know what to do with. With VLANs, however, you can minimize this flooding in more ways than one. For example, back in the "Trunking" section, you restricted VLANs from crossing a trunk with the CatOS **clear trunk** *vlan#* command and the **switchport trunk allowed** or **remove** command on IOS switches.

You can also configure VTP pruning so that unless a frame needs to cross a trunk to get to a switch belonging to the same VLAN, it doesn't. This is kind of like throwing a bridge into VTP. Use the following CatOS commands for pruning:

- **set vtp pruning enable**
- **clear vtp pruneeligible** *vlanrange*
- **set vtp pruneeligible** *vlanrange*
- **sh vtp domain** (to check pruning results)

NOTE   The default VLANs are not pruning-eligible. As previously mentioned, GVRP is the IEEE standard way of pruning.

I have mentioned quite a bit of information on VLANs. Take a few minutes to review some of the most important commands back in Table 7-1 and throughout the chapter before you continue. You may also find it helpful to review Table 6-7, Catalyst OS and IOS commands, and commands from the quick troubleshooting checklists from the preceding chapter, too.

In summary, there are three main steps for working VLANs:

1   Define and create a VTP domain:

set vtp domain *name* (up to 32 characters, cAsE sEnSiTiVe)

show vtp domain

Only trunk-connected switches learn the VTP domain, unless of course they were already configured with another VTP domain.

DTP includes the VTP domain name in the trunk negotiation, so two different domain names will not trunk.

Set the mode to server, transparent, or client. However, the domain name is *not required* if in transparent mode.

2   Create the VLAN.

3   Associate ports with the VLAN.

Now that you understand the requirements for intra-VLAN connectivity, I want to spend some time with how you can use routers to enable you to communicate from one VLAN to another.

Inter-VLAN Routing

There are three different ways to perform inter-VLAN routing. If you have the luxury of an 8500 or 12000 GSR, assigning an individual port to each VLAN is an optimal solution. If not, you can trunk between a switch and a Fast Ethernet router interface by taking advantage of subinterfaces. Alternatively, RSMs on Cat5000/5500 or MSFCs on Cat6000/6500 work just fine. This means you are inserting a router on a card into a Catalyst slot in which you session into the module number. My lab hardware lends itself more toward the router-on-a-stick approach. If you are using one of the other methods, however, you can find some great examples at Cisco.com.

Router on a Stick

Figure 7-7 illustrates the router-on-a-stick scenario in which r3 looks like a lollipop coming off of the switch. The "stick" is the physical interface on the router acting as a trunk for the inter-VLAN communications. The main fa0/2 interface on the router is divided into logical subinterfaces to facilitate routing between VLANs. Without the subinterfaces, one physical interface would be necessary for each VLAN, which works great but certainly does not scale well.

Use Figure 7-7 as a guide to configure the IP parameters for all switches, routers, and VLANs at this time (as you see starting in Example 7-29). Also set the default gateway for all the switches to the routed interface for VLAN1.

Figure 7-7   *Chapter 7 Scenario (Router on a Stick)*

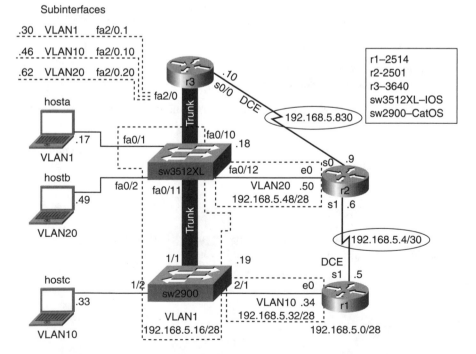

Example 7-29 *Router-on-a-Stick Switch Configuration*

```
sw3512xl#no debug all
All possible debugging has been turned off
sw3512xl#configure terminal
sw3512xl(config)#ip default-gateway 192.168.5.30
sw3512xl(config)#interface fastethernet 0/10
sw3512xl(config-if)#switchport mode trunk
sw3512xl(config-if)#end

sw2900> (enable) set ip route ?
Usage: set ip route <destination> <gateway> [metric][primary]
       (destination and gateway are IP alias or IP address in
        dot notation: a.b.c.d)
sw2900> (enable) set ip route 0.0.0.0 192.168.5.30
Route added.
```

Now that the switches are configured to support the router-on-a-stick configuration, configure the router as in Example 7-30. These subinterfaces are the default gateways you previously configured for your hosts.

Example 7-30 *Router-on-a-Stick r3 Configuration*

```
r3(config)#interface fastethernet 2/0.1
r3(config-subif)#description vlan1
r3(config-subif)#ip address 192.168.5.30 255.255.255.240
Configuring IP routing on a LAN subinterface is only allowed if that
subinterface is already configured as part of an IEEE 802.10 or ISL vLAN.
r3(config-subif)#encap isl 1
r3(config-subif)#ip address 192.168.5.30 255.255.255.240

r3(config-subif)#interface fastethernet 2/0.10
r3(config-subif)#description vlan 10
r3(config-subif)#encap isl 10
r3(config-subif)#ip address 192.168.5.46 255.255.255.240

r3(config)#interface fastethernet 2/0.20
r3(config-subif)#description vlan 20
r3(config-subif)#encap isl 20
r3(config-subif)#ip address 192.168.5.62 255.255.255.240

r3(config-subif)#interface fastethernet 2/0
r3(config-if)#no shut
r3(config-if)#end

r3#show ip interface brief
Interface               IP-Address      OK? Method Status                 Protocol
Serial0/0               unassigned      YES unset  administratively down  down
...
Serial1/7               unassigned      YES unset  administratively down  down
FastEthernet2/0         unassigned      YES unset  up                     up
FastEthernet2/0.1       192.168.5.30    YES manual up                     up
FastEthernet2/0.10      192.168.5.46    YES manual up                     up
FastEthernet2/0.20      192.168.5.62    YES manual up                     up
r3#copy running-config startup-config
```

The initial shaded output just means that you need to configure the ISL encapsulation before configuring the IP address. Although not required, I think it is easier to troubleshoot later if the VLAN number and subinterface number match as in the example. Note how I brought all the subinterfaces up simultaneously by performing a **no shut** on the main interface.

Don't forget to assign the IP addresses on r1 and r2 as in Example 7-31. Then show the VLANs on r3 to see the router on a stick in action.

Example 7-31 *IP Addresses for r1 and r2*

```
r1(config)#interface ethernet 0
r1(config-if)#ip address 192.168.5.34 255.255.255.240
r1(config-if)#no shut
r1(config-if)#interface serial 1
r1(config-if)#ip address 192.168.5.5 255.255.255.252
r1(config-if)#no shut
r1(config-if)#end
r1#copy running-config startup-config
r2(config)#interface ethernet 0
r2(config-if)#ip address 192.168.5.50 255.255.255.240
r2(config-if)#no shut
r2(config-if)#interface serial 0
r2(config-if)#ip address 192.168.5.9 255.255.255.252
r2(config-if)#no shut
r2(config-if)#interface serial 1
r2(config-if)#ip address 192.168.5.6 255.255.255.252
r2(config-if)#no shut
r2(config-if)#end
r2#copy running-config startup-config
r2#show ip interface brief
Interface            IP-Address       OK? Method Status              Protocol
Ethernet0            192.168.5.50     YES manual up                  up
Serial0              192.168.5.9      YES manual up                  up
Serial1              192.168.5.6      YES manual up                  up
r1#show ip interface brief
Interface            IP-Address       OK? Method Status              Protocol
Ethernet0            192.168.5.34     YES manual up                  up
Ethernet1            unassigned       YES unset  administratively down down
Serial0              unassigned       YES unset  administratively down down
Serial1              192.168.5.5      YES manual up                  up
```

Use the **show vlan** command on r3 as in Example 7-32 to verify your router-on-a-stick scenario at this time.

Example 7-32 *Verifying the VLAN Configuration on the Router on a Stick (r3)*

```
r3>show vlan
Virtual LAN ID:  1 (Inter Switch Link Encapsulation)
   vLAN Trunk Interface:    FastEthernet2/0.1
   Protocols Configured:    Address:            Received:       Transmitted:
      IP                    192.168.5.30        89              73
Virtual LAN ID:  10 (Inter Switch Link Encapsulation)
   vLAN Trunk Interface:    FastEthernet2/0.10
   Protocols Configured:    Address:            Received:       Transmitted:
```

Example 7-32 *Verifying the VLAN Configuration on the Router on a Stick (r3) (Continued)*

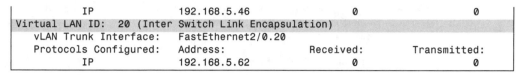

```
          IP              192.168.5.46              0                  0
Virtual LAN ID:  20 (Inter Switch Link Encapsulation)
    vLAN Trunk Interface:   FastEthernet2/0.20
  Protocols Configured:    Address:          Received:        Transmitted:
          IP              192.168.5.62              0                  0
```

All addresses should be assigned at this point. Subnet 192.168.5.0 was used across the serial links to get 192.168.5.4/30 and 192.168.5.8/30. Just remember that you performed variable-length subnet masking (VLSM) on subnet 0, so it can't be directly assigned somewhere else.

Now that you have created the VTP domain, set up your VLANs, associated them with the correct ports, configured the router on a stick, and assigned your IP addresses, perform a little testing. Start your testing from hosta, which is on VLAN1, and work your way outward as in Example 7-33.

Example 7-33 *Testing the Router-on-a-Stick Configuration from hosta*

```
C:\>remark can hosta ping the gateway?
C:\>ping 192.168.5.30
Pinging 192.168.5.30 with 32 bytes of data:
Reply from 192.168.5.30: bytes=32 time<10ms TTL=255
Reply from 192.168.5.30: bytes=32 time<10ms TTL=255
Reply from 192.168.5.30: bytes=32 time<10ms TTL=255
Reply from 192.168.5.30: bytes=32 time<10ms TTL=255
Ping statistics for 192.168.5.30:
    Packets: Sent = 4, Received = 4, Lost = 0 (0% loss),
Approximate round trip times in milli-seconds:
    Minimum = 0ms, Maximum =  0ms, Average =  0ms
C:\>remark can hosta ping the 3512xl switch?
C:\>ping 192.168.5.18
Pinging 192.168.5.18 with 32 bytes of data:
Request timed out.
Reply from 192.168.5.18: bytes=32 time<10ms TTL=255
Reply from 192.168.5.18: bytes=32 time<10ms TTL=255
Reply from 192.168.5.18: bytes=32 time<10ms TTL=255
Ping statistics for 192.168.5.18:
    Packets: Sent = 4, Received = 3, Lost = 1 (25% loss),
Approximate round trip times in milli-seconds:
    Minimum = 0ms, Maximum =  0ms, Average =  0ms
C:\>remark can hosta ping the 2900 switch?
C:\>ping 192.168.5.19
Pinging 192.168.5.19 with 32 bytes of data:
Reply from 192.168.5.19: bytes=32 time=10ms TTL=60
Reply from 192.168.5.19: bytes=32 time<10ms TTL=60
Reply from 192.168.5.19: bytes=32 time<10ms TTL=60
Reply from 192.168.5.19: bytes=32 time<10ms TTL=60
Ping statistics for 192.168.5.19:
    Packets: Sent = 4, Received = 4, Lost = 0 (0% loss),
Approximate round trip times in milli-seconds:
    Minimum = 0ms, Maximum =  10ms, Average =  2ms
C:\>remark can hosta ping r2s0?
C:\>ping 192.168.5.9
```

continues

Example 7-33   *Testing the Router-on-a-Stick Configuration from hosta (Continued)*

```
Pinging 192.168.5.9 with 32 bytes of data:
Request timed out.
Request timed out.
Request timed out.
Request timed out.
Ping statistics for 192.168.5.9:
    Packets: Sent = 4, Received = 0, Lost = 4 (100% loss),
Approximate round trip times in milli-seconds:
    Minimum = 0ms, Maximum =  0ms, Average =  0ms
C:\>remark can hosta ping r1s1?
C:\>ping 192.168.5.5
Pinging 192.168.5.5 with 32 bytes of data:
Request timed out.
Request timed out.
Request timed out.
Request timed out.
Ping statistics for 192.168.5.5:
    Packets: Sent = 4, Received = 0, Lost = 4 (100% loss),
Approximate round trip times in milli-seconds:
    Minimum = 0ms, Maximum =  0ms, Average =  0ms
```

Hosta can ping the default gateway and both switches, but not the other router interfaces. Is there anything in common with the ping targets that are successful? Can you spot the issue(s) here? Use the shaded output from the preceding example, Figure 7-7, and your troubleshooting skills to assist you with spotting the issue as I do in Example 7-34.

Example 7-34   *Why Can't You Ping Another VLAN?*

```
r1#show ip route
Codes: C - connected, S - static, I - IGRP, R - RIP, M - mobile, B - BGP
       D - EIGRP, EX - EIGRP external, O - OSPF, IA - OSPF inter area
       N1 - OSPF NSSA external type 1, N2 - OSPF NSSA external type 2
       E1 - OSPF external type 1, E2 - OSPF external type 2, E - EGP
       i - IS-IS, L1 - IS-IS level-1, L2 - IS-IS level-2, * - candidate default
       U - per-user static route, o - ODR
Gateway of last resort is not set
     192.168.5.0/24 is variably subnetted, 2 subnets, 2 masks
C       192.168.5.32/28 is directly connected, Ethernet0
C       192.168.5.4/30 is directly connected, Serial1
r1#show ip protocols
```

Hosta can ping its default gateway because it is on the same local subnet. Hosta can ping both switches because the management interfaces are set to VLAN1. Because hosta does not have a route to get to the other VLANs/subnets, it forwards the packets to its default gateway, which is fa2/0.1 on r3. Although r3 has a route to get to the majority of the other subnets, remember that the Internet Control Message Protocol (ICMP) packets need to return as well. r1 has two directly connected routes in the routing table, but no routing protocols or static routes are configured to facilitate communicating from one network to another. You should configure Open Shortest Path First (OSPF) as the routing protocol to allow inter-VLAN routing as in Example 7-35.

Example 7-35 *Configuring OSPF for Inter-VLAN Routing*

```
r1#configure terminal
r1(config)#router ospf 7
r1(config-router)#network 192.168.5.0 0.0.0.255 area 7
r1(config-router)#end
r1#copy running-config startup-config

r2(config)#router ospf 7
r2(config-router)#network 192.168.5.0 0.0.0.255 area 7
r2(config-router)#end
r2#copy running-config startup-config

r3(config)#router ospf 7
r3(config-router)#network 192.168.5.0 0.0.0.255 area 7
r3(config-router)#end
r3#copy running-config startup-config
```

Now use **show ip protocols** and **show ip route** to confirm your OSPF configuration as in Example 7-36.

Example 7-36 *Verifying OSPF*

```
r3#show ip protocols
Routing Protocol is "ospf 7"
  Sending updates every 0 seconds
  Invalid after 0 seconds, hold down 0, flushed after 0
  Outgoing update filter list for all interfaces is not set
  Incoming update filter list for all interfaces is not set
  Redistributing: ospf 7
  Routing for Networks:
    192.168.5.0
  Routing Information Sources:
    Gateway         Distance      Last Update
  Distance: (default is 110)
r3#show ip route
...
   192.168.5.0/24 is variably subnetted, 5 subnets, 2 masks
C       192.168.5.32/28 is directly connected, FastEthernet2/0.10
C       192.168.5.48/28 is directly connected, FastEthernet2/0.20
O       192.168.5.8/30
           [110/3125] via 192.168.5.34, 00:02:25, FastEthernet2/0.10
O       192.168.5.4/30
           [110/1563] via 192.168.5.34, 00:02:25, FastEthernet2/0.10
C       192.168.5.16/28 is directly connected, FastEthernet2/0.1
r2#show ip route
...
   192.168.5.0/24 is variably subnetted, 5 subnets, 2 masks
O       192.168.5.32/28 [110/1563] via 192.168.5.10, 00:02:14, Serial0
C       192.168.5.48/28 is directly connected, Ethernet0
C       192.168.5.8/30 is directly connected, Serial0
```

continues

Example 7-36 *Verifying OSPF (Continued)*

```
C        192.168.5.4/30 is directly connected, Serial1
O        192.168.5.16/28 [110/1563] via 192.168.5.10, 00:02:14, Serial0

r1#show ip route
...
     192.168.5.0/24 is variably subnetted, 5 subnets, 2 masks
C        192.168.5.32/28 is directly connected, Ethernet0
O        192.168.5.48/28 [110/1572] via 192.168.5.6, 00:02:22, Serial1
O        192.168.5.8/30 [110/3124] via 192.168.5.6, 00:02:23, Serial1
C        192.168.5.4/30 is directly connected, Serial1
O    192.168.5.16/28 [110/3125] via 192.168.5.6, 00:02:23, Serial1
```

Example 7-24 clearly shows the issues to be related to routing. Although the VLAN configurations were sufficient, keep in mind that each VLAN uses a separate IP subnet. You configured the router to route the VLAN traffic from one VLAN to another with the router-on-a-stick configuration. However, a routing protocol or static routes are still required to reach the other networks. Remember that utilities such as ping work in both directions with ICMP echos and replies; therefore, the packets not only need to know how to get to the destination, but the destination router needs a route for the return path.

Because IP is the only protocol that you are running in this scenario, I chose OSPF as the routing protocol. Area 0 was not required because there is only one area. Troubleshooting OSPF first requires that you make sure the lower layers are alright. The **show ip route** and **show ip protocols** commands certainly get you started with routing issues. It is not easy to remember all the commands, but if you can recall **show ip ospf ?** and **debug ip ospf adj**, that certainly will help immensely with troubleshooting OSPF. For instance, on r3 turn on **debug ip ospf adj**, clear the OSPF process, and monitor the activity as in Example 7-37. You can either completely remove OSPF on r3 and put it back or just clear the OSPF process.

NOTE   You must use the shortened version of **adj** for adjacency for this command to work. If you are running multiple processes of OSPF on the same box, the **clear ip ospf process #** command enables you to clear them individually (to limit the impact).

Example 7-37 *Monitoring OSPF Adjacency*

```
r3(config)#no router ospf 7
r3(config)#end
r3#debug ip ospf adj
OSPF adjacency events debugging is on
r3#configure terminal
Enter configuration commands, one per line.  End with CNTL/Z.
r3(config)#router ospf 7
r3(config-router)#network 192.168.5.0 0.0.0.255 area 7
Dec  5 03:08:14.623: OSPF: Interface FastEthernet2/0.1 going Up
Dec  5 03:08:14.623: OSPF: Interface FastEthernet2/0.10 going Up
Dec  5 03:08:14.623: OSPF: Interface FastEthernet2/0.20 going Up
```

Example 7-37 *Monitoring OSPF Adjacency (Continued)*

```
Dec  5 03:08:15.123: OSPF: Build router LSA for area 7, router ID 192.168.5.62,
  seq 0x80000001
r3(config-router)#end
r3#copy running-config startup-config
Dec  5 03:08:16.963: %SYS-5-CONFIG_I: Configured from console by console
Dec  5 03:08:19.991: OSPF: Rcv hello from 192.168.5.34 area 7 from FastEthernet2/
  0.10 192.168.5.34
Dec  5 03:08:19.991: OSPF: 2 Way Communication to 192.168.5.34 on FastEthernet2/
  0.10, state 2WAY
Dec  5 03:08:19.991: OSPF: Backup seen Event before WAIT timer on FastEthernet2/
  0.10
Dec  5 03:08:19.991: OSPF: DR/BDR election on FastEthernet2/0.10
Dec  5 03:08:19.991: OSPF: Elect BDR 192.168.5.62
Dec  5 03:08:19.991: OSPF: Elect DR 192.168.5.34
Dec  5 03:08:19.991: OSPF: Elect BDR 192.168.5.62
Dec  5 03:08:19.991: OSPF: Elect DR 192.168.5.34
Dec  5 03:08:19.991:         DR: 192.168.5.34 (Id)    BDR: 192.168.5.62 (Id)
Dec 5 03:08:19.991: OSPF: Send DBD to 192.168.5.34 on FastEthernet2/0.10 seq 0x12A
  opt 0x2 flag 0x7 len 32
Dec  5 03:08:19.991: OSPF: End of hello processing
Dec  5 03:08:19.999: OSPF: Rcv DBD from 192.168.5.34 on FastEthernet2/0.10 seq
  0x1B13 opt 0x2 flag 0x7 len 32  mtu 1500 state EXSTART
Dec  5 03:08:19.999: OSPF: First DBD and we are not SLAVE
Dec  5 03:08:19.999: OSPF: Rcv DBD from 192.168.5.34 on FastEthernet2/0.10 seq
  0x12A opt 0x2 flag 0x2 len 92  mtu 1500 state EXSTART
Dec  5 03:08:19.999: OSPF: NBR Negotiation Done. We are the MASTER
Dec 5 03:08:20.003: OSPF: Send DBD to 192.168.5.34 on FastEthernet2/0.10 seq 0x12B
opt 0x2 flag 0x3 len 52
Dec  5 03:08:20.003: OSPF: Database request to 192.168.5.34
Dec  5 03:08:20.003: OSPF: sent LS REQ packet to 192.168.5.34, length 36
Dec  5 03:08:20.007: OSPF: Rcv DBD from 192.168.5.34 on FastEthernet2/0.10 seq
  0x12B opt 0x2 flag 0x0 len 32  mtu 1500 state EXCHANGE
Dec 5 03:08:20.007: OSPF: Send DBD to 192.168.5.34 on FastEthernet2/0.10 seq 0x12C
opt 0x2 flag 0x1 len 32
Dec  5 03:08:20.011: OSPF: Rcv DBD from 192.168.5.34 on FastEthernet2/0.10 seq
  0x12C opt 0x2 flag 0x0 len 32  mtu 1500 state EXCHANGE
Dec  5 03:08:20.015: OSPF: Exchange Done with 192.168.5.34 on FastEthernet2/0.10
Dec  5 03:08:20.015: OSPF: Synchronized with 192.168.5.34 on FastEthernet2/0.10,
  state FULL
Dec  5 03:08:20.263: OSPF: Build router LSA for area 7, router ID 192.168.5.62,
  seq 0x80000006
Dec  5 03:08:25.599: OSPF: Rcv hello from 192.168.5.50 area 7 from FastEthernet2/
  0.20 192.168.5.50
Dec  5 03:08:25.599: OSPF: End of hello processing
Dec  5 03:08:29.991: OSPF: Rcv hello from 192.168.5.34 area 7 from FastEthernet2/
  0.10 192.168.5.34
Dec  5 03:08:29.991: OSPF: Neighbor change Event on interface FastEthernet2/0.10
Dec  5 03:08:29.991: OSPF: DR/BDR election on FastEthernet2/0.10
Dec  5 03:08:29.991: OSPF: Elect BDR 192.168.5.62
Dec  5 03:08:29.991: OSPF: Elect DR 192.168.5.34
Dec  5 03:08:29.991:         DR: 192.168.5.34 (Id)    BDR: 192.168.5.62 (Id)
Dec  5 03:08:29.991: OSPF: End of hello processing
Dec  5 03:08:35.599: OSPF: Rcv hello from 192.168.5.50 area 7 from FastEthernet2/
  0.20 192.168.5.50
r3#undebug all
```

Example 7-37 reviews the hello exchange and election process for the designated router/backup designated router (DR/BDR). Because all the correct information was previously in your routing table, there isn't much troubleshooting to do here. However, *always* confirm adjacency and neighbors when you suspect OSPF routing issues. Look at your neighbors in Example 7-38.

Example 7-38   *Verifying Your OSPF Neighbors*

```
r3#show ip ospf neighbor detail
 Neighbor 192.168.5.34, interface address 192.168.5.34
    In the area 7 via interface FastEthernet2/0.10
    Neighbor priority is 1, State is FULL, 6 state changes
    DR is 192.168.5.34 BDR is 192.168.5.46
    Options 2
    Dead timer due in 00:00:34
 Neighbor 192.168.5.50, interface address 192.168.5.50
    In the area 7 via interface FastEthernet2/0.20
    Neighbor priority is 1, State is INIT, 1 state changes
    DR is 192.168.5.50 BDR is 0.0.0.0
    Options 0
    Dead timer due in 00:00:30
```

Now that you have verified your routing protocols and routing tables, continue to test the chapter scenario. Confirm connectivity from hosta to the other hosts and the serial links between the routers as in Example 7-39. Also determine the path taken. No matter what you are testing, ping and trace are still the most basic tools to get you out of the toughest situations. Example 7-39 clearly displays how hosta can successfully ping the other hosts and remote networks. All pings and tracerts should be successful at this point. Continue to troubleshoot if that is not the case.

Example 7-39   *Testing from hosta*

```
Microsoft Windows 2000 [Version 5.00.2195]
 (c) Copyright 1985-2000 Microsoft Corp.
C:\>remark can hosta ping hostb?
C:\>ping 192.168.5.49
Pinging 192.168.5.49 with 32 bytes of data:
Request timed out.
Reply from 192.168.5.49: bytes=32 time<10ms TTL=127
Reply from 192.168.5.49: bytes=32 time<10ms TTL=127
Reply from 192.168.5.49: bytes=32 time<10ms TTL=127
Ping statistics for 192.168.5.49:
    Packets: Sent = 4, Received = 3, Lost = 1 (25% loss),
Approximate round trip times in milli-seconds:
    Minimum = 0ms, Maximum =  0ms, Average =  0ms
C:\>remark can hosta ping hostc?
C:\>ping 192.168.5.33
Pinging 192.168.5.33 with 32 bytes of data:
Reply from 192.168.5.33: bytes=32 time<10ms TTL=127
Reply from 192.168.5.33: bytes=32 time<10ms TTL=127
Reply from 192.168.5.33: bytes=32 time<10ms TTL=127
Reply from 192.168.5.33: bytes=32 time<10ms TTL=127
Ping statistics for 192.168.5.33:
    Packets: Sent = 4, Received = 4, Lost = 0 (0% loss),
```

Example 7-39 *Testing from hosta (Continued)*

```
Approximate round trip times in milli-seconds:
    Minimum = 0ms, Maximum =  0ms, Average =  0ms
C:\>remark can hosta ping r2s0?
C:\>ping 192.168.5.9
Pinging 192.168.5.9 with 32 bytes of data:
Reply from 192.168.5.9: bytes=32 time=20ms TTL=254
Reply from 192.168.5.9: bytes=32 time=10ms TTL=254
Reply from 192.168.5.9: bytes=32 time=10ms TTL=254
Reply from 192.168.5.9: bytes=32 time=10ms TTL=254
Ping statistics for 192.168.5.9:
    Packets: Sent = 4, Received = 4, Lost = 0 (0% loss),
Approximate round trip times in milli-seconds:
    Minimum = 10ms, Maximum =  20ms, Average =  12ms
C:\>remark can hosta ping r1s1?
C:\>ping 192.168.5.5
Pinging 192.168.5.5 with 32 bytes of data:
Reply from 192.168.5.5: bytes=32 time=10ms TTL=254
Reply from 192.168.5.5: bytes=32 time=10ms TTL=254
Reply from 192.168.5.5: bytes=32 time=10ms TTL=254
Reply from 192.168.5.5: bytes=32 time=10ms TTL=254
Ping statistics for 192.168.5.5:
    Packets: Sent = 4, Received = 4, Lost = 0 (0% loss),
Approximate round trip times in milli-seconds:
    Minimum = 10ms, Maximum =  10ms, Average =  10ms
```

Notice in Example 7-40 how in all cases, tracert illustrates that r3 VLAN1 192.168.5.30 is the first hop. All VLAN traffic passes through the router on a stick to its gateway; this is fine if the traffic is not overwhelming. A separate router with multiple ports or an RSM/MSFC is a much more scalable solution to routing inter-VLAN traffic.

Example 7-40 *Testing the Packet Path*

```
C:\>tracert 192.168.5.49
Tracing route to HOSTB [192.168.5.49]
over a maximum of 30 hops:
  1   <10 ms    <10 ms    <10 ms   192.168.5.30
  2   <10 ms    <10 ms    <10 ms   HOSTB [192.168.5.49]
Trace complete.
C:\>tracert 192.168.5.33
Tracing route to HOSTC [192.168.5.33]
over a maximum of 30 hops:
  1   <10 ms    <10 ms    <10 ms   192.168.5.30
  2   <10 ms    <10 ms    <10 ms   HOSTC [192.168.5.33]
Trace complete.
C:\>tracert 192.168.5.9
Tracing route to 192.168.5.9 over a maximum of 30 hops
  1   <10 ms    <10 ms    <10 ms   192.168.5.30
  2    10 ms     20 ms     10 ms   192.168.5.9
Trace complete.
C:\>tracert 192.168.5.5
Tracing route to 192.168.5.5 over a maximum of 30 hops
```

continues

Example 7-40 *Testing the Packet Path (Continued)*

```
  1   <10 ms   <10 ms   <10 ms   192.168.5.30
  2   <10 ms   <10 ms   <10 ms   192.168.5.50
  3    10 ms    20 ms    10 ms   192.168.5.5
Trace complete.
C:\>
```

Router Blades (RSM/MSFC)

One or more RSM/MSFCs can be inserted into a modular type of switch, such as the Cat5000 or Cat6000. This is like inserting a router blade with its own memory and IOS into the switch as a line card module.

NOTE   Although the CatOS devices automatically write the configuration to NVRAM for the main Supervisor module, this is not the case with the other modules, such as an RSM or MSFC, so remember to save your configurations at all times.

To configure the RSM/MSFC, enter the **session 15** command to take you to the router command-line interface (CLI). The result of the **session** *mod#* command is that it opens a telnet session across the backplane. The destination address is 127.0.0.*slot# plus one*. For example, slot 2 uses 127.0.0.3, and slot 3 uses 127.0.0.4. Alternatively, use the console port.

Unlike the router-on-a-stick configuration, RSMs/MSFCs do not use subinterfaces for VLANs. Instead, virtual interfaces are used, such as **interface vlan 1** or **interface vlan 2**. Because they are interfaces, you need to remember to issue a **no shut** on them. View the status of them using **show interface vlan 1** or **show interface vlan 2**. To create the VLANs on the Supervisor module, just issue the command **set vlan** *vlan# ports*.

NOTE   As far as troubleshooting RSM/MSFCs, remember they are routers on cards. Commands that you have used over and over, such as **ping**, **trace**, **debug ip icmp**, **debug ip packet**, and so on, can be used again.

Hot Standby Router Protocol (HSRP)

HSRP is used in the practical environment for default gateway redundancy and can be used to take advantage of many paths to a given destination. Hellos are sent out to 224.0.0.2, which is the all routers' multicast address. The UDP port is 1985. The basic components of HSRP include an active router, standby router, and a virtual router. The virtual router is what is configured on the hosts for the default gateway. The virtual router points to the active router when it is available. However, the standby router takes over after three missed hellos to the active router.

So, how do elections work in HSRP? The preemption process allows the router with the highest priority to take over after three missed hellos. The default priority is 100, and if priorities are the same, the tiebreaker is the highest IP address. The preempt delay feature allows the router time to populate its routing table before taking over. Use the following command where the group number is configurable depending on your hardware:

standby *group#* **priority** *priority#* **preempt delay** *#ofseconds*

When using HSRP with VLANs, consider divvying them up to help share the load. You might have separate routers, a chassis with two Supervisor cards, or two separate boxes with a Supervisor each for redundancy. Because there is no redundancy in the chapter scenario right now, use Example 7-41 to assist you with the steps of how to configure HSRP in a practical environment. The first part of the example illustrates the commands on one router and the second part on a redundant router. Any hosts of course would use the virtual address.

Example 7-41 *Configuring HSRP with VLANs*

```
RouterA Configuration
RouterA(config)#interface vlan 100
RouterA(config-if)#ip address 10.10.100.3 255.255.255.0
RouterA(config-if)#standby 100 priority 120 preempt delay 5
RouterA(config-if)#standby 100 ip 10.10.100.1

RouterA(config)#interface vlan 101
RouterA(config-if)#ip address 10.10.101.2 255.255.255.0
RouterA(config-if)#standby 101 ip 10.10.101.1

RouterB Configuration
RouterB(config)#interface vlan 100
RouterB(config-if)#ip address 10.10.100.2 255.255.255.0
RouterB(config-if)#standby 100 ip 10.10.100.1

RouterB(config)#interface vlan 101
RouterB(config-if)#ip address 10.10.101.3 255.255.255.0
RouterB(config-if)#standby 101 priority 120 preempt delay 5
RouterB(config-if)#standby 101 ip 10.10.101.1
```

Use the following commands to assist you with troubleshooting HSRP issues:

- **show standby ?**
- **standby debug** and **debug condition standby ?**

NOTE   The standards-based HSRP is Virtual Router Redundancy Protocol (VRRP).

To gain better performance for larger networks, Cisco offers multiple route switch technologies.

Route Switch Technologies

Layer 3 switching is routing any way you look at it. Devices used to be more clearly defined–bridges and switches were Layer 2 hardware-based devices, and routers were Layer 3 devices that performed their operations in software. That is history. However, you may hear others talk about *routing switches* and *switching routers*.

Routing switches are more Layer 2–oriented with some upper-layer functionality. They use hardware to route, but generally don't run routing protocols. Switching routers are primarily Layer 3 devices that can also switch, and do run routing protocols. Either way, hardware application-specific integrated circuits (ASICs) are used for switching speed and performance. Routers are not as slow as they once were, so this is really a moot point.

Routing and switching are both very important concepts that allow the hierarchical design for campus networks. Many internetworking devices today not only provide rich Layer 2 and Layer 3 functionality, but also upper-layer features to allow for making security and quality of service (QoS) decisions.

Traditional routing uses destination-based packet forwarding according to the Layer 3 header addresses. The frame passes from hop to hop according to the best path, which is normally some function of bandwidth depending on the routing protocol. By adding a NetFlow Feature Card (NFFC) and enabling multilayer switching (MLS), the Cat5000 can shortcut the process and rewrite the frame header similar to the router. Just as Layer 3 devices shortcut on IP addresses, Layer 4 devices can shortcut on port values. Shortcuts at other upper layers are often referred to as Application Layer switching.

Cisco Express Forwarding (CEF)

Back in the Chapter 1, "Shooting Trouble," the basics of routing and switching were covered. You reviewed how routers *route* to the destination network address and that they buffer and *switch* packets from the inbound interface to the outbound interface within the router. Performance is definitely affected by the switching type, but switching types have certainly improved over the years.

Fast switching (**ip route-cache**) has been the default and available since the 10.x code. The router does a route table lookup for the first packet toward a destination and caches it so that it doesn't have to do a route table lookup on each and every packet. If a router actually performs a route table lookup on each and every packet, you can imagine the overhead. This is called process switching and is used when you perform such tasks as debug commands. CEF is a switching type whereby even the first packet gets cached because the switching is performed in hardware.

CEF switching (**ip route-cache cef**) is now the default and has been available since the 11.x code. In higher-end models, such as the Cisco 12000 GSR routers and Catalyst 6500 switches with MSFC-2 cards, CEF is the default switching type. In the lower-end routers, CEF is an optional switching type and is done in software rather than hardware. You can enable CEF globally and then turn it off on any interfaces that are running features that may interfere with CEF with the following commands:

```
ip cef
  interface e0
  no ip route-cache cef
```

CEF uses a Forwarding Information Base (FIB) to make longest match destination-based switching decisions. Think of this as somewhat like the routing table for switching decisions. Each FIB entry points to its Layer 2 rewrite information in the adjacency table. You can read the FIB with the **show mls entry cef** command, view the contents of the adjacency table with **show mls entry cef adjacency**, and clear the adjacency table with **clear adjacency**. There is nothing to turn CEF on or off in its hardware-based form. However, **no ip cef** disables CEF switching globally in software. Use **show ip cef** *ipaddr* and **show adjacency** [**detail**] for troubleshooting. To see which packets were dropped or not forwarded by CEF, issue the **show cef** [**dropped**|**not-cef-switched**] command. Distributed CEF (dCEF) synchronizes the line cards to the adjacency table on the route processor; therefore, **clear adjacency** clears all. If you need to just clear the CEF information on a line card, use **clear cef linecard** *slot#* **?** instead.

NOTE   Like fast switching, CEF by default uses per-destination-based load sharing. However, you can change the default in CEF with the **ip load-sharing** [**per-packet**][**per-destination**] interface command. If you disable CEF, the next fastest switching type takes over, which is fast switching.

Multilayer Switching (MLS)

MLS is a book in itself, as previously mentioned, but Cisco provides this route switch technology on such platforms as their Cat5000 and 6000 (and now 4000). The 5000 uses the NFFC and the 6000 uses the MSFC along with a PFC.

MLS is a caching technique where the feature card remembers actions taken by the router to shortcut the router the next time. MLS does not take a Layer 2 device and turn it into a router; but it is an advanced form of switching that caches the Layer 3 information.

Multilayer Switching Protocol (MLSP) packets are hello packets sent out by the router. On a Cat5000, for example, this is how the NFFC learns about MLS-capable routers and their MAC addresses. The NFFC identifies candidate packets. It is able to do this based on pattern-matching routines as it looks for packets destined to the MAC addresses gleaned from the hellos. The NFFC identifies enable packets so that it has all the information necessary to rewrite the Layer 2 header *as the router did for the first packet*. The NFFC shortcuts future packets by rewriting the header itself instead of forwarding it to the router. It also has to decrement and test time to live (TTL) and recalculate the IP header checksum. Basically, the first packet in a flow is sent to the router/Layer 3 engine for a routing decision. If the frame is returned to the switch for forwarding (the destination is reached through another of the switch ports), the switch finishes creation of the cache entry and all other frames are forwarded by the switch without having to go to the Layer 3 engine.

MLS relies on hardware caching to basically shortcut routing, whereas switching routers such as the Cat8500 rely on hardware to perform router functions. A Reduced Instruction Set Computer (RISC)–based CPU handles routing protocols, and intelligent line cards do CEF table lookup and forwarding functions. VLAN features are not directly supported on the 8500s. This is where the ever so popular 6000 series comes in to play.

This chapter's scenario exposed you to VLANs and other related features in a step-by-step practical approach. Make sure you save all configurations and repeat any steps on which you need more practice. As you proved with the lab work, routers bring flexibility and scalability to VLANs.

Shooting Trouble with VLANs

This section is for you if you have ever whispered to yourself, "Where the heck are my VLANs?" Actually, the entire chapter is for you. Shooting trouble with VLANs requires that you understand Physical and Data Link Layer targets and well as normal switch and router operations. A physical and logical map is not just something nice to have. It is so important that I want you to take time now to draw a Layer 2 and Layer 3 map of your environment as it is. My drawings are in Figure 7-8 and Figure 7-9.

Figure 7-8 *Chapter 7 Physical Map (VLANs)*

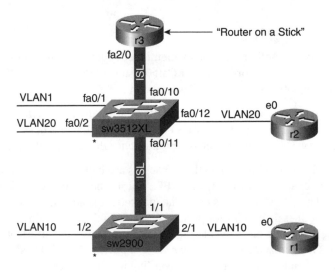

* Both switches in VLAN1

Figure 7-9   *Chapter 7 Logical Map (VLANs)*

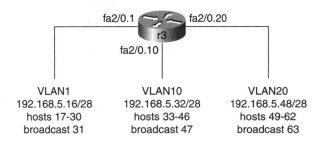

Now that you have your maps, make sure you have copies of the configuration on your routers and switches.

Regardless of the issue, you must continue to follow a consistent methodology, such as those suggested in the first part of the book, to assist you in isolating fault domains. It is probably not a bad idea to go back and review the Ethernet and switch beginning checklists and ending sections on shooting trouble. They all allude to the fact that interfaces (ports) are the main Data Link Layer targets. However, VLAN-to-VLAN communications involve routing, so it would be to your advantage to go back and review the routing chapter as well. Look at your pictures and other documentation to assist with end-to-end troubleshooting.

As with anything else, you may have a software or hardware bottleneck. Know the limitations of your transport and your devices. Use your CCO account on Cisco.com to assist with specific error messages and to take a look at sample configurations. Again, all of this systematic troubleshooting relates back to the OSI model. Do you have power? Are the power supply and fans running? Are devices turned on? Do they have link lights? Green means go. Check Layer 2 encapsulations, speed, and duplex settings. How about your route tables. Is there any filtering that is blocking what you are trying to do? Just keep moving up the stack.

With VLANs in particular, *beware* of adding new switches and the results of the default VTP server mode. Use some of the diagnostic commands, such as the following:

- **show cdp neighbors**
- **show ip interface brief**
- **show vlan**
- **show vlan brief**
- **show vtp ?**
- **show spanning-tree/show spantree**
- **show interface/show port**

- **show arp**

- **show ip cache (show ip cef / show adjacency)**

- **show vlan statistics**

The **debug vlan packet** command displays only packets with a VLAN ID that the router is not configured to support. This is good for address and encapsulation issues. Issue **debug span ?** and compare to the CatOS **show spantree** to view STP bridge protocol data units (BPDUs) in action. Alternatively, experiment with the **set trace** commands in CatOS, which are not the same as but appear to resemble debug in IOS. Again, practice a limited amount of safe debug in a practical environment.

Once again it is time for the chapter Trouble Tickets. The plan here is to give you several things to do, let you make mistakes and fix some things on your own, and to introduce other problems that you should have some experience with as a support person.

Trouble Tickets

Complete the following trouble tickets in order. Use the information and tools from this chapter and the previous chapters to analyze, test, and document as you go. Feel free to create your own Physical Layer or other problems if you need more practice in that area. Sample solutions are provided after this section.

Trouble Ticket 1

Review the VTP and VLAN configurations of both switches in their current state. Use the **reload** command on the 3512XL IOS device and the **reset system** command on the 2900 CatOS box to perform a warm boot of them. Do you anticipate any VLAN issues?

Trouble Ticket 2

Configure hosta or the 3512XL so that it will monitor the activity of port fa0/3 to fa0/5. Turn on Sniffer Pro. Create VLAN30 and associate it with port fa0/3 to fa0/5 on the 3512XL, but do not allow it to cross the trunk to the 2900. Show the VLAN database.

Trouble Ticket 3

Erase the configuration on the 3512XL. What is the impact on your VLAN environment?

Trouble Ticket 4

Paste your backup file to reload the configuration on the 3512XL.

Trouble Ticket 5

Change the 3512XL to VTP server mode with a domain name of donna. Create VLAN400 and 500 on the 3512XL. Clear the configuration on the 2900. Reset the 2900 and analyze the results.

Trouble Ticket 6

Verify that hosta and hostc can telnet to r3. Show the configuration of r3 so that you can review the router-on-a-stick configuration once again. Configure an access list to only allow hosta to telnet to r3. Verify that other devices can still ping and trace r3. Remove the ACL after your testing.

Trouble Ticket 7

Change the password and perform a password recovery on the CatOS 2900 switch. Perform the same for the 3512XL IOS switch.

Trouble Tickets Solutions

These solutions are not always the only way to perform these tasks. Compare your results or use them as guidelines to help you get started. Keep in mind that your exact results may vary according to your hardware and software.

Trouble Ticket 1 Solution

This trouble ticket gives you an opportunity to review VLANs and the effect of VTP. Use the **show vtp status** and **show vlan** commands on the 3512XL IOS box as in Example 7-42. The **show vtp domain**, **show vtp statistics**, and **show vlan** commands should give you the same type of information on the 2900 CatOS box.

Example 7-42 *IOS VTP Status*

```
sw3512xl#show vtp status
VTP Version                     : 2
Configuration Revision          : 0
Maximum VLANs supported locally : 254
Number of existing VLANs        : 9
VTP Operating Mode              : Transparent
VTP Domain Name                 : donna
VTP Pruning Mode                : Disabled
VTP V2 Mode                     : Disabled
...
sw3512xl#show vlan
VLAN Name                             Status    Ports
---- -------------------------------- --------- -------------------------------
1    default                          active    Fa0/1, Fa0/3, Fa0/4, Fa0/6,
                                                Fa0/7, Fa0/8, Fa0/9, Gi0/1,
```

continues

Example 7-42 *IOS VTP Status (Continued)*

```
                                                    Gi0/2
10   vlan10                          active
20   vlan20                          active   Fa0/2, Fa0/12
100  VLAN0100                        active   Fa0/5
200  vlan200                         active
...
sw2900> (enable) show vtp domain
Domain Name                   Domain Index VTP Version Local Mode  Password
---------------------------   ------------ ----------- ----------- ----------
donna                             1           2         server       -
Vlan-count Max-vlan-storage Config Revision Notifications
---------- ---------------- --------------- -------------
7          1023             2               disabled
Last Updater    V2 Mode  Pruning  PruneEligible on Vlans
--------------- -------- -------- -------------------------
192.168.5.19    disabled disabled 2-1000
sw2900> (enable) show vtp statistics
VTP statistics:
summary advts received          0
subset  advts received          0
request advts received          0
summary advts transmitted       600
subset  advts transmitted       2
request advts transmitted       0
No of config revision errors    0
No of config digest errors      0
VTP pruning statistics:
Trunk     Join Transmitted  Join Received  Summary advts received from
                                           non-pruning-capable device
--------  ----------------  -------------  ---------------------------
 1/1      0                 1              0
sw2900> (enable)show vlan
VLAN Name                         Status    IfIndex Mod/Ports, Vlans
---- -----------------------------  --------- ------- -----------------------
1    default                        active    5       2/2-12
10   vlan10                         active    10      1/2
                                                      2/1
100  VLAN0100                       active    11
...
```

After the warm system boots, you really shouldn't notice much difference—assuming you saved your configurations before you reloaded the boxes. You should notice some informational DTP messages in your log, such as the following, as the devices reload their configurations:

```
sw2900> (enable) %DTP-5-TRUNKPORTON:Port 1/1 has become isl trunk
%DTP-5-NONTRUNKPORTON:Port 1/1 has become non-trunk
%DTP-5-TRUNKPORTON:Port 1/1 has become isl trunk
%DTP-5-NONTRUNKPORTON:Port 1/1 has become non-trunk
%DTP-5-TRUNKPORTON:Port 1/1 has become isl trunk
```

Compare the summary advertisements in Example 7-43 to the example prior to the reset. They increased because the 2900 switch is in the default VTP server mode.

Example 7-43 *Summary Advertisements*

```
sw2900> (enable) show vtp statistics
VTP statistics:
summary advts received        0
subset  advts received        0
request advts received        0
summary advts transmitted     603
subset  advts transmitted     5
request advts transmitted     0
No of config revision errors  0
No of config digest errors    0
...
```

Turning off the 3512XL that was in VTP transparent mode was not detrimental to the other switch in the server mode or vice versa in this example. When the 3512 came back up, the shaded DTP message appeared to show the ISL trunk status between the two switches. Transparent mode means that the VLANs are local to the switch. The 3512 knew about VLAN10 and 20 before, and it still does.

Trouble Ticket 2 Solution

Port monitoring on a switch requires a little more effort on your part for setup, which in some ways is a level of security in itself. Example 7-44 illustrates configuring the activity of ports fa0/3, fa0/4, and fa0/5 to be monitored by interface fa0/1.

Example 7-44 *Port Monitoring on the 3512XL (IOS)*

```
sw3512xl#show port monitor
sw3512xl#configure terminal
sw3512xl(config)#interface fastethernet 0/1
sw3512xl(config-if)#port monitor fa0/3
sw3512xl(config-if)#port monitor fa0/4
sw3512xl(config-if)#port monitor fa0/5
FastEthernet0/1 and FastEthernet0/5 are in different vlan
sw3512xl(config-if)#end
```

You might or might not get a message similar to the shaded output in Example 7-44. However, the problem is that interface fa0/5 is in VLAN100, as you can see in Example 7-45. You can also remove VLAN100 if you didn't already.

Example 7-45 *Clearing Extraneous VLANs*

```
sw3512xl#show vlan brief
VLAN Name                             Status    Ports
---- -------------------------------- --------- -------------------------------
1    default                          active    Fa0/1, Fa0/3, Fa0/4, Fa0/6,
                                                Fa0/7, Fa0/8, Fa0/9, Gi0/1,
                                                Gi0/2
10   vlan10                           active
20   vlan20                           active    Fa0/2, Fa0/12
100  VLAN0100                         active    Fa0/5
```

continues

Example 7-45 *Clearing Extraneous VLANs (Continued)*

```
...
sw3512xl#vlan database
sw3512xl(vlan)#no vlan 100
Deleting VLAN 100...
sw3512xl(vlan)#exit
APPLY completed.
Exiting....

sw3512xl#configure terminal
sw3512xl(config)#interface fastethernet 0/1
sw3512xl(config-if)#port monitor fa0/5
FastEthernet0/1 and FastEthernet0/5 are in different vlan
```

There are still issues because the port did not automatically go back to the default VLAN1 assignment. Fix that and configure port monitoring as planned (see Example 7-46).

Example 7-46 *Port Monitoring on the 3512XL (IOS)*

```
sw3512xl(config-if)#interface fastethernet 0/5
sw3512xl(config-if)#no switchport access vlan
sw3512xl(config-if)#switchport access vlan 1
sw3512xl(config-if)#no shut

sw3512xl#show interface fastethernet 0/5 switchport
Name: Fa0/5
Switchport: Enabled
Administrative mode: static access
Operational Mode: static access
Administrative Trunking Encapsulation: isl
Operational Trunking Encapsulation: isl
Negotiation of Trunking: Disabled
Access Mode VLAN: 1 (default)
Trunking Native Mode VLAN: 1 (default)
Trunking VLANs Enabled: NONE
Pruning VLANs Enabled: NONE

sw3512xl#configure terminal
sw3512xl(config)#interface fastethernet 0/1
sw3512xl(config-if)#port monitor fa0/5
sw3512xl(config-if)#end
```

Next, you should create VLAN30 and assign the ports to be monitored (fa0/3 to 5) to this VLAN as in Example 7-47.

Example 7-47 *Creating VLAN30*

```
sw3512xl#vlan database
sw3512xl(vlan)#vlan 30 name vlan30
VLAN 30 added:
    Name: vlan30
sw3512xl(vlan)#exit
APPLY completed.
Exiting....
```

Example 7-47 *Creating VLAN30 (Continued)*

```
sw3512xl(config)#interface fastethernet 0/3
sw3512xl(config-if)#switchport access vlan 30
FastEthernet0/3 is being monitored
sw3512xl(config-if)#interface fastethernet 0/4
sw3512xl(config-if)#switchport access vlan 30
FastEthernet0/4 is being monitored
sw3512xl(config-if)#interface fastethernet 0/5
sw3512xl(config-if)#switchport access vlan 30
FastEthernet0/5 is being monitored
sw3512xl(config-if)#end
sw3512xl#show vlan
VLAN Name                             Status    Ports
---- -------------------------------- --------- -------------------------------
1    default                          active    Fa0/1, Fa0/3, Fa0/4, Fa0/5,
                                                Fa0/6, Fa0/7, Fa0/8, Fa0/9,
                                                Gi0/1, Gi0/2
10   vlan10                           active
20   vlan20                           active    Fa0/2, Fa0/12
30   vlan30                           active
...
```

VLAN 30 is active, but the ports do not display because you are monitoring them. Because the switch is in VTP transparent mode, there is no other configuration for you to perform to keep this VLAN local to the switch.

For the last part of this Trouble Ticket, you were asked to display the VLAN database (see Example 7-48).

Example 7-48 *Displaying the VLAN Database (IOS)*

```
sw3512xl#vlan database
sw3512xl(vlan)#show
  VLAN ISL Id: 1
    Name: default
    Media Type: Ethernet
    VLAN 802.10 Id: 100001
    State: Operational
    MTU: 1500
  VLAN ISL Id: 10
    Name: vlan10
    Media Type: Ethernet
    VLAN 802.10 Id: 100010
    State: Operational
    MTU: 1500
  VLAN ISL Id: 20
    Name: vlan20
    Media Type: Ethernet
    VLAN 802.10 Id: 100020
    State: Operational
    MTU: 1500
  VLAN ISL Id: 30
    Name: vlan30
    Media Type: Ethernet
```

continues

Example 7-48 *Displaying the VLAN Database (IOS) (Continued)*

```
      VLAN 802.10 Id: 100030
      State: Operational
      MTU: 1500
    VLAN ISL Id: 1002
      Name: fddi-default
      Media Type: FDDI
      VLAN 802.10 Id: 101002
      State: Operational
      MTU: 1500
      Bridge Type: SRB
      Ring Number: 0
    VLAN ISL Id: 1003
      Name: token-ring-default
      Media Type: Token Ring
      VLAN 802.10 Id: 101003
      State: Operational
      MTU: 1500
      Bridge Type: SRB
      Ring Number: 0
    VLAN ISL Id: 1004
      Name: fddinet-default
      Media Type: FDDI Net
      VLAN 802.10 Id: 101004
      State: Operational
      MTU: 1500
      STP Type: IEEE
    VLAN ISL Id: 1005
      Name: trnet-default
      Media Type: Token Ring Net
      VLAN 802.10 Id: 101005
      State: Operational
      MTU: 1500
      STP Type: IBM
```

Trouble Ticket 3 Solution

Erasing the configuration on the 3512XL does not appear to clear the VLANs in Example 7-49. However, deleting the *vlan.dat* file and reloading the router does the trick in Example 7-50.

Example 7-49 *Erasing the Configuration Does Not Clear the VLANs*

```
sw3512xl#write erase
[OK]
sw3512xl#reload
System configuration has been modified. Save? [yes/no]: n
Proceed with reload? [confirm]
%SYS-5-RELOAD: Reload requested
sw2900> (enable) %DTP-5-NONTRUNKPORTON:Port 1/1 has become non-trunk
%DTP-5-TRUNKPORTON:Port 1/1 has become isl trunk
%DTP-5-NONTRUNKPORTON:Port 1/1 has become non-trunk
%DTP-5-TRUNKPORTON:Port 1/1 has become isl trunk
```

Example 7-50 *Deleting the vlan.dat File to Completely Clear the VLANs*

```
Switch#dir flash:
Directory of flash:
  2  drwx       13888    Mar 01 1993 00:05:51  html
  4  -rwx         796    Mar 01 1993 00:24:15  vlan.dat
  5  -rwx     1273530    Mar 01 1993 00:02:49  c3500XL-c3h2s-mz-112.8.2-SA6.bin
  6  -rwx       82475    Mar 01 1993 00:03:29  c3500XL-hdiag-mz_8_1.SA6
224  -rwx         342    Mar 01 1993 00:04:40  env_vars
226  -rwx           0    Mar 01 1993 01:08:37  config.text
3612672 bytes total (1545216 bytes free)
Switch#del flash:vlan.dat
Delete filename [vlan.dat]?
Delete flash:vlan.dat? [confirm]
Switch#reload
Proceed with reload? [confirm]
%SYS-5-RELOAD: Reload requested
...
...done Initializing C3500XL flash.
C3500XL POST: System Board Test: Passed
C3500XL POST: CPU Buffer Test: Passed
C3500XL POST: CPU Notify RAM Test: Passed
C3500XL POST: CPU Interface Test: Passed
C3500XL POST: Testing Switch Core: Passed
C3500XL POST: Testing Buffer Table: Passed
C3500XL POST: Data Buffer Test: Passed
C3500XL POST: Configuring Switch Parameters: Passed
C3500XL POST: Ethernet Controller Test: Passed
C3500XL POST: MII Test: Passed
cisco WS-C3512-XL (PowerPC403) processor (revision 0x01) with 8192K/1024K bytes of
  memory.
Processor board ID 0x16, with hardware revision 0x00
Last reset from warm-reset
Processor is running Enterprise Edition Software
...
C3500XL INIT: Complete
Switch>enable
Switch#show vlan
VLAN Name                             Status    Ports
---- -------------------------------- --------- -------------------------------
1    default                          active    Fa0/1, Fa0/2, Fa0/3, Fa0/4,
                                                Fa0/5, Fa0/6, Fa0/7, Fa0/8,
                                                Fa0/9, Fa0/10, Fa0/11, Fa0/12,
                                                Gi0/1, Gi0/2
1002 fddi-default                     active
1003 token-ring-default               active
1004 fddinet-default                  active
1005 trnet-default                    active
...
```

The 2900 did not lose VLANs as a result of this; however, the trunk port between the 3512 and the 2900 is obviously not working now.

Trouble Ticket 4 Solution

I suppose I could have had you do this prior to wiping out the configuration on the 3512XL in the preceding Trouble Ticket, but sometimes when you forget to do something like that, it helps you to always remember to do it in the future. If you didn't save your preceding configuration file, you should create a backup file as in Example 7-51. If you have problems pasting, insert the appropriate modes into the file and use your terminal emulation program (SecureCRT Transfer function) to transmit the file in (because sometimes there are inconsistencies when you just paste the VLANs into a configuration).

Example 7-51   *Creating a Backup Configuration File for the 3512XL*

```
!!!begin paste
service timestamps debug datetime msec localtime
service timestamps log datetime msec localtime
hostname sw3512XL
enable secret donna
interface VLAN1
 ip address 192.168.5.18 255.255.255.240
interface FastEthernet0/1
 description sw3512xl fa0/1 to hosta
 speed 100
 duplex full
 port monitor FastEthernet0/3
 port monitor FastEthernet0/4
 port monitor FastEthernet0/5
 port monitor FastEthernet0/11
 spanning-tree portfast
 no shut
interface FastEthernet0/2
 description sw3512xl fa0/2 to hostb
 speed 10
 duplex half
 switchport access vlan 20
 spanning-tree portfast
 no shut
interface FastEthernet0/3
 no shut
interface FastEthernet0/4
 no shut
interface FastEthernet0/5
 no shut
interface FastEthernet0/10
 description sw3512xl fa0/10 to r3 fa2/0
 speed 100
 duplex full
 switchport mode trunk
 no shut
interface FastEthernet0/11
 description sw3512xl fa0/11 to sw2900 1/1
 speed 100
 duplex full
 switchport mode trunk
 no shut
```

Example 7-51 *Creating a Backup Configuration File for the 3512XL (Continued)*

```
interface FastEthernet0/12
 description sw3512xl fa0/12 to r2e0
 duplex half
 switchport access vlan 20
 no shut
ip default-gateway 192.168.5.30
no logging console
line con 0
 logging synchronous
 stopbits 1
line vty 0 4
 password donna
 login
line vty 5 15
 login
end
!!!end paste
```

Trouble Ticket 5 Solution

Hopefully, after the last Trouble Ticket you remembered to back up your configuration files before you started. Example 7-52 shows the TFTP server backup for both switches.

Example 7-52 *Copying the Configurations to a TFTP Server*

```
sw3512XL#copy run tftp
Source filename [running-config]?
Destination IP address or hostname []? 192.168.5.17
Destination filename [running-config]? sw3512xl-vlans
Building configuration...
!!
1603 bytes copied in 0.351 secs

sw2900> (enable) write network
IP address or name of remote host? 192.168.5.17
Name of configuration file? sw2900-vlans
Upload configuration to sw2900-vlans on 192.168.5.17 (y/n) [n]? y
.....
...........
...........
..
Finished network upload.  (8795 bytes)
sw2900> (enable)
```

Now that the configurations are backed up, change the VTP domain name to donna, change the VTP mode to server, and create VLAN400 and 500 on the 3512XL as in Example 7-53.

Example 7-53 *VTP and VLAN Configuration on the 3512XL (IOS)*

```
sw3512xl#vlan database
sw3512xl(vlan)#vtp domain donna
Changing VTP domain name from NULL to donna
sw3512xl(vlan)#vtp server
Setting device to VTP SERVER mode.
sw3512xl(vlan)#vlan 400 name vlan400
VLAN 400 added:
    Name: vlan400
sw3512xl(vlan)#vlan 500 name vlan500
VLAN 500 added:
    Name: vlan500
sw3512xl(vlan)#exit
APPLY completed.
Exiting....
```

Display the VLANs on both the IOS and CatOS boxes to compare the results as in Example 7-54.

Example 7-54 *Comparing the VLANs on Both Boxes*

```
sw3512XL#show vlan
VLAN Name                             Status    Ports
---- -------------------------------- --------- -------------------------------
1    default                          active    Fa0/1, Fa0/3, Fa0/4, Fa0/5,
                                                Fa0/6, Fa0/7, Fa0/8, Fa0/9,
                                                Gi0/1, Gi0/2
10   vlan10                           active
20   vlan20                           active    Fa0/2, Fa0/12
30   vlan30                           active
400  vlan400                          active
500  vlan500                          active
sw2900> (enable) sh vlan
VLAN Name                             Status    IfIndex Mod/Ports, Vlans
---- -------------------------------- --------- ------- -----------------------
1    default                          active    28      2/2-12
10   vlan10                           active    33      1/2
                                                        2/1
20   vlan20                           active    35
30   vlan30                           active    36
400  vlan400                          active    37
500  vlan500                          active    38
```

Notice how the 2900 automatically picked up all the VLANs from the 3512XL because both devices are in the VTP server mode. Next, clear the configuration on the 2900 as in Example 7-55.

Example 7-55 *Clearing the Configuration on the 2900*

```
sw2900> (enable) clear config all
This command will clear all configuration in NVRAM.
This command will cause ifIndex to be reassigned on the next system startup.
Do you want to continue (y/n) [n]? y
........
```

Example 7-55 *Clearing the Configuration on the 2900 (Continued)*

```
.................
System configuration cleared.
Console> (enable)reset system
```

When the 2900 resets, compare the VLANs again. You should find that the 3512XL VTP server mode box maintains everything it had before you reset the 2900 and that the 2900 obviously has no VLANs except for the default reserved ones. This scenario *did not wipe out* the VLANs on the 3512XL because when you cleared the configuration on the 2900, you also reset the domain name, which also resets the VTP versioning. You can prove this by issuing the **show vtp domain** and **show vtp statistics** commands, if you like.

Use the TFTP server to get your configuration back for the 2900 (**configure network**). Do this for experience in a lab such as this, but you will be fighting these two boxes forever with both of them being in VTP server mode. What I suggest at this point is leaving the VLANs as they are on the 3512XL. Bring the configuration back from the TFTP server and change the VTP mode on the 2900 to VTP client so that it will learn what it needs from the VTP server. Feel free to remove VLAN30, 400, and 500 from the VTP server. See Example 7-56 to compare the ending VLAN databases.

Example 7-56 *Correcting the VLAN Issues*

```
sw2900> (enable) configure network
...
sw2900> (enable) set vtp mode client
VTP domain donna modified
sw2900> (enable) show vlan
VLAN Name                             Status    IfIndex Mod/Ports, Vlans
---- -------------------------------- --------- ------- -----------------------
1    default                          active    5       2/2-12
10   vlan10                           active    24      1/2
                                                        2/1
20   vlan20                           active    22
30   vlan30                           active    23

sw3512XL>show vlan
VLAN Name                             Status    Ports
---- -------------------------------- --------- ------------------------------
1    default                          active    Fa0/1, Fa0/3, Fa0/4, Fa0/5,
                                                Fa0/6, Fa0/7, Fa0/8, Fa0/9,
                                                Gi0/1, Gi0/2
10   vlan10                           active
20   vlan20                           active    Fa0/2, Fa0/12
```

Test your new VTP configuration through the same ping tests you used back in Example 7-39 to make sure things are working. Save all of your ending configurations to the TFTP server as *r1-vlans*, *r2-vlans*, *r3-vlans*, *sw3512xl-vlans*, and *sw2900-vlans*. Also, save them as a file named *chapter 7 ending configs* using a terminal emulation program such as SecureCRT or HyperTerm.

The point here is "VLAN wipeout." It is a great idea to fool with VLANs and VTP in a lab environment with every possible combination. In a practical environment, the default server mode is *not* the best default for all your switches. Another word of caution: If you replace a Supervisor module with a new one that has higher revision number, you could (*you will*) delete all your existing VLANs. Make sure you reset the revision number for the Supervisor module before you insert it. An easy way to do this is to just reset the VTP domain name.

Trouble Ticket 6 Solution

You should have performed the telnet from the command prompt on hosta and hostc. It should have been successful. If not, you have a little more work than I intended for the Trouble Ticket. Example 7-57 shows the router-on-a-stick portion of the configuration.

Example 7-57 *Router-on-a-Stick Configuration*

```
hostname r3
...
interface FastEthernet2/0
 description r3 fa2/0 to sw3512xl fa0/10
 no ip address
 no ip directed-broadcast
 speed 100
 full-duplex
!
interface FastEthernet2/0.1
 description vlan1
 encapsulation isl 1
 ip address 192.168.5.30 255.255.255.240
 no ip redirects
 no ip directed-broadcast
!
interface FastEthernet2/0.10
 description vlan 10
 encapsulation isl 10
 ip address 192.168.5.46 255.255.255.240
 no ip redirects
 no ip directed-broadcast
!
interface FastEthernet2/0.20
 description vlan 20
 encapsulation isl 20
 ip address 192.168.5.62 255.255.255.240
 no ip redirects
 no ip directed-broadcast
!
router ospf 7
 network 192.168.5.0 0.0.0.255 area 7
...
end
```

Example 7-58 illustrates the access list configuration to only allow hosta to telnet to r3.

Example 7-58 *ACL Configuration*

```
r3(config)#access-list ?
  <1-99>       IP standard access list
  <100-199>    IP extended access list
  <1000-1099>  IPX SAP access list
  <1100-1199>  Extended 48-bit MAC address access list
  <1200-1299>  IPX summary address access list
  <1300-1999>  IP standard access list (expanded range)
  <200-299>    Protocol type-code access list
  <2000-2699>  IP extended access list (expanded range)
  <300-399>    DECnet access list
  <400-499>    XNS standard access list
  <500-599>    XNS extended access list
  <600-699>    Appletalk access list
  <700-799>    48-bit MAC address access list
  <800-899>    IPX standard access list
  <900-999>    IPX extended access list
  rate-limit   Simple rate-limit specific access list
r3(config)#access-list 1 ?
  deny    Specify packets to reject
  permit  Specify packets to forward
r3(config)#access-list 1 permit ?
  Hostname or A.B.C.D  Address to match
  any                  Any source host
  host                 A single host address
r3(config)#access-list 1 permit 192.168.5.17
r3(config)#access-list 1 deny any log
r3(config)#line vty 0 4
r3(config-line)#access-class 1 ?
  in   Filter incoming connections
  out  Filter outgoing connections
r3(config-line)#access-class 1 in
r3(config-line)#end
r3#copy running-config startup-config
```

Now test out the ACL as in Example 7-59.

Example 7-59 *ACL Testing*

```
sw3512xl#telnet 192.168.5.30
Trying 192.168.5.30 ...
% Connection refused by remote host

sw3512xl#ping 192.168.5.30
Type escape sequence to abort.
Sending 5, 100-byte ICMP Echos to 192.168.5.30, timeout is 2 seconds:
!!!!!
Success rate is 100 percent (5/5), round-trip min/avg/max = 1/2/3 ms

sw3512xl#trace 192.168.5.30
Type escape sequence to abort.
Tracing the route to 192.168.5.30
  1 192.168.5.30 0 msec 18 msec *
```

Hosta can still successfully telnet to r3. When another host or device attempts to telnet to r3, it should fail. Hostc says, "Could not open a connection to 192.168.5.30." The 2900 says "Unable to connect," and the 3512XL says, "Connection refused by remote host." Finally, remember to remove the access list as in Example 7-60. Depending on the IOS version, you may need to remove the individual lines of code applied to the interface, too.

Example 7-60   *Removing the ACL*

```
r3(config)#no access-list 1
r3(config)#end
r3#copy running-config startup-config
r3#show access-lists
r3#
```

Trouble Ticket 7 Solution

See Appendix B, "Troubleshooting Resources," for the solution.

You have completed the chapter Trouble Tickets when you feel comfortable with the tasks assigned and the various scenarios throughout the chapter. Review or experiment in the areas where you need more help. Understanding and troubleshooting in a simple environment is certainly the foundation for understanding more complex protocols and technologies. Check your understanding with the chapter review questions.

Review Questions

Use this chapter and your practical troubleshooting knowledge and skills to answer the following questions. The answers are located in Appendix A, "Answers to Review Questions."

1   Compare ISL to 802.1Q.

2   Can you change the management VLAN?

3   Why should you use a separate management VLAN?

4   What does a transparent mode–configured Catalyst do with a VTP update message?

5   You incorrectly associated port 8 with VLAN8, so you issue the following command: **clear vlan 8** to clear the port from VLAN8 and back to the default VLAN1. However, the port status is still showing as inactive. How can you fix this issue?

6   The lab technician was nice enough to give you his switch to replace a production switch that you were having problems with. He quickly clears all the VLANs on the switch and hands it over to you. When you plug the switch into your network, you quickly realize that all your other VLANs disappear. Where did you go wrong? Is there anything you can do to avoid such issues?

7 You want to verify that you configured portfast on the 3512XL port fa0/2. How can you accomplish this?

8 Routing provides _____ connectivity, whereas trunking provides _____ connectivity.

9 There are three major steps for working VLANs. What are they?

10 Can VLANs assist with people trying to Sniff the network?

11 In a router-on-a-stick configuration, as in the chapter scenario, what would you expect to be the first hop if hosta were to tracert to hostc?

Summary

Shooting trouble with VLANs is no different from anything else. Always have a methodical plan. Know your devices and how to maneuver the CatOS and IOS. Understand routing and switching processes. Beware of autonegotiation of speed, duplex, trunking, and so on. Create backups. Be prepared for vanishing VLANs if you didn't take the appropriate VTP design up front. Know your VTP modes. Have physical and logical maps handy and use them to help you troubleshoot not only complex end-to-end problems, but simple issues, too. Isolate problem domains. Use your tools.

Many things that used to be performed on routers are now performed on switches with router blades. Although many switches are usable the minute you take them out of the box, they are obviously a little more optimal if configured for the environment. Switching and VLAN targets are still ports and interfaces. Don't assume too much. For example, don't just try another cable or another port; try a known good one.

This chapter reviewed real-world intra- and inter-VLAN communication advantages, disadvantages, and issues. The important topics included addressing, gateways, VTP, routing, and probably the one you recall the best: vanishing VLANs. The next two chapters focus on troubleshooting WAN issues to continue to build your troubleshooting skills.

PART IV

Supporting the WAN

CHAPTER 8

Shooting Trouble with Frame Relay

Frame Relay is a Layer 2 edge technology whereby frames travel from your routers (DTE devices) through a series of Frame Relay switches to get to the proper destination. At the edge of enterprise and service provider networks, these switches are DCE devices, although this varies within the clouds. Frame is one of those technologies that is not only available in the United States, but also worldwide. The service can be carrier provided or privately owned and is a cost-effective alternative to leased lines.

This chapter begins the WAN focus of this book with shooting Frame Relay troubles. It gives practical application to a number of objectives falling under the CCNP support guidelines and more. Use familiar Cisco commands and problem isolation techniques to build the chapter scenarios and resolve the Trouble Tickets. This chapter assumes you have a good understanding of protocol characteristics and a methodical troubleshooting mindset.

With supporting the WAN, many times the battle is deciding whether the problem is in fact yours or whether it is a service provider issue. You will analyze real-world Frame Relay issues including Layer 2 and Layer 3 addressing and issues related to LMI, data-link connection identifier (DLCI) assignments, mapping statements, routing protocols, and so on. Continue to identify targets and document the results using ping, trace, show, clear, debug, and other troubleshooting commands and utilities. To gain practical experience, you may follow the many figures and examples in this chapter or use my guidelines to build it yourself.

This chapter covers the following topics:

- Scenario: Shooting Trouble with Frame Relay
- A Brief History of Frame Relay
- Frame Relay Frames
- Frame Relay Addressing
- Frame Relay at the Physical Layer
- Shooting Trouble with Frame Relay
- Trouble Tickets
- Trouble Ticket Solutions

Supporting Website Files

You can find files and links to utilities that support this book on the Cisco Press website at www.ciscopress.com/1587200570. Even if you do not have a lab, you can take advantage of the supporting configuration files including the logs to understand device input and output. The files are listed throughout the chapters in italics.

In order to be able to read and work with some of the supporting files offered at www.ciscopress.com/1587200570, you may want to download some of the programs listed in Table I-1 in the Introduction.

Scenario: Shooting Trouble with Frame Relay

In the WAN world, it is always easy to blame things on someone else. Therefore, it is important to understand a bit about what happens in the cloud and on the user ends so that you can narrow down the problem as to whether it is your problem, someone else's problem or a service provider issue. The goal in this first scenario is to configure Frame Relay in a hybrid back-to-back configuration using r1, r2, and r3, as in Figure 8-1.

Figure 8-1 *Shooting Trouble with Frame Relay (Hybrid Back-to-Back Topology)*

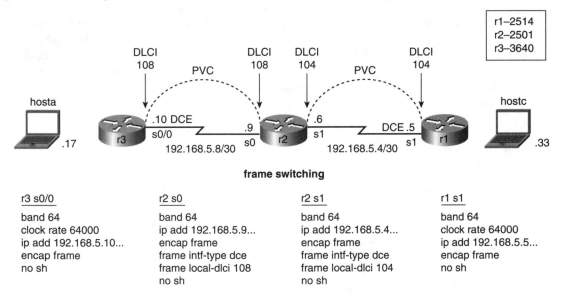

As always, there is not always one right or wrong way to achieve this task or tasks presented. The ability to obtain the end result using good practices is extremely important in any real-world network. My troubleshooting and device configurations are presented starting in

Example 8-1 so that you can compare your work and perhaps see a different approach to obtaining the end result. Use the previous checklists, your step-by-step troubleshooting methodology, and the Frame Relay checklist in Table 8-1 to assist in testing.

Table 8-1 *Frame Relay Quick Troubleshooting Checklist*

Isolating Problems	Commands and Symptoms
Check IP address, subnet mask, and routing protocols. All of these are Layer 3 or above that ride on top of Frame Relay. Keep in mind that many routing protocols are multicast/broadcast, but Frame Relay is NBMA*.	**ping** **traceroute** **show ip protocols** **show ip route**
Isolating Problems	**Commands and Symptoms**
Check interface status and encapsulation. If the point-to-point PVC** is *active*, for example, line protocol for the subinterface is up.	**show ip interface brief** **show interfaces serial 0**
Are you communicating with the provider?	**show frame-relay lmi**
Are your DLCIs *active*?	**show frame-relay map** **show frame-relay pvc** **clear frame-relay-inarp**
Look at PVC statistics. Monitor the Frame traffic.	**show frame-relay traffic**
Verify the route statements on the frame switch.	**show frame-relay route**
Watch the interface communications.	**debug serial interface**
Watch the LMI† handshake.	**debug frame-relay lmi**
Watch the packets received.	**debug frame-relay events**
Watch the packets sent.	**debug frame-relay packet**

*NBMA = nonbroadcast multiaccess
**PVC = permanent virtual circuit
†LMI = Local Management Interface

Back-to-Back Frame Relay

A Frame Relay back-to-back configuration can be quite helpful in a testing environment *once you get it to work*. Refer to Cisco.com for assistance with a true back-to-back external link Frame Relay solution using no LMI. I want you to use sort of a hybrid back-to-back situation for testing where r2 acts as a pseudo frame switch as I do Example 8-1. It is a good idea to confirm that things are not broken to begin with if you are starting from existing configurations. Back-to-back frame is tricky enough, however, so I want you to erase the configurations on the three routers and configure back-to-back frame from the beginning.

Configure the routers starting with r2 first because it is acting as a back-to-back hub device for the other routers (see Figure 8-1 and Example 8-1). For now just configure the bare-bones configuration with no descriptions or passwords to concentrate on this Layer 2 technology in action. In a practical environment, this obviously should be a requirement.

Example 8-1 *Configuring r2 as a Pseudo Frame Switch*

```
Router(config)#hostname r2
r2(config)#frame-relay switching
r2(config)#interface serial 0
r2(config-if)#bandwidth 64
r2(config-if)#ip address 192.168.5.9 255.255.255.252
r2(config-if)#encap frame-relay
r2(config-if)#frame-relay intf-type dce
r2(config-if)#frame-relay local-dlci 108
r2(config-if)#no shut
r2(config-if)#interface serial 1
r2(config-if)#bandwidth 64
r2(config-if)#encap frame
r2(config-if)#ip address 192.168.5.6 255.255.255.252
r2(config-if)#encap frame
r2(config-if)#frame-relay intf-type dce
r2(config-if)#frame-relay local-dlci 104
r2(config-if)#no shut
```

I called r2 a *pseudo frame switch* because there are no frame route statements in the configuration. The **encap frame-relay** command changed the default High-Level Data Link Control (HDLC) encapsulation on the WAN interfaces to Frame Relay so that you could configure the other Frame Relay parameters. Now look at the frame map and PVCs in Example 8-2.

Example 8-2 *Reviewing the Map and PVCs on the Frame Switch*

```
r2#show frame-relay map
r2#show frame-relay pvc
PVC Statistics for interface Serial0 (Frame Relay DCE)
DLCI = 108, DLCI USAGE = LOCAL, PVC STATUS = INACTIVE, INTERFACE = Serial0
  input pkts 0            output pkts 0           in bytes 0
  out bytes 0             dropped pkts 0          in FECN pkts 0
  in BECN pkts 0          out FECN pkts 0         out BECN pkts 0
  in DE pkts 0            out DE pkts 0
  out bcast pkts 0         out bcast bytes 0
  pvc create time 00:01:30, last time pvc status changed 00:00:53

PVC Statistics for interface Serial1 (Frame Relay DCE)
DLCI = 104, DLCI USAGE = LOCAL, PVC STATUS = INACTIVE, INTERFACE = Serial1
  input pkts 0            output pkts 0           in bytes 0
  out bytes 0             dropped pkts 0          in FECN pkts 0
  in BECN pkts 0          out FECN pkts 0         out BECN pkts 0
  in DE pkts 0            out DE pkts 0
  out bcast pkts 0         out bcast bytes 0
  pvc create time 00:00:31, last time pvc status changed 00:00:31
r2#copy running-config startup-config
```

It certainly makes sense that there is no *frame mapping* at this point because the other ends (r1 and r3) are still configured for HDLC encapsulation, the default for serial interfaces. For the same reason, the PVCs are *inactive*. The DLCIs were assigned on the main interface using the

frame-relay local-dlci command. Typically the **frame interface-dlci** command is used when using subinterfaces with LMI provided (as discussed later in this chapter).

NOTE   From a support standpoint, it is good to see the bouncing PVC state from active to inactive, because for future reference you now know this is a good indication the other end of the PVC has not been configured.

It is important to note that regardless of the physical DTE/DCE cable, Frame Relay has its own DTE/DCE configuration at Layer 2 as you witnessed with the **frame-relay intf-type dce** command for both interfaces on r2. If you issue the **show controllers** command as in Example 8-3, you will see that both are physical DTE interfaces. However, the preceding example portrays them as Frame Relay DCEs. This is absolutely correct. For there is a Layer 1 and Layer 2 DTE/DCE with this technology.

Example 8-3   **show controllers** *for the Physical DTE*

```
r2#show controllers s 0
HD unit 0, idb = 0x107EAC, driver structure at 0x10D340
buffer size 1524  HD unit 0, V.35 DTE cable
cpb = 0x1, eda = 0x48DC, cda = 0x48F0
RX ring with 16 entries at 0x4014800
...
r2#show controllers s 1
HD unit 1, idb = 0x111648, driver structure at 0x116AE0
buffer size 1524  HD unit 1, V.35 DTE cable
cpb = 0x2, eda = 0x3104, cda = 0x3118
```

NOTE   On a practical note, generating clock is also a Layer 1 DCE function and Layer 2 is not concerned with clocking.

Next configure r1 to communicate to r2 using Frame Relay as in Example 8-4. Turn on **debug service timestamps** and logging. Clear the counters to make sure you start your troubleshooting from this point on if necessary. Feel free to turn on **logging synchronous**, too. Because this is a lab, just before you bring up the interface turn on keepalive debugging to watch the goings-on.

Example 8-4   *Back-to-Back Frame Relay r1 Configuration*

```
Router(config)#hostname r1
r1(config)#service timestamps debug datetime localtime msec
r1(config)#service timestamps log datetime localtime msec
r1(config)#exit
r1#clock set 5:21:00 Dec 9 2002
r1#clear counters
r1#configure terminal
```

continues

Example 8-4   *Back-to-Back Frame Relay r1 Configuration (Continued)*

```
r1(config)#line console 0
r1(config-line)#logging synchronous
r1(config-line)#interface s1
r1(config-if)#bandwidth 64
r1(config-if)#clock rate 64000
r1(config-if)#ip address 192.168.5.5 255.255.255.252
r1(config-if)#encap frame
r1(config-if)#end
r1#debug frame-relay lmi
Frame Relay LMI debugging is on
Displaying all Frame Relay LMI data
r1#configure terminal
r1(config)#interface s1
r1(config-if)#no shut
Dec  9 05:25:31.487: %LINK-3-UPDOWN: Interface Serial1, changed state to up
Dec  9 05:25:31.527: Serial1(out): StEnq, myseq 1, yourseen 0, DTE up
Dec  9 05:25:31.531: datagramstart = 0xE22EA4, datagramsize = 14
Dec  9 05:25:31.531: FR encap = 0x00010308
Dec  9 05:25:31.535: 00 75 95 01 01 00 03 02 01 00
Dec  9 05:25:31.539:
Dec  9 05:25:31.539: Serial1(out): StEnq, myseq 1, yourseen 0, DTE up
Dec  9 05:25:31.543: datagramstart = 0xE22EA4, datagramsize = 13
Dec  9 05:25:31.543: FR encap = 0x00010308
Dec  9 05:25:31.547: 00 75 51 01 00 53 02 01 00
Dec  9 05:25:31.551:
Dec  9 05:25:31.551: Serial1(out): StEnq, myseq 1, yourseen 0, DTE up
Dec  9 05:25:31.551: datagramstart = 0xE22EA4, datagramsize = 13
Dec  9 05:25:31.555: FR encap = 0xFCF10309
Dec  9 05:25:31.555: 00 75 01 01 00 03 02 01 00
Dec  9 05:25:31.559:!!!next is the full status from the frame switch
Dec  9 05:25:31.571: Serial1(in): Status, myseq 1
Dec  9 05:25:31.575: RT IE 1, length 1, type 0
Dec  9 05:25:31.575: KA IE 3, length 2, yourseq 1 , myseq 1
Dec  9 05:25:31.579: PVC IE 0x7 , length 0x6 , dlci 104, status 0x4 , bw 0
Dec  9 05:25:31.579: %FR-5-DLCICHANGE: Interface Serial1 - DLCI 104 state changed
   to DELETED
...
Dec  9 05:25:41.607: %FR-5-DLCICHANGE: Interface Serial1 - DLCI 104 state changed
   to DELETED
Dec  9 05:25:42.519: %LINEPROTO-5-UPDOWN: Line protocol on Interface Serial1,
   changed state to up
...
Dec  9 05:26:31.543: Serial1(in): Status, myseq 7
Dec  9 05:26:31.547: RT IE 1, length 1, type 0
Dec  9 05:26:31.547: KA IE 3, length 2, yourseq 7 , myseq 7
Dec  9 05:26:31.551: PVC IE 0x7 , length 0x6 , dlci 104, status 0x2 , bw 0
r1(config)#
Dec  9 05:26:31.551: %FR-5-DLCICHANGE: Interface Serial1 - DLCI 104 state changed
   to ACTIVE
r1(config)#end
r1#undebug all
```

On r1 it was only necessary to turn on Frame Relay encapsulation. Everything else was accomplished via default Inverse Address Resolution Protocol (Inverse ARP) activity. Review the keepalive activity with the **debug frame-relay lmi** command. Notice the status inquiries going *out* from r1 to r2 (frame switch) about every 10 seconds. After six inquiries, the switch returns the DLCIs in a full status message. This is the normal LMI exchange between the local router and the Frame Relay carrier.

Regardless of troubleshooting the LAN or the WAN, **show ip interface brief** is still a quick way to show the interface status, as I do in the next example. View the interfaces, the Frame Relay mapping, and ping the other end of the PVC as in Example 8-5.

Example 8-5   *r1 Testing*

```
r1#show ip interface brief
Interface            IP-Address      OK? Method Status                Protocol
Ethernet0            unassigned      YES unset  administratively down down
Ethernet1            unassigned      YES unset  administratively down down
Serial0              unassigned      YES unset  administratively down down
Serial1              192.168.5.5     YES manual up                    up
r1#show interfaces s1
Serial1 is up, line protocol is up
  Hardware is HD64570
  Internet address is 192.168.5.5/30
  MTU 1500 bytes, BW 64 Kbit, DLY 20000 usec, rely 255/255, load 1/255
  Encapsulation FRAME-RELAY, loopback not set, keepalive set (10 sec)
  LMI enq sent  92, LMI stat recvd 93, LMI upd recvd 0, DTE LMI up
  LMI enq recvd 0, LMI stat sent  0, LMI upd sent  0
  LMI DLCI 1023  LMI type is CISCO  frame relay DTE
...
    DCD=up  DSR=up  DTR=up  RTS=up  CTS=up
r1#show frame-relay map
Serial1 (up): ip 192.168.5.6 dlci 104(0x68,0x1880), dynamic,
             broadcast,, status defined, active
r1#ping 192.168.5.6
Type escape sequence to abort.
Sending 5, 100-byte ICMP Echos to 192.168.5.6, timeout is 2 seconds:
!!!!!
Success rate is 100 percent (5/5), round-trip min/avg/max = 32/32/32 ms
r1#show frame-relay pvc
PVC Statistics for interface Serial1 (Frame Relay DTE)
DLCI = 104, DLCI USAGE = LOCAL, PVC STATUS = ACTIVE, INTERFACE = Serial1
  input pkts 5            output pkts 5          in bytes 520
  out bytes 520          dropped pkts 0          in FECN pkts 0
  in BECN pkts 0         out FECN pkts 0         out BECN pkts 0
  in DE pkts 0           out DE pkts 0
  out bcast pkts 0        out bcast bytes 0
  pvc create time 00:15:17, last time pvc status changed 00:15:18
r1#show interface s1
Serial1 is up, line protocol is up
  Hardware is HD64570
  Internet address is 192.168.5.5/30
  MTU 1500 bytes, BW 64 Kbit, DLY 20000 usec, rely 255/255, load 1/255
  Encapsulation FRAME-RELAY, loopback not set, keepalive set (10 sec)
  LMI enq sent  6, LMI stat recvd 6, LMI upd recvd 0, DTE LMI up
  LMI enq recvd 0, LMI stat sent  0, LMI upd sent  0
  LMI DLCI 1023  LMI type is CISCO  frame relay DTE
  FR SVC disabled, LAPF state down
r1#copy running-config startup-config
```

The output clearly shows that **show ip interface brief** is a quick check of the layers; however, **show interfaces s1** provides more Frame Relay details for the interface. For example, the shaded lines display not only the IP address but also the subnet mask and the LMI keepalive activity. The encapsulation is frame. The default LMI type of Cisco is talking over DLCI 1023. The status inquiries sent (out) are equal to the messages received (in), and you are looking at the Frame Relay DTE end of the PVC.

The example output also illustrates ping to be successful and rightly so. Think of the Frame Relay PVC like a PVC pipe that carries water from one end to the other. The Frame PVC transports variable-length frames from the source network to the destination network through the service provider cloud.

Frame Relay maps a Layer 2 DLCI to a Layer 3 network address, such as IP, IPX, or AppleTalk for example. When you view your ending running configuration, note the individual protocols spelled out for Frame Relay. The default method of doing this Layer 2-to-Layer 3 dynamic mapping is by a process called *Inverse ARP*. You verified the mapping with the **show frame-relay map** command in the preceding example. Each PVC shows the DLCI number assigned, the usage of local compared to global, with a status of dynamic compared to static. The DLCI number is shown in decimal, hex, and what you might expect to see on the wire. The other PVC statistics are quite helpful in supporting Frame Relay, and you will experience them more throughout this chapter.

Now configure and test r3 as in Example 8-6 to finish up your hybrid back-to-back chapter scenario. Turn on Frame Relay event debugging to watch the major happenings.

Example 8-6   *r3 Hybrid Back-to-Back Configuration*

```
Router(config)#hostname r3
r3(config)#service timestamps debug datetime localtime msec
r3(config)#service timestamps log datetime localtime msec
r3(config)#end
r3#clock set 5:50:00 Dec 9 2002
r3#clear counters
r3(config)#line console 0
r3(config-line)#logging synchronous
r3(config-line)#interface s0/0
r3(config-if)#bandwidth 64
r3(config-if)#clock rate 64000
r3(config-if)#ip address 192.168.5.10 255.255.255.252
r3(config-if)#encap frame
r3(config-if)#no shut
r3(config-if)#end
r3#copy running-config startup-config
r3#debug frame-relay events
Frame Relay events debugging is on
Dec  9 05:52:49.087: %LINEPROTO-5-UPDOWN: Line protocol on Interface Serial0/0,
changed state to up
Dec  9 05:53:38.099: %FR-5-DLCICHANGE: Interface Serial0/0 - DLCI 108 state changed
to ACTIVE
Dec  9 05:53:38.135: Serial0/0: FR ARP input
Dec  9 05:53:38.135: datagramstart = 0x240034E, datagramsize = 30
Dec  9 05:53:38.139: FR encap = 0x18C10300
Dec  9 05:53:38.139: 80 00 00 00 08 06 00 0F 08 00 02 04 00 09 00 00
```

Example 8-6   *r3 Hybrid Back-to-Back Configuration (Continued)*

```
Dec  9 05:53:38.139: C0 A8 05 09 18 C1 C0 A8 05 0A
Dec  9 05:53:38.139:
r3#undebug all
r3#copy running-config startup-config
r3#show frame-relay map
Serial0/0 (up): ip 192.168.5.9 dlci 108(0x6C,0x18C0), dynamic,
                broadcast,, status defined, active
r3#ping 192.168.5.9
Type escape sequence to abort.
Sending 5, 100-byte ICMP Echos to 192.168.5.9, timeout is 2 seconds:
!!!!!
Success rate is 100 percent (5/5), round-trip min/avg/max = 28/30/32 ms
```

Configuring r3 was as simple as configuring r1 because you used the default Inverse ARP once again. The shaded output of the **show frame-relay map** statement shows dynamic for this. The ping to r2 should be successful.

Save your configurations to a file named *hybrid back-to-back frame relay* in case you want to quickly return to the back-to-back configuration.

NOTE   There is not just one way to configure back-to-back Frame Relay. Research the topic at Cisco.com and try some of the other configurations.

In most real-world WAN applications, you configure the user ends of the PVCs that connect through the cloud in a hub-and-spoke topology using subinterfaces. You will get plenty of practice configuring and troubleshooting Frame Relay using subinterfaces throughout this chapter and in the practical environment. I want to turn your attention to using a router as a Frame Relay switch to get started.

Using a Router as a Frame Relay Switch

Many of the Cisco-certified classes have you work with Frame Relay but not all of them have you actually do this from a service provider perspective with building the frame switch. My purpose in configuring a router as the frame switch is so that you understand the cloud. What happens inside the mysterious Frame Relay cloud is really just passing the frames through some more switches depending on what the service provider is doing.

Use the following steps to set up a router as a Frame Relay switch:

1 Give the frame switch a hostname.

2 Turn on Frame Relay switching.

3 Configure bandwidth.

4 Configure clock rate if physical DCE.

5 Configure encapsulation. (Default is **cisco**, or you can set to **ietf**.)

6 Configure LMI type. (Default is **cisco**, or you can set to **ansi** or **q933a**.)

7 Configure frame interface type. (Default is **dte**, or you can set to **dce**.)

8 Configure frame route statements.

9 Troubleshoot the frame switch as needed:

show frame-relay route

show frame-relay lmi

show frame-relay pvc

show ip interface brief

no shut

Instead of completely erasing r2, modify it so that it is a frame switch as in Figure 8-2 and Example 8-7.

Figure 8-2 *Configuring r2 as a Frame Switch*

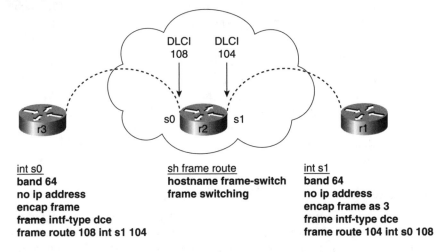

int s0
band 64
no ip address
encap frame
frame intf-type dce
frame route 108 int s1 104

sh frame route
hostname frame-switch
frame switching

int s1
band 64
no ip address
encap frame as 3
frame intf-type dce
frame route 104 int s0 108

Example 8-7   *Configuring r2 as a Frame Switch*

```
r2(config)#hostname frame switch
                      ^
% Invalid input detected at '^' marker.
r2(config)#hostname frame-switch
frame-switch(config)#interface s0
frame-switch(config-if)#encap frame
frame-switch(config-if)#frame-relay route ?
  <16-1007>  input dlci to be switched
frame-switch(config-if)#frame-relay route 108 ?
  interface  outgoing interface for pvc switching
frame-switch(config-if)#frame-relay route 108 interface s1 ?
  <16-1007>  output dlci to use when switching
frame-switch(config-if)#frame-relay route 108 interface s1 104 ?
  <cr>
frame-switch(config-if)#frame-relay route 108 interface s1 104
frame-switch(config-if)#interface s1
frame-switch(config-if)#encap frame
frame-switch(config-if)#frame route 104 interface s0 108
frame-switch(config-if)#end
frame-switch#copy running-config startup-config
```

Because **frame-relay switching** and **frame-relay intf-type dce** are already on from the back-to-back scenario, the **frame relay route** commands are really all you need to make r2 a true Frame Relay switch. These statements are interface configuration commands. Here, you route what comes in interface s0 as DLCI 108 out interface s1 as DLCI 104. For the other PVC, start at interface s1 to route what comes in s0 as DLCI 104 out interface s0 as DLCI 108.

You may not have removed the IP addresses from the previous exercise; a frame switch does not need IP addresses. In the future, you should be able to recognize whether you have an output for the **show frame-relay map** command on the frame switch as in Example 8-8. Fix this now and verify the frame switch with the **show frame-relay route command**. Feel free to remove the local DLCI statement from the preceding exercise, too, because it is no longer required.

Example 8-8   *Verifying the Frame Switch*

```
frame-switch#show frame-relay map
Serial0 (up): ip 192.168.5.10 dlci 108(0x6C,0x18C0), dynamic,
              broadcast,, status defined, active
Serial1 (up): ip 192.168.5.5 dlci 104(0x68,0x1880), dynamic,
              broadcast,, status defined, active
frame-switch#show frame-relay pvc
PVC Statistics for interface Serial0 (Frame Relay DCE)
DLCI = 108, DLCI USAGE = SWITCHED, PVC STATUS = ACTIVE, INTERFACE = Serial0
  input pkts 7            output pkts 6          in bytes 580
  out bytes 550          dropped pkts 0         in FECN pkts 0
  in BECN pkts 0         out FECN pkts 0        out BECN pkts 0
  in DE pkts 0           out DE pkts 0
  out bcast pkts 0        out bcast bytes 0          Num Pkts Switched 1
  pvc create time 01:20:18, last time pvc status changed 00:00:52
...
frame-switch#show frame-relay route
Input Intf      Input Dlci      Output Intf     Output Dlci     Status
Serial0         108             Serial1         104             active
Serial1         104             Serial0         108             active
```

NOTE	Use **?** each step of the way when configuring the frame route statements. The familiar **show frame-relay lmi**, **show frame-relay map**, and **show frame-relay pvc** commands are ready to lend a hand with supporting Frame Relay on your routers, but add **show frame-relay route** to your tool bag for troubleshooting a frame switch.

Save your r2 ending configuration to a file named *r2 as a frame switch for r1 and r3*.

Before you make too many assumptions, you better make sure the r1 and r3 configuration still work with the newly configured frame switch. Pinging from one end to the other should fail at this point with the frame switch in the middle.

You would certainly have a route and be able to ping if you add static routes as in Example 8-9 to get to the destination network. Actually for the preceding back-to-back example it would be fine, but adding static routes or routing protocols here would be very odd things to do. Remember, Frame Relay is Layer 2.

Example 8-9   *r1 and r3 Static Routes*

```
r1(config)#ip route 192.168.5.8 255.255.255.252 s1
r3(config)#ip route 192.168.5.4 255.255.255.252 s0/0
r3(config)#end
r1#ping 192.168.5.10
Type escape sequence to abort.
Sending 5, 100-byte ICMP Echos to 192.168.5.10, timeout is 2 seconds:
!!!!!
Success rate is 100 percent (5/5), round-trip min/avg/max = 56/58/60 ms
```

If you took the static route or routing protocol approach to fixing this problem, remove that portion of your configuration now. Instead, I want you to configure the IP addresses for r1s1 and r3s0/0 to be on the same subnet as in Figure 8-3 and Example 8-10. Use the existing IP address for r1.

Figure 8-3   *Configuring r1 and r3 on the Same Subnet*

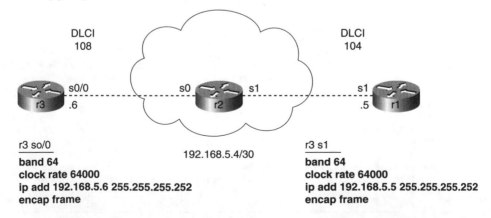

Example 8-10 *Configuring r1 and r3 on the Same Subnet*

```
r1(config)#no ip route 192.168.5.8 255.255.255.252
r1(config)#end
r1#copy running-config startup-config

r3(config)#no ip route 192.168.5.4 255.255.255.252
r3(config)#interface s0/0
r3(config-if)#ip address 192.168.5.6 255.255.255.252
r3(config-if)#end
r3#copy running-config startup-config
```

Test the Frame Relay connections from the router point of view and then from the service provider point of view as in Example 8-11.

Example 8-11 *Testing the Frame Relay Connections*

```
r1#show frame-relay map
Serial1 (up): ip 192.168.5.6 dlci 104(0x68,0x1880), dynamic,
              broadcast,, status defined, active
r1#ping 192.168.5.6
Type escape sequence to abort.
Sending 5, 100-byte ICMP Echos to 192.168.5.6, timeout is 2 seconds:
!!!!!
Success rate is 100 percent (5/5), round-trip min/avg/max = 56/57/60 ms
r1#trace 192.168.5.6
Type escape sequence to abort.
Tracing the route to 192.168.5.6
  1 192.168.5.6 28 msec 28 msec *
r1#show arp

r3#show frame-relay map
Serial0/0 (up): ip 192.168.5.5 dlci 108(0x6C,0x18C0), dynamic,
                broadcast,, status defined, active
r3#ping 192.168.5.5
Type escape sequence to abort.
Sending 5, 100-byte ICMP Echos to 192.168.5.5, timeout is 2 seconds:
!!!!!
Success rate is 100 percent (5/5), round-trip min/avg/max = 56/58/60 ms
r3#trace 192.168.5.5
Type escape sequence to abort.
Tracing the route to 192.168.5.5
  1 192.168.5.5 28 msec 28 msec *

frame-switch#show frame-relay route
Input Intf      Input Dlci     Output Intf     Output Dlci     Status
Serial0         108            Serial1         104             active
Serial1         104            Serial0         108             active
```

The shaded output clearly shows that the frame switch is transparent to r1 and r3. The pings are successful and trace shows no intermediary hops, and that is what you should expect. When you look at the output of **show frame-relay map**, think of it like looking at the ARP table in Ethernet.

For Frame Relay Inverse ARP issues, I suggest **clear frame-relay-inarp** or bouncing the serial interfaces on r1 and r3 so that they relearn the DLCI information and rebuild their maps. You may need to do that here. If the **show frame-relay lmi** command indicates timeouts, use the **debug frame-relay lmi** command after you bounce (**shut/no shut**)the interfaces to observe the communications between the router and the frame switch like in Example 8-12.

Example 8-12 *Troubleshooting the Frame Connections*

```
frame-switch(config)#interface s0
frame-switch(config-if)#shut
frame-switch(config-if)#interface s1
frame-switch(config-if)#shut
r1(config)#interface s1
r1(config-if)#shut
r3(config)#interface s0/0
r3(config-if)#shut
frame-switch(config-if)#interface s0
frame-switch(config-if)#no shut
frame-switch(config-if)#interface s1
frame-switch(config-if)#no shut
r1#debug frame-relay lmi
Frame Relay LMI debugging is on
Displaying all Frame Relay LMI data
r1#configure terminal
r1(config)#interface s1
r1(config-if)#no shut
01:13:47: %LINK-3-UPDOWN: Interface Serial1, changed state to up
01:13:47: Serial1(out): StEnq, myseq 1, yourseen 0, DTE up
01:13:47: datagramstart = 0xE22EA4, datagramsize = 14
01:13:47: FR encap = 0x00010308
01:13:47: 00 75 95 01 01 00 03 02 01 00
01:13:47:
01:13:47: Serial1(out): StEnq, myseq 1, yourseen 0, DTE up
01:13:47: datagramstart = 0xE22EA4, datagramsize = 13
01:13:47: FR encap = 0x00010308
01:13:47: 00 75 51 01 00 53 02 01 00
01:13:47:
01:13:47: Serial1(out): StEnq, myseq 1, yourseen 0, DTE up
01:13:47: datagramstart = 0xE22EA4, datagramsize = 13
01:13:47: FR encap = 0xFCF10309
01:13:47: 00 75 01 01 00 03 02 01 00
01:13:47:
01:13:47: Serial1(in): Status, myseq 1
01:13:47: RT IE 1, length 1, type 0
01:13:47: KA IE 3, length 2, yourseq 1 , myseq 1
01:13:47: PVC IE 0x7 , length 0x6 , dlci 104, status 0x2 , bw 0
01:13:47: %FR-5-DLCICHANGE: Interface Serial1 - DLCI 104 state changed to ACTIVE
01:13:48: %LINEPROTO-5-UPDOWN: Line protocol on Interface Serial1, changed state
    to up
01:13:57: Serial1(out): StEnq, myseq 2, yourseen 1, DTE up
01:13:57: datagramstart = 0xE22EA4, datagramsize = 13
01:13:57: FR encap = 0xFCF10309
01:13:57: 00 75 01 01 01 03 02 02 01
01:13:57:
```

Example 8-12 *Troubleshooting the Frame Connections (Continued)*

```
01:13:57: Serial1(in): Status, myseq 2
01:13:57: RT IE 1, length 1, type 0
01:13:57: KA IE 3, length 2, yourseq 2 , myseq 2
01:13:57: PVC IE 0x7 , length 0x6 , dlci 104, status 0x0 , bw 0
01:13:57: %FR-5-DLCICHANGE: Interface Serial1 - DLCI 104 state changed to
    INACTIVE
r3(config-if)#no shut
01:14:44: %LINK-3-UPDOWN: Interface Serial0/0, changed state to up
01:14:44: %FR-5-DLCICHANGE: Interface Serial0/0 - DLCI 108 state changed to
    ACTIVE
01:14:45: %LINEPROTO-5-UPDOWN: Line protocol on Interface Serial0/0,
    changed state to up
r3(config-if)#end
r3#show frame-relay map
Serial0/0 (up): ip 192.168.5.5 dlci 108(0x6C,0x18C0), dynamic,
              broadcast,, status defined, active
r1(config-if)#end
...
r1#undebug all
...
r1#show frame-relay map
Serial1 (up): ip 192.168.5.6 dlci 104(0x68,0x1880), dynamic,
              broadcast,, status defined, active
r1#ping 192.168.5.6
Type escape sequence to abort.
Sending 5, 100-byte ICMP Echos to 192.168.5.6, timeout is 2 seconds:
!!!!!
Success rate is 100 percent (5/5), round-trip min/avg/max = 56/57/60 ms
r3#ping 192.168.5.5
Type escape sequence to abort.
Sending 5, 100-byte ICMP Echos to 192.168.5.5, timeout is 2 seconds:
!!!!!
Success rate is 100 percent (5/5), round-trip min/avg/max = 56/58/60 ms
!!!notice the following output where you can't ping yourself
r3#ping 192.168.5.6
Type escape sequence to abort.
Sending 5, 100-byte ICMP Echos to 192.168.5.6, timeout is 2 seconds:
.....
Success rate is 0 percent (0/5)
r3#copy running-config startup-config
frame-switch#copy running-config startup-config
r1#copy running-config startup-config
```

The lessons learned from this exercise should reinforce that Frame Relay is a Layer 2 technology. Note that I turned up the frame switch interfaces first and then the spokes so that Inverse ARP would occur properly. The **show frame-relay map** command displays the Layer 2/Layer 3 mapping to assist you with why you may not be able to get to your destination. The **clear frame-relay-inarp** command should clear all the Inverse ARP learned entries so that they are relearned; if problems occur, however, you can always bounce the interfaces. If necessary, you can always change the encapsulation back to HDLC and then back to Frame Relay.

By the way, the shaded output illustrates that r1 can ping r3 and vice versa, yet r3 can't ping itself. This is the norm with multipoint interfaces in Frame Relay. If you really want it to work, you can put in a static map statement such as in Example 8-13.

Example 8-13 *Adding a Static Frame Relay Map*

```
r3(config-if)#frame-relay map ip 192.168.5.6 108
r3(config-if)#end
r3#ping 192.168.5.6
Type escape sequence to abort.
Sending 5, 100-byte ICMP Echos to 192.168.5.6, timeout is 2 seconds:
!!!!!
Success rate is 100 percent (5/5), round-trip min/avg/max = 112/114/124 ms
r3#show frame-relay pvc
PVC Statistics for interface Serial0/0 (Frame Relay DTE)
DLCI = 108, DLCI USAGE = LOCAL, PVC STATUS = ACTIVE, INTERFACE = Serial0/0
  input pkts 55          output pkts 52          in bytes 4970
  out bytes 4850         dropped pkts 0          in FECN pkts 0
  in BECN pkts 0         out FECN pkts 0         out BECN pkts 0
  in DE pkts 0           out DE pkts 0
  out bcast pkts 7        out bcast bytes 474
  pvc create time 22:52:49, last time pvc status changed 22:52:49
!!!the line above is sort of a tattle tale line:o)
r3#show frame-relay map
Serial0/0 (up): ip 192.168.5.5 dlci 108(0x6C,0x18C0), dynamic,
            broadcast,, status defined, active
Serial0/0 (up): ip 192.168.5.6 dlci 108(0x6C,0x18C0), static,
            CISCO, status defined, active
```

The preceding example shows how simple it is to add a static map in the interface configuration mode. You can ping yourself, the PVC is active, and you now have a have a static entry in your frame map table along with the previous dynamic one.

NOTE   Always check the running configuration before you remove everything because Inverse ARP may very well be turned off on a protocol-by-protocol basis.

Also note that the frame switch is not configured for routing at all. For your IP packets to get to their destination, they need a route or need to be on the same network. With such a simple example, configuring the interfaces on the same subnet or a static route is fine. In larger networks it obviously is not practical to set up everything using static routes but rather more feasible to use a routing protocol and default routes. Frame Relay has its own issues with main interfaces and routing protocols because of its nonbroadcast multiaccess (NBMA) nature. Obviously, Frame Relay can't go out and ARP everything on the WAN like in the LAN. NBMA primarily means that multiple routers are supported without broadcasting capabilities. Hence routing updates must be replicated using this type of multipoint connection.

Save your configurations. The significant parts of my ending configurations are in Example 8-14.

Example 8-14   *Shooting Trouble with Frame Relay Scenario Same Subnet Configurations*

```
r1#show running-config
interface Serial1
 bandwidth 64
 ip address 192.168.5.5 255.255.255.252
 encapsulation frame-relay
 clockrate 64000

frame-switch#show running-config
frame-relay switching
interface Serial0
 bandwidth 64
 no ip address
 encapsulation frame-relay
 frame-relay intf-type dce
 frame-relay route 108 interface Serial1 104
!
interface Serial1
 bandwidth 64
 no ip address
 encapsulation frame-relay
 frame-relay intf-type dce
 frame-relay route 104 interface Serial0 108

r3#show run
interface Serial0/0
 bandwidth 64
 ip address 192.168.5.6 255.255.255.252
 encapsulation frame-relay
 clockrate 64000
 frame-relay map ip 192.168.5.6 108
```

Keep in mind that the service provider can pretty much do what they want inside the cloud and it doesn't necessarily have to be Frame Relay. They may be doing ATM MPLS with the appropriate encapsulation on entry to the cloud and appropriate encapsulation on leaving the cloud to your destination, or just re-encapsulating in IP.

Figure 8-4 shows an example of a Frame Relay cloud with more switches to give you a better feel for the appropriate route statements in the real world. If you have multiple routers in your environment, feel free to experiment with supporting a more complex cloud.

Figure 8-4 *Multiple Switches in the Cloud*

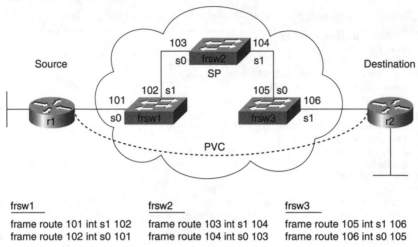

frsw1	frsw2	frsw3
frame route 101 int s1 102	frame route 103 int s1 104	frame route 105 int s1 106
frame route 102 int s0 101	frame route 104 int s0 103	frame route 106 int s0 105

Now I want to review some Frame Relay history and terminology before you move on to shooting more Frame Relay troubles. If you are already comfortable with the terminology, feel free to move directly into the "Frame Relay Frames" and "Frame Relay Addressing" sections.

A Brief History of Frame Relay

Originally Frame Relay was conceived to run over ISDN. The initial proposals went to the Consultative Committee on International Telephone and Telegraph (CCITT) in 1984. As mentioned in the initial chapters, CCITT is now known as ITU-T, for international standards, whereas American National Standards Institute (ANSI) is still known for American standards.

Standards

ITU-T approved what is known as Recommendation I.122, the framework for additional packet mode bearer services back in 1988. This was part of a series of ISDN specifications where Link Access Protocol D Channel (LAPD) carried the signaling information on the D channel. I.122 outlined how LAPD might be used in other applications besides ISDN. ANSI rapidly progressed on this recommendation and T1.606 was approved early in 1990 with complete approval in 1991. The ITU and ANSI standards for Frame Relay are in alignment with one another. ANSI T1.606 is equivalent to ITU-T I.122 for architecture, and ANSI T1.616 is equivalent to ITU-T Q.922 for data transfer.

In 1990 the Gang of Four consortium developed LMI. LMI is further discussed in the signaling section. The Gang of Four included the following:

- Cisco

- StrataCom (later acquired by Cisco)

- Northern Telecom

- DEC (later acquired by Compaq)

LMI popularized Frame Relay and the Gang of Four later formed the Frame Relay Forum that has grown to more than 300 members. The Frame Relay Forum in Figure 8-5 is at www.frforum.com. It is an excellent resource for Frame Relay.

Figure 8-5   *Frame Relay Forum*

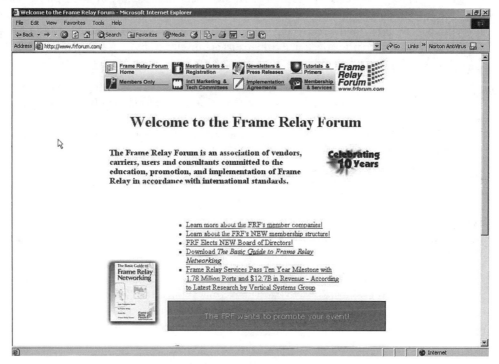

Frame Relay is a bandwidth-on-demand technology where you share bandwidth with others in the cloud on a packet-by-packet basis. Although in a PVC the logical path is up and running, no bandwidth is actually consumed until needed. This is perceptibly more cost-effective than paying for leased lines in many business applications. Frame Relay not only provides a low cost of ownership, but it is standards-based, has low overhead along with high reliability (depending on your service level agreements), and internetworks well with other services such as ATM.

Frame Relay is based on sort of a KISS principal ("Keep It Simple, Stupid!"), by letting the higher-level protocols worry with the problems. Although the technology includes signaling and congestion-notification mechanisms, they are optional. This does not affect compliance with the standards but does affect performance. Your best bet is to subscribe to the Committed Information Rate (CIR) that is right for you. This and your maximum burst rate (less than the line speed) is primarily your service level agreement (SLA) with the provider. When your frames are above the CIR, the provider can set the Discard Eligible (DE) bit to 1. This just means that DE traffic is discarded prior to frames with the DE bit set to 0 or non-DE. However, the reality of all this is *all* bits are Discard Eligible by the nature of Frame Relay. It is up to the upper layers to do the error correction. On the other hand if you have a fat enough pipe, there are times you will be able to burst to more than your CIR depending on your SLA, but not more than your physical capacity. For example, your physical pipe may be a T1 or T3, but your end-to-end CIR may only be 56 kbps.

Frame Relay is a connection-oriented data-link protocol. The virtual connection or connection identifier for the PVC is the DLCI. It offers statistical multiplexing by switching variable-length frames. Obviously, this means that traffic delays vary according to frame size. However, Frame Relay is even optimal for carrying delay-sensitive traffic such as voice. Traffic shaping and quality of service prioritization mechanisms are discussed in *CCNP Practical Studies: Remote Access* (Cisco Press).

It is getting pretty old to say Frame Relay is a more efficient X.25 replacement because it has been alive for better than 10 years now. However, Frame Relay really is an updated X.25 that leaves the slow error correction and flow control to the upper layers so as not to burden things at Layer 2. You could say Layer 2 can switch it or pitch it and let the upper layers recover anything that has been discarded, for X.25 is the *only* Layer 2 protocol to offer error correction (retransmittal). Frame Relay typical speeds are 56 kbps to 44.7 Mbps (DS3).

Terminology

Like other technologies, many terms and acronyms are associated with Frame Relay. Use Figure 8-6 to help you review them.

Frame Relay is used between the customer premises equipment (CPE) and the Frame Relay switch, but the complete path is known up front. Figure 8-6 illustrates the LMI signaling (keepalives) that occurs from your router to the local frame switch. The Frame Relay connections from r1 to r2 and r3 are through PVCs. Local DLCIs are the Layer 2 connection identifiers assigned by the service provider.

Autosensing LMI and traffic shaping are among the many significant features that have been available since 11.2 code. Congestion control may be through forward explicit congestion notification (FECN) and backward explicit congestion notification (BECN) if in fact Frame Relay is used within the service provider cloud. The DE bit is a priority discard bit, but packets within your CIR take priority. On the other hand, you may burst higher than your CIR if you have the physical capacity to do so. The following list provides a quick review of the main Frame Relay terms:

- **DLCI**—Data-link connection identifier is a number that identifies the logical *local* circuit between the router and the frame switch. My discussion of DLCIs assumes local significance, which is the norm in practical application. Think of these as circuit identifiers that are provided by the service provider.

Figure 8-6   *Frame Relay Terminology*

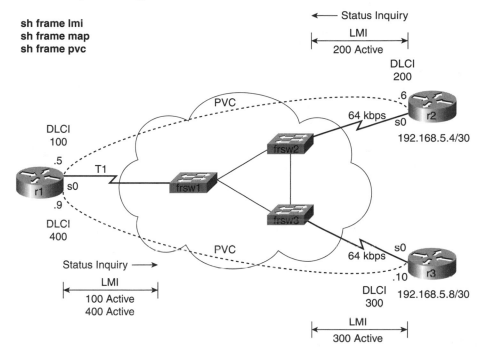

- **PVC**—Permanent virtual circuit is a virtual circuit that corresponds to an end-to-end path going through a Frame Relay cloud. It is permanently established compared to a switched virtual circuit (SVC), which is established on demand.

- **LMI**—Local Management Interface is the signaling between the local router and the local Frame Relay switch. The three types include Cisco (LMI), ANSI (Annex D), and Q933A (Annex A).

- **CIR**—Committed Information Rate is the delivery during normal conditions—minimum acceptable throughput.

- **Committed burst**—Guaranteed delivery under normal conditions.

- **Excess burst**—Bytes outside the CIR accepted by the frame switch and marked as DE eligible.

- **DE**—Discard Eligible is really a priority discard bit in case the network becomes short of resources.

- **BECN**—Backward explicit congestion notification is set in frames traveling in the opposite direction of the congested path.

- **FECN**—Forward explicit congestion notification informs the DTE device receiving the frame that congestion was experienced in the path between the source and destination.

- **SLA**—You have a service level agreement with your service provider, which includes such things as response time, availability, restoration of service, throughput, and SLA reporting. For example, physically you may have a T1 or T3 but you only pay for the subscription you need, yet you can burst to the maximum burst rate within your physical capacity if available. On the other hand, frames flagged as DE are dropped when congestion occurs. The ingress frame switch optionally performs the policing. It can drop all frames in excess of CIR plus burst or it can just mark them DE and let them proceed. This is a service provider policy choice.

- **CPE**—Customer premises equipment.

This terminology may vary according to the service provider, but these are some of the most common terms and acronyms used in the Frame Relay environment.

Now I want to look at Frame Relay frames to analyze the details of some of the terminology mentioned.

Frame Relay Frames

Because Frame Relay is primarily a Layer 2 technology, I want to spend a bit more time with the encapsulation, frame format, and signaling for purposes of supporting it.

Encapsulation

I wouldn't expect encapsulation to be a new topic for you. In this chapter you just change your WAN encapsulation or frame type from HDLC to Frame Relay to communicate using a *connection-oriented Data Link Layer technology*. With Frame Relay you communicate from DTE (router) to DTE (router) through a provider. Each data-link segment connects to the nearest Frame Relay switch (DCE). Typically the DLCI has local significance. This local significance is just like my cell phone speed dial. I have programmed number 1 to be Mom, and number 2 to be Ed, but you may have number 1 as your significant other and number 2 as your Mom or Dad. Think of the phone number as the IP address and the speed dial as the DLCI.

You can also relate DLCIs to going to the bank. Next time you are sitting at the drive-up window close to closing time, watch the tubes and dream about Frame Relay in a hub-and-spoke topology. You place your payroll check in the tube just as someone else in the next lane (using another DLCI) is doing. The tubes all go to one of the tellers (hub) working that day. When the bank teller processes your transaction, she knows who you are by the tube (PVC) you came in on and therefore gives you your cash and gives the other person hers.

Any way you look at it, some Layer 3 payload gets stuffed into a Layer 2 frame to be transported to the local provider to get it to the proper destination. Statistically you can multiplex many virtual circuits over one physical circuit but part of this efficiency is due to the error and flow control being left up to higher-layer protocols. At Layer 2 the default encapsulation type for Frame Relay is Cisco. The encapsulation possibilities are as follows:

- Cisco is the default for Cisco devices.

- IETF is for compatibility with non-Cisco devices.

NOTE   Cisco encapsulation is appropriate when both devices are Cisco routers, and Internet Engineering Task Force (IETF) encapsulation is appropriate when at least one of the devices is not.

Now look at the Frame Relay header to see where all the pieces fit.

The Frame Relay Header

Examine the Frame Relay format in Figure 8-7. The frame starts and ends with a 1-byte flag. The Layer 2 DLCIs are contained within the 2-byte address header, and the data is variable. Frame Relay does use a frame check sequence (FCS). Even though the protocol can recognize when there has been an error, there is no retransmission capability at Layer 2 to correct bad data.

Figure 8-7   *Frame Relay Header*

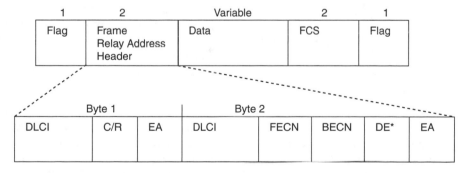

*If there is a problem, discard the data.

Think of the 10-bit DLCI like the MAC address on a LAN. Both are Layer 2 addresses, and routing requires mappings of IP next hops to Layer 2 addresses. The DLCI identifies the local connection. The Command/Response (C/R) bit is application-specific and not modified by the network, and the Extension (EA) bits allow for a 3- or 4-byte header. Current implementations use a 2-byte DLCI, but the EA bits allow room for growth in the future. The next 3 bits are used for congestion control. Figure 8-8 shows a graphical view of explicit congestion notification (ECN).

Figure 8-8 *Frame Relay ECN*

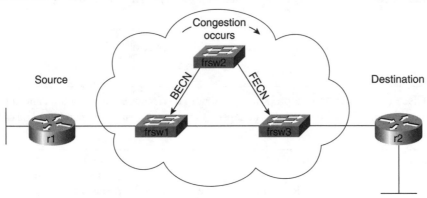

BECN – Backward Explicit Congestion Notification
Notify the source that congestion has occured in the path.

FECN – Forward Explicit Congestion Notification
Signal the next neighbor in the path toward destination that congestion has occured along the path.

FECN is forward explicit congestion notification in that it tells the receiving end that the congestion occurred in the path from the source to the destination. BECN is backward explicit congestion notification in that it is set in frames traveling in the opposite direction of the congested path. FECN notifies the destination, whereas BECN notifies the source. The DE bit is a priority-based DE bit in case the network becomes short of resources. The frame switch sets the DE bit to 1 when the frame is above your CIR (or committed burst). CPE could do the same, but it makes no sense for the CPE (router) to set DE. Why should you volunteer for packet discard compared to all the other customers?

NOTE Keep in mind that if there is a lower-layer problem, the data gets discarded (prior to any unmarked frame) and the upper layers request the retransmission. The reason for the discard may be due to errors or congestion. This is part of the efficiency of Frame Relay as a Layer 2 technology.

If you have access to a WAN sniffer, hook it up and watch what is happening. Sniffing on the WAN is quite a bit more expensive than sniffing the LAN. Our focus for analyzing the Frame

Relay header has and will continue to be with show and debug commands built in to the IOS. If you expect to see any output at all for Frame Relay, however, it relies on the connection between your router and the frame switch. This signaling or keepalive is more often referred to as LMI. When encapsulation is configured properly, the LMI keepalive activity starts between the local router and frame switch.

Signaling (LMI)

The **show frame-relay lmi** command is one you must have on the tip of your tongue when troubleshooting Frame Relay. Chevrolet may be the heartbeat of America, but LMI is the heartbeat of Frame Relay. LMI is the signaling between your router and the local frame switch. The LMI type must match on the same data link (from the router to the local frame switch), although multiple LMI types can be used from the source to the destination network. The signaling consists of a status *request* from the local router to the frame switch and a status *message* from the frame switch to the local router. Example 8-15 displays the output of **show frame-relay lmi**.

Example 8-15   show frame-relay lmi

```
r1>show frame-relay lmi
LMI Statistics for interface Serial1 (Frame Relay DTE) LMI TYPE = CISCO
   Invalid Unnumbered info 0           Invalid Prot Disc 0
   Invalid dummy Call Ref 0            Invalid Msg Type 0
   Invalid Status Message 0            Invalid Lock Shift 0
   Invalid Information ID 0            Invalid Report IE Len 0
   Invalid Report Request 0           Invalid Keep IE Len 0
   Num Status Enq. Sent 4403          Num Status msgs Rcvd 4403
   Num Update Status Rcvd 0           Num Status Timeouts 0
r1>
```

The first shaded line displays the statistics for the s1 interface that is configured as Frame Relay DTE with an LMI type of Cisco, which is the default configuration for a Frame Relay interface. The next to the last shaded line indicates the status inquiries and is equal to the messages received, which means LMI is working properly. Keep an eye on the last line for an increasing number of timeouts within the keepalive interval, which tends to lead to faulty equipment or circuit issues.

The **debug frame-relay lmi** shows the router requesting DLCIs from the frame switch and the local frame switch responding with new PVCs, deleted PVCs, and the integrity of the existing PVCs. Status inquiries always go from the router to the frame switch, which in turn replies with up-to-date PVC and DLCI information. Refer back to Figure 8-6 for a moment. If all is well, the local frame switch for r1 should return DLCI 100 and 400 both as active in that particular example. This process is dynamic like ARP is in the LAN, so you are not sending to something that does not exist. However, things are not always normal when the router receives LMI information. See Table 8-2 for possible PVC states.

Table 8-2   *PVC States*

PVC State	Description
Active	The provider's network believes that the PVC is configured and operational from edge to edge within the cloud. The remote router is configured to match.
Inactive	Local connection may be fine but the other end is not working. Perhaps it has not been configured yet, either on the router or within the provider cloud.
Deleted	The DLCI that the router is reporting to the frame switch has no validating entry in the frame route table. The DLCIs may have been reversed or the PVC may have been deleted.

Use the following commands to check the LMI status:

- **show frame-relay lmi**

- **show frame-relay pvc**

- **show interfaces**

Issue a **show interfaces s0** to check the LMI type. Cisco supports the following LMI types:

- Cisco LMI type uses DLCI 1023 as its data path.

- ANSI T1.617 Annex D LMI uses DLCI 0 as its data path.

- ITU-T Q.933 Annex A uses DLCI 0 as its data path.

Note that LMI typically runs over reserved DLCI 0 or 1023. Normally the DLCIs assigned from the service provider are in the range of 16 to 1007. You can easily remember that if you were 16 years old when you got your driver's license and if you are a James Bond fan.

What if you need to configure the LMI to be something other than the Cisco default? The service provider makes this decision in the real world, but in the private world you can certainly do what you want. Refer back to Figure 8-3 if you need to review your lab setup again. Configure r1 for ANSI LMI, and watch the keepalives until the line protocol goes down as in Example 8-16.

Example 8-16   *Configuring and Testing ANSI LMI*

```
r1#debug frame-relay lmi
Frame Relay LMI debugging is on
Displaying all Frame Relay LMI data
r1#configure terminal
r1(config)#interface s1
r1(config-if)#frame-relay lmi-type ansi
r1(config-if)#end
Dec 10 09:09:29.553: Serial1(out): StEnq, myseq 1, yourseen 0, DTE up
Dec 10 09:09:29.557: datagramstart = 0xE3F544, datagramsize = 14
Dec 10 09:09:29.557: FR encap = 0x00010308
Dec 10 09:09:29.557: 00 75 95 01 01 01 03 02 01 00
Dec 10 09:09:29.565:
```

Example 8-16   *Configuring and Testing ANSI LMI (Continued)*

```
Dec 10 09:09:29.785: %SYS-5-CONFIG_I: Configured from console by console
Dec 10 09:09:39.553: Serial1(out): StEnq, myseq 2, yourseen 0, DTE up
Dec 10 09:09:39.557: datagramstart = 0xE3F544, datagramsize = 14
Dec 10 09:09:39.557: FR encap = 0x00010308
Dec 10 09:09:39.561: 00 75 95 01 01 00 03 02 02 00
Dec 10 09:09:39.565:
r1#
Dec 10 09:09:49.553: Serial1(out): StEnq, myseq 3, yourseen 0, DTE up
Dec 10 09:09:49.557: datagramstart = 0xE3F544, datagramsize = 14
Dec 10 09:09:49.557: FR encap = 0x00010308
Dec 10 09:09:49.557: 00 75 95 01 01 00 03 02 03 00
Dec 10 09:09:49.565:
Dec 10 09:09:59.553: %FR-5-DLCICHANGE: Interface Serial1 - DLCI 104 state changed
to INACTIVE
Dec 10 09:09:59.585: Serial1(out): StEnq, myseq 1, yourseen 0, DTE down
Dec 10 09:09:59.589: datagramstart = 0xE3F544, datagramsize = 14
Dec 10 09:09:59.589: FR encap = 0x00010308
Dec 10 09:09:59.593: 00 75 95 01 01 00 03 02 01 00
Dec 10 09:09:59.597:
Dec 10 09:10:00.553: %LINEPROTO-5-UPDOWN: Line protocol on Interface Serial1,
changed state to down
r1#show frame-relay map
r1#show frame-relay pvc
PVC Statistics for interface Serial1 (Frame Relay DTE)
```

Now set s1 on the frame switch to be ANSI LMI, and continue to watch the keepalive activity on r1 as in Example 8-17.

Example 8-17   *Configuring the Frame Switch for ANSI LMI*

```
frame-switch(config)#interface s1
frame-switch(config-if)#frame-relay lmi-type ansi
frame-switch(config-if)#end
frame-switch#copy running-config startup-config
!!!status inquiry from r1 to the frame switch
Dec 10 09:30:49.553: Serial1(out): StEnq, myseq 126, yourseen 1, DTE down
Dec 10 09:30:49.557: datagramstart = 0xE3F544, datagramsize = 14
Dec 10 09:30:49.557: FR encap = 0x00010308
Dec 10 09:30:49.561: 00 75 95 01 01 01 03 02 7E 01
!!!keepalive reply from the frameswitch to r1 (full status update)
Dec 10 09:30:49.597: Serial1(in): Status, myseq 126
Dec 10 09:30:49.597: RT IE 1, length 1, type 0
Dec 10 09:30:49.601: KA IE 3, length 2, yourseen 2 , myseq 126
Dec 10 09:30:49.601: PVC IE 0x7 , length 0x3 , dlci 104, status 0x2
!!!status inquiry from r1 to the frame switch
Dec 10 09:30:59.581: Serial1(out): StEnq, myseq 127, yourseen 2, DTE up
Dec 10 09:30:59.581: datagramstart = 0xE3F544, datagramsize = 14
Dec 10 09:30:59.585: FR encap = 0x00010308
Dec 10 09:30:59.585: 00 75 95 01 01 01 03 02 7F 02
!!!keepalive reply from the frameswitch to r1
Dec 10 09:30:59.601: Serial1(in): Status, myseq 127
Dec 10 09:30:59.605: RT IE 1, length 1, type 1
```

continues

Example 8-17 *Configuring the Frame Switch for ANSI LMI (Continued)*

```
Dec 10 09:30:59.605: KA IE 3, length 2, yourseq 3 , myseq 127
Dec 10 09:31:00.553: %LINEPROTO-5-UPDOWN: Line protocol on Interface Serial1,
changed state to up
!!!status inquiry from r1 to the frame switch
Dec 10 09:31:09.553: Serial1(out): StEnq, myseq 128, yourseen 3, DTE up
Dec 10 09:31:09.557: datagramstart = 0xE3F544, datagramsize = 14
Dec 10 09:31:09.557: FR encap = 0x00010308
Dec 10 09:31:09.561: 00 75 95 01 01 01 03 02 80 03
!!!keepalive reply from the frameswitch to r1
Dec 10 09:31:09.577: Serial1(in): Status, myseq 128
Dec 10 09:31:09.577: RT IE 1, length 1, type 1
Dec 10 09:31:09.577: KA IE 3, length 2, yourseq 4 , myseq 128
!!!status inquiry from r1 to the frame switch
Dec 10 09:31:19.553: Serial1(out): StEnq, myseq 129, yourseen 4, DTE up
Dec 10 09:31:19.557: datagramstart = 0xE3F544, datagramsize = 14
Dec 10 09:31:19.557: FR encap = 0x00010308
Dec 10 09:31:19.561: 00 75 95 01 01 01 03 02 81 04
!!!keepalive reply from the frameswitch to r1
Dec 10 09:31:19.577: Serial1(in): Status, myseq 129
Dec 10 09:31:19.577: RT IE 1, length 1, type 1
Dec 10 09:31:19.577: KA IE 3, length 2, yourseq 5 , myseq 129
!!!status inquiry from r1 to the frame switch
Dec 10 09:31:29.553: Serial1(out): StEnq, myseq 130, yourseen 5, DTE up
Dec 10 09:31:29.557: datagramstart = 0xE3F544, datagramsize = 14
Dec 10 09:31:29.557: FR encap = 0x00010308
Dec 10 09:31:29.561: 00 75 95 01 01 01 03 02 82 05
!!!keepalive reply from the frameswitch to r1
Dec 10 09:31:29.577: Serial1(in): Status, myseq 130
Dec 10 09:31:29.577: RT IE 1, length 1, type 1
Dec 10 09:31:29.577: KA IE 3, length 2, yourseq 6 , myseq 130
!!!status inquiry from r1 to the frame switch
Dec 10 09:31:39.553: Serial1(out): StEnq, myseq 131, yourseen 6, DTE up
Dec 10 09:31:39.557: datagramstart = 0xE3F544, datagramsize = 14
Dec 10 09:31:39.557: FR encap = 0x00010308
Dec 10 09:31:39.561: 00 75 95 01 01 00 03 02 83 06
!!!keepalive reply from the frameswitch to r1 (full status update)
Dec 10 09:31:39.577: Serial1(in): Status, myseq 131
Dec 10 09:31:39.581: RT IE 1, length 1, type 0
Dec 10 09:31:39.581: KA IE 3, length 2, yourseq 7 , myseq 131
Dec 10 09:31:39.585: PVC IE 0x7 , length 0x3 , dlci 104, status 0x2
Dec 10 09:31:39.585: %FR-5-DLCICHANGE: Interface Serial1 - DLCI 104 state changed
to ACTIVE
r1#show frame-relay map
Serial1 (up): ip 192.168.5.6 dlci 104(0x68,0x1880), dynamic,
              broadcast,, status defined, active
r1#undebug all
```

The output of **debug frame-relay lmi** is quite helpful to show the LMI status request sent out by the router as indicated by (out) on the interface. Likewise, the (in) on the interface indicates the LMI received from the switch. Also, type 0 is a full LMI status message that includes such data as the DLCI, the status, the CIR, and any traffic-shaping type of information. The status corresponds to the active, inactive, and deleted states of DLCIs. For example, 0x0 is inactive, 0x2 is active, and 0x4 is deleted. Watch out for 0x4 (the deleted status). The DLCIs may be reversed or the PVC may have actually been deleted.

Now that the DLCI is active, view the LMI statistics, clear the interface counters so that old statistics are not in your way later, and ping the other end of the PVC as in Example 8-18.

Example 8-18   *Viewing the LMI Statistics*

```
r1#show frame-relay lmi
LMI Statistics for interface Serial1 (Frame Relay DTE) LMI TYPE = ANSI
  Invalid Unnumbered info 0           Invalid Prot Disc 0
  Invalid dummy Call Ref 0            Invalid Msg Type 0
  Invalid Status Message 0            Invalid Lock Shift 0
  Invalid Information ID 0            Invalid Report IE Len 0
  Invalid Report Request 0           Invalid Keep IE Len 0
  Num Status Enq. Sent 9675          Num Status msgs Rcvd 9549
  Num Update Status Rcvd 0           Num Status Timeouts 127
r1#
r1#clear counters s1
Clear "show interface" counters on this interface [confirm]
r1#ping 192.168.5.6
Type escape sequence to abort.
Sending 5, 100-byte ICMP Echos to 192.168.5.6, timeout is 2 seconds:
!!!!!
Success rate is 100 percent (5/5), round-trip min/avg/max = 56/58/60 ms
```

Examples 8-16 and 8-17 illustrate what it is like to have a local LMI mismatch, but how the remote end of the PVC can use a different LMI from the local end. You proved that the frame switch can handle multiple LMI types just in case it is connected to something other than a Cisco device. However, the same data link or connection between the local router and the frame switch must use the same LMI. Use the **show frame-relay lmi** command to find LMI mismatches. When you are sending and not receiving, for instance, it is kind of like you talking English and the other person talking French when neither of you happen to be bilingual. Watch for the increase in status timeouts as highlighted in the preceding example.

Frame Relay Addressing

Frame Relay Layer 2 addresses are DLCIs. I mentioned previously that the WAN DLCIs are analgous to the LAN MACs. ARP is the method I discussed for mapping IP to MAC in the LAN chapters and RARP is just the opposite of mapping MAC to IP. Frame uses Inverse ARP. Routers learn remote IP addresses to map to local DLCIs via Inverse ARP or static map statements as illustrated in Figure 8-9. Use the picture and steps covered in the next section to assist you with troubleshooting Frame Relay Inverse ARP issues.

Figure 8-9 *Inverse ARP*

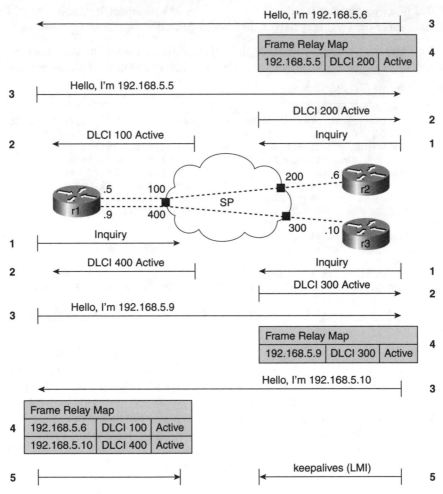

Refer to the five steps that follow in the "Inverse ARP" section.

Inverse ARP

As you have witnessed in the **debug lmi** commands, about once a minute or every six keepalives a router requests a full status response from a Frame Relay network with active DLCIs. This is the signaling or LMI between the local router and the local Frame Relay switch. The router then sends an Inverse ARP out on each PVC. The remote routers respond with their respective IP addresses. The original router then maps the IP addresses to the right DLCIs. Understanding this is critical to anyone troubleshooting Frame Relay networks. Follow along with the steps in Figure 8-9:

1 After the Physical Layer is up, the router sends a status inquiry to the local frame switch. The default keepalive activity between the router and the switch is occurring every 10 seconds. Every sixth poll (60 seconds), the router requests a full status.

2 The local frame switch replies with a status update message to the router every 10 seconds with a full update including DLCI information every 60 seconds, specifically, every sixth LMI inquiry.

3 Now that the local router knows about a PVC through an active DLCI, it can send its IP address to the other end. This is an Inverse ARP packet.

4 The remote router knows which local DLCI it received the address on and sets up a corresponding map. It is important to note that the local router uses its own DLCI, which may not be the same as the remote router is using.

5 Keepalive (LMI) activity continues to occur by default every 10 seconds between the router and the local frame switch with a full status message every 60 seconds. This dynamic nature ensures that any changes are accounted for as they occur.

NOTE   Decrease your keepalive activity by one until they stabilize if you are having trouble with flapping links.

See the previous examples for **show frame-relay map** output, but Example 8-19 and 8-20 display a couple of debug commands that can assist you capture the Inverse ARP activity.

Example 8-19 *Inverse ARP and* **debug frame-relay events**

```
r1#debug frame-relay events
Frame Relay events debugging is on
r1#configure terminal
r1(config)#interface s1
r1(config-if)#shut
r1(config-if)#no shut
01:48:12: %LINK-3-UPDOWN: Interface Serial1, changed state to up
01:48:13: %LINEPROTO-5-UPDOWN: Line protocol on Interface Serial1,
    changed state to up
01:48:22: %FR-5-DLCICHANGE: Interface Serial1 - DLCI 104 state changed to ACTIVE
01:48:23: Serial1: FR ARP input
01:48:23: datagramstart = 0xE3B384, datagramsize = 30
01:48:23: FR encap = 0x18810300
01:48:23: 80 00 00 00 08 06 00 0F 08 00 02 04 00 08 00 00
01:48:23: C0 A8 05 06 18 C1 00 00 00 00
01:48:23:
r1(config-if)#end
r1#ping 192.168.5.6
Type escape sequence to abort.
Sending 5, 100-byte ICMP Echos to 192.168.5.6, timeout is 2 seconds:
!!!!!
Success rate is 100 percent (5/5), round-trip min/avg/max = 56/58/60 ms
r1#undebug all
```

Example 8-19 shows the Inverse ARP activity when you bring up an interface. Although not recommended in a practical environment, compare the previous events received to the **debug frame-relay packet** output in Example 8-20.

Example 8-20 *Inverse ARP and* **debug frame packet**

```
r1#debug frame-relay packet
Frame Relay packet debugging is on
r1#configure terminal
r1(config)#interface s1
r1(config-if)#shut
r1(config-if)#no shut
01:49:46: %LINK-3-UPDOWN: Interface Serial1, changed state to up
01:49:47: %LINEPROTO-5-UPDOWN: Line protocol on Interface Serial1,
    changed state to up
01:49:56: %FR-5-DLCICHANGE: Interface Serial1 - DLCI 104 state changed to ACTIVE
01:49:56: Serial1(o): dlci 104(0x1881), pkt encaps 0x0300 0x8000 0x0000 0x806
    (ARP), datagramsize 30
01:49:56: FR: Sending INARP Request on interface Serial1 dlci 104 for link 7(IP)
01:49:56: broadcast dequeue
01:49:56: Serial1(o):Pkt sent on dlci 104(0x1881),
    pkt encaps 0x300  0x8000 0x0    0x806 (ARP), datagramsize 30
01:50:03: Serial1(i): dlci 104(0x1881),
    pkt encaps 0x0300 0x8000 0x0000 0x806 (ARP), datagramsize 30
01:50:03: Serial1: frame relay INARP received
01:50:03: FR: Sending INARP Reply on interface Serial1 dlci 104 for link 7(IP)
r1(config-if)#end
r1#ping 192.168.5.6
Type escape sequence to abort.
Sending 5, 100-byte ICMP Echos to 192.168.5.6, timeout is 2 seconds:
!!!!!
Success rate is 100 percent (5/5), round-trip min/avg/max = 64/64/64 ms
r1#
01:50:37: Serial1(o): dlci 104(0x1881), pkt type 0x800(IP), datagramsize 104
01:50:37: Serial1(i): dlci 104(0x1881), pkt type 0x800, datagramsize 104
01:50:37: Serial1(o): dlci 104(0x1881), pkt type 0x800(IP), datagramsize 104
...
01:50:38: Serial1(i): dlci 104(0x1881), pkt type 0x800, datagramsize 104
r1#undebug all
```

The **debug frame packet** command is excellent to watch the Inverse ARP activity for understanding. On the other hand, like any *debug packet* command, it is not too forgiving in the production environment.

As you can see, commands such as **show interfaces**, **show frame-relay lmi**, **show frame-relay pvc**, **show frame-relay map**, **show frame-relay route**, **debug frame-relay lmi**, **debug frame-relay events**, and **debug frame packet** are quite beneficial in troubleshooting Frame Relay. How many times have you made a typo on an IP address or DLCI assignment? Mistakes certainly stand out with these commands, especially if you quickly compare them to **show ip interface brief**. So far on the end-user side of the frame you have been using Inverse ARP for the Layer 2-to-Layer 3 mapping. Now I want to turn your attention to using static maps.

Static Map Statements

Static map statements in Frame Relay disable Inverse ARP. You can think of this like your routing protocols having a higher administrative distance than your static routes and the latter taking precedence. Actually, routing protocols are a good topic to discuss with Frame Relay and I cover them in the "Shooting Trouble with Frame Relay" section.

NOTE	Frame Relay is an NBMA technology, so remember to use the **broadcast** keyword with static maps so that the Layer 3 routing updates get forwarded. It allows broadcasts and multicasts over the PVC and in effect turns the broadcast into a unicast to send it out so that the other side gets the routing updates.

With Inverse ARP, the **show frame-relay map** command displays not only *dynamic* for the method of learning about the map, but also *broadcast*. However, this is not the default when you define your own static map statements.

Now I want you to turn off Inverse ARP and use static mappings for your hub-and-spoke topology from r2 to r1 and r3 as in Example 8-21.

Example 8-21 *Static Map Statements*

```
r1(config)#interface s1
r1(config-if)#frame map ip 192.168.5.6 ?
  <16-1007>  DLCI
r1(config-if)#frame map ip 192.168.5.6 104 ?
  broadcast            Broadcasts should be forwarded to this address
  cisco                Use CISCO Encapsulation
  compress             Enable TCP/IP and RTP/IP header compression
  ietf                 Use RFC1490/RFC2427 Encapsulation
  nocompress           Do not compress TCP/IP headers
  payload-compression  Use payload compression
  rtp                  RTP header compression parameters
  tcp                  TCP header compression parameters
  <cr>
r1(config-if)#frame map ip 192.168.5.6 104 broadcast
r1(config-if)#end
r1#copy running-config startup-config

r3(config)#interface s0/0
r3(config-if)#frame map ip 192.168.5.5 108 broadcast
r3(config-if)#end
r3#copy running-config startup-config
```

Configuring the static map statements automatically turned off Inverse ARP as Example 8-22 illustrates. Verify that r3 can ping the address mapped to DLCI 108.

Example 8-22 *Viewing the Static Map Configurations*

```
r1#show frame-relay map
Serial1 (up): ip 192.168.5.6 dlci 104(0x68,0x1880), static,
              broadcast,CISCO, status defined, active
r3#show frame-relay map
Serial0/0 (up): ip 192.168.5.5 dlci 108(0x6C,0x18C0), static,
              broadcast,CISCO, status defined, active
r3#ping 192.168.5.5
Type escape sequence to abort.
Sending 5, 100-byte ICMP Echos to 192.168.5.5, timeout is 2 seconds:
!!!!!
Success rate is 100 percent (5/5), round-trip min/avg/max = 56/58/60 ms
```

NOTE   Inverse ARP is enabled by default, but turned off automatically when you put in a static map
statement. To select Inverse ARP for a particular protocol, use the following interface
configuration command: **frame-relay inverse-arp** *protocol dlci#*. This is not necessary on a
point-to-point subinterface.

Other options that are available while configuring static map statements include compression,
and from a support standpoint what you are doing on one end better match what you are doing on
the other. An example of the command is **frame-relay map ip 192.168.5.6 104 broadcast payload-
compress packet-by-packet**. Feel free to experiment with compression with Frame Relay, but
remember to remove it from your configurations before you continue on with Frame Relay at
the Physical Layer.

Frame Relay at the Physical Layer

Although Frame Relay is a Layer 2 technology, it obviously depends on Layer 1, too. How
about things such as clocking, cables, controllers, and channel service units/data service units
(CSUs/DSUs)? These are all things you take for granted, but cannot forget in the support world.
Although in lab scenarios you use back-to-back serial cables with one end wired to be a
physical DTE and the other end to be a physical DCE, this works a little differently in the
practical world.

The router may directly connect to the Frame Switch or to a CSU/DSU that connects to the
frame switch. The CSU/DSU is like a modem in many respects. It converts the V.35 or EIA/
TIA-449 signals to a properly coded transmission signal necessary by the local exchange carrier
(LEC) local circuit. You receive your clock (timing) from the provider in practical application,
instead of you using the **clock rate** statement on your DCE end of the cable.

In this section I concentrate more on supporting the hub-and-spoke topology using
subinterfaces because that is probably the most common application of Frame Relay.

Topologies

As many design books discuss, there are basically three physical approaches or topologies you can adopt in Frame Relay: hub-and-spoke (star), partial mesh, and full mesh (or some hybrid thereof).

Which one you pick really boils down your redundancy needs and your pocketbook. Scalability, manageability, and optimization always seem to find their way into the goals of any internetwork design. Frame Relay is no exception. For example, you normally don't see the maximum number of DLCIs configured on an individual serial port. Instead 200 to 300 is the normal maximum, and more like 50 or less is more realistic. Take into consideration things such as what routing protocols you are using, your router CPU capacity, PVC speeds, the speed of your lines, compression, your CIR, and bursting capabilities.

A hub-and-spoke topology is normally more economical. Redundant PVCs sound like a good thing. However, you pay for each PVC, and although in many cases that is more economical than leased lines, you should use the appropriate topology and get the appropriate SLA from the provider for your requirements. My focus is really not on design here but rather on supporting the different types of Frame Relay interfaces that you may run across in the WAN.

Interfaces that support Frame Relay are multipoint and non-NBMA by default. As you have learned in your routing studies, however, many routing updates are broadcast or multicast in nature. If you have multiple neighbors off the same multipoint interface, there is a need for routing replication for each PVC. This is a big issue on the WAN with NBMA technologies. Therefore it is important for you to get lots of hands-on experience with Frame Relay over both multipoint and point-to-point subinterfaces and a variety of routing protocols.

Subinterfaces

Point-to-point subinterfaces should be used in the majority of cases regardless of protocol because packets received on one interface can be forwarded out another. This way, a single physical interface works like several logical interfaces. I like to think of each point-to-point subinterface as if it were my own dedicated leased line. Point-to-point subinterfaces require their own subnet like leased lines, but *are not* subject to the split-horizon issues of Frame Relay running on main or multipoint interfaces. Point-to-point interfaces don't need map statements. Instead interface DLCIs are assigned, because each subinterface is a separate PVC.

Multipoint subinterfaces *do not* resolve split-horizon issues, but they can save IP address space because a single subnet is used. They are more applicable to mesh topologies, whereas point-to-point subinterfaces are more applicable to hub-and-spoke topologies.

Define a subinterface in interface configuration mode using the following example: **interface serial0.1 [multipoint | point-to-point]**. The shortcut **interface s0.1 p** creates a point-to-point subinterface for s0. The shortcut **interface s0.1 m** creates a multipoint subinterface for s0. The documentation for 12.1 code and later states that there is no default as far as multipoint or point-to-point. However, a serial physical interface is in fact multipoint for Frame Relay.

It is time for some more practical application of all this. I want you to configure subinterfaces to shoot some trouble for yourself. Then I will review some common issues with routing protocols over Frame Relay, particularly regarding its NBMA nature. Use the same routers you have been working with in the chapter scenarios thus far. Configure r3 as the frame switch and the rest of the routers in a hub-and-spoke topology using r1 as the hub at the HQ site. HQ should be able to communicate with all remote locations using Frame Relay multipoint subinterfaces. All remote locations (DC and VA) should be able to communicate with HQ using multipoint subinterfaces over network 192.168.8.0/24. The service provider provides all clocking. Use r2 and r4 as the spokes or the remote locations. Draw a diagram as in Figure 8-10 for your lab and use it to shoot any troubles as you go along.

First, rewire according to the multipoint subinterfaces scenario in Figure 8-10. Then configure the frame switch, and then the hub (HQ) and spokes (DC and VA). Compare your results to the examples starting in Example 8-23.

NOTE   Make sure you put descriptions on your interfaces and passwords on your devices to enable telnet access. Using the **logging synchronous** command is a good practice, too. I saved you a few steps by eliminating these from some of the previous configurations just because this is a lab. However, bad habits are hard to break. Always do this in a practical environment to assist you with troubleshooting. I saved my configuration to a file named *r3 as frame switch for multipoint scenario* if you prefer to paste it into r1's configuration mode instead of typing.

Figure 8-10   *Multipoint Subinterface*

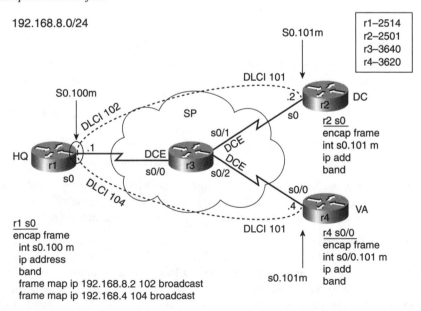

Example 8-23 *Frame Switch Configuration*

```
Router(config)#hostname frame-switch
frame-switch(config)#frame-relay switching
frame-switch(config)#interface s0/0
frame-switch(config-if)#description r3s0/0 to HQ
frame-switch(config-if)#bandwidth 64
frame-switch(config-if)#clock rate 64000
frame-switch(config-if)#encap frame
frame-switch(config-if)#frame-relay intf-type dce
frame-switch(config-if)#frame route 102 interface s0/1 101
frame-switch(config-if)#frame route 104 interface s0/2 101
frame-switch(config-if)#no shut
frame-switch(config-if)#interface s0/1
frame-switch(config-if)#description r3s0/1 to DC
frame-switch(config-if)#bandwidth 64
frame-switch(config-if)#clock rate 64000
frame-switch(config-if)#encap frame
frame-switch(config-if)#frame-relay intf-type dce
frame-switch(config-if)#frame route 101 interface s0/0 102
frame-switch(config-if)#no shut
frame-switch(config-if)#interface s0/2
frame-switch(config-if)#description r3s0/2 to VA
frame-switch(config-if)#bandwidth 64
frame-switch(config-if)#clock rate 64000
frame-switch(config-if)#encap frame
frame-switch(config-if)#frame-relay intf-type dce
frame-switch(config-if)#frame route 101 interface s0/0 104
frame-switch(config-if)#no shut
frame-switch(config-if)#exit
frame-switch(config)#line console 0
frame-switch(config-line)#logging synchronous
frame-switch(config-line)#exit
frame-switch(config)#enable secret donna
frame-switch(config)#line vty 0 4
frame-switch(config-line)#password donna
frame-switch(config-line)#end
frame-switch#copy running-config startup-config
```

The frame switch configuration is familiar to you by now although you could have accidentally configured r2 rather than r3 or ran into Physical Layer issues. This frame switch implementation is more practical than what you worked with earlier in the sense that the physical DCE ends of the cable connect you to the service provider. Verify that you set it up properly with the **show frame-relay route** command as in Example 8-24.

Example 8-24 *Verifying the New Frame Switch Configuration*

```
frame-switch#show frame-relay route
Input Intf      Input Dlci      Output Intf     Output Dlci     Status
Serial0/0       102             Serial0/1       101             inactive
Serial0/0       104             Serial0/2       101             inactive
Serial0/1       101             Serial0/0       102             inactive
Serial0/2       101             Serial0/0       104             inactive
```

The input interface/dlci columns show the interface and DLCI number the packets come in on and the output interface/dlci columns show the interface and DLCI number the packets leave on. The PVC status is inactive at the present time because you have not configured the other ends.

Next configure the hub router using a multipoint subinterface as in Figure 8-10 and Example 8-25. My file is named *r1 multipoint hub config* if you would rather just copy and paste.

Example 8-25 *Configuring the Hub Router for Multipoint Subinterfaces*

```
Router(config)#hostname r1
r1(config)#interface s0
r1(config-if)#encap frame
r1(config-if)#interface s0.100
% Incomplete command.
r1(config)#interface s0.100 multipoint
r1(config-subif)#ip address 192.168.8.1 255.255.255.0
r1(config-subif)#bandwidth 64
r1(config-subif)#frame-relay map ip 192.168.8.2 102 broadcast
r1(config-subif)#frame-relay map ip 192.168.8.4 104 broadcast
r1(config-subif)#no shut
r1(config)#line console 0
r1(config-line)#logging synchronous
r1(config-line)#exit
r1(config)#enable secret donna
r1(config)#line vty 0 4
r1(config-line)#password donna
r1(config-line)#end
r1#copy running-config startup-config
```

Finally, configure the spoke routers using multipoint subinterfaces, too, as in Example 8-26. At this time *do not* use mapping statements for r2 and r4. Once again, you can copy and paste if you prefer.

Example 8-26 *Configuring the Spoke Routers with Multipoint Subinterfaces*

```
Router(config)#hostname r2
r2(config)#interface s0
r2(config-if)#encap frame
r2(config-if)#interface s0.101 m
r2(config-subif)#bandwidth 64
r2(config-subif)#ip address 192.168.8.2 255.255.255.0
r2(config-subif)#no shut
r2(config-subif)#exit
r2(config)#line console 0
r2(config-line)#logging synchronous
r2(config-line)#exit
r2(config)#enable secret donna
r2(config)#line vty 0 4
r2(config-line)#password donna
r2(config-line)#end
r2#copy running-config startup-config

Router(config)#hostname r4
r4(config)#interface s0/0
```

Example 8-26   *Configuring the Spoke Routers with Multipoint Subinterfaces (Continued)*

```
r4(config-if)#encap frame
r4(config-if)#interface s0/0.101 m
r4(config-subif)#bandwidth 64
r4(config-subif)#ip address 192.168.8.4 255.255.255.0
r4(config-subif)#no shut
r4(config-subif)#exit
r4(config)#line console 0
r4(config-line)#logging synchronous
r4(config-line)#exit
r4(config)#enable secret donna
r4config)#line vty 0 4
r4(config-line)#password donna
r4(config-line)#end
r4#copy running-config startup-config
```

Verify connectivity. Check your interfaces, LMI, PVCs, and so on starting in Example 8-27.

Example 8-27   *Verifying Multipoint Subinterface Configurations*

```
r1#show ip interface brief
Interface              IP-Address      OK? Method Status                 Protocol
Ethernet0              unassigned      YES unset  administratively down down
Ethernet1              unassigned      YES unset  administratively down down
Serial0                unassigned      YES unset  administratively down down
Serial0.100            192.168.8.1     YES manual down                   down
Serial1                unassigned      YES unset  administratively down down
```

You may have forgot to bring up all your interfaces as I did in my copy-and-paste file, but **show ip interface brief** clearly shows you *administratively down*. Fix the r1 interface issues as in Example 8-28.

Example 8-28   *Bringing Up the Main Serial0 Interface*

```
r1(config)#interface s0
r1(config-if)#no shut
00:54:16: %LINK-3-UPDOWN: Interface Serial0, changed state to up
00:54:16: %LINEPROTO-5-UPDOWN: Line protocol on Interface Serial0.100,
    changed state to up
00:54:16: %LINEPROTO-5-UPDOWN: Line protocol on Interface Serial0.100,
    changed state to down
00:54:26: %FR-5-DLCICHANGE: Interface Serial0 - DLCI 102 state changed to ACTIVE
00:54:26: %LINEPROTO-5-UPDOWN: Line protocol on Interface Serial0.100,
    changed state to up
00:54:27: %LINEPROTO-5-UPDOWN: Line protocol on Interface Serial0,
    changed state to up
00:54:27: %FR-5-DLCICHANGE: Interface Serial0 - DLCI 104 state changed to ACTIVE
00:54:36: %FR-5-DLCICHANGE: Interface Serial0 - DLCI 104 state changed to
    INACTIVE
r1(config-if)#end
```

DLCI 104 appears to be bouncing between active and inactive. The "no shut" of the physical interface caused all subinterfaces to be optimistically "up" until the actual IOS verification method (LMI) deemed it not so. The default time and date stamps certainly aren't as useful as with the **service timestamps [debug|log] datetime localtime msec** commands, which would be helpful for troubleshooting other issues. Add those commands and set the clock for all your hub-and-spoke boxes at this time.

Configure and troubleshoot the rest of your routers until they are configured like Figure 8-10. Ensure HQ can ping DC and VA. Continue your Frame Relay testing as in Example 8-29.

Example 8-29 *Verifying the Frame Relay Multipoint Subinterface Scenario on r1*

```
r1#show frame-relay map
Serial0.100 (up): ip 192.168.8.2 dlci 102(0x66,0x1860), static,
              broadcast,
              CISCO, status defined, active
Serial0.100 (up): ip 192.168.8.4 dlci 104(0x68,0x1880), static,
              broadcast,
              CISCO, status defined, active
r1#ping 192.168.8.2
Type escape sequence to abort.
Sending 5, 100-byte ICMP Echos to 192.168.8.2, timeout is 2 seconds:
.....
Success rate is 0 percent (0/5)
r1#ping 192.168.8.4
Type escape sequence to abort.
Sending 5, 100-byte ICMP Echos to 192.168.8.4, timeout is 2 seconds:
.....
Success rate is 0 percent (0/5)
```

The **show frame-relay map** output illustrates how DLCI 102 can get to 192.168.8.2 (DC) and how DLCI 104 can get to 192.168.8.4 (VA). The PVCs are active, yet the pings are not successful. Help me determine the problem in Example 8-30.

Example 8-30 *Verifying the Frame Relay Multipoint Subinterface Scenario on r2 and r4*

```
r2#show frame-relay map
r2#
r2#clear frame-relay-inarp
r4#show frame-relay map
Serial0/0 (up): ip 0.0.0.0 dlci 101(0x65,0x1850)
              broadcast,
              CISCO, status defined, active
r4#clear frame-relay-inarp
r4#show frame-relay map
Serial0/0 (up): ip 0.0.0.0 dlci 101(0x65,0x1850)
              broadcast,
              CISCO, status defined, active
```

You just never know what to expect when you are troubleshooting. r2 shows nothing in its Inverse ARP table, and r4 has a 0.0.0.0 mapping that does not belong there. You tried clearing the Inverse ARP table, which did not seem to make a difference. The 0.0.0.0 is not a default route, but the IOS's way of saying an Inverse ARP message has not been received from the neighbor at the other end of the PVC. That's why the ping failed—it made it fine from r1 to r4, but r4 couldn't send the reply because the map was incomplete (encapsulation failed). The other end already sent its Inverse ARP message well before the r4 end was active. After r1 sent an Inverse ARP message, r4 could complete the map. DC and VA need directions on how to get to HQ. You should configure map statements like you did for r1 on r2 and r4. Verify that it works in Example 8-31.

Example 8-31   *Configuring Static Maps on r2 and r4*

```
r2(config)#interface s0.101
r2(config-subif)#frame-relay map ip 192.168.8.1 101
r4(config)#interface s0/0.101
r4(config-subif)#frame-relay map ip 192.168.8.1 101
!!!HQ to DC
r1#ping 192.168.8.2
Type escape sequence to abort.
Sending 5, 100-byte ICMP Echos to 192.168.8.2, timeout is 2 seconds:
!!!!!
Success rate is 100 percent (5/5), round-trip min/avg/max = 60/60/60 ms
!!!HQ to VA
r1#ping 192.168.8.4
Type escape sequence to abort.
Sending 5, 100-byte ICMP Echos to 192.168.8.4, timeout is 2 seconds:
!!!!!
Success rate is 100 percent (5/5), round-trip min/avg/max = 60/60/60 ms
!!!DC to HQ
r2#ping 192.168.8.1
Type escape sequence to abort.
Sending 5, 100-byte ICMP Echos to 192.168.8.1, timeout is 2 seconds:
!!!!!
Success rate is 100 percent (5/5), round-trip min/avg/max = 60/60/60 ms
!!!VA to HQ
r4#ping 192.168.8.1
Type escape sequence to abort.
Sending 5, 100-byte ICMP Echos to 192.168.8.1, timeout is 2 seconds:
!!!!!
Success rate is 100 percent (5/5), round-trip min/avg/max = 56/59/60 ms
```

This scenario does offer you a learning opportunity. The 0.0.0.0 route was stuck in the mapping somehow, and you had to reload the routers (at least the router with the 0.0.0.0 mapping) to get rid of it. In looking back, you could have changed the encapsulation back to HDLC and then reconfigured Frame Relay. Perhaps that would have been a better thing to try instead of a reload if multiple people were affected.

For the experience, verify this multipoint scenario further using all the Frame Relay commands discussed so far. Ultimately, HQ should be able to communicate with DC and VA and vice versa as was proved back in Example 8-31. However, DC should not be able to ping VA in this scenario because there is nothing in the Inverse ARP table to allow it to do so. This would require static maps like you did back in Exercise 8-12 when you wanted to ping yourself using multipoint interfaces in Frame Relay.

A good practical application of a multipoint subinterface configuration is when you are migrating from main interfaces to point-to-point subinterfaces. When doing so, take the lowest CIR times the number of PVCs to get a good bandwidth for each multipoint PVC. Point-to-point subinterfaces are by far more common in the real world, and you will work with them in Trouble Tickets.

NOTE	The **frame-relay interface-dlci** *dlci#* command is typically used with point-to-point subinterfaces. Multipoint communications make use of Inverse ARP or static mappings.

Shooting Trouble with Frame Relay

In this section I want to reinforce the general things to look for when shooting Frame Relay troubles. Also I want to cover a little more detail on shooting trouble with running routing protocols over Frame Relay, and then discuss loopback testing.

The first question to ask yourself with Frame Relay is did it ever work. You are obviously going beyond your control that you had in the LAN to the service provider cloud. However, you must still continue your layered approach to troubleshooting. Although Frame Relay is a Layer 2 technology, it does not work across a broken physical link. If these lower layers are broken, you are wasting your time troubleshooting the upper layers.

The commands **show ip interface brief**, **show interface s0**, **show controllers s 0**, as well as link lights are all invaluable Physical Layer tools. Interface resets are a good indication of queued packets that have not been transmitted, hardware problems, or clocking signals. Other error counts, such as packets input and output and carrier transitions beyond your baseline, are worthwhile to analyze. Move up the stack to check the encapsulation or frame type. Are you communicating with the frame switch? Remember that the LMI type, whether it be Cisco, ANSI, or Q933A must match with the local switch port. Look at the keepalive activity between the local router and the frame switch with **show frame-relay lmi**. Clear the interface counters and watch the Num Status Enq Sent and the Num Status Msgs Rcvd. They should be about the same. Num Status Timeouts tracks how many times the status message was not received within the keepalive window. Perhaps there is an LMI autosensing issue. The service provider provides the DLCIs so that they can do the appropriate mapping to get you to your destination. However, they are not mistake-proof. Maybe the DLCIs are reversed; review the Inverse ARP table with **show frame-relay map**.

NOTE	All unassigned DLCIs reported by the frame switch via LMI are assigned to the main physical interface as multipoint. Because providers make mistakes, and Inverse ARP and CDP are enabled by default, this may cause a security concern. Check **show frame-relay map** frequently for the appearance of unknown DLCIs.

Use **show frame-relay lmi** and **debug frame-relay lmi** like you did back in Examples 8-13 through 8-15 to see whether the router and switch are talking. This **debug** command does not have much of an impact on router operations as most **debug** commands because the output is minimal. It does a great job of showing the LMI exchange for router-to-switch inquiries and switch-to-router reply status messages. The (out)StEnq is the LMI status inquiry sent by the router, and (in)Status is the reply from the frame switch. A full LMI message contains PVC data including DLCI, status, and CIR.

Use the following commands with a little more caution:

- **debug frame-relay events** to show counts of packets received on interface

- **debug frame-relay packet** to see the packets sent out a Frame Relay interface

Possible packet types include 0x308, which is a signaling message for DLCI 0, and 0x309, which is an LMI message valid with a DLCI of 1023.

Issue a **debug serial interface** command early on to see the keepalive activity. Change the encapsulation to HDLC to see the keepalive traffic, because if LMI is down for Frame Relay the frame interface will not be able to generate keepalives. It only takes three missed keepalives in a row to take the line down. You'll look at HDLC a little closer in the next chapter, but the point here is that only Cisco HDLC encapsulation supports detection of a looped Layer 1 and still keeps the line protocol up so that you may send test traffic.

Keepalives in the WAN world are truly between you and the service provider, not just your own interface. You look at these more in the next WAN chapter. For example:

- Mineseq is the keepalive sent by the local side.

- Yourseen is the keepalive sent by the remote side.

- Mineseen is the local keepalive seen by the remote side.

NOTE   Always remember to turn off all debug processing when finished testing. Remember, **u all** is short for **undebug all** or **no debug all**.

Perhaps the issue is not with configuration at all but with performance. Take a look at the output of **show frame-relay traffic** in Example 8-32.

Example 8-32   **show frame-relay traffic**

```
r1#show frame-relay traffic
Frame Relay statistics:
        ARP requests sent 0, ARP replies sent 0
        ARP request recvd 0, ARP replies recvd
```

Any way you look at it, if the frame switch runs out of buffers it looks at the DE packets to see what it can discard. In general you can help with performance issues out of the router with priority queuing. Frame Relay traffic shaping assists with switch congestion. Relate this back to the Chapter 3, "Shooting Trouble with IP," subnetting analogy with the congestion of the cars crossing the Chesapeake Bay Bridge. The Mass Transit Authority (MTA) borrows lanes as appropriate to facilitate roadwork and east-bound and west-bound access. However, the improved EZPass system dedicates one or more lanes to local commuters.

Numerous issues relate to routing protocols, mostly broadcast or multicast in nature. Yet Frame Relay is NBMA. This creates some interesting results and is actually another book in itself. Throughout this book, I have you experiment with some of the more common issues with routing protocols. The next section speaks to running those routing protocols over the Frame Relay data link.

NOTE   Other routing reference material from Cisco Press you can read includes Henry Benjamin's *CCNP Practical Studies: Routing*; *Troubleshooting IP Routing Protocols* (Shamim, Aziz, Liu, Martey); and Jeff Doyle's *Routing TCP/IP*, Volumes I and II (Cisco Press). Another excellent book is *Advanced IP Routing in Cisco Networks* (McGraw-Hill Osborne) by Terry Slattery and Bill Burton.

Frame Relay and Routing Protocols

Routing protocols such as Open Shortest Path First (OSPF), Extended Interior Gateway Routing Protocol (EIGRP), Intermediate System-to-Intermediate System (IS-IS), and Border Gateway Protocol (BGP) all run over Frame Relay. Cisco's implementation of Frame Relay supports various Layer 3 *routed* protocols including IP, DECnet, AppleTalk, Xerox Network Systems (XNS), Internetwork Packet Exchange (IPX), Connectionless Network Service (CLNS), and so on. Whether Frame Relay or another WAN transport, if there are traffic issues or memory issues due to large routing tables, first *make sure you have properly summarized* according to the routing protocol rules. Unfortunately, the commands are all slightly different with summarizing each and every routing protocol. As I have alluded to in this chapter, with Frame Relay reachability issues exist when using multiple PVCs over a single interface. Depending on the topology, split horizon may be doing its job of reducing routing loops but causing other problems because of the NBMA nature of Frame Relay.

For example, IP split horizon is disabled by default on Frame Relay interfaces. However, this creates a problem with protocols such as IPX and AppleTalk because they rely on split horizon to work properly. To make a long story short, regardless of protocol the workaround is subinterfaces. Subinterfaces resolve many upper-layer routing issues. Multipoint and point-to-point subinterfaces were discussed back in the "Frame Relay at the Physical Layer" section.

Now I'll review EIGRP, then OSPF, then IS-IS, and finally BGP because they are all very common in the real world today. My goal is just to quickly review some of the common commands to help you recognize some of the issues of running these routing protocols over

Frame Relay to prepare you for the Trouble Tickets and practical application. Refer back to the general discussion of IP routing protocols back in Chapter 3.

EIGRP over Frame Relay

EIGRP, encapsulated in the IP header as protocol number 88, works well in the LAN and the WAN. However, the topology type has an impact on neighbor adjacencies across the WAN. EIGRP operates over multicast address 224.0.0.10, but Frame Relay is an NBMA technology by default. Nonbroadcast means no multicast either.

The big issues to review with EIGRP over Frame Relay include how EIGRP uses the bandwidth. It is crucial that you configure your bandwidth statements, because by default EIGRP can use up to half of the bandwidth. If you don't configure the bandwidth and you allow EIGRP to use 50 percent of the default 1.544 Mbps for a serial link when you really only have a 56 kbps or 64 kbps link to begin with, and you have a big topology table, and routes start flapping, you probably won't be too happy with EIGRP. You are already familiar with the bandwidth statement, but you can configure the percentage of bandwidth that EIGRP is allowed to use using the **ip bandwidth-percent eigrp** *as-number percent* command. For example, **ip bandwidth-percent eigrp 100 200** allows EIGRP autonomous system 100 to utilize 200 percent of the configured bandwidth. So if the bandwidth is configured to 25 kbps, EIGRP would be allowed to use up to 50 kbps. Obviously you need to make sure the line is provisioned appropriately. On the other hand, you may want to lessen the percent number so that the routing updates are not consuming all of your bandwidth.

Speaking of provisioning bandwidth for the WAN, the best practice is to configure the bandwidth to be the CIR of the PVC—unless, of course, you have a 0 CIR; but I guess you wouldn't have anything to complain about if that were the case. That method works just fine for point-to-point PVCs, but for multipoint, EIGRP uses the bandwidth on the main interface divided by the number of neighbors to get the neighbor bandwidth. In effect there is a single entry point with multiple exit points so that the bandwidth is equally shared. If there are varying CIRs, it is a *better practice* to convert to point-to-point subinterfaces As a workaround, you can manually configure the bandwidth by taking the lowest CIR and multiplying by the number of PVCs. Be careful not to oversubscribe yourself. Adjust the EIGRP bandwidth percent so that you have about a 1:1 ratio for the amount of bandwidth that EIGRP can use.

Another big issue with EIGRP on the WAN in general is making sure you limit the need to know through summarization, outbound route filters, and distribute lists as to not end up with Stuck in Active (SIA) routes. If a router cannot answer a query because it is too busy or has memory problems, that is one problem, but if the WAN circuit is down or only works in one direction, some packets may be lost. Although not required, a hierarchical design model increases EIGRP's scalability on the WAN.

NOTE   Just a word of caution, EIGRP can form one-way neighbor relationships, but OSPF can't.

You will configure EIGRP in the Trouble Tickets. For now, however, the discussion turns to OSPF over Frame Relay.

OSPF over Frame Relay

OSPF works over nearly every data link out there, including Frame Relay. Like EIGRP, the topology type has a big impact on how adjacencies are created. OSPF is encapsulated in the IP header as protocol number 89. Keep in mind that OSPF works over multicast addresses 224.0.0.5 and 224.0.0.6, but by default Frame Relay as well as ATM and X.25 are NBMA data-link technologies. In OSPF, if you don't have any neighbors you obviously don't have link-state advertisements (LSAs) in the link-state database or any OSPF-learned routes in the routing table.

OSPF considers Frame Relay NBMA to be like any other broadcast media for its data-link transport. The default hello interval is 30 seconds, and the default dead interval is 120 seconds. As you can review in Table 8-3, there are two RFC-compliant modes and three additional modes from Cisco to control how OSPF operates over NBMA. This is not just another table to memorize. These modes really determine how the hello protocol and flooding work. Remember that OSPF uses multicast. The big issue with OSPF over an NBMA topology is that the designated router (DR) and backup designated router (BDR) need a list of all other routers to establish adjacencies.

Table 8-3   *OSPF over NBMA Modes*

Mode	Topology	Addressing	Adjacency
RFC			
NBMA	Full mesh	One subnet	*Manual configuration DR/BDR
Point-to-multipoint	Partial mesh Hub-and-spoke	One subnet	Automatic configuration No DR/BDR
Cisco			
Broadcast	Full mesh	One subnet	Automatic configuration DR/BDR
Point-to-multipoint nonbroadcast	Partial mesh Hub-and-spoke	One subnet	*Manual configuration No DR/BDR
Point-to-point	Partial mesh Hub-and-spoke Using subinterfaces	Multiple subnets	Automatic No DR/BDR

*It is good practice to configure neighbor statements on both ends although it may work with one. You can further control OSPF on a neighbor-by-neighbor basis using the [**priority**], [**poll-interval**], and [**cost**] options.

Rather than the default NBMA multipoint connectivity, Frame Relay more commonly operates in a hub-and-spoke topology. Other topologies include partial and full mesh.

NOTE   For the modes in Table 8-3 that do elect DR/BDR, it is important for the routers elected to have a direct connection (PVC) to each of the other routers.

Configure the OSPF network modes using the **ip ospf network** interface configuration command. Interfaces and multipoint subinterfaces default to NBMA. Other interfaces can be set to the RFC-compliant NBMA mode using the **ip ospf network non-broadcast** command. Nothing defaults to the RFC point-to-multipoint mode, but the command to set it is **ip ospf network point-to-multipoint [non-broadcast]**. The [**non-broadcast**] option is for the Cisco-defined mode. The other Cisco modes are set using **ip ospf network broadcast** and **ip ospf network point-to-point**. Broadcast mode acts like Ethernet, Token Ring, or FDDI, and **point-to-point** is the default for point-to-point subinterfaces. So to summarize, either use **frame map** with the **broadcast** parameter, subinterfaces as point-to-point links, or OSPF neighbor statements.

Refer back to these commands later as you work through the rest of this book. For now move on to IS-IS over Frame Relay.

IS-IS over Frame Relay

Integrated Intermediate System-to-Intermediate System (IS-IS) is more often used in the service provider world, as is BGP. However, IS-IS is an IGP and BGP is an Exterior Gateway Protocol (EGP). It was developed by ISO to support OSI protocols (especially CLNS and CLNP) and later extended to support IP. IS-IS is *not* carried in an IP packet but rather encapsulated directly into Layer 2. However, it is more like OSPF than other routing protocols.

Similarities include the following:

* Both are link-state routing protocols that use the SPF/Dijkstra algorithm.

* Both use hello packets to form neighbor adjacencies.

* Areas form a built-in two-level hierarchy.

* Both are classless routing protocols (support variable -length subnet masking [VLSM]).

* Both support authentication.

* Both use the concept of a DR. (IS-IS called this DIS.)

Cisco routers can operate as Level 1 (L1), Level 2 (L2), or L1/L2 routers. L1s are similar to OSPF internal routers and hold a copy of the link-state database for the local area. L2s are similar to OSPF Area Border Routers (ABRs). They interconnect areas and store interarea information, both local links and information about remote areas. L1/L2 routers are similar to OSPF backbone routers. There are separate adjacencies for L1 and L2. However, adjacencies occur with all routers, not just with the DR like in OSPF.

Although OSPF and IS-IS are quite similar, a couple of things set IS-IS ahead for very large networks. For example, there is not as much confusion over the network types; IS-IS networks are either broadcast or point-to-point. With the IS-IS L1, L2, L1/L2 design, there are fewer link-state packets to process, so it is less processor intensive, too. In OSPF, the MAXAGE of an LSA starts at 0 and counts upward to a fixed value. In practice, this means the lifetime of an LSA is two hours, after which it must be refreshed and flooded across the entire area. Obviously, this causes excessive traffic in the core. If in fact you have only one huge OSPF area, every single LSA will need to be refreshed at least once every two hours. Worse yet, if a router misses one of the refreshed LSAs, there is no longer a route. LSA MAXAGE is hard coded into the protocol for OSPF. However, IS-IS counts its equivalent to MAXAGE in reverse. It starts at a number that the user defines and counts down to 0. By increasing this refresh interval, you eliminate a lot of the overhead of the protocol. Many service provider networks set the refresh interval to the maximum and run IS-IS with thousands of routers in a single level with no ill effects.

IS-IS is a viable OSPF alternative. A network service access point (NSAP) is the location where OSI network services are provided to the Transport Layer. All routers in the same area must use the same area address. Rather than the router ID that OSPF uses, IS-IS uses the OSI NSAP address. The NSAP structure includes the area identifier; the system ID/MAC; and the selector (00). The area identifier loosely equates to the network. The system ID/MAC identifies an individual device. You can think of the Selector byte kind of like an IP port. L1 and L2 routing are based on a unique system ID. Typically the system ID is the MAC address in the CLNS world and the IP address in the IP world.

When troubleshooting IS-IS over Frame Relay in particular, remember that it does not have parameters like the **ip ospf network** command. Commands such as **show isis topology**, **show clns route**, **show isis route**, **which route**, **show clns neighbor**, **show isis database**, **clear isis ***, **show frame-relay map**, and **debug isis adj packet** are quite helpful in supporting IS-IS.

As far as Frame Relay is concerned, do not configure **ip router isis** on the main interface because IS-IS will treat it like a broadcast network and adjacency will not occur. You must have full-mesh PVCs to implement IS-IS in a point-to-multipoint environment. Just as with OSPF over hub-and-spoke Frame Relay where the DR needs to be the hub router, this is true with IS-IS, too. The DR in IS-IS is called the DIS.

BGP, like IS-IS, really doesn't have as many Frame Relay-specific issues but is something you may need to support. If you are interested in more detail in the BGP area, look at *Internet Routing Architectures* by Sam Halabi (Cisco Press) and *Routing TCP/IP*, Volume II, by Jeff Doyle and Jennifer DeHaven Carroll (Cisco Press).

BGP over Frame Relay

BGP is a loop-free Application Layer connection-oriented reliable EGP that runs over TCP port 179. Instead of a single metric, there are a series of attributes. BGP runs as EBGP between autonomous systems and as IBGP within an autonomous system.

BGP runs over various data links including Frame Relay. Unlike the other routing protocols, it is encapsulated within TCP. Some of the specific issues with BGP over Frame Relay include the use of the **ebgp-multihop** command when Exterior Border Gateway Protocol (EBGP) neighbors are not directly connected. Also, when using a loopback in the neighbor statement, use **neighbor ip-address update-source loopback** *loopback#*. Network statements *don't* initialize anything like an IGP; they are what you advertise.

Although not just related to Frame Relay, next-hop-self and synchronization are two commonly misunderstood topics when deploying IBGP. IP carries traffic, but BGP carries routes—and there is no way you want BGP to advertise a bad route. BGP bad routes induce autonomous system inconsistencies and black holes into your network.

The synchronization rule says not to use (or advertise to an external neighbor) a route learned via Interior Border Gateway Protocol (IBGP) until a matching route has been learned from an Interior Gateway Protocol (IGP). Hence, BGP must wait until the IGP propagates routing information across the autonomous system, which causes BGP to be synchronized with the IGP. Only then are routes added to the IP routing table. It is practical to turn off synchronization when *all* routers within an autonomous system are running full-mesh IBGP, which is designed to propagate routes within an autonomous system to another autonomous system when another IGP is not being used.

You can relate synchronization on (the default) to being an apprentice at something. For example, I am always learning or teaching new topics. When I teach a class for the first time, it is helpful to have someone confirm what I am talking about or check my work. When I have some experience teaching a topic, however, I no longer need someone to confirm what I already know; this is the stage similar to when you would turn synchronization off in BGP.

In Figure 8-11 both r1 and r2 should have **no synchronization** in their router configurations.

Figure 8-11   *BGP Next-Hop-Self and Synchronization*

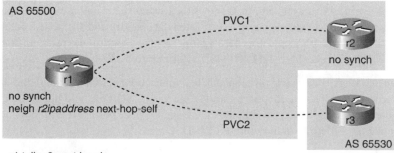

r1 tells r2 next hop is
r3 and r2 can't get there.
With next-hop-self r1 says, "Hey neighbor r2
use me to get to another autonomous system."

Figure 8-11 also illustrates the next-hop-self concept. r1 has both EBGP and IBGP neighbors. When r1 passes along an externally learned route to its internal neighbor r2, it offers r2 the convenience of going through r1 to get to the external system. The command is always configured on the router with an interface in EBGP and IBGP, and in Figure 8-11 that is r1. This command (**neighbor** *r2ipaddress* **next-hop-self**) does not replace the neighbor statement; it is an additional statement.

Remember BGP is an EGP and every change you make effects not only you but also your peers. With any BGP changes, you normally need to reset the neighbor. Although fine in a lab environment, **clear ip bgp *** can be detrimental to you and whomever you are peering with in practical application. So always replace the * with the *neighbor's IP address*, otherwise you may find out very quickly more than you ever wanted to know about network instability and service provider route dampening. In a nutshell, *dampening* is where the service provider can suppress your routes according to the criteria within the **bgp dampening ?** command. In 12.0 code and above, soft resets were introduced if your neighbor supports them. Refer to the IOS release notes for "BGP Soft Reset Enhancement."

Just as you experienced in the chapter scenarios, you really do need to think about how things work in order to support them. You will experiment with running the various routing protocols over Frame Relay in the Trouble Tickets. Obviously Layer 3 and above routing protocols still depend on Layer 2 and Layer 1.

You must take the divide-and-conquer approach on the WAN. Half the battle is determining whether it is your issue or a service provider issue; then you can work your way up the layers. If you get LMI but not your other DLCIs, for instance, you don't have much choice but to contact the service provider so that they can perform some remote loopback testing.

Frame Relay Loopback Testing

Loopback tests can help you define the extent of WAN problems in general. Your provider will certainly be happy and probably more willing to assist if you have already verified your side of things. Figure 8-12 shows four different loopback tests. Depending on your exact equipment, you can familiarize yourself with the appropriate loopback commands and menus.

The **show interfaces s0** command shows the looped status and how the keepalives continue to increment. Use an extended ping to verify the data pattern and size to test connectivity up to the CSU/DSU. If the pings are not at least 80-percent successful, the problem is physical in nature between the local router and CSU/DSU as in Figure 8-12(A).

Figure 8-12(B) shows a local loopback test to test connectivity through the local CSU/DSU. Figure 8-12 is a remote loopback through the local CSU/DSU and up to the remote CSU/DSU. Problems here indicate issues in the cloud. Figure 8-12 is an external loopback, which could indicate a problem with the remote CSU/DSU.

Figure 8-12   *Loopback Testing*

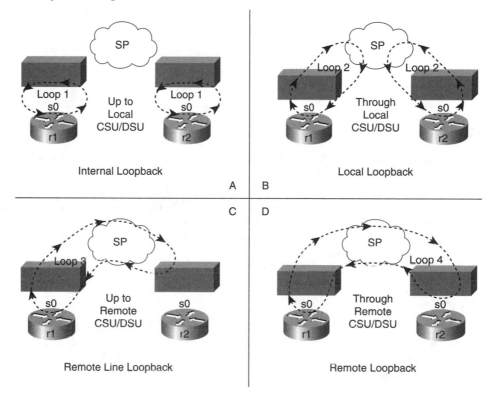

Keep in mind that timing is important in troubleshooting as well. While you are testing things out, the service provider may have already caught and fixed the problem. So don't be too stumped when you go through all of this and then the data link is up as it should have been in the first place. What I am saying is that it doesn't hurt to repeat commands that you started with in the first place.

Regardless of the loopback testing type, the best command you can run while testing is an extended ping while you monitor your serial interface with a command such as **show interfaces s0**. To get the extended ping commands, just type **ping** from privilege mode and make your selections. For example, you could set the repeat count to 100, the datagram size to 1500, and vary the data pattern. The default data pattern is 0xabcd. Try the following data patterns to help detect CSU/DSU or cable issues: 0x0000, 0x1111, 0xaaaa, and 0xffff. Extended ping was introduced back in Chapter 2, "What's in Your Tool Bag."

NOTE   Remember to restore your router back to its original setting after the loopback tests. It is also a good idea to carry a "hard" loopback plug in your tool bag to round out the possible tests.

The chapter scenarios exposed you to supporting Frame Relay by taking a layered practical methodical approach just as the other chapters did. Make sure you save all configurations and repeat any steps in which you need more practice.

Once again it is time for the chapter Trouble Tickets. The plan here is to give you several things to do, let you make mistakes and fix some things on your own, and to introduce other problems that you should have some experience with as a support person.

Trouble Tickets

Complete the following Trouble Tickets in order. Use the information and tools from this chapter and the previous chapters to analyze, test, and document as you go. Feel free to create your own Physical Layer or other problems if you need more practice in that area. I want you to shoot the troubles of using routing protocols over Frame Relay to make things a little more realistic to the practical environment. Feel free to change the routing protocol to what you actually use to troubleshoot issues specific to your needs. As always, sample solutions are provided after this section.

Trouble Ticket 1

Configure and troubleshoot BGP over Frame Relay using Figure 8-13 as a guide. Continue with the multipoint subinterfaces topology back in Figure 8-10. Just add the additional point-to-point PVC and configure BGP to allow communication among all sites. Document the issues and save all configuration changes.

Figure 8-13   *Trouble Ticket 1: BGP over Frame*

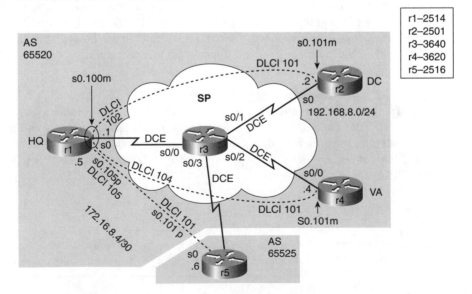

Trouble Ticket 2

Configure and troubleshoot OSPF over Frame Relay using the same physical layout as in Figure 8-13. You have the requirement to use default or static routes between r1 and r5. Add at least one loopback to each router to simulate multiple networks. Document and save all issues and configuration changes.

Trouble Ticket 3

Alternatively, you could have configured the **ip ospf network point-to-multipoint** interface command instead of manually configuring the neighbor statements in the preceding Trouble Ticket. Give it a try.

Trouble Ticket 4

Shut down the interfaces on the frame switch and observe the results on the other routers.

Trouble Ticket 5

Sometimes SPs may mix up the DLCIs for the PVCs. Perhaps they gave you the right information this time, but they incorrectly did their mapping on the frame switch. Today you are the service provider, and I want you to simulate this scenario by routing what comes in the r3 interface s0/1 as DLCI 102 out the s0/0 interface as DLCI 101. Observe the results, but be sure to fix the problem before you move on to the next Trouble Ticket.

Trouble Ticket 6

Turn on Frame Relay compression for one end of the PVC between r1 and r5. Document the results. Fix the issues without turning compression off. Then turn compression off and make sure things still work.

Trouble Ticket Solutions

These solutions are not always the only way to perform these tasks. Compare your results.

Trouble Ticket 1 Solution

First connect the physical cable between r5 and the frame switch. Then configure the frame switch to handle the new PVC, and then r1 and r5 as in Example 8-33.

Example 8-33 *Configuring the Frame Switch, r1, and r5*

```
!!!frame switch configuration for new PVC
frame-switch#configure terminal
frame-switch(config)#interface s0/3
frame-switch(config-if)#bandwidth 64
frame-switch(config-if)#clock rate 64000
frame-switch(config-if)#encap frame
frame-switch(config-if)#frame-relay intf-type dce
frame-switch(config-if)#frame route 101 interface s0/0 105
frame-switch(config-if)#no shut
frame-switch(config-if)#end
frame-switch#copy running-config startup-config
!!!r1 configuration for point-to-point PVC 105
r1#configure terminal
r1(config)#interface s0.105 p
r1(config-subif)#bandwidth 64
r1(config-subif)#ip address 172.16.8.5 255.255.255.252
r1(config-subif)#frame-relay interface-dlci 105
r1(config-fr-dlci)#no shut
r1(config-if)#end
r1#copy running-config startup-config
!!!r5 configuration for point-to-point PVC 101
Router#configure terminal
Router(config)#hostname r5
r5(config)#interface s0
r5(config-if)#encap frame
r5(config-if)#interface s0.101 p
r5(config-subif)#bandwidth 64
r5(config-subif)#ip address 172.16.8.6 255.255.255.252
r5(config-subif)#frame-relay interface-dlci 101
r5(config-fr-dlci)#exit
r5(config-if)#no shut
r5(config-if)#end
```

Then ping to test the new configuration. Because ping should be unsuccessful at this point, I do not show the output. Continue your testing as in Example 8-34.

Example 8-34 *Checking the Interfaces for r5 and r1*

```
r5#show ip interface brief
Interface          IP-Address      OK? Method Status                Protocol
BRI0               unassigned      YES unset  administratively down down
BRI0:1             unassigned      YES unset  administratively down down
BRI0:2             unassigned      YES unset  administratively down down
Ethernet0          unassigned      YES unset  administratively down down
Serial0            unassigned      YES unset  administratively down down
Serial0.101        172.16.8.6      YES manual down                  down
Serial1            unassigned      YES unset  administratively down down
r5#clock set 6:38:00 Dec 13 2002
r5#configure terminal
r5(config)#service timestamps debug datetime localtime msec
r5(config)#service timestamps log datetime localtime msec
r5(config)#enable secret donna
r5(config)#line vty 0 4
r5(config-line)#password donna
```

Example 8-34 *Checking the Interfaces for r5 and r1 (Continued)*

```
r5(config-line)#exit
r5(config)#line console 0
r5(config-line)#logging synchronous
r5(config-line)#exit
r5(config)#interface s0
r5(config-if)#no shut
r5(config-if)#end
r5#copy running-config startup-config

r1#show ip interface brief
Interface              IP-Address      OK? Method Status                 Protocol
Ethernet0              unassigned      YES unset  administratively down  down
Ethernet1              unassigned      YES unset  administratively down  down
Serial0                unassigned      YES unset  up                     up
Serial0.100            192.168.8.1     YES manual up                     up
Serial0.105            172.16.8.5      YES manual down                   down
Serial1                unassigned      YES unset  administratively down  down
r1#configure terminal
r1(config)#interface s0
r1(config-if)#no shut
Dec 13 18:40:51.930: %LINEPROTO-5-UPDOWN: Line protocol on Interface Serial0.105,
  changed state to up
Dec 13 18:40:51.938: %FR-5-DLCICHANGE: Interface Serial0 - DLCI 105 state changed
  to ACTIVE
Dec 13 18:41:01.346: %FR-5-DLCICHANGE: Interface Serial0 - DLCI 105 state changed
  to DELETED
Dec 13 18:41:01.346: %LINEPROTO-5-UPDOWN: Line protocol on Interface Serial0.105,
  changed state to down
r1(config-if)#end
r1#copy running-config startup-config
```

Although you brought the administratively down interface up, the DLCI is still in a deleted state. Look at the routers and the frame switch in Example 8-35 to determine the problem.

Example 8-35 *Troubleshooting r1, r5, and the Frame Switch*

```
r1#show run interface s0.105
...
interface Serial0.105 point-to-point
 bandwidth 64
 ip address 172.16.8.5 255.255.255.252
 no ip directed-broadcast
 frame-relay interface-dlci 105
end
r1#show frame-relay map
Serial0.100 (up): ip 192.168.8.2 dlci 102(0x66,0x1860), static,
              broadcast,
              CISCO, status defined, active
Serial0.100 (up): ip 192.168.8.4 dlci 104(0x68,0x1880), static,
              broadcast,
              CISCO, status defined, active
Serial0.105 (down): point-to-point dlci, dlci 105(0x69,0x1890), broadcast
              status deleted
r5#show frame-relay map
Serial0.101 (down): point-to-point dlci, dlci 101(0x65,0x1850), broadcast
```

continues

Example 8-35 *Troubleshooting r1, r5, and the Frame Switch (Continued)*

```
             status defined, inactive
frameswitch>show frame-relay route
Input Intf      Input Dlci     Output Intf     Output Dlci     Status
Serial0/0       102            Serial0/1       101             active
Serial0/0       104            Serial0/2       101             active
Serial0/1       101            Serial0/0       102             active
Serial0/2       101            Serial0/0       104             active
Serial0/3       101            Serial0/0       105             inactive
```

Hopefully, you see that you have a missing route statement from the frame switch, but how did you know what to look for? Instead of looking at the running configuration, you can check statuses: A good indication of this issue is the deleted status for DLCI 105 as well as the other end of the PVC being inactive. Fix these issues as in Example 8-36.

Example 8-36 *Adding the Missing Frame Route Statement*

```
frame-switch#configure terminal
frame-switch(config)#interface s0/0
frame-switch(config-if)#frame route 105 interface s0/3 101
frame-switch(config-if)#no shut
frame-switch(config-if)#
4d05h: %FR-5-DLCICHANGE: Interface Serial0/0 - DLCI 105 state changed to ACTIVE
4d05h: %FR-5-DLCICHANGE: Interface Serial0/3 - DLCI 101 state changed to ACTIVE
frame-switch(config-if)#end
frame-switch#copy running-config startup-config
```

Now that everything appears to be configured properly, show the Inverse ARP tables on each device and verify connectivity as in Example 8-37.

Example 8-37 *Testing the New PVC*

```
r1#show frame-relay map
Serial0.100 (up): ip 192.168.8.2 dlci 102(0x66,0x1860), static,
              broadcast,
              CISCO, status defined, active
Serial0.100 (up): ip 192.168.8.4 dlci 104(0x68,0x1880), static,
              broadcast,
              CISCO, status defined, active
Serial0.105 (up): point-to-point dlci, dlci 105(0x69,0x1890), broadcast
          status defined, active
r2#show frame-relay map
Serial0.101 (up): ip 192.168.8.1 dlci 101(0x65,0x1850), dynamic,
              broadcast,, status defined, active
frame-switch#show frame-relay route
Input Intf      Input Dlci     Output Intf     Output Dlci     Status
Serial0/0       102            Serial0/1       101             active
Serial0/0       104            Serial0/2       101             active
Serial0/0       105            Serial0/3       101             active
Serial0/1       101            Serial0/0       102             active
Serial0/2       101            Serial0/0       104             active
Serial0/3       101            Serial0/0       105             active
r4#show frame-relay map
```

Example 8-37 *Testing the New PVC (Continued)*

```
Serial0/0.101 (up): ip 192.168.8.1 dlci 101(0x65,0x1850), dynamic,
               broadcast,, status defined, active
r5#show frame-relay map
Serial0.101 (up): point-to-point dlci, dlci 101(0x65,0x1850), broadcast
           status defined, active
```

Active is the status you wanted to begin with on the frame switch and all the routers. Compare the findings in the preceding example to your drawing.

Save your configurations and move up the stack to work on the routing protocol. Configure BGP as in Example 8-38. r1 should advertise the 192.168.8.0 network to the other AS. r2 and r4 should be configured such that they use r1 to get to r5.

Example 8-38 *Configuring BGP over Frame Relay*

```
r1(config)#router bgp 65520
r1(config-router)#network 192.168.8.0

r1(config-router)#neighbor 192.168.8.2 remote-as 65520
r1(config-router)#neighbor 192.168.8.4 remote-as 65520
r1(config-router)#neighbor 172.16.8.6 remote-as 65525

r1(config-router)#neighbor 192.168.8.2 next-hop-self
r1(config-router)#neighbor 192.168.8.4 next-hop-self

r1(config-router)#no synchronization
r1(config-router)#end
r1#copy running-config startup-config

r2#configure terminal
r2(config)#router bgp 65520
r2(config-router)#neighbor 192.168.8.1 remote-as 65520
r2(config-router)#end
r2#copy running-config startup-config

r4#configure terminal
r4(config)#router bgp 6520
r4(config-router)#router bgp 65520
BGP is already running; AS is 6520
!!!oops I made a typo
r4(config)#no router bgp 6520
r4(config)#router bgp 65520
r4(config-router)#neighbor 192.168.8.1 remote-as 65520
r4(config-router)#end
r4#copy running-config startup-config

r5#configure terminal
r5(config)#router bgp 65525
r5(config-router)#neighbor 172.16.8.5 remote-as 65520
r5(config-router)#end
r5#copy running-config startup-config
```

While setting up the BGP process, I made a typo. Actually it is a good way to prove that that while other routing protocols (such as OSPF and EIGRP) will run multiple processes, BGP will only run a single process. It is fine to advertise the 192.168.8.0 network without the mask statement because it is on the class boundary, and the manual neighbor statements are necessary because absolutely nothing in BGP is automatic. In looking at Figure 8-13, r1 has two IBGP peers (neighbors) and one EBGP peer (neighbor). The **next-hop-self** statement is needed for the IBGP peer to use r1 to get to the other AS because r1 has an interface in both autonomous systems. On the spoke routers, only the BGP process and neighbor statements are configured.

Perform the neighbor testing in Example 8-39. What TCP or BGP state are the neighbors in? Are they receiving prefixes?

Example 8-39 *Identifying BGP Neighbors*

```
r1#show ip bgp summary
BGP router identifier 192.168.8.1, local AS number 65520
BGP table version is 2, main routing table version 2
1 network entries and 1 paths using 121 bytes of memory
1 BGP path attribute entries using 96 bytes of memory
BGP activity 1/0 prefixes, 1/0 paths

Neighbor        V    AS MsgRcvd MsgSent   TblVer  InQ OutQ Up/Down  State/PfxRcd
172.16.8.6      4 65525       5       6        2    0    0 00:02:49        0
192.168.8.2     4 65520       7       8        2    0    0 00:04:19        0
192.168.8.4     4 65520       6       7        2    0    0 00:03:42        0
```

The **show ip bgp summary** command is an excellent way to BGP statistics and your neighbors. Any number, including 0 in the State/PfxRcd column, indicates that the neighbors are ready to receive prefixes. Thus they have completed both the TCP and BGP sessions. Investigate the TCP and BGP sessions a little further in Example 8-40.

Example 8-40 *Displaying the TCP and BGP Sessions*

```
r1#debug ip bgp events
BGP events debugging is on
r1#configure terminal
r1(config)#interface s0
r1(config-if)#shut
r1(config-if)#no shut
Dec 13 20:01:06.813: %LINEPROTO-5-UPDOWN: Line protocol on Interface Serial0.100,
  changed state to down
Dec 13 20:01:06.817: %LINEPROTO-5-UPDOWN: Line protocol on Interface Serial0.105,
  changed state to down
Dec 13 20:01:07.065: BGP: 172.16.8.6 reset requested
Dec 13 20:01:07.065: BGP: 172.16.8.6 reset due to Interface flap
Dec 13 20:01:07.069: BGP: 172.16.8.6 went from Established to Idle
Dec 13 20:01:08.305: BGP: 192.168.8.2 computing updates, neighbor version 2, table
  version 3, starting at 0.0.0.0
Dec 13 20:01:08.309: BGP: 192.168.8.2 update run completed, ran for 0ms, neighbor
  version 2, start version 3, throttled to 3, check point net 0.0.0.0
Dec 13 20:01:08.313: BGP: 192.168.8.4 computing updates, neighbor version 2, table
  version 3, starting at 0.0.0.0
```

Example 8-40 *Displaying the TCP and BGP Sessions (Continued)*

```
Dec 13 20:01:08.317: BGP: 192.168.8.4 update run completed, ran for 0ms, neighbor
  version 2, start version 3, throttled to 3, check point net 0.0.0.0
Dec 13 20:01:08.809: %LINEPROTO-5-UPDOWN: Line protocol on Interface Serial0.100,
  changed state to up
Dec 13 20:01:08.813: %LINEPROTO-5-UPDOWN: Line protocol on Interface Serial0.105,
  changed state to up
Dec 13 20:01:12.837: BGP: 192.168.8.4 computing updates, neighbor version 3, table
  version 4, starting at 0.0.0.0
Dec 13 20:01:12.841: BGP: 192.168.8.4 update run completed, ran for 0ms, neighbor
  version 3, start version 4, throttled to 4, check point net 0.0.0.0
Dec 13 20:01:13.945: BGP: 192.168.8.2 computing updates, neighbor version 3, table
  version 4, starting at 0.0.0.0
Dec 13 20:01:13.949: BGP: 192.168.8.2 update run completed, ran for 0ms, neighbor
  version 3, start version 4, throttled to 4, check point net 0.0.0.0
Dec 13 20:01:27.845: BGP: 172.16.8.6 went from Idle to Active
Dec 13 20:01:40.749: BGP: scanning routing tables
Dec 13 20:01:55.969: BGP: 172.16.8.6 went from Active to OpenSent
Dec 13 20:01:56.581: BGP: 172.16.8.6 went from OpenSent to OpenConfirm
Dec 13 20:01:56.817: BGP: 172.16.8.6 went from OpenConfirm to Established
Dec 13 20:01:56.921: BGP: 172.16.8.6 computing updates, neighbor version 0, table
  version 4, starting at 0.0.0.0
Dec 13 20:01:56.925: BGP: 172.16.8.6 update run completed, ran for 0ms, neighbor
  version 0, start version 4, throttled to 4, check point net 0.0.0.0
r1(config-if)#end
r1#undebug all
r1#copy running-config startup-config
```

Although there are other commands, I find **show ip bgp summary** to be a very valuable tool.
It not only enables you to see the neighbor relationship, if there are problems it shows the actual
TCP or BGP state you are in with each neighbor. The first three states are TCP connections and
the last three are BGP connections with *established* being the Promised Land.

NOTE   *Active* sounds good—and it is, when you are talking DLCIs in Frame Relay—but in BGP
routing, it means the TCP session is not yet established, as in "actively trying."

You can very quickly look at the State/PfxRcd column to check BGP neighbor issues. Numbers
mean you are receiving prefixes; words mean you are stuck in another state for some reason. If
you do everything right the first time, it is hard to learn from your mistakes, but the **debug ip
bgp events** command clearly shows you the steps a neighbor goes through. The **show ip bgp
neighbor** command gives you specifics about the neighbor and displays the established state.
It also tells you whether the neighbor is internal or external. Compare the output of **show ip bgp
summary** in Example 8-39 to **show ip bgp neighbors** in Example 8-41.

Example 8-41 *Viewing Your BGP Neighbors on r1*

```
r1#show ip bgp neighbors
BGP neighbor is 172.16.8.6,  remote AS 65525, external link
 Index 2, Offset 0, Mask 0x4
  BGP version 4, remote router ID 172.16.8.6
  BGP state = Established, table version = 4, up for 00:15:16
  Last read 00:00:16, hold time is 180, keepalive interval is 60 seconds
  Minimum time between advertisement runs is 30 seconds
  Received 31 messages, 0 notifications, 0 in queue
  Sent 33 messages, 0 notifications, 0 in queue
  Prefix advertised 2, suppressed 0, withdrawn 0
  Connections established 2; dropped 1
  Last reset 00:16:06, due to Interface flap
  0 accepted prefixes consume 0 bytes
  0 history paths consume 0 bytes
Connection state is ESTAB, I/O status: 1, unread input bytes: 0
Local host: 172.16.8.5, Local port: 11005
Foreign host: 172.16.8.6, Foreign port: 179

Enqueued packets for retransmit: 0, input: 0  mis-ordered: 0 (0 bytes)

Event Timers (current time is 0xC4A3DA8):
Timer          Starts    Wakeups          Next
Retrans          20         0             0x0
TimeWait          0         0             0x0
AckHold          18        13             0x0
SendWnd           0         0             0x0
KeepAlive         0         0             0x0
GiveUp            0         0             0x0
PmtuAger          0         0             0x0
DeadWait          0         0             0x0

iss: 3426000199  snduna: 3426000604  sndnxt: 3426000604     sndwnd:  15980
irs: 2443213131  rcvnxt: 2443213484  rcvwnd:      16032  delrcvwnd:    352

SRTT: 487 ms, RTTO: 3830 ms, RTV: 1428 ms, KRTT: 0 ms
minRTT: 40 ms, maxRTT: 300 ms, ACK hold: 200 ms
Flags: higher precedence, nagle

Datagrams (max data segment is 1460 bytes):
Rcvd: 25 (out of order: 0), with data: 18, total data bytes: 352
Sent: 34 (retransmit: 0), with data: 19, total data bytes: 404
!!!The rest of the neighbors are IBGP peers
BGP neighbor is 192.168.8.2,  remote AS 65520, internal link
 Index 1, Offset 0, Mask 0x2
  NEXT_HOP is always this router
  BGP version 4, remote router ID 192.168.8.2
  BGP state = Established, table version = 4, up for 00:27:58
  Last read 00:00:59, hold time is 180, keepalive interval is 60 seconds
  Minimum time between advertisement runs is 5 seconds
  Received 30 messages, 0 notifications, 0 in queue
  Sent 33 messages, 0 notifications, 0 in queue
  Prefix advertised 2, suppressed 0, withdrawn 1
  Connections established 1; dropped 0
```

Example 8-41 *Viewing Your BGP Neighbors on r1 (Continued)*

```
   Last reset never
   0 accepted prefixes consume 0 bytes
   0 history paths consume 0 bytes
Connection state is ESTAB, I/O status: 1, unread input bytes: 0
Local host: 192.168.8.1, Local port: 179
Foreign host: 192.168.8.2, Foreign port: 11000
...
BGP neighbor is 192.168.8.4,  remote AS 65520, internal link
 Index 3, Offset 0, Mask 0x8
  NEXT_HOP is always this router
  BGP version 4, remote router ID 192.168.8.4
  BGP state = Established, table version = 4, up for 00:27:26
...
```

Note that the output of **show ip bgp neighbors** presents you with much more detail than **show ip bgp summary**. For example, it clearly shows the neighbor is in the established state and whether the peer is IBGP (internal) or EBGP (external). Continue to verify your neighbors from the spoke perspective in Example 8-42.

Example 8-42 *Viewing Your BGP Neighbors on r2, r4, and r5*

```
r2#show ip bgp summary
BGP router identifier 192.168.8.2, local AS number 65520
BGP table version is 4, main routing table version 4
1 network entries and 1 paths using 121 bytes of memory
1 BGP path attribute entries using 96 bytes of memory
BGP activity 1/0 prefixes, 2/1 paths
Neighbor        V    AS MsgRcvd MsgSent   TblVer  InQ OutQ Up/Down  State/PfxRcd
192.168.8.1     4 65520      43      40        4    0    0 00:37:21            1
r4#show ip bgp summary
BGP table version is 6, main routing table version 6
1 network entries (1/3 paths) using 208 bytes of memory
1 BGP path attribute entries using 104 bytes of memory
0 BGP route-map cache entries using 0 bytes of memory
0 BGP filter-list cache entries using 0 bytes of memory
Neighbor        V    AS MsgRcvd MsgSent   TblVer  InQ OutQ Up/Down  State/PfxRcd
192.168.8.1     4 65520      43      40        6    0    0 00:37:07            1
!!!the following shortcut works too
r5#sh ip bgp sum
BGP router identifier 172.16.8.6, local AS number 65525
BGP table version is 4, main routing table version 4
1 network entries and 1 paths using 121 bytes of memory
1 BGP path attribute entries using 144 bytes of memory
BGP activity 2/1 prefixes, 2/1 paths
Neighbor        V    AS MsgRcvd MsgSent   TblVer  InQ OutQ Up/Down  State/PfxRcd
172.16.8.5      4 65520      43      41        4    0    0 00:25:21            1
```

If there would have been any neighbor issues, I would have backed up to make sure I had physical connectivity and had manually configured the neighbors. Now that you have verified the BGP neighbors, confirm the BGP tables and the routing tables as in Example 8-43.

Example 8-43 *Confirming the BGP and Routing Tables*

```
r1#show ip bgp
BGP table version is 4, local router ID is 192.168.8.1
Status codes: s suppressed, d damped, h history, * valid, > best, i - internal
Origin codes: i - IGP, e - EGP, ? - incomplete
   Network          Next Hop            Metric LocPrf Weight Path
*> 192.168.8.0      0.0.0.0                  0            32768 i
r1#show ip route
Codes: C - connected, S - static, I - IGRP, R - RIP, M - mobile, B - BGP
       D - EIGRP, EX - EIGRP external, O - OSPF, IA - OSPF inter area
       N1 - OSPF NSSA external type 1, N2 - OSPF NSSA external type 2
       E1 - OSPF external type 1, E2 - OSPF external type 2, E - EGP
       i - IS-IS, L1 - IS-IS level-1, L2 - IS-IS level-2, * - candidate default
       U - per-user static route, o - ODR
Gateway of last resort is not set
C    192.168.8.0/24 is directly connected, Serial0.100
     172.16.0.0/30 is subnetted, 1 subnets
C       172.16.8.4 is directly connected, Serial0.105
r2#show ip bgp
BGP table version is 4, local router ID is 192.168.8.2
Status codes: s suppressed, d damped, h history, * valid, > best, i - internal
Origin codes: i - IGP, e - EGP, ? - incomplete
   Network          Next Hop            Metric LocPrf Weight Path
*>i192.168.8.0      192.168.8.1              0    100     0 i
r2#show ip route
...
C    192.168.8.0/24 is directly connected, Serial0.101
r4#show ip bgp
BGP table version is 6, local router ID is 192.168.8.4
Status codes: s suppressed, d damped, h history, * valid, > best, i - internal
Origin codes: i - IGP, e - EGP, ? - incomplete
   Network          Next Hop           Metric LocPrf Weight Path
*>i192.168.8.0      192.168.8.1              0    100     0 i
r4#show ip route
...
C    192.168.8.0/24 is directly connected, Serial0/0.101
r5#show ip bgp
BGP table version is 4, local router ID is 172.16.8.6
Status codes: s suppressed, d damped, h history, * valid, > best, i - internal
Origin codes: i - IGP, e - EGP, ? - incomplete
   Network          Next Hop           Metric LocPrf Weight Path
*> 192.168.8.0      172.16.8.5               0         0 65520 i
r5#show ip route
...
B    192.168.8.0/24 [20/0] via 172.16.8.5, 00:33:30
     172.16.0.0/30 is subnetted, 1 subnets
C       172.16.8.4 is directly connected, Serial0.101
```

The only routing table that has BGP routes is r5. Many times routes are in the BGP table but just can't make it to the routing table, particularly with IBGP. As discussed earlier, when all routers in an AS are running BGP you can safely turn off synchronization. Do that now for r1, r2, and r4 as in Example 8-44. Then reset the BGP table.

Example 8-44 *No Synchronization*

```
r1(config)#router bgp 65520
r1(config-router)#no synchronization
r1(config-router)#end
r1#copy running-config startup-config

!!!no synch is short for no synchronization
r2(config)#router bgp 65520
r2(config-router)#no synch
r2(config-router)#end
r2#copy running-config startup-config

r4(config)#router bgp 65520
r4(config-router)#no synch
r4(config-router)#end
r4#copy running-config startup-config

r1#clear ip bgp *
```

A word of caution before you perform more testing: For an IBGP peer to propagate routes to another IBGP peer, or EBGP peer for that matter, full-mesh connectivity is required. That is not too scalable in the practical service provider world, so they tend to use route reflectors or confederations for this purpose. Route reflectors allow routes to *bounce* or reflect from one IBGP peer to another. You can think of them as rubber routers if you like. Confederations are like mini-autonomous systems to make all neighbors appear as if they are EBGP so that there are no IBGP issues.

Instead of having every router peer with every router for a full-mesh topology, set up r1 as a route reflector to clients r2 and r4 (IBGP peers) as in Example 8-45. This time reset BGP for only the affected peers.

Example 8-45 *Configuring r1 as a Route Reflector*

```
r1(config)#router bgp 65520
r1(config-router)#neighbor 192.168.8.2 route-reflector-client
r1(config-router)#neighbor 192.168.8.4 route-reflector-client
r1(config-router)#end
r1#clear ip bgp 192.168.8.2
r1#clear ip bgp 192.168.8.4
r1#copy running-config startup-config
```

Test your hybrid point-to-point multipoint hub-and-spoke topology in Example 8-46.

Example 8-46 *Testing the Hub and Spokes*

```
!!!r1 pings r2
r1#ping 192.168.8.2
Type escape sequence to abort.
Sending 5, 100-byte ICMP Echos to 192.168.8.2, timeout is 2 seconds:
!!!!!
Success rate is 100 percent (5/5), round-trip min/avg/max = 60/60/60 ms
```

continues

Example 8-46 *Testing the Hub and Spokes (Continued)*

```
!!!r1 pings r4
r1#p 192.168.8.4
Type escape sequence to abort.
Sending 5, 100-byte ICMP Echos to 192.168.8.4, timeout is 2 seconds:
!!!!!
Success rate is 100 percent (5/5), round-trip min/avg/max = 56/56/60 ms
!!!r2 pings r1
r2>p 192.168.8.1
Type escape sequence to abort.
Sending 5, 100-byte ICMP Echos to 192.168.8.1, timeout is 2 seconds:
!!!!!
Success rate is 100 percent (5/5), round-trip min/avg/max = 60/60/60 ms
!!!r2 pings r4
r2>p 192.168.8.4
Type escape sequence to abort.
Sending 5, 100-byte ICMP Echos to 192.168.8.4, timeout is 2 seconds:
.....
Success rate is 0 percent (0/5)
!!!r2 pings r5
r2#p 172.16.8.6
Type escape sequence to abort.
Sending 5, 100-byte ICMP Echos to 172.16.8.6, timeout is 2 seconds:
.....
Success rate is 0 percent (0/5)
```

NOTE   On many devices, *p* is a shortcut for ping.

Compare the output of the last couple of examples to Figure 8-13 to determine the problems. Recall back in Example 8-43 that there were no BGP learned routes in r1, r2, and r4. Even after you turn synchronization off in Example 8-44, these routes do not appear in either the BGP or routing table because the 172.16.8.4/30 prefix has not been advertised. That is a very likely reason as to why r2 can't ping r5 in Example 8-46. Fix this in Example 8-47.

Example 8-47 *Advertising the 172.16.8.4 Network*

```
r1(config)#router bgp 65520
r1(config-router)#network 172.16.8.4 mask 255.255.255.252
r1(config-router)#end
r1#copy running-config startup-config
r1#clear ip bgp *
r1#show ip bgp
r1#show ip bgp
r1#show ip bgp
```

Note that in the preceding example the mask had to be typed in for the network statement because it differs from the classful mask. It is easy to forget to type the word mask, but in the Cisco software you can always rely on the question mark (**?**) for help.

NOTE   You must have patience to support BGP. Everything is manual in operation, and although convergence is relatively fast, sometimes things just take a little more time to appear than what you would expect. That is why you see an empty BGP table in Example 8-47; get used to the Up Arrow key to repeat the last command.

It is important to not configure the network statement on each and every router like you are used to with an IGP routing protocol. Remember that BGP is an EGP. You manually configure your neighbors and don't need a network statement for adjacency to occur. In an example like Figure 8-13, however, it was pretty important to advertise the 192.168.8.0 network out to the other AS and vice versa. Static and default routes would probably have been more appropriate if you were running another IGP inside AS 65520 or if you had multiple networks involved.

Advertising the 172.16.8.4 network into AS 65520 should allow r2 and r4 to be able to ping r5 in the remote AS. First look at the BGP table on r1 in Example 8-48, then look at the BGP and routing tables on r2 to see whether this is in fact possible. Verify with ping.

Example 8-48   *Testing the Network Advertisement*

```
r1>show ip bgp
BGP table version is 3, local router ID is 192.168.8.1
Status codes: s suppressed, d damped, h history, * valid, > best, i - internal
Origin codes: i - IGP, e - EGP, ? - incomplete
   Network          Next Hop          Metric LocPrf Weight Path
*> 172.16.8.4/30    0.0.0.0                0          32768 i
*> 192.168.8.0      0.0.0.0                0          32768 i
r2>show ip bgp
BGP table version is 13, local router ID is 192.168.8.2
Status codes: s suppressed, d damped, h history, * valid, > best, i - internal
Origin codes: i - IGP, e - EGP, ? - incomplete
   Network          Next Hop          Metric LocPrf Weight Path
*>i172.16.8.4/30    192.168.8.1            0    100      0 i
*>i192.168.8.0      192.168.8.1            0    100      0 i
r2>show ip route
...
C    192.168.8.0/24 is directly connected, Serial0.101
     172.16.0.0/30 is subnetted, 1 subnets
B        172.16.8.4 [200/0] via 192.168.8.1, 00:06:15
!!!r2 pings r5 via EBGP
r2>ping 172.16.8.6
Type escape sequence to abort.
Sending 5, 100-byte ICMP Echos to 172.16.8.6, timeout is 2 seconds:
!!!!!
Success rate is 100 percent (5/5), round-trip min/avg/max = 116/116/120 ms
!!!r2 pings r4 via IBGP
r2>ping 192.168.8.4
Type escape sequence to abort.
Sending 5, 100-byte ICMP Echos to 192.168.8.4, timeout is 2 seconds:
.....
Success rate is 0 percent (0/5)
```

Example 8-48 shows how r2 can now reach r5 via EBGP, yet it can't reach r4 via IBGP. The remaining issue is that the spoke routers can reach the hub (r1) but not each other. Do not be so quick to blame this one on BGP, although it appears that everything is working except the route reflectors. By definition the IBGP routes from r2 should bounce off of r1 to r4 and vice versa. That is not happening here; the ping fails from r2 to r4. Review the examples throughout this Trouble Ticket and Figure 8-13 for some hints.

This is a Frame Relay issue because now you want DC to talk to VA and VA to talk to DC through HQ. This was not a requirement in any of the chapter scenarios or Trouble Tickets thus far. Currently, there are no physical or logical connections between DC and VA. Program your spoke routers in Example 8-49 so that the remote sites can talk to one another.

Example 8-49 *Configuring Static Maps for the Spoke Routers*

```
r2#show frame-relay map
Serial0.101 (up): ip 192.168.8.1 dlci 101(0x65,0x1850), dynamic,
              broadcast,, status defined, active
r2#configure terminal
r2(config)#interface s0.101
r2(config-subif)#frame map ip 192.168.8.1 101 broadcast
r2(config-subif)#frame map ip 192.168.8.4 101 broadcast
r2(config-subif)#end
!!!remove any extraneous dynamic mappings
r2#clear frame-relay-inarp
r2#copy running-config startup-config

r4#configure terminal
r4(config)#interface s0/0.101
r4(config-subif)#frame map ip 192.168.8.1 101 broadcast
r4(config-subif)#frame map ip 192.168.8.2 101 broadcast
r4(config-subif)#end
!!!the next command is short for clear frame-relay-inarp
r4#clear frame
r4#copy running-config startup-config
```

Look at the Inverse ARP table on r2 and r4. Verify connectivity as in Example 8-50.

Example 8-50 *Testing the Spoke Routers*

```
r2#show frame-relay map
Serial0.101 (up): ip 192.168.8.1 dlci 101(0x65,0x1850), static,
              broadcast,
              CISCO, status defined, active
Serial0.101 (up): ip 192.168.8.4 dlci 101(0x65,0x1850), static,
              broadcast,
              CISCO, status defined, active

r2#ping 192.168.8.4
Type escape sequence to abort.
Sending 5, 100-byte ICMP Echos to 192.168.8.4, timeout is 2 seconds:
!!!!!
Success rate is 100 percent (5/5), round-trip min/avg/max = 116/118/128 ms
```

Example 8-50 *Testing the Spoke Routers (Continued)*

```
r4#ping 192.168.8.2
Type escape sequence to abort.
Sending 5, 100-byte ICMP Echos to 192.168.8.2, timeout is 2 seconds:
!!!!!
Success rate is 100 percent (5/5), round-trip min/avg/max = 112/116/124 ms

r2#show ip bgp sum
BGP router identifier 192.168.8.2, local AS number 65520
BGP table version is 3, main routing table version 3
2 network entries and 2 paths using 242 bytes of memory
1 BGP path attribute entries using 96 bytes of memory
BGP activity 2/0 prefixes, 2/0 paths
Neighbor        V     AS MsgRcvd MsgSent   TblVer  InQ OutQ Up/Down  State/PfxRcd
192.168.8.1     4 65520      23      21        3    0    0 00:18:37          2
```

Having a route to get to your destination and the physical transport, too, is obviously pretty important. Originally you set up your Frame Relay connection with a PVC from HQ to DC and VA as well as another from HQ to the other AS using multipoint subinterfaces. However, you were relying on Inverse ARP to get you through r1 to the other IBGP peer. Instead you needed not only the route reflector configuration but static map statements, too.

NOTE   Patience is the answer for BGP any way you configure it. I am not undermining it by any means, but from a support standpoint, take time for a cup of tea and check your configurations again. Always remember to use **clear ip bgp** with a specific address where possible every time you make a change. On the other hand, check those layers.

Now that things are working all the way up the stack, glimpse at the BGP updates as in Example 8-51 so that you see what is going on when you issue **clear ip bgp** *. Feel free to show the clock periodically to see the timing of things or just look at the time and date stamps from the **service timestamps debug** output that you previously configured.

Example 8-51 *BGP Routing Updates*

```
r1#debug ip bgp updates
BGP updates debugging is on
r1#show clock
22:08:39.825 UTC Fri Dec 13 2002
r1#clear ip bgp *
Dec 13 22:09:08.113: BGP: 192.168.8.2 computing updates, neighbor version 0, table
  version 1, starting at 0.0.0.0
Dec 13 22:09:08.117: BGP: 192.168.8.2 update run completed, ran for 0ms, neighbor
  version 0, start version 1, throttled to 1, check point net 0.0.0.0
Dec 13 22:09:08.121: BGP: 192.168.8.4 computing updates, neighbor version 0, table
  version 1, starting at 0.0.0.0
Dec 13 22:09:08.125: BGP: 192.168.8.4 update run completed, ran for 0ms, neighbor
  version 0, start version 1, throttled to 1, check point net 0.0.0.0
```

continues

Example 8-51   *BGP Routing Updates (Continued)*

```
Dec 13 22:09:29.681: BGP: 172.16.8.6 computing updates, neighbor version 0, table
   version 1, starting at 0.0.0.0
Dec 13 22:09:29.685: BGP: 172.16.8.6 update run completed, ran for 0ms, neighbor
   version 0, start version 1, throttled to 1, check point net 0.0.0.0
Dec 13 22:09:57.957: BGP: nettable_walker 172.16.8.4/30 route sourced locally
Dec 13 22:09:57.961: BGP: nettable_walker 192.168.8.0/24 route sourced locally
Dec 13 22:09:57.961: BGP: 192.168.8.2 computing updates, neighbor version 1, table
   version 3, starting at 0.0.0.0
Dec 13 22:09:57.965: BGP: 192.168.8.2 send UPDATE 172.16.8.4/30, next 192.168.8.1,
   metric 0, path
Dec 13 22:09:57.969: BGP: 192.168.8.2 send UPDATE 192.168.8.0/24 (chgflags: 0x8),
   next 192.168.8.1, path  (before routemap/aspath update)
Dec 13 22:09:57.977: BGP: 192.168.8.2 1 updates enqueued (average=60, maximum=60)
Dec 13 22:09:57.977: BGP: 192.168.8.2 update run completed, ran for 12ms, neighbor
   version 1, start version 3, throttled to 3, check point net 0.0.0.0
Dec 13 22:09:57.981: BGP: 192.168.8.4 computing updates, neighbor version 1, table
   version 3, starting at 0.0.0.0
Dec 13 22:09:57.985: BGP: 192.168.8.4 send UPDATE 172.16.8.4/30, next 192.168.8.1,
   metric 0, path
Dec 13 22:09:57.993: BGP: 192.168.8.4 send UPDATE 192.168.8.0/24 (chgflags: 0x8),
   next 192.168.8.1, path  (before routemap/aspath update)
Dec 13 22:09:57.997: BGP: 192.168.8.4 1 updates enqueued (average=60, maximum=60)
Dec 13 22:09:58.001: BGP: 192.168.8.4 update run completed, ran for 12ms, neighbor
   version 1, start version 3, throttled to 3, check point net 0.0.0.0
Dec 13 22:09:59.101: BGP: 172.16.8.6 computing updates, neighbor version 1, table
   version 3, starting at 0.0.0.0
Dec 13 22:09:59.105: BGP: 172.16.8.6 send UPDATE 172.16.8.4/30, next 172.16.8.5,
   metric 0, path 65520
Dec 13 22:09:59.109: BGP: 172.16.8.6 send UPDATE 192.168.8.0/24 (chgflags: 0x8),
   next 172.16.8.5, path  (before routemap/aspath update)
Dec 13 22:09:59.117: BGP: 172.16.8.6 1 updates enqueued (average=57, maximum=57)
Dec 13 22:09:59.117: BGP: 172.16.8.6 update run completed, ran for 12ms, neighbor
   version 1, start version 3, throttled to 3, check point net 0.0.0.0
r1#undebug all
```

After you have watched the BGP routing update process for a few minutes, you should have a couple of occurrences of the nettable walker process. It runs about every minute to populate the routing table from the BGP table. Save your configurations to a file named *tt1 bgp configs*.

Congratulations. You have successfully configured BGP over Frame Relay NBMA.

Trouble Ticket 2 Solution

Assuming you are continuing from the preceding Trouble Ticket, first remove BGP and configure the loopbacks in Example 8-52.

Example 8-52   *Removing BGP and Configuring Loopback Addresses*

```
r1(config)#no router bgp 65520
r1(config)#interface loopback 8
r1(config-if)#ip address 1.1.1.1 255.255.255.0
```

Example 8-52   *Removing BGP and Configuring Loopback Addresses (Continued)*

```
r1(config-if)#no shut
r1(config-if)#end
r1#show ip protocols

r2(config)#no router bgp 65520
!!!lo8 is short for loopback 8
r2(config)#interface lo8
r2(config-if)#ip address 2.2.2.2 255.255.255.0
r2(config-if)#no shut
r2(config-if)#end
r2#show ip protocols

r4(config)#no router bgp 65520
r4(config)#interface lo8
r4(config-if)#ip address 4.4.4.4 255.255.255.0
r4(config-if)#no shut
r4(config-if)#end
r4#show ip protocols

r5(config)#no router bgp 65525
r5(config)#interface lo8
r5(config-if)#ip address 5.5.5.5 255.255.255.0
r5(config-if)#no shut
r5(config-if)#end
r5#show ip protocols
```

Now that you have completely removed BGP and verified that with the old-faithful **show ip protocols** command, configure OSPF, including the loopbacks, as in Example 8-53.

Example 8-53   *Configuring OSPF*

```
r1(config)#router ospf 1
r1(config-router)#network 192.168.8.0 0.0.0.255 area 8
r1(config-router)#network 1.1.1.0 0.0.0.255 area 8
r1(config-router)#end
r1#copy running-config startup-config

r2(config)#router ospf 1
r2(config-router)#network 192.168.8.0 0.0.0.255 area 8
r2(config-router)#network 2.2.2.0 0.0.0.255 area 8
r2(config-router)#end
r2#copy running-config startup-config

r4(config)#router ospf 1
r4(config-router)#network 192.168.8.0 0.0.0.255 area 8
r4(config-router)#network 4.4.4.0 0.0.0.255 area 8
r4(config-router)#end
r4#copy running-config startup-config
```

Verify OSPF connectivity between the routers in network 192.168.8.0 as in Example 8-54.

Example 8-54 *Verifying OSPF*

```
r1#show ip ospf neighbor
r1#!!!no neighbors so no sense in looking for routes
r1#show ip ospf interface s0
r1#!!!appears that opsf not configured on int s0
r1#show run
...
interface Loopback8
 ip address 1.1.1.1 255.255.255.0
 no ip directed-broadcast
...
router ospf 1
 network 1.1.1.0 0.0.0.255 area 8
 network 192.168.8.0 0.0.0.255 area 8
end
r1#clear ip ospf process
Reset ALL OSPF processes? [no]: y
r1#show ip ospf interface
Loopback8 is up, line protocol is up
  Internet Address 1.1.1.1/24, Area 8
  Process ID 1, Router ID 1.1.1.1, Network Type LOOPBACK, Cost: 1
  Loopback interface is treated as a stub Host
Serial0.100 is up, line protocol is up
  Internet Address 192.168.8.1/24, Area 8
  Process ID 1, Router ID 1.1.1.1, Network Type NON_BROADCAST, Cost: 1562
  Transmit Delay is 1 sec, State WAITING, Priority 1
  No designated router on this network
  No backup designated router on this network
  Timer intervals configured, Hello 30, Dead 120, Wait 120, Retransmit 5
    Hello due in 00:00:18
    Wait time before Designated router selection 00:01:39
  Neighbor Count is 0, Adjacent neighbor count is 0
  Suppress hello for 0 neighbor(s)
r1#
```

For better or worse, I assume Layer 2 is alright because you just finished the preceding Trouble Ticket. Like Example 8-54 illustrates, the next step is to see whether you have any OSPF neighbors and if not, why not. Next I checked to make sure OSPF was configured on the interface with the **show ip ospf interface** command, but actually I just looked at s0. Alternatively, you could use **show run**. It looks like things are configured properly, so I issued a **clear ip ospf process** and, sure enough, that did the trick. Well, almost. Look back at the output of **show ip ospf interface** to find the real issue and fix it as in Example 8-55.

Example 8-55 *OSPF Neighbors*

```
r1#show ip ospf neighbor
r1#configure terminal
r1(config)#router ospf 1
r1(config-router)#neighbor 192.168.8.2 ?
  cost              OSPF cost for point-to-multipoint neighbor
```

Example 8-55 *OSPF Neighbors (Continued)*

```
     database-filter  Filter OSPF LSA during synchronization and flooding for
                      point-to-multipoint neighbor
     poll-interval    OSPF dead-router polling interval
     priority         OSPF priority of non-broadcast neighbor
     <cr>
r1(config-router)#neighbor 192.168.8.2
r1(config-router)#neighbor 192.168.8.4
r1(config-router)#end
r1#show ip ospf neighbor
Neighbor ID     Pri   State          Dead Time   Address         Interface
N/A              0    ATTEMPT/DROTHER 00:01:48    192.168.8.4     Serial0.100
N/A              0    ATTEMPT/DROTHER 00:01:46    192.168.8.2     Serial0.100
r1#show ip ospf neighbor
Neighbor ID     Pri   State          Dead Time   Address         Interface
N/A              0    ATTEMPT/DROTHER 00:01:44    192.168.8.4     Serial0.100
2.2.2.2          1    FULL/DR         00:01:58    192.168.8.2     Serial0.100
r1#!!!things are starting to happen now
r1#show ip ospf neighbor
Neighbor ID     Pri   State          Dead Time   Address         Interface
N/A              0    ATTEMPT/DROTHER 00:01:40    192.168.8.4     Serial0.100
2.2.2.2          1    FULL/DR         00:01:59    192.168.8.2     Serial0.100
r1#show ip ospf neighbor
Neighbor ID     Pri   State          Dead Time   Address         Interface
4.4.4.4          1    FULL/DR         00:01:59    192.168.8.4     Serial0.100
2.2.2.2          1    FULL/DROTHER    00:01:56    192.168.8.2     Serial0.100
r1#show ip ospf neighbor detail
 Neighbor 4.4.4.4, interface address 192.168.8.4
    In the area 8 via interface Serial0.100
    Neighbor priority is 1, State is FULL, 7 state changes
    DR is 192.168.8.4 BDR is 192.168.8.1
    Poll interval 60
    Options 2
    Dead timer due in 00:01:32
 Neighbor 2.2.2.2, interface address 192.168.8.2
    In the area 8 via interface Serial0.100
    Neighbor priority is 1, State is FULL, 7 state changes
    DR is 192.168.8.2 BDR is 192.168.8.1
    Poll interval 60
    Options 2
    Dead timer due in 00:01:54
```

Yes, there are issues with running OSPF over Frame Relay NBMA, as mentioned earlier in the chapter. Personally, I would rather just configure point-to-point subinterfaces and be done with it, but there are workarounds. One method is to manually specify the neighbor statements. Notice that I only configured the neighbor statement on one end. However, it is a much better practice to configure the neighbor statements on both ends so as not to leave anything to chance. Speaking of leaving anything to chance, you do not have a full-mesh configuration here, so it is pretty important that the hub router be the DR. Force r1 to be the DR for the serial interfaces by making the other routers ineligible to become the DR as in Example 8-56. Configure the other neighbor statements while you are at it. Watch the election process on r4.

Example 8-56 *Forcing r1 to Become the DR*

```
r2#show ip ospf neighbor
Neighbor ID     Pri   State          Dead Time    Address         Interface
1.1.1.1           1   FULL/BDR       00:01:45     192.168.8.1     Serial0.101
r2#configure terminal
r2(config)#router ospf 1
r2(config-router)#neighbor 192.168.8.1
r2(config-router)#interface s0.101
r2(config-subif)#ip ospf priority 0
r2(config-subif)#end

r4#configure terminal
r4(config)#router ospf 1
r4(config-router)#neighbor 192.168.8.1
r4(config-router)#interface s0/0.101
r4(config-subif)#ip ospf priority 0
r4(config-subif)#end
r4#debug ip ospf adj
OSPF adjacency events debugging is on
Dec 13 23:37:18.150: OSPF: Rcv hello from 1.1.1.1 area 8 from Serial0/0.101
  192.168.8.1
Dec 13 23:37:18.150: OSPF: Neighbor change Event on interface Serial0/0.101
Dec 13 23:37:18.154: OSPF: DR/BDR election on Serial0/0.101
Dec 13 23:37:18.154: OSPF: Elect BDR 1.1.1.1
Dec 13 23:37:18.154: OSPF: Elect DR 1.1.1.1
Dec 13 23:37:18.154:        DR: 1.1.1.1 (Id)    BDR: 1.1.1.1 (Id)
Dec 13 23:37:18.154: OSPF: Send DBD to 1.1.1.1 on Serial0/0.101 seq 0xFDD opt 0x2
  flag 0x7 len 32
Dec 13 23:37:18.154: OSPF: End of hello processing
Dec 13 23:37:18.190: OSPF: Rcv DBD from 1.1.1.1 on Serial0/0.101 seq 0xDB6 opt 0x2
  flag 0x7 len 32 state EXSTART
Dec 13 23:37:18.190: OSPF: First DBD and we are not SLAVE
Dec 13 23:37:18.654: OSPF: Build router LSA for area 8, router ID 4.4.4.4
Dec 13 23:37:23.154: OSPF: Retransmitting DBD to 1.1.1.1 on Serial0/0.101
Dec 13 23:37:23.154: OSPF: Send DBD to 1.1.1.1 on Serial0/0.101 seq 0xFDD opt 0x2
  flag 0x7 len 32
Dec 13 23:37:23.190: OSPF: Rcv DBD from 1.1.1.1 on Serial0/0.101 seq 0xDB6 opt 0x2
  flag 0x7 len 32 state EXSTART
Dec 13 23:37:23.190: OSPF: First DBD and we are not SLAVE
Dec 13 23:37:23.222: OSPF: Rcv DBD from 1.1.1.1 on Serial0/0.101 seq 0xFDD opt 0x2
  flag 0x2 len 132 state EXSTART
Dec 13 23:37:23.222: OSPF: NBR Negotiation Done. We are the MASTER
Dec 13 23:37:23.222: OSPF: Send DBD to 1.1.1.1 on Serial0/0.101 seq 0xFDE opt 0x2
  flag 0x3 len 132
Dec 13 23:37:23.286: OSPF: Rcv DBD from 1.1.1.1 on Serial0/0.101 seq 0xFDE opt 0x2
  flag 0x0 len 32 state EXCHANGE
Dec 13 23:37:23.286: OSPF: Send DBD to 1.1.1.1 on Serial0/0.101 seq 0xFDF opt 0x2
  flag 0x1 len 32
Dec 13 23:37:23.322: OSPF: Rcv DBD from 1.1.1.1 on Serial0/0.101 seq 0xFDF opt 0x2
  flag 0x0 len 32 state EXCHANGE
Dec 13 23:37:23.326: OSPF: Exchange Done with 1.1.1.1 on Serial0/0.101
Dec 13 23:37:23.326: OSPF: Synchronized with 1.1.1.1 on Serial0/0.101, state FULL
Dec 13 23:37:23.654: OSPF: Build router LSA for area 8, router ID 4.4.4.4
Dec 13 23:37:28.654: OSPF: Build router LSA for area 8, router ID 4.4.4.4
```

Example 8-56 *Forcing r1 to Become the DR (Continued)*

```
r4#show ip ospf neighbor
Neighbor ID     Pri   State         Dead Time   Address        Interface
1.1.1.1           1   FULL/DR        00:01:46   192.168.8.1    Serial0/0.101
Dec 13 23:37:48.270: OSPF: Rcv hello from 1.1.1.1 area 8 from Serial0/0.101
   192.168.8.1
Dec 13 23:37:48.270: OSPF: Neighbor change Event on interface Serial0/0.101
Dec 13 23:37:48.270: OSPF: DR/BDR election on Serial0/0.101
Dec 13 23:37:48.270: OSPF: Elect BDR 0.0.0.0
Dec 13 23:37:48.274: OSPF: Elect DR 1.1.1.1
Dec 13 23:37:48.274:        DR: 1.1.1.1 (Id)    BDR: none
Dec 13 23:37:48.274: OSPF: End of hello processing
Dec 13 23:37:48.774: OSPF: Build router LSA for area 8, router ID 4.4.4.4
r4#undebug all
r1#show ip ospf neighbor
Neighbor ID     Pri   State         Dead Time   Address        Interface
4.4.4.4           0   FULL/DROTHER   00:01:46   192.168.8.4    Serial0.100
2.2.2.2           0   FULL/DROTHER   00:01:38   192.168.8.2    Serial0.100
```

Observe the preceding output of **show ip ospf neighbor** on each of the routers to note that both r2 and r4 are in a full state with the DR (r1). Likewise, from r1's perspective it is in a full state with the DRothers. The **clear ip ospf process** command was not necessary here because changing the priority to 0 forced the election to occur. Had you set r1 with a higher priority, clearing the OSPF process or bouncing the interface would have been an effective way to trigger the election. However, on r4 the version of code doesn't support the **clear ip ospf** command anyway. The **debug ip ospf adj** command enabled you to watch the stages of the election process.

I find it more helpful for troubleshooting to manually configure the router ID (RID). In the preceding example, the loopbacks should take precedence unless OSPF was configured before you created them. The problem with making changes to the RID is that it normally doesn't take effect until you reload the router (or restart the OSPF process). I can get away with that in a test environment, but that is not always a choice in a practical environment. Example 8-57 illustrates how to hard code the RIDs.

Example 8-57 *Hard Coding the RIDs*

```
r1(config)#router ospf 1
r1(config-router)#router-id ?
  A.B.C.D   OSPF router-id in IP address format
r1(config-router)#router-id 1.1.1.1
Reload or use "clear ip ospf process" command, for this to take effect
r1(config-router)#end
r1#copy running-config startup-config

r2(config)#router ospf 1
r2(config-router)#router-id 2.2.2.2
Reload or use "clear ip ospf process" command, for this to take effect
r2(config-router)#end
r2#copy running-config startup-config
```

continues

Example 8-57 *Hard Coding the RIDs (Continued)*

```
r4(config)#router ospf 1
r4(config-router)#router-id 4.4.4.4
                            ^
% Invalid input detected at '^' marker.
r4(config-router)#end
r4#show ver
Cisco Internetwork Operating System Software
IOS (tm) 3600 Software (C3620-D-M), Version 11.3(9)T,  RELEASE SOFTWARE (fc1)
r4#!!!ios version issue
```

After hard coding the RID in Example 8-57, the IOS told you to reload or clear the OSPF process for the new RID to take effect. Alternatively, you could try a **no router ospf 1** instead in cases where the IOS version does not support the **clear ip ospf process** command. Review your neighbors and OSPF tables in Example 8-58 after your OSPF processes reset.

Example 8-58 *Viewing OSPF Neighbors, Processes, and Databases*

```
r1#show ip ospf neighbor
Neighbor ID     Pri   State         Dead Time   Address         Interface
4.4.4.4           0   FULL/DROTHER  00:01:44    192.168.8.4     Serial0.100
2.2.2.2           0   FULL/DROTHER  00:01:48    192.168.8.2     Serial0.100
r2#show ip ospf neighbor
Neighbor ID     Pri   State         Dead Time   Address         Interface
1.1.1.1           1   FULL/DR       00:01:57    192.168.8.1     Serial0.101
r4#show ip ospf neighbor
Neighbor ID     Pri   State         Dead Time   Address         Interface
1.1.1.1           1   FULL/DR       00:01:52    192.168.8.1     Serial0/0.101
r4#show ip ospf neighbor detail
 Neighbor 1.1.1.1, interface address 192.168.8.1
    In the area 8 via interface Serial0/0.101
    Neighbor priority is 1, State is FULL
    DR is 192.168.8.1 BDR is 0.0.0.0
    Poll interval 60
    Options 2
    Dead timer due in 00:01:48
r4>
r1#show ip ospf
 Routing Process "ospf 1" with ID 1.1.1.1
 Supports only single TOS(TOS0) routes
 SPF schedule delay 5 secs, Hold time between two SPFs 10 secs
 Minimum LSA interval 5 secs. Minimum LSA arrival 1 secs
 Number of external LSA 0. Checksum Sum 0x0
 Number of DCbitless external LSA 0
 Number of DoNotAge external LSA 0
 Number of areas in this router is 1. 1 normal 0 stub 0 nssa
    Area 8
        Number of interfaces in this area is 2
        Area has no authentication
        SPF algorithm executed 4 times
        Area ranges are
        Number of LSA 7. Checksum Sum 0x30C32
        Number of DCbitless LSA 0
```

Example 8-58 *Viewing OSPF Neighbors, Processes, and Databases (Continued)*

```
          Number of indication LSA 0
          Number of DoNotAge LSA 0
r1#show ip ospf database
      OSPF Router with ID (1.1.1.1) (Process ID 1)
            Router Link States (Area 8)
Link ID          ADV Router       Age        Seq#        Checksum Link count
1.1.1.1          1.1.1.1          711        0x80000002 0x1FF1    2
2.2.2.2          2.2.2.2          706        0x80000008 0x3FA     2
4.4.4.4          4.4.4.4          195        0x8000000A 0xDE03    2
            Net Link States (Area 8)
Link ID          ADV Router       Age        Seq#        Checksum
192.168.8.1      1.1.1.1          711        0x80000001 0xE4BE
```

The first shaded output shows the new RID in the Neighbor ID column, then the neighbor priority, the DR state, the timers, and the actual neighbor interface address is listed in the Address column with the corresponding neighbor interface to the right. After I analyzed the neighbors, I looked at how OSPF was configured with **show ip ospf** and the link-state database with **show ip ospf database**. With serial interfaces, each interface is considered a link rather than just the wire between them, which is why you see two links in the database for each address. When supporting OSPF, you must have neighbors and link states before you get any OSPF routes in your routing table.

Next configure a default route in Example 8-59 on r1 to get to the outside world (meaning the other AS). Have OSPF advertise a default route to r2 and r4 as in Example 8-58, but do not configure a default route on r2 and r4 themselves.

Example 8-59 *Configuring a Default Route on r1*

```
r1#configure terminal
r1(config)#ip route 0.0.0.0 0.0.0.0 s0.105
r1(config)#end
r1#copy running-config startup-config
r1#show ip route
...
Gateway of last resort is 0.0.0.0 to network 0.0.0.0
     1.0.0.0/24 is subnetted, 1 subnets
C       1.1.1.0 is directly connected, Loopback8
     2.0.0.0/32 is subnetted, 1 subnets
O       2.2.2.2 [110/1563] via 192.168.8.2, 00:12:22, Serial0.100
C    192.168.8.0/24 is directly connected, Serial0.100
     4.0.0.0/32 is subnetted, 1 subnets
O       4.4.4.4 [110/1563] via 192.168.8.4, 00:12:22, Serial0.100
     172.16.0.0/30 is subnetted, 1 subnets
C       172.16.8.4 is directly connected, Serial0.105
S*   0.0.0.0/0 is directly connected, Serial0.105
```

You configured the default route on r1 to send all unknown packets out interface s0.105. This resulted in setting the gateway of last resort and the **S*** entry in the routing table. Although r1 now has a route to get to the other networks, the remote devices do not have a return route. Now have r1 advertise a default route via OSPF into the spoke routers r2 and r4 in Example 8-60.

Example 8-60 *Advertising Default Routes into the Spoke Routers*

```
r1#configure terminal
r1(config)#router ospf 1
r1(config-router)#default-information originate ?
  always        Always advertise default route
  metric        OSPF default metric
  metric-type   OSPF metric type for default routes
  route-map     Route-map reference
  <cr>
r1(config-router)#default-information originate always
r1(config-router)#end
r1#copy running-config startup-config
r1#clear ip ospf process
Reset ALL OSPF processes? [no]: y
```

View the OSPF external routes (E2) in the routing tables of r2 and r4, as in Example 8-61.

Example 8-61 *Advertising Default Routes into the Spoke Routers*

```
r2#show ip route
Codes: C - connected, S - static, I - IGRP, R - RIP, M - mobile, B - BGP
       D - EIGRP, EX - EIGRP external, O - OSPF, IA - OSPF inter area
       N1 - OSPF NSSA external type 1, N2 - OSPF NSSA external type 2
       E1 - OSPF external type 1, E2 - OSPF external type 2, E - EGP
       i - IS-IS, L1 - IS-IS level-1, L2 - IS-IS level-2, * - candidate default
       U - per-user static route, o - ODR
Gateway of last resort is 192.168.8.1 to network 0.0.0.0
     1.0.0.0/32 is subnetted, 1 subnets
O       1.1.1.1 [110/1563] via 192.168.8.1, 00:00:15, Serial0.101
     2.0.0.0/24 is subnetted, 1 subnets
C       2.2.2.0 is directly connected, Loopback8
C    192.168.8.0/24 is directly connected, Serial0.101
     4.0.0.0/32 is subnetted, 1 subnets
O       4.4.4.4 [110/1563] via 192.168.8.4, 00:00:15, Serial0.101
O*E2 0.0.0.0/0 [110/1] via 192.168.8.1, 00:00:15, Serial0.101

r4#show ip route
...
Gateway of last resort is 192.168.8.1 to network 0.0.0.0
     1.0.0.0/32 is subnetted, 1 subnets
O       1.1.1.1 [110/1563] via 192.168.8.1, 00:02:07, Serial0/0.101
     2.0.0.0/32 is subnetted, 1 subnets
O       2.2.2.2 [110/1563] via 192.168.8.2, 00:02:07, Serial0/0.101
C    192.168.8.0/24 is directly connected, Serial0/0.101
     4.0.0.0/24 is subnetted, 1 subnets
C       4.4.4.0 is directly connected, Loopback8
O*E2 0.0.0.0/0 [110/1] via 192.168.8.1, 00:02:07, Serial0/0.101
```

Now that the spoke routers have learned a default route via OSPF, they should be able to ping outside of the specific networks in their routing tables. Ping is a two-way street, however, and you need to make sure the echo replies can return. Therefore, in Example 8-62 configure a static route on r5 to get to the 192.168.8.0 network using r1 as the next hop before you start your ping testing.

Example 8-62 *Configuring a Static Route on r5*

```
r5#configure terminal
r5(config)#ip route 192.168.8.0 255.255.255.0 172.16.8.5
r5(config)#end
r5#show ip route
...
Gateway of last resort is not set
S    192.168.8.0/24 [1/0] via 172.16.8.5
      5.0.0.0/24 is subnetted, 1 subnets
C        5.5.5.0 is directly connected, Loopback8
      172.16.0.0/30 is subnetted, 1 subnets
C        172.16.8.4 is directly connected, Serial0.101
```

Fix any other issues, save your configurations, and test things out using the loopbacks as in Example 8-63.

Example 8-63 *Testing the OSPF Configurations*

```
r1#copy running-config startup-config
r1#ping 2.2.2.2
Type escape sequence to abort.
Sending 5, 100-byte ICMP Echos to 2.2.2.2, timeout is 2 seconds:
!!!!!
Success rate is 100 percent (5/5), round-trip min/avg/max = 60/60/60 ms
r1#ping 4.4.4.4
Type escape sequence to abort.
Sending 5, 100-byte ICMP Echos to 4.4.4.4, timeout is 2 seconds:
!!!!!
Success rate is 100 percent (5/5), round-trip min/avg/max = 56/59/60 ms
r1#p 5.5.5.5
Type escape sequence to abort.
Sending 5, 100-byte ICMP Echos to 5.5.5.5, timeout is 2 seconds:
!!!!!
Success rate is 100 percent (5/5), round-trip min/avg/max = 56/59/60 ms

r2#copy running-config startup-config
r2#ping 1.1.1.1
Type escape sequence to abort.
Sending 5, 100-byte ICMP Echos to 1.1.1.1, timeout is 2 seconds:
!!!!!
Success rate is 100 percent (5/5), round-trip min/avg/max = 60/60/60 ms
r2#ping 4.4.4.4
Type escape sequence to abort.
Sending 5, 100-byte ICMP Echos to 4.4.4.4, timeout is 2 seconds:
!!!!!
Success rate is 100 percent (5/5), round-trip min/avg/max = 116/118/128 ms
r2#ping 5.5.5.5
Type escape sequence to abort.
```

continues

Example 8-63 *Testing the OSPF Configurations (Continued)*

```
Sending 5, 100-byte ICMP Echos to 5.5.5.5, timeout is 2 seconds:
!!!!!
Success rate is 100 percent (5/5), round-trip min/avg/max = 116/116/116 ms

r4#copy running-config startup-config
r4#ping 1.1.1.1
Type escape sequence to abort.
Sending 5, 100-byte ICMP Echos to 1.1.1.1, timeout is 2 seconds:
!!!!!
Success rate is 100 percent (5/5), round-trip min/avg/max = 56/59/60 ms
r4#ping 2.2.2.2
Type escape sequence to abort.
Sending 5, 100-byte ICMP Echos to 2.2.2.2, timeout is 2 seconds:
!!!!!
Success rate is 100 percent (5/5), round-trip min/avg/max = 116/118/128 ms
r4#ping 5.5.5.5
Type escape sequence to abort.
Sending 5, 100-byte ICMP Echos to 5.5.5.5, timeout is 2 seconds:
!!!!!
Success rate is 100 percent (5/5), round-trip min/avg/max = 112/114/116 ms

r5#copy running-config startup-config
r5#ping 1.1.1.1
Type escape sequence to abort.
Sending 5, 100-byte ICMP Echos to 1.1.1.1, timeout is 2 seconds:
.....
Success rate is 0 percent (0/5)
```

Looks like everything is fine until you get to r5. Analyze the routing table, fix the problem, and
continue testing in Example 8-64.

Example 8-64 *Analyzing, Fixing, and Testing r5*

```
r5#show ip route
Gateway of last resort is not set
S    192.168.8.0/24 [1/0] via 172.16.8.5
     5.0.0.0/24 is subnetted, 1 subnets
C       5.5.5.0 is directly connected, Loopback8
     172.16.0.0/30 is subnetted, 1 subnets
C       172.16.8.4 is directly connected, Serial0.101
r5#configure terminal
r5(config)#ip route 0.0.0.0 0.0.0.0 s0.101
r5(config)#end
r5#show ip route
Gateway of last resort is 0.0.0.0 to network 0.0.0.0
S    192.168.8.0/24 [1/0] via 172.16.8.5
     5.0.0.0/24 is subnetted, 1 subnets
C       5.5.5.0 is directly connected, Loopback8
     172.16.0.0/30 is subnetted, 1 subnets
C       172.16.8.4 is directly connected, Serial0.101
S*   0.0.0.0/0 is directly connected, Serial0.101
r5#show ip protocols
```

Example 8-64 *Analyzing, Fixing, and Testing r5 (Continued)*

```
r5#ping 1.1.1.1
Type escape sequence to abort.
Sending 5, 100-byte ICMP Echos to 1.1.1.1, timeout is 2 seconds:
!!!!!
Success rate is 100 percent (5/5), round-trip min/avg/max = 60/60/60 ms
r5#ping 2.2.2.2
Type escape sequence to abort.
Sending 5, 100-byte ICMP Echos to 2.2.2.2, timeout is 2 seconds:
!!!!!
Success rate is 100 percent (5/5), round-trip min/avg/max = 116/116/120 ms
r5#ping 4.4.4.4
Type escape sequence to abort.
Sending 5, 100-byte ICMP Echos to 4.4.4.4, timeout is 2 seconds:
!!!!!
Success rate is 100 percent (5/5), round-trip min/avg/max = 112/113/116 ms
```

You would have been successful had you used the 192.168.8.0 network for your ping tests. Remember that r5 is not running a routing protocol at all and is relying on static and default routes to get to the couple of networks it needs to communicate with. In Example 8-65, perform a traceroute from r5 to r4 to see once again how the frame switch is transparent to routing.

Example 8-65 *Trace from r5 to r4*

```
r5#trace 4.4.4.4
Type escape sequence to abort.
Tracing the route to 4.4.4.4
  1 172.16.8.5 28 msec 28 msec 28 msec
  2 192.168.8.4 56 msec 56 msec *
```

Save your configurations to a file named *tt2 ospf configs*.

Congratulations. You have successfully configured OSPF over Frame Relay NBMA using static neighbor statements.

Trouble Ticket 3 Solution

Instead of using static neighbor statements in the preceding Trouble Ticket, you could have configured the **ip ospf network** type as in Example 8-66.

Example 8-66 *Configuring the **ip ospf network** Type*

```
r1(config)#router ospf 1
r1(config-router)#no neighbor 192.168.8.2
r1(config-router)#no neighbor 192.168.8.4
r1(config)#end
r1#configure terminal
r1(config)#interface s0.100
r1(config-subif)#ip ospf network ?
  broadcast               Specify OSPF broadcast multi-access network
  non-broadcast           Specify OSPF NBMA network
```

continues

Example 8-66 *Configuring the* **ip ospf network** *Type (Continued)*

```
       point-to-multipoint  Specify OSPF point-to-multipoint network
       point-to-point       Specify OSPF point-to-point network
    r1(config-subif)#ip ospf network point-to-multipoint
    r1(config-subif)#end
    r1#copy running-config startup-config

    r2#configure terminal
    r2(config)#router ospf 1
    r2(config-router)#no neighbor 192.168.8.1
    r2#configure terminal
    r2(config)#interface s0.101
    r2(config-subif)#ip ospf network point-to-multipoint
    r2(config-subif)#end
    r2#copy running-config startup-config

    r4#configure terminal
    r4(config)#router ospf 1
    r4(config-router)#no neighbor 192.168.8.1
    r4#configure terminal
    r4(config)#interface s0/0.101
    r4(config-subif)#ip ospf network point-to-multipoint
    r4(config-subif)#end
    r4#copy running-config startup-config
```

First I removed the static neighbor statements and then added the **ip ospf network point-to-point** command to r1, r2, and r4. This is not necessary on r5 because it has a point-to-point subinterface rather than multipoint. Verify your OSPF neighbors and ensure your pings still work as in Example 8-67.

Example 8-67 *Verifying OSPF Neighbors*

```
r1#show ip ospf neighbor
Neighbor ID     Pri   State      Dead Time   Address        Interface
2.2.2.2           0   FULL/  -   00:01:59    192.168.8.2    Serial0.100
4.4.4.4           0   FULL/  -   00:01:59    192.168.8.4    Serial0.100
```

Using this method does not require manual neighbor statements or a DR/BDR election. All ping tests should succeed. During this Trouble Ticket, I made a mistake and created an extraneous subinterface. Remove it in Example 8-68.

Example 8-68 *Deleting a Subinterface*

```
r1#show ip interface brief
Interface         IP-Address      OK? Method Status                Protocol
Ethernet0         unassigned      YES unset  administratively down down
Ethernet1         unassigned      YES unset  administratively down down
Loopback8         1.1.1.1         YES NVRAM  up                    up
Serial0           unassigned      YES unset  up                    up
Serial0.100       192.168.8.1     YES NVRAM  up                    up
Serial0.101       unassigned      YES unset  up                    up
Serial0.105       172.16.8.5      YES NVRAM  up                    up
```

Example 8-68   *Deleting a Subinterface (Continued)*

```
Serial1                 unassigned     YES unset  administratively down down
r1#configure terminal
r1(config-if)#no interface s0.101
% Not all config may be removed and may reappear after reactivating the
    sub-interface
r1(config)#end
r1#show ip interface brief
Interface           IP-Address     OK? Method Status              Protocol
Ethernet0           unassigned     YES unset  administratively down down
Ethernet1           unassigned     YES unset  administratively down down
Loopback8           1.1.1.1        YES NVRAM  up                  up
Serial0             unassigned     YES unset  up                  up
Serial0.100         192.168.8.1    YES NVRAM  up                  up
Serial0.101         unassigned     YES unset  deleted             down
Serial0.105         172.16.8.5     YES NVRAM  up                  up
Serial1             unassigned     YES unset  administratively down down
r1#copy running-config startup-config
r1#reload
Proceed with reload? [confirm]
01:09:21: %SYS-5-RELOAD: Reload requested
...
r1>show ip interface brief
Interface           IP-Address     OK? Method Status              Protocol
Ethernet0           unassigned     YES unset  administratively down down
Ethernet1           unassigned     YES unset  administratively down down
Loopback8           1.1.1.1        YES NVRAM  up                  up
Serial0             unassigned     YES unset  up                  up
Serial0.100         192.168.8.1    YES NVRAM  up                  up
Serial0.105         172.16.8.5     YES NVRAM  up                  up
Serial1             unassigned     YES unset  administratively down down
```

The moral of this story is that you have to reload the router to completely get rid of the unwanted subinterface. Save your configurations to a file named *tt3 ospf configs*.

Trouble Ticket 4 Solution

Example 8-69 starts by making sure all DLCIs are active before any changes are made. Shut down the serial interfaces on r3 (the frame switch) and observe the results .

Example 8-69   *Observing Service Provider Issues with the Frame Switch Shut Down*

```
r1#show frame-relay map
Serial0.100 (up): ip 192.168.8.2 dlci 102(0x66,0x1860), static,
              broadcast,
              CISCO, status defined, active
Serial0.100 (up): ip 192.168.8.4 dlci 104(0x68,0x1880), static,
              broadcast,
              CISCO, status defined, active
Serial0.105 (up): point-to-point dlci, dlci 105(0x69,0x1890), broadcast
          status defined, active
```

continues

Example 8-69 *Observing Service Provider Issues with the Frame Switch Shut Down (Continued)*

```
frameswitch#configure terminal
frameswitch(config)#interface s0/0
frameswitch(config-if)#shut
frameswitch(config-if)#interface s0/1
frameswitch(config-if)#shut
frameswitch(config-if)#interface s0/2
frameswitch(config-if)#shut
frameswitch(config-if)#interface s0/3
frameswitch(config-if)#shut

r1#show frame-relay map
Serial0.100 (down): ip 192.168.8.2 dlci 102(0x66,0x1860), static,
            broadcast,
            CISCO, status deleted
Serial0.100 (down): ip 192.168.8.4 dlci 104(0x68,0x1880), static,
            broadcast,
            CISCO, status deleted
Serial0.105 (down): point-to-point dlci, dlci 105(0x69,0x1890), broadcast
            status deleted

r2#show frame-relay map
Serial0.101 (down): ip 192.168.8.1 dlci 101(0x65,0x1850), static,
            broadcast,
            CISCO, status deleted
Serial0.101 (down): ip 192.168.8.4 dlci 101(0x65,0x1850), static,
            broadcast,
            CISCO, status deleted
```

Notice how I tested to make sure things worked to begin with before I started experimenting. The key word here is *deleted*. This is a service provider issue. The DLCIs were once there but no longer are or perhaps they were never configured. Bring only the s0/0 interface up and observe the results in Example 8-70.

Example 8-70 *Observing Service Provider Issues with s0/0 Up*

```
frame-switch(config)#interface s0/0
frame-switch(config-if)#no shut
frame-switch(config-if)#end
!!!first look at the r1 end for dlci 102
r1#show frame-relay map
Serial0.100 (down): ip 192.168.8.2 dlci 102(0x66,0x1860), static,
            broadcast,
            CISCO, status defined, inactive
Serial0.100 (down): ip 192.168.8.4 dlci 104(0x68,0x1880), static,
            broadcast,
            CISCO, status defined, inactive
Serial0.105 (down): point-to-point dlci, dlci 105(0x69,0x1890), broadcast
            status defined, inactive
!!!then look at the r2 end for the same pvc
r2#show frame-relay map
Serial0.101 (down): ip 192.168.8.1 dlci 101(0x65,0x1850), static,
```

Example 8-70 *Observing Service Provider Issues with s0/0 Up (Continued)*

```
               broadcast,
               CISCO, status deleted
Serial0.101 (down): ip 192.168.8.4 dlci 101(0x65,0x1850), static,
               broadcast,
               CISCO, status deleted
```

The effect of bringing up the s0/0 interface on the frame switch changed the DLCI to an inactive state on the local r1 side. However, the other end of the PVC on r2 is still deleted. Make sure you bring all the interfaces up again before you start the next Trouble Ticket.

Trouble Ticket 5 Solution

First you should play the role of the service provider and mix up the DLCIs as in Example 8-71. Remove the correct route statement and then route what comes in the r3 interface s0/1 as DLCI 102 out the s0/0 interface as DLCI 101.

Example 8-71 *Misconfiguring the DLCIs*

```
frame-switch#configure terminal
frame-switch(config)#interface s0/1
frame-switch(config-if)#no frame route 101 interface s0/0 102
frame-switch(config-if)#frame route 102 interface s0/0 101
!!!first look at the frame switch for dlci 102
frame-switch#show frame-relay route
Input Intf      Input Dlci      Output Intf     Output Dlci     Status
Serial0/0       102             Serial0/1       101             inactive
Serial0/0       104             Serial0/2       101             active
Serial0/0       105             Serial0/3       101             active
Serial0/1       102             Serial0/0       101             inactive
Serial0/2       101             Serial0/0       104             active
Serial0/3       101             Serial0/0       105             active
!!!now look at the r1 end for dlci 102
r1#show frame-relay map
Serial0.100 (up): ip 192.168.8.2 dlci 102(0x66,0x1860), static,
               broadcast,
               CISCO, status defined, inactive
Serial0.100 (up): ip 192.168.8.4 dlci 104(0x68,0x1880), static,
               broadcast,
               CISCO, status defined, active
Serial0.105 (up): point-to-point dlci, dlci 105(0x69,0x1890), broadcast
          status defined, active
r1#show frame-relay pvc 102
PVC Statistics for interface Serial0 (Frame Relay DTE)
DLCI = 102, DLCI USAGE = LOCAL, PVC STATUS = INACTIVE, INTERFACE = Serial0.100
  input pkts 49          output pkts 45          in bytes 4108
  out bytes 3944         dropped pkts 0          in FECN pkts 0
  in BECN pkts 0         out FECN pkts 0         out BECN pkts 0
  in DE pkts 0           out DE pkts 0
  out bcast pkts 0        out bcast bytes 0
  pvc create time 00:13:55, last time pvc status changed 00:01:15
```

continues

Example 8-71 *Misconfiguring the DLCIs (Continued)*

```
!!!now look at the r2 end for dlci 102
r2#show frame-relay map
Serial0.101 (down): ip 192.168.8.1 dlci 101(0x65,0x1850), static,
               broadcast,
               CISCO, status deleted
Serial0.101 (down): ip 192.168.8.4 dlci 101(0x65,0x1850), static,
               broadcast,
               CISCO, status deleted
```

The frame switch shows inactive frame routes for PVC 102. r1 shows an inactive state, too. However, r2 is more local to the problem in the cloud and shows a deleted state for DLCI 102. You know it was once there because you configured it, but something mysteriously happened in the cloud. Fix the service provider issues in Example 8-72.

Example 8-72 *Fixing the Frame Route Statement in the Cloud*

```
frame-switch(config)#interface s0/1
frame-switch(config-if)#frame route 101 interface s0/0 102
frameswitch(config-if)#no frame route 102 interface s0/0 101
frameswitch(config-if)#end

r1#show frame-relay map
Serial0.100 (up): ip 192.168.8.2 dlci 102(0x66,0x1860), static,
               broadcast,
               CISCO, status defined, active
Serial0.100 (up): ip 192.168.8.4 dlci 104(0x68,0x1880), static,
               broadcast,
               CISCO, status defined, active
Serial0.105 (up): point-to-point dlci, dlci 105(0x69,0x1890), broadcast
           status defined, active

r2#show frame-relay map
Serial0.101 (up): ip 192.168.8.1 dlci 101(0x65,0x1850), static,
               broadcast,
               CISCO, status defined, active
Serial0.101 (up): ip 192.168.8.4 dlci 101(0x65,0x1850), static,
               broadcast,
               CISCO, status defined, active
```

Trouble Ticket 6 Solution

Turn on Frame Relay compression on r1 as in Example 8-73.

Example 8-73 *Frame Relay Compression on r1*

```
r1(config)#interface s0.105
r1(config-subif)#frame-relay payload-compression packet-by-packet
r1(config-subif)#end
r1#show frame-relay map
Serial0.100 (up): ip 192.168.8.2 dlci 102(0x66,0x1860), static,
               broadcast,
               CISCO, status defined, active
Serial0.100 (up): ip 192.168.8.4 dlci 104(0x68,0x1880), static,
```

Example 8-73 *Frame Relay Compression on r1 (Continued)*

```
                    broadcast,
                    CISCO, status defined, active
Serial0.105 (up): point-to-point dlci, dlci 105(0x69,0x1890), broadcast
          status defined, active
r1#ping 5.5.5.5
Type escape sequence to abort.
Sending 5, 100-byte ICMP Echos to 5.5.5.5, timeout is 2 seconds:
.....
Success rate is 0 percent (0/5)
r5#show frame-relay map
Serial0.101 (up): point-to-point dlci, dlci 101(0x65,0x1850), broadcast
          status defined, active
r5#ping 1.1.1.1
Type escape sequence to abort.
Sending 5, 100-byte ICMP Echos to 1.1.1.1, timeout is 2 seconds:
.....
Success rate is 0 percent (0/5)
```

The frame maps look fine, but mismatched compression types do not enable you to communicate. Turn compression on for r5, the other end of the PVC, as in Example 8-74.

Example 8-74 *Frame Relay Compression on Both Ends of the PVC*

```
r5#configure terminal
r5(config)#interface s0.101
r5(config-subif)#frame-relay payload-compression packet-by-packet
r5(config-subif)#end
r5#ping 1.1.1.1
Type escape sequence to abort.
Sending 5, 100-byte ICMP Echos to 1.1.1.1, timeout is 2 seconds:
!!!!!
Success rate is 100 percent (5/5), round-trip min/avg/max = 36/36/36 ms
```

Now that things are successful, turn frame compression off as in Example 8-75.

Example 8-75 *Removing Frame Relay Compression on Both Ends*

```
r5#configure terminal
r5(config)#interface s0.101
r5(config-subif)#no frame-relay payload-compression packet-by-packet
r5(config-subif)#end
r1#configure terminal
r1(config)#interface s0.105
r1(config-subif)#no frame-relay payload-compression packet-by-packet
r1(config-subif)#end
!!!making sure you can ping
r1#ping 5.5.5.5
Type escape sequence to abort.
Sending 5, 100-byte ICMP Echos to 5.5.5.5, timeout is 2 seconds:
!!!!!
Success rate is 100 percent (5/5), round-trip min/avg/max = 60/60/60 ms
```

Compression works if configured the same on both ends, but many times it works best not configured at all.

Review Questions

Use this chapter and your practical troubleshooting knowledge and skills to answer the following questions. The answers are located in Appendix A, "Answers to Review Questions."

1 Can a single Frame Relay PVC be assigned different DLCIs on each end of a virtual circuit?

2 What are the three possible states for a Frame Relay PVC? Explain.

3 What is the result if one end of the PVC is set to the default Cisco LMI type and the other end is set to ANSI or Q933A?

4 Can you ping yourself in Frame Relay? Why or why not?

5 Headquarters is connected to several branch office routers through a Frame Relay cloud. You know for a fact that the hub router is version 12.1, but you are not sure about all the remotes. Keepalive activity is occurring at most of the remote offices but not all of them. What should you check?

6 Headquarters is connected to several branch office routers through a Frame Relay cloud. The engineer at one of the branch offices is having problems communicating with another branch office. How can you help him out?

7 Explain the output of **show frame-relay map** in the following example:

```
r1#show frame-relay map
Serial1 (up): ip 192.168.5.6 dlci 104(0x68,0x1880), dynamic,
              broadcast,, status defined, active
```

8 You have decided to contact your service provider about getting a higher CIR to allocate more bandwidth because you have been experiencing consistent problems with dropped packets due to congestion on the PVC. What command did you use to determine this?

9 In an all-Cisco-shop Frame Relay, Cisco encapsulation is fine. What Frame Relay encapsulation type is available for other vendors?

10 Point-to-point subinterfaces are often used in configuring Frame Relay to avoid the routing issues with main interfaces and multipoint configurations. Do you need an IP address on the main interface if using point-to-point subinterfaces?

11 How does a router get a DLCI?

12 You are attempting to fix a bad IP address on a Frame Relay interface, but the mapping is still showing the old address. What should you do?

Summary

Layer 2 WAN issues boil down to some pretty basic troubleshooting. Interfaces and controllers are the main targets. For example, if serial x is down and the line protocol is down, check the following:

- Cable

- Interface

- CSU/DSU

- Service provider issues

If serial x is up and the line protocol is down, check the following:

- Clocking and DTE/DCE cable/interface

- Encapsulation

- LMI type

- Other Frame Relay configuration

- Loopback tests

- Service provider issues

Frame Relay is a Layer 2 edge technology that is economic, scalable, manageable, and optimal for the public or private WAN. Connections are through virtual circuits. The entire path is known up front (PVC), and the big advantage to this is not having to set up and tear down the circuits. Unlike its predecessor, X.25, Frame Relay has error detection at Layer 2 but leaves the error correction up to the upper layers. Figure 8-14 shows a pictorial review of troubleshooting Frame Relay.

Figure 8-14   *Frame Relay Troubleshooting Review*

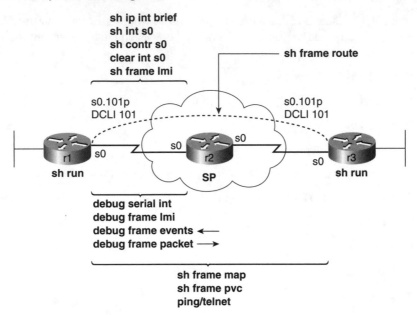

This chapter focused on real-world WAN issues relating to Frame Relay at Layer 2 with specific routing protocol issues at the upper layers as a result of the NBMA topology. The next chapter continues to focus on troubleshooting WAN issues to continue to build your troubleshooting skills.

CHAPTER 9

Shooting Trouble with HDLC, PPP, ISDN BRI, and Dial Backup

This chapter addresses various CCNP Support WAN topics. It includes scenarios and Trouble Tickets for High-Level Data Link Control (HDLC), Point-to-Point Protocol (PPP), Integrated Services Digital Network Basic Rate Interface (ISDN BRI), and Dial Backup. It is assumed you have internetworking experience particularly with IP and routing protocols in the WAN. You will analyze these WAN technologies individually and together for more practical application. This chapter in combination with the previous chapters prepares you for the next chapter and practical internetwork support where you must integrate various skills and predefined troubleshooting methods to solve numerous issues.

In supporting the WAN, many times the battle is deciding whether the problem is in fact yours or whether it is a service provider issue. You will analyze real-world WAN issues, identify troubleshooting targets, and document the results using ping, trace, show, clear, debug and other troubleshooting utilities. Gain practical experience by following the text, figures, and examples or use my guidelines to build the scenarios and Trouble Tickets yourself.

This chapter covers the following topics:

- Scenario: Shooting Trouble on the WAN
- WAN Terminology
- HDLC
- PPP
- ISDN BRI
- Dial-on-Demand Routing
- Dial Backup
- Trouble Tickets
- Trouble Ticket Solutions

Supporting Website Files

You can find files and links to utilities that support this book on the Cisco Press website at www.ciscopress.com/1587200570. Even if you do not have a lab, you can take advantage of the supporting configuration files including the logs to understand device input and output. The files are listed throughout the chapters in italics.

In order to be able to read and work with some of the supporting files offered at www.ciscopress.com/1587200570, you may want to download some of the programs listed in Table I-1 in the Introduction.

Scenario: Shooting Trouble on the WAN

This chapter uses some of the same devices you have been working with throughout the book. First you need to adjust your physical topology as shown in Figure 9-1. You will then work on Layer 2, Layer 3, and so on. The Trouble Tickets in Chapter 8, "Shooting Trouble with Frame Relay," covered Open Shortest Path First (OSPF), Border Gateway Protocol (BGP), and Frame Relay troubles using multipoint and point-to-point subinterfaces. For a little variety, you will work with Enhanced Interior Gateway Routing Protocol (EIGRP) and Intermediate System-to-Intermediate System (IS-IS) on the WAN in this chapter.

Figure 9-1 *Shooting Trouble on the WAN*

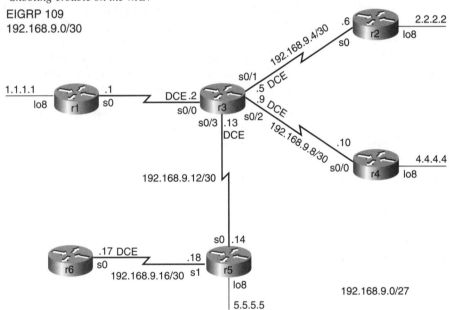

EIGRP 109
192.168.9.0/30

NOTE Do your homework up front if you plan to set up the ISDN labs. Unfortunately, there is no back-to-back cable plan for ISDN, so you need an ISDN switch or ISDN simulator of some type. Keep in mind that if your BRI ports are S/T, which most 2500 ports are, you need NT1s depending on the specific capabilities of your ISDN switch or simulator. For more details, see the "ISDN BRI" section. One of the most economical solutions I found for a simulator is at www.cheapisdn.com.

The scenario goal is for you to modify your existing configuration or start from scratch to build a scenario that you can continue to build off of with the various WAN topics. Do that now using the following guidelines. Add router 6 (r6), and redeploy r1 through r5 so that they are best utilized for the appropriate LAN and WAN interface requirements. Just remember to label your devices as in Figure 9-1 if you make any physical changes so that you can follow along with the chapter. Connect r5s1 to r6s1 using a back-to-back serial cable. My r6 is a 2520. However, you can use whatever has the correct number of interfaces for the scenarios. It is preferred that r5 and r6 both have an ISDN BRI interface for later use. All data links should be using the default encapsulation type to transport IP and EIGRP autonomous system 109. I am restricting you to subnet 0; 192.168.9.0/27 for now.

Draw a picture of the physical layout and label the pertinent items as in Figure 9-1. After the physical connectivity, configure all routers starting with r1. My instructions start from the ending configurations of Chapter 8. Change the routing protocol from OSPF to EIGRP, the encapsulation from Frame Relay to HDLC, and account for the new routers and addresses as in Example 9-1.

There is not always one right or wrong way to accomplish the tasks presented. The ability to obtain the end result using good practices is extremely important in any real-world network. My troubleshooting and device configurations are presented starting in Example 9-1 so that you can compare your work and perhaps see a different approach to obtaining the end result. Use the previous checklists, your step-by-step troubleshooting methodology, and the WAN checklist in Table 9-1 to assist in testing. Frame Relay is not included in this checklist but was covered back in Chapter 8.

Table 9-1   *WAN Quick Troubleshooting Checklist*

Isolating Problems	Commands and Symptoms
Ping is a quick initial test for any troubleshooting. Extended ping gives you more options.	**ping**
Trace is ping's companion test for connectivity and performance. Extended trace gives you more options.	**traceroute**
Check Physical Layer status and clocking.	**show controllers s 0** **show controllers bri 0** **show controllers t 1**

Check interface status and encapsulation.	**show ip interface brief**
	show interfaces [*interface*]
	    show interfaces s0
	    show interfaces bri0 [1 | 2]
	show ip interfaces [*interface*]
	show cdp neighbors [detail]
	clear interface ?
	clear counters

Monitor using date and time stamps for logging and debug activity.	**service timestamps debug datetime localtime msec** **service timestamps log datetime localtime msec**

continues

Table 9-1 *WAN Quick Troubleshooting Checklist (Continued)*

Isolating Problems	Commands and Symptoms
Are you communicating with the provider? Have you ever communicated with the provider? If Layer 1 is deactivated, check your switch type configuration, SPIDs, and configuration.	**show isdn status** **show dialer** **debug dialer** **show dialer interface bri 0** **show isdn history** **debug serial interface**
Check your Layer 2/Layer3 mapping. ISDN has its own Layer 2 and Layer 3. Layer 3 is for signaling and has nothing to do with the bearer payload being IP Layer 3.*	**show dialer map** **show isdn status**
Analyze ISDN Layer 2 communications between you and the local switch (local loop).	**show isdn status** **debug isdn q921**
Analyze ISDN Layer 3 activity (end-to-end signaling).	**show isdn status** **debug isdn q931**
Verify end-to-end PPP authentication.	**debug ppp negotiation** **debug ppp authentication**
Verify configuration.	**show run interface bri0**
Communicate with the service provider.	

*Q931 deals with ISDN end-to-end call setup, but there is no Layer 3 address. The E.164 phone number would be like your MAC address on the LAN, which technically makes ISDN part of the Layer 2 data-link realm.

Example 9-1 illustrates the router configurations for r1 through r3 according to this chapter's section "Shooting Trouble on the WAN Scenario." Example 9-2 shows the same for r4 through r6.

Example 9-1 *Shooting Trouble on the WAN r1 Through r3 Configuration*

```
r1(config)#interface s0
r1(config-if)#shut
r1(config-if)#encap hdlc
r1(config-if)#bandwidth 64
r1(config-if)#ip address 192.168.9.1 255.255.255.252
r1(config-if)#no shut
r1(config-if)#no router ospf 1
r1(config)#router eigrp 109
r1(config-router)#network 192.168.9.0
r1(config-router)#end
r1#copy running-config startup-config
r2(config)#interface s0
r2(config-if)#shut
r2(config-if)#encap hdlc
r2(config-if)#bandwidth 64
r2(config-if)#ip address 192.168.9.6 255.255.255.252
```

Example 9-1   *Shooting Trouble on the WAN r1 Through r3 Configuration (Continued)*

```
r2(config-if)#no shut
r2(config-if)#no router ospf 1
r2(config)#router eigrp 109
r2(config-router)#network 192.168.9.0
r2(config-router)#end
r2#copy running-config startup-config
frame-switch(config)#hostname r3
r3(config)#interface s0/0
r3(config-if)#shut
r3(config-if)#encap hdlc
r3(config-if)#bandwidth 64
r3(config-if)#clock rate 64000
r3(config-if)#ip address 192.168.9.2 255.255.255.252
r3(config-if)#no shut
r3(config-if)#interface s0/1
r3(config-if)#shut
r3(config-if)#encap hdlc
r3(config-if)#bandwidth 64
r3(config-if)#clock rate 64000
r3(config-if)#ip address 192.168.9.5 255.255.255.252
r3(config-if)#no shut
r3(config-if)#interface s0/2
r3(config-if)#shut
r3(config-if)#encap hdlc
r3(config-if)#bandwidth 64
r3(config-if)#clock rate 64000
r3(config-if)#ip address 192.168.9.9 255.255.255.252
r3(config-if)#no shut
r3(config-if)#interface s0/3
r3(config-if)#shut
r3(config-if)#encap hdlc
r3(config-if)#bandwidth 64
r3(config-if)#clock rate 64000
r3(config-if)#ip address 192.168.9.13 255.255.255.252
r3(config-if)#no shut
r3(config-if)#router eigrp 109
r3(config-router)#network 192.168.9.0
r3(config-router)#end
r3#copy running-config startup-config
```

Example 9-2   *Shooting Trouble on the WAN r4 Through r6 Configuration*

```
r4(config)#interface s0/0
r4(config-if)#shut
r4(config-if)#encap hdlc
r4(config-if)#bandwidth 64
r4(config-if)#ip address 192.168.9.10 255.255.255.252
r4(config-if)#no shut
r4(config-if)#no router ospf 1
r4(config)#router eigrp 109
r4(config-router)#network 192.168.9.0
r4(config-router)#end
r4#copy running-config startup-config
```

continues

Example 9-2   *Shooting Trouble on the WAN r4 Through r6 Configuration (Continued)*

```
r5(config)#interface s0
r5(config-if)#shut
r5(config-if)#encap hdlc
r5(config-if)#bandwidth 64
r5(config-if)#ip address 192.168.9.14 255.255.255.252
r5(config-if)#no shut
r5(config)#interface s1
r5(config-if)#shut
r5(config-if)#encap hdlc
r5(config-if)#bandwidth 64
r5(config-if)#ip address 192.168.9.18 255.255.255.252
r5(config-if)#no shut
r5(config-if)#no router ospf 1
r5(config)#router eigrp 109
r5(config-router)#network 192.168.9.0
r5(config-router)#exit
r5#copy running-config startup-config
Router(config)#hostname r6
r6(config)#interface s0
r6(config-if)#bandwidth 64
r6(config-if)#clock rate 64000
r6(config-if)#ip address 192.168.9.17 255.255.255.252
r6(config-if)#no shut
r6(config-if)#router eigrp 109
r6(config-router)#network 192.168.9.0
r6(config-router)#end
r6(config)#enable secret donna
r6(config)#line console 0
r6(config-line)#logging synchronous
r6(config-line)#end
r6#copy running-config startup-config
```

NOTE   Although it is not a requirement to shut down the interfaces as in the previous examples, it is a best practice.

Even though you took a router-by-router approach to configuration, take a layer-by-layer approach to testing and troubleshooting the scenario. First check your controllers, interfaces, and devices as in Example 9-3.

Example 9-3   *Testing Controllers, Interfaces, and Devices*

```
r1#show controllers s 0
HD unit 0, idb = 0x10DB70, driver structure at 0x113008
buffer size 1524  HD unit 0, V.35 DTE cable
...
r1#show ip interface brief
Interface          IP-Address      OK? Method Status               Protocol
Ethernet0          unassigned      YES unset  administratively down down
Ethernet1          unassigned      YES unset  administratively down down
```

Example 9-3   *Testing Controllers, Interfaces, and Devices (Continued)*

```
Loopback8                1.1.1.1          YES manual up                        up
Serial0                  192.168.9.1      YES manual up                        up
Serial0.100              192.168.8.1      YES manual deleted                   down
Serial0.105              172.16.8.5       YES manual deleted                   down
Serial1                  unassigned       YES unset  administratively down down

r1#show cdp neighbors
Capability Codes: R - Router, T - Trans Bridge, B - Source Route Bridge
                  S - Switch, H - Host, I - IGMP, r - Repeater
Device ID       Local Intrfce     Holdtme     Capability  Platform  Port ID
r3              Ser 0             143             R       3640      Ser 0/0
r1#show cdp neighbors detail
-------------------------
Device ID: r3
Entry address(es):
  IP address: 192.168.9.2
Platform: cisco 3640,  Capabilities: Router
Interface: Serial0,  Port ID (outgoing port): Serial0/0
Holdtime : 134 sec
Version :
Cisco Internetwork Operating System Software
IOS (tm) 3600 Software (C3640-JS-M), Version 12.0(13), RELEASE SOFTWARE (fc1)
Copyright  1986-2000 by cisco Systems, Inc.
Compiled Tue 05-Sep-00 21:39 by linda


r2>show controllers s 0
HD unit 0, idb = 0x107EAC, driver structure at 0x10D340
buffer size 1524  HD unit 0, V.35 DTE cable
...
r2>show ip interface brief
Interface                IP-Address       OK? Method Status                  Protocol
Ethernet0                unassigned       YES unset  administratively down down
Loopback8                2.2.2.2          YES manual up                        up
Serial0                  192.168.9.6      YES manual up                        up
Serial0.101              192.168.8.2      YES manual deleted                   down
Serial1                  unassigned       YES unset  administratively down down
r2>show cdp neighbors detail
Device ID: r3
Entry address(es):
  IP address: 192.168.9.5
Platform: cisco 3640,  Capabilities: Router
Interface: Serial0,  Port ID (outgoing port): Serial0/1
Holdtime : 172 sec
Version :
Cisco Internetwork Operating System Software
IOS (tm) 3600 Software (C3640-JS-M), Version 12.0(13), RELEASE SOFTWARE (fc1)
Copyright  1986-2000 by cisco Systems, Inc.
Compiled Tue 05-Sep-00 21:39 by linda
```

My output in Example 9-3 only shows r1 and r2. However, you should complete the same steps for all your devices. The commands **show controllers**, **show ip interface brief**, and **show cdp**

neighbors detail are once again quite helpful for targeting lower-level issues. The r3 and r6 serial interfaces are DCE, whereas all others are DTE. All used interfaces are *up and up*, and **show cdp neighbors** displays the appropriate neighbors. After all of that, however, r6 cannot ping r1. Bounce the interfaces (**shut/no shut**) if needed because you made so many changes. You might want to reload to get rid of all the extraneous deleted subinterfaces. This is the only way to truly get rid of deleted subinterfaces from the Interface Descriptor Block (IDB) table. Continue testing up the stack as in Example 9-4.

Example 9-4   *Continue Testing up the Stack*

```
r6#ping 192.168.9.1
Sending 5, 100-byte ICMP Echos to 192.168.9.1, timeout is 2 seconds:
!!!!!
Success rate is 100 percent (5/5), round-trip min/avg/max = 84/84/88 ms
r6#ping 192.168.9.6
Sending 5, 100-byte ICMP Echos to 192.168.9.6, timeout is 2 seconds:
!!!!!
Success rate is 100 percent (5/5), round-trip min/avg/max = 88/88/88 ms
r6#ping 192.168.9.10
Sending 5, 100-byte ICMP Echos to 192.168.9.10, timeout is 2 seconds:
!!!!!
Success rate is 100 percent (5/5), round-trip min/avg/max = 84/86/88 ms
r6#ping 192.168.9.14
Sending 5, 100-byte ICMP Echos to 192.168.9.14, timeout is 2 seconds:
!!!!!
Success rate is 100 percent (5/5), round-trip min/avg/max = 32/32/32 ms
r1#ping 192.168.9.17
Sending 5, 100-byte ICMP Echos to 192.168.9.17, timeout is 2 seconds:
!!!!!
Success rate is 100 percent (5/5), round-trip min/avg/max = 84/86/88 ms
r1#ping 192.168.9.6
Sending 5, 100-byte ICMP Echos to 192.168.9.6, timeout is 2 seconds:
!!!!!
Success rate is 100 percent (5/5), round-trip min/avg/max = 56/56/60 ms
r1#ping 192.168.9.10
Sending 5, 100-byte ICMP Echos to 192.168.9.10, timeout is 2 seconds:
!!!!!
Success rate is 100 percent (5/5), round-trip min/avg/max = 56/58/60 ms
```

The testing from r6 to the other addresses and from r1 to the other addresses appears to be fine. Check your lower-layer troubleshooting targets (controllers and interfaces) and troubleshoot as required.

NOTE Make sure there are no leftovers from the previous chapters that are causing problems if things are not working as written. It is always a good practice to know what is in your configurations and why, so now is just as good of a time as any to check that.

Now create loopback9 6.6.6.6/32 on r6. Advertise all the loopbacks in EIGRP as in Example 9-5. Then review the routing tables in Example 9-6.

Example 9-5   *Advertising the Loopbacks in EIGRP*

```
r6(config)#interface loopback 9
r6(config-if)#ip address 6.6.6.6 255.255.255.255
r6(config-if)#router eigrp 109
r6(config-router)#network 6.6.6.6
r6(config-router)#end
r6#copy running-config startup-config
r1(config)#router eigrp 109
r1(config-router)#network 1.1.1.1
r1(config-router)#end
r1#copy running-config startup-config
r2(config)#router eigrp 109
r2(config-router)#network 2.2.2.2
r2(config-router)#end
r2#copy running-config startup-config
r3(config)#router eigrp 109
r3(config-router)#network 3.3.3.3
r3(config-router)#end
r3#copy running-config startup-config
...
1d16h: %DUAL-5-NBRCHANGE: IP-EIGRP 109: Neighbor 192.168.9.6 (Serial0/1) is
    up: new adjacency
1d16h: %DUAL-5-NBRCHANGE: IP-EIGRP 109: Neighbor 192.168.9.14 (Serial0/3) is
    up: new adjacency
1d16h: %DUAL-5-NBRCHANGE: IP-EIGRP 109: Neighbor 192.168.9.10 (Serial0/2) is
    up: new adjacency
r4(config)#router eigrp 109
r4(config-router)#network 4.4.4.4
r4(config-router)#end
r4#copy running-config startup-config
r5(config)#router eigrp 109
r5(config-router)#network 5.5.5.5
r5(config-router)#end
r5#copy running-config startup-config
```

Example 9-5 illustrates creating the new loopback on r6 and assumes that the other loopbacks are already in place. Then they are added to EIGRP autonomous system 109. Note the log messages shown on r3. They tell you that the router has been up for 1 day and 16 hours (1d16h); however, it is helpful to have more accurate date and time stamps associated with your log messages. To assist with that, configure the following statements on your devices:

```
clock set ?
service timestamps debug datetime localtime msec
service timestamps log datetime localtime msec
```

Ensure you set the clock and put in the previous **timestamps** commands above before you continue. Check the results of advertising the loopbacks into EIGRP by reviewing your routing tables in Example 9-6.

Example 9-6   *Reviewing the Routing Tables*

```
r6#show ip route
...
D    1.0.0.0/8 [90/41664000] via 192.168.9.18, 00:00:19, Serial0
D    2.0.0.0/8 [90/41664000] via 192.168.9.18, 00:00:19, Serial0
D    4.0.0.0/8 [90/41664000] via 192.168.9.18, 00:00:19, Serial0
     192.168.9.0/24 is variably subnetted, 6 subnets, 2 masks
D       192.168.9.0/30 [90/41536000] via 192.168.9.18, 00:00:20, Serial0
D       192.168.9.0/24 is a summary, 00:01:49, Null0
D       192.168.9.4/30 [90/41536000] via 192.168.9.18, 00:00:20, Serial0
D       192.168.9.8/30 [90/41536000] via 192.168.9.18, 00:00:20, Serial0
D       192.168.9.12/30 [90/41024000] via 192.168.9.18, 00:00:20, Serial0
C       192.168.9.16/30 is directly connected, Serial0
D    5.0.0.0/8 [90/40640000] via 192.168.9.18, 00:00:21, Serial0
     6.0.0.0/8 is variably subnetted, 2 subnets, 2 masks
C       6.6.6.6/32 is directly connected, Loopback9
D       6.0.0.0/8 is a summary, 00:01:49, Null0
```

Hopefully, the 1.0.0.0/8, 2.0.0.0/8, 4.0.0.0/8, and 5.0.0.0/8 with a missing 3.0.0.0 looked strange to you compared to the directly connected loopback routing table entry of 6.6.6.6/32. Fix the issue as in Example 9-7 so that the loopbacks are shown as a /32 in the routing tables and so you can see network 3.3.3.3.

Example 9-7   *Fixing the Loopbacks*

```
r1(config)#router eigrp 109
r1(config-router)#no auto-summary
r1(config-router)#end
r1#copy running-config startup-config
Dec 21 04:07:28.723: %SYS-5-CONFIG_I: Configured from console by console
```

Example 9-7 only illustrates the **no auto-summary** command on r1, but you should configure this router config mode command on all your devices. Note how the logging changes to show you the time and date stamp of the configuration change.

When you entered the loopback network statements in Example 9-5 as hosts (6.6.6.6) without a mask, a classful mask was applied to them. The previous routing table entry for 6.0.0.0/8 pointing to null0 illustrated that.

Remember that although you can summarize on any interface you want with EIGRP that the default **auto-summary** configuration summarizes on the classful boundary. Now view the routing tables once again in Example 9-8.

Example 9-8   *Viewing the Routing Tables*

```
r6#show ip route
...
     1.0.0.0/24 is subnetted, 1 subnets
D       1.1.1.0 [90/41664000] via 192.168.9.18, 00:00:18, Serial0
     2.0.0.0/24 is subnetted, 1 subnets
D       2.2.2.0 [90/41664000] via 192.168.9.18, 00:00:18, Serial0
```

Example 9-8   *Viewing the Routing Tables (Continued)*

```
      4.0.0.0/24 is subnetted, 1 subnets
D        4.4.4.0 [90/41664000] via 192.168.9.18, 00:00:18, Serial0
!!!if you have more than 5 subnets you may have missed a no auto-sum
      192.168.9.0/30 is subnetted, 5 subnets
D        192.168.9.0 [90/41536000] via 192.168.9.18, 00:00:18, Serial0
D        192.168.9.4 [90/41536000] via 192.168.9.18, 00:00:18, Serial0
D        192.168.9.8 [90/41536000] via 192.168.9.18, 00:00:18, Serial0
D        192.168.9.12 [90/41024000] via 192.168.9.18, 00:00:18, Serial0
C        192.168.9.16 is directly connected, Serial0
      5.0.0.0/24 is subnetted, 1 subnets
D        5.5.5.0 [90/40640000] via 192.168.9.18, 00:00:19, Serial0
      6.0.0.0/32 is subnetted, 1 subnets
C        6.6.6.6 is directly connected, Loopback9
```

It is not important that all loopbacks are named loopback9 for this chapter. That is a good approach if you are configuring from scratch. If you are just modifying the Chapter 8 configurations as I am, use the existing loopback8 interfaces. Remember to configure a loopback9 for r3 because it was acting as a frame switch in the preceding chapter and for r6 because it was added in this chapter scenario. Example 9-9 shows what the loopback looks like in the *running-config*.

Example 9-9   *Viewing the Loopbacks in the running-config File*

```
r1#sh run interface loopback 8
...
interface Loopback8
 ip address 1.1.1.1 255.255.255.0
 no ip directed-broadcast
```

Experiment a bit to see the results of typing the loopbacks in as host routes with a mask of 255.255.255.255 as in Example 9-10.

Example 9-10   *Configuring Loopbacks as Host Routes*

```
r1(config)#interface loopback 8
r1(config-if)#ip address 1.1.1.1 255.255.255.255
r2(config)#interface loopback 8
r2(config-if)#ip address 2.2.2.2 255.255.255.255
r3(config)#interface loopback 9
r3(config-if)#ip address 3.3.3.3 255.255.255.255
r4(config)#interface loopback 8
r4(config-if)#ip address 4.4.4.4 255.255.255.255
r5(config)#interface loopback 8
r5(config-if)#ip address 5.5.5.5 255.255.255.255
r6(config)#interface loopback 9
r6(config-if)#ip address 6.6.6.6 255.255.255.255
```

Now observe the output of the *running-config* file and the routing table in Example 9-11.

Example 9-11 *Observe the Host Routes*

```
r6#show run interface lo9
Building configuration...
Current configuration:
interface Loopback9
 ip address 6.6.6.6 255.255.255.255
 no ip directed-broadcast
end
r6#show ip route
...
     1.0.0.0/32 is subnetted, 1 subnets
D       1.1.1.1 [90/41664000] via 192.168.9.18, 00:02:21, Serial0
     2.0.0.0/32 is subnetted, 1 subnets
D       2.2.2.2 [90/41664000] via 192.168.9.18, 00:02:01, Serial0
     3.0.0.0/32 is subnetted, 1 subnets
D       3.3.3.3 [90/41152000] via 192.168.9.18, 00:01:42, Serial0
     4.0.0.0/32 is subnetted, 1 subnets
D       4.4.4.4 [90/41664000] via 192.168.9.18, 00:01:24, Serial0
     192.168.9.0/30 is subnetted, 5 subnets
D       192.168.9.0 [90/41536000] via 192.168.9.18, 00:20:17, Serial0
D       192.168.9.4 [90/41536000] via 192.168.9.18, 00:20:17, Serial0
D       192.168.9.8 [90/41536000] via 192.168.9.18, 00:20:17, Serial0
D       192.168.9.12 [90/41024000] via 192.168.9.18, 00:20:17, Serial0
C       192.168.9.16 is directly connected, Serial0
     5.0.0.0/32 is subnetted, 1 subnets
D       5.5.5.5 [90/40640000] via 192.168.9.18, 00:01:04, Serial0
     6.0.0.0/32 is subnetted, 1 subnets
C       6.6.6.6 is directly connected, Loopback9
```

As a support person, you may need to understand routing. With EIGRP you need to know how to turn off the default **auto-summary** and manually summarize as appropriate to limit your queries in the search of feasible successors. Remember to use **show ip route** or **show ip route eigrp** to analyze the routing table. However, **show protocols** and **show ip protocols** are quite helpful in troubleshooting routing issues, too. EIGRP is one of the fastest converging protocols; therefore, when you finished the configuration on r6, the routing tables had already caught up to you.

Save your configurations and then review the next section to become more familiar with the WAN.

WAN Terminology

Now that you have a working scenario with r1 to r6, I want to discuss WAN concerns and terminology a bit more. The Telecommunications Act of 1996 drastically changed the way of the WAN. However, there are still three main concerns when connecting your sites:

- Availability
- Bandwidth
- Cost

Whether you select leased lines, circuit-switched networks, packet-switched networks, cell-switched networks, Digital Subscriber Lines (DSL), cable modems, or wireless, you must interface with the provider(s). Interfacing with the provider is a big part of supporting the WAN. The central office (CO) is the entry point of the cloud for calling devices and the exit point of the cloud for called devices. It is the switching point for calls that traverse the service provider's toll network. The last mile or local loop extends from the demarcation point (demarc) to the CO. Essentially the demarc is known in the support world as the "line of blame." Customer premises equipment (CPE) resides at the customer location, although it may be owned by the subscriber or leased from the provider. More than one provider may be involved for your various primary, sectional, regional, and international trunks and switches. Knowing who to call for what is an important part of troubleshooting methodology.

Use Figure 9-2 to review the DTE/DCE specifications and Table 9-2 to review WAN connection types and encapsulations.

NOTE   Although the lab scenarios and Trouble Tickets you work through in this book (and in any lab for that matter) make use of back-to-back serial cables, in a practical environment you must order the appropriate cable. One end is the standard DB60, but the other end could be EIA/TIA-232, EIA/TIA-449, EIA/TIA-530, V.35, X.21, and so on. Figure 9-2 shows an example of the Physical Layer DTE/DCE requirements in the lab compared to the practical application of such.

Figure 9-2   *Serial DTE/DCE Connections*

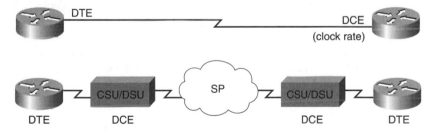

Table 9-2   *WAN Connections*

Layer 1 Connection Types	Layer 2 Encapsulations	Examples
Leased line Synchronous serial	HDLC PPP SLIP*	Point-to-point or dedicated connections (pre-established path) Private use No service provider (no cloud)

continues

Table 9-2 *WAN Connections (Continued)*

Layer 1 Connection Types	Layer 2 Encapsulations	Examples
Circuit switched Asynchronous serial Synchronous serial (legacy 56 kbps)	HDLC PPP SLIP	Phone call (dedicated for the call duration) ISDN (totally synchronous) Service provider
Packet switched Synchronous serial	Frame Relay ATM X.25	Store and forward Service provider (Share physical connections to reduce cost, virtual circuits)

*SLIP = Serial Line Internet Protocol

HDLC is the first of this chapter's specific WAN topics I want to focus on. The section starts with a brief overview, then looks at the layers, and finishes up with shooting HDLC troubles.

HDLC

High-Level Data Link Control (HDLC) started in the 1970s. IBM Synchronous Data Link Control (SDLC) was created in the mid-1970s for Systems Network Architecture (SNA). SDLC is a bit-oriented synchronous data-link protocol that the ISO modified into HDLC. The Consultative Committee for Telegraph and Telephone (CCITT), now the ITU-T, modified HDLC to create Link Access Procedure (LAP) and Link Access Procedure Balanced (LAPB) for X.25. IEEE modified HDLC, too, for its IEEE 802.2.

HDLC is the default WAN encapsulation type between two Cisco devices. Example 9-12 clears the counters and displays the output of **show interfaces serial 0** for r6.

Example 9-12 *Clear the Counters and Show the Serial Interfaces*

```
r6#clear counters serial 0
Clear "show interface" counters on this interface [confirm]
r6#show interfaces s0
Serial0 is up, line protocol is up
  Hardware is HD64570
  Internet address is 192.168.9.17/30
  MTU 1500 bytes, BW 64 Kbit, DLY 20000 usec, rely 255/255, load 1/255
  Encapsulation HDLC, loopback not set, keepalive set (10 sec)
  Last input 00:00:00, output 00:00:03, output hang never
  Last clearing of "show interface" counters 00:00:07
  Queueing strategy: fifo
  Output queue 0/40, 0 drops; input queue 0/75, 0 drops
```

Example 9-12 *Clear the Counters and Show the Serial Interfaces (Continued)*

```
      5 minute input rate 0 bits/sec, 0 packets/sec
      5 minute output rate 0 bits/sec, 0 packets/sec
         3 packets input, 150 bytes, 0 no buffer
         Received 1 broadcasts, 0 runts, 0 giants, 0 throttles
         0 input errors, 0 CRC, 0 frame, 0 overrun, 0 ignored, 0 abort
         1 packets output, 64 bytes, 0 underruns
         0 output errors, 0 collisions, 0 interface resets
         0 output buffer failures, 0 output buffers swapped out
         0 carrier transitions
         DCD=up  DSR=up  DTR=up  RTS=up  CTS=up
```

View the *running-config* for interface s0. Shut down the s0 interface in Example 9-13 so that you can observe the effect.

Example 9-13 *Administratively Shut Down*

```
r6#show run interface s0
interface Serial0
 bandwidth 64
 ip address 192.168.9.17 255.255.255.252
 no ip directed-broadcast
 no ip mroute-cache
 no fair-queue
 clockrate 64000
end
!!!although hdlc is the current encapsulation type
!!!you do not see it in the config because it is the default
r6#configure terminal
r6(config)#interface s0
r6(config-if)#shut
Dec 21 05:12:52.259: %LINK-5-CHANGED: Interface Serial0, changed state to
administratively down
Dec 21 05:12:53.259: %LINEPROTO-5-UPDOWN: Line protocol on Interface Serial0,
changed state to down
r6(config-if)#end
Dec 21 05:13:13.107: %SYS-5-CONFIG_I: Configured from console by console
!!!note the interface status below
r6#show interfaces s0
Serial0 is administratively down, line protocol is down
  Hardware is HD64570
  Internet address is 192.168.9.17/30
  MTU 1500 bytes, BW 64 Kbit, DLY 20000 usec, rely 255/255, load 1/255
  Encapsulation HDLC, loopback not set, keepalive set (10 sec)
  Last input 00:00:47, output 00:00:42, output hang never
  Last clearing of "show interface" counters 00:07:04
  Queueing strategy: fifo
  Output queue 0/40, 0 drops; input queue 0/75, 0 drops
  5 minute input rate 0 bits/sec, 0 packets/sec
  5 minute output rate 0 bits/sec, 0 packets/sec
     127 packets input, 7810 bytes, 0 no buffer
     Received 44 broadcasts, 0 runts, 0 giants, 0 throttles
     0 input errors, 0 CRC, 0 frame, 0 overrun, 0 ignored, 0 abort
```

continues

Example 9-13 *Administratively Shut Down (Continued)*

```
      128 packets output, 7818 bytes, 0 underruns
      0 output errors, 0 collisions, 0 interface resets
      0 output buffer failures, 0 output buffers swapped out
      0 carrier transitions
      DCD=down  DSR=down  DTR=up  RTS=up  CTS=down
```

Administratively down always means you need to issue a **no shut** command on the specific interface. Note the time you last cleared the counters. Also, the Data Carrier Detect (DCD) and Data Set Ready (DSR) are in a down state when the interface is administratively shut down.

Change the encapsulation, and **no shut** the interface as in Example 9-14. Review the results so that you know what to look for when troubleshooting. Pay close attention to the interface status and encapsulation mismatches logs. This example assumes the other end of the data link to be correctly configured for HDLC.

Example 9-14 *Encapsulation Mismatches*

```
r6(config)#interface s0
r6(config-if)#encap frame
r6(config-if)#no shut
Dec 21 05:14:11.447: %LINK-3-UPDOWN: Interface Serial0, changed state to up
Dec 21 05:14:22.479: %LINEPROTO-5-UPDOWN: Line protocol on Interface Serial0,
changed state to up
Dec 21 05:14:52.479: %LINEPROTO-5-UPDOWN: Line protocol on Interface Serial0,
changed state to down
r6(config-if)#end
Dec 21 05:15:11.515: %SYS-5-CONFIG_I: Configured from console by console
r6#show interfaces s0
Serial0 is up, line protocol is down
  Hardware is HD64570
  Internet address is 192.168.9.17/30
  MTU 1500 bytes, BW 64 Kbit, DLY 20000 usec, rely 255/255, load 1/255
  Encapsulation FRAME-RELAY, loopback not set, keepalive set (10 sec)
  LMI enq sent   6, LMI stat recvd 0, LMI upd recvd 0, DTE LMI down
...
      0 output errors, 0 collisions, 3 interface resets
      0 output buffer failures, 0 output buffers swapped out
      6 carrier transitions
      DCD=up  DSR=up  DTR=up  RTS=up  CTS=up
```

The s0 physical interface is up, but the line protocol is down. This symptom should definitely make you check the encapsulation on both ends of the data link. Also note the three interface resets and six carrier transitions. Interface resets occur when the interface has been completely reset, which normally is from cabling or signaling issues. The system resets the interface automatically if it sees that the physical interface is up but the line protocol is down. Carrier transitions occur when there is an interruption in signal. If DCD goes down and then back up, for instance, that is two transitions. If they continue to increase, check the cabling or other attached hardware. If output drops also increase, the problem may be congestion. Fix the encapsulation mismatch in Example 9-15, as you anticipate the increased number of transitions and resets.

Example 9-15 *Fixing Encapsulation Mismatches*

```
r6(config)#interface s0
r6(config-if)#shut
Dec 21 05:15:48.551: %LINK-5-CHANGED: Interface Serial0, changed state to
administratively down
r6(config-if)#encap hdlc
r6(config-if)#no shut
r6(config-if)#end
r6#copy running-config startup-config
Dec 21 05:15:57.783: %LINK-3-UPDOWN: Interface Serial0, changed state to up
Dec 21 05:15:58.895: %LINEPROTO-5-UPDOWN: Line protocol on Interface Serial0,
changed state to up
Dec 21 05:15:58.907: %SYS-5-CONFIG_I: Configured from console by console
r6#show interfaces s0
Serial0 is up, line protocol is up
  Hardware is HD64570
  Internet address is 192.168.9.17/30
  MTU 1500 bytes, BW 64 Kbit, DLY 20000 usec, rely 255/255, load 1/255
  Encapsulation HDLC, loopback not set, keepalive set (10 sec)
  Last input 00:00:03, output 00:00:01, output hang never
  Last clearing of "show interface" counters 01:10:58
  Queueing strategy: fifo
  Output queue 0/40, 0 drops; input queue 0/75, 0 drops
  5 minute input rate 0 bits/sec, 0 packets/sec
  5 minute output rate 0 bits/sec, 0 packets/sec
     1382 packets input, 87139 bytes, 0 no buffer
     Received 477 broadcasts, 0 runts, 0 giants, 0 throttles
     0 input errors, 0 CRC, 0 frame, 0 overrun, 0 ignored, 0 abort
     1377 packets output, 85541 bytes, 0 underruns
     0 output errors, 0 collisions, 8 interface resets
     0 output buffer failures, 0 output buffers swapped out
     8 carrier transitions
     DCD=up  DSR=up  DTR=up  RTS=up  CTS=up
r6#clear counters s0
Clear "show interface" counters on this interface [confirm]
```

The **show interfaces** command not only shows encapsulation type, but also keepalive activity, bandwidth, carrier transitions, and data terminal settings to assist you with troubleshooting serial interfaces. Carrier transitions can occur with bad modems, bad cables, noisy lines, and so on. So it means misconfigured lines will look the same, too. Some other things may be better tested with **show controllers s 0** and by looking at the clocking state. From your testing, you now know how important it is to clear you interface counters to observe the activity over a certain period of time.

The Layers

Look at Figure 9-3 to put the layers into perspective.

Figure 9-3 *HDLC Frame Format*

Flag 7E	Address (Circuit ID)	Control	Proprietary	Data	FCS	Flag 7E
1 Byte	1 Byte	1 Byte			2 Bytes	1 Byte

HDLC has absolutely no built-in authentication mechanisms like PPP's Password Authentication Protocol (PAP) and Challenge Handshake Authentication Protocol (CHAP). It starts and ends with a 1-byte Flag field. HDLC consists of an Address and Control field, the data, and an frame check sequence (FCS) for error detection. Cisco's HDLC contains a proprietary field to carry multiple Layer 3 protocols.

NOTE The ISO implementation of HDLC only supports one protocol, whereas Cisco includes a proprietary field that can carry multiple Layer 3 protocols.

Shooting Trouble with HDLC

When shooting trouble with HDLC or any WAN encapsulation, it is often helpful to capture and analyze some background traffic on the WAN. Just as you did on the LAN, identify the different types of messages when things are working to assist you when things are not working.

Turn on commands such as **terminal monitor (term mon)** to view debug output over telnet sessions if needed. Remember to set the clock and add the **service timestamps** commands to put a time stamp on debug and log messages. This time stamp can be an uptime or a date and time indicator. Use local time-zone information and the Network Time Protocol (NTP) in practical application.

For now, concentrate on r5 and r6 to analyze the HDLC traffic. On both routers, turn on **debug serial interface** as in Example 9-7. This assumes you have **term mon** enabled if needed. Also **service timestamps debug datetime localtime msec** and **service timestamps log datetime localtime msec** are quite useful if your router time is correct. Configure that now if you haven't already. Watch the activity for a couple of minutes to identify the messages. Capture the activity to a file for more detailed review. The pertinent parts are presented in Example 9-16.

Example 9-16 *Debug Serial Interface*

```
r5#clear counters
r5#terminal monitor
% Console already monitors
r5#debug serial interface
Serial network interface debugging is on

r6#clear counters
r6#terminal monitor
% Console already monitors
r6#debug serial interface
Serial network interface debugging is on
r6#
Dec 21 06:24:27.991: Serial0: HDLC myseq 410, mineseen 410*, yourseen 410, line up
Dec 21 06:24:37.999: Serial0: HDLC myseq 411, mineseen 411*, yourseen 411, line up
Dec 21 06:24:48.007: Serial0: HDLC myseq 412, mineseen 412*, yourseen 412, line up
```

What you should have gleaned from this exercise is that HDLC messages are keepalives on the
WAN. These keepalives go to the other end and allow the line protocol status to state up. These
keepalives occur by default every 10 seconds. For example, look at the time stamps from r6:
6:24:27, 6:24:37, 6:24:48, and so on. Keepalives in the WAN world are truly between you and
the service provider, not just your own interface as in the LAN. Relate the preceding shaded
output to the following information about WAN keepalives:

- mineseq is the keepalive sent by the local side.

- yourseen is the keepalive sent by the remote side.

- mineseen is the local keepalive seen by the remote side.

The yourseen is actually the last one I (r6) saw from you plus one (that is, the one I expect to
see from you next). The mineseen is the last received yourseen, which should match the myseq
going out so that what I'm sending and what you expect to see are the same.

Missing three keepalives in a row on the WAN takes the line protocol down. To spot such issues,
always check your Layer 1 modem control leads as you did previously with **show interfaces
s0**. The interface resets would also have incremented. Although it takes 20 to 30 seconds for the
interface to go down, it comes back up almost immediately.

Take a few minutes and try this out as in Example 9-17. Make sure things are up and running
from the preceding exercise, such as **term mon,** the **service timestamps** commands, and the
debug serial interface command. Turn off the keepalives on r6s0 and monitor the results. Turn
them back on and monitor the results until things are working again.

Example 9-17 *Debug Serial Interface with Keepalive Issues*

```
r6#show debug
Generic serial:
  Serial network interface debugging is on
r6#configure terminal
r6(config)#interface s0
```

continues

Example 9-17   *Debug Serial Interface with Keepalive Issues (Continued)*

```
Dec 21 06:33:09.175: Serial0: HDLC myseq 462, mineseen 462*, yourseen 462, line up
r6(config-if)#no keepalive
Dec 21 06:33:24.659: Serial0 - Got keepalive with none configured
Dec 21 06:33:34.775: HD(0): got an interrupt state = 0x8055
Dec 21 06:33:34.779: HD(0): New serial state = 0x0055
Dec 21 06:33:34.779: HD(0): DTR is down.
Dec 21 06:33:34.783: HD(1): New serial state = 0x0600
Dec 21 06:33:34.783: HD(1): Cable is unplugged.
Dec 21 06:33:34.787: HD(0): got an interrupt state = 0x8057
Dec 21 06:33:34.791: HD(0): New serial state = 0x0057
Dec 21 06:33:34.791: HD(0): DTR is up.
Dec 21 06:33:34.795: HD(1): New serial state = 0x0600
Dec 21 06:33:34.795: HD(1): Cable is unplugged.
Dec 21 06:33:34.795: HD(0): got an interrupt state = 0x805F
Dec 21 06:33:34.799: HD(0): New serial state = 0x005F
Dec 21 06:33:34.799: HD(0): DTR is up.
Dec 21 06:33:34.803: HD(1): New serial state = 0x0600
Dec 21 06:33:34.803: HD(1): Cable is unplugged.
Dec 21 06:33:34.807: Serial0 - Got keepalive with none configured
...
r6#show interface s0
Serial0 is up, line protocol is up
  Hardware is HD64570
  Internet address is 192.168.9.17/30
  MTU 1500 bytes, BW 64 Kbit, DLY 20000 usec, rely 255/255, load 1/255
  Encapsulation HDLC, loopback not set, keepalive not set
  Last input 00:00:05, output 00:00:04, output hang never
...
     0 output errors, 0 collisions, 0 interface resets
     0 output buffer failures, 0 output buffers swapped out
     6 carrier transitions
     DCD=up  DSR=up  DTR=up  RTS=up  CTS=up
r6#configure terminal
r6(config-if)#keepalive 10
Dec 21 06:34:39.295: Serial0: HDLC myseq 0, mineseen 463*, yourseen 471, line up
Dec 21 06:34:45.859: HD(0): got an interrupt state = 0x8055
Dec 21 06:34:45.859: HD(0): New serial state = 0x0055
Dec 21 06:34:45.863: HD(0): DTR is down.
Dec 21 06:34:45.863: HD(1): New serial state = 0x0600
Dec 21 06:34:45.863: HD(1): Cable is unplugged.
Dec 21 06:34:45.871: HD(0): got an interrupt state = 0x8057
Dec 21 06:34:45.871: HD(0): New serial state = 0x0057
Dec 21 06:34:45.875: HD(0): DTR is up.
Dec 21 06:34:45.875: HD(1): New serial state = 0x0600
Dec 21 06:34:45.875: HD(1): Cable is unplugged.
Dec 21 06:34:45.879: HD(0): got an interrupt state = 0x805F
Dec 21 06:34:45.879: HD(0): New serial state = 0x005F
Dec 21 06:34:45.883: HD(0): DTR is up.
Dec 21 06:34:45.883: HD(1): New serial state = 0x0600
Dec 21 06:34:45.883: HD(1): Cable is unplugged.
Dec 21 06:34:49.295: Serial0: HDLC myseq 1, mineseen 1*, yourseen 472, line up
Dec 21 06:34:59.295: Serial0: HDLC myseq 2, mineseen 2*, yourseen 1, line up
Dec 21 06:35:09.419: Serial0: HDLC myseq 3, mineseen 3*, yourseen 2, line up
r6(config-if)#end
```

Use Example 9-17 to review the normal handshake-like activity of the WAN sequence numbers again. Keepalives are sequence numbers and acknowledgments that go to the other end of the point-to-point link. This is why you witnessed the "got keepalive with none configured" message. The up, down, up, down interface reset activity (flapping link) was a good indication of no keepalives. The shaded output of the sequence numbers shows how they restart after the interface has been brought back to the up status. If the line protocol does not come back to the up status and the keepalive activity still does not occur, I would suspect a hardware problem.

Now turn off all debugging and examine r6s0 in Example 9-18. Clear the counters to remove the interface resets and carrier transition activity. Look at the routing tables and test connectivity with ping as in Example 9-19.

Example 9-18 *Cleaning Up*

```
r5#undebug all
r6#undebug all
r6#show interfaces s0
Serial0 is up, line protocol is up
  Hardware is HD64570
  Internet address is 192.168.9.17/30
  MTU 1500 bytes, BW 64 Kbit, DLY 20000 usec, rely 255/255, load 1/255
  Encapsulation HDLC, loopback not set, keepalive set (10 sec)
  Last input 00:00:02, output 00:00:01, output hang never
  Last clearing of "show interface" counters 00:26:25
  Queueing strategy: fifo
  Output queue 0/40, 0 drops; input queue 0/75, 0 drops
  5 minute input rate 0 bits/sec, 0 packets/sec
  5 minute output rate 0 bits/sec, 0 packets/sec
     521 packets input, 33073 bytes, 0 no buffer
     Received 187 broadcasts, 0 runts, 0 giants, 0 throttles
     0 input errors, 0 CRC, 0 frame, 0 overrun, 0 ignored, 0 abort
     526 packets output, 33082 bytes, 0 underruns
     0 output errors, 0 collisions, 0 interface resets
     0 output buffer failures, 0 output buffers swapped out
     8 carrier transitions
     DCD=up  DSR=up  DTR=up  RTS=up  CTS=up

r6#clear counters s0
Clear "show interface" counters on this interface [confirm]
Dec 21 06:50:12.259: %CLEAR-5-COUNTERS: Clear counter on interface Serial0 by
console
```

Example 9-19 *Testing the HDLC Scenario*

```
r6#show ip route
...
Gateway of last resort is not set
     1.0.0.0/32 is subnetted, 1 subnets
D       1.1.1.1 [90/41664000] via 192.168.9.18, 00:16:40, Serial0
     2.0.0.0/32 is subnetted, 1 subnets
D       2.2.2.2 [90/41664000] via 192.168.9.18, 00:16:40, Serial0
     3.0.0.0/32 is subnetted, 1 subnets
D       3.3.3.3 [90/41152000] via 192.168.9.18, 00:16:40, Serial0
```

continues

Example 9-19 *Testing the HDLC Scenario (Continued)*

```
        4.0.0.0/32 is subnetted, 1 subnets
D          4.4.4.4 [90/41664000] via 192.168.9.18, 00:16:40, Serial0
        192.168.9.0/30 is subnetted, 5 subnets
D          192.168.9.0 [90/41536000] via 192.168.9.18, 00:16:40, Serial0
D          192.168.9.4 [90/41536000] via 192.168.9.18, 00:16:40, Serial0
D          192.168.9.8 [90/41536000] via 192.168.9.18, 00:16:40, Serial0
D          192.168.9.12 [90/41024000] via 192.168.9.18, 00:16:41, Serial0
C          192.168.9.16 is directly connected, Serial0
        5.0.0.0/32 is subnetted, 1 subnets
D          5.5.5.5 [90/40640000] via 192.168.9.18, 00:16:42, Serial0
        6.0.0.0/32 is subnetted, 1 subnets
C          6.6.6.6 is directly connected, Loopback9

r6#ping 1.1.1.1
Sending 5, 100-byte ICMP Echos to 1.1.1.1, timeout is 2 seconds:
!!!!!
Success rate is 100 percent (5/5), round-trip min/avg/max = 84/87/92 ms
r6#ping 2.2.2.2
Sending 5, 100-byte ICMP Echos to 2.2.2.2, timeout is 2 seconds:
!!!!!
Success rate is 100 percent (5/5), round-trip min/avg/max = 88/88/88 ms
r6#ping 3.3.3.3
Sending 5, 100-byte ICMP Echos to 3.3.3.3, timeout is 2 seconds:
!!!!!
Success rate is 100 percent (5/5), round-trip min/avg/max = 56/57/60 ms
r6#ping 4.4.4.4
Sending 5, 100-byte ICMP Echos to 4.4.4.4, timeout is 2 seconds:
!!!!!
Success rate is 100 percent (5/5), round-trip min/avg/max = 84/92/112 ms
r6#ping 5.5.5.5
Sending 5, 100-byte ICMP Echos to 5.5.5.5, timeout is 2 seconds:
!!!!!
Success rate is 100 percent (5/5), round-trip min/avg/max = 32/32/32 ms
r6#ping 6.6.6.6
Sending 5, 100-byte ICMP Echos to 6.6.6.6, timeout is 2 seconds:
!!!!!
Success rate is 100 percent (5/5), round-trip min/avg/max = 4/4/4 ms
r6#ping 192.168.9.1
Sending 5, 100-byte ICMP Echos to 192.168.9.1, timeout is 2 seconds:
!!!!!
Success rate is 100 percent (5/5), round-trip min/avg/max = 88/88/88 ms
```

When you have thoroughly tested your scenario, save all configurations to a file named *hdlc ending configurations*.

NOTE   Frame Relay is covered in the preceding chapter. When shooting trouble with Frame Relay, issue a **debug serial interface** command early on to see the keepalive activity. Change the encapsulation to HDLC to see the keepalive traffic, because if LMI is down for Frame Relay, the frame interface will not be able to generate keepalives. Remember, it only takes three missed keepalives to take the line down.

HDLC is the default encapsulation for serial links. If you are using multiple vendors, multiple Layer 3 protocols, or need authentication, however, HDLC is not the solution. PPP was created to eliminate some of the issues, such as running multiple protocols and authentication with HDLC, but *Cisco HDLC* handles multiplexing of Layer 3 protocols just fine.

PPP

PPP was designed in the 1980s as a point-to-point Internet encapsulation protocol. In addition to that, it overcomes the standards limitations on serial connectivity, including addressing, encapsulation, and multiple protocol support through Link Control Protocols (LCPs) and Network Control Protocols (NCPs). PPP includes router-to-router and host-to-host type connections over synchronous and asynchronous circuits.

The Layers

PPP offers secure access over any WAN Physical Layer interface, including asynchronous/ synchronous serial, HSSI, and ISDN. It uses LCPs to negotiate and set up data-link parameters and NCPs to encapsulate multiple protocols, as illustrated in Figure 9-4.

Figure 9-4 *PPP Layers*

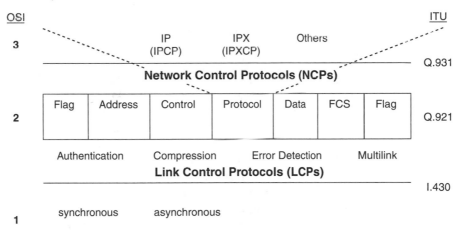

The frame structure is very similar to ISO's HDLC with an added Protocol field, as you can see in Figure 9-5. However, it is a bit more than Cisco's HDLC because it has authentication and other capabilities.

Figure 9-5   *PPP Frame Format*

| Flag
7E | Address
FF | Control
03 | Protocol | Data | FCS | Flag
7E |
|---|---|---|---|---|---|---|
| 1 Byte | 1 Byte | 1 Byte | 2 Bytes | | 2 or 4
Bytes | 1 Byte |

The beginning or ending flag is 7E or 01111110 in binary. The Address field is the broadcast address of all Fs in hex or all 1s in binary because station addresses are not assigned. The Control field is much like LLC Type 1. The Protocol field encapsulates the upper-layer protocols. The default maximum length of the Data field is 1500 bytes, although other values are allowed by adjusting the maximum transmission unit (MTU) size. The FCS is normally 2 bytes but can be 4 bytes to improve the error-detection capabilities.

PPP is a connectionless link service that goes through four LCP phases, as follows:

1 Link establishment and configuration (ACK frame has been sent and received)

2 Link quality determination

3 NCP configuration negotiation to support multiple Layer 3 protocols

4 Link termination (user request or physical problem)

There are also four LCP configuration options, as follows:

- **Authentication**—No authentication is the default, but PAP, CHAP, and Microsoft Challenge Handshake Authentication Protocol (MSCHAP) are available. PAP is only done upon the initial link establishment; it is a *one-way challenge* performed *one time*. The hostname/username and password are sent in clear text, and the peer (calling router) is in control of the attempts. Hostnames and passwords are CaSe SeNsItIvE. The PAP security level is better than nothing but not always the best option. I tend to agree with whoever coined the phrase "pathetic authentication protocol" on this one. CHAP is preferred and is an IETF standard. CHAP is a three-way challenge that randomly happens for the length of the call. It uses a shared secret password that is known only to the communicating routers. This shared secret is an MD5 hash. A hash is a one-way algorithm, so the actual password is never sent across the link. For simplicity's sake, think of the hash being equal to "MyName+Password" when challenged, and you would compare it to your table of username commands with passwords to see whether the value you get of "Username+Password" matches the value I sent. It is a bit more complicated than that in reality, but that covers the concept. If you prefer, you can think of the hash algorithm like turning potatoes into hash browns or a pig into sausage. It is kind of difficult to reverse these activities.

NOTE	The challenge sent by the called router contains a block of data. The calling router uses its password to calculate an MD5 hash of the data block that is sent in the response. The called router uses its password for the connection to also calculate an MD5 hash of the data block and compares the results to determine whether to accept or deny. Thus, the password is not sent on the communications link.

- **Compression**—Offered through the Cisco Control Protocol (CCP) using Stacker or Predictor.

- **Error detection**—Monitor data drops with a quality number and avoid frame looping with the magic number.

- **Multilink**—Bundling multiple links to use them as one using the Multilink Protocol (MP). This is referred to as Multilink Point-to-Point Protocol (MPPP).

From a support standpoint, take the KISS (Keep It Simple, Stupid!) approach. This means make sure you can communicate and then augment with authentication and other options. Refer back to the scenario in Figure 9-1 to make sure you configure all the interfaces. The configuration of r1 is in Example 9-20 to get you started.

Example 9-20 *r1 PPP Encapsulation*

```
r1(config)#interface s0
r1(config-if)#shut
r1(config-if)#encap ppp
r1(config-if)#no shut
r1(config-if)#end
r1#copy running-config startup-config
```

Next you should verify that PPP is in fact the encapsulation being used and that you can ping from end to end as in Example 9-21. Look for LCP Open followed by open CPs for each payload type. If necessary, you can carefully use **debug ppp negotiation**.

Example 9-21 *Verifying PPP Encapsulation*

```
r6#show interfaces s0
Serial0 is up, line protocol is up
  Hardware is HD64570
  Internet address is 192.168.9.17/30
  MTU 1500 bytes, BW 64 Kbit, DLY 20000 usec, rely 255/255, load 1/255
  Encapsulation PPP, loopback not set, keepalive set (10 sec)
  LCP Open
  Open: IPCP, CDPCP

r6#ping 1.1.1.1
Type escape sequence to abort.
Sending 5, 100-byte ICMP Echos to 1.1.1.1, timeout is 2 seconds:
!!!!!
Success rate is 100 percent (5/5), round-trip min/avg/max = 88/88/92 ms
```

Although only shown on r6 in Example 9-21, all routers are set to PPP encapsulation and the pings work in both directions. Note the shaded output of the Layer 2 LCP open and the Layer 3 IPCP and CDPCP. This indicates that the link establishment phase is operational and that the Network Layer protocol phase is sending NCP packets for IP and CDP.

Shooting Trouble with PPP

Shooting trouble with PPP normally does not involve solely PPP as it is configured here. PPP issues *normally* involve authentication and other LCP options.

Configure an appropriate username and password statement on r5 and r6 and configure CHAP authentication with me in Example 9-22. First configure r5, then turn on **debug ppp authentication** on r6, and then configure r6. Note the incoming challenge expected values as you configure r6.

Example 9-22 *PPP Encapsulation with CHAP Authentication*

```
r5(config)#username r6 password donna
r5(config)#interface s1
r5(config-if)#shut
r5(config-if)#ppp authentication ?
  chap     Challenge Handshake Authentication Protocol (CHAP)
  ms-chap  Microsoft Challenge Handshake Authentication Protocol (MS-CHAP)
  pap      Password Authentication Protocol (PAP)
r5(config-if)#ppp authentication chap
r5(config-if)#no shut
r5(config-if)#end
r5#copy running-config startup-config

r6#debug ppp authentication
r6#configure terminal
r6(config)#user
!!!note the incoming challenges here
Dec 21 07:37:12.391: Se0 PPP: Phase is AUTHENTICATING, by the peer
Dec 21 07:37:12.399: Se0 CHAP: I CHALLENGE id 57 len 23 from "r5"
Dec 21 07:37:12.403: Se0 CHAP: Username r5 not found
Dec 21 07:37:12.407: Se0 CHAP: Unable to authenticate for peer
r6(config)#username r5 pa
Dec 21 07:37:16.431: Se0 PPP: Phase is AUTHENTICATING, by the peer
Dec 21 07:37:16.439: Se0 CHAP: I CHALLENGE id 58 len 23 from "r5"
Dec 21 07:37:16.443: Se0 CHAP: Username r5 not found
Dec 21 07:37:16.447: Se0 CHAP: Unable to authenticate for peer
r6(config)#username r5 password donna
Dec 21 07:37:18.519: Se0 PPP: Phase is AUTHENTICATING, by the peer
Dec 21 07:37:18.531: Se0 CHAP: I CHALLENGE id 59 len 23 from "r5"
Dec 21 07:37:18.535: Se0 CHAP: Username r5 not found
Dec 21 07:37:18.539: Se0 CHAP: Unable to authenticate for peer
Dec 21 07:37:22.563: Se0 PPP: Phase is AUTHENTICATING, by the peer
Dec 21 07:37:22.571: Se0 CHAP: I CHALLENGE id 60 len 23 from "r5"
Dec 21 07:37:22.575: Se0 CHAP: O RESPONSE id 60 len 23 from "r6"
Dec 21 07:37:22.591: Se0 CHAP: I SUCCESS id 60 len 4s
r6(config)#interface s0
Dec 21 07:37:23.551: %LINEPROTO-5-UPDOWN: Line protocol on Interface Serial0,
changed state to up
```

Example 9-22 *PPP Encapsulation with CHAP Authentication (Continued)*

```
r6(config-if)#shut
Dec 21 07:37:29.243: %LINK-5-CHANGED: Interface Serial0, changed state to
administratively down
Dec 21 07:37:30.243: %LINEPROTO-5-UPDOWN: Line protocol on Interface Serial0,
changed state to down
r6(config-if)#ppp authentication chap
r6(config-if)#no shut
r6(config-if)#end
Dec 21 07:37:49.131: %SYS-5-CONFIG_I: Configured from console by console
Dec 21 07:37:49.747: %LINK-3-UPDOWN: Interface Serial0, changed state to up
Dec 21 07:37:49.779: Se0 PPP: Treating connection as a dedicated line
Dec 21 07:37:49.795: Se0 PPP: Phase is AUTHENTICATING, by both
Dec 21 07:37:49.799: Se0 CHAP: O CHALLENGE id 1 len 23 from "r6"
Dec 21 07:37:49.803: Se0 CHAP: I CHALLENGE id 61 len 23 from "r5"
Dec 21 07:37:49.811: Se0 CHAP: O RESPONSE id 61 len 23 from "r6"
Dec 21 07:37:49.815: Se0 CHAP: I RESPONSE id 1 len 23 from "r5"
Dec 21 07:37:49.819: Se0 CHAP: O SUCCESS id 1 len 4
Dec 21 07:37:49.823: Se0 CHAP: I SUCCESS id 61 len 4
Dec 21 07:37:50.827: %LINEPROTO-5-UPDOWN: Line protocol on Interface Serial0,
changed state to up
r6#copy running-config startup-config
r6#u all
```

When you configure authentication only on r5, it shuts down the line protocol. Because both routers are configured, you are seeing the authentication process for both. This is one of those processes that is pretty entertaining to watch (when it is successful). (Sometimes we support people get excited over the little things.) The **debug ppp authentication** output is fairly simple to understand. Review the ending authentication by both parties and the input (I) and output (O) challenge, response, and success lines.

You can perform two-way CHAP between routers, which may be initiated in either direction or both. Alternatively, it may just be a one-way CHAP between an end system and a router. After link establishment occurs, the called router sends a challenge to the calling router. The calling router sends a response. Then the called router can either accept or reject. These challenges continue to occur but on a random interval depending on the local router or a third-party authentication server, such as Terminal Access Controller Access Control System (TACACS) or Remote Authentication Dial-in User Service (RADIUS), if one is used.

Follow through Example 9-23 for mismatched authentication issues. Change the router r6 connection to PAP authentication and continue to watch the output of **debug ppp authentication**.

Example 9-23 *PPP with Mismatched Authentication*

```
r6#debug ppp authentication
PPP authentication debugging is on
r6#configure terminal
r6(config)#interface s0
r6(config)#shut
Dec 21 07:49:10.091: %LINK-5-CHANGED: Interface Serial0, changed state to
administratively down
```

continues

Example 9-23 *PPP with Mismatched Authentication (Continued)*

```
r6(config-if)#ppp authentication pap
Dec 21 07:49:11.091: %LINEPROTO-5-UPDOWN: Line protocol on Interface Serial0,
changed state to down
r6(config-if)#no shut
Dec 21 07:49:18.939: %LINK-3-UPDOWN: Interface Serial0, changed state to up
Dec 21 07:49:18.971: Se0 PPP: Treating connection as a dedicated line
r6(config-if)#end
Dec 21 07:49:51.519: %SYS-5-CONFIG_I: Configured from console by console
!!!not much is happening on r6
!!!yet r5 has flapping links
Dec 21 07:48:39.427: %LINK-3-UPDOWN: Interface Serial1, changed state to up
Dec 21 07:48:43.515: %LINK-3-UPDOWN: Interface Serial1, changed state to down
Dec 21 07:49:01.515: %LINK-3-UPDOWN: Interface Serial1, changed state to up
Dec 21 07:49:09.603: %LINK-3-UPDOWN: Interface Serial1, changed state to down
Dec 21 07:49:23.603: %LINK-3-UPDOWN: Interface Serial1, changed state to up
Dec 21 07:49:29.691: %LINK-3-UPDOWN: Interface Serial1, changed state to down
Dec 21 07:49:35.691: %LINK-3-UPDOWN: Interface Serial1, changed state to down
```

Now that you have worked with this for yourself, it should be much easier to recognize the up, down, up, down status or flapping link as a likely authentication problem. Change the PPP authentication of r6s0 back to CHAP and monitor the results in Example 9-24. Turn off all debug output using the shortcut.

Example 9-24 *Debug PPP Authentication*

```
r6(config-if)#shut
Dec 21 08:01:56.039: %LINK-5-CHANGED: Interface Serial0, changed state to
administratively down
r6(config-if)#ppp authentication chap
r6(config-if)#no shut
Dec 21 08:02:33.635: %LINK-3-UPDOWN: Interface Serial0, changed state to up
Dec 21 08:02:33.667: Se0 PPP: Treating connection as a dedicated line
Dec 21 08:02:33.679: Se0 PPP: Phase is AUTHENTICATING, by both
Dec 21 08:02:33.683: Se0 CHAP: O CHALLENGE id 2 len 23 from "r6"
Dec 21 08:02:33.687: Se0 CHAP: I CHALLENGE id 62 len 23 from "r5"
Dec 21 08:02:33.695: Se0 CHAP: O RESPONSE id 62 len 23 from "r6"
Dec 21 08:02:33.699: Se0 CHAP: I RESPONSE id 2 len 23 from "r5"
Dec 21 08:02:33.707: Se0 CHAP: O SUCCESS id 2 len 4
Dec 21 08:02:33.711: Se0 CHAP: I SUCCESS id 62 len 4
Dec 21 08:02:34.711: %LINEPROTO-5-UPDOWN: Line protocol on Interface Serial0,
changed state to up
r6(config-if)#end
r6#u all
```

Now that everything is working again, perform similar testing with the **debug ppp negotiation** command in Example 9-25. I wanted you to get used to the **no debug** shortcut to prepare yourself for when the router is too busy to let you type the full command. Consider typing **u all** before you start any debug activity so that you can quickly use the Up Arrow key to turn it off in a pinch.

Example 9-25 *Debug PPP Negotiation*

```
r6#u all
r6#debug ppp negotiation
r6#configure terminal
r6(config)#interface s0
r6(config-if)#shut
Dec 21 08:09:26.355: %LINK-5-CHANGED: Interface Serial0, changed state to
administratively down
Dec 21 08:09:26.387: Se0 IPCP: State is Closed
Dec 21 08:09:26.387: Se0 CDPCP: State is Closed
Dec 21 08:09:26.391: Se0 PPP: Phase is TERMINATING
Dec 21 08:09:26.391: Se0 LCP: State is Closed
Dec 21 08:09:26.395: Se0 PPP: Phase is DOWN
Dec 21 08:09:26.399: Se0 IPCP: Remove route to 192.168.9.18
Dec 21 08:09:27.355: %LINEPROTO-5-UPDOWN: Line protocol on Interface Serial0,
changed state to down
r6(config-if)#ppp authentication pap
r6(config-if)#no shut
Dec 21 08:09:57.935: %LINK-3-UPDOWN: Interface Serial0, changed state to up
Dec 21 08:09:57.967: Se0 PPP: Treating connection as a dedicated line
Dec 21 08:09:57.967: Se0 PPP: Phase is ESTABLISHING, Active Open
r6#u all
Dec 21 08:09:57.971: Se0 LCP: O CONFREQ [Closed] id 62 len 14
Dec 21 08:09:57.975: Se0 LCP:    AuthProto PAP (0x0304C023)
Dec 21 08:09:57.979: Se0 LCP:    MagicNumber 0x10ABD744 (0x050610ABD744)
Dec 21 08:09:57.983: Se0 LCP: I CONFREQ [REQsent] id 189 len 15
Dec 21 08:09:57.987: Se0 LCP:    AuthProto CHAP (0x0305C22305)
Dec 21 08:09:57.991: Se0 LCP:    MagicNumber 0x003C1F4F (0x0506003C1F4F)
Dec 21 08:09:57.991: Se0 LCP: O CONFACK [REQsent] id 189 len 15
Dec 21 08:09:57.995: Se0 LCP:    AuthProto CHAP (0x0305C22305)
Dec 21 08:09:57.999: Se0 LCP:    MagicNumber 0x003C1F4F (0x0506003C1F4F)
Dec 21 08:09:58.003: Se0 LCP: I CONFNAK [ACKsent] id 62 len 9
```

The **debug ppp negotiation** command illustrates LCP authentication and error detection as well NCP addressing in quite a bit more detail than **debug ppp authentication**. It was intriguing trying to issue any other commands. At the beginning of the output, IPCP and CDPCP were closed and PPP was terminating. *Pay attention* to the Os and Is for outgoing and incoming challenges. r6 sent out PAP and wanted to agree on a magic number, but that didn't happen. As a result, the 192.168.9.18 route was removed. Then there was an incoming request for CHAP. Notice the couple of REQsents followed by the CONFNAK [Negative ACK sent] rather than a CONFACK. The connection finally closes because the remote host won't authenticate.

NOTE   More detail means more overhead, so be sure to turn off all debug output when you are finished troubleshooting.

Next make sure the authentication between r5 and r6 is set back to CHAP. Turn on **debug ppp negotiation** to watch the normal activity as in Example 9-26. Follow the Outgoing and Incoming debugs.

Example 9-26 *Debug PPP Negotiation*

```
r6#show ip interface brief
Interface             IP-Address      OK? Method Status            Protocol
...
Loopback9             6.6.6.6         YES manual up                up
Serial0               192.168.9.17    YES manual up                down
...
r6#show interfaces s0
Serial0 is up, line protocol is down
  Hardware is HD64570
  Internet address is 192.168.9.17/30
  MTU 1500 bytes, BW 64 Kbit, DLY 20000 usec, rely 255/255, load 1/255
  Encapsulation PPP, loopback not set, keepalive set (10 sec)
  LCP Listen
  Closed: LEXCP, DECCP, OSICP, VINESCP, XNSCP, IPCP, CCP, CDPCP, BRIDGECP
          LLC2, ATCP, IPXCP, NBFCP, BACP
...
r6#configure terminal
r6(config)#interface s0
r6(config-if)#shut
Dec 21 08:20:40.411: %LINK-5-CHANGED: Interface Serial0, changed state to
  administratively down
r6(config-if)#ppp authentication chap
r6(config-if)#end
Dec 21 08:21:13.303: %SYS-5-CONFIG_I: Configured from console by console
r6#u all
All possible debugging has been turned off
r6#debug ppp negotiation
PPP protocol negotiation debugging is on
r6#configure terminal
r6(config)#interface s0
r6(config-if)#no shut
r6(config-if)#end
Dec 21 08:21:45.187: %SYS-5-CONFIG_I: Configured from console by console
Dec 21 08:21:46.227: %LINK-3-UPDOWN: Interface Serial0, changed state to up
Dec 21 08:21:46.259: Se0 PPP: Treating connection as a dedicated line
Dec 21 08:21:46.259: Se0 PPP: Phase is ESTABLISHING, Active Open
Dec 21 08:21:46.263: Se0 LCP: O CONFREQ [Closed] id 93 len 15
Dec 21 08:21:46.267: Se0 LCP:    AuthProto CHAP (0x0305C22305)
Dec 21 08:21:46.271: Se0 LCP:    MagicNumber 0x10B6A853 (0x050610B6A853)
Dec 21 08:21:46.275: Se0 LCP: I CONFREQ [REQsent] id 254 len 15
Dec 21 08:21:46.279: Se0 LCP:    AuthProto CHAP (0x0305C22305)
Dec 21 08:21:46.279: Se0 LCP:    MagicNumber 0x0046EF5C (0x05060046EF5C)
Dec 21 08:21:46.283: Se0 LCP: O CONFACK [REQsent] id 254 len 15
Dec 21 08:21:46.287: Se0 LCP:    AuthProto CHAP (0x0305C22305)
Dec 21 08:21:46.291: Se0 LCP:    MagicNumber 0x0046EF5C (0x05060046EF5C)
Dec 21 08:21:46.295: Se0 LCP: I CONFACK [ACKsent] id 93 len 15
Dec 21 08:21:46.295: Se0 LCP:    AuthProto CHAP (0x0305C22305)
Dec 21 08:21:46.299: Se0 LCP:    MagicNumber 0x10B6A853 (0x050610B6A853)
Dec 21 08:21:46.303: Se0 LCP: State is Open
Dec 21 08:21:46.303: Se0 PPP: Phase is AUTHENTICATING, by both
```

Example 9-26 *Debug PPP Negotiation (Continued)*

```
Dec 21 08:21:46.307: Se0 CHAP: O CHALLENGE id 3 len 23 from "r6"
Dec 21 08:21:46.311: Se0 CHAP: I CHALLENGE id 63 len 23 from "r5"
Dec 21 08:21:46.319: Se0 CHAP: O RESPONSE id 63 len 23 from "r6"
Dec 21 08:21:46.323: Se0 CHAP: I RESPONSE id 3 len 23 from "r5"
Dec 21 08:21:46.331: Se0 CHAP: O SUCCESS id 3 len 4
Dec 21 08:21:46.335: Se0 CHAP: I SUCCESS id 63 len 4
Dec 21 08:21:46.335: Se0 PPP: Phase is UP
Dec 21 08:21:46.339: Se0 IPCP: O CONFREQ [Closed] id 5 len 10
Dec 21 08:21:46.343: Se0 IPCP:    Address 192.168.9.17 (0x0306C0A80911)
Dec 21 08:21:46.347: Se0 CDPCP: O CONFREQ [Closed] id 5 len 4
Dec 21 08:21:46.351: Se0 IPCP: I CONFREQ [REQsent] id 5 len 10
Dec 21 08:21:46.355: Se0 IPCP:    Address 192.168.9.18 (0x0306C0A80912)
Dec 21 08:21:46.359: Se0 IPCP: O CONFACK [REQsent] id 5 len 10
Dec 21 08:21:46.363: Se0 IPCP:    Address 192.168.9.18 (0x0306C0A80912)conf t
r6#u all
Dec 21 08:21:46.367: Se0 CDPCP: I CONFREQ [REQsent] id 5 len 4
Dec 21 08:21:46.367: Se0 CDPCP: O CONFACK [REQsent] id 5 len 4
Dec 21 08:21:46.371: Se0 IPCP: I CONFACK [ACKsent] id 5 len 10
Dec 21 08:21:46.375: Se0 IPCP:    Address 192.168.9.17 (0x0306C0A80911)
Dec 21 08:21:46.379: Se0 IPCP: State is Open
Dec 21 08:21:46.383: Se0 CDPCP: I CONFACK [ACKsent] id 5 len 4
Dec 21 08:21:46.383: Se0 CDPCP: State is Open
Dec 21 08:21:46.395: Se0 IPCP: Install route to 192.168.9.18
Dec 21 08:21:47.335: %LINEPROTO-5-UPDOWN: Line protocol on Interface Serial0,
   changed state to up
All possible debugging has been turned off
```

NOTE If you are certain you have typed everything correctly in the configuration, remove (**no out**) the authentication statements to verify you can communicate without them. Then put them back and verify again.

I think this example speaks for itself, and you can follow the link establishment, authentication, and network phase very easily. Be sure to remove any **username all** statements that you may have accidentally put in by typing the shortcut **u all** (for **undebug all**) while in configuration mode. Compare your ending saved configurations to the output in my *ppp ending configs* file.

Note that in both PAP and CHAP authentication methods, the password still shows up in the configuration. Actually this depends on the IOS version. Prior to IOS 11.2, the passwords were encrypted. If you want them encrypted in the configuration now, you can use the **service password-encryption** global configuration command. The passwords will then show as encryption type number 7 in the configuration. However, only PAP passwords are sent across the wire in the clear, not CHAP.

PPP is used not only for serial interfaces but over Integrated Services Digital Network (ISDN) connections as well. My focus in the next WAN topic is ISDN BRI. You may or may not have the equipment to perform the hands-on exercises and Trouble Tickets for this topic, but I have included the examples in this book and the appropriate files are available for your review.

ISDN BRI

Originally it was thought that ISDN would replace every phone line in the United States. However, this service has transitioned through periods where some people just did not appreciate its digital advantages, including quality, speed, and call setup. ISDN provides voice, data, video, and other services for the small office/home office (SOHO) and telecommuter environments as well as backup services and contingency plans for others. Depending on the availability, bandwidth, and cost of other services, it may still be a viable alternative.

Although my primary focus here is BRI as displayed in Figure 9-6, there are two flavors of ISDN:

- Basic Rate Interface (BRI)
    - 2 B (64 kbps) for data, voice, video
        - Bearer channels
    - 1 D (16 kbps) for out-of-band control and signaling
        - Delta channel
    - Total bit rate is 144 kbps
    - 2B + D
- Primary Rate Interface (PRI)
    - 23 B (64 kbps) for data, voice, video
    - 1 D (64 kbps) for out-of-band control and signaling
    - 23 B + D
    - Total bit rate is 1.536 Mbps
    - 30 B + 1 D for a total bit rate of 2.048 Mbps in Europe, Australia, and Japan

---

NOTE   Japan uses a J1, which is equivalent to a T1 PRI (23 B + D)

NOTE   The BRI interface creates the 2 B channels (128 kbps) and the D channel (16 kbps) to total 144 kbps. If you add the other 48 kbps of overhead (synchronization and framing), the total becomes 192 kbps.

The ISDN network components in Figure 9-7 include the terminal equipment, termination devices, reference, and function points.

Figure 9-6   *ISDN BRI*

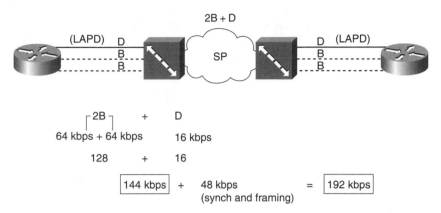

Figure 9-7   *ISDN Network Components*

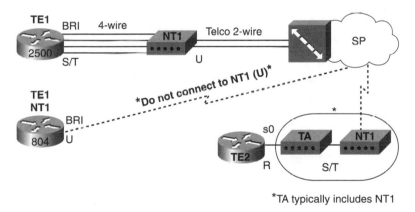

Terminal equipment includes the following:

- **TE1**—Native ISDN terminal, such as a router or telephone

- **TE2**—Non-native ISDN terminal, such as a router or PC; needs a terminal adapter (TA)

Network termination devices include the following:

- **NT1**—CPE in North America; carrier provided elsewhere. It is the device responsible for the time-division multiplexing (TDM) between the four-wire connection from the router to the two-wire connection to the telco. *The NT1 applies power to the line*.

- **NT2**—Typically found in private branch exchanges (PBXs). There is an NT1/2 available to provide the function of both the NT1 and NT2. Not always used.

A line termination (LT) is a physical connection to an ISDN switch, whereas reference points are more like conceptual interfaces. They are just letters of the alphabet that don't stand for anything, but they do happen to go in alphabetic order toward the service provider: R, S, T, U. Pictures are quite helpful here, and these concepts appear to be pretty significant on all Cisco exams. Figure 9-8 gives you a block diagram review of the ISDN functions and the following reference points:

- **R**—Between non-ISDN equipment (TE2) and TA
- **S**—Between user terminals and NT2
- **T**—Between NT1 and NT2
- **U**—Between NT1 and the carrier network
- **V**—Between ISDN switches within the carrier cloud

Figure 9-8   *ISDN Functions and Reference Points*

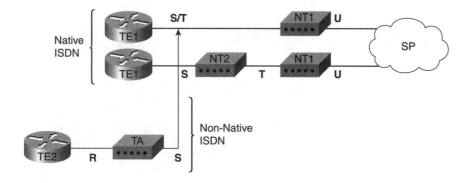

NOTE   Do not connect a U reference point on a router into an NT1 or you may find out what blue smoke (that is, a fried device) smells like. By the same token, do not plug a powered NT1 cable into an Ethernet or console port. As shown in Figure 9-8, the U includes the NT1 and the NT1 is what applies the 48V DC power to the line.

In the United States, the NT1 is the responsibility of the subscriber, whereas in Europe it is typically provided by the service provider. ISDN is an international service, but services, providers, and switch types vary by region and country.

Although there are many different switch types, it is possible to have one emulate another. For example, I can take an Adtran switch, which defaults to basic-ni1, and have it emulate a basic-5ess, which is what a Madge switch uses. Table 9-3 lists some of the major ISDN switch types.

An ISDN simulator may be more cost-effective for labs and may be what you are using here. However, you still need to be familiar with the switch types and how to configure them.

Table 9-3   *ISDN Switch Types*

Switch Type	Location
Basic-5ess*	AT&T (U.S. and Canada)
Basic-dms100	North America
Basic-ni1	National ISDN-1 (North America)
Basic-ts013	Australia
Basic-net3	United Kingdom and Europe
Ntt	Japan

*IOS 12.0 code sets the ISDN switch type to basic-5ess as the default.

The basic-ni1 uses Service Profile Identifiers (SPIDs), and the basic-5ess doesn't. SPIDs are an optional feature that may or may not be utilized depending on the provider (and in fact frequently is dependent on the switch type used by the provider). Typically, SPIDs include the E.164 10-digit (area code + number) in addition to extra ID codes. National ISDN will have 14 digits (fqn + 0101), and DMS will have 12 digits (01 + fqn).

NOTE   IOS 12.0 and above sets the global ISDN switch type to basic-5ess by default. All interfaces inherit the global switch type unless one is specifically configured on the interface.

As you can see, ISDN is available in different parts of the world. Cisco ISDN standards are based on the international standards. The ITU-T standard encompasses Layer 1 through Layer 3, and is further defined as follows:

- **E series**—For telephone, network, and ISDN, including numbering plans and addressing.

- **I series**—For concepts, structures, and terminology for devices.

- **Q series**—For switching and signaling with LAPD (Q.921) for the D channel and Q.931 Network Layer between the ISDN switch and the terminal device.

NOTE   To help you commit the ISDN standards to memory, think of them as such: E for *existing*; I for *information*; and Q for *signaling*. (Admittedly, the Q is harder to remember than the others; perhaps you can think of it like the q933a for LMI signaling in Frame Relay.)

Just as the standards suggest, ISDN call processing takes a layered approach. It uses Link Access Protocol D (LAPD) for control and signaling on the D channel. In many instances, the 16-kbps D channel *appears to always be up*, which is why call setup takes less than a few seconds. Normally, the common signaling between the local ISDN switch and the remote ISDN switch (in the cloud) is Signaling System 7 (SS7). However, SS7 is beyond the scope of this book. The B channels are mostly used for circuit-switched data encapsulated as either HDLC or PPP, whereas the D channel is used for signaling.

The Layers

At the Physical Layer, an RJ-45 connector is wired as follows for the S/T interface at the TA end, whereas a U interface is pins 4/5 only for tip/ring.

- Pins 1 (green) and 2 (green/white) for power source
- Pins 7 (brown) and 8 (brown/white) for power sink
- Pins 3 (orange/white) and 6 (orange) for Tx
- Pins 4 (blue/white) and 5 (blue) for Rx

NOTE   An unused ISDN port is a good place for a cutoff or blank RJ-45 connector, so you don't accidentally plug into the port something you shouldn't.

This is a good time to physically connect r5 and r6 to the NT1 S/T ports as in Figure 9-9. Also connect the ISDN switch or simulator to the NT1 U ports. Based on the D-channel sync bits, the ports on the ISDN simulator should be green, whereas the NT1 is flashing ready (green) for the physical connections. If not, you will continue to troubleshoot as you walk through the ISDN scenario. Figure 9-9 and Figure 9-10 show the physical views. Do not program your devices for ISDN yet.

Figure 9-9   *Scenario: Shooting Trouble with ISDN BRI*

```
isdn switch-type basic-ni
dialer-list 1 protocol ip permit
int bri0
    dialer-group 1
    dialer idle-ti 55
    ip address 192.168.9.21 255.255.255.252
    dialer map ip 192.168.9.22 name r5 8358662
    dialer map ip 192.168.9.22 name r5 8358664
```

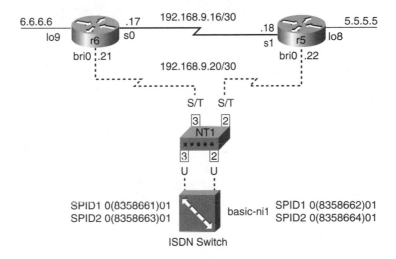

Figure 9-10 *ISDN Simulator and NT1*

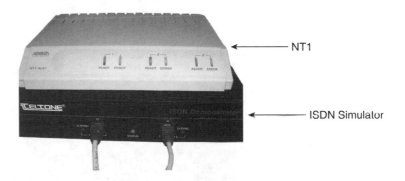

Because you can't always physically inspect things, controller and interface commands help you walk through the layers. For example, **show controllers bri 0** shows the Physical Layer statistics. However, **show isdn status** offers the most help at this point.

Take a look at the Physical Layer statistics as in Example 9-27.

Example 9-27 *ISDN Physical Layer Statistics*

```
r5#show controllers bri 0
BRI unit 0
D Chan Info:
Layer 1 is ACTIVATING
r5#show isdn status
 **** No Global ISDN Switchtype currently defined ****
ISDN BRI0 interface
        dsl 0, interface ISDN Switchtype = none
    Layer 1 Status:
        DEACTIVATED
    Layer 2 Status:
        Layer 2 NOT Activated
    Layer 3 Status:
        0 Active Layer 3 Call(s)
    Activated dsl 0 CCBs = 0
    The Free Channel Mask:  0x80000003
    Total Allocated ISDN CCBs = 0
```

I cut the majority of the output in Example 9-27 except for the item you should look for in the **show controllers bri 0** output. The BRI controllers should be *activated* not *activating*. The output of **show isdn status** clearly tells you the problem. I must say this is the most useful command in supporting ISDN. Fix this Physical Layer problem in Example 9-28 on both ISDN routers before you continue.

Example 9-28 *Configuring ISDN BRI at the Physical Layer*

```
r5#configure terminal
r5(config)#isdn switch-type ?
  basic-1tr6     1TR6 switch type for Germany
  basic-5ess     AT&T 5ESS switch type for the U.S.
  basic-dms100   Northern DMS-100 switch type
  basic-net3     NET3 switch type for UK and Europe
  basic-ni       National ISDN switch type
  basic-ts013    TS013 switch type for Australia
  ntt            NTT switch type for Japan
  vn3            VN3 and VN4 switch types for France
  <cr>
r5(config)#isdn switch-type basic-ni

r6(config)#isdn switch-type basic-ni
r6(config)#end
r6#show isdn status
Global ISDN Switchtype = basic-ni
ISDN BRI0 interface
        dsl 0, interface ISDN Switchtype = basic-ni
    Layer 1 Status:
        DEACTIVATED
...
r6#configure terminal
r6(config)#interface bri0
```

Example 9-28 *Configuring ISDN BRI at the Physical Layer (Continued)*

```
r6(config-if)#no shut
Dec 22 01:01:52.987: %LINK-3-UPDOWN: Interface BRI0:1, changed state to down
Dec 22 01:01:53.019: %LINK-3-UPDOWN: Interface BRI0:2, changed state to down
Dec 22 01:01:53.119: %LINK-3-UPDOWN: Interface BRI0, changed state to up
Dec 22 01:01:53.327: %ISDN-6-LAYER2UP: Layer 2 for Interface BR0, TEI 99 changed
  to up

r5(config)#interface bri0
r5(config-if)#no shut
Dec 22 01:02:14.267:  isdn_Call_disconnect()
Dec 22 01:02:14.267: %LINK-3-UPDOWN: Interface BRI0:1, changed state to down
Dec 22 01:02:14.303:  isdn_Call_disconnect()
Dec 22 01:02:14.303: %LINK-3-UPDOWN: Interface BRI0:2, changed state to down
Dec 22 01:02:14.399: %LINK-3-UPDOWN: Interface BRI0, changed state to up
Dec 22 01:02:14.607: %ISDN-6-LAYER2UP: Layer 2 for Interface BR0, TEI 100 changed
  to up
r5(config-if)#end
r5#show isdn status
Global ISDN Switchtype = basic-ni
ISDN BRI0 interface
        dsl 0, interface ISDN Switchtype = basic-ni
    Layer 1 Status:
        ACTIVE
    Layer 2 Status:
        TEI = 100, Ces = 1, SAPI = 0, State = MULTIPLE_FRAME_ESTABLISHED
    Layer 3 Status:
        0 Active Layer 3 Call(s)
    Activated dsl 0 CCBs = 0
    The Free Channel Mask:  0x80000003
    Total Allocated ISDN CCBs = 0
```

You took the right steps in Example 9-28 to configure the ISDN switch type, but you need to bring up the BRI interfaces, too. Analyze the BRI LEDs on the routers, the NT1, and the simulator. They should all be green. Now that you know the equipment and the links are working, you can concentrate on the configuration.

NOTE   Many international ISDN connections do not use the full ISDN signaling, and the interswitch connections may limit the speed to 56 kbps. However, the receiving end thinks this is a 64-kbps call. Configure the 56 kbps call using the **isdn not-end-to-end 56** command. In addition, dialer maps enable you to specify the speed for the outgoing call, but the default is 64 kbps.

Although not practical (due to expense and security reasons), next I want you to configure ISDN to allow *all IP-related traffic* to bring up the link between r5 and r6. Assign IP addresses and configure the connection so that it will time out if idle for more than 55 seconds. Use the

ISDN configuration commands in Figure 9-9 for r6 as a guide, although you must modify them to configure r5 as Example 9-29 illustrates.

Example 9-29 *Configuring IP Addresses and ISDN Traffic*

```
r5(config)#dialer-list 1 protocol ip permit
r5(config)#interface bri0
r5(config-if)#shut
r5(config-if)#dialer-group 1
!!!note that all the dialer map parameters are for the destination
r5(config-if)#dialer map ip 192.168.9.21 name r5 8358661
r5(config-if)#dialer map ip 192.168.9.21 name r5 8358663
r5(config-if)#dialer idle-timeout 55
r5(config-if)#ip address 192.168.9.22 255.255.255.252
r5(config-if)#no shut
Dec 22 01:27:06.003: %ISDN-6-LAYER2DOWN: Layer 2 for Interface BRI0, TEI 100
  changed to down
Dec 22 01:27:06.007: %ISDN-6-LAYER2DOWN: Layer 2 for Interface BR0, TEI 100 changed
  to down
Dec 22 01:27:08.107: %SYS-5-CONFIG_I: Configured from console by console
Dec 22 01:27:08.175: %ISDN-6-LAYER2UP: Layer 2 for Interface BR0, TEI 101 changed
  to up
r5(config-if)#end
!!!follow figure 9-9 for I entered the wrong map statements
r5#configure terminal
r5(config)#interface bri0
r5(config-if)#no dialer map ip 192.168.9.21 name r5 8358661
r5(config-if)#no dialer map ip 192.168.9.21 name r5 8368663
!!!now for the correct ones
r5(config-if)#dialer map ip 192.168.9.21 name r6 8358661
r5(config-if)#dialer map ip 192.168.9.21 name r6 8358663
r5(config-if)#no shut
Dec 22 01:34:22.943:  isdn_Call_disconnect()
Dec 22 01:34:22.947:  isdn_Call_disconnect()
Dec 22 01:34:23.011:  isdn_Call_disconnect()
Dec 22 01:34:23.011:  isdn_Call_disconnect()
Dec 22 01:34:23.355: %ISDN-6-LAYER2DOWN: Layer 2 for Interface BRI0, TEI 101
  changed to down
Dec 22 01:34:23.359: %ISDN-6-LAYER2DOWN: Layer 2 for Interface BR0, TEI 101 changed
  to down
Dec 22 01:34:25.523: %ISDN-6-LAYER2UP: Layer 2 for Interface BR0, TEI 102 changed
  to up
r5#copy running-config startup-config

r6(config)#dialer-list 1 protocol ip permit
r6(config)#interface bri0
r6(config-if)#shut
r6(config-if)#dialer-group 1
r6(config-if)#dialer map ip 192.168.9.22 name r5 8358662
r6(config-if)#dialer map ip 192.168.9.22 name r5 8358664
r6(config-if)#dialer idle-timeout 55
r6(config-if)#ip address 192.168.9.21 255.255.255.252
r6(config-if)#no shut
Dec 22 01:46:30.223: %LINK-3-UPDOWN: Interface BRI0:1, changed state to down
Dec 22 01:46:30.259: %LINK-3-UPDOWN: Interface BRI0:2, changed state to down
```

Example 9-29 *Configuring IP Addresses and ISDN Traffic (Continued)*

```
Dec 22 01:46:30.351: %LINK-3-UPDOWN: Interface BRI0, changed state to up
r6(config-if)#
Dec 22 01:46:30.523: %ISDN-6-LAYER2DOWN: Layer 2 for Interface BRI0, TEI 99 changed
  to down
Dec 22 01:46:30.527: %ISDN-6-LAYER2DOWN: Layer 2 for Interface BR0, TEI 99 changed
  to down
r6(config-if)#
Dec 22 01:46:32.687: %ISDN-6-LAYER2UP: Layer 2 for Interface BR0, TEI 103 changed
  to up
r6(config-if)#end
r6#copy running-config startup-config
```

Now that you have configured ISDN, I want to talk about the configuration a bit before you test it. One of the requirements given prior to Example 9-29 was for you to allow all IP traffic to bring up the link. Although **dialer-list 1 protocol ip permit** is frequently good in the lab and testing environment, in live networks you almost always want a more restrictive policy. Otherwise, you may be paying for ISDN usage charges every time *any* IP traffic brings up the link. This command is actually the default. However, it doesn't give you any problems until you apply the global **dialer-list 1** command using the interface **dialer-group 1** command.

The **dialer map** command handles the Layer 2 and Layer 3 mapping, similar to the **frame-relay map** you learned about in the preceding chapter. I think of it like a static route to configure it. "Where do you want to go and how will you get there?" is what I ask myself. The "where do you want to go?" part is the destination IP and router name. The "how will you get there?" part is the phone number you must dial. Compare this to the **dialer map** statements you typed back in Example 9-29.

At this point, you have configured the IP addresses, dialer timeout, and dialer map, but not the phone numbers. The phone number in ISDN is like the data-link connection identifier (DLCI) in Frame Relay or the MAC address on a LAN. With SPIDs the phone numbers are typically included; if not, you must configure the local directory number (LDN). Keep in mind that if you are given SPIDs they should be configured. Add the SPIDs that were provided by the service provider, as indicated in Figure 9-9 and Example 9-30.

NOTE   In my case the SPIDs and LDNs were provided by the manufacturer of the ISDN demonstrator in my lab (and appear a little different if you are using an ISDN switch). Thanks to my friend Chris Heffner, a Cisco instructor and CCIE for Global Knowledge Network, for lending it to me. You can get more information on this device at www.teltone.com by searching for "isdn demonstrator."

Example 9-30 *Configuring the SPIDs*

```
r5(config)#interface bri0
r5(config-if)#shut
r5(config-if)#isdn ?
  all-incoming-calls-v120  Answer all incoming calls as V.120
  answer1                  Specify Called Party number and subaddress
  answer2                  Specify Called Party number and subaddress
  caller                   Specify incoming telephone number to be verified
  calling-number           Specify Calling Number included for outgoing calls
  fast-rollover-delay      Delay between fastrollover dials
  incoming-voice           Specify options for incoming calls.
  not-end-to-end           Specify speed when calls received are not isdn end
                           to end
  outgoing-voice           Specify information transfer capability for voice
                           calls
  send-alerting            Specify if Alerting message to be sent out before
                           Connect message
  sending-complete         Specify if Sending Complete included in outgoing
                           SETUP message
  spid1                    Specify Service Profile IDentifier
  spid2                    Specify Service Profile IDentifier
  static-tei               Specify a Static TEI for ISDN BRI
  switch-type              Select the Interface ISDN switch type
  tei-negotiation          Set when ISDN TEI negotiation should occur
  timeout-signaling        Flush D channel if a signaling packet can't be
                           transmitted in 1 second
r5(config-if)#isdn spid1 ?
  WORD  spid1 string
r5(config-if)#isdn spid1 0835866201 ?
  WORD  local directory number
  <cr>
r5(config-if)#isdn spid1 0835866201 8358662
r5(config-if)#isdn spid2 0835866401 8358664
r5(config-if)#no shut
Dec 22 02:12:46.175:  isdn_Call_disconnect()
Dec 22 02:12:46.175: %LINK-3-UPDOWN: Interface BRI0:1, changed state to down
Dec 22 02:12:46.207:  isdn_Call_disconnect()
Dec 22 02:12:46.207: %LINK-3-UPDOWN: Interface BRI0:2, changed state to down
Dec 22 02:12:46.303: %LINK-3-UPDOWN: Interface BRI0, changed state to up
Dec 22 02:12:46.471: %ISDN-6-LAYER2DOWN: Layer 2 for Interface BRI0, TEI 102
  changed to down
Dec 22 02:12:46.475: %ISDN-6-LAYER2DOWN: Layer 2 for Interface BR0, TEI 102 changed
  to down
Dec 22 02:12:48.643: %ISDN-6-LAYER2UP: Layer 2 for Interface BR0, TEI 104 changed
  to up
Dec 22 02:12:48.811: %ISDN-6-LAYER2UP: Layer 2 for Interface BR0, TEI 105 changed
  to up
r5(config-if)#end
r5#copy running-config startup-config

r6#configure terminal
r6(config)#interface bri0
r6(config-if)#shut
r6(config-if)#isdn spid1 0835866101 8358661
```

Example 9-30 *Configuring the SPIDs (Continued)*

```
r6(config-if)#isdn spid2 0835866301 8358663
r6(config-if)#no shut
Dec 22 02:14:28.855: %LINK-3-UPDOWN: Interface BRI0:1, changed state to down
Dec 22 02:14:28.887: %LINK-3-UPDOWN: Interface BRI0:2, changed state to down
Dec 22 02:14:28.983: %LINK-3-UPDOWN: Interface BRI0, changed state to up
Dec 22 02:14:29.151: %ISDN-6-LAYER2DOWN: Layer 2 for Interface BRI0, TEI 103
  changed to down
Dec 22 02:14:29.155: %ISDN-6-LAYER2DOWN: Layer 2 for Interface BR0, TEI 103 changed
  to down
Dec 22 02:14:31.319: %ISDN-6-LAYER2UP: Layer 2 for Interface BR0, TEI 106 changed
  to up
Dec 22 02:14:31.487: %ISDN-6-LAYER2UP: Layer 2 for Interface BR0, TEI 107 changed
  to up
r6(config-if)#end
r6#copy running-config startup-config
```

As you can verify in Figure 9-30, my SPIDs contain the LDN, so the LDN configuration is really optional; however, it doesn't hurt to configure it. Keep in mind as you work through my examples that my SPID configuration is for an ISDN simulator, not an ISDN switch, so your SPID format may differ a bit. As always, use the question mark to help you configure the information you are given.

Now review the BRI interface status and statistics with **show ip interface brief** and with **show interfaces bri** to see the D channel. Although it is probably not present in your lab, help me determine the issue in Example 9-31.

Example 9-31 *ISDN Interface Statistics*

```
r5#show ip interface brief
Interface              IP-Address      OK? Method Status                Protocol
BRI0                   192.168.9.22    YES manual up                    up
BRI0:1                 unassigned      YES unset  down                  down
BRI0:2                 unassigned      YES unset  down                  down
...
r5#configure terminal
r5(config)#interface bri0
r5(config-if)#no shut
5d15h:  isdn_Call_disconnect()
5d15h:  isdn_Call_disconnect()
5d15h:  isdn_Call_disconnect()
5d15h:  isdn_Call_disconnect()
5d15h: %ISDN-6-LAYER2DOWN: Layer 2 for Interface BRI0, TEI 121 changed to down
5d15h: %ISDN-6-LAYER2DOWN: Layer 2 for Interface BR0, TEI 121 changed to down
5d15h: %ISDN-6-LAYER2UP: Layer 2 for Interface BR0, TEI 123 changed to up
5d15h: %ISDN-4-INVALID_SPID: Interface BR0, Spid1 was rejected
5d15h:  isdn_Call_disconnect()
5d15h:  isdn_Call_disconnect()
5d15h: %ISDN-6-LAYER2DOWN: Layer 2 for Interface BRI0, TEI 123 changed to down
5d15h: %ISDN-6-LAYER2DOWN: Layer 2 for Interface BR0, TEI 123 changed to down
5d15h: %ISDN-6-LAYER2UP: Layer 2 for Interface BR0, TEI 124 changed to up
5d15h: %ISDN-6-LAYER2UP: Layer 2 for Interface BR0, TEI 125 changed to up
```

Now it is time for a little troubleshooting, and the problem is not just the lack of time and date stamps. The invalid SPID message made me double check my physical wiring. I started there because I'm following troubleshooting methods presented in the earlier chapters. The methodology indicates that it helps to start at the bottom and work your way up. Sure enough, the BRI cables on the routers were reversed. This would have been the same result on r6, but I decided to take care of this issue by swapping the cables. Feel free to duplicate my problem and analyze the issues before you continue. This was a matter of right cable, wrong router. The same types of issues exist here as with shooting any Physical Layer or Data Link Layer trouble. Your key troubleshooting focus is on the local loop, which is terminated on the NT1 device.

In your lab, verify that the D channel is up, shut down the serial interfaces between r5 and r6, and review the BRI configuration as in Example 9-32. Observe both B channels with **show interfaces bri0 1 2**.

Example 9-32 *Verifying the D Channel and BRI Configuration*

```
r5#show ip interface brief
Interface              IP-Address      OK? Method Status              Protocol
BRI0                   192.168.9.22    YES manual up                  up
BRI0:1                 unassigned      YES unset  down                down
BRI0:2                 unassigned      YES unset  down                down
...
r5#configure terminal
r5(config)#interface s1
r5(config-if)#shut
r5(config-if)#end
r5#show interface bri0
BRI0 is up, line protocol is up (spoofing)
  Hardware is BRI
  Internet address is 192.168.9.22/30
  MTU 1500 bytes, BW 64 Kbit, DLY 20000 usec, rely 255/255, load 1/255
  Encapsulation HDLC, loopback not set
  Last input 00:00:00, output 00:00:00, output hang never
  Last clearing of "show interface" counters never
  Input queue: 0/75/0 (size/max/drops); Total output drops: 0
  Queueing strategy: weighted fair
  Output queue: 0/1000/64/0 (size/max total/threshold/drops)
     Conversations  0/1/256 (active/max active/max total)
     Reserved Conversations 0/0 (allocated/max allocated)
  5 minute input rate 0 bits/sec, 0 packets/sec
  5 minute output rate 0 bits/sec, 0 packets/sec
     142 packets input, 638 bytes, 0 no buffer
     Received 13 broadcasts, 0 runts, 0 giants, 0 throttles
     0 input errors, 0 CRC, 0 frame, 0 overrun, 0 ignored, 0 abort
     140 packets output, 623 bytes, 0 underruns
     0 output errors, 0 collisions, 11 interface resets
     0 output buffer failures, 0 output buffers swapped out
     5 carrier transitions

r5#show interfaces bri0 1 2
BRI0:1 is down, line protocol is down
  Hardware is BRI
  MTU 1500 bytes, BW 64 Kbit, DLY 20000 usec, rely 255/255, load 1/255
```

Example 9-32 *Verifying the D Channel and BRI Configuration (Continued)*

```
   Encapsulation HDLC, loopback not set, keepalive set (10 sec)
   Last input never, output never, output hang never
   Last clearing of "show interface" counters never
...
BRI0:2 is down, line protocol is down
   Hardware is BRI
   MTU 1500 bytes, BW 64 Kbit, DLY 20000 usec, rely 255/255, load 1/255
   Encapsulation HDLC, loopback not set, keepalive set (10 sec)
   Last input never, output never, output hang never
   Last clearing of "show interface" counters never
...
```

Note the output of **show interfaces bri0** above for the 16 kbps D channel. It shows (spoofing). Spoofing is just what it sounds like. The interface lies to the Layer 3 so that there will be a routing entry maintained in the router to allow dial-on-demand routing (DDR) to wake up and trigger a call when required. The B channels are not up all the time as you verified with **show interfaces bri0 1 2** because they need some interesting traffic to bring them up.

Next look at the dialer configuration with **show dialer interface bri0** and **show dialer map** as in Example 9-33. Verify your dial strings and statements. Fix them if necessary.

Example 9-33 *ISDN Dial Strings and Maps*

```
r5#show dialer interface bri0
BRI0 - dialer type = ISDN
Dial String      Successes    Failures    Last called    Last status
8358663                 0           0      never                   -
8358661                 0           0      never                   -
0 incoming call(s) have been screened.
0 incoming call(s) rejected for callback.
BRI0:1 - dialer type = ISDN
Idle timer (55 secs), Fast idle timer (20 secs)
Wait for carrier (30 secs), Re-enable (15 secs)
Dialer state is idle
BRI0:2 - dialer type = ISDN
Idle timer (55 secs), Fast idle timer (20 secs)
Wait for carrier (30 secs), Re-enable (15 secs)
Dialer state is idle

r5#show dialer map
!!!read this as to get to r6(B-channel 1) dial 8358661
Static dialer map ip 192.168.9.21 name r6 (8358661) on BR0
!!!read this as to get to r6(B-channel 2) dial 8358663
Static dialer map ip 192.168.9.21 name r6 (8358663) on BR0
```

The best test is to bring up the connection in Example 9-34. Analyze your interfaces while the ISDN connection is up and running.

Example 9-34 *Bringing Up the ISDN Connection*

```
r5#ping 192.168.9.21
Sending 5, 100-byte ICMP Echos to 192.168.9.21, timeout is 2 seconds:
.!!!!
Success rate is 80 percent (4/5), round-trip min/avg/max = 36/37/40 ms
Dec 22 02:59:38.827: %LINK-3-UPDOWN: Interface BRI0:1, changed state to up
Dec 22 02:59:39.867: %LINEPROTO-5-UPDOWN: Line protocol on Interface BRI0:1,
  changed state to up
Dec 22 02:59:44.863: %ISDN-6-CONNECT: Interface BRI0:1 is now connected to 8358661 r6
r5#show interfaces bri0 1 2
BRI0:1 is up, line protocol is up
  Hardware is BRI
  MTU 1500 bytes, BW 64 Kbit, DLY 20000 usec, rely 255/255, load 1/255
  Encapsulation HDLC, loopback not set, keepalive set (10 sec)
  Time to interface disconnect:  idle 00:00:47
  Last input 00:00:07, output 00:00:06, output hang never
  Last clearing of "show interface" counters never
  Input queue: 0/75/0 (size/max/drops); Total output drops: 0
  Queueing strategy: weighted fair
  Output queue: 0/1000/64/0 (size/max total/threshold/drops)
     Conversations  0/1/256 (active/max active/max total)
     Reserved Conversations 0/0 (allocated/max allocated)
  5 minute input rate 0 bits/sec, 0 packets/sec
  5 minute output rate 0 bits/sec, 0 packets/sec
     14 packets input, 964 bytes, 0 no buffer
     Received 6 broadcasts, 0 runts, 0 giants, 0 throttles
     0 input errors, 0 CRC, 0 frame, 0 overrun, 0 ignored, 0 abort
     14 packets output, 964 bytes, 0 underruns
     0 output errors, 0 collisions, 13 interface resets
     0 output buffer failures, 0 output buffers swapped out
     3 carrier transitions
BRI0:2 is down, line protocol is down
...
r5#show ip interface brief
Interface          IP-Address      OK? Method Status                Protocol
BRI0               192.168.9.22    YES manual up                    up
BRI0:1             unassigned      YES unset  up                    up
BRI0:2             unassigned      YES unset  down                  down
Ethernet0          unassigned      YES unset  administratively down down
Loopback8          5.5.5.5         YES NVRAM  up                    up
Serial0            192.168.9.14    YES NVRAM  up                    up
Serial1            192.168.9.18    YES NVRAM  administratively down down
Dec 22 03:00:35.595: %ISDN-6-DISCONNECT: Interface BRI0:1  disconnected from
  8358661 r6, call lasted 56 seconds
Dec 22 03:00:35.707:  isdn_Call_disconnect()
Dec 22 03:00:35.707: %LINK-3-UPDOWN: Interface BRI0:1, changed state to down
Dec 22 03:00:36.707: %LINEPROTO-5-UPDOWN: Line protocol on Interface BRI0:1,
  changed state to down
```

The **ping** command is just as good as anything else to bring up the ISDN B channel because it requires IP. **protocol IP permit** was part of your dialer list and dialer map statements. Your time and date stamps are quite informative here to let you know that BRI0:1 is up and connected to r6 using the phone number 835-8661. The output of **show interfaces bri0 1 2** shows you that the first B channel is up, the default encapsulation is HDLC, and that you have 47 seconds until disconnect. You can also see that the interface counters have never been cleared. If you see an IP address, you are looking at the D channel instead. Perhaps you typed **show interfaces bri0** without the 1 or 2 at the end. The output of **show ip interface brief** also clearly shows the D channel and B channel as being up for the line and protocol. Although only one B channel is used by default, you can configure the other one with the **dialer threshold** command. You will do this in the "Trouble Tickets" section. Note the ending shaded call disconnect where your **dialer idle-timeout** configuration of 55 seconds took effect.

NOTE   Any errors with the dialer commands should lead you to verifying your **dialer list**, **dialer group**, **dialer map**, and **dialer string** commands.

Next bring the link up again to verify the layers with **show isdn status** as in Example 9-35.

Example 9-35   show isdn status *Command Output*

```
r5#ping 192.168.9.21
Sending 5, 100-byte ICMP Echos to 192.168.9.21, timeout is 2 seconds:
.!!!!
Success rate is 80 percent (4/5), round-trip min/avg/max = 36/36/36 ms
Dec 22 03:25:28.799: %LINK-3-UPDOWN: Interface BRI0:1, changed state to up
Dec 22 03:25:28.835: %ISDN-6-CONNECT: Interface BRI0:1 is now connected to 8358661
Dec 22 03:25:29.843: %LINEPROTO-5-UPDOWN: Line protocol on Interface BRI0:1,
changed state to up
r5#show isdn status
Global ISDN Switchtype = basic-ni
ISDN BRI0 interface
        dsl 0, interface ISDN Switchtype = basic-ni
    Layer 1 Status:
        ACTIVE
    Layer 2 Status:
        TEI = 104, Ces = 1, SAPI = 0, State = MULTIPLE_FRAME_ESTABLISHED
        TEI = 105, Ces = 2, SAPI = 0, State = MULTIPLE_FRAME_ESTABLISHED
    Spid Status:
        TEI 104, ces = 1, state = 5(init)
            spid1 configured, spid1 sent, spid1 valid
            Endpoint ID Info: epsf = 0, usid = 2, tid = 1
        TEI 105, ces = 2, state = 5(init)
            spid2 configured, spid2 sent, spid2 valid
            Endpoint ID Info: epsf = 0, usid = 4, tid = 1
    Layer 3 Status:
        1 Active Layer 3 Call(s)
    Activated dsl 0 CCBs = 1
        CCB:callid=0x8003, sapi=0x0, ces=0x1, B-chan=1
    The Free Channel Mask:  0x80000002
Dec 22 03:25:34.839: %ISDN-6-CONNECT: Interface BRI0:1 is now connected to 8358661 r6
    Total Allocated ISDN CCBs = 1
```

As previously mentioned, the **show isdn status** command is an extremely useful command in troubleshooting the layers with ISDN BRI. However, it helps to understand the frame format in Figure 9-11 to assist you in interpreting what you are looking at with the output of this command and similar ones. After I review the ISDN LAPD framing, I will move into shooting more ISDN troubles.

Figure 9-11   *ISDN LAPD Frame Format*

Flag	Address	Control	Information	FCS	Flag
1 Byte	1 or 2 Bytes	1 or 2 Bytes	(Layer 3)	2 or 4 Bytes	1 Byte

At Layer 1, the terminal endpoint (TE) is required before Layer 2 setup can occur. This is not end-to-end, but rather router (TE) to the local ISDN switch. An example of this is when I had the cables reversed on the routers and the controllers were activating rather than activated. As you can observe in Figure 9-12, there are two key fields in the LAPD address: TEI and SAPI.

Figure 9-12   *The LAPD Address Field*

8	7	6	5	4	3	2	1
SAPI						C/R	EA 0
TEI							EA 1

At Layer 2, ISDN operates much like HDLC. Check your terminal endpoint identifiers (TEIs). A TEI uniquely defines a terminal. 0 through 63 are not automatically assigned to user equipment, 64 through 126 are dynamically assigned, and TEI 127 is used for a broadcast. Although the ISDN switches may remove TEIs, the routers keep track of them. If you need to remove a router's TEIs, you need to **reload** the router to do so. The **shut/no shut** approach or **clear interface bri0** is not enough. However, that will increment the TEIs automatically and fixes many ISDN issues, too. Note that the TEIs of 104 (r5 SPID1) and 105 (r5 SPID2) are dynamically assigned in Example 9-35.

The service access point identifier (SAPI) defines the message type for the related ISDN Layer 3 management. SAPI 0 indicates call control procedures or ISDN Layer 3 signaling. SAPI 1 through 15 and 17 through 31 are reserved for future standardization. SAPI 16 is for X.25 procedures. SAPI 63 indicates Layer 2 management including TEI assignment, and SAPI 64 is used for call control.

The Command/Response (C/R) bit shows a value of 0 or 1 depending on the network side or the user side and whether a command or response:

- Network to user

  1 = Command

  0 = Response

- User to network

  0 = Command

  1 = Response

NOTE   For more details on the LAPD frame, refer to the ITU standards. I really like the protocol reference guides offered by DigiNet Corporation at www.diginet.com. I think you will find them very worthwhile for a nominal fee. They are not only for ISDN but also for supporting other technologies.

Now that you understand more of the ISDN Layer 2 technical details, take time to use the **debug isdn q921** command. Outside of **show isdn status**, it is the primary ISDN Layer 2 tool. You can use it to check TEI handling, call setup, information transfer, data-link monitoring, and disconnects. Issue it now on r5 and bring up the connection to watch the normal activity of ISDN Layer 2 as in Example 9-36. Wait for the call to disconnect before you turn off the **debug** command.

Example 9-36   **debug isdn q921** *Command*

```
r5#debug isdn q921
ISDN Q921 packets debugging is on
Dec 22 04:06:03.183: ISDN BR0: TX -> RRp sapi = 0  tei = 108 nr = 1
Dec 22 04:06:03.211: ISDN BR0: RX <- RRf sapi = 0  tei = 108  nr = 1
Dec 22 04:06:03.351: ISDN BR0: TX -> RRp sapi = 0  tei = 109 nr = 1
Dec 22 04:06:03.375: ISDN BR0: RX <- RRf sapi = 0  tei = 109  nr = 1
r5#ping 192.168.9.21
Sending 5, 100-byte ICMP Echos to 192.168.9.21, timeout is 2 seconds:
.!!!!
Success rate is 80 percent (4/5), round-trip min/avg/max = 36/36/36 ms
Dec 22 04:06:15.787: ISDN BR0: TX -> INFOc sapi = 0  tei = 108  ns = 1  nr = 1  i
 = 0x0801040504028890180183C20738333538363631
Dec 22 04:06:15.999: ISDN BR0: RX <- INFOc sapi = 0  tei = 108  ns = 1  nr = 2  i
 = 0x08018402180189952A1B809402603D8307383335383636318E0B2054656C746F6E65203120
Dec 22 04:06:16.015: ISDN BR0: TX -> RRr sapi = 0  tei = 108  nr = 2
Dec 22 04:06:16.127: ISDN BR0: RX <- INFOc sapi = 0  tei = 108  ns = 2  nr = 2  i
 = 0x08018407
Dec 22 04:06:16.139: ISDN BR0: TX -> RRr sapi = 0  tei = 108  nr = 3
Dec 22 04:06:16.143: %LINK-3-UPDOWN: Interface BRI0:1, changed state to up
Dec 22 04:06:16.179: %ISDN-6-CONNECT: Interface BRI0:1 is now connected to 8358661
```

continues

Example 9-36 debug isdn q921 *Command (Continued)*

```
Dec 22 04:06:16.187: ISDN BR0: TX -> INFOc sapi = 0  tei = 108  ns = 2  nr = 3  i
  = 0x0801040F
Dec 22 04:06:16.231: ISDN BR0: RX <- RRr sapi = 0  tei = 108  nr = 3
Dec 22 04:06:17.187: %LINEPROTO-5-UPDOWN: Line protocol on Interface BRI0:1,
  changed state to up
Dec 22 04:06:22.183: %ISDN-6-CONNECT: Interface BRI0:1 is now connected to 8358661 r6
Dec 22 04:06:33.379: ISDN BR0: TX -> RRp sapi = 0  tei = 109 nr = 1
Dec 22 04:06:33.403: ISDN BR0: RX <- RRf sapi = 0  tei = 109  nr = 1
Dec 22 04:06:46.235: ISDN BR0: TX -> RRp sapi = 0  tei = 108 nr = 3
Dec 22 04:06:46.259: ISDN BR0: RX <- RRf sapi = 0  tei = 108  nr = 3
Dec 22 04:07:03.407: ISDN BR0: TX -> RRp sapi = 0  tei = 109 nr = 1
Dec 22 04:07:03.435: ISDN BR0: RX <- RRf sapi = 0  tei = 109  nr = 1
Dec 22 04:07:12.887: %ISDN-6-DISCONNECT: Interface BRI0:1  disconnected from
  8358661 r6, call lasted 56 seconds
Dec 22 04:07:12.899: ISDN BR0: TX -> INFOc sapi = 0  tei = 108  ns = 3  nr = 3  i
  = 0x0801044508028090
Dec 22 04:07:12.991: ISDN BR0: RX <- INFOc sapi = 0  tei = 108  ns = 3  nr = 4  i
  = 0x0801844D
Dec 22 04:07:12.999: ISDN BR0: TX -> RRr sapi = 0  tei = 108  nr = 4
Dec 22 04:07:13.011:  isdn_Call_disconnect()
Dec 22 04:07:13.011: %LINK-3-UPDOWN: Interface BRI0:1, changed state to down
Dec 22 04:07:13.043: ISDN BR0: TX -> INFOc sapi = 0  tei = 108  ns = 4  nr = 4  i
  = 0x0801045A
Dec 22 04:07:13.111: ISDN BR0: RX <- RRr sapi = 0  tei = 108  nr = 5
Dec 22 04:07:14.011: %LINEPROTO-5-UPDOWN: Line protocol on Interface BRI0:1,
  changed state to down
r5#no debug isdn q921
ISDN Q921 packets debugging is off
```

Follow along with the output of Example 9-36 to look at the call control procedures over SAPI 0, the dynamic assignment of the TEIs, and the Tx and Rx for the C/R activity. I have shaded the changes in the BRI interface status so that you can follow the steps. The **debug bri** command enables you to watch the actual TEI negotiation.

It is often helpful to know whether call setup has ever occurred for troubleshooting purposes. Review the history of calls in Example 9-37.

Example 9-37 show isdn history *Command Output*

```
r5#show isdn history
--------------------------------------------------------------------------------
                            ISDN CALL HISTORY
--------------------------------------------------------------------------------
History table has a maximum of 100 entries.
History table data is retained for a maximum of 15 Minutes.
--------------------------------------------------------------------------------
Call    Calling     Called      Remote  Seconds Seconds Seconds Charges
Type    Number      Number      Name    Used    Left    Idle    Units/Currency
--------------------------------------------------------------------------------
Out                 8358661     r6      56                      0
--------------------------------------------------------------------------------
```

Example 9-37 **show isdn history** *Command Output*

```
r5#ping 192.168.9.21
Sending 5, 100-byte ICMP Echos to 192.168.9.21, timeout is 2 seconds:
.!!!!
...
r5#show isdn history
-------------------------------------------------------------------------------
                               ISDN CALL HISTORY
-------------------------------------------------------------------------------
History table has a maximum of 100 entries.
History table data is retained for a maximum of 15 Minutes.
-------------------------------------------------------------------------------
Call    Calling     Called      Remote  Seconds Seconds Seconds Charges
Type    Number      Number      Name    Used    Left    Idle    Units/Currency
-------------------------------------------------------------------------------
Out                 8358661     r6      56                      0
Out                 8358661     r6      10      46      8       0
-------------------------------------------------------------------------------
```

This router has always been on the initiating side of setting up the ISDN call parameters. Feel free to go to r6 to initiate the call and then repeat the **history** command on r6 to see the difference. It should add an additional inbound call. Another similar command is **show isdn active** to see just the active call.

NOTE   Remember that ISDN has its own Layer 2 and Layer 3. ISDN Layer 3 is for signaling and has nothing to do with the bearer payload being IP Layer 3. Q931 deals with end-to-end call setup, but there is no Layer 3 address. The E.164 phone number would be like your MAC address on the LAN, which technically makes ISDN part of the Layer 2 Data Link Layer realm.

Just like **debug isdn q921** shows the details of ISDN Layer 2, you can troubleshoot ISDN Layer 3 information with **debug isdn q931**. Use it to check call setup parameters such as SPIDs and phone numbers. In Example 9-38, issue it on r5 to watch the normal activity of ISDN Layer 3.

Example 9-38 **debug isdn q931** *Command Output*

```
r5#debug isdn q931
ISDN Q931 packets debugging is on
r5#ping 192.168.9.21
Sending 5, 100-byte ICMP Echos to 192.168.9.21, timeout is 2 seconds:
.!!!!
Success rate is 80 percent (4/5), round-trip min/avg/max = 36/36/36 ms
Dec 22 04:53:23.275: ISDN BR0: TX ->  SETUP pd = 8  callref = 0x06
Dec 22 04:53:23.279:         Bearer Capability i = 0x8890
Dec 22 04:53:23.279:         Channel ID i = 0x83
Dec 22 04:53:23.283:         Keypad Facility i = '8358661'
Dec 22 04:53:23.491: ISDN BR0: RX <-  CALL_PROC pd = 8  callref = 0x86
Dec 22 04:53:23.491:         Channel ID i = 0x89
```

continues

Example 9-38 debug isdn q931 *Command Output (Continued)*

```
Dec 22 04:53:23.495:           Locking Shift to Codeset 5
Dec 22 04:53:23.499:           Codeset 5 IE 0x2A  i = 0x809402, '`=', 0x8307, '8358661',
  0x8E0B20, 'Teltone', 0x20, '1', 0x20
Dec 22 04:53:23.619: ISDN BR0: RX <-  CONNECT pd = 8  callref = 0x86
Dec 22 04:53:23.635: %LINK-3-UPDOWN: Interface BRI0:1, changed state to up
Dec 22 04:53:23.667: %ISDN-6-CONNECT: Interface BRI0:1 is now connected to 8358661
Dec 22 04:53:23.679: ISDN BR0: TX ->  CONNECT_ACK pd = 8  callref = 0x06
Dec 22 04:53:24.675: %LINEPROTO-5-UPDOWN: Line protocol on Interface BRI0:1,
  changed state to up
Dec 22 04:53:29.671: %ISDN-6-CONNECT: Interface BRI0:1 is now connected to 8358661 r6
!!!active call in progress
r5#show isdn status
Global ISDN Switchtype = basic-ni
ISDN BRI0 interface
        dsl 0, interface ISDN Switchtype = basic-ni
    Layer 1 Status:
        ACTIVE
    Layer 2 Status:
        TEI = 108, Ces = 1, SAPI = 0, State = MULTIPLE_FRAME_ESTABLISHED
        TEI = 109, Ces = 2, SAPI = 0, State = MULTIPLE_FRAME_ESTABLISHED
    Spid Status:
        TEI 108, ces = 1, state = 5(init)
            spid1 configured, spid1 sent, spid1 valid
            Endpoint ID Info: epsf = 0, usid = 2, tid = 1
        TEI 109, ces = 2, state = 5(init)
            spid2 configured, spid2 sent, spid2 valid
            Endpoint ID Info: epsf = 0, usid = 4, tid = 1
    Layer 3 Status:
        1 Active Layer 3 Call(s)
    Activated dsl 0 CCBs = 1
        CCB:callid=0x8006, sapi=0x0, ces=0x1, B-chan=1
    The Free Channel Mask:  0x80000002
    Total Allocated ISDN CCBs = 1
r5#
Dec 22 04:54:20.375: %ISDN-6-DISCONNECT: Interface BRI0:1  disconnected from
  8358661 r6, call lasted 56 seconds
Dec 22 04:54:20.387: ISDN BR0: TX ->  DISCONNECT pd = 8  callref = 0x06
Dec 22 04:54:20.391:           Cause i = 0x8090 - Normal call clearing
Dec 22 04:54:20.495: ISDN BR0: RX <-  RELEASE pd = 8  callref = 0x86
Dec 22 04:54:20.511:  isdn_Call_disconnect()
Dec 22 04:54:20.515: %LINK-3-UPDOWN: Interface BRI0:1, changed state to down
Dec 22 04:54:20.547: ISDN BR0: TX ->  RELEASE_COMP pd = 8  callref = 0x06
Dec 22 04:54:21.511: %LINEPROTO-5-UPDOWN: Line protocol on Interface BRI0:1,
  changed state to down
!!!after the call tear down
r5#show isdn status
Global ISDN Switchtype = basic-ni
ISDN BRI0 interface
        dsl 0, interface ISDN Switchtype = basic-ni
    Layer 1 Status:
        ACTIVE
    Layer 2 Status:
```

Example 9-38 debug isdn q931 *Command Output (Continued)*

```
            TEI = 108, Ces = 1, SAPI = 0, State = MULTIPLE_FRAME_ESTABLISHED
            TEI = 109, Ces = 2, SAPI = 0, State = MULTIPLE_FRAME_ESTABLISHED
        Spid Status:
            TEI 108, ces = 1, state = 5(init)
                spid1 configured, spid1 sent, spid1 valid
                Endpoint ID Info: epsf = 0, usid = 2, tid = 1
            TEI 109, ces = 2, state = 5(init)
                spid2 configured, spid2 sent, spid2 valid
                Endpoint ID Info: epsf = 0, usid = 4, tid = 1
        Layer 3 Status:
            0 Active Layer 3 Call(s)
        Activated dsl 0 CCBs = 0
        The Free Channel Mask:  0x80000003
        Total Allocated ISDN CCBs = 0
r5#undebug all
```

The call reference parameters help to distinguish between the different calls. For example, the reason for the preceding disconnect is *normal call clearing*. See the shaded output after the 56-second disconnect in Example 9-38.

Now that you have looked at the LAPD frame format and experimented with some of the commands on a layer-by-layer basis, I want to focus on shooting ISDN BRI troubles.

Shooting Trouble with ISDN BRI

Although you have already performed some pretty intensive ISDN troubleshooting, I want to reinforce the general things to look for when shooting ISDN BRI troubles. Also I want to cover a little more detail on defining interesting traffic and running routing protocols over ISDN links.

Several show, debug, and clear IOS commands are available to help you understand and support ISDN. Example 9-39 illustrates the ISDN show commands.

Example 9-39 *ISDN Show Commands*

```
r5#show isdn ?
  active    ISDN active calls
  history   ISDN call history
  memory    ISDN memory information
  status    ISDN Line Status
  timers    ISDN Timer values
```

The **show isdn active** command shows calls in progress, but if there is not a call in progress perhaps you should try **show isdn history** to see whether there was ever a call placed. Refer back to the previous examples for the output of these commands. The **show isdn memory** command shows ISDN memory pool statistics and what is in use. The **show isdn timers** shows the switch type and other Layer 2 and Layer 3 values.

The commands **show ip interface brief**, **show interface bri0 [1 | 2]**, **show controllers bri 0** as well as link lights are all invaluable Physical Layer tools. Without **1** or **2**, **show interface bri0** shows the D-channel activity; with the **1** or **2** you are looking at the B channels. Error counts such as packets input and output and carrier transitions beyond your baseline are worthwhile to analyze. Move up the stack to check the encapsulation or frame type. Are you communicating with the ISDN switch? Remember that the switch type must match between your router and the local ISDN switch. Get this information from the provider. Look at the keepalive activity (D-channel signaling) between the local router and the ISDN switch with **show interfaces bri0**. Be sure to clear the interface with **clear interface bri0** to reset the hardware logic and re-establish the TEI before you call it a day. As with other technologies, clear the interface counters using **clear counters bri0** to establish what you are looking at from this point on (so that you are not confused by previous interface resets, for instance).

Use **show isdn status** to see the switch type and a summary of what is going on with the layers. This is by far the most informative command for supporting ISDN. ISDN Layer 3 depends on Layer 2 and Layer 2 depends on Layer 1, but that shouldn't be any big surprise by now. The incorrect switch type is a very common problem; expect Layer 1 and Layer 2 to be *deactivated* if this is the issue. Use **debug isdn q921** to further define issues with the telco switch and **debug isdn q931** to further pinpoint call setup issues. Q921 will help when a cable is unplugged or help determine whether the cable is bad (and by the same logic, when nothing is going through).

Other common targets are dialer configuration, encapsulation, and authentication issues. Phone numbers, SPIDs, and the map statements to get to the other end are all things to look at with the dialer. Review Example 9-40 for dialer troubleshooting. Refer back to the "Shooting Trouble with PPP" section for assistance with PPP encapsulation and or authentication troubleshooting.

Example 9-40   *Dialer Troubleshooting*

```
r5>show dialer ?
  interface  Show dialer information on one interface
  maps       Show dialer maps
  <cr>
r5>show dialer
BRI0 - dialer type = ISDN
Dial String      Successes   Failures    Last called   Last status
8358663                  0          0    never              -
8358661                  6          0    00:20:01      successful
0 incoming call(s) have been screened.
0 incoming call(s) rejected for callback.
BRI0:1 - dialer type = ISDN
Idle timer (55 secs), Fast idle timer (20 secs)
Wait for carrier (30 secs), Re-enable (15 secs)
Dialer state is idle
BRI0:2 - dialer type = ISDN
Idle timer (55 secs), Fast idle timer (20 secs)
Wait for carrier (30 secs), Re-enable (15 secs)
Dialer state is idle
r5>show dialer maps
Static dialer map ip 192.168.9.21 name r6 (8358661) on BR0
Static dialer map ip 192.168.9.21 name r6 (8358663) on BR0
```

Example 9-40   *Dialer Troubleshooting (Continued)*

```
r5>ping 192.168.9.21
Type escape sequence to abort.
Sending 5, 100-byte ICMP Echos to 192.168.9.21, timeout is 2 seconds:
.!!!!
Success rate is 80 percent (4/5), round-trip min/avg/max = 36/36/36 ms
Dec 22 05:16:37.326: %LINK-3-UPDOWN: Interface BRI0:1, changed state to up
Dec 22 05:16:37.358: %ISDN-6-CONNECT: Interface BRI0:1 is now connected to 8358661
Dec 22 05:16:38.366: %LINEPROTO-5-UPDOWN: Line protocol on Interface BRI0:1,
  changed state to up
r5>show dialer
BRI0 - dialer type = ISDN
Dial String      Successes    Failures    Last called    Last status
8358663                  0           0    never          -
8358661                  7           0    00:00:05        successful
0 incoming call(s) have been screened.
0 incoming call(s) rejected for callback.
BRI0:1 - dialer type = ISDN
Idle timer (55 secs), Fast idle timer (20 secs)
Wait for carrier (30 secs), Re-enable (15 secs)
Dialer state is data link layer up
!!!note that it tells you why the call was made
Dial reason: ip (s=192.168.9.22, d=192.168.9.21)
Time until disconnect 51 secs
Connected to 8358661 (r6)
BRI0:2 - dialer type = ISDN
Idle timer (55 secs), Fast idle timer (20 secs)
Wait for carrier (30 secs), Re-enable (15 secs)
Dialer state is idle
Dec 22 05:16:43.362: %ISDN-6-CONNECT: Interface BRI0:1 is now connected to 8358661 r6
```

Dialer commands such as those illustrated in Example 9-40 are useful in spotting ISDN or other dialup issues. Find out why the call was made or terminated to begin with. Narrow down the dialer issues by specifying a particular interface to see phone numbers, successes, failures, and per B-channel timers and dialer states. Clear the dialer statistics to start from now on with **clear dialer interface bri0**. Dialer maps map the Layer 2 phone numbers to the destination IP addresses, and the **show dialer map** command displays them quite nicely. Perhaps you forgot the **broadcast** keyword on the **map** statement for your routing protocol updates or maybe you didn't mean for routing updates to cross the ISDN link. It is very easy to make typos in this area, especially when phone numbers only vary by one or two digits. The **show run interface bri0** command in Example 9-41 helps you quickly spot issues with your bri0 interface configuration to check for missed statements and typos.

Example 9-41   **show run interface bri0** *Command Output*

```
r5#show run interface bri0
Building configuration...
Current configuration:
!
interface BRI0
```

continues

Example 9-41 **show run interface bri0** *Command Output (Continued)*

```
 ip address 192.168.9.22 255.255.255.252
 no ip directed-broadcast
 dialer idle-timeout 55
 dialer map ip 192.168.9.21 name r6 8358661
 dialer map ip 192.168.9.21 name r6 8358663
 dialer-group 1
 isdn switch-type basic-ni
 isdn spid1 0835866201 8358662
 isdn spid2 0835866401 8358664
end

r6#show run interface bri0
Building configuration...
Current configuration:
!
interface BRI0
 ip address 192.168.9.21 255.255.255.252
 no ip directed-broadcast
 dialer idle-timeout 55
 dialer map ip 192.168.9.22 name r5 8358662
 dialer map ip 192.168.9.22 name r5 8358664
 dialer-group 1
 isdn switch-type basic-ni
 isdn spid1 0835866101 8358661
 isdn spid2 0835866301 8358663
end
```

If you are trying to narrow down why you can't dial, give **debug dialer events** a try as in Example 9-42. Note the reason for the dial and dial attempts.

Example 9-42 **debug dialer events** *Command*

```
r5#debug dialer events
Dial on demand events debugging is on
r5#ping 192.168.9.21
Sending 5, 100-byte ICMP Echos to 192.168.9.21, timeout is 2 seconds:
.!!!!
Success rate is 80 percent (4/5), round-trip min/avg/max = 36/36/36 ms
Dec 22 05:28:43.190: BR0 DDR: Dialing cause ip (s=192.168.9.22, d=192.168.9.21)
Dec 22 05:28:43.194: BR0 DDR: Attempting to dial 8358661
Dec 22 05:28:43.546: %LINK-3-UPDOWN: Interface BRI0:1, changed state to up
Dec 22 05:28:43.578: %ISDN-6-CONNECT: Interface BRI0:1 is now connected to 8358661
Dec 22 05:28:43.590: BR0:1 DDR: dialer protocol up
Dec 22 05:28:44.586: %LINEPROTO-5-UPDOWN: Line protocol on Interface BRI0:1,
  changed state to up
Dec 22 05:28:49.582: %ISDN-6-CONNECT: Interface BRI0:1 is now connected to 8358661 r6
```

NOTE   Figure 9-13 in the "Summary" section at the end of this chapter reviews of many of these commands to assist you with troubleshooting ISDN issues before you call Cisco Technical Assistance Center (TAC).

Perhaps the issue is not with configuration at all but with performance. What is the load on the line? Maybe you need to adjust the threshold to bring up another B channel or configure multilink. Perhaps you need to analyze the type of traffic traversing the link. How about issues relating to routing protocols on the ISDN link?

Dial-on-Demand Routing

DDR is dynamic routing on an as-needed basis to reduce WAN communication costs. It is good for periodic connections that transfer small amounts of data. It obviously is not a solution for today's e-commerce sites. Typically, static or default routes are used. After specifying the route (if needed), define the traffic that brings up the link. It is *critical* to remember that any traffic, whether interesting or not, can traverse the link while it is up. The exception is broadcast/multicast unless it is specified in the dialer map. You have already configured this. The idea is to resolve a next-hop address to a phone number, which you did with the dialer map statements.

Assuming you have a route, you must next specify interesting traffic to enable the connection. Access lists give you much more granular control than the $24,000 default **dialer-list 1 protocol ip permit** global command. Analyze your running configuration; this is how things are configured right now. Although the **protocol ip permit** command works well for testing in a lab, there are horror stories about this in the real world. People have configured ISDN to allow any IP traffic to bring up the link and keep it up for that matter in practical application. Can you imagine having your ISDN link up for a month or so and getting a $24,000 phone bill for the usage charges of ISDN? It has happened, but I bet not twice in the same place. So, preferably you should point the dialer list to an access list in the real world. If you do not want telnet to bring up the ISDN link, for example, you can configure that with an access list. Do that next in Example 9-43.

Example 9-43 *Dialer List Pointing to an Access List*

```
r5#configure terminal
r5(config)#interface bri0
r5(config-if)#no dialer-group 1
r5(config-if)#exit

r5(config)#dialer-list 9 protocol ip list ?
  <1-199>      IP access list
  <1300-2699>  IP expanded access list
r5(config)#dialer-list 9 protocol ip list 109

r5(config)#access-list 109 deny tcp any any eq ?
  <0-65535>    Port number
  bgp          Border Gateway Protocol (179)
  chargen      Character generator (19)
  cmd          Remote commands (rcmd, 514)
  daytime      Daytime (13)
  discard      Discard (9)
  domain       Domain Name Service (53)
  echo         Echo (7)
  exec         Exec (rsh, 512)
  finger       Finger (79)
```

continues

Example 9-43 *Dialer List Pointing to an Access List (Continued)*

```
   ftp          File Transfer Protocol (21)
   ftp-data     FTP data connections (used infrequently, 20)
   gopher       Gopher (70)
   hostname     NIC hostname server (101)
   ident        Ident Protocol (113)
   irc          Internet Relay Chat (194)
   klogin       Kerberos login (543)
   kshell       Kerberos shell (544)
   login        Login (rlogin, 513)
   lpd          Printer service (515)
   nntp         Network News Transport Protocol (119)
   pim-auto-rp  PIM Auto-RP (496)
   pop2         Post Office Protocol v2 (109)
   pop3         Post Office Protocol v3 (110)
   smtp         Simple Mail Transport Protocol (25)
   sunrpc       Sun Remote Procedure Call (111)
   syslog       Syslog (514)
   tacacs       TAC Access Control System (49)
   talk         Talk (517)
   telnet       Telnet (23)
   time         Time (37)
   uucp         Unix-to-Unix Copy Program (540)
   whois        Nicname (43)
   www          World Wide Web (HTTP, 80)

r5(config)#access-list 109 deny tcp any any eq telnet ?
   ack          Match on the ACK bit
   eq           Match only packets on a given port number
   established  Match established connections
   fin          Match on the FIN bit
   gt           Match only packets with a greater port number
   log          Log matches against this entry
   log-input    Log matches against this entry, including input interface
   lt           Match only packets with a lower port number
   neq          Match only packets not on a given port number
   precedence   Match packets with given precedence value
   psh          Match on the PSH bit
   range        Match only packets in the range of port numbers
   rst          Match on the RST bit
   syn          Match on the SYN bit
   tos          Match packets with given TOS value
   urg          Match on the URG bit
   <cr>
!!!the following two commands are all that are necessary
!!!to create the acl
r5(config)#access-list 109 deny tcp any any eq telnet log
r5(config)#access-list 109 permit ip any any

!!!the following command ties the dialer to the acl
r5(config)#dialer-list 9 protocol ip list 109

!!!now you must apply the acl to the bri interface
r5(config)#interface bri0
```

Example 9-43 *Dialer List Pointing to an Access List (Continued)*

```
r5(config-if)#dialer-group ?
  <1-10>  Dialer list number
r5(config-if)#dialer-group 9
r5(config-if)#end
```

Creating the access list is only one part of minimizing interesting traffic. The dialer list ties the access list to the dialer, but it does not take effect until the statement is applied to the interface with the **dialer-group** command. Think of this like access list (**global create**) and access group (**interface apply**). Go back and review the protocol, port and keyword details that are available. This is a great way to find a frequently used port number that you are unsure of as well.

NOTE

After the call has been triggered by interesting traffic, all traffic is allowed to use the connection. If interesting traffic stops, however, the other traffic may stop in the midst of things.

Repeat the **access list**, **dialer list**, and **dialer group** commands on r6. Use **debug dialer** to verify interesting traffic as in Example 9-44.

Example 9-44 *Debug Dialer to Verify Interesting Traffic*

```
r5#debug dialer
Dial on demand events debugging is on
r6#telnet 192.168.9.22
Trying 192.168.9.22 ...
% Connection timed out; remote host not responding
Dec 22 07:14:46.034: %SEC-6-IPACCESSLOGP: list 109 denied tcp 192.168.9.21(11001)
   -> 192.168.9.22(23), 1 packet
r6#ping 192.168.9.22
Sending 5, 100-byte ICMP Echos to 192.168.9.22, timeout is 2 seconds:
.!!!!
Success rate is 80 percent (4/5), round-trip min/avg/max = 36/36/36 ms
Dec 22 07:15:42.882: BR0 DDR: Dialing cause ip (s=192.168.9.21, d=192.168.9.22)
Dec 22 07:15:42.886: BR0 DDR: Attempting to dial 8358662
Dec 22 07:15:43.238: %LINK-3-UPDOWN: Interface BRI0:1, changed state to up
Dec 22 07:15:43.274: %ISDN-6-CONNECT: Interface BRI0:1 is now connected to 8358662
Dec 22 07:15:43.286: BR0:1 DDR: dialer protocol up
Dec 22 07:15:44.282: %LINEPROTO-5-UPDOWN: Line protocol on Interface BRI0:1,
   changed state to up
Dec 22 07:15:49.278: %ISDN-6-CONNECT: Interface BRI0:1 is now connected to 8358662 r5
r6#telnet 192.168.9.22
Trying 192.168.9.22 ... Open
User Access Verification
Password:
r5>en
Password:
r5#!!!note that I can telnet after the link is up
r5#!!!but not to bring the link up
r5#!!!no matter what I a
```

The gist of the preceding example is that with a dialer list you only control what type of traffic brings up the link. The initial telnet was denied and you can see the shaded log line as to why. However, telnet was allowed when the link was already up. When it was time for teardown, no matter what you were doing related to uninteresting traffic, it terminated immediately. That is what I was trying to tell you in the last line, when my telnet session got cut off.

NOTE   Depending on how you pay for your ISDN services, consider adjusting **dialer load-threshold** and **dialer idle-timeout**. Use **show isdn history** and look at the interface statistics to monitor what has happened to see whether you need to adjust. The **dialer idle-timeout** default is 120 seconds, for example, which could be a long time to wait if you are paying by the minute. On the other hand, if you are paying by the call you may need to increase it.

The are many ways to configure dial applications. I highly recommend Bill Burton's *Remote Access for Cisco Networks* (McGraw-Hill Professional) and the sample configurations at Cisco.com. Cook up your own concoctions with CCO's Access Dial Configuration Cookbook.

Next I briefly review dial backup from a support viewpoint, and then move on to the Trouble Tickets.

Dial Backup

Dial backup is available in three varieties:

- Backup interface
- Floating static routes
- Dialer watch

Regardless of the method, you need to know what the primary and backup links are and what interfaces are involved. The type of interface as well as your overall routing design are influential factors as to which method may work best for you. For example, **backup interface** is not designed for running on a Frame Relay physical interface, but it works just fine if using subinterfaces. *Always* make sure the primary and backup links work individually without getting fancy. What I mean is, make sure both links work to begin with before you have one try to back up another.

Use the **backup interface** command to configure the ISDN link to be the backup for the serial link between r5 and r6 as in Example 9-45.

Example 9-45 *Backup Interface*

```
r5(config)#interface s1
r5(config-if)#no shut
r6(config)#interface s0
r6(config-if)#no shut
r6(config-if)#end
r6#show ip interface brief
Interface              IP-Address      OK? Method Status                 Protocol
BRI0                   192.168.9.21    YES manual up                     up
BRI0:1                 unassigned      YES unset  down                   down
BRI0:2                 unassigned      YES unset  down                   down
Ethernet0              unassigned      YES unset  administratively down  down
Loopback9              6.6.6.6         YES manual up                     up
Serial0                192.168.9.17    YES manual up                     up
Serial1                unassigned      YES unset  down                   down
Serial2                unassigned      YES unset  administratively down  down
Serial3                unassigned      YES unset  administratively down  down
r6#!!!the serial and bri interfaces are up

r6#configure terminal
r6(config)#interface s0
r6(config-if)#backup interface bri0
Dec 22 07:51:53.102: %ISDN-6-LAYER2DOWN: Layer 2 for Interface BRI0, TEI 116
  changed to down
Dec 22 07:51:53.106: %ISDN-6-LAYER2DOWN: Layer 2 for Interface BRI0, TEI 117
  changed to down
Dec 22 07:51:53.150: %LINK-5-CHANGED: Interface BRI0, changed state to standby mode
r6(config-if)#end
```

Now that the backup interface is configured, view the s0 interface in Example 9-46 to see the differences.

Example 9-46 *Viewing the Backup Interface*

```
r6#show interface s0
Serial0 is up, line protocol is up
  Hardware is HD64570
  Internet address is 192.168.9.17/30
  Backup interface BRI0, failure delay 0 sec, secondary disable delay 0 sec,
  kickin load not set, kickout load not set
  MTU 1500 bytes, BW 64 Kbit, DLY 20000 usec, rely 255/255, load 1/255
  Encapsulation PPP, loopback not set, keepalive set (10 sec)
  LCP Open
  Open: IPCP, CDPCP
  Last input 00:00:02, output 00:00:04, output hang never
  Last clearing of "show interface" counters never
  Queueing strategy: fifo
  Output queue 0/40, 0 drops; input queue 0/75, 0 drops
  5 minute input rate 0 bits/sec, 0 packets/sec
  5 minute output rate 0 bits/sec, 0 packets/sec
     2622 packets input, 135193 bytes, 0 no buffer
     Received 0 broadcasts, 0 runts, 0 giants, 0 throttles
     1 input errors, 1 CRC, 0 frame, 0 overrun, 0 ignored, 1 abort
     2634 packets output, 133687 bytes, 0 underruns
```

continues

Example 9-46 *Viewing the Backup Interface (Continued)*

```
        0 output errors, 0 collisions, 634 interface resets
        0 output buffer failures, 0 output buffers swapped out
        7 carrier transitions
        DCD=up  DSR=up  DTR=up  RTS=up  CTS=up
r6#clear counters s0
```

For practical application of this, assume that ISDN was put in between r5 and r6 because it is critical that r6 be able to communicate with r3 even if the serial link between r5 and r6 is down. The serial link is using a routing protocol, however, and the ISDN link is not. There are specific commands to assist with running particular routing protocols over DDR links, but here a default route is very appropriate. On the other hand, maybe you don't want all traffic going over the link anyway. You can restrict this with a floating static route as in Example 9-47.

NOTE   Common methods of configuring a routing protocol over DDR links include the following:

- RIP/IGRP—Snapshot routing

- OSPF—IP OSPF demand circuit

- EIGRP—Can redistribute on-demand routing (ODR)

Example 9-47 *Floating Static Route*

```
r6#show ip protocols
Routing Protocol is "eigrp 109"
  Outgoing update filter list for all interfaces is not set
  Incoming update filter list for all interfaces is not set
  Default networks flagged in outgoing updates
  Default networks accepted from incoming updates
  EIGRP metric weight K1=1, K2=0, K3=1, K4=0, K5=0
  EIGRP maximum hopcount 100
  EIGRP maximum metric variance 1
  Redistributing: eigrp 109
  Automatic network summarization is not in effect
  Routing for Networks:
    6.0.0.0
    192.168.9.0
  Routing Information Sources:
    Gateway         Distance      Last Update
    (this router)          5      1w1d
    192.168.9.18          90      00:17:25
  Distance: internal 90 external 170

r6#configure terminal
r6(config)#ip route 192.168.9.12 255.255.255.252 192.168.9.22 ?
  <1-255>    Distance metric for this route
  permanent  permanent route
```

Example 9-47 *Floating Static Route (Continued)*

```
tag          Set tag for this route
<cr>
r6(config)#ip route 192.168.9.12 255.255.255.252 192.168.9.22 200
```

In Example 9-47 I issued the **show ip protocols** command to verify the administrative distance for EIGRP, the routing protocol that is running on r6. Notice that I set the administrative distance for the floating static route to a number higher than the administrative distance for EIGRP. You might consider setting it to 201 in practical application to take care of BGP as well. Remember, the lower the administrative distance, the more believable the route.

The **shut** command will not trigger dial-backup interfaces, so physically disconnect the serial cable on r6 to test this. Monitor the results in Example 9-48. After verifying that things work, plug the serial cable back in to verify that it is still the primary link. The ISDN link should return to standby automatically.

Example 9-48 *Testing the Backup Interface and Floating Static*

```
r6#show ip interface brief
Interface              IP-Address      OK? Method Status                 Protocol
BRI0                   192.168.9.21    YES manual standby mode           down
BRI0:1                 unassigned      YES unset  administratively down down
BRI0:2                 unassigned      YES unset  administratively down down
...
Serial0                192.168.9.17    YES manual up                     up
...
r6#!!!physically unplug the serial cable from r6
Dec 22 09:24:31.625: %LINK-3-UPDOWN: Interface Serial0, changed state to down
Dec 22 09:24:31.661: %LINK-3-UPDOWN: Interface BRI0:1, changed state to down
Dec 22 09:24:31.693: %LINK-3-UPDOWN: Interface BRI0:2, changed state to down
Dec 22 09:24:31.777: %LINK-3-UPDOWN: Interface BRI0, changed state to up
Dec 22 09:24:32.097: %ISDN-6-LAYER2UP: Layer 2 for Interface BR0, TEI 126 changed
  to up
Dec 22 09:24:32.261: %ISDN-6-LAYER2UP: Layer 2 for Interface BR0, TEI 65 changed
  to up
Dec 22 09:24:32.625: %LINEPROTO-5-UPDOWN: Line protocol on Interface Serial0,
  changed state to down

!!!the D-Channel is up
r6#show ip interface brief
Interface              IP-Address      OK? Method Status                 Protocol
BRI0                   192.168.9.21    YES manual up                     up
BRI0:1                 unassigned      YES unset  down                   down
BRI0:2                 unassigned      YES unset  down                   down
Ethernet0              unassigned      YES unset  administratively down down
Loopback9              6.6.6.6         YES NVRAM  up                     up
Serial0                192.168.9.17    YES NVRAM  down                   down
...
!!!the floating static route is in the table
r6#show ip route
...
    192.168.9.0/30 is subnetted, 2 subnets
```

continues

Example 9-48 *Testing the Backup Interface and Floating Static (Continued)*

```
S        192.168.9.12 [200/0] via 192.168.9.22
C        192.168.9.20 is directly connected, BRI0
     6.0.0.0/32 is subnetted, 1 subnets
C        6.6.6.6 is directly connected, Loopback9

!!!send some interesting traffic to open the B-Channel
r6#ping 192.168.9.13
Sending 5, 100-byte ICMP Echos to 192.168.9.13, timeout is 2 seconds:
.!!!!
Success rate is 80 percent (4/5), round-trip min/avg/max = 60/63/64 ms
Dec 22 09:25:23.289: %LINK-3-UPDOWN: Interface BRI0:1, changed state to up
Dec 22 09:25:23.325: %ISDN-6-CONNECT: Interface BRI0:1 is now connected to 8358662
Dec 22 09:25:24.333: %LINEPROTO-5-UPDOWN: Line protocol on Interface BRI0:1,
   changed state to up
Dec 22 09:25:29.329: %ISDN-6-CONNECT: Interface BRI0:1 is now connected to 8358662 r5

!!!the first B-Channel is up
r6#show ip interface brief
Interface           IP-Address      OK? Method Status                Protocol
BRI0                192.168.9.21    YES manual up                    up
BRI0:1              unassigned      YES unset  up                    up
BRI0:2              unassigned      YES unset  down                  down
Ethernet0           unassigned      YES unset  administratively down down
Loopback9           6.6.6.6         YES NVRAM  up                    up
Serial0             192.168.9.17    YES NVRAM  down                  down
...
r6#!!!now plug the cable back in
Dec 22 09:26:20.133: %ISDN-6-DISCONNECT: Interface BRI0:1  disconnected from
   8358662 r5, call lasted 56 seconds
Dec 22 09:26:20.245: %LINK-3-UPDOWN: Interface BRI0:1, changed state to down
Dec 22 09:26:21.245: %LINEPROTO-5-UPDOWN: Line protocol on Interface BRI0:1,
   changed state to down
!!!s0 automatically comes up
Dec 22 09:26:33.661: %LINK-3-UPDOWN: Interface Serial0, changed state to up
Dec 22 09:26:34.729: %LINEPROTO-5-UPDOWN: Line protocol on Interface Serial0,
   changed state to up
Dec 22 09:26:34.745: %ISDN-6-LAYER2DOWN: Layer 2 for Interface BRI0, TEI 126
   changed to down
Dec 22 09:26:34.749: %ISDN-6-LAYER2DOWN: Layer 2 for Interface BRI0, TEI 65 changed
   to down
r6#!!!bri0 automatically goes back to standby
Dec 22 09:26:34.789: %LINK-5-CHANGED: Interface BRI0, changed state to standby mode
```

Note that it was only necessary to configure the backup interface on one side. When s0 was down, r6 needed a route to get to the r3 destination, which the floating static provides. Verify the state of your interfaces and routing table under normal circumstances to help you recognize abnormalities (see Example 9-49).

Example 9-49 *Verifying the Normal Interfaces and Routing Table*

```
r6#show ip interface brief
Interface            IP-Address      OK? Method Status                 Protocol
BRI0                 192.168.9.21    YES manual standby mode           down
BRI0:1               unassigned      YES unset  administratively down  down
BRI0:2               unassigned      YES unset  administratively down  down
Ethernet0            unassigned      YES unset  administratively down  down
Loopback9            6.6.6.6         YES NVRAM  up                     up
Serial0              192.168.9.17    YES NVRAM  up                     up

r6#show ip route
Codes: C - connected, S - static, I - IGRP, R - RIP, M - mobile, B - BGP
       D - EIGRP, EX - EIGRP external, O - OSPF, IA - OSPF inter area
       N1 - OSPF NSSA external type 1, N2 - OSPF NSSA external type 2
       E1 - OSPF external type 1, E2 - OSPF external type 2, E - EGP
       i - IS-IS, L1 - IS-IS level-1, L2 - IS-IS level-2, * - candidate default
       U - per-user static route, o - ODR
Gateway of last resort is not set
     1.0.0.0/32 is subnetted, 1 subnets
D       1.1.1.1 [90/41664000] via 192.168.9.18, 00:17:15, Serial0
     2.0.0.0/32 is subnetted, 1 subnets
D       2.2.2.2 [90/41664000] via 192.168.9.18, 00:17:16, Serial0
     3.0.0.0/32 is subnetted, 1 subnets
D       3.3.3.3 [90/41152000] via 192.168.9.18, 00:17:16, Serial0
     4.0.0.0/32 is subnetted, 1 subnets
D       4.4.4.4 [90/41664000] via 192.168.9.18, 00:17:16, Serial0
     192.168.9.0/24 is variably subnetted, 11 subnets, 2 masks
D       192.168.9.1/32 [90/41536000] via 192.168.9.18, 00:17:16, Serial0
D       192.168.9.0/30 [90/41536000] via 192.168.9.18, 00:17:16, Serial0
D       192.168.9.4/30 [90/41536000] via 192.168.9.18, 00:17:16, Serial0
D       192.168.9.6/32 [90/41536000] via 192.168.9.18, 00:17:16, Serial0
D       192.168.9.8/30 [90/41536000] via 192.168.9.18, 00:17:16, Serial0
D       192.168.9.10/32 [90/41536000] via 192.168.9.18, 00:17:18, Serial0
D       192.168.9.13/32 [90/41024000] via 192.168.9.18, 00:17:18, Serial0
D       192.168.9.12/30 [90/41024000] via 192.168.9.18, 00:17:18, Serial0
C       192.168.9.16/30 is directly connected, Serial0
C       192.168.9.18/32 is directly connected, Serial0
D       192.168.9.20/30 [90/41024000] via 192.168.9.18, 00:17:18, Serial0
     5.0.0.0/32 is subnetted, 1 subnets
D       5.5.5.5 [90/40640000] via 192.168.9.18, 00:17:18, Serial0
     6.0.0.0/32 is subnetted, 1 subnets
C       6.6.6.6 is directly connected, Loopback9
```

Note that the s0 interface is once again up and up. The BRI D channel is in standby, and the BRI B channels are administratively shut down. The routing table knows how to get to r3 because it has an EIGRP learned route. The floating static was only inserted when needed, hence the name floating static. Feel free to remove the **backup interface** command and try this exercise with just the floating static. Just ping to bring up the ISDN link and check your routing table.

Assuming everything is configured properly, this is a very smooth operation. A console message was generated to let you know that the BRI is out of standby mode. If you do not see this console message, you may need to adjust the **backup delay** enable timer. Another common problem is not having a route to your destination network(s) when using the backup link. However, you had that covered with the floating static route. You might experience issues with the primary coming back up and the backup not going back to standby; check your **backup delay** disable timer. The syntax to enable/disable timers is as follows:

```
backup delay enabletimer disabletimer
```

For example, **backup delay 10 60** says that the backup link will be up 10 seconds after the primary link fails and the backup link will go down 60 seconds after the primary comes back up. These timers may also be the reason for flapping links, but you should always verify physical connectivity in that respect as well. Commands such as **show ip route**, **show dialer**, and **debug dialer** are helpful in troubleshooting DDR issues.

You have gained lots of practical experience with the first two dial-backup solutions: backup interface and floating static routes. Another practical dial-backup solution for EIGRP is dialer watch. Dialer watch monitors a specified route, and when the route is no longer present it initiates the backup link. One of the advantages of dialer watch is the capability to monitor more than one route and to activate the backup when the all the monitored routes are out of the table. The traditional floating static route triggers only if the single specified route goes away.

Remove the **backup interface** statement from r6. Configure dialer watch in its place as in Example 9-50 to watch the 192.168.9.8 and 192.168.9.12 links. Delay disconnecting the backup interface for 20 seconds after the primary link is up again.

Example 9-50 *Dialer Watch*

```
r6(config)#interface s0
r6(config-if)#no backup interface
r6(config-if)#exit

r6(config)#dialer watch?
watch-list
r6(config)#dialer watch-list ?
  <1-30>  Dialer watch group number
r6(config)#dialer watch-list 9 ?
  ip  IP
r6(config)#dialer watch-list 9 ip ?
  A.B.C.D  IP address
r6(config)#dialer watch-list 9 ip 192.168.9.8 255.255.255.252
r6(config)#dialer watch-list 9 ip 192.168.9.12 255.255.255.252
r6(config)#interface bri0
r6(config-if)#shut
r6(config-if)#dialer ?
  callback-secure       Enable callback security
  caller                Specify telephone number to be screened
  enable-timeout        Set length of time an interface stays down before it
                        is available for dialing
  fast-idle             Set idle time before disconnecting line with an
                        unusually high level of contention
  hold-queue            Configure output hold queue
  idle-timeout          Specify idle timeout before disconnecting line
```

Example 9-50 *Dialer Watch (Continued)*

```
   load-threshold        Specify threshold for placing additional calls
   map                   Define multiple dial-on-demand numbers
   pool-member           Specify dialer pool membership
   priority              Specify priority for use in dialer group
   rotary-group          Add to a dialer rotary group
   snapshot              Specify snapshot sequence number for Dialer Profiles
   string                Specify telephone number to be passed to DCE device
   wait-for-carrier-time How long the router will wait for carrier
   watch-disable         Time to wait before bringing down watched route link
   watch-group           Assign interface to dialer-watch-list
r6(config-if)#dialer watch-group 9
r6(config-if)#dialer watch-disable ?
  <1-2147483>  Watch route disable time in seconds
r6(config-if)#dialer watch-disable 20
r6(config-if)#no shut
r6(config-if)#end
r6#copy running-config startup-config
```

Dialer watch is certainly easy to configure and understand. See whether it works by removing the serial cable from r6 as you did with the backup interface method. If you are not successful, it could be a version issue. Cisco recommends that you use IOS 12.1(7) or higher to fix the current nonfeatures (more commonly known as *bugs*) with dialer watch.

These backup methods are very useful but are a lot more scalable with dialer profiles. For more flexibility with DDR, consider deploying dialer profiles. Dialer profiles separate the logical configurations from the physical interfaces. The big advantage is that the configuration for the dialer interface is re-usable on more than one physical interface. The main components include dialer interfaces, dialer pool, and physical interfaces. There are also optional **dialer map-class** statements to supply other configuration parameters to the logical dialer interfaces.

To apply the components to practical application, first you create a virtual interface (**interface dialer 0**). Assign the IP address and encapsulation method just as if it were any physical interface. By assigning the dialer interface to a dialer pool (**dialer pool 1**), the logical interface now has many physical interfaces from which it may draw. As far as the physical interface configuration, make it a dialer pool member (**dialer-pool member 1**) and specify the encapsulation type. This places the physical interface into a dialer pool to point the physical interface to the logical interface configuration.

After the major components have been configured, you can also use these logical interfaces in situations such as in static routes (**ip route 192.168.9.8 255.255.255.252 dialer 0**). You can also **passive-interface** a dialer interface to keep routing protocols from continuously bringing up an ISDN link. For examples and application, go to Cisco.com, login and search for "Configuring ISDN DDR with Dialer Profiles." Another great reference is the Bill Burton book mentioned previously, *Remote Access for Cisco Networks*.

Take some time to clean up your configurations. At a minimum, remove all **access group**, **dialer group**, and **backup interface** commands applied to interfaces. Check your final configurations against the file *isdn ending configs* to ensure you are prepared for the Trouble Tickets. Troubleshoot as necessary to make sure you have a working scenario before moving on to the Trouble Tickets.

Once again it is time for the chapter Trouble Tickets. The plan here is to give you several things to do, to let you make mistakes and fix some things on your own, and to introduce other problems that you should have some experience with as a support person.

Trouble Tickets

Complete the following Trouble Tickets in order. Use the information and tools from this chapter and the previous chapters to analyze, test, and document as you go. Create your own Physical Layer problems or other problems if you need more practice in that area. Modify the Trouble Tickets to make them more applicable to fit your individual needs. Sample solutions are provided after this section.

Trouble Ticket 1

Turn on **debug bri** on r5 to watch the TEI negotiation. Unplug the BRI0 cable to the router and monitor the results. Check the output of **show isdn status**. Plug the cable back in and monitor the results.

Trouble Ticket 2

You are in the midst of troubleshooting your ISDN connection. Look at the following output to decide what the issues are and what to do next:

```
r5#show isdn status
 **** No Global ISDN Switchtype currently defined ****
ISDN BRI0 interface
        dsl 0, interface ISDN Switchtype = none
    Layer 1 Status:
        DEACTIVATED
    Layer 2 Status:
        Layer 2 NOT Activated
    Layer 3 Status:
        0 Active Layer 3 Call(s)
    Activated dsl 0 CCBs = 0
    The Free Channel Mask:  0x80000003
  Total Allocated ISDN CCBs = 0
```

Trouble Ticket 3

Remove the SPID1 configuration from r5. What results do you expect to see with **show isdn status** now? Compare your results to the solution provided. Add the SPID back and verify things before you continue to Trouble Ticket 4.

Trouble Ticket 4

Change the encapsulation to PPP with PAP authentication for the ISDN link between r5 and r6. Troubleshoot as required and verify connectivity to a remote network. Compare your configurations and troubleshooting to the solution provided.

Trouble Ticket 5

Configure and troubleshoot IS-IS over HDLC using the same physical layout that you have now. r1 through r5 should still run EIGRP, but r5 and r6 should run IS-IS. End-to-end connectivity is required.

Trouble Ticket 6

Many times performance is an issue with only one B channel handling the load. Bring up the second B channel if the load on the first one is more than 10 percent. I know that 10 percent is a very low number and 50 to 80 may be more practical. However, with 10 percent there is no need to assert a very heavy load on the line to witness the same results. Feel free to make the number lower than 10 percent for lab purposes.

Trouble Ticket Solutions

These solutions are not always the only way to perform these tasks. Compare your results.

Trouble Ticket 1 Solution

Turn on the **debug bri** command in Example 9-51 to watch the TEI negotiation.

Example 9-51 *TEI Negotiation*

```
r5#debug bri
Basic Rate network interface debugging is on
r5#!!!unplug the cable
Dec 23 06:51:14.784: BRI: write_sid: scp = 0, wrote = E
Dec 23 06:51:14.792: BRI: write_sid: scp = 0, wrote = E
Dec 23 06:51:14.792: BRI: write_sid: scp = 0, wrote = E
Dec 23 06:51:25.404: BRI: write_sid: scp = 0, wrote = 92
Dec 23 06:51:25.404: BRI: write_sid: scp = 90, wrote = 93
Dec 23 06:51:25.408: BRI0: ACTIVATED, state F2, event DI
Dec 23 06:51:25.408: BRI: T4 timer started DEACT timer expired
Dec 23 06:51:26.012: BRI: write_sid: scp = 0, wrote = 92
Dec 23 06:51:26.012: BRI: write_sid: scp = 90, wrote = 93
Dec 23 06:51:26.016: BRI: write_sid: scp = 0, wrote = 1
Dec 23 06:51:26.016: BRI: write_sid: scp = 0, wrote = 0
Dec 23 06:51:26.020:   isdn_Call_disconnect()
Dec 23 06:51:26.020:   isdn_Call_disconnect()
Dec 23 06:51:26.024: BRI: disable channel B1
```

continues

Example 9-51 *TEI Negotiation (Continued)*

```
Dec 23 06:51:26.024: BRI: disable channel B2

r5#show isdn status
Global ISDN Switchtype = basic-ni
ISDN BRI0 interface
        dsl 0, interface ISDN Switchtype = basic-ni
    Layer 1 Status:
        DEACTIVATED
    Layer 2 Status:
        TEI = 118, Ces = 1, SAPI = 0, State = TEI_ASSIGNED
        TEI = 119, Ces = 2, SAPI = 0, State = TEI_ASSIGNED
    Spid Status:
        TEI 118, ces = 1, state = 5(init)
            spid1 configured, spid1 sent, spid1 valid
            Endpoint ID Info: epsf = 0, usid = 2, tid = 1
        TEI 119, ces = 2, state = 5(init)
            spid2 configured, spid2 sent, spid2 valid
            Endpoint ID Info: epsf = 0, usid = 4, tid = 1
...
r5#!!!plug cable back in
Dec 23 06:52:11.132: BRI: write_sid: scp = 0, wrote = 92
Dec 23 06:52:11.132: BRI: write_sid: scp = 80, wrote = 93
Dec 23 06:52:11.132: BRI0: DEACTIVATED, state F1, event LSD
Dec 23 06:52:11.136: BRI: write_sid: scp = 0, wrote = 1B
Dec 23 06:52:11.140: BRI: write_sid: scp = 0, wrote = 20
Dec 23 06:52:11.200: BRI: write_sid: scp = 0, wrote = 92
Dec 23 06:52:11.200: BRI: write_sid: scp = A0, wrote = 93
Dec 23 06:52:11.204: BRI0: DEACTIVATED, state F3, event AP
Dec 23 06:52:11.204: BRI: write_sid: scp = 0, wrote = 3
Dec 23 06:52:11.216: BRI: write_sid: scp = 0, wrote = 92
Dec 23 06:52:11.216: BRI: write_sid: scp = E0, wrote = 93
Dec 23 06:52:11.216: BRI0: PENDING, state F7, event AI
Dec 23 06:52:11.220: BRI: Received activation indication.
Dec 23 06:52:11.232: BRI: write_sid: scp = 0, wrote = E
Dec 23 06:52:11.388: %ISDN-6-LAYER2DOWN: Layer 2 for Interface BRI0, TEI 118
  changed to down
Dec 23 06:52:11.388: %ISDN-6-LAYER2DOWN: Layer 2 for Interface BRI0, TEI 119
  changed to down
Dec 23 06:52:11.392: %ISDN-6-LAYER2DOWN: Layer 2 for Interface BR0, TEI 118 changed
  to down
Dec 23 06:52:11.420: BRI: write_sid: scp = 0, wrote = E
Dec 23 06:52:13.420: BRI: write_sid: scp = 0, wrote = E
Dec 23 06:52:13.532: BRI: write_sid: scp = 0, wrote = E
Dec 23 06:52:13.556: %ISDN-6-LAYER2UP: Layer 2 for Interface BR0, TEI 70 changed
  to up
Dec 23 06:52:13.564: BRI: write_sid: scp = 0, wrote = E
Dec 23 06:52:13.644: BRI: write_sid: scp = 0, wrote = E
Dec 23 06:52:13.664: BRI: write_sid: scp = 0, wrote = E
Dec 23 06:52:13.700: BRI: write_sid: scp = 0, wrote = E
Dec 23 06:52:13.724: %ISDN-6-LAYER2UP: Layer 2 for Interface BR0, TEI 71 changed
  to up
Dec 23 06:52:13.732: BRI: write_sid: scp = 0, wrote = E
Dec 23 06:52:13.816: BRI: write_sid: scp = 0, wrote = E
r5#no debug bri
```

This is a little more output than you want occurring on a regular basis, so keep that in mind to find the best time to issue the command. The output continuously displays **write sid**, which is an internal command written to the interface controller subunit identifier (SID). With the cable unplugged, the activation timer (T3) expired and the status was F2. The timers deactivated, the call terminated, and both B channels went down. Also note the Layer2Down messages. In summary, if there are quick BRI interface changes, always check the Physical Layer, such as the cable or interface. Unless you want to see all the TEI negotiation in the background, however, **show isdn status** is still the best tool for troubleshooting ISDN layers.

Trouble Ticket 2 Solution

The obvious issue is the missing ISDN switch type or mismatch that **show isdn status** reveals quite nicely. When Layer 1 is deactivated, you should immediately suspect a bad cable or the switch type. You might want to take a few minutes and remove your switch type as in the following output and then fix the issues. Glance at the output of **show isdn status** in Example 9-52 before you make any changes. Note any complications.

Example 9-52   **show isdn status** *Command Output*

```
r5#show isdn status
Global ISDN Switchtype = basic-ni
ISDN BRI0 interface
        dsl 0, interface ISDN Switchtype = basic-ni
    Layer 1 Status:
        ACTIVE
    Layer 2 Status:
        TEI = 70, Ces = 1, SAPI = 0, State = MULTIPLE_FRAME_ESTABLISHED
        TEI = 71, Ces = 2, SAPI = 0, State = MULTIPLE_FRAME_ESTABLISHED
    Spid Status:
        TEI 70, ces = 1, state = 5(init)
            spid1 configured, spid1 sent, spid1 valid
            Endpoint ID Info: epsf = 0, usid = 2, tid = 1
        TEI 71, ces = 2, state = 5(init)
            spid2 configured, spid2 sent, spid2 valid
            Endpoint ID Info: epsf = 0, usid = 4, tid = 1
    Layer 3 Status:
        0 Active Layer 3 Call(s)
    Activated dsl 0 CCBs = 0
    The Free Channel Mask:  0x80000003
    Total Allocated ISDN CCBs = 0
```

Now remove both the global interface switch types for r5 in Example 9-53.

Example 9-53   *Removing the ISDN Switch Types*

```
r5(config)#interface bri0
r5(config-if)#no isdn switch-type
Warning: No ISDN switch-type defined.  No calls possible.
r5(config-if)#exit
```

continues

Example 9-53 *Removing the ISDN Switch Types (Continued)*

```
Dec 23 07:09:52.456: %ISDN-6-LAYER2DOWN: Layer 2 for Interface BR0, TEI 70 changed
    to down
Dec 23 07:09:52.460: %ISDN-6-LAYER2DOWN: Layer 2 for Interface BRI0, TEI 70 changed
    to down
Dec 23 07:09:52.628: %ISDN-6-LAYER2DOWN: Layer 2 for Interface BR0, TEI 71 changed
    to down
Dec 23 07:09:52.632: %ISDN-6-LAYER2DOWN: Layer 2 for Interface BRI0, TEI 71 changed
    to down
r5(config)#no isdn switch-type
Warning: No ISDN switch-type defined.  No calls possible, unless switchtype defined
Globally and/or per interface.
This change will take full effect upon reload.
r5(config)#end
r5#copy running-config startup-config
r5#reload
r5#show isdn status
 **** No Global ISDN Switchtype currently defined ****
ISDN BRI0 interface
        dsl 0, interface ISDN Switchtype = none
    Layer 1 Status:
        DEACTIVATED
!!!now define your switch type and test
r5#configure terminal
r5(config)#isdn switch-type basic-ni
Dec 23 07:17:13.171: %ISDN-6-LAYER2UP: Layer 2 for Interface BR0, TEI 72 changed
    to up
Dec 23 07:17:13.339: %ISDN-6-LAYER2UP: Layer 2 for Interface BR0, TEI 73 changed
    to up
r5(config)#end
r5#copy running-config startup-config
```

The main complication to note is that when you completely remove the ISDN switch type the router warns you that no calls are possible. It also does not take effect until you reload the router. Just like other features, however, you may run into slight differences with the version of code.

Trouble Ticket 3 Solution

First remove your SPIDs from r5 as in Example 9-54. Then clear the BRI interface and show the ISDN status.

Example 9-54 *Removing SPIDs*

```
r5#show run interface bri0
interface BRI0
 ip address 192.168.9.22 255.255.255.252
 no ip directed-broadcast
 dialer idle-timeout 55
 dialer map ip 192.168.9.21 name r6 8358661
 dialer map ip 192.168.9.21 name r6 8358663
 isdn switch-type basic-ni
```

Example 9-54 *Removing SPIDs (Continued)*

```
 isdn spid1 0835866201 8358662
 isdn spid2 0835866401 8358664
end

r5#configure terminal
r5(config)#interface bri0
r5(config-if)#no isdn spid1 0835866201 8358662
r5(config-if)#no isdn spid2 0835866401 8358664
r5(config-if)#end
r5#clear interface bri0
Dec 23 07:24:13.107:  isdn_Call_disconnect()
Dec 23 07:24:13.111:  isdn_Call_disconnect()
Dec 23 07:24:13.299: %ISDN-6-LAYER2DOWN: Layer 2 for Interface BRI0, TEI 72 changed
  to down
Dec 23 07:24:13.303: %ISDN-6-LAYER2DOWN: Layer 2 for Interface BRI0, TEI 73 changed
  to down
Dec 23 07:24:13.307: %ISDN-6-LAYER2DOWN: Layer 2 for Interface BR0, TEI 72 changed
  to down
Dec 23 07:24:14.111: %LINEPROTO-5-UPDOWN: Line protocol on Interface BRI0:1,
  changed state to down
Dec 23 07:24:14.115: %LINEPROTO-5-UPDOWN: Line protocol on Interface BRI0:2,
  changed state to down
Dec 23 07:24:15.475: %ISDN-6-LAYER2UP: Layer 2 for Interface BR0, TEI 74 changed
  to up
r5#show isdn status
Global ISDN Switchtype = basic-ni
ISDN BRI0 interface
        dsl 0, interface ISDN Switchtype = basic-ni
    Layer 1 Status:
        ACTIVE
    Layer 2 Status:
        TEI = 74, Ces = 1, SAPI = 0, State = MULTIPLE_FRAME_ESTABLISHED
    Layer 3 Status:
        0 Active Layer 3 Call(s)
    Activated dsl 0 CCBs = 0
    The Free Channel Mask:  0x80000003
    Total Allocated ISDN CCBs = 0
```

Note how I first issued the **show run interface bri0** command so that I had the commands right in front of me that I wanted to delete. I used **clear interface bri0** to clear the interface so that this would take effect. TEI was not assigned as you can see by the SPID status. Now add one SPID back at a time and observe the results in Example 9-55.

Example 9-55 *Configuring SPIDs (First B Channel)*

```
r5#!!!add one SPID back at a time
r5#configure terminal
r5(config)#interface bri0
r5(config-if)#isdn spid1 0835866201 8358662
r5(config-if)#end
r5#clear interface bri0
r5#show isdn status
```

continues

Example 9-55 *Configuring SPIDs (First B Channel) (Continued)*

```
Global ISDN Switchtype = basic-ni
ISDN BRI0 interface
        dsl 0, interface ISDN Switchtype = basic-ni
    Layer 1 Status:
        ACTIVE
    Layer 2 Status:
        TEI = 75, Ces = 1, SAPI = 0, State = MULTIPLE_FRAME_ESTABLISHED
    Spid Status:
        TEI 75, ces = 1, state = 5(init)
            spid1 configured, spid1 sent, spid1 valid
            Endpoint ID Info: epsf = 0, usid = 2, tid = 1
    Layer 3 Status:
        0 Active Layer 3 Call(s)
    Activated dsl 0 CCBs = 0
    The Free Channel Mask:  0x80000003
    Total Allocated ISDN CCBs = 0
```

Focus on the ISDN Layer 2 status. Your key is the MULTIPLE_FRAME_ESTABLISHED state for each B channel. When you removed both SPIDs and added one back, however, you only saw one MULTIPLE_FRAME_ESTABLISHED. Add the other SPID back in Example 9-56 and observe the results.

Example 9-56 *Configuring SPIDs (Second B Channel)*

```
r5#!!!now add the other SPID
r5#configure terminal
r5(config)#interface bri0
r5(config-if)#isdn spid2 0835866401 8358664
r5(config-if)#end
r5#clear interface bri0
r5#show isdn status
Global ISDN Switchtype = basic-ni
ISDN BRI0 interface
        dsl 0, interface ISDN Switchtype = basic-ni
    Layer 1 Status:
        ACTIVE
    Layer 2 Status:
        TEI = 76, Ces = 1, SAPI = 0, State = MULTIPLE_FRAME_ESTABLISHED
        TEI = 77, Ces = 2, SAPI = 0, State = MULTIPLE_FRAME_ESTABLISHED
    Spid Status:
        TEI 76, ces = 1, state = 5(init)
            spid1 configured, spid1 sent, spid1 valid
            Endpoint ID Info: epsf = 0, usid = 2, tid = 1
        TEI 77, ces = 2, state = 5(init)
            spid2 configured, spid2 sent, spid2 valid
            Endpoint ID Info: epsf = 0, usid = 4, tid = 1
```

The moral of this ticket is MULTIPLE_FRAME_ESTABLISHED and valid SPIDs. The tool is **show isdn status**.

Trouble Ticket 4 Solution

Configure PPP encapsulation with PAP authentication on the ISDN bri0 interfaces to produce the configurations in Example 9-57.

Example 9-57 *Configuring PPP Encapsulation and PAP Authentication*

```
r5#show running-config
hostname r5
enable password cisco
username r6 password 0 donna
ip subnet-zero
isdn switch-type basic-ni
...
interface Loopback8
 ip address 5.5.5.5 255.255.255.255
 no ip directed-broadcast
!
interface Serial0
 bandwidth 64
 ip address 192.168.9.14 255.255.255.252
 no ip directed-broadcast
 encapsulation ppp
 no ip mroute-cache
!
interface Serial1
 bandwidth 64
 ip address 192.168.9.18 255.255.255.252
 no ip directed-broadcast
 encapsulation ppp
 ppp authentication chap
!
interface BRI0
 ip address 192.168.9.22 255.255.255.252
 no ip directed-broadcast
 encapsulation ppp
 dialer idle-timeout 55
 dialer map ip 192.168.9.21 name r6 8358661
 dialer map ip 192.168.9.21 name r6 8358663
 dialer-group 1
 isdn switch-type basic-ni
 isdn spid1 0835866201 8358662
 isdn spid2 0835866401 8358664
 ppp authentication pap callin
 ppp pap sent-username paplady password 7 0117090A550A
...
end

r6#show running-config
hostname r6
!
username r5 password 0 donna
username paplady password 0 donna
ip subnet-zero
isdn switch-type basic-ni
```

continues

Example 9-57 *Configuring PPP Encapsulation and PAP Authentication (Continued)*

```
!
interface Loopback9
 ip address 6.6.6.6 255.255.255.255
 no ip directed-broadcast
!
interface Serial0
 bandwidth 64
 ip address 192.168.9.17 255.255.255.252
 no ip directed-broadcast
 encapsulation ppp
 no ip mroute-cache
 clockrate 64000
 ppp authentication chap
!
...
interface BRI0
 ip address 192.168.9.21 255.255.255.252
 no ip directed-broadcast
 encapsulation ppp
 dialer idle-timeout 55
 dialer map ip 192.168.9.22 name r5 8358662
 dialer map ip 192.168.9.22 name r5 8358664
 dialer-group 1
 isdn switch-type basic-ni
 isdn spid1 0835866101 8358661
 isdn spid2 0835866301 8358663
 ppp authentication pap
...
end
```

Turn on the **debug ppp negotiation** command to watch the authentication process in Example 9-58.

Example 9-58 *Debug PPP Negotiation over ISDN*

```
r5#debug ppp negotiation
PPP protocol negotiation debugging is on
r5#ping 192.168.9.21
Type escape sequence to abort.
Sending 5, 100-byte ICMP Echos to 192.168.9.21, timeout is 2 seconds:
.!!!!
Success rate is 80 percent (4/5), round-trip min/avg/max = 36/37/40 ms
Dec 23 08:11:17.355: %LINK-3-UPDOWN: Interface BRI0:1, changed state to up
Dec 23 08:11:17.391: %ISDN-6-CONNECT: Interface BRI0:1 is now connected to 8358661
Dec 23 08:11:17.399: BR0:1 PPP: Treating connection as a callout
Dec 23 08:11:17.399: BR0:1 PPP: Phase is ESTABLISHING, Active Open
Dec 23 08:11:17.403: BR0:1 PPP: No remote authentication for call-out
Dec 23 08:11:17.403: BR0:1 LCP: O CONFREQ [Closed] id 3 len 10
Dec 23 08:11:17.407: BR0:1 LCP:    MagicNumber 0x0042EEFD (0x05060042EEFD)
Dec 23 08:11:17.423: BR0:1 LCP: I CONFREQ [REQsent] id 3 len 14
Dec 23 08:11:17.427: BR0:1 LCP:    AuthProto PAP (0x0304C023)
Dec 23 08:11:17.431: BR0:1 LCP:    MagicNumber 0x172FC497 (0x0506172FC497)
Dec 23 08:11:17.431: BR0:1 LCP: O CONFACK [REQsent] id 3 len 14
Dec 23 08:11:17.435: BR0:1 LCP:    AuthProto PAP (0x0304C023)
```

Example 9-58 *Debug PPP Negotiation over ISDN (Continued)*

```
Dec 23 08:11:17.439: BR0:1 LCP:    MagicNumber 0x172FC497 (0x0506172FC497)
Dec 23 08:11:17.443: BR0:1 LCP: I CONFACK [ACKsent] id 3 len 10
Dec 23 08:11:17.443: BR0:1 LCP:    MagicNumber 0x0042EEFD (0x05060042EEFD)
Dec 23 08:11:17.447: BR0:1 LCP: State is Open
Dec 23 08:11:17.451: BR0:1 PPP: Phase is AUTHENTICATING, by the peer
Dec 23 08:11:17.459: BR0:1 PAP: O AUTH-REQ id 3 len 18 from "paplady"
Dec 23 08:11:17.475: BR0:1 PAP: I AUTH-ACK id 3 len 5
Dec 23 08:11:17.479: BR0:1 PPP: Phase is UP
Dec 23 08:11:17.483: BR0:1 IPCP: O CONFREQ [Closed] id 3 len 10
Dec 23 08:11:17.487: BR0:1 IPCP:    Address 192.168.9.22 (0x0306C0A80916)
Dec 23 08:11:17.491: BR0:1 CDPCP: O CONFREQ [Closed] id 3 len 4
Dec 23 08:11:17.495: BR0:1 IPCP: I CONFREQ [REQsent] id 3 len 10
Dec 23 08:11:17.495: BR0:1 IPCP:    Address 192.168.9.21 (0x0306C0A80915)
Dec 23 08:11:17.499: BR0:1 IPCP: O CONFACK [REQsent] id 3 len 10
Dec 23 08:11:17.503: BR0:1 IPCP:    Address 192.168.9.21 (0x0306C0A80915)
Dec 23 08:11:17.507: BR0:1 CDPCP: I CONFREQ [REQsent] id 3 len 4
Dec 23 08:11:17.511: BR0:1 CDPCP: O CONFACK [REQsent] id 3 len 4
Dec 23 08:11:17.515: BR0:1 IPCP: I CONFACK [ACKsent] id 3 len 10
Dec 23 08:11:17.519: BR0:1 IPCP:    Address 192.168.9.22 (0x0306C0A80916)
Dec 23 08:11:17.519: BR0:1 IPCP: State is Open
Dec 23 08:11:17.523: BR0:1 CDPCP: I CONFACK [ACKsent] id 3 len 4
Dec 23 08:11:17.527: BR0:1 CDPCP: State is Open
Dec 23 08:11:17.535: BR0 IPCP: Install route to 192.168.9.21
Dec 23 08:11:18.479: %LINEPROTO-5-UPDOWN: Line protocol on Interface BRI0:1,
  changed state to up
Dec 23 08:11:23.395: %ISDN-6-CONNECT: Interface BRI0:1 is now connected to 8358661 r6
!!!now for the disconnect
Dec 23 08:12:14.115: %ISDN-6-DISCONNECT: Interface BRI0:1  disconnected from
8358661 r6, call lasted 56 seconds
Dec 23 08:12:14.227:  isdn_Call_disconnect()
Dec 23 08:12:14.227: %LINK-3-UPDOWN: Interface BRI0:1, changed state to down
Dec 23 08:12:14.259: BR0:1 IPCP: State is Closed
Dec 23 08:12:14.263: BR0:1 CDPCP: State is Closed
Dec 23 08:12:14.263: BR0:1 PPP: Phase is TERMINATING
Dec 23 08:12:14.267: BR0:1 LCP: State is Closed
Dec 23 08:12:14.267: BR0:1 PPP: Phase is DOWN
Dec 23 08:12:14.271: BR0 IPCP: Remove route to 192.168.9.21
Dec 23 08:12:15.227: %LINEPROTO-5-UPDOWN: Line protocol on Interface BRI0:1,
  changed state to down
r5#u all
```

PAP is a one-way challenge performed one time. Notice the authentication request and acknowledgment. The commands **debug ppp authentication** and **debug ppp negotiation** are quite helpful in troubleshooting authentication issues. In my test, r5 was the calling router and r6 was the called router. Reference the CCO "Configuring and Troubleshooting PAP" Tech Note at Cisco.com for more detail.

Trouble Ticket 5 Solution

Refer back to the initial chapter scenario in Figure 9-1 for the physical layout of your lab. Use Figure 9-9 as a more detailed view of r5 and r6. Configure IS-IS on r5 and r6 as in Example 9-59. If you want to see more of what is going on you can log the adjacency changes for IS-IS.

Example 9-59 *Configuring IS-IS on r5 and r6*

```
r5#configure terminal
r5(config)#router isis
r5(config-router)#net ?
  XX.XXXX. ... .XXX.XX  Network entity title (NET)
r5(config-router)#net 49.0001.5555.5555.00
r5(config-router)#interface s1
r5(config-if)#ip router isis
Dec 23 08:20:26.927: Se1 PPP: Outbound clns_es packet dropped, OSICP is Closed
  [starting negotiations]
Dec 23 08:20:26.927: Se1 OSICP: State is Listen
Dec 23 08:20:26.931: Se1 OSICP: TIMEout: State Listen
Dec 23 08:20:26.935: Se1 OSICP: O CONFREQ [Listen] id 1 len 4
Dec 23 08:20:26.947: Se1 LCP: I PROTREJ [Open] id 47 len 10 protocol OSICP
  (0x802301010004)
Dec 23 08:20:26.947: Se1 OSICP: State is Closed
Dec 23 08:20:27.083: Se1 PPP: Outbound clns_is packet dropped, OSICP is Closed
  [starting negotiations]
Dec 23 08:20:27.087: Se1 OSICP: State is Closed
Dec 23 08:20:27.091: Se1 OSICP: TIMEout: State Closed
Dec 23 08:20:27.091: Se1 OSICP: State is Listen
r5(config-if)#interface loopback 8
r5(config-if)#ip router isis
r5(config-if)#router eigrp 109
!!!no need to send any eigrp advertisements on s1 or lo8
r5(config-router)#passive-interface s1
r5(config-router)#passive-interface lo8
r5(config-router)#end
r5#copy running-config startup-config

r6#configure terminal
r6(config)#no router eigrp 109
r6(config)#router isis
r6(config-router)#net 49.0001.6666.6666.00
r6(config-router)#interface s0
r6(config-if)#ip router isis
r6(config-if)#interface loopback 9
r6(config-if)#ip router isis
r6(config-if)#end
r6#copy running-config startup-config
```

Now that IS-IS is configured, view your neighbors, the topology, the database, and your interfaces in Example 9-60.

Example 9-60   *Verifying IS-IS*

```
r6#show clns neighbors
System Id       Interface   SNPA              State  Holdtime  Type Protocol
0001.5555.5555 Se0         *PPP*             Up     28        L1L2 IS-IS

r6#show isis ?
  database      IS-IS link state database
  mesh-groups   IS-IS mesh groups
  route         IS-IS level-1 routing table
  spf-log       IS-IS SPF log
  topology      IS-IS paths to Intermediate Systems

r6#show isis topology
IS-IS paths to level-1 routers
System Id       Metric  Next-Hop        Interface    SNPA
0001.5555.5555  10      0001.5555.5555  Se0          *PPP*
0001.6666.6666  --


IS-IS paths to level-2 routers
System Id       Metric  Next-Hop        Interface    SNPA
0001.5555.5555  10      0001.5555.5555  Se0          *PPP*
0001.6666.6666  --

r6#show isis database
IS-IS Level-1 Link State Database
LSPID                 LSP Seq Num  LSP Checksum  LSP Holdtime  ATT/P/OL
0001.5555.5555.00-00  0x00000004   0x58C6        1043          0/0/0
0001.5555.5555.01-00  0x00000001   0x3DF8        934           0/0/0
0001.6666.6666.00-00* 0x00000004   0x8FFE        1053          0/0/0
0001.6666.6666.01-00* 0x00000001   0x0AA3        1057          0/0/0

IS-IS Level-2 Link State Database
LSPID                 LSP Seq Num  LSP Checksum  LSP Holdtime  ATT/P/OL
0001.5555.5555.00-00  0x00000005   0x68C5        1053          0/0/0
0001.6666.6666.00-00* 0x00000005   0x18CC        1058          0/0/0
r6#

r6#show ip interface brief
Interface           IP-Address       OK? Method Status                Protocol
BRI0                192.168.9.21     YES manual up                    up
BRI0:1              unassigned       YES unset  down                  down
BRI0:2              unassigned       YES unset  down                  down
Ethernet0           unassigned       YES unset  administratively down down
Loopback9           6.6.6.6          YES NVRAM  up                    up
Serial0             192.168.9.17     YES NVRAM  up                    up
Serial1             unassigned       YES unset  administratively down down
Serial2             unassigned       YES unset  administratively down down
Serial3             unassigned       YES unset  administratively down down

r6#show clns interface s0
Serial0 is up, line protocol is up
  Checksums enabled, MTU 1500, Encapsulation PPP
  ERPDUs enabled, min. interval 10 msec.
  RDPDUs enabled, min. interval 100 msec., Addr Mask enabled
```

continues

Example 9-60 *Verifying IS-IS (Continued)*

```
Congestion Experienced bit set at 4 packets
CLNS fast switching enabled
CLNS SSE switching disabled
DEC compatibility mode OFF for this interface
Next ESH/ISH in 49 seconds
Routing Protocol: IS-IS
  Circuit Type: level-1-2
  Interface number 0x0, local circuit ID 0x100
  Level-1 Metric: 10, Priority: 64, Circuit ID: 0001.6666.6666.00
  Number of active level-1 adjacencies: 1
  Level-2 Metric: 10, Priority: 64, Circuit ID: 0001.6666.6666.00
  Number of active level-2 adjacencies: 1
  Next IS-IS Hello in 5 seconds
```

If for some reason you do not have neighbors or adjacencies, don't assume it is an IS-IS issue. You have made lots of encapsulation changes in this chapter, and I would expect that to be a major target here. The **debug isis adj-packets** command in Example 9-61 can help you determine such issues.

Example 9-61 **debug isis adj-packets**

```
r5#debug isis adj-packets
IS-IS Adjacency related packets debugging is on
r5#
Jul 20 07:10:34: ISIS-Adj: Sending L2 IIH on Loopback8
Jul 20 07:10:34: ISIS-Adj: Sending L1 IIH on Loopback8
Jul 20 07:10:36: ISIS-Adj: Sending L1 IIH on Loopback8
Jul 20 07:10:37: ISIS-Adj: Sending L2 IIH on Loopback8
Jul 20 07:10:38: ISIS-Adj: Encapsulation failed on serial IIH (Serial1)
...
r5#undebug all
```

Change the encapsulation of r5s1 and r6s0 to HDLC as in Example 9-62. If you did not experience the "encapsulation failed" message in Example 9-61, you certainly can force that to happen here between your configuration of r5 and r6. Display the routing tables on both r5 and r6 to verify reachability information to all subnets in Example 9-63.

Example 9-62 *HDLC Encapsulation*

```
r5(config)#interface s1
r5(config-if)#shut
r5(config-if)#encap hdlc
r5(config-if)#no shut

r6(config)#interface s0
r6(config-if)#shut
r6(config-if)#encap hdlc
r6(config-if)#no shut
```

Example 9-63 *Routing Tables*

```
r5#show ip route
     1.0.0.0/32 is subnetted, 1 subnets
D       1.1.1.1 [90/41152000] via 192.168.9.13, 00:01:33, Serial0
     2.0.0.0/32 is subnetted, 1 subnets
D       2.2.2.2 [90/41152000] via 192.168.9.13, 00:01:33, Serial0
     3.0.0.0/32 is subnetted, 1 subnets
D       3.3.3.3 [90/40640000] via 192.168.9.13, 00:01:33, Serial0
     4.0.0.0/32 is subnetted, 1 subnets
D       4.4.4.4 [90/41152000] via 192.168.9.13, 00:01:33, Serial0
     192.168.9.0/24 is variably subnetted, 10 subnets, 2 masks
D       192.168.9.1/32 [90/41024000] via 192.168.9.13, 00:01:33, Serial0
D       192.168.9.0/30 [90/41024000] via 192.168.9.13, 00:01:33, Serial0
D       192.168.9.4/30 [90/41024000] via 192.168.9.13, 00:01:34, Serial0
D       192.168.9.6/32 [90/41024000] via 192.168.9.13, 00:01:34, Serial0
D       192.168.9.8/30 [90/41024000] via 192.168.9.13, 00:01:34, Serial0
D       192.168.9.10/32 [90/41024000] via 192.168.9.13, 00:01:35, Serial0
C       192.168.9.13/32 is directly connected, Serial0
C       192.168.9.12/30 is directly connected, Serial0
C       192.168.9.16/30 is directly connected, Serial1
C       192.168.9.20/30 is directly connected, BRI0
     5.0.0.0/32 is subnetted, 1 subnets
C       5.5.5.5 is directly connected, Loopback8
     6.0.0.0/32 is subnetted, 1 subnets
i L1    6.6.6.6 [115/20] via 192.168.9.17, Serial1

r6#show ip route
     192.168.9.0/30 is subnetted, 2 subnets
C       192.168.9.16 is directly connected, Serial0
C       192.168.9.20 is directly connected, BRI0
     5.0.0.0/32 is subnetted, 1 subnets
i L1    5.5.5.5 [115/20] via 192.168.9.18, Serial0
     6.0.0.0/32 is subnetted, 1 subnets
C       6.6.6.6 is directly connected, Loopback9
```

Instead of redistributing between IS-IS and EIGRP on r5, have r5 advertise a default route via IS-IS as in Example 9-64. Verify connectivity via the loopbacks.

Example 9-64 *Advertising a Default Route*

```
r5#configure terminal
r5(config)#router isis
r5(config-router)#default-information originate
r5(config-router)#end
r6#show ip route
Gateway of last resort is 192.168.9.18 to network 0.0.0.0
     192.168.9.0/30 is subnetted, 2 subnets
C       192.168.9.16 is directly connected, Serial0
C       192.168.9.20 is directly connected, BRI0
     5.0.0.0/32 is subnetted, 1 subnets
i L1    5.5.5.5 [115/20] via 192.168.9.18, Serial0
     6.0.0.0/32 is subnetted, 1 subnets
C       6.6.6.6 is directly connected, Loopback9
```

continues

Example 9-64 *Advertising a Default Route (Continued)*

```
i*L2 0.0.0.0/0 [115/10] via 192.168.9.18, Serial0

r6#ping 1.1.1.1
Type escape sequence to abort.
Sending 5, 100-byte ICMP Echos to 1.1.1.1, timeout is 2 seconds:
!!!!!
Success rate is 100 percent (5/5), round-trip min/avg/max = 88/88/92 ms
= 4/4/4 ms
r6#copy running-config startup-config
r5#copy running-config startup-config
```

In your earlier testing, you should have noticed that r6 did not have a route to get to the remote networks. With the **default-information originate** command, IS-IS sent a default route to the others regardless of whether a default route existed in the routing table.

Remove the IS-IS **default-information originate** and any other static/default routes in r5 and r6. Configure one-way redistribution from EIGRP into IS-IS on r5 as in Example 9-65.

Example 9-65 *Redistributing EIGRP into IS-IS*

```
r5(config-router)#redistribute eigrp 109 metric ?
  <0-63>  ISIS default metric
r5(config-router)#redistribute eigrp 109 metric 50
r5(config-router)#end

r5#show ip route
Codes: C - connected, S - static, I - IGRP, R - RIP, M - mobile, B - BGP
       D - EIGRP, EX - EIGRP external, O - OSPF, IA - OSPF inter area
       N1 - OSPF NSSA external type 1, N2 - OSPF NSSA external type 2
       E1 - OSPF external type 1, E2 - OSPF external type 2, E - EGP
       i - IS-IS, L1 - IS-IS level-1, L2 - IS-IS level-2, * - candidate default
       U - per-user static route, o - ODR
Gateway of last resort is not set
     1.0.0.0/32 is subnetted, 1 subnets
D       1.1.1.1 [90/41152000] via 192.168.9.13, 00:07:53, Serial0
     2.0.0.0/32 is subnetted, 1 subnets
D       2.2.2.2 [90/41152000] via 192.168.9.13, 00:07:54, Serial0
     3.0.0.0/32 is subnetted, 1 subnets
D       3.3.3.3 [90/40640000] via 192.168.9.13, 00:07:54, Serial0
     4.0.0.0/32 is subnetted, 1 subnets
D       4.4.4.4 [90/41152000] via 192.168.9.13, 00:07:54, Serial0
     192.168.9.0/24 is variably subnetted, 9 subnets, 2 masks
D       192.168.9.1/32 [90/41024000] via 192.168.9.13, 00:07:54, Serial0
D       192.168.9.0/30 [90/41024000] via 192.168.9.13, 00:07:54, Serial0
D       192.168.9.4/30 [90/41024000] via 192.168.9.13, 00:07:54, Serial0
D       192.168.9.6/32 [90/41024000] via 192.168.9.13, 00:07:54, Serial0
D       192.168.9.8/30 [90/41024000] via 192.168.9.13, 00:07:54, Serial0
D       192.168.9.10/32 [90/41024000] via 192.168.9.13, 00:07:55, Serial0
C       192.168.9.12/30 is directly connected, Serial0
C       192.168.9.16/30 is directly connected, Serial1
C       192.168.9.20/30 is directly connected, BRI0
     5.0.0.0/32 is subnetted, 1 subnets
```

Example 9-65 *Redistributing EIGRP into IS-IS (Continued)*

```
C        5.5.5.5 is directly connected, Loopback8
     6.0.0.0/32 is subnetted, 1 subnets
i L1     6.6.6.6 [115/20] via 192.168.9.17, Serial1

r6#show ip route
     1.0.0.0/32 is subnetted, 1 subnets
i L2     1.1.1.1 [115/60] via 192.168.9.18, Serial0
     2.0.0.0/32 is subnetted, 1 subnets
i L2     2.2.2.2 [115/60] via 192.168.9.18, Serial0
     3.0.0.0/32 is subnetted, 1 subnets
i L2     3.3.3.3 [115/60] via 192.168.9.18, Serial0
     4.0.0.0/32 is subnetted, 1 subnets
i L2     4.4.4.4 [115/60] via 192.168.9.18, Serial0
     192.168.9.0/24 is variably subnetted, 9 subnets, 2 masks
i L2     192.168.9.1/32 [115/60] via 192.168.9.18, Serial0
i L2     192.168.9.0/30 [115/60] via 192.168.9.18, Serial0
i L2     192.168.9.4/30 [115/60] via 192.168.9.18, Serial0
i L2     192.168.9.6/32 [115/60] via 192.168.9.18, Serial0
i L2     192.168.9.8/30 [115/60] via 192.168.9.18, Serial0
i L2     192.168.9.10/32 [115/60] via 192.168.9.18, Serial0
S        192.168.9.12/30 [1/0] via 192.168.9.22
C        192.168.9.16/30 is directly connected, Serial0
C        192.168.9.20/30 is directly connected, BRI0
     5.0.0.0/32 is subnetted, 1 subnets
i L1     5.5.5.5 [115/20] via 192.168.9.18, Serial0
     6.0.0.0/32 is subnetted, 1 subnets
C        6.6.6.6 is directly connected, Loopback9
```

The issues with this Trouble Ticket were not so much IS-IS issues but mismatched encapsulation issues and lower-level WAN interface targets. However, the **debug isis adj-packets** command quickly identified encapsulation issues. Like OSPF, in IS-IS if you don't have neighbors that in turn means no routes either. Hence looking for neighbors is a good place to start your IS-IS troubleshooting. Use the following commands to assist with shooting other IS-IS troubles:

- **show ip protocols**
- **show protocols**
- **show ip route**
- **clear isis ***
- **log-adjacency-changes**
- **show clns neighbors** [**detail**] to verify the status of adjacencies
- **show clns interface** to verify the configuration of the interface
- **show isis database** to list the packets in the link-state database
- **show isis topology** to list the system IDs of known IS-IS routers

- **show isis spf-log** to display shortest path first events
- **debug isis adj-packets**
- **debug isis update-packets**
- **debug isis spf-events**

Common IS-IS issues include misconfiguration, mismatched Level 1/Level 2 interfaces, area misconfiguration, and duplicate system IDs. Always check your neighbors and your logs. If you have turned on **log-adjacency-changes** remember to do a **show logging** to see the results. You may need to increase your logging buffer as well.

Now that IS-IS is working and you have full connectivity via the serial link between r5 and r6, modify the ISDN configuration to use CHAP authentication as in Example 9-66.

Example 9-66 *Configuring CHAP Authentication*

```
r5(config)#interface bri0
r5(config-if)#encap ppp
r5(config-if)#ppp authentication chap
r5(config-if)#username r6 pass donna
r5(config)#end

r6(config)#interface bri0
r6(config-if)#encap ppp
r6(config-if)#ppp authentication chap
r6(config-if)#username r5 pass donna
r6(config)#end
r5#copy running-config startup-config
r6#copy running-config startup-config
```

Ping to verify that your new configuration is operational. Shut down or remove the serial cable between r5 and r6 to make sure that the ISDN connection is used. Alternatively, configure the ISDN connection as an automatic backup to the serial link. If you want to look at the CHAP challenge again, issue the **debug ppp authentication** command.

Trouble Ticket 6 Solution

Thus far you have worked with the ISDN D channel for call setup and signaling and the one B channel for data traffic. Example 9-67 illustrates how to automatically bring up the second B channel if the load on the first one is more than 10 percent. To see the effect, repeat the exercise with the load at five percent if you experience problems.

Example 9-67 *Configuring the* **dialer load-threshold**

```
r5#clear dialer
r5#clear counters
r5#configure terminal
r5(config)#interface bri0
r5(config-if)#dialer load-threshold 25 either
```

Example 9-67   *Configuring the* **dialer load-threshold** *(Continued)*

```
r5(config-if)#end
r5#copy running-config startup-config

r6#clear dialer
r6#clear counters
r6(config)#interface bri0
r6(config-if)#dialer load-threshold 25 either
r6(config-if)#end
r6#copy running-config startup-config
```

Now that things are configured, test it as in Example 9-68.

Example 9-68   *Bringing Up the Second B Channel*

```
r5#ping
Protocol [ip]:
Target IP address: 6.6.6.6
Repeat count [5]: 100
Datagram size [100]: 1500
Timeout in seconds [2]:
Extended commands [n]: y
Source address or interface:
Type of service [0]:
Set DF bit in IP header? [no]:
Validate reply data? [no]:
Data pattern [0xABCD]:
Loose, Strict, Record, Timestamp, Verbose[none]: verbose
Loose, Strict, Record, Timestamp, Verbose[V]:
Sweep range of sizes [n]: y
Sweep min size [36]:
Sweep max size [18024]:
Sweep interval [1]:
Type escape sequence to abort.
Sending 1798900, [36..18024]-byte ICMP Echos to 6.6.6.6, timeout is 2 seconds:
Request 0 timed out (size 36)
Reply to request 1 (20 ms) (size 37)
...
Reply to request 26 (28 ms) (size 62)
Dec 24 05:49:46: %LINEPROTO-5-UPDOWN: Line protocol on Interface BRI0:1,
    changed state to up
Reply to request 27 (32 ms) (size 63)
...
Reply to request 127 (52 ms) (size 163)
Reply to request 128 (52 ms) (size 164)
Dec 24 05:49:51: %ISDN-6-CONNECT: Interface BRI0:1 is now connected to
    8358661 r6
...
Reply to request 425 (124 ms) (size 461)
Dec 24 05:50:19: BR0 DDR: rotary group to 8358661 overloaded (27)
Dec 24 05:50:19: BR0 DDR: Attempting to dial 8358661
Dec 24 05:50:20: %LINK-3-UPDOWN: Interface BRI0:2, changed state to up
Dec 24 05:50:20: %ISDN-6-CONNECT: Interface BRI0:1 is now connected to
    8358661 r6
```

continues

Example 9-68 *Bringing Up the Second B Channel (Continued)*

```
...
Dec 24 05:50:20: BR0:2 DDR: dialer protocol up
Dec 24 05:50:21: %LINEPROTO-5-UPDOWN: Line protocol on Interface BRI0:2,
    changed state to up
Reply to request 434 (128 ms) (size 470)
...
Reply to request 440 (128 ms) (size 476)
Dec 24 05:50:21: BR0 DDR: rotary group to 8358661 underloaded (14),
    starting load activity timer
...
Dec 24 05:50:26: %ISDN-6-CONNECT: Interface BRI0:2 is now connected to
    8358661 r6
...
```

As you can see in Example 9-68, extended ping is a powerful traffic generator for getting the threshold to a level to bring up the second B channel. A ping sweep of 36 to 1500 bytes is a good initial test when installing or troubleshooting devices. Over 1500 bytes doesn't buy you a whole lot, because the MTU size is 1500, but small sizes are good for latency issues. Sending 1500 bytes with a data pattern of all 1s or all 0s is a good practical test, too. The Windows default is 32 bytes, but you can use the **ping -l** parameter to adjust this on the PC. On the other hand, the very large ping size buys me a lot in this ticket. The packets are over 1500 bytes, so they must be fragmented, and I want to hurry up and get a load on the line to bring up the needed second B channel.

I stopped the output instead of waiting for it to finish. Verify that the second B channel was truly brought up as in Example 9-69.

Example 9-69 *Verifying the Second B Channel*

```
r5#show dialer
Dial on demand events debugging is on
BRI0 - dialer type = ISDN
Dial String      Successes    Failures    Last called   Last status
8358663          0            0           never         -
8358661          2            0           00:00:44      successful
0 incoming call(s) have been screened.
0 incoming call(s) rejected for callback.

BRI0:1 - dialer type = ISDN
Idle timer (55 secs), Fast idle timer (20 secs)
Wait for carrier (30 secs), Re-enable (15 secs)
Dialer state is data link layer up
Dial reason: ip (s=192.168.9.22, d=6.6.6.6)
Time until disconnect 10 secs
Connected to 8358661 (r6)

BRI0:2 - dialer type = ISDN
Idle timer (55 secs), Fast idle timer (20 secs)
Wait for carrier (30 secs), Re-enable (15 secs)
Dialer state is data link layer up
```

Example 9-69 *Verifying the Second B Channel (Continued)*

```
Dial reason: Dialing on overload
Time until disconnect 51 secs
Connected to 8358661 (r6)

r5#show interface bri0 1 2
BRI0:1 is up, line protocol is up
  Hardware is BRI
  MTU 1500 bytes, BW 64 Kbit, DLY 20000 usec, rely 255/255, load 1/255
  Encapsulation PPP, loopback not set, keepalive set (10 sec)
  Time to interface disconnect:  idle 00:00:02
  LCP Open
  Open: IPCP, CDPCP
  Last input 00:00:03, output 00:00:03, output hang never
  Last clearing of "show interface" counters 00:02:19
  Input queue: 0/75/0 (size/max/drops); Total output drops: 0
  Queueing strategy: weighted fair
  Output queue: 0/1000/64/0 (size/max total/threshold/drops)
     Conversations  0/1/256 (active/max active/max total)
     Reserved Conversations 0/0 (allocated/max allocated)
  5 minute input rate 0 bits/sec, 0 packets/sec
  5 minute output rate 0 bits/sec, 0 packets/sec
     447 packets input, 105642 bytes, 0 no buffer
     Received 0 broadcasts, 0 runts, 0 giants, 0 throttles
     0 input errors, 0 CRC, 0 frame, 0 overrun, 0 ignored, 0 abort
     447 packets output, 105642 bytes, 0 underruns
     0 output errors, 0 collisions, 2 interface resets
     0 output buffer failures, 0 output buffers swapped out
     1 carrier transitions
BRI0:2 is up, line protocol is up
  Hardware is BRI
  MTU 1500 bytes, BW 64 Kbit, DLY 20000 usec, rely 255/255, load 27/255
  Encapsulation PPP, loopback not set, keepalive set (10 sec)
  Time to interface disconnect:  idle 00:00:41
  LCP Open
  Open: IPCP, CDPCP
  Last input 00:00:05, output 00:00:05, output hang never
Dec 24 05:51:15: BR0:1 DDR: idle timeout
Dec 24 05:51:15: BR0:1 DDR: disconnecting call
Dec 24 05:51:15: %ISDN-6-CONNECT: Interface BRI0:2 is now connected to 8358661 r6
Dec 24 05:51:15: %ISDN-6-DISCONNECT: Interface BRI0:1  disconnected from 8358661
r6, call lasted 89 seconds
r5#copy running-config startup-config
```

Both B channels were in fact up but are disconnecting due to the idle timeout.

Because the load went up to about 27, the second B channel came up. 255/255 is 100-percent load. For anything less than 255, you can divide the numerator by the denominator to get the load as a percentage. You set the dialer threshold to 25, which is about .10 times 255 or 25/255.

Compare your final saved fixed configurations to the *chapter 9 ending configs* file. Update your documentation and fix anything that is broken. You have completed the chapter Trouble Tickets when you feel comfortable with the tasks assigned and the various scenarios throughout the chapter. Review or experiment in the areas where you need more help. Understanding and troubleshooting in a lab is certainly the basis for configuring devices in the real world. Check your understanding with the chapter review questions.

Review Questions

Use this chapter and your practical troubleshooting knowledge and skills to answer the following questions. The answers are located in Appendix A, "Answers to Review Questions."

1 Why do interface resets occur?

2 True or false: The ISDN signaling protocol is LAPB for the D channel.

3 The modem control leads on **show interfaces s0** are quite helpful for troubleshooting. DCD keeps changing state. What else on the interface statistics would you expect to be increasing? Look at Example 9-13 if you need to see a display of the modem control leads.

4 Your router has a native ISDN BRI port. Is this device a TE1 or TE2?

5 What is the difference between Multilink PPP and dial backup?

6 Use the first HDLC scenario as a guide. Can you spot the issue in the following output:

```
r3#
03:03:49: IP-EIGRP: Neighbor 192.168.9.18 not on common subnet for Serial0/3
03:04:03: IP-EIGRP: Neighbor 192.168.9.18 not on common subnet for Serial0/3
03:04:18: IP-EIGRP: Neighbor 192.168.9.18 not on common subnet for Serial0/3
03:04:32: IP-EIGRP: Neighbor 192.168.9.18 not on common subnet for Serial0/3

r5#show ip interface brief
Interface          IP-Address      OK? Method Status                Protocol
BRI0               unassigned      YES unset  administratively down down
BRI0:1             unassigned      YES unset  administratively down down
BRI0:2             unassigned      YES unset  administratively down down
Ethernet0          unassigned      YES unset  administratively down down
Loopback8          5.5.5.5         YES manual up                    up
Serial0            192.168.9.18    YES manual up                    up
Serial0.101        172.16.8.6      YES manual deleted               down
Serial1            unassigned      YES unset  administratively down down
r5#
03:04:01: IP-EIGRP: Neighbor 192.168.9.13 not on common subnet for Serial0
03:04:15: IP-EIGRP: Neighbor 192.168.9.13 not on common subnet for Serial0
03:04:29: IP-EIGRP: Neighbor 192.168.9.13 not on common subnet for Serial0
```

7 Throughout the chapter you experienced multiple carrier transitions. What command is very helpful in helping you figure out the issues with this problem?

8   You have a high-speed Ethernet that is sending packets faster than the ISDN link can keep up with. How can you improve performance?

9   When are floating static routes appropriate?

10   When using the **backup interface** method to back up a circuit, do you place the **backup interface** command under the primary or secondary interface?

11   You are controlling the backup interface using the **backup delay 10 60** command. What do the numbers 10 and 60 correspond to?

12   Your ISDN phone bill is a lot more than you expected, but you have interesting traffic set appropriately with an access list. It seems that when you finish transferring your files over the ISDN link, the link doesn't go down. It stays up until you manually bring it down. What did you forget?

13   Including synchronization and framing, what is the total bandwidth for ISDN BRI?

14   Can you use one 64 kbps B channel to handle backup for multiple T1s?

Summary

Take a divide-and-conquer layered approach to supporting the WAN. Determine whether the trouble is with you or the service provider. After verifying that interfaces and controllers are functioning properly, you can move on to Layer 3 and above. Extended ping and traceroute are wonderful tools to assist you with both connectivity and performance issues. Service time stamps are invaluable for understanding debug and log output. Clearing interface counters and statistics are important to start monitoring the data-link activity for a certain time period.

This chapter covered HDLC, PPP, and ISDN WAN technologies. PPP has several advantages over HDLC but a little more troubleshooting to go with it. Authentication is the key target. In supporting ISDN, **show isdn status** is by far the most informative command. If there are issues, however, you may need to analyze the switch type, the dialer, q921, q931, and authentication issues. Refer to Figure 9-13 for a pictorial review of troubleshooting the WAN.

Figure 9-13 *WAN Troubleshooting Review*

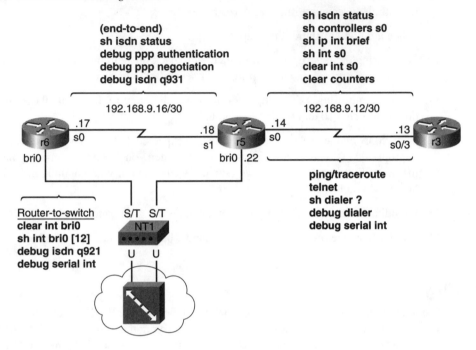

This completes the individual topic troubleshooting chapters. The next chapter is meant as a comprehensive review. It is full of troubles for you to dissect. Leverage off of your skills, methods, experiences, and what you have learned throughout this book to complete the hands-on Trouble Tickets in Chapter 10, "Trouble Tickets: The Sum of All Fears."

Comprehensive Troubleshooting Exercises

CHAPTER 10

Trouble Tickets:
The Sum of All Fears

This final chapter offers you a practical comprehensive troubleshooting review. Part I of this book covers protocol characteristics, methodology, and tools. Part II focuses on supporting the IP and IPX protocols as well as some other interesting topics such as upgrades and password recovery. The focus of Part III is Ethernet, switching, and VLANs. Part IV is about supporting the WAN. I take a slightly different approach in this chapter. In this part, I present you with a new physical scenario and several Trouble Tickets. You first need to discover the topology and get a good baseline. Then you work through the Trouble Tickets *on your own one-by-one* to spot and fix any issues.

This chapter covers the following topics:

- Scenario: Shooting Trouble Review

- Trouble Ticket 1 Discovery Lab

- Trouble Ticket 2 Documentation Lab

- Trouble Ticket 3 OSPF Lab

- Trouble Ticket 4 RIP/OSPF/EIGRP Redistribution Lab

- Trouble Ticket 5 Frame Relay/ISDN Backup Lab

- Trouble Ticket 6 VLAN and Spanning Tree Lab

Supporting Website Files

You can find files and links to utilities that support this book on the Cisco Press website at www.ciscopress.com/1587200570. Even if you do not have a lab, you can take advantage of the supporting configuration files including the logs to understand device input and output. The files are listed throughout the chapters in italics.

In order to be able to read and work with some of the supporting files offered at www.ciscopress.com/1587200570, you may want to download some of the programs listed in Table I-1 in the Introduction.

Scenario: Shooting Trouble Review

In addition to the terminal server, six routers, three switches, and three PCs you have been working with throughout the book, you need another router with a minimum of two serial interfaces to complete the Trouble Tickets in this chapter. It doesn't need to do much more than act as a Frame Relay switch for two other routers. I also have a Microsoft box, a Novell box, and an 804 router on the backbone. The 804 is primarily used as a ping target and could be used as a TFTP server or a route generator. However, it is not required because you can certainly use your Microsoft box for this purpose. The Novell server is optional as well.

As always, there is not just one right or wrong way to accomplish the tasks presented. The ability to obtain the end result using good practices is extremely important in any real-world network. At a minimum you should "spot the issues" that are printed in the Trouble Ticket solutions sections following each Trouble Ticket. Think methodically. Put your tools to practice. Use the knowledge gained from the previous chapters, your own troubleshooting experiences, and a step-by-step approach to quickly get a grip on the troubles before they get a grip on you. Compare your work against the supporting files. The files *required* for this chapter include the following:

- *tt1 layer 2 configuration*
- *tt1 layer 3 configuration*
- *tt1 layer 3 testing*
- *tt1 final configs*
- *tt2 testing*
- *tt2 syslog*
- *tt2 copying configs to the tftp server*
- *tt3 troubled configs*
- *tt3 testing*
- *tt3 fixed configs*
- *tt4 troubled configs*
- *tt4 fixed configs*
- *tt4 copying configs to the tftp server*
- *tt5 troubled configs*
- *tt5 fixed configs*
- *tt6 troubled configs*
- *tt6 new hosts file*
- *tt6 fixed configs*

NOTE	If you paste in my files instead of configuring everything yourself, remember to modify my supporting troubled files for your lab environment. For example, the first serial interface on my duck router is s0, whereas yours may be s0/0. My backbone is connected via e0; yours may be fa0/0.

Trouble Ticket 1 Discovery Lab

Ideally, you should use Figure 10-1 as a physical starting point, discover the network on your own, and update your drawing accordingly. To make this a true discovery lab, you should have someone else do the cabling and load the preconfigured files for you. They are in the file called *tt1 layer 2 configuration*. Alternatively, erase all the configurations yourself, power the devices down, and wire the new scenario as in Figure 10-2. Then you can paste in the configurations from the file provided (or configure, if you prefer).

Figure 10-1   *Chapter 10 Discovery*

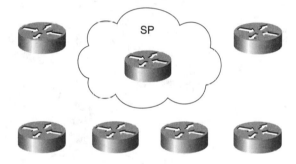

Have the person setting up the lab use Figure 10-2 as a guide to build and configure Layer 1 and Layer 2. If you are discovering everything for yourself, I expect you to draw a diagram similar to Figure 10-2 rather than just look at mine.

NOTE	Give yourself the benefit of breaking and fixing things. Do not just paste in my *troubled files*, and then turn around and paste in my *fixed files*. Instead, use my *troubled files* to break things. Use the methodology, tools, and resources covered throughout the book and in your practical experiences to "spot the issues" and then fix them.

After you have discovered (or configured) and tested the lower layers, use Figure 10-3 to configure the IP addressing, hosts files, and routing protocols. Alternatively, paste the configurations in from the *tt1 layer 3 configuration* file. In this Trouble Ticket, configure anything that is missing on your devices to ensure end-to-end connectivity as in Figure 10-2. Don't forget to configure your hosts.

Figure 10-2 *Lower-Layer Discovery/Configuration*

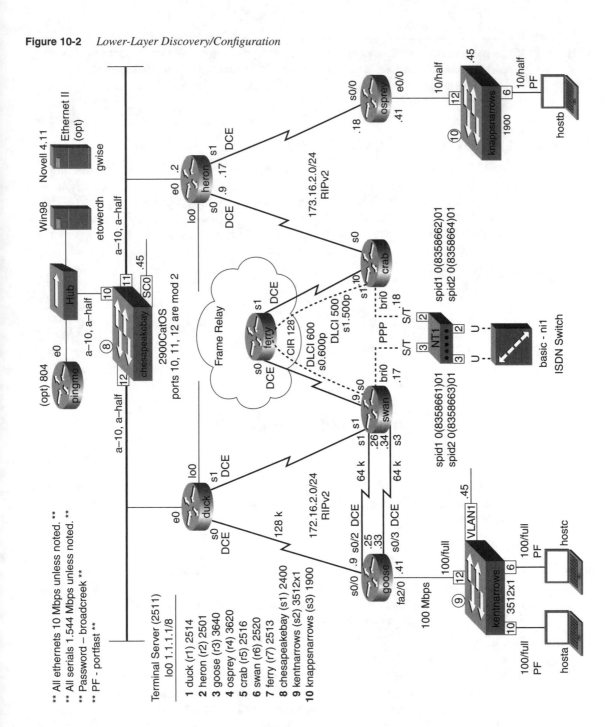

Figure 10-3 *Upper-Layer Discovery/Configuration*

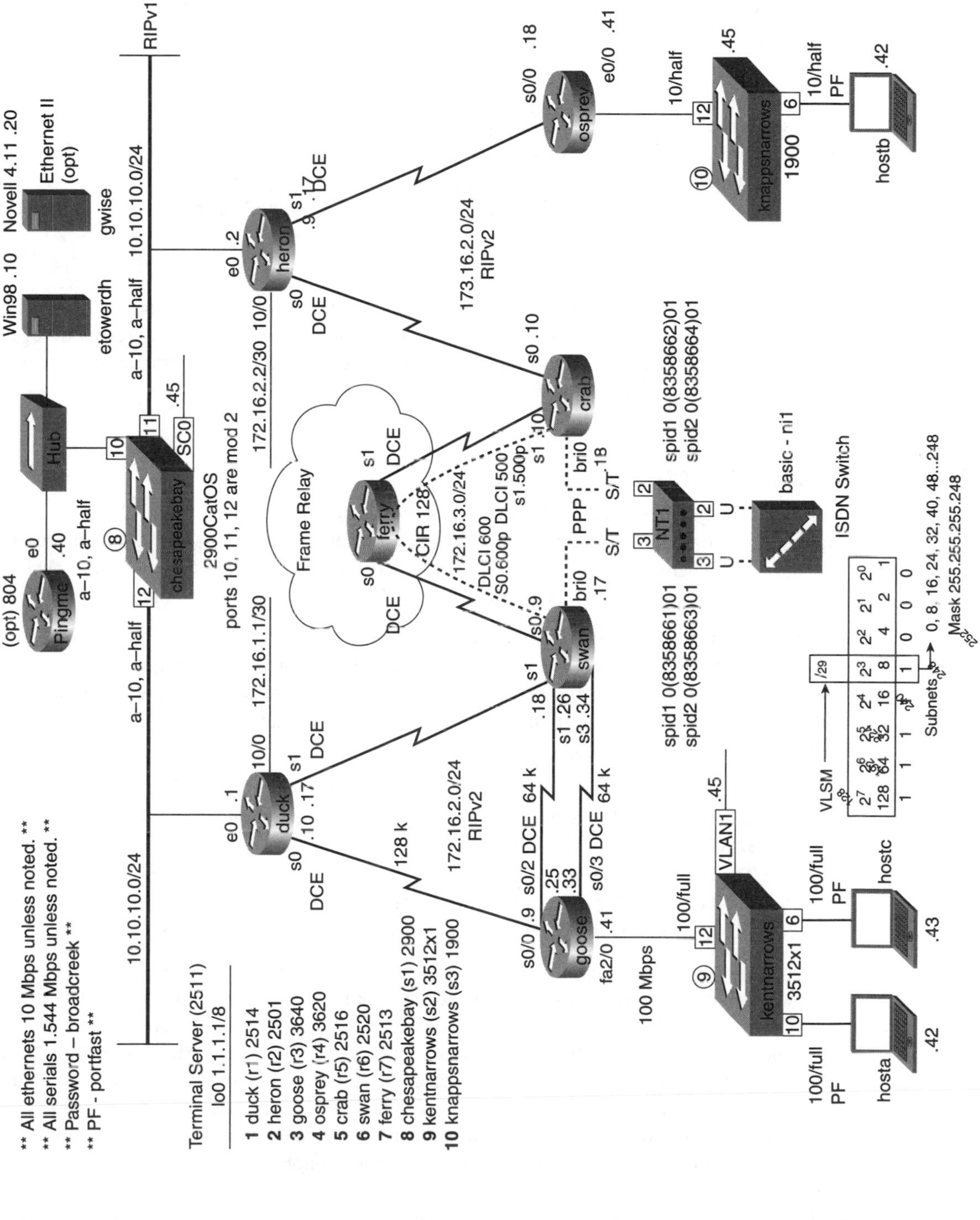

Test and fix any minor issues and move directly into the documentation lab. Compare your final configurations to the output in the "Trouble Ticket 10-1 Discovery Lab Solution" section and the *tt1 layer 3 testing* and *tt1 final configs* files.

NOTE   More so than the other chapters, you *must* thoroughly review the figures, examples, and configuration files provided to gain practical experience from this chapter. Even if you don't have the equipment handy, you can walk through the chapter and supporting documentation as if you did. If you think you are *just* at that comfortable level, do the labs anyway! You may still learn something.

Make sure you have a working configuration and take time to update your documents and tables to assist with troubleshooting later. No access lists or filters are in place at the present time, and all passwords that are configured should be broadcreek. Simple ping and trace tests via your hosts tables are sufficient at this point.

Trouble Ticket 1 Discovery Lab Solution

At a minimum you should have discovered the topology like that in Figure 10-2 and 10-3. In a practical environment, you should use a program that automatically discovers the devices and keeps track of changes for you, too. I am thinking of network management programs such as CiscoWorks, HP OpenView, Cisco Info Center (CIC), Visio 2000, and so on.

The device names are not just r1, r2, r3, and so on. Instead, I wanted to remind you to take the naming of devices a little more seriously in a practical environment. Having a plan for naming and addressing is important and makes it easier for you to spot things that are out of the ordinary. After working through the solution, use Trouble Ticket 2 as a reminder that you need to document your new topology.

Remember that the troubleshooting targets at the lower layers are interfaces and controllers. I assume that in your baseline you verified and documented items such as model number, serial number, RAM/Flash memory, IOS version, configuration register settings, bandwidth/speed, clocking, encapsulation, duplex, descriptions, addresses, passwords, spanning-tree portfast, VLANs, and the like. Other things that are valuable to document in practical application include the detailed location of equipment down to the wiring closet, rack, and position.

The shaded output in Examples 10-1 through 10-3 are the types of things you should have discovered and recorded on your drawing or table for the Layer 2 baseline. To support Cisco you need to adjust the commands slightly according to the CatOS or IOS command sets. Example 10-1 illustrates the types of things to look for on your routers. Much of my output has been omitted from the printed text but is included in the sample files. However, you should include everything in your baseline. For the ISDN and Frame Relay devices, refer back to those chapters for information about commands such as **show frame map**, **show frame lmi**, **show isdn status**, and so on. I concentrate more on them in Trouble Ticket 5.

Example 10-1   *Building a Layer 2 Baseline for the Routers*

```
duck>show version
Cisco Internetwork Operating System Software
IOS (tm) 2500 Software (C2500-JS-L), Version 12.0(21a), RELEASE SOFTWARE (fc1)
Copyright  1986-2002 by cisco Systems, Inc.
Compiled Sat 02-Feb-02 02:08 by nmasa
Image text-base: 0x030520E0, data-base: 0x00001000
ROM: System Bootstrap, Version 5.2(8a), RELEASE SOFTWARE
BOOTFLASH: 3000 Bootstrap Software (IGS-RXBOOT), Version 10.2(8a), RELEASE
SOFTWARE (fc1)
duck uptime is 7 hours, 34 minutes
System restarted by power-on
System image file is "flash:c2500-js-l.120-21a.bin"
cisco 2500 (68030) processor (revision L) with 14336K/2048K bytes of memory.
Processor board ID 03074719, with hardware revision 00000000
Bridging software.
X.25 software, Version 3.0.0.
SuperLAT software (copyright 1990 by Meridian Technology Corp).
TN3270 Emulation software.
2 Ethernet/IEEE 802.3 interface(s)
2 Serial network interface(s)
32K bytes of non-volatile configuration memory.
16384K bytes of processor board System flash (Read ONLY)
Configuration register is 0x2102

duck>show flash
System flash directory:
File  Length   Name/status
  1   10253564  c2500-js-l.120-21a.bin
[10253628 bytes used, 6523588 available, 16777216 total]
16384K bytes of processor board System flash (Read ONLY)

duck>show interfaces
Ethernet0 is up, line protocol is up
  Hardware is Lance, address is 0000.0c8d.6705 (bia 0000.0c8d.6705)
  Description: duck to chesapeakebay backbone
  MTU 1500 bytes, BW 10000 Kbit, DLY 1000 usec, rely 255/255, load 1/255
  Encapsulation ARPA, loopback not set, keepalive set (10 sec)
  ARP type: ARPA, ARP Timeout 04:00:00
  Last input 00:00:13, output 00:00:03, output hang never
  Last clearing of "show interface" counters never
Queueing strategy: fifo
  Output queue 0/40, 0 drops; input queue 0/75, 0 drops
  5 minute input rate 0 bits/sec, 0 packets/sec
  5 minute output rate 0 bits/sec, 0 packets/sec
     1060 packets input, 119692 bytes, 0 no buffer
     Received 1060 broadcasts, 0 runts, 0 giants, 0 throttles
     0 input errors, 0 CRC, 0 frame, 0 overrun, 0 ignored, 0 abort
     0 input packets with dribble condition detected
     2098 packets output, 194947 bytes, 0 underruns
     0 output errors, 0 collisions, 15 interface resets
     0 babbles, 0 late collision, 0 deferred
     0 lost carrier, 0 no carrier
     0 output buffer failures, 0 output buffers swapped out
```

continues

Example 10-1 *Building a Layer 2 Baseline for the Routers (Continued)*

```
Ethernet1 is administratively down, line protocol is down
  Hardware is Lance, address is 0000.0c8d.6706 (bia 0000.0c8d.6706)
  MTU 1500 bytes, BW 10000 Kbit, DLY 1000 usec, rely 252/255, load 1/255
  Encapsulation ARPA, loopback not set, keepalive set (10 sec)
  ARP type: ARPA, ARP Timeout 04:00:00
...
Serial0 is up, line protocol is up
  Hardware is HD64570
  Description: duck to goose
  MTU 1500 bytes, BW 1544 Kbit, DLY 20000 usec, rely 255/255, load 1/255
  Encapsulation HDLC, loopback not set, keepalive set (10 sec)
  Last input 00:00:05, output 00:00:05, output hang never
  Last clearing of "show interface" counters never
...
Serial1 is up, line protocol is up
  Hardware is HD64570
  Description: duck to swan
  MTU 1500 bytes, BW 1544 Kbit, DLY 20000 usec, rely 255/255, load 1/255
  Encapsulation HDLC, loopback not set, keepalive set (10 sec)
  Last input 00:00:02, output 00:00:09, output hang never
  Last clearing of "show interface" counters never
...
!!!check your interfaces if they do not match the output
!!!problems mean physical or data link issues at this point
!!!fix any controller or interface issues on all devices before you continue
duck>enable
Password:
duck#clear counters
Clear "show interface" counters on all interfaces [confirm]
duck#show ip interface brief
Interface             IP-Address      OK? Method Status                Protocol
Ethernet0             unassigned      YES unset  up                    up
Ethernet1             unassigned      YES unset  administratively down down
Serial0               unassigned      YES unset  up                    up
Serial1               unassigned      YES unset  up                    up
duck#show cdp neighbor detail
-------------------------
Device ID: swan
Entry address(es):
Platform: cisco 2520,  Capabilities: Router
Interface: Serial1,  Port ID (outgoing port): Serial1
Holdtime : 173 sec
Version :
Cisco Internetwork Operating System Software
IOS (tm) 2500 Software (C2500-JS-L), Version 12.0(9), RELEASE SOFTWARE (fc1)
Copyright  1986-2000 by cisco Systems, Inc.
Compiled Mon 24-Jan-00 22:30 by bettyl
-------------------------
Device ID: 005352782(chesapeakebay)
Entry address(es):
  IP address: 10.10.10.45
Platform: WS-C2900,  Capabilities: Trans-Bridge Switch
Interface: Ethernet0,  Port ID (outgoing port): 2/12
```

Example 10-1   *Building a Layer 2 Baseline for the Routers (Continued)*

```
Holdtime : 170 sec
Version :
WS-C2900 Software, Version McpSW: 4.4(1) NmpSW: 4.4(1)
Copyright  1995-1999 by Cisco Systems
------------------------
Device ID: goose
Entry address(es):
Platform: cisco 3640,  Capabilities: Router
Interface: Serial0,  Port ID (outgoing port): Serial0/0
Holdtime : 176 sec
Version :
Cisco Internetwork Operating System Software
IOS (tm) 3600 Software (C3640-JS-M), Version 12.0(13), RELEASE SOFTWARE (fc1)
Copyright  1986-2000 by cisco Systems, Inc.
Compiled Tue 05-Sep-00 21:39 by linda

duck#show cdp neighbors
Capability Codes: R - Router, T - Trans Bridge, B - Source Route Bridge
                  S - Switch, H - Host, I - IGMP, r - Repeater
Device ID        Local Intrfce     Holdtme    Capability  Platform  Port ID
swan                    Ser 1      165           R         2520      Ser 1
005352782(chesapeakcEth 0          163           T S       WS-C2900  2/12
goose                   Ser 0      171           R         3640      Ser 0/0
```

If your output differs from that in Example 10-1, go back and examine the Physical and Data Link Layers. For example, check link lights, controllers and clock, speed and duplex, encapsulation mismatches, interface issues, cables, and so on. Example 10-2 illustrates what to look for on your CatOS-based switch to assist with building your Layer 1 and Layer 2 baseline.

Example 10-2   *Building a Layer 2 Baseline for the CatOS Switches*

```
chesapeakebay>show version
WS-C2900 Software, Version McpSW: 4.4(1) NmpSW: 4.4(1)
Copyright  1995-1999 by Cisco Systems
NMP S/W compiled on Jan  6 1999, 18:05:22
MCP S/W compiled on Jan 06 1999, 17:50:33
System Bootstrap Version: 2.2(2)
Hardware Version: 2.3  Model: WS-C2900  Serial #: 005352782
Mod Port Model        Serial #    Versions
--- ---- ---------    ---------   -------------------------------------------
1    2   WS-X2900     005352782 Hw : 2.3
                                Fw : 2.2(2)
                                Fw1: 2.2(1)
                                Sw : 4.4(1)
2   12   WS-X2901     008675483 Hw : 1.4
                                Fw : 3.1(1)
                                Sw : 4.4(1)
        DRAM                   FLASH                   NVRAM
Module Total   Used    Free    Total   Used    Free    Total Used  Free
------ ------- ------- ------- ------- ------- ------- ----- ----- -----
1       20480K  9972K  10508K   4096K   3584K   512K    256K  112K  144K
Uptime is 0 day, 7 hours, 37 minutes

chesapeakebay>show interface
```

continues

Example 10-2 *Building a Layer 2 Baseline for the CatOS Switches (Continued)*

```
sl0: flags=51<UP,POINTOPOINT,RUNNING>
        slip 0.0.0.0 dest 0.0.0.0
sc0: flags=63<UP,BROADCAST,RUNNING>
        vlan 1 inet 10.10.10.45 netmask 255.255.255.0 broadcast 10.10.10.255

chesapeakebay>show port
Port  Name                 Status      Vlan    Level  Duplex Speed Type
----- -------------------- ----------- ------- ------ ------ ----- ------------
 1/1                       notconnect 1        normal half    100 100BaseTX
 1/2                       notconnect 1        normal half    100 100BaseTX
 2/1                       notconnect 1        normal auto   auto 10/100BaseTX
...
 2/10                      connected  1        normal a-half a-10 10/100BaseTX
 2/11 to heron             connected  1        normal a-half a-10 10/100BaseTX
 2/12 to duck              connected  1        normal a-half a-10 10/100BaseTX
...
chesapeakebay> enable
Enter password:
chesapeakebay> (enable)set port name 2/10 to hub
Port 2/10 name set.
chesapeakebay> (enable)show port capabilities
Model                      WS-X2900
Port                       1/1
Type                       100BaseTX
Speed                      100
Duplex                     half,full
Trunk encap type           ISL
Trunk mode                 on,off,desirable,auto,nonegotiate
Channel                    no
Broadcast suppression      no
Flow control               no
Security                   yes
Membership                 static,dynamic
Fast start                 yes
Rewrite                    no
...
----------------------------------------------------------------
Model                      WS-X2901
Port                       2/10
Type                       10/100BaseTX
Speed                      auto,10,100
Duplex                     half,full
Trunk encap type           ISL
Trunk mode                 on,off,desirable,auto,nonegotiate
Channel                    no
Broadcast suppression      pps(0-150000)
Flow control               no
Security                   yes
Membership                 static,dynamic
Fast start                 yes
Rewrite                    no
----------------------------------------------------------------
chesapeakebay> (enable)show cdp neighbor detail
Device-ID: 804
Device Addresses:
```

Example 10-2   *Building a Layer 2 Baseline for the CatOS Switches (Continued)*

```
   IP Address: 10.10.10.40
Holdtime: 152 sec
Capabilities: ROUTER
Version:
  Cisco Internetwork Operating System Software
  IOS (tm) C800 Software (C800-G3-MW), Version 12.0(1)XB1,
     RELEASE SOFTWARE (fc1)
  TAC:Home:SW:IOS:Specials for info
  Copyright  1986-1998 by cisco Systems, Inc.
Platform: Cisco C804
Port-ID (Port on Device): Ethernet0
Port (Our Port): 2/10

Device-ID: duck
Device Addresses:
Holdtime: 153 sec
Capabilities: ROUTER
Version:
  Cisco Internetwork Operating System Software
  IOS (tm) 2500 Software (C2500-JS-L), Version 12.0(21a), RELEASE SOFTWARE (fc1)
  Copyright  1986-2002 by cisco Systems, Inc.
Platform: cisco 2500
Port-ID (Port on Device): Ethernet0
Port (Our Port): 2/12

Device-ID: heron
Device Addresses:
Holdtime: 124 sec
Capabilities: ROUTER
Version:
  Cisco Internetwork Operating System Software
  IOS (tm) 2500 Software (C2500-JS-L), Version 12.0(21a), RELEASE SOFTWARE (fc1)
  Copyright  1986-2002 by cisco Systems, Inc.
Platform: cisco 2500
Port-ID (Port on Device): Ethernet0
Port (Our Port): 2/11

chesapeakebay> (enable)show cdp neighbors
Capability Codes: R - Router, T - Trans Bridge, B - Source Route Bridge
                  S - Switch, H - Host, I - IGMP, r - Repeater
Port      Device-ID                  Port-ID            Platform           Capability
--------  -----------------------    ----------------   ----------------   ----------
 2/10     804                        Ethernet0          Cisco C804             R
 2/11     duck                       Ethernet0          cisco 2500             R
 2/12     heron                      Ethernet0          cisco 2500             R

chesapeakebay> (enable)show cam dynamic
* = Static Entry. + = Permanent Entry. # = System Entry. R = Router Entry.
    X = Port Security Entry
VLAN  Dest MAC/Route Des  Destination Ports or VCs / [Protocol Type]
----  ------------------  -------------------------------------------------------
1       00-00-0c-38-a0-5d   2/11 [ALL]
1       00-00-0c-8d-67-05   2/12 [ALL]
1       00-50-73-07-d0-76   2/10 [ALL]
Total Matching CAM Entries Displayed = 3
```

NOTE   Some differences exist between the CatOS and Cisco IOS. Refer back to Chapter 6, "Shooting Trouble with CatOS and IOS," and Chapter 7, "Shooting Trouble with VLANs on Routers and Switches," for a quick review.

Example 10-2 illustrates some commands to get you started on baselining the 2900 CatOS-based switch. Example 10-3 does the same for kentnarrows, your IOS-based switch. However, the IOS commands are very similar to the router, so most of them are not repeated here. Interfaces, modules, trunks, ports, Address Resolution Protocol (ARP) tables, switch tables, caching, memory and CPU statistics, Hot Standby Router Protocol (HSRP), utilization, VLANs, and so on are good data to capture for future comparison.

Example 10-3   *Building a Layer 2 Baseline for the IOS Switches*

```
kentnarrows#show mac-address-table
Dynamic Address Count:                    1
Secure Address (User-defined) Count:      0
Static Address (User-defined) Count:      0
System Self Address Count:                37
Total MAC addresses:                      38
Maximum MAC addresses:                    8192
Non-static Address Table:
Destination Address  Address Type  VLAN  Destination Port
------------------   -----------   ----  ------------------
00b0.6481.e300       Dynamic       1     FastEthernet0/12
```

NOTE   Improvements are always being made. If you are used to typing **show mac** for short, be aware that this doesn't work in the most current Catalyst IOS. **show mac** is now treated as an incomplete command. One must enter **show mac address** (note, no hyphen).

The main point I wanted to make with reiterating the output of commands you should already be familiar with is for you not to rely only on **show running-config** or **show config**. Go back and review all the checklists and ending reviews in each and every chapter for assistance with the individual commands.

The **show running-config** and **show startup-config/show config** commands are great to get a handle on how things are configured and what you need to type in for configuration purposes. They are also quite helpful to give you a starting point for copying and pasting to speed up configuring multiple devices. However, the object of mastering the troubleshooting game is that you really need to know how to interpret the output of various other commands, not just **show running-config**.

Paste in the configurations from *tt1 layer 3 configuration* or configure the Layer 3 data as in Figure 10-3. My Layer 3 and above baseline starts in Example 10-4. Verify yours now.

Example 10-4   *Building a Layer 3 and Above Baseline from the duck Router*

```
duck#ping goose
Sending 5, 100-byte ICMP Echos to 172.16.1.9, timeout is 2 seconds:
!!!!!
Success rate is 100 percent (5/5), round-trip min/avg/max = 16/16/16 ms
duck#ping swan
Sending 5, 100-byte ICMP Echos to 172.16.3.9, timeout is 2 seconds:
!!!!!
Success rate is 100 percent (5/5), round-trip min/avg/max = 4/5/8 ms
duck#ping kentnarrows
Sending 5, 100-byte ICMP Echos to 172.16.1.45, timeout is 2 seconds:
!!!!!
Success rate is 100 percent (5/5), round-trip min/avg/max = 16/18/20 ms
duck#ping chesapeakebay
Sending 5, 100-byte ICMP Echos to 10.10.10.45, timeout is 2 seconds:
!!!!!
Success rate is 100 percent (5/5), round-trip min/avg/max = 4/5/8 ms
duck#ping knappsnarrows
Sending 5, 100-byte ICMP Echos to 172.16.2.45, timeout is 2 seconds:
.!!!!
Success rate is 80 percent (4/5), round-trip min/avg/max = 4/8/12 ms
duck#trace knappsnarrows
Tracing the route to knappsnarrows (172.16.2.45)
  1 heron (10.10.10.2) 4 msec 4 msec 4 msec
  2 osprey (172.16.2.18) 4 msec 4 msec 4 msec
  3 knappsnarrows (172.16.2.45) 8 msec 4 msec 8 msec
duck#trace kentnarrows
Tracing the route to kentnarrows (172.16.1.45)
  1 goose (172.16.1.9) 8 msec 8 msec 8 msec
  2 kentnarrows (172.16.1.45) 8 msec * 8 msec
duck#show arp
Protocol  Address          Age (min)  Hardware Addr   Type   Interface
Internet  10.10.10.2           13     0000.0c38.a05d  ARPA   Ethernet0
Internet  10.10.10.1            -     0000.0c8d.6705  ARPA   Ethernet0
Internet  10.10.10.40          1      0050.7307.d076  ARPA   Ethernet0
Internet  10.10.10.45          10     0010.ffe5.17ff  ARPA   Ethernet0
```

Example 10-4 displays the successful results of ping and trace output from the duck router, which I used as a starting point. It is not good to assume that this type of testing works from the other devices; therefore, you should repeat Example 10-4 from every device for your baseline. You may have started from hosta and worked your way around to hostb; that is an appropriate method of testing and baselining as well.

Do not continue until you can ping every device, as in Example 10-4. Check your Physical Layer and interfaces if you run into any problems.

Example 10-5 displays the interfaces on the duck router. This time not only can you check the line and protocol status but also the IP addresses. To display the masks or see other statistics, you need to look at the individual interfaces, routing tables, and **show protocols** command output.

Example 10-5 *Building a Layer 3 and Above Baseline from the duck Router (Interfaces)*

```
duck#show ip interface brief
Interface           IP-Address      OK? Method Status                Protocol
Ethernet0           10.10.10.1      YES manual up                    up
Ethernet1           unassigned      YES unset  administratively down down
Loopback10          172.16.1.1      YES manual up                    up
Serial0             172.16.1.10     YES manual up                    up
Serial1             172.16.1.17     YES manual up                    up

duck#show interfaces e0
Ethernet0 is up, line protocol is up
  Hardware is Lance, address is 0000.0c8d.6705 (bia 0000.0c8d.6705)
  Description: duck to chesapeakebay backbone
  Internet address is 10.10.10.1/24
  MTU 1500 bytes, BW 10000 Kbit, DLY 1000 usec, rely 255/255, load 1/255
  Encapsulation ARPA, loopback not set, keepalive set (10 sec)
...
duck#show interfaces s0
Serial0 is up, line protocol is up
  Hardware is HD64570
  Description: duck to goose
  Internet address is 172.16.1.10/29
  MTU 1500 bytes, BW 1544 Kbit, DLY 20000 usec, rely 255/255, load 1/255
  Encapsulation HDLC, loopback not set, keepalive set (10 sec)
...
duck#show interfaces s1
Serial1 is up, line protocol is up
  Hardware is HD64570
  Description: duck to swan
  Internet address is 172.16.1.17/29
  MTU 1500 bytes, BW 1544 Kbit, DLY 20000 usec, rely 255/255, load 1/255
  Encapsulation HDLC, loopback not set, keepalive set (10 sec)
...
duck#show protocols
Global values:
  Internet Protocol routing is enabled
Ethernet0 is up, line protocol is up
  Internet address is 10.10.10.1/24
Ethernet1 is administratively down, line protocol is down
Loopback10 is up, line protocol is up
  Internet address is 172.16.1.1/30
Serial0 is up, line protocol is up
  Internet address is 172.16.1.10/29
Serial1 is up, line protocol is up
  Internet address is 172.16.1.17/29
```

Note the preceding **show protocols** output. It is quite helpful, because it very quickly shows you whether the routing process is on or off. This command also gives you the line and protocol status, as well as the IP address and mask, all in an easy-to-read format. Example 10-6 illustrates the IP protocols and routing tables on duck.

Example 10-6   *Building a Layer 3 and Above Baseline from the duck Router (Protocols)*

```
duck#show ip protocols
Routing Protocol is "rip"
  Sending updates every 30 seconds, next due in 12 seconds
  Invalid after 180 seconds, hold down 180, flushed after 240
  Outgoing update filter list for all interfaces is not set
  Incoming update filter list for all interfaces is not set
  Redistributing: rip
  Default version control: send version 2, receive version 2
    Interface         Send  Recv   Key-chain
    Ethernet0         1 2   1 2
    Loopback10        2     2
    Serial0           2     2
    Serial1           2     2
  Routing for Networks:
    10.0.0.0
    172.16.0.0
  Routing Information Sources:
    Gateway          Distance      Last Update
    10.10.10.2          120        00:00:14
    172.16.1.18         120        00:00:18
    172.16.1.9          120        00:00:19
  Distance: (default is 120)

duck#show ip route
Codes: C - connected, S - static, I - IGRP, R - RIP, M - mobile, B - BGP
       D - EIGRP, EX - EIGRP external, O - OSPF, IA - OSPF inter area
       N1 - OSPF NSSA external type 1, N2 - OSPF NSSA external type 2
       E1 - OSPF external type 1, E2 - OSPF external type 2, E - EGP
       i - IS-IS, L1 - IS-IS level-1, L2 - IS-IS level-2, * - candidate default
       U - per-user static route, o - ODR
Gateway of last resort is not set
     172.16.0.0/16 is variably subnetted, 11 subnets, 2 masks
R       172.16.1.40/29 [120/1] via 172.16.1.9, 00:00:24, Serial0
R       172.16.2.40/29 [120/2] via 10.10.10.2, 00:00:20, Ethernet0
R       172.16.1.32/29 [120/1] via 172.16.1.9, 00:00:24, Serial0
                       [120/1] via 172.16.1.18, 00:00:24, Serial1
R       172.16.1.24/29 [120/1] via 172.16.1.9, 00:00:24, Serial0
                       [120/1] via 172.16.1.18, 00:00:24, Serial1
C       172.16.1.16/29 is directly connected, Serial1
R       172.16.2.16/29 [120/1] via 10.10.10.2, 00:00:20, Ethernet0
C       172.16.1.8/29 is directly connected, Serial0
R       172.16.2.8/29 [120/1] via 10.10.10.2, 00:00:21, Ethernet0
R       172.16.3.8/29 [120/1] via 172.16.1.18, 00:00:24, Serial1
C       172.16.1.0/30 is directly connected, Loopback10
R       172.16.2.0/30 [120/1] via 10.10.10.2, 00:00:21, Ethernet0
     10.0.0.0/8 is variably subnetted, 2 subnets, 2 masks
R       10.0.0.0/8 [120/7] via 172.16.1.18, 00:00:04, Serial1
                   [120/7] via 10.10.10.2, 00:00:26, Ethernet0
C       10.10.10.0/24 is directly connected, Ethernet0
```

The preceding routing table shows 11 subnets for 172.16.0.0, but there should be 12. I have identified 172.16.3.16 to be the missing route, which is the ISDN network in Figure 10-3. I brought my interfaces up and then had 12 routes. It is not important that ISDN is operational in this ticket, as long as your Frame Relay link is up and running. If the 172.16.3.8 network is in your routing table, it is.

Example 10-7 displays the hosts table that is on duck and the other devices for ease of ping, trace, and telnet operations.

Example 10-7   *Building a Layer 3 and Above Baseline from the duck Router (hosts table)*

```
duck#show hosts
Default domain is not set
Name/address lookup uses domain service
Name servers are 255.255.255.255
Host                  Flags         Age Type    Address(es)
duck                  (perm, OK)    8   IP      10.10.10.1   172.16.1.10
                                                172.16.1.17
heron                 (perm, OK)    0   IP      10.10.10.2   172.16.2.9
                                                172.16.2.17
goose                 (perm, OK)    0   IP      172.16.1.9   172.16.1.25
                                                172.16.1.33   172.16.1.41
osprey                (perm, OK)    0   IP      172.16.2.18   172.16.2.41
crab                  (perm, OK)    8   IP      172.16.2.10   172.16.3.10
                                                172.16.3.18
swan                  (perm, OK)    0   IP      172.16.3.9   172.16.1.18
                                                172.16.1.26   172.16.1.34
                                                172.16.3.17
chesapeakebay         (perm, OK)    0   IP      10.10.10.45
kentnarrows           (perm, OK)    0   IP      172.16.1.45
knappsnarrows         (perm, OK)    0   IP      172.16.2.45
pingme                (perm, OK)    8   IP      10.10.10.40
gwise                 (perm, OK)    8   IP      10.10.10.20
Host                  Flags         Age Type    Address(es)
novell                (perm, OK)    8   IP      10.10.10.20
etowerdh              (perm, OK)    8   IP      10.10.10.10
win98                 (perm, OK)    8   IP      10.10.10.10
hosta                 (perm, OK)    8   IP      172.16.1.42
hostc                 (perm, OK)    8   IP      172.16.1.43
hostb                 (perm, OK)    8   IP      172.16.2.42
cat2900               (perm, OK)    8   IP      10.10.10.45
cat3512               (perm, OK)    8   IP      172.16.1.45
cat1900               (perm, OK)    8   IP      172.16.2.45
```

Example 10-8 goes on to test things from the heron router's perspective.

Example 10-8   *Building a Layer 3 and Above Baseline from the heron Router*

```
heron#trace kentnarrows
Tracing the route to kentnarrows (172.16.1.45)
  1 duck (10.10.10.1) 208 msec 124 msec 56 msec
  2 goose (172.16.1.9) 12 msec 12 msec 8 msec
  3 kentnarrows (172.16.1.45) 12 msec *  8 msec
heron#trace knappsnarrows
Tracing the route to knappsnarrows (172.16.2.45)
```

Example 10-8 *Building a Layer 3 and Above Baseline from the heron Router (Continued)*

```
  1 osprey (172.16.2.18) 0 msec 4 msec 0 msec
  2 knappsnarrows (172.16.2.45) 12 msec 4 msec 8 msec
heron#show ip interface brief
Interface            IP-Address      OK? Method Status          Protocol
Ethernet0            10.10.10.2      YES manual up              up
Loopback10           172.16.2.2      YES manual up              up
Serial0              172.16.2.9      YES manual up              up
Serial1              172.16.2.17     YES manual up              up
```

Continue to baseline the other devices in the Trouble Ticket. Compare your ending configurations to the *tt1 final configs* file. If you want to see more of my testing, refer to the *tt1 layer 3 testing* file.

Note that I separated discovering Layer 1 and Layer 2 from Layer 3 in this Trouble Ticket. I wanted to once more emphasize a layered approach to discovery, configuration, and troubleshooting. It is helpful to understand whether you have a Layer 2 or Layer 1 issue causing the problem or if in fact it is something at Layer 3 or above.

NOTE   The **ping** command is a quick test to help you decide whether you have connectivity or data-link issues when you can't physically access equipment; it is a quick test of Layer 3 and below. The Cisco and UNIX **traceroute** command tests up through Layer 4 via User Datagram Protocol (UDP) packets, whereas Microsoft **tracert** command tests through Layer 3 with Internet Control Message Protocol (ICMP) echos.

If you need more practice after completing the discovery lab, feel free to turn this Trouble Ticket into a configuration lab or vice versa. Actually, I highly recommend it. Practice makes perfect. You can erase the configurations on all devices and configure them from scratch as in Figure 10-3.

Trouble Ticket 2 Documentation Lab

Baselining and documentation are very important prerequisites to supporting and continuing to support networks. Add any additional notes to your drawings and tables and take time to redraw them if necessary. Often colored pens/pencils enable you to highlight different encapsulations, protocols, addresses, settings, and such.

Logging and time stamps are extremely helpful for documentation purposes. Tools such as Network Time Protocol (NTP), syslog, TFTP, FTP, and Simple Network Management Protocol (SNMP) are quite valuable when it comes to supporting internetworks. Put some of these tools to practical use as you perform the following tasks:

- Set up the duck router as the master timekeeper and have the other devices get their time from duck.

- Configure the devices so that they display log and debug output with a time and date stamp in milliseconds.

- Set up a syslog server such as the free 3CDaemon on hosta and configure the other devices to send their informational logs to the syslog server.

- Increase the size of your logging buffers.

- Perform a **show tech-support** and other baseline commands on your routers.

- Save all configurations. Send them to a TFTP/FTP server of your choice. This could be part of the 3CDaemon that is running on hosta. Alternatively, you can set up one of your routers as a TFTP server.

- Make sure you know where to locate specific data on Cisco's website to properly support all of your devices. Go back and review Chapter 2, "What's in Your Tool Bag?" for more specifics. For now, research the differences between a manual memory dump and an exception dump. Manually generate a memory dump from the duck router to the existing TFTP server.

- Don't forget about your hosts and servers. Make sure you know Layer 2 and Layer 3 addresses, gateways, routes, frame types, protocols, and so on. Refer back to the previous chapters to assist you with this. Add this information to your diagram or create a separate table.

- (Optional) Use a protocol analyzer such as Sniffer for your baseline. Use the Sniffer as well as **show** and **debug** commands where you can to analyze all background traffic on your network. You need to know what normal is for your environment. Refer back to Chapter 2 for a refresher on protocol analysis with Sniffer Pro.

Look at the "Trouble Ticket 2 Documentation Lab Solution." Can you spot the issues? Better yet, can you fix the issues? Make a list of each issue that you fix to compare it to the issue list and ending configuration in the sample solutions. Fix everything you identify, and use ping and trace to test all connectivity. For example, my 804 (pingme router) is a good ping target on the backbone, but use what you have. If you are really struggling, this Trouble Ticket includes sample output in a file named *tt2 testing*, and so does the next. Use this as a last resort. Now is your chance to apply methods and tools on your own.

Trouble Ticket 2 Documentation Lab Solution

Look at Figure 10-3. Because the drawing is getting a little crowded, you may want to take the information gathered and compile it into a table such as in Figure 10-4. This method to collect data is what I used in Chapter 5, "Shooting Trouble with Ethernet." Refer back to it for the templates to use for your devices and make any necessary changes for this scenario.

Figure 10-4   *Chapter 10 Discovery Baseline*

Hostname:*duc*   **Model:** *2514*
IOS: *12.0(21a)*   **Filename:** *c2500-js-l.120-21a.bin*
RAM: *14336K/2048K*   **Flash:** *16384K*   **Config register:** *0x2102*
Routing protocols: *IP RIPv1 and v2*
Redistribution:
Bridging:
Other notes:
Neighbors are chesapeakebay, goose, and swan

Interface	MAC Address	IP Address	IP Encap	IPX Address	IPX Encap	Serial Encap
e0 10M/half	0000.0c8d.6705	10.10.10.1/24	ARPA			
s0 128K/DTE		172.16.1.10/29				HDLC
s1 1544K/DTE		172.16.1.17/29				HDLC

*For a switch I would include the management IP address, STP, Portfast, and Trunk State as well as VLAN and VTP data. If you are not using IPX or another routed protocol, you can remove those columns to make things easier to read.

k

Examine the examples and the supporting files for this chapter's Trouble Ticket 1 and Trouble Ticket 2. Review the ending configurations in the preceding chapter and the following examples to get more familiar with the environment you will be supporting in this chapter. NTP, time stamps, logging, and TFTP configuration start in Example 10-9 (and go through Example 10-17). Open the supporting file for more detailed data, including the configuration and a **show tech-support** output for the devices (*tt2 testing*). The TFTP server ending configurations for this Trouble Ticket are available in case you have the need to use TFTP to copy them to your devices.

Example 10-9   *Document the duck Router*

```
duck#clock set 9:59:00 July 30 2002
duck#configure terminal
duck(config)#service timestamps debug datetime msec
duck(config)#service timestamps log datetime msec
duck(config)#logging 172.16.1.42
duck(config)#logging trap ?
  <0-7>            Logging severity level
  alerts           Immediate action needed           (severity=1)
  critical         Critical conditions               (severity=2)
  debugging        Debugging messages                (severity=7)
  emergencies      System is unusable                (severity=0)
  errors           Error conditions                  (severity=3)
  informational    Informational messages            (severity=6)
  notifications    Normal but significant conditions (severity=5)
  warnings         Warning conditions                (severity=4)
  <cr>
duck(config)#logging trap informational
duck(config)#logging buffer 500000
duck(config)#ntp ?
  access-group        Control NTP access
  authenticate        Authenticate time sources
  authentication-key  Authentication key for trusted time sources
  broadcastdelay      Estimated round-trip delay
  clock-period        Length of hardware clock tick
  master              Act as NTP master clock
  max-associations    Set maximum number of associations
  peer                Configure NTP peer
  server              Configure NTP server
  source              Configure interface for source address
  trusted-key         Key numbers for trusted time sources
duck(config)#ntp master
duck(config)#end
duck#copy running-config startup-config
```

Set up your syslog server before you configure the other routers. Figure 10-5 displays the 3CDaemon free syslog server running on hosta.

Figure 10-5   *3CDaemon Syslog on hosta*

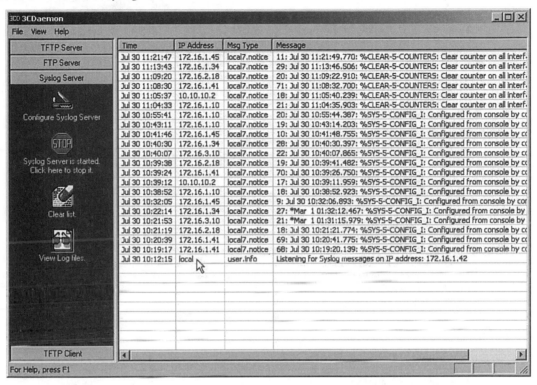

Example 10-10   *Document the heron Router*

```
heron(config)#service timestamps debug datetime msec
heron(config)#service timestamps log datetime msec
heron(config)#ntp server 172.16.1.1
heron(config)#ntp source e0
heron(config)#end
heron#show ntp status
Clock is synchronized, stratum 9, reference is 172.16.1.1
nominal freq is 250.0000 Hz, actual freq is 250.0000 Hz, precision is 2**19
reference time is C0F0E5E3.EBC9E623 (10:16:03.921 UTC Tue Jul 30 2002)
clock offset is -0.1268 msec, root delay is 6.52 msec
root dispersion is 0.21 msec, peer dispersion is 0.05 msec
heron#configure terminal
heron(config)#logging 172.16.1.42
heron(config)#logging trap informational
heron(config)#logging buffer 500000
heron(config)#end
heron#copy running-config startup-config
```

Example 10-11 *Document the goose Router*

```
goose(config)#logging 172.16.1.42
goose(config)#logging trap informational
goose(config)#logging buffer 500000
goose(config)#service timestamps debug datetime msec
goose(config)#service timestamps log datetime msec
goose(config)#ntp server 172.16.1.1
goose(config)#ntp source s0/0
goose(config)#end
goose#show clock
10:19:32.447 UTC Tue Jul 30 2002
goose#copy running-config startup-config
```

Example 10-12 *Document the osprey Router*

```
osprey(config)#logging 172.16.1.42
osprey(config)#logging trap info
osprey(config)#logging buffer 500000
osprey(config)#service timestamps debug datetime msec
osprey(config)#service timestamps log datetime msec
osprey(config)#ntp server 172.16.1.1
osprey(config)#ntp source s0/0
osprey(config)#end
osprey#copy running-config startup-config
```

Example 10-13 *Document the crab Router*

```
crab(config)#logging 172.16.1.42
crab(config)#logging trap informational
crab(config)#logging buffer 500000
crab(config)#service timestamps debug datetime msec
crab(config)#service timestamps log datetime msec
crab(config)#ntp server 172.16.1.1
crab(config)#ntp source s0
crab(config)#end
crab#copy running-config startup-config
```

Example 10-14 *Document the swan Router*

```
swan(config)#logging 172.16.1.42
swan(config)#logging trap informational
swan(config)#logging buffer 500000
swan(config)#service timestamps debug datetime msec
swan(config)#service timestamps log datetime msec
swan(config)#ntp server 172.16.1.1
swan(config)#ntp source s1
swan(config)#end
swan#copy running-config
```

Example 10-15   *Document the ferry Router (Frame Relay Switch)*

```
ferry(config)#logging 172.16.1.42
Cannot open logging port to 172.16.1.42
ferry(config)#logging trap informational
ferry(config)#logging buffer 500000
ferry(config)#service timestamps debug datetime msec
ferry(config)#service timestamps log datetime msec
ferry(config)#ntp server 172.16.1.1
ferry(config)#ntp source s0
ferry(config)#end
ferry#copy running-config startup-config
```

Example 10-16   *Document the chesapeakebay Switch (2900 CatOS)*

```
chesapeakebay> (enable)set logging server 172.16.1.42
172.16.1.42 added to System logging server table.
chesapeakebay> (enable)set logging timestamp enable
System logging messages timestamp will be enabled.
chesapeakebay> (enable)set logging buffer 500000
Usage: set logging buffer <buffer_size>
       (buffer_size = 1..500)
chesapeakebay> (enable)set logging buffer 500
System logging buffer size set to <500>
chesapeakebay> (enable)set ntp server 172.16.1.1
NTP server 172.16.1.1 added.
chesapeakebay> (enable)show ntp
Current time: Tue Jul 30 2002, 10:48:28
Timezone: '', offset from UTC is 0 hours
Summertime: '', disabled
Last NTP update:
Broadcast client mode: disabled
Broadcast delay: 3000 microseconds
Client mode: disabled
NTP-Server
----------------------------------------
172.16.1.1
```

Example 10-17   *Document the kentnarrows Switch (3512XL IOS)*

```
kentnarrows(config)#logging 172.16.1.42
kentnarrows(config)#logging trap informational
kentnarrows(config)#logging buffer 500000
kentnarrows(config)#service timestamps debug datetime msec
kentnarrows(config)#service timestamps log datetime msec
kentnarrows(config)#ntp server 172.16.1.1
kentnarrows(config)#ntp source vlan1
kentnarrows(config)#end
kentnarrows#show ntp status
Clock is synchronized, stratum 9, reference is 172.16.1.1
nominal freq is 381.4697 Hz, actual freq is 381.4697 Hz, precision is 2**17
reference time is C0F0E9A4.9AD26EC9 (10:32:04.604 UTC Tue Jul 30 2002)
clock offset is 4.1159 msec, root delay is 15.59 msec
root dispersion is 7.81 msec, peer dispersion is 3.68 msec
kentnarrows#copy running-config startup-config
!!! the output of the 1900 is not shown for this trouble ticket
```

Now that you have some common documentation tools configured, such as NTP, time stamps, logging, and syslog, you should continue to use these tools to assist you with supporting the network. Verify that NTP is working on duck in Example 10-18 and then be sure to save all your configurations.

Example 10-18 *Viewing NTP on duck*

```
duck#show ntp associations
      address          ref clock       st  when  poll reach  delay  offset   disp
*~127.127.7.1      127.127.7.1        7    15    64  377    0.0   0.00    0.0
  * master (synced), # master (unsynced), + selected, - candidate, ~ configured
duck#show ntp status
Clock is synchronized, stratum 8, reference is 127.127.7.1
nominal freq is 250.0000 Hz, actual freq is 250.0000 Hz, precision is 2**19
reference time is C0F0EC36.D3096102 (10:43:02.824 UTC Tue Jul 30 2002)
clock offset is 0.0000 msec, root delay is 0.00 msec
root dispersion is 0.02 msec, peer dispersion is 0.02 msec
```

Example 10-19 shows the copying of the configurations to the TFTP server that I have running on hosta. I did not bother with the 1900 or 804 because they would be just as easy to reconfigure as to download the configuration.

Example 10-19 *Copying the Configurations to the TFTP Server*

```
duck#copy running-config tftp
Address or name of remote host []? 172.16.1.42
Destination filename [tt2duck-confg]?
!!
1936 bytes copied in 8.744 secs (242 bytes/sec)
heron#copy running-config tftp
Address or name of remote host []? 172.16.1.42
Destination filename [tt2heron-confg]?
!!
1963 bytes copied in 7.676 secs (280 bytes/sec)
goose#copy running-config tftp
Address or name of remote host []? 172.16.1.42
Destination filename [goose-confg]? tt2goose-confg
!!
2880 bytes copied in 1.664 secs (2880 bytes/sec)
osprey#copy running-config tftp
Remote host []? 172.16.1.42
Name of configuration file to write [osprey-confg]? tt2osprey-confg
Write file tt2osprey-confg on host 172.16.1.42? [confirm]
Building configuration...
Writing tt2osprey-confg !! [OK]
crab#copy running-config tftp
Address or name of remote host []? 172.16.1.42
Destination filename [crab-confg]? tt2crab-confg
!!
2695 bytes copied in 10.64 secs (269 bytes/sec)
swan#copy running-config tftp
Address or name of remote host []? 172.16.1.42
Destination filename [swan-confg]? tt2swan-confg
!!
2333 bytes copied in 12.356 secs (194 bytes/sec)
```

Example 10-19 *Copying the Configurations to the TFTP Server (Continued)*

```
ferry#copy running-config tftp
Address or name of remote host []? 172.16.1.42
Destination filename [ferry-confg]? tt2ferry-confg
%Error opening tftp://172.16.1.42/tt2ferry-confg (Socket error)
ferry#!!!ip is not running on the frame switch
ferry#!!!use your terminal program to get a copy of that config

chesapeakebay>enable
Enter password:
chesapeakebay> (enable)copy ?
Usage: copy tftp flash
       copy flash tftp
chesapeakebay> (enable)write ?
Usage: write network
       write terminal
       write <host> <file>
chesapeakebay> (enable)write network
IP address or name of remote host? 172.16.1.42
Name of configuration file? tt2chesapeakebay-confg
Upload configuration to tt2chesapeakebay-confg on 172.16.1.42 (y/n) [n]? y
...
Finished network upload.  (7861 bytes)
chesapeakebay> (enable)

kentnarrows#copy running-config tftp
Source filename [running-config]?
Destination IP address or hostname []? 172.16.1.42
Destination filename [running-config]? tt2kentnarrows-confg
Building configuration...
!!
1952 bytes copied in 0.322 secs
```

My supporting TFTP files are included as well. Reference their names in Example 10-19.

Another task in this Trouble Ticket is the memory dump. Example 10-20 displays the output of
the memory dump to the TFTP server, which takes some time if you plan on letting it finish.

Example 10-20 *Memory Dump to TFTP*

```
duck#ping 172.16.1.42
Type escape sequence to abort.
Sending 5, 100-byte ICMP Echos to 172.16.1.42, timeout is 2 seconds:
!!!!!
Success rate is 100 percent (5/5), round-trip min/avg/max = 16/16/20 ms
duck#write core
Remote host [0.0.0.0]? 172.16.1.42
Base name of core files to write [duck-core]?
writing uncompressed tftp://172.16.1.42/duck-core
 !!!!!!!!!!!!!!!!!!!!!!!!!!!!!!!!!!!!!!!!!!!!!!!!!!!!!!!!!!!!!!!!!!!!!!!!!!!!!!!!!!
 !!!!!!!!!!!!!!!!!!!!!!!!!!!!!!!!!!!!!!!!!!!!!!!!!!!!!!!!!!!!!!!!!!!!!!!!!!!!!!!!!!
 !!!!!!!!!!!!!!!!!!!!!!!!!!!!!!!!!!!!!!!!!!!!!!!!!!!!!!!!!!!!!!!!!!!!!!!!!!!!!!!!!!
 ...
writing uncompressed tftp://172.16.1.42/duck-coreiomem
```

The core dump created two files on the TFTP server for the duck router:

- *duck-core*
- *duck-coreiomem*

NOTE Cisco is moving away from relying on writing an exception dump to an external TFTP/FTP server. Whenever there is sufficient space in boot flash or on a Flash PC card, a *crashinfo* file is usually written. This includes the output of **show stack** and **show tech-support**, as well as the most recent exec mode and config mode commands.

You should also create a table to document your hosts as in Table 10-1. If you are the server/workstation group rather than the network group, your table will probably look a lot more detailed than what this provides. The point here is that troubleshooting is end to end. Normally this means from host to host with any switches and routers in between. The main tools on Windows hosts include **ipconfig/winipcfg** and the network property sheet. Ensure you can ping, trace, and telnet to every device from each host before you proceed to the other Trouble Tickets.

Table 10-1 *Hosts*

hosta: Win2K WinBook (172.16.1.42/29) (3Com PCMCIA NIC 00104BA5AE50) IP-arpa/IPX-sap 100Mbps/full Client for Microsoft and NetWare Networks
hostb: Win98 Toshiba (172.16.2.42/29) (Xircom CE-IIps NIC 0080C7AAC887) IP-arpa/IPX-sap 10Mbps/half Client for Microsoft and NetWare Networks File and Printer Sharing for Microsoft
hostc: Win98 Dell (172.16.1.43/29) (3Com PCMCIA NIC 005004DF5F3C) IP-arpa 100Mbps/full Client for Microsoft File and Printer Sharing for Microsoft Networks

Documentation and baselining are extremely important but are very time-consuming. In a practical environment, it many times gets put off until later, and later never comes. However, supporting the LAN and WAN is much easier when you have done your homework up front.

NOTE You can never have too much documentation. Now that you have it, consider experimenting a bit. If you really want to verify your configurations, erase them all on your devices. Be brave and reload them, too. Then set up your devices for basic IP connectivity to the TFTP server and download your previously saved configurations.

Now that you are quite familiar with the scenario through discovering or configuring it, supporting it, and documenting it, be prepared for some more challenging Trouble Tickets. The name of the Trouble Ticket obviously gives you a hint of *some* (not all) of the issues. You need to "spot the issues" *on your own* instead of following my lead page by page, step by step. Issue lists are provided after each Trouble Ticket so that you can make sure you at least found the issues I intended.

Trouble Ticket 3 OSPF Lab

Paste in the configuration changes from my *tt3 troubled configs* file to get started. In this Trouble Ticket, the routing protocol changes from Routing Information Protocol (RIP) to Open Shortest Path First (OSPF). Update your drawings accordingly. When you are certain everything is working (and it is not right now), display the OSPF configuration on the swan router and perform a trace to the goose router. Explain why goose takes the path it chooses. Save your corrected configurations to the TFTP server. All hosts should be able to ping and trace a device on the backbone.

The chesapeakebay backbone switch and the Frame Relay ferry router should both be operational. I would much prefer to have a Gigabit Ethernet or even a 100-Mbps backbone, but it is not necessary for you to go to that expense for lab purposes. In the practical environment, that is another issue. It is also not intended for you to configure ISDN in this ticket unless you want to. OSPF is running on all routers except the 804 on the backbone, in which the particular IOS doesn't support OSPF. Instead of upgrading the IOS, use default routes. All telnets to knappsnarrows are blocked, but ping, trace, and HTTP access should work in this scenario. Make sure you are able to ping all loopbacks, and then move on to the rest of the intended solution.

Trouble Ticket 3 OSPF Lab Solution

Many times fixing one thing can break another or lead you to another issue, which is why I referred to this as the intended solution. However, you must keep a methodical mindset and divide and conquer to find the real issues. Hopefully, the practical nature of this book thus far has helped shape you into someone who has the methodology, tools, and know-how to do some troubleshooting on your own. That is your task for the rest of the Trouble Tickets in this book. You should have already pasted in the troubled configurations from the *tt3 troubled configs* file, but if not, you can do that now. Review your documentation that you should have been updating throughout the chapter, peek at Figure 10-6 if you must, and fix any issues at this time. Document your findings.

NOTE If you have problems pasting in the configurations, you may need to adjust the options such as the Line Send Delay in your terminal program.

Use the following notes to make sure you found and fixed all the issues I planned for the OSPF Trouble Ticket. (There may be others, too, but you'll need to find them as you go along.)

hosta issues:

- Wrong subnet mask of 255.255.255.252. You may not have had this problem, but you can configure it to observe the results.

duck (r1) issues:

- Multiple OSPF routing processes are not needed here. (You need to redistribute if you leave this unless you want completely separate routing processes.) OSPF 2 uses a subnet mask rather than a wildcard mask. Depending on your IOS version, the IOS may autocorrect this into a wildcard mask.

- My intent was for you to remove the router OSPF 2 configuration, not redistribute.

- Missing network 172.16.1.0 statement under OSPF 1, so you can't reach the two 64 kbps links between goose and swan.

heron (r2) issues:

- Password recovery.

- Clock on s0 and s1.

- Loopback 10 administratively shut down.

- No IP subnet zero.

- OSPF configuration.

goose (r3) issues:

- Speed on fa2/0.

- Duplex on fa2/0.

- The access list should block hosta and hostc from telnetting to knappsnarrows. However, ping and HTTP should still work.

- There are only **deny** statements in the access list. Every ACL needs at least one **permit** statement.

- The access list should be inbound on goose fa2/0.

osprey (r4) issues:

- Incorrect hostname (egret rather than osprey).

- OSPF was incorrectly configured for area 2. Just because the duck router has a route to the osprey router doesn't mean that osprey has a return trip back to duck.

crab (r5) issues:

- The OSPF statement for interfaces 0.0.0.0 255.255.255.255 is set to area 0. It should be area 1, but this incorrect OSPF statement causes a nice virtual link reminder on the crab router.

swan (r6) issues:

- There are individual OSPF statements for the interfaces, but there is an incorrect address on the last one.

chesapeakebay (s1) issues:

- Ports incorrectly set to VLAN 10.

- VTP mode was set to transparent with a VTP domain name of tt3.

kentnarrows (s2) issues:

- Speed on fa0/12.

If you need assistance with testing and finding the issues, the file *tt3 testing* may help; I have annotated it in several places to help you understand some of the issues. The fun of all this is if you did not find all the issues in one Trouble Ticket, they may still be there waiting for you in the next one. On the other hand, if you are totally frustrated, you can paste in the necessary portions of the *tt3 fixed configs* file.

Next use Example 10-21 to answer the question about the swan-to-goose trace.

Example 10-21   *swan-to-goose Trace*

```
swan#trace goose
Type escape sequence to abort.
Tracing the route to goose (172.16.1.9)
  1 duck (172.16.1.17) 4 msec 4 msec 4 msec
  2 goose (172.16.1.9) 12 msec *  8 msec

swan#show ip ospf interface
Serial1 is up, line protocol is up
  Internet Address 172.16.1.18/29, Area 1
    Process ID 1, Router ID 172.16.3.9, Network Type POINT_TO_POINT, Cost: 64
  Transmit Delay is 1 sec, State POINT_TO_POINT,
  Timer intervals configured, Hello 10, Dead 40, Wait 40, Retransmit 5
    Hello due in 00:00:03
  Neighbor Count is 1, Adjacent neighbor count is 1
    Adjacent with neighbor 172.16.1.1
  Suppress hello for 0 neighbor(s)
Serial2 is up, line protocol is up
  Internet Address 172.16.1.26/29, Area 1
```

continues

Example 10-21 *swan-to-goose Trace (Continued)*

```
     Process ID 1, Router ID 172.16.3.9, Network Type POINT_TO_POINT, Cost: 1562
    Transmit Delay is 1 sec, State POINT_TO_POINT,
    Timer intervals configured, Hello 10, Dead 40, Wait 40, Retransmit 5
      Hello due in 00:00:00
    Neighbor Count is 1, Adjacent neighbor count is 1
      Adjacent with neighbor 172.16.1.41
    Suppress hello for 0 neighbor(s)
  Serial3 is up, line protocol is up
    Internet Address 172.16.1.34/29, Area 1
     Process ID 1, Router ID 172.16.3.9, Network Type POINT_TO_POINT, Cost: 1562
    Transmit Delay is 1 sec, State POINT_TO_POINT,
    Timer intervals configured, Hello 10, Dead 40, Wait 40, Retransmit 5
      Hello due in 00:00:03
    Neighbor Count is 1, Adjacent neighbor count is 1
      Adjacent with neighbor 172.16.1.41
    Suppress hello for 0 neighbor(s)
  swan#!!!compare the costs to the bandwidths
```

Compare your final saved fixed configurations to the *tt3 fixed configs* file. Compare your updated drawing to Figure 10-6.

NOTE   On the practical side of things, you may consider breaking up OSPF area 1 into two separate areas. For example, looking at Figure 10-6, 172.16.1.0/24 could be left as it is in OSPF area 1 and 172.16.2.0/24 could easily be its own area 2.

Congratulations are most definitely in order for completing this Trouble Ticket. Move along to the next or save the challenge for another day.

Trouble Ticket 4 RIP/OSPF/EIGRP Redistribution Lab

Redistribution is trouble in itself, and you should never really plan to use it permanently. However, everyone does. It is a quick way to get multiple routing protocols talking and also a quick way to insert routing loops or feedback without the proper filtering. Preferably, if you must redistribute you should redistribute in one direction and use static or default routes in the other instead of mutually redistributing.

Paste in the configuration changes from my *tt4 troubled configs* file to get started. In this Trouble Ticket, the routing protocol changes once again. Use Figure 10-7 as a guide to understand the routing domains so that you can shoot the troubles with Trouble Ticket 10-4. As you can see in Example 10-22, a syslog server was running when some of the issues occurred.

Figure 10-6   *Trouble Ticket 3 OSPF*

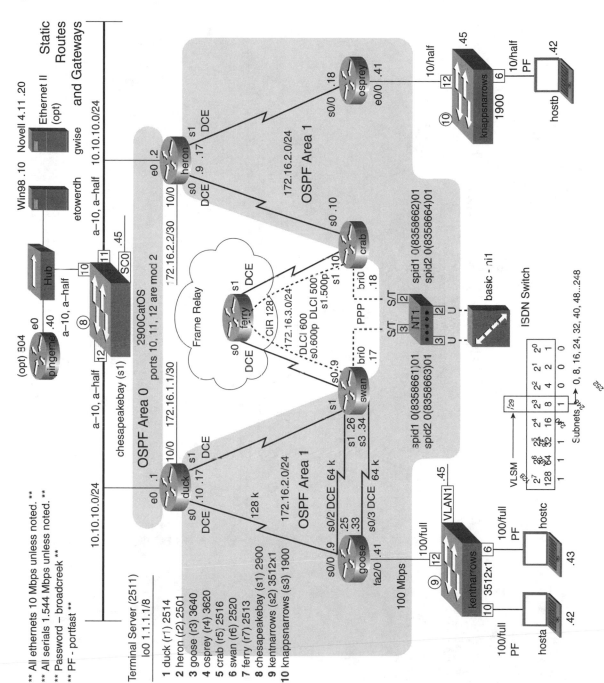

Figure 10-7 *Trouble Ticket 4 RIP/OSPF/EIGRP Redistribution*

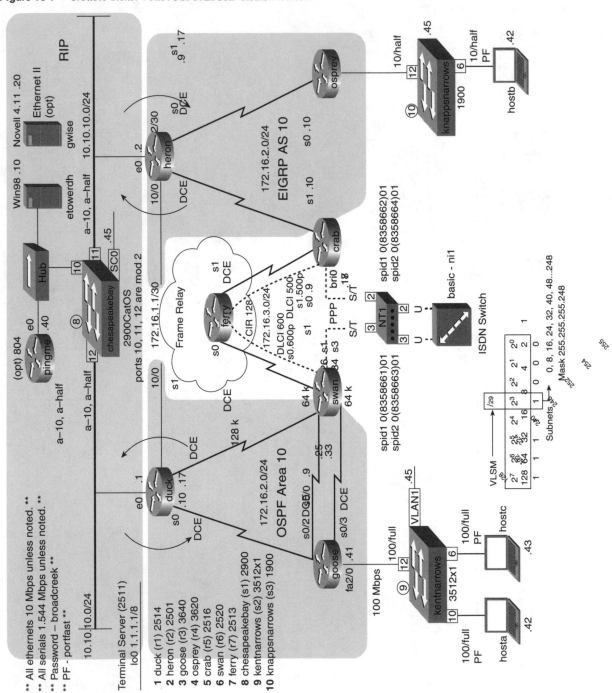

Example 10-22 *Syslog Output*

```
Jul 31 19:22:08 local Listening for Syslog messages on IP address: 172.16.1.42
Jul 31 19:23:23 172.16.1.41 125: Jul 31 07:23:47.352: %LINEPROTO-5-UPDOWN:
    Line protocol on Interface Serial0/0, changed state to down
Jul 31 19:23:25 172.16.1.41 126: Jul 31 07:23:49.076: %LINK-3-UPDOWN:
    Interface Serial0/0, changed state to up
Jul 31 19:23:25 172.16.1.41 127: Jul 31 07:23:50.076: %LINEPROTO-5-UPDOWN:
    Line protocol on Interface Serial0/0, changed state to up
Jul 31 19:23:36 172.16.1.41 128: Jul 31 07:24:00.456: %OSPF-5-ADJCHG:
    Process 1, Nbr 172.16.1.1 on Serial0/0 from FULL to DOWN, Neighbor Down
Jul 31 19:23:53 172.16.1.41 129: Jul 31 07:24:17.376: %LINEPROTO-5-UPDOWN:
    Line protocol on Interface Serial0/0, changed state to down
Jul 31 19:25:27 10.10.10.1 64: Jul 31 07:25:48.218: %SYS-5-CONFIG_I:
    Configured from console by console
Jul 31 19:26:07 172.16.2.2 34: Jul 31 07:26:31.402: %DUAL-5-NBRCHANGE:
    IP-EIGRP 10: Neighbor 172.16.2.10 (Serial0) is down: interface passive
Jul 31 19:26:18 172.16.2.10 37: Jul 31 07:26:42.003: %DUAL-5-NBRCHANGE:
    IP-EIGRP 10: Neighbor 172.16.2.9 (Serial0) is down: holding time expired
Jul 31 19:36:04 172.16.1.41 130: .Jul 31 07:36:28.471: %SYS-5-CONFIG_I:
    Configured from console by console
```

Once upon a time everything was working, but not anymore. Look at Example 10-22 to help determine what is wrong. The swan router should use the Frame Relay circuit to get to the Extended Interior Gateway Protocol (EIGRP) domain. The crab router should use the Frame Relay circuit to get to the OSPF domain. When you have addressed all the issues, copy your working configurations to the TFTP server.

Trouble Ticket 4 RIP/OSPF/EIGRP Redistribution Lab Solution

You should have pasted in the configuration changes from my *tt4 troubled configs* file. Fix the issues and document your findings. Use the following list to make sure you found and fixed all the issues I planned. There may be others, too.

duck (r1) issues:

- Aliases were set for the **show** command (and its shortcuts) to "not.this.time." However, you can use **write terminal** in place of **show run** to see and change the alias commands.

- RIP is only sending version 1, which doesn't understand discontiguous subnets.

- Network 10.10.10.0 advertised in both RIP and OSPF and redistributed.

- Route filtering.

- Router OSPF 10 not needed.

- Encapsulation mismatch on s0.

heron (r2) issues:

- Passive interface on s0 under EIGRP.

- The EIGRP **ip summary-address** statement gives the same effect as the default **auto-summary** feature.

- Incorrect subnet mask on e0.

goose(r3) issues:

- Password recovery.

- OSPF is broken after the password recovery. You had to bring the interfaces up, too, because they were all in a shutdown state.

- Duplicate IP with hostc.

osprey (r4) issues:

- Duplicate MAC with hostb.

swan (r6) issues:

- The default route is 0.0.0.0 255.255.255.255 rather than 0.0.0.0 0.0.0.0.

chesapeakebay (s1) issues:

- Module 2 is in a shutdown state.

Compare your final saved fixed configurations to the *tt4 fixed configs* file. Add any additional notes to your drawing and/or tables.

Trouble Ticket 5 Frame Relay/ISDN Backup Lab

On the WAN you are interfacing with service providers no matter what service you use. When it is critical that remote offices communicate with headquarters or each other, normally some type of automatic failover is in place until the network recovers. Redundancy is one thing; problem diagnosis is another.

Suppose you get a call from a user indicating that "things are slow." Slow compared to what? Is the underlying cause a throughput issue or that of response time. A large file transfer will be limited by bandwidth, for example, whereas a transaction processing system will be limited by latency (lots of end-to-end trips). Ultimately, you must characterize whether you are dealing with a user complaint or an application requirement. To do that, it is important to understand the behavior of the application and the protocol stack from end to end.

This is not intended to be a design book, but internetworks clearly operate more efficiently if they are designed well. My point is that your issues on the WAN may not just be configuration-oriented. Finding faults and understanding why they occurred may mean you have performance issues that traffic sharing and quality of service (QoS) can assist with or you may in fact need more bandwidth. Many times we think bandwidth solves all, when in fact it doesn't shrink geography. These issues are beyond the scope of the book but are becoming more and more important in everyday network support. Ensure you properly design your networks to begin with and that you are prepared to support them with the right tools in your tool bag.

In this Trouble Ticket, you must play the role of the end user and the service provider and take care of all issues. Verify that Frame Relay is working and using the ISDN link for a backup. Start your testing with hosta and work your way around to hostb to spot the issues to draw you closer to the real problem areas.

The physical devices and wires have not changed, but the logical topology has been adjusted somewhat. Update your drawing as per Figure 10-8 after you discover the new changes.

The swan keeps passing packets to the duck router to get to kentnarrows. I want you to assume the T1 between swan and duck is quite saturated, however. Send all packets from swan to kentnarrows and its hosts by way of the goose router. Likewise, packets coming from hosta and hostb should not go through the chesapeakebay switch to get to the swan router. In addition, chesapeakebay should take the shortest route to the hosts.

Congratulate yourself when you can successfully console and telnet to kentnarrows, chesapeakebay, and knappsnarrows from hosta. A current syslog capture display is in Example 10-23 if it can be of any help.

Example 10-23 *Trouble Ticket 5 Syslog Capture*

```
Aug 01 13:37:41 local Listening for Syslog messages on IP address:
    172.16.1.42
Aug 01 13:38:45 172.16.2.9 58: Aug  1 01:39:09.524: %SYS-5-CONFIG_I:
    Configured from console by console
Aug 01 13:40:34 172.16.1.41 82: Aug  1 01:40:59.069: %SYS-5-CONFIG_I:
    Configured from console by console
Aug 01 13:41:53 172.16.1.18 136: Aug  1 01:42:17.984: %SYS-5-CONFIG_I:
    Configured from console by console
Aug 01 13:42:25 172.16.1.18 137: Aug  1 01:42:46.992: %SYS-5-CONFIG_I:
    Configured from console by console
Aug 01 13:44:59 172.16.3.10 68: Aug  1 01:45:24.693: %LINK-3-UPDOWN:
    Interface BRI0:1, changed state to down
Aug 01 13:44:59 172.16.3.10 69: Aug  1 01:45:24.725: %LINK-3-UPDOWN:
    Interface BRI0:2, changed state to down
Aug 01 13:44:59 172.16.3.10 70: Aug  1 01:45:24.817: %LINK-3-UPDOWN:
    Interface BRI0, changed state to up
Aug 01 13:45:00 172.16.3.10 71: Aug  1 01:45:25.029: %ISDN-6-LAYER2UP:
    Layer 2 for Interface BR0, TEI 102 changed to up
Aug 01 13:45:00 172.16.3.10 72: Aug  1 01:45:25.201: %ISDN-6-LAYER2UP:
    Layer 2 for Interface BR0, TEI 103 changed to up
Aug 01 13:45:23 172.16.3.10 73: Aug  1 01:45:48.729: %ISDN-6-LAYER2DOWN:
    Layer 2 for Interface BRI0, TEI 102 changed to down
Aug 01 13:45:23 172.16.3.10 74: Aug  1 01:45:48.733: %ISDN-6-LAYER2DOWN:
    Layer 2 for Interface BRI0, TEI 103 changed to down
Aug 01 13:45:23 172.16.3.10 75: Aug  1 01:45:48.773: %LINK-5-CHANGED:
    Interface BRI0, changed state to standby mode
```

continues

Example 10-23   *Trouble Ticket 5 Syslog Capture (Continued)*

```
Aug 01 13:45:23 172.16.3.10 76: Aug  1 01:45:48.805: %LINK-3-UPDOWN:
   Interface BRI0:1, changed state to down
Aug 01 13:45:24 172.16.3.10 77: Aug  1 01:45:48.837: %LINK-3-UPDOWN:
   Interface BRI0:2, changed state to down
Aug 01 13:46:00 172.16.3.10 78: Aug  1 01:46:24.885: %SYS-5-CONFIG_I:
   Configured from console by console
Aug 01 13:47:27 172.16.3.10 80: Aug  1 01:47:51.733: %FR-5-DLCICHANGE:
   Interface Serial1 - DLCI 600 state changed to ACTIVE
Aug 01 13:47:27 172.16.3.10 81: Aug  1 01:47:51.733: %LINEPROTO-5-UPDOWN:
   Line protocol on Interface Serial1.500, changed state to up
Aug 01 13:47:48 172.16.3.10 87: Aug  1 01:48:13.345: %SYS-5-CONFIG_I:
   Configured from console by console
Aug 01 13:50:16 172.16.3.10 88: Aug  1 01:50:38.612: %SYS-5-CONFIG_I:
   Configured from console by console
Aug 01 13:58:38 172.16.1.18 138: Aug  1 01:59:00.391: %SYS-5-CONFIG_I:
   Configured from console by console
Aug 01 14:00:25 172.16.3.10 89: Aug  1 02:00:49.985: %FR-5-DLCICHANGE:
   Interface Serial1 - DLCI 500 state changed to DELETED
Aug 01 14:00:36 172.16.1.18 139: Aug  1 02:01:00.914: %FR-5-DLCICHANGE:
   Interface Serial0 - DLCI 600 state changed to INACTIVE
Aug 01 14:00:36 172.16.1.18 140: Aug  1 02:01:00.914: %LINEPROTO-5-UPDOWN:
   Line protocol on Interface Serial0.600, changed state to down
Aug 01 14:00:45 172.16.1.18 141: Aug  1 02:01:11.014: %LINK-3-UPDOWN:
   Interface BRI0:1, changed state to down
Aug 01 14:00:45 172.16.1.18 142: Aug  1 02:01:11.046: %LINK-3-UPDOWN:
   Interface BRI0:2, changed state to down
Aug 01 14:00:45 172.16.1.18 143: Aug  1 02:01:11.134: %LINK-3-UPDOWN:
   Interface BRI0, changed state to up
Aug 01 14:00:46 172.16.1.18 144: Aug  1 02:01:11.358: %ISDN-6-LAYER2UP:
   Layer 2 for Interface BR0, TEI 104 changed to up
Aug 01 14:00:46 172.16.1.18 145: Aug  1 02:01:11.522: %ISDN-6-LAYER2UP:
   Layer 2 for Interface BR0, TEI 105 changed to up
Aug 01 14:01:36 172.16.1.18 146: Aug  1 02:02:00.903: %FR-5-DLCICHANGE:
   Interface Serial0 - DLCI 600 state changed to DELETED
Aug 01 14:01:36 172.16.1.18 147: Aug  1 02:02:01.899: %LINEPROTO-5-UPDOWN:
   Line protocol on Interface Serial0, changed state to down
```

NOTE   At this point, you should be putting to practice many of the CatOS/IOS commands you have worked with throughout the book. Once again, your solution should not just be to compare running configurations, but rather use a methodical plan. Use the divide-and-conquer layered approach and practice commands such as **ping**, **trace**, **show**, **clear**, and **debug**.

Figure 10-8 *Trouble Ticket 5 Frame Relay/ISDN Backup*

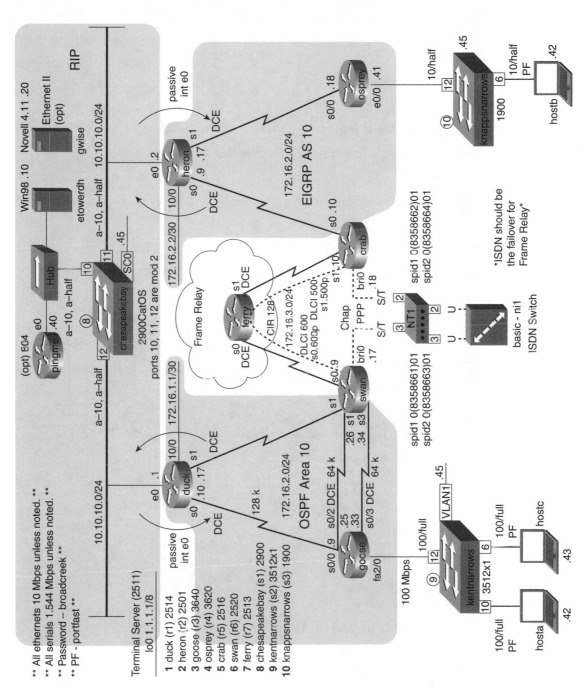

Trouble Ticket 5 Frame Relay/ISDN Backup Lab Solution

Use the following list to make sure you found and fixed all the issues I planned. There may be others, too.

heron (r2) issues:

- The **no ip split-horizon** statement on s1.

goose (r3) issues:

- You need to add an **ip ospf cost** statement to interface s0/2.
- The access list is preventing hosta from telnetting to knappsnarrows.

crab (r5) issues:

- The **backup interface** command was on the main s1 interface rather than the subinterface.
- ISDN switch type on interface.
- Data-link connection identifiers (DLCIs).
- Missing service profile identifier (SPID).

swan (r6) issues:

- Username statement.
- Authentication was Password Authentication Protocol (PAP) rather than Challenge Handshake Authentication Protocol (CHAP).
- Frame Relay compression.
- DLCIs.
- Missing **dialer-group** statement, so no interesting traffic was defined.
- **ip ospf cost** statement is too high of a cost.

ferry (r7) frame switch issues:

- Incorrect frame DCE statement on s0.
- Route statements.

chesapeakebay (s1) issues:

- Password recovery.

kentnarrows (s2) issues:

- Password recovery for secret and telnet passwords.

When you can successfully console to all devices and telnet to kentnarrows, chesapeakebay, and knappsnarrows from hosta, congratulations are in order. Remember to make sure the other initial requirements are operational, too.

NOTE   I realize that you are used to telnetting from one device to another, but part of the requirement for the remaining Trouble Tickets is for you to console directly to devices as well. Please do that to make sure you find all the issues I intended.

Compare your final saved fixed configurations to the *tt5 fixed configs* file. Add any additional notes to your drawing and tables.

Trouble Ticket 6 VLAN and Spanning-Tree Lab

Just as loops can occur in the upper layers because of mutual redistribution and improper filtering, they can also occur at Layer 2. Back in Chapters 6 and 7 I spent some time on the Spanning Tree Protocol (STP). STP assists with bridge/switch loops and it is normally not the best practice to just turn it off. As a matter of fact, Cisco performs a per-VLAN STP. VLANs help you segment your broadcast domains and use a lesser number of routers while doing so. However, the ideal design is still hierarchical in nature.

In this Trouble Ticket, you are just starting to implement VLANs and are thinking about upgrading your 1900 switch. For now, knappsnarrows and hostb are both in the default VLAN 1, which requires no configuration on the 1900 on your part except for management IP addressing.

To prepare for Trouble Ticket 6 you need to make a minor physical change to the topology by shutting down the e0/0 interface on the osprey router and port 12 on the knappsnarrows switch. *Alternatively, just remove the cable between them.* Two additional connections are required between kentnarrows and knappsnarrows as shown in Figure 10-9.

Start your testing from hosta to work toward any major issues. When you can successfully telnet to kentnarrows, chesapeakebay, and knappsnarrows from hosta, hostb, and hostc, that is definitely an accomplishment. You have finished the labs when you can console directly into the devices and copy the configurations to the TFTP server.

Figure 10-9 *Trouble Ticket 10-6 VLANs and STP*

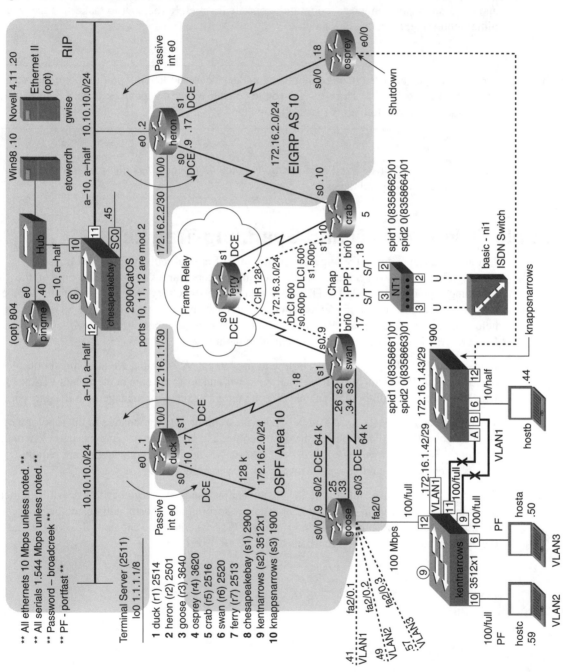

Trouble Ticket 6 VLAN and Spanning-Tree Lab Solution

Use the following list to make sure you found and fixed all the issues I planned. Obviously there may have been others, too.

General issues:

- Physically you need two crossover cables between the two switches for redundancy.

- Hosts tables.

- Leftovers from previous Trouble Tickets.

goose (r3) issues:

- Console speed set to 2400. Change your terminal program settings or telnet in to change it back to the 9600 default.

- fa2/0 administratively shut down.

- fa2/0 speed.

- fa2/0 duplex.

kentnarrows (s2) issues:

- fa0/12 is missing the **switchport mode trunk** statement for kentnarrows. Use the **show interfaces fa0/12 switchport** command to verify.

- No default gateway.

- VLAN1 address should be 172.16.1.42/29.

- fa0/12 speed.

- fa0/12 duplex.

- No STP on VLAN1, so what will take care of the Layer 2 redundancy between kentnarrows and knappsnarrows? Turn it back on with the **spanning-tree vlan 1** command.

Compare your final saved fixed configurations to the *tt6 fixed configs* file. Add any additional notes to your drawing and tables.

Now that you have completed these challenging Trouble Tickets, go back and review all your documentation. I highly recommend you print the supporting files for this chapter and "swim" through the Trouble Tickets once again. Practice makes perfect. Shooting internetworking troubles is not just something you can pick up a book on and expect to be successful. To alleviate your fears, you must put your theory to practical use.

Review Questions

Use this chapter and your practical troubleshooting knowledge and skills to answer the following questions. The answers are located in Appendix A, "Answers to Review Questions."

1   The following output was captured during Trouble Ticket 6. Why is fa0/9 in a blocking state?

```
kentnarrows#show spanning-tree vlan 1
Spanning tree 1 is executing the IEEE compatible Spanning Tree protocol
  Bridge Identifier has priority 32768, address 00d0.7968.8484
  Configured hello time 2, max age 20, forward delay 15
  Current root has priority 32768, address 0090.922a.7680
  Root port is 24, cost of root path is 19
  Topology change flag not set, detected flag not set, changes 1
  Times:  hold 1, topology change 35, notification 2
          hello 2, max age 20, forward delay 15
  Timers: hello 0, topology change 0, notification 0
Interface Fa0/1 (port 13) in Spanning tree 1 is down
  Port path cost 100, Port priority 128
  Designated root has priority 32768, address 0090.922a.7680
  Designated bridge has priority 32768, address 00d0.7968.8484
  Designated port is 13, path cost 19
  Timers: message age 0, forward delay 0, hold 0
  BPDU: sent 0, received 0
Interface Fa0/2 (port 14) in Spanning tree 1 is down
  Port path cost 100, Port priority 128
  Designated root has priority 32768, address 0090.922a.7680
  Designated bridge has priority 32768, address 00d0.7968.8484
  Designated port is 14, path cost 19
  Timers: message age 0, forward delay 0, hold 0
  BPDU: sent 0, received 0
Interface Fa0/3 (port 15) in Spanning tree 1 is down
  Port path cost 100, Port priority 128
  Designated root has priority 32768, address 0090.922a.7680
  Designated bridge has priority 32768, address 00d0.7968.8484
  Designated port is 15, path cost 19
  Timers: message age 0, forward delay 0, hold 0
  BPDU: sent 0, received 0
Interface Fa0/4 (port 16) in Spanning tree 1 is down
  Port path cost 100, Port priority 128
  Designated root has priority 32768, address 0090.922a.7680
  Designated bridge has priority 32768, address 00d0.7968.8484
  Designated port is 16, path cost 19
  Timers: message age 0, forward delay 0, hold 0
  BPDU: sent 0, received 0
Interface Fa0/5 (port 17) in Spanning tree 1 is down
  Port path cost 100, Port priority 128
  Designated root has priority 32768, address 0090.922a.7680
  Designated bridge has priority 32768, address 00d0.7968.8484
  Designated port is 17, path cost 19
  Timers: message age 0, forward delay 0, hold 0
  BPDU: sent 0, received 0
Interface Fa0/7 (port 19) in Spanning tree 1 is down
  Port path cost 100, Port priority 128
```

```
Designated root has priority 32768, address 0090.922a.7680
Designated bridge has priority 32768, address 00d0.7968.8484
Designated port is 19, path cost 19
Timers: message age 0, forward delay 0, hold 0
BPDU: sent 0, received 0
Interface Fa0/8 (port 20) in Spanning tree 1 is down
Port path cost 100, Port priority 128
Designated root has priority 32768, address 0090.922a.7680
Designated bridge has priority 32768, address 00d0.7968.8484
Designated port is 20, path cost 19
Timers: message age 0, forward delay 0, hold 0
BPDU: sent 0, received 0
Interface Fa0/9 (port 22) in Spanning tree 1 is BLOCKING
Port path cost 19, Port priority 128
Designated root has priority 32768, address 0090.922a.7680
Designated bridge has priority 32768, address 0090.922a.7680
Designated port is 27, path cost 0
Timers: message age 3, forward delay 0, hold 0
BPDU: sent 11, received 333
Interface Fa0/11 (port 24) in Spanning tree 1 is FORWARDING
Port path cost 19, Port priority 128
Designated root has priority 32768, address 0090.922a.7680
Designated bridge has priority 32768, address 0090.922a.7680
Designated port is 26, path cost 0
Timers: message age 2, forward delay 0, hold 0
BPDU: sent 3, received 346
Interface Fa0/12 (port 25) in Spanning tree 1 is FORWARDING
Port path cost 19, Port priority 128
Designated root has priority 32768, address 0090.922a.7680
Designated bridge has priority 32768, address 00d0.7968.8484
Designated port is 25, path cost 19
Timers: message age 0, forward delay 0, hold 0
BPDU: sent 345, received 0
```

2 Using the same data in the preceding question, why are fa0/6 and fa0/10 missing?

3 While troubleshooting Trouble Ticket 6, I unplugged the dongle attached to the network interface card (NIC) to see which port the host was connected to. According to the following output and Figure 10-9, which host did I perform this on?

```
kentnarrows(config)#
.Mar  1 03:47:25.507: %LINK-3-UPDOWN: Interface FastEthernet0/10,
    changed state to down
.Mar  1 03:47:25.735: %LINEPROTO-5-UPDOWN: Line protocol on
    Interface FastEthernet0/10, changed state to down
.Mar  1 03:47:43.858: %LINK-3-UPDOWN: Interface FastEthernet0/10,
    changed state to up
.Mar  1 03:47:44.773: %LINEPROTO-5-UPDOWN: Line protocol on
    Interface FastEthernet0/10, changed state to up
```

4   Refer to the following output. Are there any potential issues?

```
chesapeakebay> (enable)show port status
Port  Name                 Status      Vlan        Level  Duplex Speed Type
----- -------------------- ----------  ----------  ------ ------ ----- -----------
1/1                        notconnect 1            normal half    100 100BaseTX
1/2                        notconnect 1            normal half    100 100BaseTX
2/1                        disabled   1            normal auto    auto 10/100BaseTX
2/2                        disabled   1            normal auto    auto 10/100BaseTX
2/3                        disabled   1            normal auto    auto 10/100BaseTX
2/4                        disabled   1            normal auto    auto 10/100BaseTX
2/5                        disabled   1            normal auto    auto 10/100BaseTX
2/6                        disabled   1            normal auto    auto 10/100BaseTX
2/7                        disabled   1            normal auto    auto 10/100BaseTX
2/8                        disabled   1            normal auto    auto 10/100BaseTX
2/9                        disabled   1            normal auto    auto 10/100BaseTX
2/10  to hub               disabled   1            normal auto    auto 10/100BaseTX
2/11  to heron             disabled   1            normal auto    auto 10/100BaseTX
2/12  to duck              disabled   1            normal auto    auto 10/100BaseTX
```

5   What is likely to be the issue with the following output that was captured during Trouble Ticket 4?

```
goose#trace hostc
Tracing the route to hostc (172.16.1.43)
  1 hostc (172.16.1.43) 0 msec
*Mar  1 00:10:20.670: IP: s=172.16.1.43 (local), d=172.16.1.43
    (FastEthernet2/0), len 28, sending
*Mar  1 00:10:20.670: IP: s=172.16.1.43 (FastEthernet2/0), d=172.16.1.43,
    len 28, rcvd 0
*Mar  1 00:10:20.670: IP: s=172.16.1.43 (local), d=172.16.1.43
    (FastEthernet2/0), len 56, sending
*Mar  1 00:10:20.670: IP: s=172.16.1.43 (FastEthernet2/0), d=172.16.1.43
    (FastEthernet2/0), len 56, rcvd 3
*Mar  1 00:10:20.670: IP: s=172.16.1.43 (local), d=172.16.1.43
    (FastEthernet2/0), len 28, sending
*Mar  1 00:10:20.674: IP: s=172.16.1.43 (FastEthernet2/0), d=172.16.1.43,
    len 28, rcvd 0 *  0 msec
```

6   Often trace is very much a complementary tool to ping. What is likely to be the issue with the following output that was captured during Trouble Ticket 4?

```
swan#trace kentnarrows
Tracing the route to kentnarrows (172.16.1.45)
  1 duck (172.16.1.17) 4 msec 4 msec 4 msec
  2 heron (10.10.10.2) 16 msec 12 msec 16 msec
  3 crab (172.16.2.10) 16 msec 16 msec 16 msec
  4 swan (172.16.3.9) 12 msec 12 msec 12 msec
  5 duck (172.16.1.17) 8 msec 12 msec 12 msec
  6 heron (10.10.10.2) 20 msec 20 msec 20 msec
  7 crab (172.16.2.10) 20 msec 20 msec 20 msec
  8 swan (172.16.3.9) 16 msec 16 msec 20 msec
```

```
 9 duck (172.16.1.17) 16 msec 20 msec 16 msec
10 heron (10.10.10.2) 24 msec 24 msec 28 msec
11 crab (172.16.2.10) 28 msec 28 msec 28 msec
12 swan (172.16.3.9) 24 msec 24 msec 24 msec
13 duck (172.16.1.17) 24 msec 24 msec 20 msec
14 heron (10.10.10.2) 32 msec 32 msec 32 msec
15 crab (172.16.2.10) 32 msec 32 msec 32 msec
16 swan (172.16.3.9) 28 msec 28 msec 28 msec
```

7 Analyze the following issue that occurred during Trouble Ticket 4.

```
osprey#show arp
Protocol  Address        Age (min)  Hardware Addr    Type   Interface
Internet  172.16.2.45        202     0090.922a.7680  ARPA   Ethernet0/0
Internet  172.16.2.42          0     Incomplete      ARPA
Internet  172.16.2.41          -     0080.c7aa.c887  ARPA   Ethernet0/0
```

8 The swan (2520) and crab (2516) routers both have ISDN BRI ports. Are they S/T or U?

9 What tool enables you to send traps to a network management system?

10 What steps does Cisco recommend in supporting your internetwork?

Summary

This chapter offers you an opportunity to give yourself a comprehensive, hands-on review of many of the LAN and WAN topics discussed throughout this book. This is a good pre-test and post-test exercise for supporting internetworks at the CCNA/CCNP level. It is not and was not intended to be at the CCIE level, but perhaps CCIEs will enjoy reliving some issues they have already spotted. On the other hand, it wasn't intended to give you page-by-page step-by-step instructions either. People learn by doing, and troubleshooting takes practice. It is not just something you can read and memorize. You must divide and conquer. Finding the problem you are trying to solve is a real battle. If you know you can't ping or trace from or to a particular device or host, for instance, start your troubleshooting there. *Define* the problem, then *isolate*, and then *correct*.

In this book I have identified many tools and resources along with some helpful troubleshooting checklists and sample command outputs. Put them to practical use and continue to identify new troubleshooting tools that help you with your real-world problems. Think methodology. Leverage off of your experiences and the experiences of others to prosper in troubleshooting Cisco routers and switches.

Now for the final question...*do you shoot trouble or does trouble shoot you?*

Appendixes

Answers to Review Questions

Chapter 1's Review Questions

1 The Transport Layer is the host-to-host layer in the OSI model and the TCP/IP suite. It is in-between the upper and lower layers and depending on the protocol is responsible for delivery, error detection, and correction. Describe the upper layers of the OSI model and include examples.

Answer: The upper layers of the OSI model include the following:

- **L7 Application—Service use and advertisement (file and print services, e-mail)**

- **L6 Presentation—Translation, encryption, and compression (character codes, public/private key, ASCII, JPEG)**

- **L5 Session—Dialog, session administration, connection establishment, and data transfer (NetBIOS, Sockets, drive mappings)**

2 Describe the lower layers of the OSI model and include examples.

Answer: The lower layers of the OSI model include the following:

- **L3 Network—Logical addressing and routing (IP, ARP, RARP, ICMP, and routers)**

- **L2 Data Link—Physical addressing, media access, and frame formats (Ethernet, Token Ring, Frame Relay, and switches)**

- **L1 Physical—0s and 1s, cabling, and signaling (Category 5, RJ-45, HSSI, coax, fiber, and hubs)**

3 Draw a picture showing the differences between OSI layers and TCP/IP layers.

Answer: Refer to Figure 1-16, Figure 1-17, and Figure 1-18 for pictures illustrating the differences between the OSI seven-layer model and the DoD five-layer TCP/IP suite.

4 Explain encapsulation using the appropriate protocol data unit terminology.

Answer: For a TCP/IP-based application, data gets encapsulated in a TCP segment, which gets encapsulated in an IP packet, which gets encapsulated in an Ethernet frame in order to get to the Physical Layer bits for transmission across the medium.

5   Explain de-encapsulation, including how Layer 2 hands off to Layer 3, how Layer 3 hands off to Layer 4, and so on.

Answer: De-encapsulation is like opening envelopes or presents. Each layer reads and carries out the instructions from its peer layer, discards the header, and sends the packets up the stack for further processing. The Physical Layer passes bits in frames to the Data Link Layer. The Data Link Layer uses a type code or SAP to determine which Layer 3 protocol to hand off to. The Network Layer uses a protocol number to pass to the Layer 4 protocol. The Transport Layer uses a port number to send to an upper-layer application.

6   What is the difference between a hub, switch, and router?

Answer: A hub is a Layer 1 device that does absolutely no filtering (it spits bits). A switch is a Layer 2 device that can assist with collisions and make filtering decisions based on physical addresses. A router is a Layer 3 device that can assist with collisions and broadcasts and can make filtering decisions based on logical addresses. A Layer 3 switch is really a router.

7   What is the difference between routed and routing protocols? Give examples of each.

Answer: Routing protocols exchange routes with other routers. Examples include OSPF, BGP, RIP, and EIGRP. Routed protocols deliver packets; they send user data. Examples include IP and IPX.

8   Describe packet flows through routers.

Answer: Packet flow is an important concept. Routers *route* to the destination network address. They buffer and *switch* packets from the inbound interface to the outbound interface within the router. Performance is definitely affected by the switching type. *Fast switching* refers to when a router does a route table lookup for the first packet toward a destination and caches it so that it doesn't have to perform a route table lookup on each and every packet. (Imagine the overhead if a router actually performs a route table lookup on each and every packet, which is called *process switching* and is used when you perform such tasks as debug commands.) Newer devices offer Cisco Express Forwarding (CEF) as a switching type, whereby even the first packet gets cached. Remember these important points: Routers *route* hop-to-hop, and routers *switch* from the inbound interface to the outbound interface of the router at Layer 3.

9   How can the OSI model assist in troubleshooting?

Answer: The OSI model helps you take a layered, systematic approach to troubleshooting. The OSI model provides other benefits as well (such as inter-operability, standardization, and it enables you to subdivide developer tasks without having to alter other layers). For example, those making network interface cards (NICs) really don't want to be concerned with what upper-layer applications and

protocols run over the hardware. However, NIC vendors must be concerned with LAN technologies such as Ethernet and Token Ring and what physical specifications (cable and connectors) to follow.

10 List the seven steps of the Cisco troubleshooting model?

Answer: The Cisco troubleshooting model is as follows:

1   **Define the problem.**

2   **Gather the facts.**

3   **Consider possibilities (based on facts).**

4   **Create an action plan.**

5   **Implement action plan.**

6   **Observe results.**

7   **Document the solution.**

Chapter 2's Review Questions

1 CDP sends and receives neighbor advertisements over multicast address 01-00-0c-cc-cc and uses a proprietary HDLC type value. CDP must run on media that supports what?

Answer: CDP must run on media that supports SNAP.

2 To match up the following buffer pools with the appropriate sizes (small, middle, big, very big, large, and huge), what IOS command would you use?

104 bytes

600 bytes

1524 bytes

4520 bytes

5024 bytes

18,024 bytes

Answer: You would use the show buffers command to show the output of the buffer pools and their sizes.

3 Which support tool can monitor up to all seven layers and is the least stressful on the router?

A Network monitor

B Protocol analyzer

C debug

D ping

Answer: A protocol analyzer can monitor up to all seven layers and is not as stressful as some other tools on the router.

4 List the five categories of network management and give a Cisco example of an NMS.

Answer: ISO has five categories of network management: fault, accounting, configuration and name, performance, and security management. CiscoWorks is the Cisco example of an NMS.

5 What NMS feature of Cisco's product is a replacement for CWSI? List at least four other features that this product is responsible for.

Answer: The LAN Management Solution (LMS) contains nGenius Real Time Monitor, Campus Manager, Device Fault Manager, Content Flow Monitor, CiscoView, and Resource Manager Essentials. LMS is part of the CiscoWorks family of products for fault and configuration management and troubleshooting of campus LANs and is a follow-on to the CiscoWorks for Switched Internetworks (CWSI) bundle.

6 What type of support tool records, displays, and analyzes how a protocol operates and gives a layer-by-layer decode? Give an example.

Answer: A protocol analyzer such as Sniffer Pro or EtherPeek, records, displays, and analyzes how a protocol operates and gives a layer-by-layer decode.

7 Cable testers (scanners) can be used to test physical connectivity. Many cable testers include TDR functionality. What type of device is used to test signal loss with fiber cable?

Answer: An optical time domain reflectometer (OTDR) is used to test signal loss with fiber cable.

8 What support tool is useful for baselining and continuously tracks packets but doesn't decode them?

Answer: A network monitor is useful for baselining and continuously tracks packets but doesn't decode them.

9 List at least two proactive and two reactive CCO tools?

Answer: Proactive (all could be reactive, too) tools:

- **IOS Upgrade Planner**

- **Hardware-Software Compatibility Matrix**

- **IOS Roadmap**

- **Documentation CD-ROM**

- **MarketPlace**

- **Cisco Technical Assistance Center (TAC)**

Reactive tools:

- **Bug Navigator (could be proactive, too)**

- **Output Interpreter**

- **Troubleshooting Assistant**

- **Stack Decoder**

10 Use the numbers 1–4 to match the priority levels with the following severity level.

Information needed on product

Production network severely degraded

Network performance degraded

Production network down

Answer: The correct levels follow:

Priority	Severity
1	Production network down
2	Production network severely degraded
3	Network performance degraded
4	Information needed on product

11 Escalation to Cisco support requires certain tasks. The **show tech-support** command is helpful. You need your equipment and service contract information, and you should open a case with specific priority level and case number. What CCO tool enables you to open, query, and update a case with TAC?

Answer: Use the case management toolkit to open, query, and update a case with TAC.

12 The Cisco Dynamic Configuration tool enables you to look up the specifics of a WSC1924A you bought off of eBay. You should quickly find that it is a 24-port 10-MB switch with two 100BASE-TX ports and it is upgradeable to the Enterprise Edition. Under which category would you find this on the website?

Answer: MarketPlace allowed me to look up the specifics of a device using the Configuration Tool. Marketplace is also where you can purchase a sweater with the Cisco logo.

Chapter 3's Review Questions

1 In the RIP scenario, why were you successful with using RIPv2 rather than RIPv1?

Answer: RIPv2 is classless, and RIPv1 is classful. Classless routing protocols such as RIPv2, EIGRP, OSPF, and IS-IS support VLSM and summarization. All routing protocols support summarization, but the classful ones do that in a fixed manner at the class boundary.

2 A Cisco router maintains ARP entries much longer than most PCs. How can you remove all entries from the ARP cache on a Cisco router? It would be less detrimental to all to just remove an entry associated with a given interface. Can you do that on a router? On a Windows-based PC?

Answer: On a router, clear arp does not truly clear the table; instead, it refreshes it. Unless in a test environment where it doesn't matter who you affect, you should use shut/no shut to remove the entries associated with a given interface. The command arp -d *ip address* **on a Windows-based machine allows you to remove an entry at a time.**

3 Draw a table comparing TCP/IP layers, protocols, applications, and utilities to the OSI model.

Answer: See Table 3-2.

4 On a Cisco router, **show ip route** displays the routing table. What are the numbers in brackets [ ]?

Answer: The numbers in brackets are [*administrative distance/composite metric*].

5 Subnetting, aggregation, VLSM, CIDR, supernetting, and summarization are all about moving bit boundaries. Which one(s) move the network mask bit boundary to the right?

Answer: Subnetting and VLSM.

6 Assume you moved into apartment 172.16.3.10 (host address) located at 172.16 Broad Creek Drive (network address). Other floors in the apartment building are numbered 172.16.1.0, 172.16.2.0, and 172.16.4.0. What floor (subnet) are you on? What are all the available hosts on that subnet? What is the directed broadcast address of your subnet?

Answer: Because the other subnets are 172.16.1.0, 172.16.2.0, and 172.16.4.0, you must be on subnet 172.16.3.0. If you perform the binary math, you would in fact prove that you are on subnet (floor) 3. The hosts (other apartments on your floor) are as follows: 172.16.3.1 through 172.16.3.254. 172.16.3.255 is the directed broadcast address for your subnet. Again, if you work out the binary, you will see that the first available host is the subnet plus one, the directed broadcast is all 1s for the host bits, and the last available host is the broadcast address minus one.

7 Compare the protocol and port numbers for telnet, RIP, FTP, and TFTP.

Answer: RIP (port 520) and TFTP (port 69) are both based on UDP, which is IP protocol number 17. Telnet (port 23) and FTP (ports 20, 21) are both based on TCP, which is protocol number 6. Refer to Figure 3-13 for more assistance.

8 You can ping by the IP address but not by the hostname. What is a very likely problem?

Answer: Hostname resolution. Check your hosts files and DNS servers. You can test this now if you really want.

9 You need to forward DHCP requests to another subnet, but you do not want to forward NetBIOS communications. Is this possible?

Answer: The command ip helper-address [*DHCP_server_address*] is required on your local router interface. By default, however, it allows TFTP, DNS, Time, two NetBIOS ports, two DHCP ports, and TACACS. You must specify which ports you want to forward and then the ports that you don't want to forward. To forward fewer than the eight default ports that IP helper opens up, you can use the ip forward-protocol udp [*port*] command for the ports you want to forward followed by the no ip forward-protocol udp [*port*] command for the ports you do not want to forward.

10 What IOS command enables you to verify that RIP sends broadcast routing updates? To what address are broadcast updates sent?

Answer: debug ip rip shows you that routing updates are sent to 255.255.255.255.

11 Using 192.168.5.0/24, address the network according to the following requirements: three LAN segments—one with 125 hosts, one with 50 hosts, and one with 25 hosts—and at least two and maybe more WAN segments.

Answer: I recommended that you start with host requirements, then work on your LAN requirements, and then work on the WAN requirements for VLSM. Remember that when you are solving for host bits, they are 0 bits. You should draw this out like Figure A-1 to understand the scenario and to truly see the bits:

- **Start with the maximum number of hosts and solve for x. $2^x >= 125$ hosts is 7 host bits. Note the seven 0 host bits in Figure A-1 where I assign 192.168.5.128/25 to the 125-host subnet.**

- **Use VLSM for subnet 0 to continue. Solve for x. $2^x >= 50$ hosts to arrive at 6 host bits. Note the six host 0 bits in Figure A-1 where I assign 192.168.64.0/26 to the 50-host subnet.**

- **Use VLSM for subnet 0 to continue. Solve for x. $2^x >= 25$ hosts to arrive at 5 host bits. Note the five host 0 bits in Figure A-1 where I assign 192.168.32.0/27 to the 25-host subnet.**

- **Now that you have calculated the host and LAN segement requirements, use VLSM subnet 0 out to a /30 mask to maximize the WAN links. The WAN links can use 192.168.5.0/30, 192.168.5.4/30, 192.168.5.8/30, and so on as illustrated in Figure A-1.**

Figure A-1

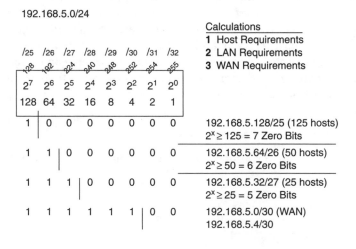

12 You are having a problem with three subnets connected via two Cisco routers. Each router can ping its own interfaces but can't get to the far side of the other router. So you decide to put in the appropriate default route statement, but things still are not operational. You are not running routing protocols because default routes serve this scenario well. Can you spot the issue?

Answer: You should draw this out and label the subnets to give you a picture of the problem. Alternatively, you can assume the scenario to be hosta connected to r1, r1 connected to r3, and hostc connected to r3. Obviously, this could be any number of things, and I would like to stress once more to use a structured approach such as in Chapter 1 and to divide and conquer to help you spot the particular issue. In looking at your configurations, you found no IP classless, so in effect your default routes were not working. After you turned on IP classless, you could route.

Chapter 4's Review Questions

1 What IOS command assists in determining detailed information if the router is propagating RIP updates?

Answer: debug ipx routing activity

2 What IOS command assists in determining detailed information if the router is propagating SAP updates?

Answer: debug ipx sap activity

3 What is the difference between the Novell internal IPX number and the Novell external IPX number?

Answer: The internal IPX number is a logical network inside the Novell server. Think of it like the loopback on a Cisco router. The internal network can also be configured on Cisco routers and must be for certain features such as IPXWAN or NLSP. The external IPX number is the wire ID analogous to IP subnets.

4 Fill in the following table with the missing Cisco and Novell encapsulation names.

Cisco Encapsulation	Novell Frame Type	Description	Novell Version Default
ARPA	Ethernet_II	EtherType pointer to Layer 3	NetWare 6.x NetWare 5.x
SAP		Length field 802.2 LLC SAP pointer to Layer 3	NetWare 3.12 through NetWare 4.x
Novell-Ether		Length field	≤ NetWare 3.11
	Ethernet_SNAP	Length field 802.2 LLC SAP SNAP header	SNAP default for Token Ring and FDDI
		Serial links	All versions for serial links

> **Answer: See Table 4-5**

5 What type of packet does Figure A-2 display? What form of Cisco encapsulation is used?

Figure A-2 *Review Question 5*

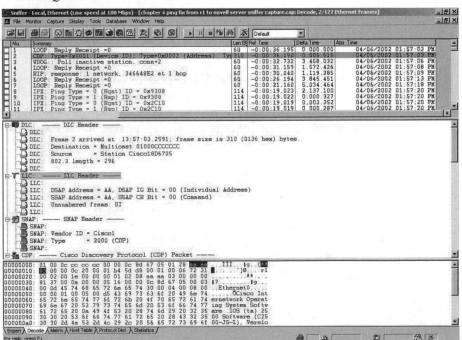

> **Answer: Frame 2 is a CDP multicast packet. The encapsulation is Cisco SNAP, which is 802.3 with 802.2 LLC, and SNAP headers.**

6 Explain the difference between Cisco ping and IPX ping. Which one is the default? Why would you change the default? How do you change the default?

Answer: The default ping is a Cisco ping that uses *IPX protocol number 2*. The IPX official ping uses *socket number 0x9086*. Cisco ping works fine for your Cisco devices, but your IPX devices do not understand its proprietary nature.

7 MTU is negotiated by NCP. It is 1500 for a local Ethernet segment and 576 bytes for the internetwork. How can you verify this?

Answer: Technically, MTU is not being negotiated; rather, it is a per-interface attribute. But via the optional "big packet" request/response, the end-to-end NCP segment size is negotiated. However, the show interfaces (see the following output) or show tech-support commands display it.

```
----------------- show interfaces -----------------
 Ethernet0 is up, line protocol is up
Hardware is Lance, address is 0000.0c8d.6705 (bia 0000.0c8d.6705)
   Description: r1e0 to hosta and hostb
  MTU 1500 bytes, BW 10000 Kbit, DLY 1000 usec, rely 255/255, load 1/255
```

8 The **route print** command displays the routing table on a PC. How can you see this information on a router running IPX RIP? How about on a Novell server?

Answer: View the routing table using the show ipx route command on the router and display networks on the Novell server.

9 How do you configure IPX RIP on a Cisco router?

Answer: Configure the ipx routing global command and specify the wire IDs on the interface using the ipx network [*wireid*] command for each directly connected network.

10 Why doesn't IPX need ARP?

Answer: ARP is not needed in IPX because the host address is already part of the network address in IPX: *Network.node:socket*.

11 Explain the following address:

12345678.0000.0000.0001:0451

Answer: Internal IPX address:socket.

12 How does IPX RIP find the best path to another network? How does this differ from IP RIP?

Answer: IPX RIP metrics are ticks/hops. IP metrics are hops. Both are limited to 15 hops.

13 In the chapter scenario, hosta is a Windows 2000 box. What command gives you the display in Figure A-3?

Figure A-3   *Review Question 13*

```
NWLink IPX Routing and Source Routing Control Program v2.00

Num  Name                        Network    Node            Frame
==================================================================
1.   IpxLoopbackAdapter          00000516   00104ba5ae50    [802.2]
2.   Local Area Connection       00000516   00104ba5ae50    [802.2]
3.   NDISWANIPX                  00000000   e0fc20524153    [EthII]  -
```

Answer: Type ipxroute config at the hosta command prompt to see the network addresses, MAC address, and frame type information on the IPX client.

Chapter 5's Review Questions

1 How would a user complain to you about an incorrect frame type issue?

Answer: For an incorrect frame type issue, I would expect to hear things from the user such as, "I can't print," "I can't get to my file," "I don't see anything in Network Neighborhood," "My screen says invalid drive specification," "I don't have a drive F," and so on.

2 What is the EtherType and SAP for Novell IPX? How does the receiving station recognize an 802.3 Novell-Ether frame?

Answer: EtherType is 8137, and SAP is e0. The checksum hex bytes 0xFFFF are for receiving station recognition. (See Figure A-4 and Figure A-5.)

Figure A-4   *IPX EtherType*

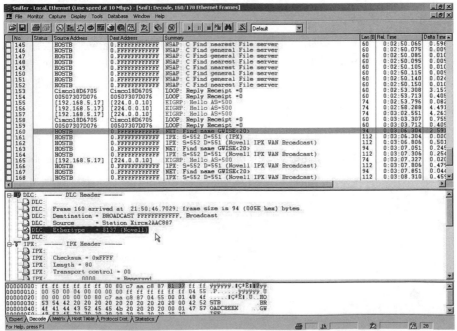

Figure A-5   *IEEE SAPs*

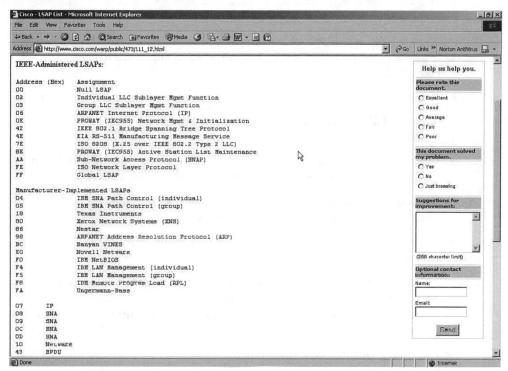

3 How do you know when an Ethernet network needs to be upgraded?

> **Answer: Yes, your users will tell you, but I hope you are one step ahead of that because you have been monitoring the load with a good network management program. You should be tracking the addition of multiple users, protocols, other devices, and all application requirements. Upgrading the bandwidth is always a good thing to do, but good use of switches to segment your existing environment into multiple collision domains assists in the cost of the upgrade process, too. Know your network and its utilization, throughput, and capacity. Look at your interface statistics and calculate the collision rate by dividing collisions by the output packets. This is a tough question to answer in just a few sentences, and obviously you should plan for upgrades.**

4 What does the following error message indicate: "%CDP-4-DUPLEXMISMATCH:Full/half duplex mismatch detected"?

> **Answer: CDP detected a duplex mismatch between Cisco devices, but it is up to you to fix it.**

5 Will communications occur if the port on one side of the link is set to full-duplex and the other side is set to half-duplex? How about if there is a speed mismatch?

Answer: Yes, it will probably work, but this situation of mismatched duplex settings is prone to performance issues. On the other hand, mismatched speeds will not communicate at all.

6 True or false: Fast Ethernet can carry more than 1500 bytes of data in the payload.

Answer: False. Unfortunately Fast Ethernet does not increase the data packet size for Ethernet.

7 What types of housekeeping traffic would you expect on the wire with Ethernet in a network similar to the chapter scenario? (Refer back to Figure 5-1.)

Answer: Routing protocol traffic such as the EIGRP hellos via multicast address 224.0.0.10, CDP updates, and keepalives at a minimum.

8 When should you clear the counters on an Ethernet interface? How do you clear the counters for interface e0?

Answer: Clear counters when you want to look at what is happening for a specific period of time or after fixing problems. Use the Cisco IOS command clear counters to clear all interface counters or the command clear counters e0 to clear just the counters for the e0 interface.

9 Compare DIX Ethernet to IEEE Ethernet

Answer: DIX Ethernet (or Ethernet II) uses a 2-byte type field to link to Layer 3. IEEE 802.3 Ethernet uses a valid length field but uses an IEEE SAP to point to Layer 3. (Refer back to Figure 5-3.)

10 What frame type carries CDP packets? How do you know?

Answer: CDP uses IEEE 802.3 frame format with a SNAP header. (Refer back to Figure 5-15.)

11 What command shows you the Layer 2 address for Ethernet on a Microsoft client? On a Cisco router?

Answer: Issue winipcfg or ipconfig /all on the client for the IP parameters and MAC address. Issue show interfaces [*interface*] on a Cisco router to see the MAC and other statistics.

12 Are collisions an issue in full-duplex Ethernet? Why or why not?

Answer: No. Collisions are not an issue in full-duplex Ethernet because the shared media is removed. A point-to-point connection, whether via a crossover cable or to a switch, is required to eliminate taking turns on the medium.

Chapter 6's Review Questions

1 On the 1900, portfast is enabled on the 10-Mbps ports and disabled on the uplink ports. Can you change this? If so, how? Give a practical example of using portfast.

Answer: Portfast is enabled by default on the 10-Mbps ports in the assumption that they are host ports on the 1900. It is not enabled on the 100-Mbps uplink ports (ports A and B) assuming they connect to another switch or server. The commands on the 1900 are as follows: menu, p for port, *select a port*, and then h for portfast mode. Refer back to Table 6-7 for portfast commands on other devices. All host ports should be enabled for portfast. Specific examples include a host that can't find a domain controller or a DHCP server or a Novell client who never gets a login screen.

2 What command outputs the following on a 2900 CatOS:

```
* = Static Entry. + = Permanent Entry. # = System Entry. R = Router Entry.
   X = Port Security Entry
VLAN  Dest MAC/Route Des  Destination Ports or VCs / [Protocol Type]
----  ----------------    ------------------------------------------
1        00-90-92-2a-76-9a   1/1 [ALL]
1        00-80-c7-aa-c8-87   1/2 [ALL]
1        00-50-04-df-5f-3c   1/2 [ALL]
1        00-d0-79-68-84-8d   1/2 [ALL]
1        00-b0-64-81-e3-00   2/3 [ALL]
```

Answer: The command is show cam dynamic on a CatOS box.

3 What command outputs the following on an IOS-based switch:

```
Dynamic Address Count:              7
Secure Address (User-defined) Count:   0
Static Address (User-defined) Count:   0
System Self Address Count:          37
Total MAC addresses:                44
Maximum MAC addresses:              8192
Non-static Address Table:
Destination Address  Address Type  VLAN  Destination Port
-------------------  ------------  ----  ----------------
0010.4ba5.ae50       Dynamic          1  FastEthernet0/12
0010.ffe5.17fd       Dynamic          1  FastEthernet0/12
0010.ffe5.17ff       Dynamic          1  FastEthernet0/12
0050.04df.5f3c       Dynamic          1  FastEthernet0/1
0080.c7aa.c887       Dynamic          1  FastEthernet0/11
0090.922a.769b       Dynamic          1  FastEthernet0/11
00b0.6481.e300       Dynamic          1  FastEthernet0/12
```

Answer: The command is show mac-address-table on an IOS box.

4 Is a port receiving traffic if it is in the STP blocking state?

Answer: Yes, a port is receiving traffic if it is in the blocking state, but it does not learn source MACs or forward any frames. The port is blocked by STP as to not cause a loop at Layer 2. However, it must still listen for BPDUs so that it can automatically become active if another port or device fails.

5 What are the STP state transitions?

Answer: See Figure 6-6 for the following STP state transitions: disabled, blocking, listening, learning, and forwarding. Compare STP to RSTP in Table 6-6.

6 How do you view the speed and duplex settings on a router or IOS-based switch? On a CatOS-based switch?

Answer: See Table 6-7. show interface on an IOS based switch, and show port on a CatOS based switch.

7 It is common practice to use loopbacks for testing. Can you be sure that a loopback address is always up?

Answer: The following output shows sending the log to an internal buffer on r3, bouncing lo10 (shut/no shut), and then reviewing the log. This type of logging is quite helpful in troubleshooting and less overhead on the device than logging to the console. It clearly displays that it is possible to shut down a loopback.

```
r3#configure terminal
r3(config)#line console 0
r3(config-line)#logging buffered
r3(config-line)#interface loopback 10
r3(config-if)#shut
r3(config-if)#end
r3#show ip interface brief
Interface            IP-Address      OK? Method Status               Protocol
...
FastEthernet2/0      192.168.5.97    YES NVRAM  up                   up
Loopback10           192.168.6.100   YES NVRAM  administratively down down
r3#show log
Syslog logging: enabled (0 messages dropped, 0 flushes, 0 overruns)
    Console logging: level debugging, 69 messages logged
    Monitor logging: level debugging, 0 messages logged
    Buffer logging: level debugging, 7 messages logged
    Trap logging: level informational, 73 message lines logged
Log Buffer (4096 bytes):
03:46:39: %SYS-5-CONFIG_I: Configured from console by vty0 (192.168.5.99)
03:46:55: %LINEPROTO-5-UPDOWN: Line protocol on Interface Loopback10, changed state
  to up
03:46:57: %LINK-3-UPDOWN: Interface Loopback10, changed state to up
03:46:57: %SYS-5-CONFIG_I: Configured from console by vty0 (192.168.5.99)
03:47:22: %LINK-5-CHANGED: Interface Loopback10, changed state to administratively
  down
03:47:23: %LINEPROTO-5-UPDOWN: Line protocol on Interface Loopback10, changed state
  to down
03:47:34: %SYS-5-CONFIG_I: Configured from console by vty0 (192.168.5.99)
r3#!!!ouch someone can shut down a loopback
r3#configure terminal
r3(config)#interface loopback 10
r3(config-if)#no shut
r3(config-if)#end
r3#show ip interface loopback 10
Loopback10 is up, line protocol is up
  Internet address is 192.168.6.100/28
  Broadcast address is 255.255.255.255
  Address determined by non-volatile memory
  MTU is 1514 bytes
```

8 I issued the following **show interface** command on the 2900 CatOS box to view the management IP address and its parameters. What is the 192.168.5.111 address?

```
sw2900> (enable) show interface
sl0: flags=51<UP,POINTOPOINT,RUNNING>
        slip 0.0.0.0 dest 0.0.0.0
sc0: flags=63<UP,BROADCAST,RUNNING>
        vlan 1 inet 192.168.5.98 netmask 255.255.255.240 broadcast 192.168.5.111
```

Answer: Do the math. 192.168.5.111 is the broadcast address for subnet 192.168.5.96/28. The mask is 240 in the last octet, which means 4 bits were borrowed. The lowest 1 bit is 16, which is the increment for the subnets. You are using subnet 96. The first address on the subnet belongs to the router, which is .97. If you add 16 to the subnet, the next subnet is 112. One less than the next subnet is the broadcast address for the current subnet. Remember that all the host bits are 1s for the broadcast address.

9 Encoded Address Recognition Logic (EARL) is an ASIC that works with the bus arbitration for packet transfers in a Catalyst 5000. Ethernet ports use a custom ASIC called _____. Other ports use a custom ASIC called _____.

Answer: Ethernet uses SAINT and other ports use SAGE.

10 You are at a host and attempt to telnet to a switch. The following message appears:

```
Password required, but none set
Connection to host lost.
```

What's the issue?

Answer: No vty password has been set. Although a password is not required on the console, it normally is required for telnet access. This is because login is the default on vty lines. You can fix the issue by supplying a password or by removing the login on the vty lines with the no login command.

11 Assume your environment to be what it is now for the chapter scenario. On hosta you type the command **tracert 192.168.5.103**. How many hops to the destination?

Answer: Hops are router hops. Everything on this side of the router is on the same network hop (broadcast domain) although there are different collision domains. The following trace output illustrates the one hop:

```
C:\>tracert 192.168.5.103
Tracing route to HOSTC [192.168.5.103]
over a maximum of 30 hops:
  1    <10 ms   <10 ms   <10 ms  HOSTC [192.168.5.103]
Trace complete.
```

Chapter 7's Review Questions

1 Compare ISL to 802.1Q.

Answer: When a frame goes out an ISL trunk, it gets encapsulated by tagging it with a 26-byte ISL header and another 4-byte CRC trailer. Therefore, it is possible for an Ethernet frame to be 1518 + 30 = 1548 bytes. ISL trunks can carry not only Ethernet traffic, but also Token Ring and FDDI, due to the *reserved field* in the ISL header.

Unlike the Cisco proprietary ISL, IEEE 802.1Q offers multivendor VLAN multiplexing support. As shown in Figure 7-5, ISL is more of an encapsulation (external tagging), whereas 802.1Q is an internal frame tagging method of VLAN identification.

2 Can you change the management VLAN?

Answer: Yes, you can change the management VLAN. However, some switches require it to be VLAN1. For example, on a CatOS box, use the set int sc0 *vlan# ipaddress subnetmask* command.

3 Why should you use a separate management VLAN?

Answer: Always use a separate management VLAN to isolate user problems. If a broadcast storm occurs, it could spread throughout the entire VLAN. On the management VLAN, this would eventually cause drastic CPU overload. Protocol traffic such as CDP, VTP, and PAgP use VLAN1. You do not want your other management traffic such as telnet, SNMP, VMPS, Syslog to interfere if you can help it. The management traffic uses whatever VLAN that is assigned to the sc0 port. STP is sent on each VLAN. If the Supervisor CPU is saturated by processing broadcasts in the management VLAN, it may not be able to keep up with STP BPDUs.

4 What does a transparent mode-configured Catalyst do with a VTP update message?

Answer: A transparent mode-configured Catalyst ignores VTP update messages unless it has trunk ports configured so that it can act as an intermediary and flood the frame to other switches.

5 You incorrectly associated port 8 with VLAN8, so you issue the following command: **clear vlan 8** to clear the port from VLAN8 and back to the default VLAN1. However, the port status is still showing as inactive. How can you fix this issue?

Answer: You need to associate port 8 with VLAN1. Although all ports originally start in VLAN1, when you change them to another VLAN they do not automatically go back to VLAN1. Instead they are sitting in an inactive state.

6 The lab technician was nice enough to give you his switch to replace a production switch that you were having problems with. He quickly clears all the VLANs on the switch and hands it over to you. When you plug the switch into your network, you quickly realize that all your other VLANs disappear. Where did you go wrong? Is there anything you can do to avoid such issues?

Answer: Evidently, the lab switch had the highest revision number; therefore, you just learned how to play "vlan wipeout" and have lots of unhappy users. Sounds like lots of work, but perhaps beforehand you should have made sure your switches were either using all VTP transparent mode or a couple of VTP servers with mostly VTP clients. If you would have just reset the VTP domain name on the lab switch, you would have been fine.

7 You want to verify that you configured portfast on the 3512XL port fa0/2. How can you accomplish this?

Answer: sh spanning-tree int fa0/2. Alternatively, you could look at the configuration file. Likewise on the 2900 CatOS switch, you could check the portfast status of hostc using sh port spantree 1/2.

8 Routing provides _____ connectivity, whereas trunking provides _____ connectivity.

Answer: Routing provides inter-VLAN connectivity, whereas trunking provides intra-VLAN connectivity.

9 There are three major steps for working VLANs. What are they?

Answer: 1. Create and define a VTP domain. 2. Create the VLAN. 3. Associate a port(s) with the VLAN.

10 Can VLANs assist with people trying to Sniff the network?

Answer: Yes, VLANs can assist with people trying to Sniff the network. Remember VLANs are subnets. The VLAN ports are switch ports, which in fact have a certain level of security on their own. You must configure port monitoring before you can run a protocol analyzer.

11 In a router-on-a-stick configuration, as in the chapter scenario, what would you expect to be the first hop if hosta were to tracert to hostc?

Answer: In a router-on-a-stick configuration, all inter-VLAN traffic goes through the stick. Therefore, in the chapter scenario that is 192.168.5.30 for VLAN1.

Chapter 8's Review Questions

1   Can a single Frame Relay PVC be assigned different DLCIs on each end of a virtual circuit?

Answer: Yes. The term *to know* **is "locally significant," which means that a particular DLCI is significant only on the link between two frame devices. Think of DLCIs as the speed-dial numbers stored in your cell phone.**

2   What are the three possible states for a Frame Relay PVC? Explain.

Answer: Refer to Table 8-2 and Trouble Ticket 4. The three possible states for a PVC are active, inactive, and deleted.

3   What is the result if one end of the PVC is set to the default Cisco LMI type and the other end is set to ANSI or Q933A?

Answer: As long as the Frame Relay switch attached to the local router is configured for the same LMI, the PVC works just fine. Remember that LMI is the signaling between the router and local frame switch, not an end-to-end function.

4   Can you ping yourself in Frame Relay? Why or why not?

Answer: On point-to-point interfaces, yes. On multipoint interfaces, however, Frame Relay is NBMA, and in a hub-and-spoke topology there is no mapping for yourself. Certainly you could put in a map statement for yourself if you really wanted to make this happen.

5   Headquarters is connected to several branch office routers through a Frame Relay cloud. You know for a fact that the hub router is version 12.1 but you are not sure about all the remotes. Keepalive activity is occurring at most of the remote offices but not all of them. What should you check?

Answer: Work through the layers. The physical connection is fine, but you are not receiving any kind of signal from a couple of pretty old existing sites. Perhaps the remote routers are something less than IOS 11.2 and need LMI configured on them. The command is frame-relay lmi-type [cisco | ansi | q933].

6   Headquarters is connected to several branch office routers through a Frame Relay cloud. The engineer at one of the branch offices is having problems communicating with another branch office. How can you help him out?

Answer: Determine how the branch office is communicating. Determine whether the engineer can ping the other branch offices. Take a methodical approach and work through the layers, addressing the following points:

- **Find out whether the interfaces are up.**

- **Check ports and cables.**

- **Are you getting LMI?**

- **Is there an encapsulation mismatch?**

- **Are the DLCIs active and assigned properly?**

- **Is there a static or dynamic mapping problem?**

- **Did you forget the broadcast keyword for the routing updates?**

- **Do you have a route?**

- **Do you have split-horizon issues?**

- **Are there any ACLs?**

7 Explain the output of **show frame-relay map** in the following example:

```
r1#show frame-relay map
Serial1 (up): ip 192.168.5.6 dlci 104(0x68,0x1880), dynamic,
               broadcast,, status defined, active
```

Answer: The show frame-relay map example indicates that s1 is up. DLCI 104 (68 in hex) maps to 192.168.5.6 using Inverse ARP. It displays dynamic, broadcast by the default nature of Inverse ARP and the PVC is active.

8 You have decided to contact your service provider about getting a higher CIR to allocate more bandwidth because you have been experiencing consistent problems with dropped packets due to congestion on the PVC. What command did you use to determine this?

Answer: The show frame-relay pvc command is helpful in checking dropped packets and FECNs and BECNs. The presence of FECNs and BECNs does not necessarily indicate that frames were dropped by the service provider. That depends on how they police. If the service provider is generous and only marks excess frames as DE, you may make out fine.

9 In an all-Cisco-shop Frame Relay, Cisco encapsulation is fine. What Frame Relay encapsulation type is available for other vendors?

Answer: The Frame Relay encapsulation types are the default Cisco and IETF for other vendors.

10 Point-to-point subinterfaces are often used in configuring Frame Relay to avoid the routing issues with main interfaces and multipoint configurations. Do you need an IP address on the main interface if using point-to-point subinterfaces?

Answer: You should not configure an IP address on the main interface when configuring Frame Relay point-to-point subinterfaces. If one is configured, you can use no ip address to remove it and configure each subinterface with an address from a different subnet.

11 How does a router get a DLCI?

Answer: Data-link connection identifiers (DLCIs) can be learned via Inverse ARP or manually configured. If manually assigned, you get the DLCI assignments from the service provider.

12 You are attempting to fix a bad IP address on a Frame Relay interface, but the mapping is still showing the old address. What should you do?

Answer: The clear frame-relay-inarp command clears the dynamic Inverse ARP table.

Chapter 9's Review Questions

1 Why do interface resets occur?

Answer: Interface resets occur when the interface has been completely reset, which normally is from cabling or signaling issues. The system resets the interface automatically if it sees that the physical interface is up, but the line protocol is down. Carrier transitions occur when an interruption in signal occurs. If DCD goes down and then back up, for example, that is two transitions. If they continue to increase, check the cabling or other attached hardware. If output drops also increase, the problem may be congestion.

2 True or false: The ISDN signaling protocol is LAPB for the D channel.

Answer: False. LAPB is for X.25. LAPD is the signaling protocol for the ISDN D channel. The ISDN B channels are for data, voice, and video and use HDLC or PPP encapsulation.

3 The modem control leads on **show interfaces s0** are quite helpful for troubleshooting. DCD keeps changing state. What else on the interface statistics would you expect to be increasing? Look at Example 9-13 if you need to see a display of the modem control leads.

Answer: The modem control leads are quite helpful for troubleshooting. If the DCD keeps changing state, the carrier transitions may in turn drop and reset the line due to the failure to output queued packets.

4 Your router has a native ISDN BRI port. Is this device a TE1 or TE2?

Answer: If your router has a native ISDN port, it is a TE1. A TE2 is a router or PC without an ISDN port that connects via a terminal adapter. Review Figure 9-7 and Figure 9-8.

5 What is the difference between Multilink PPP and dial backup?

Answer: Multilink PPP is used to aggregate traffic over multiple channels simultaneously. Dial backup is having a secondary link for when the primary fails. They are not the same.

6 Use the first HDLC scenario as a guide. Can you spot the issue in the following output:

```
r3#
03:03:49: IP-EIGRP: Neighbor 192.168.9.18 not on common subnet for Serial0/3
03:04:03: IP-EIGRP: Neighbor 192.168.9.18 not on common subnet for Serial0/3
03:04:18: IP-EIGRP: Neighbor 192.168.9.18 not on common subnet for Serial0/3
03:04:32: IP-EIGRP: Neighbor 192.168.9.18 not on common subnet for Serial0/3

r5#show ip interface brief
Interface           IP-Address      OK? Method Status                  Protocol
BRI0                unassigned      YES unset  administratively down    down
BRI0:1              unassigned      YES unset  administratively down    down
BRI0:2              unassigned      YES unset  administratively down    down
Ethernet0           unassigned      YES unset  administratively down    down
Loopback8           5.5.5.5         YES manual up                      up
Serial0             192.168.9.18    YES manual up                      up
Serial0.101         172.16.8.6      YES manual deleted                 down
Serial1             unassigned      YES unset  administratively down    down
r5#
03:04:01: IP-EIGRP: Neighbor 192.168.9.13 not on common subnet for Serial0
03:04:15: IP-EIGRP: Neighbor 192.168.9.13 not on common subnet for Serial0
03:04:29: IP-EIGRP: Neighbor 192.168.9.13 not on common subnet for Serial0
```

Answer: s0 was configured for .18 rather than .14. Obviously both ends of a wire must be on the same subnet:

```
r5#configure terminal
r5(config)#interface s1
r5(config-if)#shut
03:04:43: IP-EIGRP: Neighbor 192.168.9.13 not on common subnet for Serial0
r5(config-if)#encapsulation hdlc
r5(config-if)#ip address 192.168.9.18 255.255.255.2
03:04:57: IP-EIGRP: Neighbor 192.168.9.13 not on common subnet for Serial052
r5(config-if)#no shut
r5(config-if)#end
r5#show ip interface brief
03:05:04: %SYS-5-CONFIG_I: Configured from console by console
03:05:05: %LINK-3-UPDOWN: Interface Serial1, changed state to up
Interface           IP-Address      OK? Method Status                  Protocol
BRI0                unassigned      YES unset  administratively down    down
BRI0:1              unassigned      YES unset  administratively down    down
BRI0:2              unassigned      YES unset  administratively down    down
Ethernet0           unassigned      YES unset  administratively down    down
Loopback8           5.5.5.5         YES manual up                      up
Serial0             192.168.9.14    YES manual up                      up
Serial0.101         172.16.8.6      YES manual deleted                 down
Serial1             unassigned      YES unset  administratively down    down
```

7 Throughout the chapter you experienced multiple carrier transitions. What command is very helpful in helping you figure out the issues with this problem?

Answer: To assist with finding the issues related to carrier transitions, you should target the lower layers. First, look at show interfaces, and controllers may be of some help. You can watch the actual keepalive activity with the debug serial interface command.

8 You have a high-speed Ethernet that is sending packets faster than the ISDN link can keep up with. How can you improve performance?

Answer: There are many ways to improve performance. You could try bringing up the second B channel for ISDN. If necessary you can disable fast switching.

9 When are floating static routes appropriate?

Answer: Floating statics are used as a backup static route to a routing protocol. The administrative distance is set higher than the routing protocol so that the floating static is not used unless the routing protocol entry is not in the table.

10 When using the **backup interface** method to back up a circuit, do you place the **backup interface** command under the primary or secondary interface?

Answer: The backup interface command goes under the primary interface configuration. Refer to Example 9-31.

11 You are controlling the backup interface using the **backup delay 10 60** command. What do the numbers 10 and 60 correspond to?

Answer: The backup delay 10 60 command says that the backup link will be up 10 seconds after the primary link fails and the backup link will go down 60 seconds after the primary comes back up.

12 Your ISDN phone bill is a lot more than you expected, but you have interesting traffic set appropriately with an access list. It seems that when you finish transferring your files over the ISDN link, the link doesn't go down. It stays up until you manually bring it down. What did you forget?

Answer: Configure the dialer idle-timeout command.

13 Including synchronization and framing, what is the total bandwidth for ISDN BRI?

Answer: There are two B channels that are 64 kbps each, which equals 128 kbps. Add the D channel at 16 kbps to give you 144 kbps. Add the 48 kbps for synchronization and framing for a total of 192 kbps.

14 Can you use one 64 kbps B channel to handle backup for multiple T1s?

Answer: Yes, you can you use one 64-kbps B channel to handle backup for multiple T1s by way of dialer profiles. Dialer profiles give you this type of flexibility by separating the logical configurations from the physical interfaces.

Chapter 10's Review Questions

1 The following output was captured during Trouble Ticket 6. Why is fa0/9 in a blocking state?

```
kentnarrows#show spanning-tree vlan 1
Spanning tree 1 is executing the IEEE compatible Spanning Tree protocol
  Bridge Identifier has priority 32768, address 00d0.7968.8484
  Configured hello time 2, max age 20, forward delay 15
  Current root has priority 32768, address 0090.922a.7680
  Root port is 24, cost of root path is 19
  Topology change flag not set, detected flag not set, changes 1
  Times:  hold 1, topology change 35, notification 2
          hello 2, max age 20, forward delay 15
  Timers: hello 0, topology change 0, notification 0
Interface Fa0/1 (port 13) in Spanning tree 1 is down
   Port path cost 100, Port priority 128
   Designated root has priority 32768, address 0090.922a.7680
   Designated bridge has priority 32768, address 00d0.7968.8484
   Designated port is 13, path cost 19
   Timers: message age 0, forward delay 0, hold 0
   BPDU: sent 0, received 0
Interface Fa0/2 (port 14) in Spanning tree 1 is down
   Port path cost 100, Port priority 128
   Designated root has priority 32768, address 0090.922a.7680
   Designated bridge has priority 32768, address 00d0.7968.8484
   Designated port is 14, path cost 19
   Timers: message age 0, forward delay 0, hold 0
   BPDU: sent 0, received 0
Interface Fa0/3 (port 15) in Spanning tree 1 is down
   Port path cost 100, Port priority 128
   Designated root has priority 32768, address 0090.922a.7680
   Designated bridge has priority 32768, address 00d0.7968.8484
   Designated port is 15, path cost 19
   Timers: message age 0, forward delay 0, hold 0
   BPDU: sent 0, received 0
Interface Fa0/4 (port 16) in Spanning tree 1 is down
   Port path cost 100, Port priority 128
   Designated root has priority 32768, address 0090.922a.7680
   Designated bridge has priority 32768, address 00d0.7968.8484
   Designated port is 16, path cost 19
   Timers: message age 0, forward delay 0, hold 0
   BPDU: sent 0, received 0
Interface Fa0/5 (port 17) in Spanning tree 1 is down
   Port path cost 100, Port priority 128
   Designated root has priority 32768, address 0090.922a.7680
   Designated bridge has priority 32768, address 00d0.7968.8484
   Designated port is 17, path cost 19
   Timers: message age 0, forward delay 0, hold 0
   BPDU: sent 0, received 0
Interface Fa0/7 (port 19) in Spanning tree 1 is down
   Port path cost 100, Port priority 128
   Designated root has priority 32768, address 0090.922a.7680
   Designated bridge has priority 32768, address 00d0.7968.8484
   Designated port is 19, path cost 19
   Timers: message age 0, forward delay 0, hold 0
   BPDU: sent 0, received 0
Interface Fa0/8 (port 20) in Spanning tree 1 is down
   Port path cost 100, Port priority 128
   Designated root has priority 32768, address 0090.922a.7680
   Designated bridge has priority 32768, address 00d0.7968.8484
   Designated port is 20, path cost 19
   Timers: message age 0, forward delay 0, hold 0
   BPDU: sent 0, received 0
```

```
Interface Fa0/9 (port 22) in Spanning tree 1 is BLOCKING
    Port path cost 19, Port priority 128
    Designated root has priority 32768, address 0090.922a.7680
    Designated bridge has priority 32768, address 0090.922a.7680
    Designated port is 27, path cost 0
    Timers: message age 3, forward delay 0, hold 0
    BPDU: sent 11, received 333
Interface Fa0/11 (port 24) in Spanning tree 1 is FORWARDING
    Port path cost 19, Port priority 128
    Designated root has priority 32768, address 0090.922a.7680
    Designated bridge has priority 32768, address 0090.922a.7680
    Designated port is 26, path cost 0
    Timers: message age 2, forward delay 0, hold 0
    BPDU: sent 3, received 346
Interface Fa0/12 (port 25) in Spanning tree 1 is FORWARDING
    Port path cost 19, Port priority 128
    Designated root has priority 32768, address 0090.922a.7680
    Designated bridge has priority 32768, address 00d0.7968.8484
    Designated port is 25, path cost 19
    Timers: message age 0, forward delay 0, hold 0
    BPDU: sent 345, received 0
```

Answer: fa0/9 (port 22) is in a blocking state because there are redundant Layer 2 links. Look at Figure 10-9 to see the two additional cables added to build in this redundancy. When there is a topology change, this port may no longer be blocked.

2 Using the same data in the preceding question, why are fa0/6 and fa0/10 missing?

Answer: Fa0/6 and fa0/10 are missing because they are not in VLAN1. They are in VLAN3 and VLAN2, respectively.

3 While troubleshooting Trouble Ticket 6, I unplugged the dongle attached to the network interface card (NIC) to see which port the host was connected to. According to the following output and Figure 10-9, which host did I perform this on?

```
kentnarrows(config)#
.Mar  1 03:47:25.507: %LINK-3-UPDOWN: Interface FastEthernet0/10,
    changed state to down
.Mar  1 03:47:25.735: %LINEPROTO-5-UPDOWN: Line protocol on
    Interface FastEthernet0/10, changed state to down
.Mar  1 03:47:43.858: %LINK-3-UPDOWN: Interface FastEthernet0/10,
    changed state to up
.Mar  1 03:47:44.773: %LINEPROTO-5-UPDOWN: Line protocol on
    Interface FastEthernet0/10, changed state to up
```

Answer: While troubleshooting Trouble Ticket 6, I unplugged the dongle attached to the hosta NIC to see which port it was connected to. I had configured the VLAN1 interface on kentnarrows with a duplicate IP of its gateway. The results were quite interesting; goose could get to hosta, but kentnarrows could not. I found the issue when I tried to copy the configurations to the TFTP server when things were supposedly fixed.

4 Refer to the following output. Are there any potential issues?

```
chesapeakebay> (enable)show port status
Port  Name               Status     Vlan       Level  Duplex Speed Type
----- ------------------ ---------- ---------- ------ ------ ----- -----------
 1/1                     notconnect 1          normal half   100 100BaseTX
 1/2                     notconnect 1          normal half   100 100BaseTX
```

```
2/1                        disabled   1            normal   auto   auto 10/100BaseTX
2/2                        disabled   1            normal   auto   auto 10/100BaseTX
2/3                        disabled   1            normal   auto   auto 10/100BaseTX
2/4                        disabled   1            normal   auto   auto 10/100BaseTX
2/5                        disabled   1            normal   auto   auto 10/100BaseTX
2/6                        disabled   1            normal   auto   auto 10/100BaseTX
2/7                        disabled   1            normal   auto   auto 10/100BaseTX
2/8                        disabled   1            normal   auto   auto 10/100BaseTX
2/9                        disabled   1            normal   auto   auto 10/100BaseTX
2/10 to hub                disabled   1            normal   auto   auto 10/100BaseTX
2/11 to heron              disabled   1            normal   auto   auto 10/100BaseTX
2/12 to duck               disabled   1            normal   auto   auto 10/100BaseTX
```

**Answer: The output displays the show port status command on the 2900 CatOS box.
The ports are all disabled as it appears, but nothing happens if you enable the ports.
The real issue is that the ports are on module 2. If you were to issue a show modules,
you would see that module 2 is disabled. To fix the issue, you can type set module 2
enable on the chesapeakebay CatOS switch.**

5 What is likely to be the issue with the following output that was captured during Trouble
   Ticket 4?

```
goose#trace hostc
Tracing the route to hostc (172.16.1.43)
  1 hostc (172.16.1.43) 0 msec
*Mar  1 00:10:20.670: IP: s=172.16.1.43 (local), d=172.16.1.43
   (FastEthernet2/0), len 28, sending
*Mar  1 00:10:20.670: IP: s=172.16.1.43 (FastEthernet2/0), d=172.16.1.43,
   len 28, rcvd 0
*Mar  1 00:10:20.670: IP: s=172.16.1.43 (local), d=172.16.1.43
   (FastEthernet2/0), len 56, sending
*Mar  1 00:10:20.670: IP: s=172.16.1.43 (FastEthernet2/0), d=172.16.1.43
   (FastEthernet2/0), len 56, rcvd 3
*Mar  1 00:10:20.670: IP: s=172.16.1.43 (local), d=172.16.1.43
   (FastEthernet2/0), len 28, sending
*Mar  1 00:10:20.674: IP: s=172.16.1.43 (FastEthernet2/0), d=172.16.1.43,
   len 28, rcvd 0 *  0 msec
```

**Answer: The output shows the source and the destination address to be one and the
same. I suspect there was a duplicate IP issue.**

6 Often trace is very much a complementary tool to ping. What is likely to be the issue with
   the following output that was captured during Trouble Ticket 4?

```
swan#trace kentnarrows
Tracing the route to kentnarrows (172.16.1.45)
   1 duck (172.16.1.17) 4 msec 4 msec 4 msec
   2 heron (10.10.10.2) 16 msec 12 msec 16 msec
   3 crab (172.16.2.10) 16 msec 16 msec 16 msec
   4 swan (172.16.3.9) 12 msec 12 msec 12 msec
   5 duck (172.16.1.17) 8 msec 12 msec 12 msec
   6 heron (10.10.10.2) 20 msec 20 msec 20 msec
   7 crab (172.16.2.10) 20 msec 20 msec 20 msec
   8 swan (172.16.3.9) 16 msec 16 msec 20 msec
   9 duck (172.16.1.17) 16 msec 20 msec 16 msec
  10 heron (10.10.10.2) 24 msec 24 msec 28 msec
  11 crab (172.16.2.10) 28 msec 28 msec 28 msec
  12 swan (172.16.3.9) 24 msec 24 msec 24 msec
  13 duck (172.16.1.17) 24 msec 24 msec 20 msec
  14 heron (10.10.10.2) 32 msec 32 msec 32 msec
  15 crab (172.16.2.10) 32 msec 32 msec 32 msec
  16 swan (172.16.3.9) 28 msec 28 msec 28 msec
```

Answer: When trace continues to list the same routers over and over, you can bet there is a loop somewhere. This particular issue dealt with the mutual redistribution and lack of filtering. Distribute lists, passive interfaces, and route maps are helpful to eliminate these types of issues.

7 Analyze the following issue that occurred during Trouble Ticket 4.

```
osprey#show arp
Protocol  Address            Age (min)  Hardware Addr   Type   Interface
Internet  172.16.2.45          202      0090.922a.7680  ARPA   Ethernet0/0
Internet  172.16.2.42            0      Incomplete      ARPA
Internet  172.16.2.41            -      0080.c7aa.c887  ARPA   Ethernet0/0
```

Answer: When the osprey router looked for 172.16.2.42, it did not find it. The MAC address for 172.16.2.41, which was osprey e0/0 at the time, was manually configured with the MAC address of hostb.

8 The swan (2520) and crab (2516) routers both have ISDN BRI ports. Are they S/T or U?

Answer: The swan (2520) and crab (2516) routers both have ISDN S/T BRI ports. They both connect into an NT1. When an external NT1 is used, the router ports are S/T, which connect to the NT1, which connects via the U ports to an ISDN switch. Alternatively in my scenario, the 804 could have been used for ISDN. It has U port and would plug directly into the ISDN switch.

9 What tool enables you to send traps to a network management system?

Answer: SNMP enables you to send traps to a network management system. You can configure communities, enable traps, and identify the SNMP server via IP address.

10 What steps does Cisco recommend in supporting your internetwork?

Answer: Cisco recommends the following methodology for troubleshooting internetworks:

- **Define the problem.**
- **Gather the facts.**
- **Consider possibilities based on facts.**
- **Create an action plan.**
- **Implement the action plan.**
- **Observe the results.**
- **Document the solution.**

Troubleshooting Resources

This appendix contains useful information you may find helpful both in understanding how things work and in the troubleshooting process. The information here is intended to supplement the chapters in this book and give you more detail regarding the following topics:

- Rebooting a Router
- Configuration Register Fields
- Password Recovery Procedures
- Software Upgrades

Rebooting a Router

Supporting Cisco devices requires that you understand how the devices actually work (and boot, for that matter). At the CCNA and CCNP level, you have become very familiar with the different modes of operation: user mode, privileged mode, global configuration mode, interface mode, router configuration mode, and so on. That is not enough. Depending on the device, different things occur at boot time.

This section is not at all meant as a replacement for Cisco.com but instead is intended to give you a general idea of what happens when you reboot a router. For troubleshooting purposes, for instance, you need to know how to display boot parameters, know what configuration file and software image the device is looking for upon startup, and know how to manually adjust this.

Figure B-1 is taken directly from Cisco.com and gives you a flowchart approach as to what happens when you boot a router. You can find this and more detailed boot information at www.cisco.com/univercd/cc/td/doc/product/software/ios120/12cgcr/fun_c/fcprt2/fcreboot.htm#xtocid114470.

Figure B-1 *Rebooting a Router*

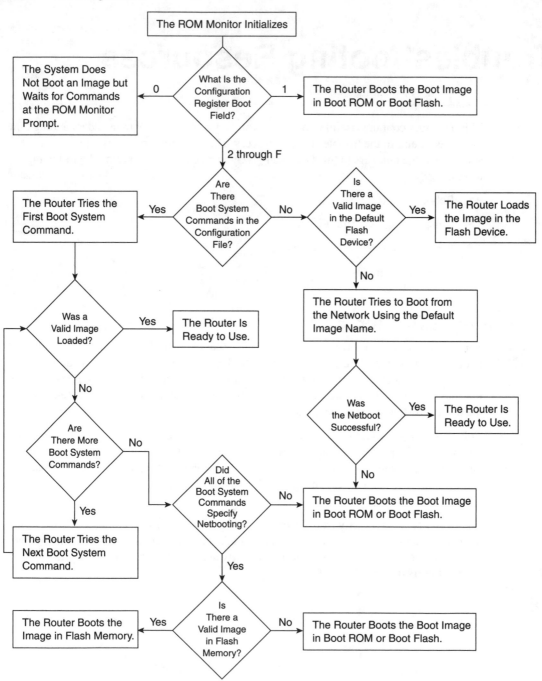

Figure B-2 displays configuration register settings. Configuration register changes today are primarily made in software, whereas in older days you had to remove the cover and set hardware DIP switches. The Boot field (lowest and rightmost 4 bits of the 16-bit register) determines whether the router loads an operating system image, and if so, where it obtains the IOS or OS image as follows:

- **0x0**—ROMMON

- **0x1**—RxBoot (or bootflash memory on higher-end models)

- **0x2 to 0xF**—Normal router boot. Looks at boot system commands in the startup configuration first and then the first file in Flash memory.

You can force the router to stop booting and enter ROMMON mode, where you can set the configuration register to boot the router manually. Assuming the Break key has not been turned off, you can issue the *break sequence* within the first 60 seconds from a console or telnet session. It is always good practice to learn exactly where the Break key is located on the PC you are using and to test the break sequence with the terminal emulator software you choose.

View the configuration register with **show version**, **confreg**, or if in ROMMON use the **o** parameter. Use the **config-register** global command to change how the router boots. To schedule a reload of the system image to occur at a later time to avoid interrupting operations immediately (within 24 hours), you can use one of the following methods:

- **reload in** *hh:mm* [*text*]

- **reload at** *hh:mm* [*month day*|*day month*] [*text*]

NOTE   The command **reload at** requires the system clock to be set. Issue a **show reload** to display the reload schedule. You can cancel with **reload cancel**.

Configuration Register Fields

Understanding the boot parameters is pretty important for support tasks such as enabling or disabling the Break key, setting the baud rate, booting an alternative image, password recovery, and upgrading the image software. Take a few minutes to review the configuration register bits in Figure B-2. Use **show version** to see what your config-register is set to and lookup the value in Figure B-2.

Figure B-2 *Cisco Config-Register Fields*

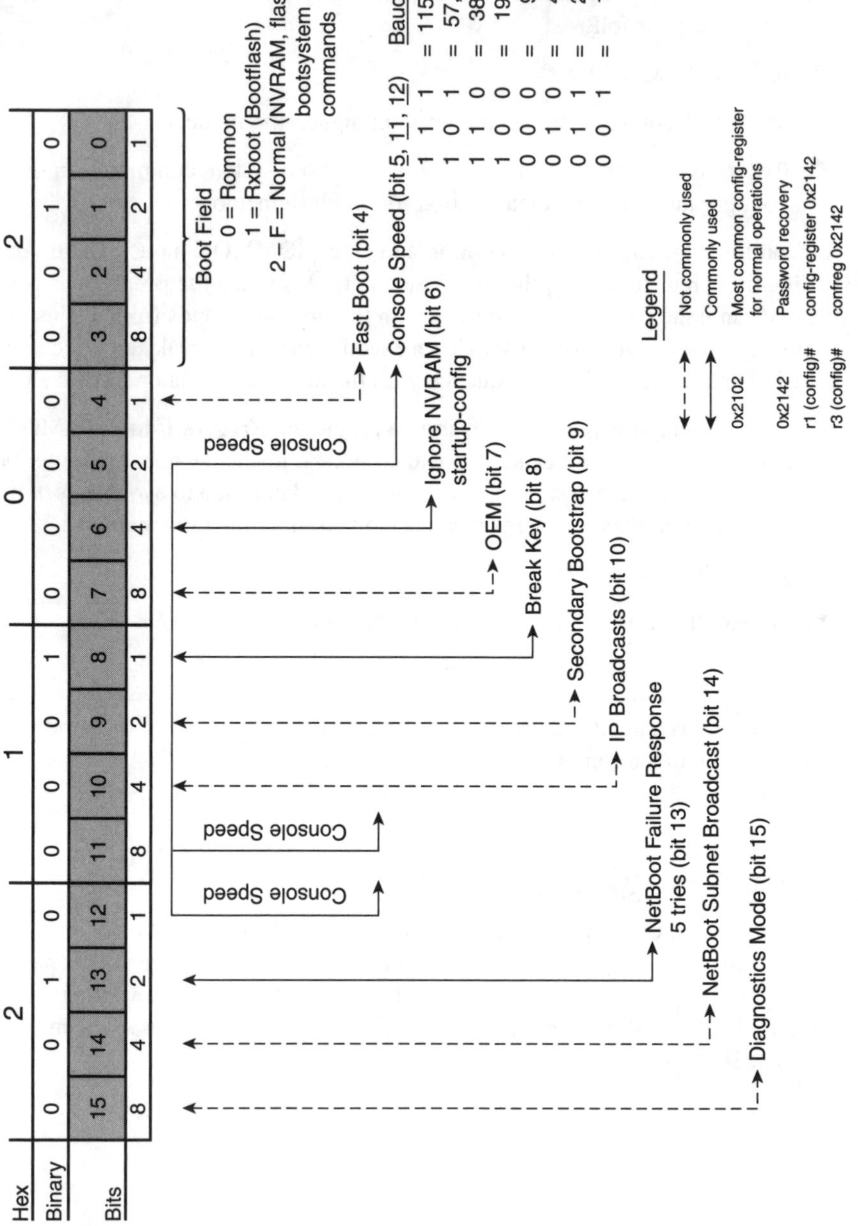

The config-register Boot field determines how the router boots. ROMMON and RxBoot (bootflash) are two different implementations of the IOS subset. Be aware, however, that not all models have RxBoot to act as a boot helper. ROMMON performs a diagnostic check and either keeps the device in ROMMON (> or rommon>) or loads RxBoot (router(boot)>). ROMMON only provides you with one-letter commands. Boot helper mode keeps the device in rxboot or bootflash, where it has host-mode functionality and checks the startup-config or loads the fully functional IOS (router>).

Password Recovery Procedures

Password recovery procedures are very well documented at Cisco.com, but I have included a step-by-step procedure for the devices used throughout this book and more for your convenience. On a practical note, the most common problem with password recovery on any device is issuing the correct break sequence from your particular terminal emulation software. See www.cisco.com/warp/public/701/61.html for a very informative table of break sequences for many terminal emulation programs. Other issues relate to understanding the modes of the device, the configuration register settings, the hardware/software particulars for the different devices, and more importantly having console access.

NOTE   You can find detailed password recovery procedures at www.cisco.com/warp/public/474/index.shtml.

Cisco 2500, 3000, 4000, 7000 Series Devices

For such devices as the Cisco 2000, 2500, 3000, 4000, AccessPro, 7000 (RP), AGS, IGS, and STS-10x platforms, the password recovery procedure is as follows:

1 Establish a console session using the following settings:

  • Speed 9600 bits per second

  • 8 data bits

  • 0 parity bits

  • 1 stop bit

  • No flow control

2 Turn off the router, and then turn it back on using the power switch.

3 Execute the break sequence (such as Ctrl+Break) within the first 60 seconds of startup to force the router into ROMMON mode.

> **NOTE**   While practicing password recovery, you must be able to issue a break
> sequence for successful password recovery. It is critical you know how your
> terminal emulator issues a break. For example, HyperTerm and SecureCRT use
> the Ctrl+Break key sequence, whereas ProComm and TeraTerm use Alt+B.
> Some versions of Windows NT have a problem sending a break signal using
> older versions of HyperTerm; visit www.hilgraeve.com for upgrades.

4 View the configuration register by typing the letter **o** at the > prompt. Usually the
   configuration register is 0x2102 or 0x102, but you should record the value so that you can
   change it back later.

5 Change the configuration register to ignore the startup-config (contents of NVRAM,
   nonvolatile random-access memory) and initialize the router by issuing the following
   commands:

```
r1>o/r 0x2142
r1>i
```

6 The router should reboot and go into setup where it ignores the startup configuration all
   together. Press Ctrl+C to break out of setup. Go to enable mode using the **enable**
   command, but do *not* exit yet.

> **NOTE**   It is best practice to copy your configuration to Notepad or another editor
> in case you were to lose it.

7 Type **copy startup-config running-config** or **config memory**. Do *not* type **copy run start**
   or **write mem** or you will lose your entire configuration.

8 Now you can hack the password by viewing the running configuration with **show
   running-config** or **write terminal**. Unencrypted passwords can be re-used, whereas
   encrypted ones need to be replaced.

> **NOTE**   During a password recovery procedure, you may or may not be able to view
> your passwords in clear text. If the **enable secret** was configured, for
> instance, the only recovery is to configure a new value due to the MD5
> encryption. If the **enable password** was configured (and **service
> password-encryption** is off), however, password recovery is merely a
> visual inspection of the existing password. Also note that all of your
> interfaces are shut down during the password recovery procedures.

9   Make the necessary changes, including changing your passwords, changing the
    configuration register back to normal, bringing up your interfaces, and saving your
    configuration as follows:

```
r1#configure terminal
r1(config)#enable secret <password>
r1(config)#config-register 0x2102
r1(config)#interface ethernet 0
r1(config-if)#no shut
r1(config-if)#interface ethernet 1
r1(config-if)#no shut
r1(config-if)#interface serial 0
r1(config-if)#no shut
r1(config-if)#interface serial 1
r1(config-if)#no shut
r1(config-if)#end
r1#copy running-config startup-config
```

10 Verify that it works by reloading and testing the various passwords. It is possible that you
    may have to hack more than one password, such as the **enable secret**, the **enable
    password**, the user-mode password (**line con 0**), the telnet password (**line vty 0 4**), or the
    auxiliary password (**line aux 0**).

11 For more information, Cisco has great documentation on password recovery
    www.cisco.com/warp/public/474/index.shtml.

Cisco 1600, 1700, 2600, 3600, 4500, 4700, 5500, and 6000 IOS Series Devices

For such devices as the Cisco 1600, 1700, 2600, 3600, 4500, 4700, 5500RSM, and 6x00
platforms, the password recovery procedure is as follows:

1   Establish a console session using the following settings:

    • Speed 9600 bits per second

    • 8 data bits

    • 0 parity bits

    • 1 stop bit

    • No flow control

2   View the configuration register by typing **show version** if possible. Usually the
    configuration register is 0x2102 or 0x102, but you should record the value so that you can
    change it back later.

3   Turn off the router, and then turn it back on using the power switch.

4   Execute the break sequence (such as Ctrl+Break) within the first 60 seconds of startup to
    force the router into ROMMON mode.

NOTE	While practicing password recovery, you must be able to issue a break sequence for successful password recovery. It is critical you know how your terminal emulator issues a break. HyperTerm and SecureCRT use the Ctrl+Break key sequence, for example, whereas ProComm and TeraTerm use Alt+B. Some versions of Windows NT have a problem sending a break signal using older versions of HyperTerm; visit www.hilgraeve.com for upgrades. In the practical environment, you should maintain backup configurations as a routine to prepare for the unexpected.

5 Change the configuration register to ignore the startup-config (contents of NVRAM) by typing **confreg 0x2142** at the ROMMON prompt.

NOTE	On the Catalyst 6000 running native IOS after you power cycle the box, the switch processor (SP) boots up first, and then after a short amount of time (about 25 seconds) it transfers console ownership to the route processor (RP or Multilayer Switch Feature Card [MSFC]). You must issue the break sequence just after the SP has given over control of the console to the RP; otherwise, you end up in ROMMON mode on the SP, which is not where you should be. Send the break after you see the following message on the console: **00:00:03: %OIR-6-CONSOLE: Changing console ownership to route processor** Then the password recovery is the same as a router.

6 Type **reset** so that the router reboots with the full IOS but ignores the startup configuration.

7 Be sure to answer **no** to all setup questions or just press Ctrl+C to break out of the setup after the router reboots. Go to enable mode using the **enable** command, but do *not* exit yet.

8 Type **copy startup-config running-config** or **config memory**. Do *not* type **copy run start** or **write mem** or you will lose your entire configuration.

NOTE	It is best practice to copy your configuration to Notepad or another editor in case you were to lose it.

9 Now you can hack the password by viewing the running configuration with **show running-config** or **write terminal**. Unencrypted passwords can be re-used, whereas encrypted ones need to be replaced.

> **NOTE** During a password recovery procedure, you may or may not be able to view your passwords in clear text. If the **enable secret** was configured, for example, the only recovery is to configure a new value due to the MD5 encryption. If the **enable password** was configured (and **service password-encryption** is off), however, password recovery is merely a visual inspection of the existing password. Also note that all of your interfaces are shut down during the password recovery procedures.

10 Make the necessary changes, including changing your passwords, changing the configuration register back to normal, bringing up your interfaces, and saving your configuration.

11 Verify that it works by reloading and testing the various passwords. It is possible that you may have to hack more than one password, such as the **enable secret**, the **enable password**, the user mode (**line con 0**) password, the telnet password (**line vty 0 4**), or the auxiliary (**line aux 0**) password.

12 For more information, Cisco has great documentation on password recovery at www.cisco.com/warp/public/474/index.shtml

Cisco 2900, 5000, and 6000 CatOS Series Devices

For such devices as the Cisco 2900, 5000, and 6000 CatOS platforms, the password recovery procedure is as follows:

1 Establish a console session using the following settings:

- Speed 9600 bits per second
- 8 data bits
- 0 parity bits
- 1 stop bit
- No flow control

2 Be sure to have all password data handy because you only have 30 seconds to enter the data after you start. You can copy and paste your responses if that is faster.

3 Turn the device off, and then turn it back on using the power switch.

4 At the Catalyst console press the Enter key to enter a null password. You only have 30 seconds to do so.

5 Type **enable** to enter enable mode. Once again, press the Enter key to enter a null password. This is still part of the first 30 seconds.

6 Change the passwords using the following commands:

- **Set pass**

  Press the Enter key for the old password, and then type in what you want the new password to be. Type the new password again when prompted to verify it.

- **Set enable**

  Press the Enter key for the old password, and then type in what you want the new password to be. Type the new password again when prompted to verify it.

NOTE   Because time is of the essence, I recommend you use the shortened versions of **set password** and **set enablepass** as listed in Steps 5 and 6. Keep in mind that you can put in anything for the new passwords during the recovery process and then change them after the fact. If you exceed the time limit, you must reboot the device and start over.

---

7 These devices automatically write their changes to NVRAM, so to test them out you can just return to user mode and then try your new passwords.

8 For more information, Cisco has great documentation on password recovery at www.cisco.com/warp/public/474/index.shtml.

Cisco 2900XL, 3500XL, 2950,and 3950 IOS Series Devices

For such devices as the Cisco 2900XL, 3500XL, 2950, and 3550 IOS platforms, the password recovery procedure is as follows:

1 Establish a console session using the following settings:

- Speed 9600 bits per second

- 8 data bits

- 0 parity bits

- 1 stop bit

- No flow control

2 Unplug the power cable from the back of the switch. Press and hold the mode button on the left side of the front panel while reconnecting the power cable.

3 Release the mode button a couple of seconds after the LED above the first port on the switch is no longer illuminated. You should get a message about the system being interrupted prior to the Flash file system initializing. (With a 1900 switch, the steps are similar up to this point.)

NOTE   If you feel like you are hugging your equipment rack with one hand on the power cord and the other on the mode button, chances are you are performing this operation correctly. If you had previously enabled **boot enable-break** on the switch, however, it will respond to a break like a router.

---

4 Type **flash_init** to reset the console speed to 9600.

5 Type **load_helper**.

6 List the files in Flash memory by typing **dir flash:**. The default configuration is config.text. Type **more flash:config.text** to view the configuration. If your passwords are not encrypted, you can enter them as normal and you are done. If they are encrypted, continue to the next step.

7 Rename the configuration file using the following syntax: **rename flash:config.text flash:config.old**.

8 Now boot the system with the **boot** command.

9 Answer **n** for no to start the setup and continue the configuration. Go to enable mode using the **enable** command, but do *not* exit yet.

10 Rename the configuration file back to what it was originally: **rename flash:config.old flash:config.text.**

11 Copy the configuration file to memory with **config mem** or **copy flash:config.text system:running-config**. Accept config.text as the source and running-config as the destination filenames.

12 Change your passwords as appropriate using the global configuration commands such as **enable password** *newpassword* or **enable secret** *newpassword*.

13 Save your configuration using **write memory** or **copy running-config startup-config**.

14 For more information, Cisco has great documentation on password recovery at www.cisco.com/warp/public/474/index.shtml.

As you can see, password recovery takes some coordination for it to work properly, especially for you not to lose your existing configuration. I compiled the basic steps for the most common

Cisco router and switch devices into Table B-1. Download this from the website for this book and keep it with all your other documentation.

Table B-1   *Donna's Password Recovery Guidelines*

Donna's Cisco Password Recovery Guidelines
www.cisco.com/warp/public/474/index.shtlm
		*Break Key Sequence
		HyperTerm/SecureCRT
		  Ctrl+Break
		ProComm/TeraTerm
		  Alt+B

2000, 2500, 3000, 4000, 7000	1600, 1700, 2600, 3600, 4500, 4700, 5500, 6000, 7500	CatOS 2900, 5000, 6000 Switches
1. Establish console session. 9600b, 8d, 0p, 1s, no flow control.	1. Establish console session. 9600b, 8d, 0p, 1s, no flow control.	1. Establish console session. 9600b, 8d, 0p, 1s, no flow control.
2. Power cycle and press Break key* within first 60 seconds.	2. Power cycle and press Break key* within first 60 seconds.	2. Power cycle. Within first 30 seconds press Enter for user password, get into enable mode, and also press Enter for enable password.
3. Observe and record config-register. Normally 0x2102. **>o**	3. Observe and record config-register. Normally 0x2102. rommon1**>confreg**	3. Change the passwords as usual using **set pass** and **set enablepass**.
4. Change config-register to ignore startup-config (NVRAM). **>o/r 0x2142** Then initialize with **>i**	4. Change config register to ignore startup-config (NVRAM). **>confreg 0x2142** **>reset**	4. Since these devices write their config automatically you should only need to test your passwords.
5. Press Ctrl+C to break out of setup mode.	5. Follow Steps 5–9 for the 2000, 2500, 3000, 4000, and 7000 to the left.	
6. From enable mode, type **copy start run** but do not exit. (Old command is **config mem**.)	2900XL, 3500XL, 2950, 3550 Switches	
7. Restore the config-register and bring up all interfaces. r1(config)#**config-reg 0x2102** r1(config)#**int s0** r1(config-if)#**no shut**	1. Establish console session. 9600b, 8d, 0p, 1s, no flow control (If you had previously enabled **boot-enable break**, the device would respond like a router and you could follow the procedures from there.)	

Table B-1   *Donna's Password Recovery Guidelines (Continued)*

8. Record or change the passwords. r1#**sh run** (or **sh config**) r1#**config t** r1(config)#**enable pass** *donna* r1(config)#**enable secret** *harrington* r1(config)#**line vty 0 4** r1(config-line)#**pass** *donna* r1(config-line)#**end**	2. Unplug the power cable from back of switch. Reconnect while you hold the front panel mode button. Release the mode button a couple seconds after the first port on the switch is no longer illuminated. You should see a message about the system being interrupted prior to the Flash memory file system initializing.
9. Save the configuration and reload. r1#**copy run start** (or **wr mem**) r1#**reload** r1#**sh version**	3. Type **flash_init** and then type **load_helper**. You can list the files in flash with **dir flash:**, and the default configuration is config.text.
	4. Type **more flash:config.text** to view the passwords. If not encrypted, you are done. If encrypted, go to Step 5.
	5. Rename the configuration file as follows: **rename flash:config.text flash:config.old.**
	6. Boot the system with the **boot** command. Answer **n** for no to start setup. Go to enable mode by typing **enable**, but do not exit.
	7. Rename the configuration file to its original name as follows: **rename flash:config.old flash:config.text.**
	8. Copy the configuration file to memory with the **config mem** or **copy flash:config.text system:running-config** command. Accept config.text as the source and running-config as the destination filenames.
	9. Change the passwords. **enable password** *donna* **enable secret** *harrington*
	10. Save your configurations. **copy run start** (or **wr mem**)

Use my password recovery guidelines to get comfortable with performing this procedure on your lab devices now. It is best to have done this a few times at leisure instead of when you are under time constraints. Examples B-1 through B-4 illustrate four of my devices.

Sample Password Recovery on a 2520 Router

Example B-1 *Password Recovery on a 2520*

```
!!!console to r6 via terminal server
!!!power cycle and press Ctrl+Break
r6#System Bootstrap, Version 11.0(10c), SOFTWARE
Copyright  1986-1996 by cisco Systems
2500 processor with 6144 Kbytes of main memory
Abort at 0x11195C6 (PC)
!!!this is rommon mode
>?
$          Toggle cache state
B [filename] [TFTP Server IP address ¦ TFTP Server Name]
           Load and execute system image from ROM or from TFTP server
C [address]  Continue execution [optional address]
D /S M L V  Deposit value V of size S into location L with modifier M
E /S M L   Examine location L with size S with modifier M
G [address]  Begin execution
H          Help for commands
I          Initialize
K          Stack trace
L [filename] [TFTP Server IP address ¦ TFTP Server Name]
           Load system image from ROM or from TFTP server, but do not
           begin execution
O          Show configuration register option settings
P          Set the break point
S          Single step next instruction
T function  Test device (? for help)

Deposit and Examine sizes may be B (byte), L (long) or S (short).
Modifiers may be R (register) or S (byte swap).
Register names are: D0-D7, A0-A6, SS, US, SR, and PC
>o
Configuration register = 0x2102 at last boot
Bit#   Configuration register option settings:
15     Diagnostic mode disabled
14     IP broadcasts do not have network numbers
13     Boot default ROM software if network boot fails
12-11  Console speed is 9600 baud
10     IP broadcasts with ones
08     Break disabled
07     OEM disabled
06     Ignore configuration disabled
03-00  Boot file is cisco2-2500 (or 'boot system' command)

>o/r 0x2142
>i
System Bootstrap, Version 11.0(10c), SOFTWARE
Copyright  1986-1996 by cisco Systems
2500 processor with 6144 Kbytes of main memory
F3: 10001304+224024+561968 at 0x3000060
              Restricted Rights Legend
Use, duplication, or disclosure by the Government is
...
Cisco Internetwork Operating System Software
IOS (tm) 2500 Software (C2500-JS-L), Version 12.0(9), RELEASE SOFTWARE (fc1)
!!!this is setup mode, press Ctrl+Break to get out of it
          --- System Configuration Dialog ---
```

Example B-1 *Password Recovery on a 2520 (Continued)*

```
Would you like to enter the initial configuration dialog? [yes/no]:
Press RETURN to get started!
!!!note that all interfaces are down
00:01:07: %LINK-5-CHANGED: Interface BRI0, changed state to administratively down
00:01:07: %LINK-5-CHANGED: Interface Ethernet0, changed state to administratively down
00:01:07: %LINK-5-CHANGED: Interface Serial0, changed state to administratively down
00:01:07: %LINK-5-CHANGED: Interface Serial1, changed state to administratively down
00:01:07: %LINK-5-CHANGED: Interface Serial2, changed state to administratively down...
Router>en
Router#!!!this is a router of the box config
Router#copy start run
Destination filename [running-config]?
1818 bytes copied in 11.320 secs (165 bytes/sec)
r6#!!!do not exit or you will lose your config and have to start over
r6#conf t
r6(config)#config-register 0x2102
r6(config)#int s0
r6(config-if)#no sh
r6(config-if)#int s1
r6(config-if)#no sh
r6(config-if)#int e0
r6(config-if)#no sh
r6(config-if)#end
r6#clock set 8:28:00 Dec 29 2002
!!!view the passwords
r6#sh run
...
enable secret 5 $1$YfpO$nxSLFSgyqcUzwObhDyCfV0
...
line con 0
 logging synchronous
 transport input none
line aux 0
line vty 0 4
 password recoverme
 login
!
end
r6#conf t
r6(config)#enable secret donna
r6(config)#line vty 0 4
r6(config-line)#pass donna
r6(config-line)#end
r6#copy running-config startup-config
r6#sh ver
...
Configuration register is 0x2142 (will be 0x2102 at next reload)
r6#reload
Proceed with reload? [confirm]
...
Press RETURN to get started!
...
r6>sh ver
...
Configuration register is 0x2102
```

Sample Password Recovery on a 3620 Router

Example B-2 *Password Recovery on a 3620*

```
r3#!!!console to r3 via terminal server
r3#!!!power cycle and press Ctrl+Break
r3#System Bootstrap, Version 11.1(20)AA2, EARLY DEPLOYMENT RELEASE SOFTWARE (fc1)
oPC = 0xbfc0a024, Cause = 0x2000, Status Reg = 0x3041f003
C3600 processor with 49152 Kbytes of main memory
Main memory is configured to 64 bit mode with parity disabled
PC = 0xbfc0a024, Cause = 0x2000, Status Reg = 0x3041f003
monitor: command "boot" aborted due to user interrupt
rommon 1 > !!!this is rommon mode
rommon 2 > confreg
    Configuration Summary
enabled are:
load rom after netboot fails
console baud: 9600
boot: image specified by the boot system commands
       or default to: cisco2-C3600
do you wish to change the configuration? y/n  [n]:
rommon 3 > confreg 0x2142
You must reset or power cycle for new config to take effect
rommon 4 > reset
System Bootstrap, Version 11.1(20)AA2, EARLY DEPLOYMENT RELEASE SOFTWARE (fc1)
oC3600 processor with 49152 Kbytes of main memory
Main memory is configured to 64 bit mode with parity disabled
program load complete, entry point: 0x80008000, size: 0x678bd4
Self decompressing the image :
################################################################################
################
...
         --- System Configuration Dialog ---
Would you like to enter the initial configuration dialog? [yes/no]:
Press RETURN to get started!
00:00:10: %LINK-3-UPDOWN: Interface Serial1/0, changed state to down
00:00:10: %LINK-3-UPDOWN: Interface Serial1/1, changed state to down
00:00:10: %LINK-3-UPDOWN: Interface Serial1/2, changed state to down
...
Router>!!!this is router out of the box config
Router>!!!all interfaces are shutdown
Router>!!!I used Ctrl+C to quit out of setup mode
Router>en
Router#copy start run
Destination filename [running-config]?
2260 bytes copied in 1.76 secs (2260 bytes/sec)
r3#conf t
r3(config)#config-reg 0x2102
r3(config)#int s0/1
r3(config-if)#no sh
r3(config-if)#int s0/2
r3(config-if)#no sh
r3(config-if)#end
r3#sh run
Building configuration...
...
```

Example B-2   *Password Recovery on a 3620 (Continued)*

```
enable secret 5 $1$cVmo$6uFnZdDlQ5TttrZR06w.9/
...
line con 0
 logging synchronous
 transport input none
line aux 0
line vty 0 4
 password donna
 login
!
end
r3#conf t
r3(config)#enable secret donna
r3(config)#end
r3#copy running-config startup-config
r3#sh ver
Cisco Internetwork Operating System Software
IOS (tm) 3600 Software (C3640-JS-M), Version 12.0(13), RELEASE SOFTWARE (fc1)
...
Configuration register is 0x2142 (will be 0x2102 at next reload)
r3#reload
Proceed with reload? [confirm]
...
r3>sh ver
Configuration register is 0x2102
```

Sample Password Recovery on a 2901 CatOS Switch

Example B-3   *Password Recovery on a 2901 CatOS Switch*

```
chesapeakebay> en
Enter password:
Sorry
chesapeakebay> !!!power cycle
chesapeakebay> !!!quickly press Enter for passwords to null them out
chesapeakebay> !!!the diagnostic tests have been eliminated here
...
Uncompressing NMP image.  This will take a minute...
Cisco Systems Console
Enter password:
chesapeakebay> en
Enter password:
chesapeakebay> (enable) set pass donna
Usage: set password
chesapeakebay> (enable) set pass
Enter old password:
Enter new password: donna
Retype new password: donna
Password changed.
chesapeakebay> (enable) set enablepass
Enter old password:
Enter new password: harrington
Retype new password: harrington
Password changed.
```

Sample Password Recovery on a 3512XL IOS Switch

Example B-4 *Password Recovery on a 3512XL IOS Switch*

```
Password:
% Bad secrets
kentnarrows>!!!unplug power cable
kentnarrows>!!!reconnect while holding mode button on front panel
kentnarrows>!!!release mode button after first port no longer lit
kentnarrows>C3500XL Boot Loader (C3500-HBOOT-M) Version 11.2(8.1)SA6, MAINTENANCE
  INTERIM SOFTWARE
Compiled Fri 14-May-99 17:59 by jchristy
 starting...
Base ethernet MAC Address: 00:d0:79:68:84:80
Xmodem file system is available.
The system has been interrupted prior to initializing the
flash filesystem.  The following commands will initialize
the flash filesystem, and finish loading the operating
system software:
    flash_init
    load_helper
    boot
switch: flash_init
Initializing Flash...
flashfs[0]: 221 files, 4 directories
flashfs[0]: 0 orphaned files, 0 orphaned directories
flashfs[0]: Total bytes: 3612672
flashfs[0]: Bytes used: 2070016
flashfs[0]: Bytes available: 1542656
flashfs[0]: flashfs fsck took 3 seconds.
...done Initializing Flash.
Boot Sector Filesystem (bs:) installed, fsid: 3
Parameter Block Filesystem (pb:) installed, fsid: 4
switch: load_helper
switch: dir flash:
Directory of flash:/
2    drwx   13888     <date>           html
5    -rwx   1273530   <date>           c3500XL-c3h2s-mz-112.8.2-SA6.bin
6    -rwx   82475     <date>           c3500XL-hdiag-mz_8_1.SA6
224  -rwx   342       <date>           env_vars
225  -rwx   796       <date>           vlan.dat
226  -rwx   2069      <date>           config.text
1542656 bytes available (2070016 bytes used)
switch: more flash:config.text
!!!look for passwords
...
enable secret 5 $1$WC9A$Ki5sCa.zi3oQtXBGEfU6D/
line con 0
 stopbits 1
line vty 0 4
password broadcreek
 login
line vty 5 15
 login
```

Example B-4   *Password Recovery on a 3512XL IOS Switch (Continued)*

```
switch: rename flash:config.text flash:config.old
switch: boot
Loading "flash:c3500XL-c3h2s-mz-112.8.2-
SA6.bin"...#######################################################################
  #######
...
Initializing C3500XL flash...
!!!the diagnostic tests have been eliminated here
Last reset from power-on
...
Press RETURN to get started!
        --- System Configuration Dialog ---
At any point you may enter a question mark '?' for help.
Use ctrl-c to abort configuration dialog at any prompt.
Default settings are in square brackets '[]'.
Continue with configuration dialog? [yes/no]:
%SYS-5-RESTART: System restarted --
Cisco Internetwork Operating System Software
IOS (tm) C3500XL Software (C3500XL-C3H2S-M), Version 11.2(8.2)SA6, MAINTENANCE INTERIM
SOFTWARE
Copyright  1986-1999 by cisco Systems, Inc.
Compiled Wed 23-Jun-99 18:32 by boba
C3500XL INIT: Complete
% Please answer 'yes' or 'no'.
Continue with configuration dialog? [yes/no]: n
Press RETURN to get started.
Switch>en
Switch#rename flash:config.old config.text
Source filename [config.old]?
%Error parsing config.text (No such device)
Switch#rename flash:config.old flash:config.text
Source filename [config.old]?
Destination filename [config.text]?
Switch#copy flash:config.text system:running-config
Source filename [config.text]?
Destination filename [running-config]?
2069 bytes copied in 0.574 secs
kentnarrows#conf t
kentnarrows(config)#enable pass donna
kentnarrows(config)#enable secret harrington
kentnarrows(config)#end
kentnarrows#copy run start
```

Just as you should familiarize yourself with password recovery procedures for your devices, you also must do the same for upgrading the operating system software. The next section provides some guidelines.

Software Upgrades

Throughout the book I have given many references to assist you with upgrading your Cisco software images. You may do this to run a new feature not available in the release you have, to fix a current bug, to improve performance or security issues such as Simple Network Management Protocol (SNMP) vulnerabilities, or to meet your own in-house standards. Ultimately, consistency makes troubleshooting easier, and software versions are no exception to the rule.

Chapter 4, "Shooting Trouble with Novell IPX," should perhaps have been called "Shooting Trouble with Novell IPX and More," because IPX was just not available using the software image installed on the routers in my lab. I used different methods to upgrade, including PC-based TFTP (PumpKin, 3CDaemon, Cisco) and FTP (3CDaemon) programs as well as setting up a router as a TFTP server to serve the image. I gave you examples with Flash load helper where the configuration register stuff is kind of in the background. It is important to be familiar with different methods because many times you must work with the tools at hand. Most people can make use of a TFTP server, for example; if your images are larger than 16 MB, however, typically you need to look at alternative methods such as FTP. If you skipped Chapter 4 because it had IPX in the title, perhaps you should go back and review it now, for I had you experiment first hand.

Follow along with the general procedures for upgrading your image software using a router as a TFTP, using third-party TFTP software, and using third-party FTP software.

For specific software installation and upgrade procedures, go to Cisco.com. The following URLs are great starting points:

- www.cisco.com/warp/customer/130/upgrade_index.shtml
- www.cisco.com/kobayashi/sw-center/

If you need assistance with downloading the file from Cisco.com, see www.cisco.com/public/sw-center/sw_download_guide/sw_download_guide.shtml. However, you need the appropriate maintenance contract, partner agreement, or special file access to download. A CCO account is a very valuable resource.

Serving an Image from a Router Configured as a TFTP Server

The software installation and upgrade procedures for Run From Flash devices such as 1600, 2000, 2500, 3000, AS5100, and AS5200 are as follows:

1 Set up a TFTP server and specify the directory where files are stored. Examples include PumpKin, 3CDaemon, and Cisco TFTP servers. Alternatively, you can serve the IOS image from a router configured as a TFTP server as follows:

```
r1(config)#tftp-server flash:c2500-js-l.120-21a.bin
r1(config)#interface ethernet 1
r1(config-if)#ip address 192.168.5.33 255.255.255.240
r1(config-if)#no shut
r1(config-if)#end
r1#copy running-config startup-config
```

2 Verify RAM, Flash memory, and feature set requirements. Copy the appropriate IOS image to the TFTP server.

3 Establish a console (preferred) or telnet session to the router using the following settings:

- Speed 9600 bits per second
- 8 data bits
- 0 parity bits
- 1 stop bit
- No flow control

4 Use **show version** to check the configuration register setting. Typically it is 0x2102, but you should document the current value.

5 Add the appropriate IP information, such as IP address, subnet mask, and default gateway if needed, and verify connectivity to the TFTP server through a simple ping. It is a good practice to copy your existing configuration files to the TFTP using **copy running-config tftp**.

NOTE   You may need to partition Flash memory if the file is larger than one partition. If the file is 10 MB, for example, and you have two 8-MB Flash modules; you can issue the **partition flash 1** command to partition the Flash.

---

6 Change the router to RxBoot (bootflash) mode by setting the configuration register to the value 0x2101 as follows:

```
Router(config)#config-register 0x2101
Router(config)#end
Router#copy running-config startup-config
Router#reload
```

NOTE   Setting the configuration register to 0x2101 puts the router in RxBoot (bootflash) mode after the reload with the following prompt:

```
Router(boot)#
```

To avoid overwriting your configuration, do *not* save any commands while in this mode. If you are connected through a telnet session, it is lost after the reload. You need to wait a few minutes and try again. If, when connected to the router through the console port, you get a > or rommon> prompt, your router is in ROMMON mode. If this happens, consult Cisco.com's boot failure recovery procedures for Xmodem. However, you will put that to practice if you follow along.

---

7   Restore the configuration register back to the original setting, or 0x2102 if you are not sure what to use.

```
r1(boot)(config)#config-register 0x2102
```

8   Copy the new Cisco IOS Software image from the TFTP server to the router, as follows:

```
Router(boot)#copy tftp flash
```

NOTE   When prompted, enter the IP address of the TFTP server, the source IOS filename, and the destination IOS filename. It is recommended to keep the IOS filename as is when you download it so that you can always look up the feature set information. Depending on the amount of space, you may need to erase Flash memory before writing the new image. Each exclamation point (!) indicates that UDP segments have been successfully transferred. A checksum verification of the image occurs after the image is written to Flash, and the router reloads itself with the new image when the software upgrade is complete.

---

9   Verify the IOS upgrade and reload if necessary without saving the configuration. A good indication of needing to reload is if you issue a **show version** and it says "router will be 0x2102 at next reload." Make sure that you are back to the normal router mode with a prompt of *hostname>* upon a reload.

Example B-5 displays a sample 2514 upgrade output.

Example B-5   *Upgrading the IOS on a 2514 (Run from Flash Device)*

```
r1(config)#config-register 0x2101
r1(config)#end
...
r1#reload
Proceed with reload? [confirm]
00:18:07: %SYS-5-RELOAD: Reload requested
...
r1(boot)#copy tftp flash
System flash directory:
File  Length    Name/status
  1   5726508   c2500-i-l.120-9
[5726572 bytes used, 11050644 available, 16777216 total]
Address or name of remote host [255.255.255.255]? 192.168.5.18
Source file name? c2500-js-l.120-21a.bin
Destination file name [c2500-js-l.120-21a.bin]?
Accessing file 'c2500-js-l.120-21a.bin' on 192.168.5.18...
Loading c2500-js-l.120-21a.bin from 192.168.5.18 (via Ethernet0): ! [OK]
Erase flash device before writing? [confirm]
Flash contains files. Are you sure you want to erase? [confirm]
Copy 'c2500-js-l.120-21a.bin' from server
  as 'c2500-js-l.120-21a.bin' into Flash WITH erase? [yes/no]y
Erasing device... eeeeeeeeeeeeeeeeeeeeeeeeeeeeeeeeeeeeeeeeeeeeeeeeeeeeeeeeeeeeee
    eeee ...erased
Loading c2500-js-l.120-21a.bin from 192.168.5.18 (via Ethernet0):
```

Example B-5   *Upgrading the IOS on a 2514 (Run from Flash Device) (Continued)*

```
      !!!!!!!!!!!!!!!!!!!!!!!!!!!!!!!!!!!!!!!!!!!!!!!!!!!!!!!!!!!!!!!!!!!!!!!
...
 [OK - 10253564/16777216 bytes]
Verifying checksum...  OK (0xFA32)
Flash copy took 0:05:55 [hh:mm:ss]
r1(boot)#show flash
System flash directory:
File  Length   Name/status
   1  10253564  c2500-js-l.120-21a.bin
[10253628 bytes used, 6523588 available, 16777216 total]
16384K bytes of processor board System flash (Read/Write)
r1(boot)#configure terminal
r1(boot)(config)#config-register 0x2102
r1(boot)(config)#end
r1(boot)#reload
System configuration has been modified. Save? [yes/no]: n
Proceed with reload? [confirm]
```

Upgrading Software Images with TFTP Programs and Flash Cards, Including an Xmodem Recovery

Follow the same concepts as in the preceding section to upgrade software images using a PC-based TFTP program rather than a router set up as a TFTP server. Learn the specifics of the application you choose to use, such as PumpKin, 3CDaemon, Cisco, or another program. Then copy the file from Cisco.com to the right directory location and make sure the TFTP application is up and running. Verify that your IP parameters (address, mask, gateway) are set up properly on your TFTP server and the router/switch device. Perform the upgrade as in the following examples.

Example B-6 uses a PC Card (PCMCIA) in slot 1 to perform this upgrade. Some devices have extra slots to ease this operation. However, you must make sure that the Flash memory on the card is partitioned and formatted for the appropriate device. This exercise is also intended to show you how to recover when you accidentally upgrade to an IOS that your physical RAM does not support.

Example B-6   *Viewing the Flash on the 3620*

```
r4#show slot1:
PCMCIA Slot1 flash directory:
File  Length   Name/status
   1  13459880  c3620-is-mz.122-8.T.bin
   2  893       startup-config [deleted]
   3  6945008   c3620-io3-mz.122-8.T4.bin
[20405976 bytes used, 565544 available, 20971520 total]
20480K bytes of processor board PCMCIA Slot1 flash (Read/Write)
r4#show flash
System flash directory:
File  Length   Name/status
   1  3971288   c3620-d-mz.113-9.T
[3971352 bytes used, 12805864 available, 16777216 total]
16384K bytes of processor board System flash (Read/Write)
```

Slot1: is among the many different types of Flash available. Others include slot0:, flash:, bootflash:, sup-bootflash:, slavesup-bootflash:, and so on. Use the **show flash [all]** command to determine the type and status for your particular device. Alternatively, think of slot0: and slot1: as hard drives and issue the **dir slot0:** or **dir slot1:** commands to check their contents. If the Flash is read-only, you can't write to it from the current mode. This is the reason that on a run-from-Flash device such as the 2500 series routers, you must drop back to RxBoot mode by setting the configuration register to 0x2101. Other routers that don't have RxBoot mode as a boot helper may have a bootflash: mode instead. If not, you can still perform the upgrade procedures from ROMMON mode, but they are much more time-consuming.

NOTE   There are many variances with equipment and flash types. For example, the flash card may have existing files and rather than format the entire card you can erase a file using the **delete** command. However, in many cases you must then issue the **squeeze** command to actually delete the space taken up by the deleted file. Research your specific requirements using your CCO account on Cisco.com.

I have physical connectivity (via a crossover cable) between my PC (hosta) that I am using as a TFTP server and the router that needs the upgrade. Alternatively, you must configure your IP settings, including the default gateway, to ensure IP communications before you can upgrade. This is one of the big advantages of using PC Cards for slot0: or slot1: because you can easily transfer the image to the internal Flash without all the IP configuration. However, you need to first get the image to the PC Card, in which a TFTP/FTP server and IP can be quite helpful. Other features that are of assistance when upgrading Cisco images include the boot system commands. For example, you can test an image by booting to an image on a PC Card or a TFTP server prior to the actual upgrade. These boot system commands are read first with the configuration register set to the default of 0x2102 because they are part of your startup configuration (NVRAM). An example of a boot system command is as follows:

```
boot system flash slot1:c3620-is-mz.122-8.T.bin
```

NOTE   Always analyze your existing configuration for existing boot system commands. Without them, the first file in flash is read. However, you can use boot system commands to load a more up-to-date larger operating system from either a tftp server or a flash card if you do not have the internal flash memory available. If there are multiple boot system commands they are read in order. You can type **no boot system** to erase them all or you can type **no** in front of each one to delete them individually. Remember to save your running-config to the startup-config after any changes to the boot system commands.

I configured my e0 interface as 10.1.1.1 255.255.255.0 and hosta (the TFTP server) as 10.1.1.2 255.255.255.0 to simplify the IP configuration. I then brought up the 3CDaemon TFTP server on hosta. As a precaution, I copied my existing configuration and the Flash image to the TFTP server as in Example B-7.

Example B-7   *Backing Up the Configuration and Software Image*

```
r4#copy run tftp
Remote host []? 10.1.1.2
Name of configuration file to write [r4-confg]?
Write file r4-confg on host 10.1.1.2? [confirm]
Building configuration...
Writing r4-confg .!! [OK]
r4#copy flash tftp
System flash directory:
File  Length    Name/status
   1  3971288   c3620-d-mz.113-9.T
[3971352 bytes used, 12805864 available, 16777216 total]
Address or name of remote host [255.255.255.255]? 10.1.1.2
Source file name? c3620-d-mz.113-9.T
Destination file name [c3620-d-mz.113-9.T]?
Verifying checksum for 'c3620-d-mz.113-9.T' (file # 1)...  OK
Copy 'c3620-d-mz.113-9.T' from Flash to server
  as 'c3620-d-mz.113-9.T'? [yes/no]y
!!!!!!!!!!!!!!!!!!!!!!!!!!!!!!!!!!!!!!!!!!!!!!!!!!!!!!!!!!!!!!!!!!!!!!!!!!!!!!!!!!!!
!!!!!!!!!!!!!!!!!!!!!!!!!!!!!!!!!!!!!!!!!!!!!!!!!!!!!
...
Upload to server done
Flash device copy took 00:00:23 [hh:mm:ss]
```

Now review the files that were previously copied to the Flash card and upgrade the internal Flash to 12.2-8T as in Example B-8. This is a good place to copy and paste the filename rather than type it.

Example B-8   *Upgrading the Internal Flash from Slot1:*

```
r4#sh slot1:
PCMCIA Slot1 flash directory:
File  Length    Name/status
   1  13459880  c3620-is-mz.122-8.T.bin
   2  893       startup-config [deleted]
   3  6945008   c3620-io3-mz.122-8.T4.bin
[20405976 bytes used, 565544 available, 20971520 total]
20480K bytes of processor board PCMCIA Slot1 flash (Read/Write)

r4#copy slot1:c3620-is-mz.122-8.T.bin flash:
System flash directory:
File  Length    Name/status
   1  3971288   c3620-d-mz.113-9.T
[3971352 bytes used, 12805864 available, 16777216 total]
Destination file name [c3620-is-mz.122-8.T.bin]?
Verifying checksum for 'c3620-is-mz.122-8.T.bin' (file # 1)...  OK
Erase flash device before writing? [confirm]
```

continues

Example B-8   *Upgrading the Internal Flash from Slot1: (Continued)*

```
Flash contains files. Are you sure you want to erase? [confirm]
Copy 'c3620-is-mz.122-8.T.bin' from slot1: device
  as 'c3620-is-mz.122-8.T.bin' into flash: device WITH erase? [yes/no]y
Erasing device... eeeeeeeeeeeeeeeeeeeeeeeeeeeeeeeeeeeeeeeeeeeeeeeeeeeeeeeeeeeeee
...erased
!!!!!!!!!!!!!!!!!!!!!!!!!!!!!!!!!!!!!!!!!!!!!!!!!!!!!!!!!!!!!!!!!!!!!!!!!!!!!!!!!!!
...
[OK - 13459880/16777216 bytes]
Flash device copy took 00:02:16 [hh:mm:ss]
Verifying checksum...  OK (0x7A7B)
r4#reload
Proceed with reload? [confirm]
System Bootstrap, Version 11.1(20)AA2, EARLY DEPLOYMENT RELEASE SOFTWARE (fc1)
C3600 processor with 32768 Kbytes of main memory
Main memory is configured to 32 bit mode with parity disabled
program load complete, entry point: 0x80008000, size: 0xcd608c
Error : memory requirements exceed available memory
Memory required     : 0x02193BAC
*** System received a Software forced crash ***
signal= 0x17, code= 0x4, context= 0x0
PC = 0x800080d4, Cause = 0x20, Status Reg = 0x3041f003
```

Although you followed the correct procedures for copying a file from slot1: to the internal
Flash, you forgot some important prerequisites. You must *always* verify you have enough RAM
and Flash memory available for the image in which you want to upgrade. That's all right,
however, because now you can experience Xmodem first hand, because that is how to recover.
First, go back to Cisco.com and download the appropriate image for the features you require
and the RAM and Flash that you have. In my lab, IP and IPX are required, so I downloaded the
appropriate image to hosta (a PC). Example B-9 starts after you break out of the repeating error
message and end up in ROM monitor mode. Although not required, it will certainly speed
things up if you increase the console speed using **confreg** on the router and the terminal settings
on the terminal emulator program. If you see garbage, you know you have a speed mismatch.

Example B-9   *Changing the Console Speed on the Router*

```
confreg
    Configuration Summary
enabled are:
load rom after netboot fails
console baud: 9600
boot: image specified by the boot system commands
      or default to: cisco2-C3600
do you wish to change the configuration? y/n  [n]:  y
enable  "diagnostic mode"? y/n  [n]:  n
enable  "use net in IP bcast address"? y/n  [n]:  n
disable "load rom after netboot fails"? y/n  [n]:  n
enable  "use all zero broadcast"? y/n  [n]:  n
enable  "break/abort has effect"? y/n  [n]:  n
```

Example B-9   *Changing the Console Speed on the Router (Continued)*

```
enable  "ignore system config info"? y/n  [n]: n
change console baud rate? y/n  [n]:  y
enter rate: 0 = 9600,  1 = 4800,  2 = 1200,  3 = 2400
4 = 19200, 5 = 38400, 6 = 57600, 7 = 115200 [0]:  7
change the boot characteristics? y/n  [n]:  n
    Configuration Summary
enabled are:
load rom after netboot fails
console baud: 115200
boot: image specified by the boot system commands
      or default to: cisco2-C3600
do you wish to change the configuration? y/n  [n]:  n
You must reset or power cycle for new config to take effect
rommon 2 > reset
```

Continue the Xmodem download in Example B-10.

Example B-10   *Using Xmodem on the 3620 to Download an Image from the PC*

```
rommon 13 > xmodem -c c3620-d-mz.121-18.bin
Do not start the sending program yet...
        File size          Checksum    File name
 10506692 bytes (0xa051c4)    0x2b5d    c3620-js-mz.121-17
WARNING: All existing data in flash will be lost!
Invoke this application only for disaster recovery.
Do you wish to continue? y/n  [n]:  y
Ready to receive file c3620-d-mz.121-18.bin ...
```

Now that the Xmodem procedures are initialized on the router, do the same through the terminal emulator program on the PC. For this example, I used HyperTerm, as illustrated in Figure B-3.

Figure B-3   *Starting Xmodem on HyperTerm*

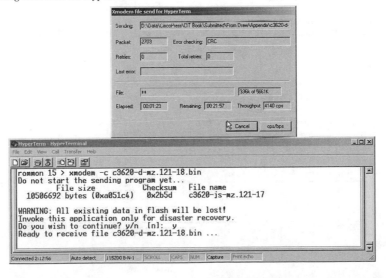

Select **Transfer> Send** from the HyperTerm menu. Specify the image name and location and start the transfer. You can expect to see console messages about erasing Flash at various memory locations, programming Flash at various memory locations. When successful you should see the following:

```
Download Complete!
program load complete, entry point: 0x80008000, size: 0x587050
Self decompressing the image :
###################################################################################
###################################################################################
###################################################################################
###################################################################################
###################################################################################
###############
# [OK]
```

The router should then boot up as normal. You can use the **config-register** command to set the register from 0x3922 back to 0x2102 (or what it was prior to the download). Reload and then test things as in Example B-11. Copy the new image from Flash to slot1: for the future. Although not illustrated here, also ensure your boot code is current. This may require a software upgrade similar to the preceding exercise or it may in fact require a new boot ROM chip itself.

Example B-11 *Verifying the Xmodem Download*

```
r4#dir flash:
Directory of flash:/
    1  -rw-      5796204            <no date>  c3620-d-mz.121-18.bin
16777216 bytes total (10980948 bytes free)
r4#copy flash slot1:
Source filename [c3620-d-mz.121-18.bin]?
Destination filename [c3620-d-mz.121-18.bin]?
Erase slot1: before copying? [confirm]
Erasing the slot1 filesystem will remove all files! Continue? [confirm]
Erasing device...
eeeeeeeeeeeeeeeeeeeeeeeeeeeeeeeeeeeeeeeeeeeeeeeeeeeeeeeeeeeeeeeeeeeeeeeeeeeeeeeeeee
eeeeeeeeeeeeeeeeeeeeeeeeeeeeeeeeeeeeeeeeeeeeeeeeeeeeeeeeeeeeeeeeeeeeeeeee ...erased
Erase of slot1: complete
Copy in
progress...CCCCCCCCCCCCCCCCCCCCCCCCCCCCCCCCCCCCCCCCCCCCCCCCCCCCCCCCCCCCCCCCCCCCCCC
CCCCCCCCCCCCCCCCCCCCCCCCCCCCCCCCCCCCCCCCCCCCCCCCCCCCCCCCCCCCCCCCCCCCCCCCCCCCCCCCCC
...
Verifying checksum...  OK (0xF693)
5796204 bytes copied in 87.200 secs (66623 bytes/sec)
r4#sh slot1:
PCMCIA Slot0 flash directory:
File  Length    Name/status
   1  5796204   c3620-d-mz.121-18.bin  [invalid checksum]
   2  5796204   c3620-d-mz.121-18.bin
[11592536 bytes used, 9378984 available, 20971520 total]
20480K bytes of processor board PCMCIA Slot0 flash (Read/Write)
r4#copy run start
```

NOTE	Refer to www.cisco.com/warp/public/130/xmodem_generic.html for detailed instructions on Xmodem and other recovery procedures.

Working with Modular Devices

Now that you are comfortable with upgrading the software on fixed devices, examine how to do the same for modular devices that contain such cards as a supervisor line card, router, and other modules.

Downloading Supervisor Engine Images Using TFTP

Downloading to a modular device—for example, a 6509 that includes a Supervisor, router, and other line cards—is not much different from downloading to a fixed device. The basics are the same, and the device should remain operational while the image downloads. Set up your TFTP/FTP server, console/telnet session, and IP parameters as mentioned previously. Verify RAM, Flash, and any special feature set requirements. Copy the appropriate image file to the TFTP/FTP server or Flash card. Enter the **copy tftp flash** command. Enter the IP address of the TFTP server, the name of the file to download, the Flash device to which to copy the file, and the destination filename when prompted. So that the new image boots when you issue the **reset system** command you need to modify the boot environment variable as follows:

```
set boot system flashdevice:filename prepend
```

In this example, *flashdevice* may be something like sup-bootflash: or slavesup-bootflash: and the filename the name of the software image. When you reset the switch, it is normal for your telnet session to disconnect. During the switch startup, however, the Supervisor Engine loads the new code into RAM. Verify this with **show version** when you reconnect via the console or telnet.

Because there are minor differences according to your hardware, research the specifics at Cisco.com before you start. With redundant Supervisors, for example, you can't download directly from the TFTP server to the standby Supervisor Flash. Instead, the standby automatically synchronizes with the new image on the active (primary) Supervisor card.

Downloading Switching Module Images Using TFTP

Set up your TFTP/FTP server, console/telnet session, and IP parameters as previously mentioned. Verify RAM, Flash, and any special feature set requirements. Copy the appropriate image file to the TFTP/FTP server or Flash card. Assuming that you want to copy the image to one module, or if there are multiple modules of the same type that you want to upgrade, enter the **copy tftp flash** command. On the other hand, if there are multiple modules of the same type, but you only want to upgrade a single one, enter the **copy tftp** *module#***/bootflash:** command. You can use **show modules** to find the particular card before you begin. Next enter the IP address of the TFTP server, the name of the file to download, the Flash device to which to copy the file, and the destination filename when prompted. All modules should remain operational during the image download. Reset the appropriate modules using the **reset** *module#* command from the Supervisor prompt. Use the **show version** *module#* command to verify the new version of code.

You can find examples of upgrading the code and for password recovery on modular devices such as the 6509 at Cisco.com. For example, check out www.cisco.com/univercd/cc/td/doc/product/lan/cat6000/sft_6_1/configgd/images.htm.

Upgrading Software Images with FTP Programs

An image may exceed the 16-MB limitation for TFTP; therefore, FTP is a workaround. Follow the TFTP procedures except for the username and password information for FTP. TFTP does not use username and passwords, but FTP does. You must follow how the FTP server is actually set up. Typically, FTP anonymous access enables you to log in with a username of anonymous with your e-mail address for the password. Example B-12 illustrates the FTP login and the command to copy the IOS or OS from an FTP server to Flash.

Example B-12 *Copying from an FTP Server to Flash*

```
r1(config)#ip ftp username anonymous
r1(config)#ip ftp password donna@shoretraining.com
r1(config)#end
r1#copy running-config startup-config
r1#copy ftp flash
!!!follow the previous tftp example for the rest of the copy
```

These are not the only methods and procedures because there are differences according to platform. Go to Cisco.com for assistance and current details.

Summary

Know your resources and where to get current information. The last thing you want to do is perform a password recovery, figure out config-register fields, or upgrade software live without ever attempting these procedures in a lab. Take a proactive approach and get acquainted with your devices before you put them into production.

Equipment Reference

Obtaining equipment can be expensive, but following along and building your own lab as I do is definitely the best way to utilize this book.

If you are unable to get the equipment, do not despair; you can still utilize this book. You just need to think aloud and pay more attention to the figures, explanations, and examples. Little changes are hidden throughout the book, and although the chapters take on a structured approach and I recommend a structured approach to troubleshooting, you will learn more if you read the fine details within the chapters so that you are prepared for the unknown.

Start with a pad of paper and document the network. Draw and redraw the networks as you work through the exercises throughout this book. Color-code your routing domains, addresses, devices, ports, terminal server connections, and so on. Download the files to get more detail on what is truly happening for the various scenarios and Trouble Tickets. Perform some research at Cisco.com as you progress through the book. Create tables and lists so that you can put yourself in the position of someone who is configuring and troubleshooting the various LAN and WAN technologies.

Support Equipment Used in This Book

Figure C-1 shows a physical diagram of the equipment used throughout this book. I would have preferred to use more up-to-date higher-end boxes such as Catalyst 6509s and the like. Keep in mind that just wasn't practical for my home lab either.

Figure C-1   *Equipment Used in This Book*

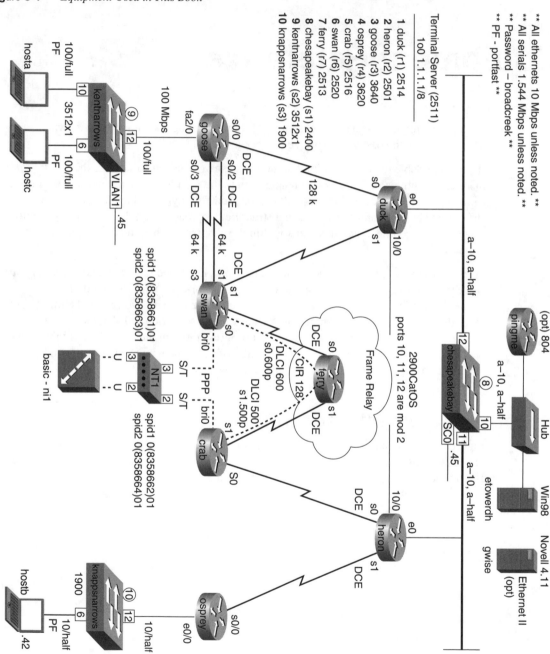

A list of equipment I used follows. Alternatively, you can use other equipment, assuming you have enough interfaces to perform the chapter scenarios and Trouble Tickets. Look at the first figure at the beginning of each chapter to get a feel for the exact equipment used on a chapter-by-chapter basis. I thought it necessary to have coverage of both the Cisco IOS and CatOS on fixed and modular devices.

The routers and switches in Figure C-1 are as follows:

- r1—2514
- r2—2501
- r3—3640
- r4—3620
- r5—2516
- r6—2520
- r7—2513
- s1—2901 CatOS
- s2—3512XL IOS (2900XL will suffice)
- s3—1900 Standard Edition (It may be more practical to use another IOS-based switch in place of the 1900 since Cisco courses are dropping the 1900s from their curriculum.)

NOTE   For the most part, IP-only images are acceptable images for your devices. Extensive feature sets are not required, so there is no need to spend lots of money upgrading RAM/Flash memory for the practical exercises. The exception to this is if you want to go through the IPX scenarios and tickets. If so, you need an image that supports the IPX protocol, too.

Other equipment I use throughout the book includes:

- A 2511 terminal server and octal cables make life much easier for getting to the console of the devices. Refer to the section on "Configuring a Terminal Server (2511)," for details.
- An 804 on the backbone as a ping target, but this is not required.
- The hub on the backbone is not required. It is not a Cisco hub.
- Category 5 straight-through and crossover cables for the Ethernets and ISDN.
- Transceivers are needed on the r1 and r2 Ethernets where there are AUI DB15 connections.

- The serial WAN connections are possible via V.35 DTE/DCE back-to-back DB60 cables. You can find them at www.stonewallcable.com.

- Power cords, power strips, and an uninterruptible power supply (UPS). Be sure you have enough power to run the equipment.

Where to Buy Equipment

I purchased most of my equipment for my lab off of eBay. If you don't have access to equipment at work or remote labs, take a look at the following sites to start your own home, work, or classroom lab:

- www.stores.ebay.com—Categories such as computers, networking and telecom, and routers and switches will take you to a vast list of merchants.

- www.ebay.com

- www.comstarinc.com

- www.netfix.com

- www.iqsale.com

- www.optsys.net

- www.cheapisdn.com

- www.cccmn.com

- www.symmic.com

- www.computergate.com

- www.cdw.com

- www.microwarehouse.com

Configuring a Terminal Server (2511)

Although a terminal server (2511) is an optional piece of equipment for the lab, it provides convenience and alleviates the frustration of swapping console cables. Yes, it is true that you can telnet from device to device. However, telnet requires IP, and you are constantly making changes in the scenarios to where you do not just automatically always have in-band (IP-based) management. The terminal server provides out-of-band management, which is totally separate from your IP configuration. Figure C-2 illustrates a 2511 (an example of a terminal server) and the octal cable connections from the asynchronous interface to the router/switch console ports.

Figure C-2   *Terminal Server (2511)*

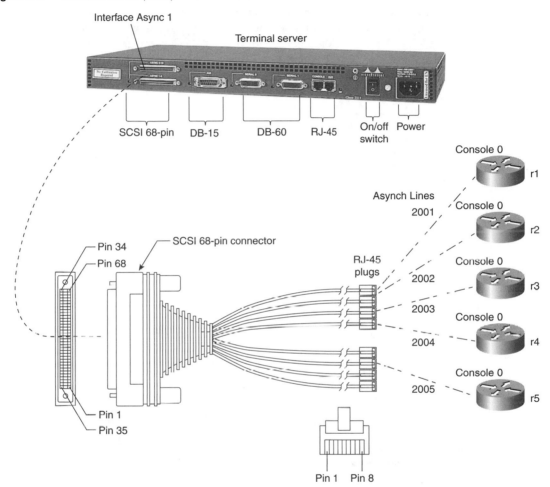

A terminal server works via a reverse telnet operation. Physically make your connections as in Figure C-1 to get started. Next, connect the asynchronous octal cable(s) to the 2511's 68-pin SCSI interface(s). Then connect a rolled console cable from the COM1 port (serial) on your PC to the console port on the terminal server. Power the device on and use a terminal emulator such as HyperTerm to connect. Set up your terminal settings as follows:

- 9600 bps

- 8 data bits

- 0 parity bits

- 1 stop bit

- No flow control

Now you are ready to program the 2511 just as if it were any other router. Assign a hostname and passwords. Create a loopback address, set up a hosts table, and allow telnet, at a minimum, as the transport across the asynchronous lines 1 through 16. Example C-1 illustrates this configuration for Chapter 3, "Shooting Trouble with IP," where you first use the terminal server.

Example C-1   *Terminal Server Configuration*

```
Router>enable
Router#configure terminal
Router(config)#hostname ts
ts(config)#enable password donna
ts(config)#line vty 0 4
ts(config-line)#login
ts(config-line)#password donna
ts(config-line)#logging synchronous
ts(config-line)#exec-timeout 30
ts(config-line)#exit
ts(config)#interface loopback 0
ts(config-if)#ip address 1.1.1.1 255.0.0.0
ts(config-if)#no shut
ts(config-if)#exit
ts(config)#ip host ?
  WORD  Name of host
ts(config)#ip host r1 ?
  <0-65535>  Default telnet port number
  A.B.C.D    Host IP address (maximum of 8)
ts(config)#ip host r1 1.1.1.1 ?
  A.B.C.D  Host IP address (maximum of 8)
  <cr>
ts(config)#ip host r1 ?
  <0-65535>  Default telnet port number
  A.B.C.D    Host IP address (maximum of 8)
ts(config)#ip host r1 2001 1.1.1.1
ts(config)#ip host r2 2002 1.1.1.1
ts(config)#ip host r3 2003 1.1.1.1
ts(config)#ip host r4 2004 1.1.1.1
ts(config)#ip host r5 2005 1.1.1.1
ts(config)#line 1 16
ts(config-line)#transport input ?
  all    All protocols
  lat    DEC LAT protocol
  mop    DEC MOP Remote Console Protocol
  nasi   NASI protocol
  none   No protocols
  pad    X.3 PAD
  rlogin Unix rlogin protocol
  telnet TCP/IP Telnet protocol
  v120   Async over ISDN
ts(config-line)#transport input all
ts(config-line)#no exec
```

Save and display the terminal server (**ts**) final configuration. The pertinent parts are in Example C-2.

Example C-2   *Terminal Server running-config*

```
ts#copy running-config startup-config
ts#show running-config
hostname ts
enable password donna
ip host r1 2001 1.1.1.1
ip host r2 2002 1.1.1.1
ip host r3 2003 1.1.1.1
ip host r4 2004 1.1.1.1
ip host r5 2005 1.1.1.1
interface Loopback0
 ip address 1.1.1.1 255.0.0.0
line con 0
 transport input none
line 1 16
 transport input all
 no exec
line aux 0
line vty 0 4
 password donna
 exec timeout 30 0
 password donna
 logging synchronous
 login
end
```

Now that the terminal server is configured, verify its operation. The terminal server essentially connects to its own loopback address via telnet by initiating the connection out an asynchronous line. Refer back to Figure C-2 for an illustration of the asynchronous line numbers starting with 2001 and incrementing by 1. Use the hosts table to connect to all devices as in Example C-3. Without a hosts table on the terminal server, you need to issue the following commands to connect to the five devices shown:

```
!!!to connect to r1
ts#telnet 1.1.1.1 2001
!!!to connect to r2
ts#telnet 1.1.1.1 2002
!!!to connect to r3
ts#telnet 1.1.1.1 2003
!!!to connect to r4
ts#telnet 1.1.1.1 2004
!!!to connect to r5
ts#telnet 1.1.1.1 2005
```

Example C-3   *Opening the Terminal Server Connections*

```
ts#show sessions
% No connections open
ts#show hosts
Default domain is not set
Name/address lookup uses domain service
Name servers are 255.255.255.255
Host                    Flags      Age Type   Address(es)
```

continues

Example C-3   *Opening the Terminal Server Connections (Continued)*

```
r1                        (perm, OK)  4   IP   1.1.1.1
r2                        (perm, OK)  4   IP   1.1.1.1
r3                        (perm, OK)  4   IP   1.1.1.1
r4                        (perm, OK)  4   IP   1.1.1.1
r5                        (perm, OK)  4   IP   1.1.1.1

ts#r1
Trying r1 (1.1.1.1, 2001)... Open
r1>
r1>!!!I am pressing Ctrl+Shift+6,x to return to the ts console

ts#r2
Trying r2 (1.1.1.1, 2002)... Open
r2>
r2>!!!I am pressing Ctrl+Shift+6,x to return to the ts console

ts#r3
Trying r3 (1.1.1.1, 2003)... Open
r3>
r3>!!!I am pressing Ctrl+Shift+6,x to return to the ts console

ts#r4
Trying r4 (1.1.1.1, 2004)... Open
r4>
r4>!!!I am pressing Ctrl+Shift+6,x to return to the ts console

ts#r5
Trying r5 (1.1.1.1, 2005)... Open
r5>
r5>!!!I am pressing Ctrl+Shift+6,x to return to the ts console
ts#
```

Notice that I typed the hostname of each device to open a connection to it. Although not a necessity, this renders the troubleshooting easier because I aligned r1 with async line 1 (2001), r2 with async line 2 (2002), and so on. The command sequence to leave the connection open, but return to the terminal server is Ctrl+Shift+6,x. If you want to disconnect, you can issue **disconnect** *session#*. View the open sessions in Example C-4.

Example C-4   *Viewing the Open Terminal Server Connections*

```
ts#show sessions
Conn Host               Address          Byte  Idle Conn Name
   1 r1                 1.1.1.1             0     8 r1
   2 r2                 1.1.1.1             0     8 r2
   3 r3                 1.1.1.1            48     8 r3
   4 r4                 1.1.1.1            51     8 r4
*  5 r5                 1.1.1.1             0     7 r5
```

Example C-4 shows that r1 through r5 are currently open sessions and that r5 is the default because the asterisk (*) displays to the left of it. The default session is the one you end up in if you press the Enter key as I do in the following output.

```
ts#
[Resuming connection 5 to r5 ... ]
r5>
```

This time, type **r5** from the terminal server rather than just the number 5 as in Example C-5.

Example C-5   *Connection Refused by Remote Host*

```
ts#r5
Trying r5 (1.1.1.1, 2005)...
% Connection refused by remote host

ts#show line
  Tty Typ     Tx/Rx     A Modem  Roty AccO AccI   Uses   Noise   Overruns   Int
*   0 CTY                -    -     -    -    -      5       0      0/0       -
*   1 TTY    9600/9600   -    -     -    -    -      1       0      0/0       -
*   2 TTY    9600/9600   -    -     -    -    -      1       0      0/0       -
*   3 TTY    9600/9600   -    -     -    -    -      1       0      0/0       -
*   4 TTY    9600/9600   -    -     -    -    -      1       0      0/0       -
*   5 TTY    9600/9600   -    -     -    -    -      1       0      0/0       -
    6 TTY    9600/9600   -    -     -    -    -      0       0      0/0       -
    7 TTY    9600/9600   -    -     -    -    -      0       0      0/0       -
*   8 TTY    9600/9600   -    -     -    -    -      0      11    424/1283    -
*   9 TTY    9600/9600   -    -     -    -    -      0      20    413/1239    -
   10 TTY    9600/9600   -    -     -    -    -      0      52    332/997     -
```

Line 5 is already open, but you really only needed to type 5 to get to it in the first place. However, it looks like something was already using line 8 and line 9 in the previous example. Clear these lines as in Example C-6 so that they are available for use.

Example C-6   *Connection Refused by Remote Host*

```
ts#clear line 8
[confirm]
 [OK]
ts#clear line 9
[confirm]
 [OK]
ts#show line
  Tty Typ     Tx/Rx     A Modem  Roty AccO AccI   Uses   Noise   Overruns   Int
*   0 CTY                -    -     -    -    -      5       0      0/0       -
*   1 TTY    9600/9600   -    -     -    -    -      1       0      0/0       -
*   2 TTY    9600/9600   -    -     -    -    -      1       0      0/0       -
*   3 TTY    9600/9600   -    -     -    -    -      1       0      0/0       -
*   4 TTY    9600/9600   -    -     -    -    -      1       0      0/0       -
*   5 TTY    9600/9600   -    -     -    -    -      1       0      0/0       -
    6 TTY    9600/9600   -    -     -    -    -      0       0      0/0       -
    7 TTY    9600/9600   -    -     -    -    -      0       0      0/0       -
    8 TTY    9600/9600   -    -     -    -    -      0      59    433/1312    -
    9 TTY    9600/9600   -    -     -    -    -      0     115    423/1270    -
```

continues

Example C-6 *Connection Refused by Remote Host (Continued)*

```
 10 TTY   9600/9600   -    -        -      -     -     0     52    332/997    -
 11 TTY   9600/9600   -    -        -      -     -     0      0      0/0      -
 12 TTY   9600/9600   -    -        -      -     -     0      0      0/0      -
 13 TTY   9600/9600   -    -        -      -     -     0      0      0/0      -
 14 TTY   9600/9600   -    -        -      -     -     0      0      0/0      -
 15 TTY   9600/9600   -    -        -      -     -     0      0      0/0      -
 16 TTY   9600/9600   -    -        -      -     -     0      0      0/0      -
 17 AUX   9600/9600   -    -        -      -     -     0      0      0/0      -
 18 VTY               -    -        -      -     -     0      0      0/0      -
 19 VTY               -    -        -      -     -     0      0      0/0      -
 20 VTY               -    -        -      -     -     0      0      0/0      -
 21 VTY               -    -        -      -     -     0      0      0/0      -
Tty Typ   Tx/Rx     A Modem    Roty AccO AccI  Uses  Noise  Overruns   Int
 22 VTY               -    -        -      -     -     0      0      0/0      -
```

INDEX

Numerics

A

D

G

GD (General Deployment), 73, 238
Get Nearest Server (GNS), 261
Gigabit EtherChannel (BEC), 448
Gigabit Ethernet, 321
global positioning system (GPS), 42
GNS (Get Nearest Server), 261
goose routers, documentation, 700
GPS (global positioning system), 42

H

hard code speed, 384
hardware
    support, 102
    tools, 113
Hayes command, 8
HDLC (High-Level Data Link Control), 68, 235, 498,
    598–601
    layers, 602
    troubleshooting, 602–607
headers
    Frame Relay, 517–519
    IP, 163, 165
    IPX, 266
    layers, 13
heron router documentation, 699
hex place values, 35
hierarchies, autonegotiation, 342
High Speed Study Group (HSSG), 322
High-Level Data Link Control. *See* HDLC
High-Speed Serial Interface (HSSI), 64
history of Frame Relay, 512–516
hops, TTL, 87
hosta
    CDaemon Syslog, 699
    testing, 379
hosta IP configuration, 376
hostnames
    command, 368
    ping command, 159
hosts, 21–22, 187
    2900 switch ping command, 376
    routes, 596
    scenario configuration, 368
    subnets, 198
    Windows 2000, 188

host-to-host connectivity, testing, 159
host-to-host delivery, 15
HSRP (Hot Standby Router Protocol), 470–471
HSSG (High Speed Study Group), 322
HSSI (High-Speed Serial Interface), 64
HTTP (Hypertext Transport Protocol), 190, 365
hubs, 36, 380, 532
hybrid back-to-back configuration, 502

I

IAB (Internet Architecture Board), 8
IANA (Internet Assigned Numbers Authority), 8
ICMP type values and codes, 97
IDB (Interface Description Block), 592
IEEE 802.1Q, 447
IEEE 802.3 Ethernet evolution, 323–324
IESG (Internet Engineering Steering Group), 8
IETF (Internet Engineering Task Force), 8
IGRP (Interior Gateway Routing Protocol), 206–208
infrastructure, 113
Integrated Services Digital Network. *See* ISDN
Interface Descriptor Block (IDB), 592
interface vlan # command, 372
interfaces
    backup, 644, 647
    bouncing, 442
    BRI, 628
    CLI, 394
        CatOS-based switches, 395–400
        IOS-based switches, 400
    default settings, 313
    HSSI, 64
    IP, 145
    ISDN BRI, 616–620
        layers, 620–637
        troubleshooting, 637-641
    MII, 337
    NIC, 10
    normal, 649
    serial
        debugging, 603
        keepalives, 603
        Trouble Tickets, 680–681
        viewing, 598
    shut down, 599
    Sniffer Pro, 115
        applying, 118–122
        starting, 116–117

K

keepalives, 603
kentnarrows switch, documentation, 701
Kermit protocol, 8
keywords, logging, 92

L

LAN Management Solution (LMS), 109
LANE (LAN Emulation), 109
LAPD (Link Access Procedure D), 620
LAPD (Link Access Protocol), 512
Layer 1, 36
Layer 2, 30, 685
Layer 3, 16, 691
Layer 4, 15
Layer 5, 15
Layer 6, 14
layers
    Access, 46
    Application, 14
    Core, 46
    Data Link, 30
    discovery labs, 682
    Distribution, 46
    Ethernet, 297
    HDLC, 602
    headers, 13
    Internet (Novell), 261–272
    ISDN BRI, 620–637
    Network, 16
    OSI, 11. *See also* OSI
    Physical, 36
        Ethernet, 337
        Frame Relay, 528–536
    PPP, 607–610
    Presentation, 14
    Session, 15
    TCP/IP, 160–162
        Internet, 162–167
        Transport, 168–176
        upper-layer, 176–192
    Transport, 15, 272–273
    troubleshooting, 44–45
    Upper (Novell), 274–276
LDN (local directory number), 625

leaks, memory, 79
learning states, 388
least significant bit (LSB), 35
LECs (Local Exchange Carrier), 528
LEDs (light emitting diodes), 405
levels, logging, 92
life cycles, IOS, 74
like devices, 40
line termination (LT), 618
Link Access Protocol Channel D (LAPD), 512, 620
link-state advertisement (LSA), 209
listening states, 387
lists
    access, 641
    ACL. *See* ACL
    dialers, 641
little-endian systems, 34
LLC (Logical Link Control), 30
LMI (Local Management Interface), 515, 519–523
LMS (LAN Management Solution), 109
load monitor command, 257
loading drivers, 258
local directory number (LDN), 625
Local Exchange Carrier (LEC), 528
Local Management Interface (LMI), 515, 519–523
local multicast addresses, 170
logging
    commands, 92, 530
    configuring, 93
    keywords, 92
    levels, 92
    trace commands, 88
logical bridges
    VLANs, 433
logical bus networks, 319
Logical Link Control (LLC), 30
logon, Microsoft Client, 260
loopbacks
    EIGRP
        advertising, 593
        Frame Relay, 544–546
        troubleshooting, 594
        viewing, 595
lower layer discovery configuration, 682
LSA (link-state advertisement), 209
LSB (least significant bit), 35
LT (line termination), 618

Q-R

S

U